POETRY

READING > REACTING > WRITING

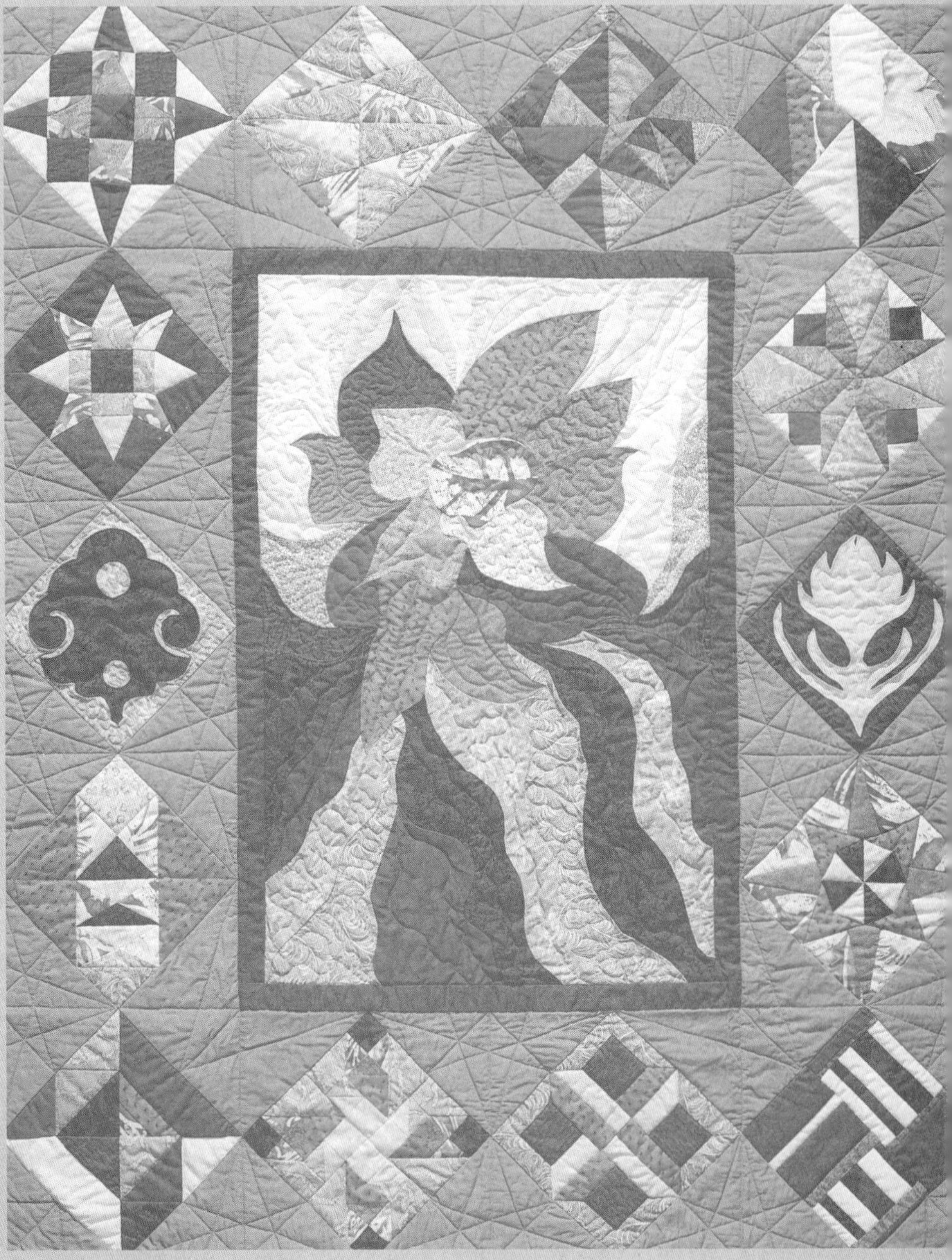

POETRY

Reading > Reacting > Writing

Laurie G. Kirszner
Philadelphia College of Pharmacy and Science

Stephen G. Mandell
Drexel University

HARCOURT BRACE COLLEGE PUBLISHERS
Fort Worth Philadelphia San Diego New York Orlando Austin San Antonio
Toronto Montreal London Sydney Tokyo

Editor-in-Chief: **Ted Buchholz**
Acquisitions Editor: **Michael Rosenberg**
Development Editor: **Camille Adkins**
Project Editor: **Barbara Moreland**
Production Manager: **Cynthia Young**
Book Designer: **Garry Harman**

Cover Artwork by: **Greta Vaught**

ISBN 0-15-501015-8
Library of Congress Card Number 93-79505

Copyright © 1994 by Harcourt Brace Jovanovich, Inc.

All rights reserved. No part of this publication may be reproduced or transmitted in any form or by any means, electronic or mechanical, including photocopy, recording, or any information storage and retrieval system, without permission in writing from the publisher.

Requests for permission to make copies of any part of the work should be mailed to: Permissions Department, Harcourt Brace College Publishers, 8th Floor, Orlando, Florida 32887

Address editorial correspondence to:
301 Commerce St., Suite 3700
Fort Worth, TX 76102

Address orders to:
6277 Sea Harbor Dr.
Orlando, FL 32887
1-800-782-4479 (outside Florida)
1-800-433-0001 (inside Florida)

Acknowledgments begin on page 513.

Printed in the United States of America

4567890123   090   987654321

PREFACE

The first edition of *Literature: Reading, Reacting, Writing* broke new ground and, perhaps as a result, received praise from both students and instructors. When we began work on the first edition, our goal was to move away from the predictability and familiarity that characterize traditional literature anthologies. In the process we wanted to demonstrate that a literature anthology could reflect the exciting changes taking place in literary studies. We also wanted to combine the study of literature with writing instruction based on the latest research from the field of composition. The success of the first edition demonstrates that the direction we chose was the right one.

In response to many requests from instructors, we have made the fiction and poetry sections of the second edition of *Literature: Reading, Reacting, Writing* available as separate volumes. These books make it possible for instructors who do not need or want a full sized literature anthology to have all the innovative features of *Literature: Reading, Reacting, Writing* in a format suited to their specific needs.

Poetry: Reading, Reacting, Writing begins with a chapter called "Understanding Literature," which helps students gain an appreciation of the complex issues surrounding the expansion of the literary canon. After surveying conventional literary themes, this chapter summarizes the reasons why many students of literature believe that the traditional canon needs to be revised. It then discusses the processes of interpreting and evaluating literature, placing special emphasis on how the personal responses of readers affect meaning. Finally, it examines the role of literary criticism and considers how it offers students perspectives that can help them expand their literary horizons.

Chapter 2, "Reading and Writing about Literature," offers a detailed discussion of writing about literature. As experienced writing teachers, and as coauthors of seven other writing texts, we know that writing about literature presents special problems for students. For this reason, we discuss the processes of reading and writing in the context of literature before we specifically discuss reading and writing about poetry. We demonstrate how students discover ideas about literature through a complex process of reading, rereading, questioning, and discussing as well as writing and rewriting. To help students see writing about literature as a process of exploring and testing ideas, of growing into a point of view or a critical stance, and of participating in an ongoing critical debate, we include writing instruction not as an afterthought, tucked away in an appendix, but in a full chapter that examines the writing process as it applies to all literature.

In Chapter 3, "Understanding Poetry," we introduce students to some of the special characteristics of poetry. Beginning with three poems that attempt to define poetry, we lead students through a general discussion of the genre and introduce them to traditional as well as experimental poems. Brief discussions of reading poetry, narrative and lyrical poetry, and poetic themes follow. The chapter concludes with a diverse collection of poems about the parent–child relationship and an exercise that involves students in discovering themes in poetry.

In Chapter 4, "Reading and Writing about Poetry," we narrow our focus to follow the progress of a student as she moves through the process of writing about two poems, Robert Hayden's "Those Winter Sundays" (p. 50) and Seamus Heaney's "Digging" (p. 51). We discuss concepts familiar to composition teachers and students of writing—gathering and arranging ideas, drafting and so on—and explain and illustrate how to apply these concepts to writing about poetry. In each of three drafts of the student essay, we show how revision and editing help strengthen an essay, making it clearer, more precise, and more compelling.

Of course, the heart of *Poetry: Reading, Reacting, Writing* is its reading selections. Throughout the book (in separate chapters focusing on voice; diction; imagery; figures of speech; sound; form; and symbolism, allegory, allusion, and myth, as well as in the Poems for Further Reading section) we include a significant number of established favorites—those poems recognized by many instructors as excellent. Students and teachers like and expect to see these works, and their familiarity makes them good starting points for introducing students to poetry. We wanted, however, to include more than the "approved" readings—and, in fact, to do more than supplement the approved list with a few token selections representing contemporary voices.

We recognize that the literary canon has expanded to include an exciting diversity of contexts, cultures, and viewpoints, and we welcome this trend as long overdue. Accordingly, we have included high-quality representatives of these diverse voices. As a result of our efforts, this anthology includes poetry by noted writers from many regions and ethnic backgrounds in the United States, Canada, and the British Isles, as well as selections by writers from various countries in Asia, Africa, Latin America, and the Caribbean. In addition, we have sought younger writers whose reputations are still developing, and a significant number of poems by women, minorities, and non-Western writers.

Many anthologies, eager to include such works because of their obvious merit and appeal, are nevertheless reluctant to look too different; therefore, they may include "new" works that are new only to their text, not to the canon, choosing "safe" minority or foreign writers whose works, already given the stamp of approval by the critical hierarchy, have been anthologized frequently. Alternately, editors may limit the number of new works to a sprinkling, or even relegate "nontraditional" or "contemporary" works to separate sections of the text. Our practice has been to place such works where they belong, alongside the "classics": to integrate new with old, familiar with unfamiliar, inviting students simultaneously to discover new works and to see familiar works in new contexts. Our goal in this anthology is not just to expand the literary canon, but also to expand the personal canons of both students and instructors.

Following the readings is a Casebook that is unique to this book. Although the student essay-in-progress in Chapter 4 does not make use of source-based research, we recognize that many literary essays do, including those assigned in introductory literature courses. At the same time, we know that instructors may be reluctant to assign such essays because of the limitations of library facilities or because they are not certain that students will be able to evaluate or even locate useful sources on their own. Still, we realize that learning to make use of critical, historical, and bibliographic sources can help students develop critical thinking skills, learn to make judgments about the validity and relevance of various ideas, and formulate critical positions of their own. For this reason, we have assembled a Casebook designed to supplement students' reading of a selection of poems by Gwendolyn Brooks. In this Casebook we include articles by literary critics, contemporary biographical and critical material from a variety of sources, and a complete student research paper based on this source material. Following the Casebook is a detailed appendix on MLA documentation format. The result is a self-contained resource that will enable students to write thoughtful critical essays on Brooks's poetry—and, eventually, on other poems as well.

Each of the features described above is designed to serve the text's dual goals: to encourage students to appreciate poems representing diverse literary subjects, styles, and perspectives, and to recognize their own role in bringing these diverse works into an expanded literary canon by reading, reacting to, and writing about them. We anticipate that students' responses will take a variety of forms: class discussion, collaborative activities, journals, informal essays, source-based literary criticism, and possibly even original poetry. Nevertheless, our goal in this text is not to turn students into literary critics or poets. If this anthology can encourage students to respond spontaneously and enthusiastically to what they read and to see their responses as involving them in an ongoing and stimulating (if sometimes unpredictable) dialogue—with peers, with critics, with instructors, with themselves, and with the work itself—then we will have accomplished our purpose.

From start to finish, this text has been a true collaboration for us, not only with each other, but also with our students and colleagues. We have worked hard on the book, and many people at Harcourt Brace have worked along with us. Camille Adkins, Shana Lum, and Michael Rosenberg gave us their time, support, and encouragement. Others at Harcourt Brace who were important to the book are Barbara Moreland, Margaret Allyson, Shelia Shutter, Garry Harmon, and Cindy Young. In addition, we would like to thank Carol Lea Clark, University of Texas at El Paso; Todd Stebbins, University of South Carolina; Gloria Underwood, Savannah College of Art and Design; Wayne Cox, Anderson College; Miriam Moore, University of South Carolina; Shelia Tombe, University of South Carolina; and Rudy Eastman, Jubilee Theatre, Fort Worth, Texas. We also appreciate the work of Anne Lesser, Carla Hahn-Clardy, and Publications Development Company.

We would like to thank all the reviewers who made valuable contributions through several drafts of the text. Reviewers of the second edition were Deborah Barberbousse, Horry-Georgetown Technical College; Bob Mayberry, University of Nevada Las Vegas; Shireen Carroll, University of Miami; Stephen Wright, Seminole Community College; Robert Dees, Orange Coast College; Larry Gray, Southeastern Louisiana University; Nancy Rayl, Cypress College; James Clemmer, Austin Peay State University; Roberta Kramer, Nassau Community College.

We would also like to thank our families—Mark, Adam, and Rebecca Kirszner and Demi, David, and Sarah Mandell—for being there when we needed them. And finally, we each thank the person on the other side of the ampersand for making our collaboration work one more time.

Detailed Contents

CHAPTER 1

UNDERSTANDING LITERATURE 1
WHAT IS LITERATURE? *1*
- IMAGINATIVE LITERATURE *1*
- CONVENTIONAL THEMES *3*
- THE LITERARY CANON *4*
  - Wole Soyinka, "Telephone Conversation" **6**

THINKING CRITICALLY *7*
- INTERPRETING LITERATURE *7*
- EVALUATING LITERATURE *10*
- THE FUNCTION OF LITERARY CRITICISM *13*

CHAPTER 2

READING AND WRITING ABOUT LITERATURE 15
READING LITERATURE *15*
- PREVIEWING *15*
- HIGHLIGHTING *16*
  - Maya Angelou, "My Arkansas" **18**
- ANNOTATING *18*

WRITING ABOUT LITERATURE *19*
- PLANNING AN ESSAY *19*
- Considering Your Audience *19*
- Understanding Your Purpose *20*
  - Writing to Respond *20*
  - Writing to Interpret *20*
  - Writing to Evaluate *20*
- Choosing a Topic *20*
- Finding Something to Say *22*
  - Brainstorming *22*
  - Keeping a Journal *23*
  - Listing *23*
- Deciding on a Thesis *25*
- Preparing an Outline *25*
- DRAFTING *26*
- REVISING AND EDITING *28*
- Strategies for Revision *28*
- The Revision Process *28*
  - Thesis *28*
  - Supporting Ideas *29*
  - Introduction *29*
  - Conclusion *30*

ix

Topic Sentences 30
Sentences and Words 31
Source Material and Documentation 32
Editing 32

CHAPTER 3

UNDERSTANDING POETRY 33
NIKKI GIOVANNI, "POETRY" 33
ARCHIBALD MACLEISH, "ARS POETICA" 34
MARIANNE MOORE, "POETRY" 35
DEFINING POETRY 36
William Shakespeare, "That Time of Year Thou Mayst in Me Behold" **38**
Louis Zukofsky, "I Walk in the Old Street" **38**
E. E. Cummings, "1(a" **39**
A NOTE ON READING POETRY 40
RECOGNIZING KINDS OF POETRY 40
NARRATIVE POETRY 40
LYRIC POETRY 41
DISCOVERING THEMES IN POETRY 42
Adrienne Rich, "A Woman Mourned by Daughters" **42**
Raymond Carver, "Photograph of My Father in His Twenty-Second Year" **44**
Judith Ortiz Cofer, "My Father in the Navy: A Childhood Memory" **45**
EXERCISE: DISCOVERING THEMES IN POETRY 46
Theodore Roethke, "My Papa's Waltz" **46**
Dylan Thomas, "Do Not Go Gentle into That Good Night" **47**
Simon J. Ortiz, "My Father's Song" **47**
Colleen J. McElroy, "My Father's Wars" **48**
Lucille Clifton, "My Mama Moved among the Days" **50**
Robert Hayden, "Those Winter Sundays" **50**
Seamus Heaney, "Digging" **51**

CHAPTER 4

READING AND WRITING ABOUT POETRY 52
READING POETRY 52
ACTIVE READING 53
PREVIEWING 53
HIGHLIGHTING AND ANNOTATING 53
WRITING ABOUT POETRY 55
PLANNING AN ESSAY 55
Choosing a Topic 55
Finding Something to Say 56
Brainstorming 56

Deciding on a Thesis 57
Preparing an Outline 57
DRAFTING 58
A COMPARISON OF TWO POEMS ABOUT FATHERS (FIRST DRAFT) 59
FIRST DRAFT: COMMENTARY 61
A COMPARISON OF TWO POEMS ABOUT FATHERS (SECOND DRAFT) 63
SECOND DRAFT: COMMENTARY 66
DIGGING FOR MEMORIES (FINAL DRAFT) 67
FINAL DRAFT: COMMENTARY 71

CHAPTER 5

VOICE 72
EMILY DICKINSON, "I'M NOBODY! WHO ARE YOU?" 72
THE PERSON IN THE POEM 72
  Louise Glück, "Gretel in Darkness" **73**
  Leonard Adamé, "My Grandmother Would Rock Quietly and Hum" **75**
  Langston Hughes, "Negro" **77**
  Robert Browning, "My Last Duchess" **78**
POEMS FOR FURTHER READING: THE PERSON IN THE POEM 80
  Leslie Marmon Silko, "Where Mountain Lion Lay Down with Deer" **80**
    * *Reading and Reacting* 81
  Janice Mirikitani, "Suicide Note" **81**
    * *Reading and Reacting* 83
THE TONE OF THE POEM 83
  Robert Frost, "Fire and Ice" **84**
  Thomas Hardy, "The Man He Killed" **85**
  Amy Lowell, "Patterns" **86**
POEMS FOR FURTHER READING: TONE 89
  Simon J. Ortiz, "Speaking" **89**
    * *Reading and Reacting* 90
  William Wordsworth, "The World Is Too Much with Us" **90**
    * *Reading and Reacting* 90
  Sylvia Plath, "Morning Song" **91**
    * *Reading and Reacting* 91
  Robert Herrick, "To the Virgins, to Make Much of Time" **92**
    * *Reading and Reacting* 92
A SPECIAL CASE OF TONE: IRONY 92
  Robert Browning, "Porphyria's Lover" **93**
  Percy Bysshe Shelly, "Ozymandias" **95**
  Ariel Dorfman, "Hope" **96**

POEMS FOR FURTHER READING: IRONY 98
    W. H. Auden, "The Unknown Citizen" **98**
        * Reading and Reacting 99
    Anne Sexton, "Cinderella" **99**
        * Reading and Reacting 102
    Dudley Randall, "Ballad of Birmingham" **102**
        * Reading and Reacting 103
        ✓ Checklist for Writing about Voice 104
    Writing Suggestions: Voice 104

CHAPTER 6

WORD CHOICE, WORD ORDER **106**
SIPHO SEPAMLA, "WORDS, WORDS, WORDS" 106
WORD CHOICE 107
    Walt Whitman, "When I Heard the Learn'd Astronomer" **108**
    William Stafford, "For the Grave of Daniel Boone" **110**
POEMS FOR FURTHER READING: WORD CHOICE 112
    Russell Endo, "Susumu, My Name" **112**
        * Reading and Reacting 112
    Adrienne Rich, "Living in Sin" **113**
        * Reading and Reacting 113
    Karl Shapiro, "Auto Wreck" **114**
        * Reading and Reacting 114
    E. E. Cummings, "in Just—" **115**
        * Reading and Reacting 116
    Theodore Roethke, "I Knew A Woman" **116**
        * Reading and Reacting 117
EXERCISE: REVISIONS AND WORD CHOICE 118
    Robert Frost, "In White" **118**
    Robert Frost, "Design" **119**
LEVELS OF DICTION 119
    FORMAL DICTION 119
    Margaret Atwood, "The City Planners" **120**
    INFORMAL DICTION 121
    Jim Sagel, "Baca Grande" **121**
POEMS FOR FURTHER READING: LEVELS OF DICTION 124
    Barbara L. Greenburg, "The Faithful Wife" **124**
        * Reading and Reacting 124
    Richard Wilbur, "For the Student Strikers" **125**
        * Reading and Reacting 125
    Charles Bukowski, "Dog Fight" **126**
        * Reading and Reacting 127
    DIALECT 127
    Fay Kicknosway, "Gracie" **127**

POEMS FOR FURTHER READING: DIALECT *129*
    Robert Burns, "John Anderson My Jo, John" ***129***
        * *Reading and Reacting 129*
    Gwendolyn Brooks, "We Real Cool" ***130***
        * *Reading and Reacting 130*
WORD ORDER *130*
    Edmund Spenser, "One Day I Wrote Her Name upon the Strand" ***131***
    E. E. Cummings, "anyone lived in a pretty how town" ***132***
POEMS FOR FURTHER READING: WORD ORDER *134*
    Edna St. Vincent Millay, "Elegy before Death" ***134***
        * *Reading and Reacting 134*
    W. H. Auden, "Look, Stranger" ***135***
        * *Reading and Reacting 135*
        ✓ *Checklist for Writing about Word Choice and Word Order 136*
    Writing Suggestions: Word Choice, Word Order *136*

CHAPTER 7

IMAGERY 138
JANE FLANDERS, "CLOUD PAINTER" *138*
William Carlos Williams, "Red Wheelbarrow" ***140***
Ezra Pound, "In a Station of the Metro" ***141***
Gary Snyder, "Some Good Things to be Said for the Iron Age" ***142***
Suzanne E. Berger, "The Meal" ***143***
William Carlos Williams, "The Great Figure" ***144***
POEMS FOR FURTHER READING: IMAGERY *146*
Dennis Brutus, "On the Island" ***146***
    * *Reading and Reacting 147*
Michelle Cliff, "A Visit to the Secret Annex" ***147***
    * *Reading and Reacting 150*
Eric Chock, "Chinese Fireworks Banned in Hawaii" ***150***
    * *Reading and Reacting 152*
Matsuo Basho, "Four Haiku" ***152***
    * *Reading and Reacting 152*
Carolyn Kizer, "After Basho" ***153***
    * *Reading and Reacting 153*
Richard Wilbur, "Sleepless at Crown Point" ***153***
    * *Reading and Reacting 154*
Jean Toomer, "Reapers" ***154***
    * *Reading and Reacting 154*
Wilfred Owen, "Dulce et Decorum Est" ***155***
    * *Reading and Reacting 155*
    ✓ *Checklist for Writing about Imagery 156*
Writing Suggestions: Imagery *156*

CHAPTER 8

FIGURES OF SPEECH 158
WILLIAM SHAKESPEARE, "SHALL I COMPARE THEE TO A SUMMER'S DAY?" 158
SIMILE, METAPHOR, AND PERSONIFICATION 159
Langston Hughes, "Dream Deferred" **159**
Lawrence Ferlinghetti, "Constantly Risking Absurdity" **160**
Audre Lorde, "Rooming Houses Are Old Women" **162**
POEMS FOR FURTHER READING: SIMILE, METAPHOR, AND PERSONIFICATION 163
Robert Burns, "Oh, My Love Is Like a Red, Red Rose" **163**
  * Reading and Reacting 164
John Updike, "Ex-Basketball Player" **164**
  * Reading and Reacting 165
Adrienne Rich, "The Roofwalker" **165**
  * Reading and Reacting 166
Randall Jarrell, "The Death of the Ball Turret Gunner" **166**
  * Reading and Reacting 167
Marge Piercy, "The Secretary Chant" **167**
  * Reading and Reacting 168
John Donne, "A Valediction: Forbidding Mourning" **168**
  * Reading and Reacting 169
HYPERBOLE AND UNDERSTATEMENT 169
Sylvia Plath, "Daddy" **170**
David Huddle, "Holes Commence Falling" **173**
POEMS FOR FURTHER READING: HYPERBOLE AND UNDERSTATEMENT 175
Anne Bradstreet, "To My Dear and Loving Husband" **175**
  * Reading and Reacting 175
Andrew Marvell, "To His Coy Mistress" **175**
  * Reading and Reacting 177
Robert Frost, "Out, Out—" **177**
  * Reading and Reacting 178
Donald Hall, "My Son, My Executioner" **178**
  * Reading and Reacting 179
Margaret Atwood, "You Fit into Me" **179**
  * Reading and Reacting 179
METONYMY AND SYNECDOCHE 180
Richard Lovelace, "To Lucasta Going to the Wars" **180**
POEM FOR FURTHER READING: METONYMY AND SYNECDOCHE 181
Dylan Thomas, "The Hand That Signed the Paper" **181**
  * Reading and Reacting 181

APOSTROPHE *181*
Sonia Sanchez, "On Passing thru Morgantown, PA." ***182***
POEMS FOR FURTHER READING: APOSTROPHE *183*
Allen Ginsberg, "A Supermarket in California" ***183***
　* *Reading and Reacting 184*
Walt Whitman, "A Noiseless Patient Spider" ***184***
　* *Reading and Reacting 185*
　✓ *Checklist for Writing about Figures of Speech 185*
Writing Suggestions: Figures of Speech *185*

CHAPTER 9

SOUND *187*
WALT WHITMAN, "HAD I THE CHOICE" *187*
RHYTHM *187*
Gwendolyn Brooks, "Sadie and Maud" ***188***
METER *189*
Samuel Taylor Coleridge, "Metrical Feet" ***192***
Emily Dickinson, "I Like to See It Lap the Miles" ***193***
POEMS FOR FURTHER READING: RHYTHM AND METER *196*
Adrienne Rich, "Aunt Jennifer's Tigers" ***196***
　* *Reading and Reacting 196*
Etheridge Knight, "For Malcolm, A Year After" ***197***
　* *Reading and Reacting 197*
ALLITERATION AND ASSONANCE *198*
Alfred, Lord Tennyson, "The Eagle" ***199***
N. Scott Momaday, "Comparatives" ***199***
Robert Herrick, "Delight in Disorder" ***201***
RHYME *202*
Ogden Nash, "The Lama" ***203***
Richard Wilbur, "A Sketch" ***204***
POEMS FOR FURTHER READING: ALLITERATION, ASSONANCE, AND RHYME *206*
Alice Walker, "Revoluntionary Petunias" ***206***
　* *Reading and Reacting 207*
Gerard Manley Hopkins, "Pied Beauty" ***207***
　* *Reading and Reacting 208*
Denise Levertov, "The Ache of Marriage" ***208***
　* *Reading and Reacting 208*
William Shakespeare, "Fear No More the Heat o' the Sun" ***209***
　* *Reading and Reacting 210*
Lewis Carroll, "Jabberwocky" ***210***
　* *Reading and Reacting 211*
　✓ *Checklist for Writing about Sound 211*
Writing Suggestions: Sound *212*

CHAPTER 10

FORM 213
JOHN KEATS, "ON THE SONNET" *213*
CLOSED FORM *214*
BLANK VERSE *215*
STANZA *215*
TRADITIONAL FORMS *217*
The Sonnet *217*
William Shakespeare, "When, in Disgrace with Fortune and Men's Eyes" **218**
Claude McKay, "The White City" **219**
   * *Reading and Reacting* *219*
John Keats, "On First Looking into Chapman's Homer" **220**
   * *Reading and Reacting* *220*
Gwendolyn Brooks, "First Fight. Then Fiddle" **221**
   * *Reading and Reacting* *221*
The Sestina *221*
Alberto Alvaro Rios, "Nani" **222**
Elizabeth Bishop, "Sestina" **223**
   * *Reading and Reacting* *224*
The Villanelle *225*
Theodore Roethke, "The Waking" **225**
William Meredith, "In Memory of Donald A. Stauffer" **226**
   * *Reading and Reacting* *227*
The Epigram *227*
Samuel Taylor Coleridge, "What Is an Epigram?" **228**
William Blake, "Her Whole Life Is an Epigram" **228**
Haiku *228*
Richard Brautigan, "Widow's Lament" **229**
Richard Wright, "Hokku Poems" **229**
   * *Reading and Reacting* *230*

OPEN FORM *230*
Carl Sandburg, "Chicago" **231**
Louise Glück, "Life Is a Nice Place" **233**
E. E. Cummings, "the sky was can dy" **234**
POEMS FOR FURTHER READING: OPEN FORM *235*
Walt Whitman, from *Out of the Cradle Endlessly Rocking* **235**
   * *Reading and Reacting* *236*
Diane Wakoski, "Sleep" **236**
   * *Reading and Reacting* *236*
Robert Hayden, "Monet's 'Waterlilies'" **237**
   * *Reading and Reacting* *238*
William Carlos Williams, "Spring and All" **238**
   * *Reading and Reacting* *239*

Lawrence Ferlinghetti, "Don't Let That Horse Eat
  That Violin" **239**
    * *Reading and Reacting* 240
Lucia Perillo, "Jury Selection" **240**
    * *Reading and Reacting* 242
CONCRETE POETRY 242
May Swenson, "Women" **243**
  POEMS FOR FURTHER READING: CONCRETE POETRY 244
George Herbert, "Easter Wings" **244**
    * *Reading and Reacting* 244
Robert Hollander, "You Too? Me Too—Why Not? Soda
  Pop" **245**
    * *Reading and Reacting* 246
    ✓ *Checklist for Writing about Form* 246
  Writing Suggestions: Form 246

CHAPTER 11

SYMBOL, ALLEGORY, ALLUSION, MYTH 248
WILLIAM BLAKE, "THE SICK ROSE" 248
SYMBOL 248
Robert Frost, "For Once, Then, Something" **249**
Jim Simmerman, "Child's Grave, Hale County,
  Alabama" **250**
Emily Dickinson, "Volcanoes Be in Sicily" **252**
  POEMS FOR FURTHER READING: SYMBOL 253
Langston Hughes, "Island" **253**
    * *Reading and Reacting* 253
Theodore Roethke, "Night Crow" **253**
    * *Reading and Reacting* 254
Howard Nemerov, "The Goose Fish" **254**
    * *Reading and Reacting* 255
ALLEGORY 255
Christina Rossetti, "Uphill" **256**
  POEM FOR FURTHER READING: ALLEGORY 257
Adrienne Rich, "Diving into the Wreck" **257**
    * *Reading and Reacting* 259
ALLUSION 259
Wole Soyinka, "Future Plans" **260**
William Meredith, "Dreams of Suicide" **261**
  POEM FOR FURTHER READING: ALLUSION 262
Delmore Schwartz, "The True-Blue American" **262**
    * *Reading and Reacting* 263
MYTH 264
Countee Cullen, "Yet Do I Marvel" **265**

POEMS FOR FURTHER READING: MYTH   266
Joseph Brodsky, "The Star of the Nativity"   266
  * Reading and Reacting   266
Louise Erdrich, "Windigo"   267
  * Reading and Reacting   267
William Butler Yeats, "Leda and the Swan"   268
  * Reading and Reacting   268
Derek Walcott, "Sea Grapes"   269
  * Reading and Reacting   269
W. H. Auden, "Musée des Beaux Arts"   270
  * Reading and Reacting   271
  ✓ Checklist for Writing about Symbol, Allegory, Allusion, Myth   271
Writing Suggestions: Symbol, Allegory, Allusion, Myth   272

POEMS FOR FURTHER READING

Anna Akhmatova, "He Loved Three Things Alone"   274
Anonymous, "Bonnie Barbara Allan"   274
Anonymous, "Sir Patrick Spence"   275
Anonymous, "Western Wind"   277
Imamu Amiri Baraka [Leroi Jones], "Watergate"   277
John Berryman, "Dream Song #14"   278
Elizabeth Bishop, "The Fish"   278
William Blake, "The Chimney Sweeper"   280
William Blake, "The Lamb"   281
William Blake, "London"   282
William Blake, "The Tyger"   282
Robert Bly, "Snowfall in the Afternoon"   283
Louise Bogan, "Women"   283
Elizabeth Barrett Browning, "How Do I Love Thee?"   284
Christopher Buckley, "Why I'm in Favor of a Nuclear Freeze"   285
George Gordon, Lord Byron, "She Walks in Beauty"   286
Thomas Campion, "There Is a Garden in Her Face"   287
Raymond Carver, "Gravy"   287
Geoffery Chaucer, from *The Canterbury Tales*   288
Judith Ortiz Cofer, "Lessons of the Past"   290
Samuel Taylor Coleridge, "Kubla Khan"   291
Hart Crane, "To Brooklyn Bridge"   293
Victor Hernandez Cruz, "Anonymous"   294
Countee Cullen, "For a Lady I Know"   295
E. E. Cummings, "Buffalo Bill's"   295
E. E. Cummings, "next to of course god america i"   295
James Dickey, "Adultery"   296
Emily Dickinson, "Because I Could Not Stop for Death"   297

Emily Dickinson, "I Heard a Fly Buzz—When I Died" *298*
Emily Dickinson, "I Taste a Liquor Never Brewed" *298*
Emily Dickinson, "The Soul Selects Her Own Society" *299*
Emily Dickinson, "Wild Nights—Wild Nights!" *299*
John Donne, "Batter My Heart, Three-Personed God" *300*
John Donne, "Death Be Not Proud" *300*
John Donne, "Song" *301*
Rita Dove, "The Satisfaction Coal Company" *301*
Michael Drayton, "Since There's No Help" *303*
Paul Laurence Dunbar, "We Wear the Mask" *304*
T. S. Eliot, "Journey of the Magi" *304*
T. S. Eliot, "The Love Song of J. Alfred Prufrock" *306*
James A. Emanuel, "Emmett Till" *310*
Louise Erdrich, "Dear John Wayne" *310*
Robert Francis, "Pitcher" *311*
Robert Frost, "Acquainted with the Night" *312*
Robert Frost, "Birches" *312*
Robert Frost, "Mending Wall" *314*
Robert Frost, "The Road Not Taken" *315*
Robert Frost, "Stopping by Woods on a Snowy Evening" *315*
Nikki Giovanni, "Nikki-Rosa" *316*
Thomas Gray, "Elegy Written in a Country Churchyard" *317*
Thomas Hardy, "Channel Firing" *321*
Robert Hayden, "Homage to the Empress of the Blues" *323*
Linda Hogan, "Heritage" *323*
Garrett Kaoru Hongo, "The Hongo Store" *325*
Gerard Manley Hopkins, "God's Grandeur" *326*
Gerard Manley Hopkins, "The Windhover" *326*
A. E. Houseman, "Terence, This Is Stupid Stuff" *327*
A. E. Houseman, "To an Athlete Dying Young" *329*
Ben Jonson, "On My First Son" *330*
Ben Jonson, "To Celia" *330*
Donald Justice, "On the Death of Friends in Childhood" *331*
John Keats, "La Belle Dame Sans Merci: A Ballad" *331*
John Keats, "Ode on a Grecian Urn" *333*
John Keats, "Ode to a Nightingale" *335*
John Keats, "When I Have Fears" *338*
Maxine Kumin, "Morning Swim" *338*
Philip Larkin, "Aubade" *339*
Denise Levertov, "What Were They Like?" *340*
Stephen Shu-ning Liu, "My Father's Martial Art" *341*
Robert Lowell, "For the Union Dead" *342*
Christopher Marlowe, "The Passionate Shepherd to His Love" *344*

Claude McKay, "If We Must Die" **345**
Edna St. Vincent Millay, "What Lips My Lips Have Kissed" **346**
John Milton, "When I Consider How My Light Is Spent" **346**
Janice Mirikitani, "Breaking Silence" **347**
N. Scott Momaday, "Earth and I Gave You Turquoise" **350**
Pat Mora, "Elena" **351**
Howard Nemerov, "The Air Force Museum at Dayton" **352**
Pablo Neruda, "The United Fruit Co." **353**
Hilton Obenzinger, "Yes, We Have No Bananas" **354**
Sharon Olds, "The One Girl at the Boys Party" **355**
Linda Pastan, "Ethics" **356**
Boris Pasternak, "In Everything I Want to Get" **356**
Sylvia Plath, "Metaphors" **357**
Ezra Pound, "The River-Merchant's Wife: A Letter" **358**
Sir Walter Raleigh, "The Nymph's Reply to the Shepherd" **359**
John Crowe Ransom, "Bells for John Whiteside's Daughter" **359**
Henry Reed, "Naming of Parts" **360**
Edward Arlington Robinson, "Miniver Cheevy" **361**
Edward Arlington Robinson, "Mr. Flood's Party" **362**
Edward Arlington Robinson, "Richard Cory" **364**
Theodore Roethke, "Child on Top of a Greenhouse" **364**
Sonia Sanchez, "right on: white america" **365**
Carl Sandburg, "Fog" **366**
Mongone Wally Serote, "For Don M.—Banned" **366**
William Shakespeare, "Let Me Not to the Marriage of True Minds" **366**
William Shakespeare, "My Mistress' Eyes Are Nothing Like the Sun" **367**
William Shakespeare, "Not Marble, Nor the Gilded Monuments" **367**
Percy Bysshe Shelley, "Ode to the West Wind" **368**
Sir Philip Sidney, "Astrophel and Stella" **371**
Charles Simic, "Birthday Star Atlas" **371**
Boris Slutsky, "How Did They Kill My Grandmother?" **373**
Stevie Smith, "Not Waving But Drowning" **374**
Cathy Song, "Lost Sister" **374**
Gary Soto, "Black Hair" **376**
Gary Soto, "History" **377**
Barry Spacks, "Finding a Yiddish Paper on the Riverside Line" **379**
Stephen Spender, "An Elementary Classroom in a Slum" **379**
Bruce Springsteen, "My Hometown" **380**
William Stafford, "Traveling through the Dark" **381**

Dona Stein, "Putting Mother By" *382*
Wallace Stevens, "Anecdote of the Jar" *383*
Wallace Stevens, "Disillusionment of Ten O'Clock" *383*
Wallace Stevens, "The Emperor of Ice-Cream" *384*
Mark Strand, "Pot Roast" *384*
Andrew Suknaski, "The Bitter Word" *386*
Alfred, Lord Tennyson, "Ulysses" *387*
Dylan Thomas, "Fern Hill" *389*
Margaret Walker, "Lineage" *390*
Edmund Waller, "Go, Lovely Rose" *391*
Tom Wayman, "Wayman in Quebec" *392*
Phyllis Weatley, "On Being Brought from Africa to America" *392*
Walt Whitman, "Cavalry Crossing a Ford" *393*
Walt Whitman, from *Song of Myself* *393*
Richard Wilbur, "Museum Piece" *395*
William Carlos Williams, "This Is Just to Say" *395*
William Wordsworth, "Composed upon Westminster Bridge" *396*
William Wordsworth, "I Wandered Lonely as a Cloud" *396*
William Wordsworth, "She Dwelt among the Untrodden Ways" *397*
James Wright, "A Blessing" *397*
William Butler Yeats, "Crazy Jane Talks with the Bishop" *398*
William Butler Yeats, "An Irish Airman Foresees His Death" *399*
William Butler Yeats, "The Lake Isle of Innisfree" *399*
William Butler Yeats, "Sailing to Byzantium" *400*
William Butler Yeats, "The Second Coming" *401*
Yevgeny Yevtushenko, "Lies" *402*

POETRY CASEBOOK ... 403

Gwendolyn Brooks, "The Ballad of Chocolate Mabbie" *405*
Gwendolyn Brooks, "A Song in the Front Yard" *406*
Gwendolyn Brooks, "People Who Have No Children Can Be Hard" *407*
Gwendolyn Brooks, "What Shall I Give My Children?" *407*
Gwendolyn Brooks, "The Bean Eaters" *407*
Gwendolyn Brooks, "The *Chicago Defender* Sends a Man to Little Rock" *408*
Gwendolyn Brooks, "The Blackstone Rangers" *410*
Gwendolyn Brooks, "The Ballad of Rudolph Reed" *412*
Gwendolyn Brooks, "Medgar Evers" *413*
Gwendolyn Brooks, "The Boy Died in My Alley" *414*
Gwendolyn Brooks, "An Interview with Myself" *415*

Gwendolyn Brooks, from *Report from Part One* **419**
Houston A. Baker, Jr., "The Achievement of Gwendolyn Brooks" **421**
George Stavros, "An Interview with Gwendolyn Brooks" **428**
Gary Smith, "Gwendolyn Brooks's 'Children of the Poor', Metaphysical Poetry and the Inconditions of Love" **430**
Maria K. Mootry, "'Chocolate Mabbie' and 'Pearl May Lee': Gwendolyn Brooks and the Ballad Tradition" **439**
Gary Smith, "Gwendolyn Brooks's *A Street in Bronzeville*, The Harlem Renaissance and the Mythologies of Black Women" **446**
Questions *452*
Student Paper: "Racial Consciousness in 'The Ballad of Rudolph Reed'" *454*

APPENDICES

Appendix A   Documenting Sources **461**

Sample Literature Paper with MLA Documentation: "Rudolfo Anaya's *Bless Me, Ultima:* A Microcosmic Representation of Chicano Literature" **470**

Appendix B   Literary History: Aristotle to the Twentieth Century **476**

Appendix C   Twentieth-Century Literary Theories **483**

Glossary of Literary Terms *504*

Acknowledgments *513*

Index of Authors, Titles, and First Lines of Poetry *523*

Index of Key Terms *537*

CHAPTER 1

UNDERSTANDING LITERATURE

WHAT IS LITERATURE?

IMAGINATIVE LITERATURE

Imaginative literature begins with a writer's need to convey his or her personal vision to readers. Even when writers use factual material—historical documents, newspaper stories, personal experience—their primary purpose is to give a unique view of experience, one that has significance beyond the moment. As the poet Ezra Pound said, "Literature is the news that *stays* news." To convey their views of experience, writers of imaginative literature frequently manipulate facts—change dates, invent characters, and create dialogue. For example, when the nineteenth-century American author Herman Melville wrote his novella *Benito Cereno,* he drew many of his facts from an eighteenth-century journal that gave an account of an actual slave revolt. In his story he reproduces court records and plot details from this primary source, but he leaves out many incidents that the original dwells on at length, and he adds material of his own. The result is an original work of literature with an emphasis that serves the author's purpose. Wanting to do more than tell the original story, Melville used the factual material as "a skeleton of actual reality" upon which to build a story that examines the nature of the truth.

Imaginative literature is more likely than other types of writing to include words chosen not only because they communicate the writer's ideas in a clear and straightforward manner, but also because they are memorable. Using vivid imagery and evocative comparisons, writers of imaginative literature strive to stretch language to its limits. By relying on the multiple connotations of words and images, a work of imaginative literature can evoke many possible meanings and interpretations. Thus imaginative literature encourages readers to see the possibilities of language and to move beyond the factual account of an event. Consider, for example, how William Wordsworth uses language in the following lines from his poem "Composed upon Westminster Bridge" (p. 396).

> This City now doth, like a garment, wear
> The beauty of the morning; silent, bare,
> Ships, towers, domes, theaters, and temples lie
> Open unto the fields, and to the sky;
> All bright and glittering in the smokeless air.

Notice that Wordsworth does not present a picture of London that is scientifically or sociologically accurate. By comparing the city at dawn to a person wearing a beautiful garment, Wordsworth creates a striking picture that has its own kind of truth, one that enables readers to participate in the speaker's imaginative experience. The city, traditionally the antithesis of nature, is "open unto the fields, and to the sky" and is therefore a part of nature. By using a strikingly original comparison, the poet is able to convey the unity of the city, nature, and himself—an idea that is not easily communicated.

Even though imaginative literature can be divided into types—fiction, poetry, and drama—called **genres,** the nature of these literary forms varies from culture to culture. In fact, some literary forms that readers in the West take very much for granted are quite alien to those familiar with other literary traditions. For example, the poetic forms of non-Western literature are quite different from those of Western Europe and North America. The sonnet, although quite common in the West, is not a conventional literary form in Chinese or Arabic poetry. Similarly, the most popular theatrical entertainment in Japan since the mid-seventeenth century, the kabuki play, does not follow many of the dramatic conventions Western audiences have come to expect and has no exact counterpart in the West. In a kabuki play, which includes stories, scenes, dances, music, acrobatics, and elaborate costumes and stage settings, all of the actors are men, some of whom play the parts of females. Many of the kabuki plays have little plot and seem to be primarily concerned with spectacle. One feature of this form of drama is a walkway that extends from the stage through the audience to the back of the theater.

Finally, conventions of narrative organization and character development can vary considerably, especially in literature descended from an oral tradition. For example, narrative organization in some Native American stories (and, even more commonly, in some African stories) can be very different from what modern readers are accustomed to. Events may be arranged spatially instead of chronologically: First a story presents all the events that happened in one place, then it presents everything that happened in another location, and so on. Character development is also much less important in some traditional African and Native American stories than in modern short fiction. In fact, a character's name, description, and personality can change dramatically (and without warning) in the course of a story.

Despite such differences, the imaginative literature of all cultures has similar effects on readers. A short story, a play, or a poem can arrest readers' attention and cause them to marvel. Lifelike characters, vivid descriptions, imaginative use of language, and intricately developed plots can fascinate and delight readers. Finally, literature can take readers where they have never been before and, in so doing, can create a sense of wonder and adventure.

At another level, however, readers find more than just pleasure or escape in literature. Beyond transporting readers out of their lives and times, literature can enable readers to see their lives and times more clearly. Whether a work of imaginative literature depicts the effect of a domineering father on his daughter, as in Sylvia Plath's poem "Daddy" (p. 170), or examines the effect of discrimination on a black African who is looking for an apartment, as in Wole Soyinka's poem "Telephone Conversation" (p. 6), it can enlighten readers and help them to understand their own experiences and the experiences of others. In this sense, literature offers readers increased insight and awareness. As the Chilean poet Pablo Neruda says, works of imaginative literature fulfill "the most ancient rites of our conscience in the awareness of being human and of believing in a common destiny."

CONVENTIONAL THEMES

The **theme** of a work of literature is its central or dominant idea. This idea is seldom stated explicitly; rather, it is conveyed through the selection and arrangement of details, through the emphasis of certain events or images, and through the actions and reactions of the characters.

Although one central theme may seem to dominate a literary work, most works explore a number of different themes or ideas. For example, the central theme of Mark Twain's *The Adventures of Huckleberry Finn* might be the idea that an individual's innate sense of right and wrong is superior to society's artificial and sometimes unnatural values. The main character, Huck, gains a growing awareness of this idea by witnessing feuds, duels, and all manner of human folly. As a result he makes a decision to help his friend Jim escape from slavery despite the fact that society, as well as his own conscience, condemns this action. However, *The Adventures of Huckleberry Finn* also examines other themes. Throughout his novel Twain criticizes many of the ideas that prevailed in the pre–Civil War South, such as the evils of slavery and the hypocrisy of the traditional religious values that dominated the towns along the Mississippi.

A literary work can explore any theme, but certain ideas occur so frequently that they have become conventions. These themes express ideas that have meaning to many individuals regardless of the time or place in which they live. One theme frequently explored in literature, a character's loss of innocence, appears in the biblical story of Adam and Eve and later finds its way into works such as Nathaniel Hawthorne's 1835 short story "Young Goodman Brown" and James Joyce's 1914 short story "Araby." Another conventional theme—the conflict between an individual's values and the values of society—is examined in the ancient Greek play *Antigone,* by Sophocles. Almost two thousand years later Norwegian playwright Henrik Ibsen deals with the same theme in *A Doll House*.

Other themes frequently examined in literary works include the individual's quest for spiritual enlightenment, the *carpe diem* ("seize the day") theme, the making of the artist, the nostalgia for a vanished past, the disillusionment of adulthood, the beauty of love, the subjugation of women, the conflict between parents and children, the clash between civilization and the wilderness, the evils of unchecked ambition, the inevitability of fate, the impact of the past on the present, the conflict between human beings and machines, and the tension between the ideal and the actual realms of experience. Modern works of literature sometimes treat such traditional themes in new ways. For example, in *1984* George Orwell explores the negative consequences of unchecked power by creating a nightmare world in which technology is used to control and dehumanize a population. Even though Orwell's novel is set in an imaginary future (it was written in 1948), its theme echoes ideas frequently examined in the plays of both Sophocles and Shakespeare.

Nearly every culture explores themes similar to those just mentioned, but writers from different cultures may develop these themes differently. A culture's history, a particular region's geography, or a country's social structure can suggest a unique way of developing a conventional theme. The assumptions, concerns, values, ideals, and beliefs of a particular country or society—or of a particular group within that society—can have an impact on the themes writers choose to explore and on the manner in which they do so.

Themes occurring repeatedly in North American literature include the loss of innocence, rites of passage, childhood epiphanies, coming to self-awareness, and the ability (or inability) to form relationships. American writers of color, in addition to exploring these themes, also develop themes that reflect their unique perspectives. African-American and Latino writers, for example, may express their frustration with the racism of the dominant society or celebrate their cultural identities. Even when they explore conventional themes, writers of color in North America may choose to do so in the context of their own experience. For example, the theme of loss of innocence may be presented as a first encounter with racial prejudice; a conflict between the individual and society may be presented as a conflict between a minority view and the values of the dominant group; and the theme of failure or aborted relationships may revolve around language difficulties or cultural misunderstandings.

THE LITERARY CANON

Originally the term *canon* referred to the authoritative or accepted list of books that made up the Christian Bible. The term was extended to include the **literary canon,** a group of works generally agreed upon by critics to be masterpieces. As standards change, the definition of what is "good" literature changes, and the canon is modified accordingly. For example, at different times Shakespeare's plays were thought by critics to be either mundane, immoral, commonplace, or brilliant. The eighteenth-century critic Samuel Johnson says of Shakespeare that "in his comick scenes he is seldom very successful" and in tragedy "his performance seems constantly to be worse, as his labor is more." Many people find it difficult to believe that a writer whose name today is synonymous with great literature could ever have been judged so harshly. But like all aesthetic works, the plays of Shakespeare affect individuals in different periods of history or in different societies in various ways.

In recent years, educators and literary scholars have charged that the traditional literary canon, like a restricted club, admits some authors and closes out all others. This fact is borne out, they say, by an examination of the literature curriculum that until recently was found at many North American colleges and universities. This curriculum typically began with Homer, Plato, Dante, and Chaucer, progressed to Shakespeare, Milton, the eighteenth-century novel, the Romantics, and the Victorians, and ended with some of the classics of modern British and American literature. Most of the writers of these works are white and male, and their writing reflects only their Western values. In educational institutions in other countries, the situation has been much the same: Students have typically studied works that reflect and reinforce their society's or their country's values.

In the United States during the past decade, critics of the traditional canon have sought to revise it to include more works by women, people of color, and writers from a variety of cultures. These additions are meant to open up the curriculum and redefine the standards by which literature is judged. For many years, literature courses in North American universities have overlooked South American, African, and Asian writers. Students of literature were not encouraged to consider the perspectives of women or of Latinos, Native Americans, or other ethnic or racial groups (let alone the perspectives of gay writers or those with disabilities). Now this situation is beginning to change. By revising and updating the list of works to be studied, critics of the traditional canon believe that we not only convey the diversity of both American and world cultures, but also expand the definition of great literature.

Consider the following poem by the Nigerian poet and playwright Wole Soyinka, a writer whose works are not yet part of the traditional European and American literary canon. The subject of his poem, which is rooted in a society that discriminates on the basis of shades of skin color, may not seem "relevant" to European audiences, and the language ("pillar-box," "omnibus") may not be clear to North Americans. Although such a poem probably would not be included in a traditional syllabus at many North American universities, it does have literary value.

Wole Soyinka
(1934–   )

TELEPHONE CONVERSATION
(1962)

The price seemed reasonable, location
Indifferent. The landlady swore she lived
Off premises. Nothing remained
But self-confession. "Madam," I warned
5 "I hate a wasted journey—I am—African."
Silence. Silenced transmission of
Pressurized good-breeding. Voice, when it came,
Lip-stick coated, long gold-rolled
Cigarette-holder pipped. Caught I was, foully.
10 "HOW DARK?" . . . I had not misheard . . .
 "ARE YOU LIGHT
OR VERY DARK?" Button B. Button A. Stench
Of rancid breath of public-hide-and-speak.
Red booth. Red pillar-box. Red double-tiered
15 Omnibus squelching tar. It *was* real! Shamed
By ill-mannered silence, surrender
Pushed dumbfoundment to beg simplification.
Considerate she was, varying the emphasis—
"ARE YOU DARK? OR VERY LIGHT?" Revelation came.
20 "You mean—like plain or milk chocolate?"
Her assent was clinical, crushing in its light,
Impersonality. Rapidly, wave-length adjusted,
I chose, "West African sepia"—and as an afterthought,
"Down in my passport." Silence for spectroscopic
25 Flight of fancy, till truthfulness clanged her accent
Hard on the mouthpiece. "WHAT'S THAT?" conceding
"DON'T KNOW WHAT THAT IS." "Like brunette."
"THAT'S DARK, ISN'T IT?" "Not altogether.
"Facially, I am brunette, but madam, you should see
30 The rest of me. Palm of my hand, soles of my feet
Are a peroxide blond. Friction, caused—
Foolishly madam—by sitting down, has turned
My bottom raven black—One moment madam!"—sensing
Her receiver rearing on the thunder clap
35 About my ears—"Madam," I pleaded, "Wouldn't you rather
See for yourself?"

Certainly canon revision is not without its problems. Some critics point out that inherent in canon revision is the danger of including a work more for political reasons than for literary merit. Nevertheless, if the debate about the literary canon has accomplished anything, it has revealed that the canon is not fixed and that many works formerly excluded from the canon—African-American slave narratives and eighteenth-century women's diaries, for example—deserve to be included.

This is an exciting time in literary studies, and as the debate about the canon continues, new questions and new answers will continue to emerge. Some of the works included in this anthology are considered part of the traditional canon, and others reflect the diversity of the expanding literary canon.

THINKING CRITICALLY

INTERPRETING LITERATURE

When you *interpret* a literary work, you attempt to understand its various meanings. One commonly held idea about reading a literary work is that its meaning lies buried somewhere within it, waiting to be unearthed. This reasoning suggests that a clever reader has only to discover the author's intent to find out what a story or poem means. The one actual meaning of a work is, therefore, hidden between the lines, unaffected by a reader's experiences or interpretations. More recently, however, a different model of the reading process—one that takes into consideration the reader as well as the work he or she is interpreting—has emerged.

Many contemporary critics recognize that the reading process is *interactive:* Meaning comes about through the interaction between a reader and a text. The meaning of a particular work comes alive in the imagination of an individual reader, and no reader can determine a work's meaning without considering his or her reaction to the text. Meaning, therefore, is created partly by what is supplied by a work and partly by what is supplied by the reader.

The most obvious kind of meaning a work supplies is factual, the information that enables a reader to follow the plot of a story, the action of a play, or the development of a poem. For instance, the work itself will provide some factual details about the setting; the characters' names, ages, and appearances; the sequence of events; and the emotions and attitudes of a poem's speaker, a story's narrator, or the characters in a play or story. This factual information cannot be ignored: If a play's stage directions identify its setting as nineteenth-century Norway or the forest of Arden, that is where it is set.

In addition to facts, a work also conveys the social, political, class, and gender attitudes of the writer. Thus a work may have an overtly feminist or class bias or a subtle political agenda; it may confirm or challenge contemporary attitudes; it may communicate a writer's nostalgia for a vanished past or his or her outrage at a corrupt present; it may take an elitist, distant view of characters and events or present a sympathetic, involved perspective. A reader's understanding of these attitudes will contribute to his or her interpretation of the work.

Finally, a work also contains assumptions about literary conventions. A poet, for example, may have definite ideas about whether a poem should be rhymed or unrhymed or about whether a particular subject is appropriate for poetic treatment. A knowledge of the literary conventions of a particular period or the preferences of a particular writer may provide a starting point for your interpretation of literature.

As a reader you also bring to a work your own personal perspectives. Your experiences, your ideas about the issues discussed in the work, and your assumptions about literature color your interpretations; so do your religious, social, and cultural beliefs. In fact, virtually every literary work means different things to different people, depending on their age, gender, nationality, political and religious beliefs, ethnic background, social and economic class, education, knowledge, and experiences. Depending on your religious beliefs, for instance, you can react to a passage from the Old Testament as literal truth, symbolic truth, or fiction. Depending on your race, where you live, your biases, and the nature of your experience, a story about racial discrimination can strike you as accurate and realistic, exaggerated for dramatic effect, or understated and restrained.

In a real sense, then, the process of determining meaning is like a conversation, one in which both you and the text have a voice. Sometimes, by clearly dictating the terms of the discussion, the text determines the direction of the conversation; at other times, by using your knowledge and experience to interpret the text, you dominate. Because every reading of a literary work is actually an interpretation, it is a mistake to look for a single "correct" reading of a text.

The 1923 poem "Stopping by Woods on a Snowy Evening" (p. 315) by the American poet Robert Frost illustrates the flexibility of the process of interpretation. Readers may interpret the poem as being about the inevitability of death; as suggesting that the poet is tired or world weary; or as making a comment about duty and the need to persevere, or about the conflicting pulls of life and art. Beyond these possibilities, readers' own associations of snow with quiet and sadness could lead them to define the mood of the poem as sorrowful or melancholy. Information about Robert Frost's life or his ideas about poetry could add to readers' appreciation of the poem, and they might even develop ideas about the poem that are quite different from the poet's. In fact, on several occasions when he spoke about "Stopping by Woods on a Snowy Evening," Frost himself gave strikingly different, even contradictory, interpretations of the poem, sometimes insisting the poem had no hidden meaning and at other times saying that it required a good deal of explication. Literary critics also disagree about its meaning. When reading a work of literature, then, keep in mind that the meaning of the text is not fixed. Your best strategy is to open yourself up to the text's many possibilities and to explore the full range of your responses.

Although no single reading of a literary work is "correct," some readings are more plausible than others. Like a scientific theory, a literary interpretation must have a basis in fact, and the text supplies the facts against which your interpretations should be judged. For example, after reading Shirley Jackson's "The Lottery," a 1948 short story in which a randomly chosen victim is stoned to death by her neighbors, you could reasonably conclude that the ceremonial aspects of the lottery suggest a contemporary pagan ritual. Your understanding of what a pagan ritual is, combined with your observation that a number of specific details in the text suggest ancient fertility ceremonies, might lead you to this conclusion. Another possibility is that "The Lottery" provides a commentary on mob psychology. The way characters reinforce one another's violent tendencies lends support to this interpretation. However, the interpretation that the ritual of the lottery is a comment on the death penalty would be difficult to support. Certainly a character in the story is killed, but she is not accused of a crime, nor is she tried or convicted. The killing is random and seemingly without motivation. Still, although seeing the "The Lottery" as an endorsement of the death penalty may be far-fetched, this interpretation is a good beginning. A second, closer reading of the story will most likely lead you in different directions, allowing you to explore other, more plausible, interpretations.

As you read, do not be afraid to take chances and present unusual or creative interpretations of a work. "Safe" readings of a work often result in dull papers that simply state the obvious. An aggressive or "strong" reading of a work, however, can raise issues that lead to interesting and intellectually challenging conclusions. Even if your reading differs from established interpretations of a work, you should not assume it has no merit. Your special knowledge of the material discussed in the text—a regional practice, an ethnic custom, an attitude toward gender—may give you a unique perspective from which to view the work. Whatever interpretation you make, be sure that you justify it by supporting your assertions with specific references to the text. If your interpretation is based on your own experiences, explain those experiences and relate them clearly to the work you are discussing. As long as you can make a reasonable case, you have the right (and perhaps the obligation) to present your ideas. By doing so you may provide your fellow students and your instructor with a reading that gives them new insight into the work.

It is important to keep in mind, however, that some interpretations are *not* reasonable. Readers may contribute ideas based on their own perspectives, but they cannot ignore or contradict evidence in the text to suit their own biases. As you read and reread a text, continue to question and reexamine your judgments. The conversation between reader and text should be a dialogue, not a monologue or a shouting match.

EVALUATING LITERATURE

When you *evaluate* a work of literature, you do more than interpret it; you make a judgment about it. You reach conclusions concerning the work—not simply that the work is good or bad, but also how effectively the work presents itself to you, the reader. To evaluate a work, you *analyze* it, breaking it apart and considering its individual elements. As you evaluate a work of literature, remember that different works are designed to fulfill different needs—for entertainment, education, enlightenment, and so on. When you begin to evaluate a work, make certain that you determine its purpose and apply reasonable standards. Consider the following guidelines:

Begin your evaluation by considering how various elements function individually within a work. For instance, fiction may use dialogue and symbols. Plays are divided into scenes and acts and employ dialogue and special staging techniques. Poems may be arranged in regularly ordered groups of lines and use poetic devices such as rhyme and meter. Understanding the choices writers make can lead you to new insights and can help you make judgments about the work. For example, why does a short story writer use a first-person narrator? Would the story have been different had it been told in the third person by a narrator who is not a participant in the action? How does unusual staging contribute to the effect achieved in a play? Would a realistic setting change the work? How would an unusual stanzaic form such as the one in E. E. Cummings's poem "Buffalo Bill's" affect your reactions to the work? Naturally, you cannot and should not focus on every aspect of a particular story, poem, or play. But you can and should focus on those that play a major role in determining your responses to a work.

As you read, ask yourself some questions. Do the characters in a short story seem real, or do they seem like cardboard cutouts? Are the stage directions of a play clear or ambiguous? Are the images in a poem original and thought-provoking, or are they clichéd?

As you continue your evaluation, decide whether or not the literary elements of a work interact to achieve a common goal. Well-crafted literary works are aesthetically pleasing, fitting together in a way that conceals the craft of the writer. Good writers are like master cabinetmakers; their skill makes it possible for them to disguise the actual work that goes into the process of creation. Consider the following stanza from the 1862 poem "Echo" by Christina Rosetti:

> Come to me in the silence of the night;
>   Come to me in the speaking silence of a dream;
> Come with soft round cheeks and eyes as bright
>   As sunlight on a stream;
>   Come back in tears,
> O memory, hope, love of finished years.

Throughout this stanza Rossetti repeats words (Come to me. . . . /Come with soft. . . . /Come back. . . .) and initial consonants (speaking silence/sunlight on a stream) to create an almost hypnotic mood. The rhyme scheme is so subtle that it is hardly noticeable. Even so, the rhymes (*night/bright, dream/stream,* and *tears/years*) reinforce the mood by creating a musical undercurrent that extends throughout the poem. This stanza is effective because its sounds and rhyme scheme work together to create a single lyrical effect.

The chorus in *Antigone* by Sophocles also illustrates how the elements of a well-crafted work of literature function together. In ancient Greece plays were performed by masked male actors who played various roles—both male and female. A chorus of fifteen men would remain in a central circle called the *orchestra* and comment on and react to the action taking place around them. Along with the dialogue, characterization, and staging, the chorus contributes to the total effect of *Antigone.* It not only expresses the moral judgment of the community, but it also acts as a guide for the audience. Once modern audiences become accustomed to the presence of the chorus, it becomes an integral part of the play. It neither distracts the audience nor intrudes upon the action. In fact, eliminating the chorus would diminish the impact of the play.

Next, consider whether a work reinforces or calls into question your ideas about the world. The 1985 short story "Gryphon" by Charles Baxter is one that may lead readers to question their assumptions. It presents a boy in a rural town whose sick teacher is replaced by an eccentric substitute. In her idiosyncratic, even exotic, way, the substitute introduces the boy to a whole new range of intellectual possibilities. Because we, like the children in the story, have learned to expect substitute teachers to be dull and conventional, the story challenges our basic assumptions about substitute teachers and, by extension, about education itself.

Works of popular fiction—those aimed at a mass audience—usually do little more than reassure readers that what they believe is correct. Catering to people's prejudices, or to their desires (for wealth or success, for example), or to their fears, these works serve as escapes from life. Serious fiction, however, goes against the grain, challenging cherished beliefs and leading readers to reexamine long-held assumptions. In James Alan McPherson's 1977 short story "A Loaf of Bread," the protagonist, a white grocer, struggles with the conflict between his desire to fight the black customers who are protesting his high prices and his wife's view that he should settle the conflict by giving all his merchandise to his customers. His reluctance to follow his wife's advice underscores his conflict with the values of those who live in the neighborhood near his store. Serious literature provokes readers to confront and question their values and beliefs, just as the grocer does.

Then, consider whether or not a work is intellectually challenging. The extended comparison between a compass and two people in love in "A Valediction: Forbidding Mourning" by the seventeenth-century English poet John Donne (p. 168) illustrates how an intellectually challenging image can communicate ideas to a reader. Compressed into the comparison are ideas about the perfection of love, the pain of enforced separation, and the difference between sexual and spiritual love. As complex as the extended comparison is, it is nonetheless accessible to the careful reader. After all, many people have used a compass to draw a circle and, therefore, are able to understand the relationship between the two points of the compass and the two lovers.

A fine line exists, however, between works that are intellectually challenging and those that are intellectually obscure. An *intellectually challenging work* makes readers think; it requires some effort on the readers' part to unlock ideas that enrich and expand their understanding of themselves and the world. Although it is complex, the work gives readers a sense that they have gained something by putting forth the effort to read and interpret it. An *intellectually obscure work,* however, seems to exist solely to display a writer's erudition or intellectual idiosyncrasies. In such works allusions to other works and events are so numerous and arcane that the work seems more like a private code than an effort to communicate with or enlighten readers. Consider the following excerpt from "Canto LXXVI" by the twentieth-century American poet Ezra Pound:

  Le Paradis n'est pas artificiel
    States of mind are inexplicable to us.
   δακρυων δακρυων δακρυων
L. P. gli onesti
    J'ai eu pitié des autres
probablement pas assez, and at moments that suited my own
   convenience
     Le paradis n'est pas artificiel,
      l'enfer non plus.
Came Eurus as comforter
and at sunset la pastorella dei suini
   driving the pigs home, benecomata dea
     under the two-winged cloud
      as of less and more than a day

This segment contains lines in French, Greek, and Italian; a reference to Eurus, the ancient Greek personification of the east wind; and the initials L.P. (Loomis Pound?). Admittedly this passage demands a lot from readers; the question is whether the reward is worth the effort. No hard and fast rule exists for determining whether a work is intellectually challenging or simply obscure. Just as a poem has no fixed meaning, it also has no fixed value. Some readers would say that the passage is good, even great, poetry. Others might argue that these lines do not yield enough pleasure and insight to justify the work needed to analyze them. As a careful reader, you must draw your own conclusions and justify them in a clear and reasonable way. Do not assume that just because a work is difficult, it is obscure. (Nor should you assume that all difficult works are great literature or that all accessible literature is trivial.) Some of the most beautiful and inspiring literary works demand a great deal of effort from readers. Most readers would agree, however, that the time spent exploring such works yields tremendous rewards.

Finally, and perhaps most importantly, consider whether a work gives you pleasure. One of the primary reasons that literature endures is that it gives readers enjoyment. As subjective as this assessment is, it is a starting point for critical judgment. When readers ask themselves what they liked about a work, why they liked it, or what they learned, they begin the process of evaluation. Although this process is largely uncritical, it can lead to an involvement with the work and to a critical response. When you encounter great literature, with all its complexities, you may lose sight of the idea of literature as a source of pleasure. But literature should touch you on a deep emotional or intellectual level, and if it does not—despite its technical perfection—it has failed to achieve one of its primary aims.

THE FUNCTION OF LITERARY CRITICISM

Sometimes your personal reactions and knowledge cannot give you enough insight into a literary work. For example, archaic language, obscure references, historical allusions, and textual inconsistencies can make reading a work particularly difficult. Similarly, an intellectual or philosophical movement such as Darwinism, Marxism, naturalism, structuralism, or feminism may influence a work, and if this is the case, you will need some knowledge of the movement before you can interpret the work (see Appendix C, Twentieth-Century Literary Theories). In addition, you may not have the background to appreciate the technical or historical dimension of a work. To widen the context of your reading, you may choose to read **literary criticism**—books and journal articles written by experts who describe, analyze, interpret, or evaluate a work of literature. Reading literary criticism not only enables you to expand your knowledge of a particular work, but also allows you to participate in the public dialogue about literature. In a sense you become part of a community of scholars who share their ideas and who are connected to one another through their writing.

Just because literary criticism is written by experts, do not assume you must accept it automatically. You have to evaluate literary criticism just as you do any new opinion that you encounter. Not all criticism is valid, timely, or responsible, and not all literary criticism is pertinent to your assignment or useful for your purposes. Some critical comments will strike you as plausible, but others will seem unfounded or biased. Quite often two critics will reach strikingly different conclusions about the skill or importance of the same work or writer, or interpret a character, a symbol, or even the entire work quite differently. The Poetry Casebook that closes this text contains articles in which critics disagree in just this fashion. One critic, for example, sees Gwendolyn Brooks primarily as a sonneteer, while another says her most important poems are ballads. Still another critic challenges Brooks's own assertion that before 1967 she did not write any poems that sufficiently reflected her blackness.

As you can see, critics may disagree, but even conflicting ideas can help you to reach your own conclusions about a work. It is up to you to sort out the various opinions and decide which have merit and which do not. The following questions can help you to evaluate literary criticism:

- What is the main point of the critical article you are reading?
- Does the critic supply enough examples to support his or her conclusions?
- Does the critic acknowledge and refute the most obvious arguments against his or her position?
- Does the critic ignore any information in the text that might call his or her conclusions into question?
- Does the critic present historical information? Biographical information? Literary information? How does this information shed light on significant aspects of the work or works being discussed?
- Does the critic exhibit any prejudices or beliefs that might interfere with his or her critical judgment?
- Does the critic slant the facts, or does he or she offer a fair and objective reading of the text?
- Does the critical book or article support its assertions with documentation? Does it contain a list of works cited? Are these works current? Are explanatory notes included where necessary?
- Do other critical works mention the book or article you are reading? What do they say about its conclusions?

With your instructor's help, you might also try to answer these questions:

- Does the critic identify with a particular critical school of thought—deconstruction, Marxism, or feminism, for example? What unique perspective does this school of thought provide?
- Is the critic well known and respected or unknown?
- Does the critic take into consideration the most important critical books and articles on his or her subject? Are there works that should have been mentioned that were not? Do these gaps cast doubts on the critic's conclusions?
- Is the critical work's publication date of any significance?

CHAPTER 2

READING AND WRITING ABOUT LITERATURE

READING LITERATURE

The process of writing about literature actually starts the moment you begin to read. At that point you begin interacting with a work and start to discover ideas about the text. As soon as you decide to write about a work, you should start recording your reactions to it. These reactions will not only help you to interpret the material, but they will also enable you to organize your ideas into a clear and logical paper.

Three strategies in particular will help you to become a more effective reader: *previewing, highlighting,* and *annotating*. As you engage in these activities, remember that the process of reading and responding to what you read is not an orderly or a sequential one. You will most likely find yourself simultaneously engaging in more than one of the strategies described here—annotating at the same time you highlight, for example. For the sake of clarity, however, we discuss each strategy separately in the pages that follow.

PREVIEWING

The first time you encounter a text you should **preview** it to get a general sense of what to look for later, when you read it more carefully. At this stage you simply want to glance through the work, looking for physical characteristics that can help you to identify some of its most noteworthy features.

These physical characteristics, which can call attention to a stylistic, structural, or even a thematic feature of a work, are often fairly easy to identify. For example, a glance is enough to identify a play's cast of characters or to show a short story's brevity. Literary texts also exhibit a wide variety of experiments with form. For example, a contemporary short story may be presented entirely in a question and answer format, it may be organized as diary entries, or it may be divided into sections by headings. Previewing may identify poems that seem to lack formal structure, such as E. E. Cummings's unconventional "l(a" (p. 39); those written in traditional forms (such as sonnets), or in experimental forms, such as the numbered list of questions and answers in Denise

Levertov's "What Were They Like?" (p. 340); or concrete poems such as George Herbert's "Easter Wings" (p. 244).

Other physical characteristics—such as the breaks between sections of stories, stanzas of poems, chapters of books, and acts and scenes of plays—are also easy to identify. Perhaps the most physically distinctive element of a text is its title. Not only can the title give you an idea what a work is about, but it can also introduce a word or phrase that is central to the work, or it can be a symbol or an allusion to another work. For example, the title of a James Joyce story called "Counterparts" places emphasis on the corresponding roles played by the central characters, and *The Sound and the Fury,* the title of a novel by William Faulkner, alludes to a speech from Shakespeare's *Macbeth* that reinforces the major theme of the novel.

Other, more subtle, physical elements—such as paragraphing, capitalization, italics, and punctuation—can also provide clues about how to read a work. In William Faulkner's 1939 short story "Barn Burning," for instance, previewing would reveal passages in italic type, indicating the protagonist's thoughts, which occasionally interrupt the narrator's story.

Previewing is a useful strategy because it suggests questions to ask later as you read more closely—for instance, *why* does Faulkner use italics in "Barn Burning"? Remember, however, that although physical elements such as those described above may be noticeable even as you preview, they are likely to be more obvious as you read more carefully and review your notes.

HIGHLIGHTING

When you go on to read a work closely, you notice stylistic features, thematic patterns, and other elements that you may want to examine further. At this point, you should begin **highlighting**—physically marking the text to identify key points and to note relationships among ideas.

What should you highlight? As you read, ask yourself whether repeated words or phrases form a pattern. Repeated words and phrases are particularly important in poetry. In Dylan Thomas's "Do Not Go Gentle into That Good Night" (p. 47), for example, the repetition of two of the poem's nineteen lines four times each enhances the effect of the poem's rhythmic, almost monotonous, cadence. As you read, then, you should highlight your text to identify such repeated words and phrases.

You should also pay particular attention at this stage to images that occur repeatedly in a work; such repeated images may form patterns that can help you to interpret the work, and for this reason they should be highlighted. During the previewing stage, you may have been able only to identify repeated images. When you reread the work, however, you can begin to determine the pattern the images form and perhaps try to decide how this pattern enhances the work's ideas. When previewing Robert Frost's "Stopping By Woods on a Snowy Evening" (p. 315), for instance, you might simply have made a mental note of the poem's related images of silence, cold, and darkness. Now you can highlight those images so that later you can consider their significance.

When you highlight, you emphasize portions of the text with a system of symbols. As you become experienced with the techniques of active reading, you will develop the system of shorthand that works best for you. For the time being, however, you can experiment with the symbols listed here:

- <u>Underline</u> important ideas that you should read again.
- Box or circle repeated words, phrases, or images.
- Question (?) confusing segments, unfamiliar references, or words that need to be defined.
- Draw lines or arrows to connect related ideas or images.
- Number incidents that occur in sequence.
- Set off a long portion of the text with a vertical line in the margin.
- Star (*) a particularly important idea.

The following poem by Maya Angelou has been highlighted by a student preparing to write about it. Notice how the student uses symbols to help him identify stylistic features, key points, and patterns of repetition that he may want to examine later.

This student identifies repeated words and phases ("brooding"; "it writhes") and places question marks beside the two words ("pend" and "rent") whose meanings he plans to look up in a dictionary. He also questions the possible meanings of "old crimes" and "ante-bellum lace," two references he needs to think more about. Finally, he stars what he tentatively identifies as the poem's key ideas. When he rereads the poem, his highlighting will make it easier for him to react to and interpret the writer's ideas.

18 Reading and Writing about Literature

Maya Angelou
(1928–   )

MY ARKANSAS
(1978)

There is a deep brooding
in Arkansas.
Old crimes like moss pend
from poplar trees.
5   The sullen earth
is much too
red for comfort.

Sunrise seems to hesitate
and in that second
10 lose its
incandescent aim, and
dusk no more shadows
than the noon.
The past is brighter yet.

15 Old hates and
ante-bellum lace are rent
but not discarded.
Today is yet to come
in Arkansas.
20 It writhes. It writhes in awful
waves of brooding.

ANNOTATING

At the same time you highlight a text, you also **annotate,** making marginal notes on the page. By engaging in this activity, you record your reactions and perhaps begin to map out a preliminary plan for your paper. Your notes may define new words, identify allusions, identify patterns of language or imagery, summarize complex plot relationships, list a work's possible themes, suggest the motivations of certain characters, or examine the possible significance of particular images or symbols. You may also use annotations to record questions that occur to you as you read. Many works contain unresolved issues that you must try to explain. For example, what motivates Sammy to quit his job at the end of John Updike's 1961 short story "A&P"? The following paragraph from "A&P" was highlighted and annotated by a student in an introduction to literature course who was writing an essay in response to this question:

Lengel sighs and begins to look very patient and old and gray. He's been a friend of my parents for years. "Sammy,

[Annotations in margins:]
Action does not seem to be the result of thought.
Sammy reacts to the girls' embarrassment
need for a clean exit — reinforce immature romantic ideas

you don't want to do this to your Mom and Dad," he tells me. It's true, I don't. <u>But it seems to me that once you begin a gesture it's fatal not to go through with it.</u> I fold the apron, "Sammy" stitched in red on the pocket, and put it on the counter, and drop the bow tie on top of it. The bow tie is theirs, if you've ever wondered. <u>"You'll feel this for the rest of your life," Lengel says, and I know that's true, too, but remembering how he made the pretty girl blush makes me so scrunchy inside I punch the No Sale tab and the machine whirs "pee-pul" and the drawer splats out.</u> One advantage to this scene taking place in summer, I can follow this up with a clean exit, there's no fumbling around getting your coat and galoshes, I just <u>saunter</u> into the electric eye in <u>my white shirt that my mother ironed the night before,</u> and the door heaves itself open, and outside the sunshine is skating around on the asphalt.

[Annotation: Cowboy — John Wayne]
[Annotation: Romantic cowboy, but his mother irons his shirt. Irony.]

Because the student's instructor had discussed the story in class and because the student had a specific assignment—to explain Sammy's actions at the end of the story—her annotations are quite focused. In addition to highlighting important information in this paragraph, she notes her reactions to the story and tries to interpret Sammy's actions. Sometimes, however, you may annotate before you have decided on a topic—in fact, the process of reading and responding to your text can help you to focus on a topic. In the absence of a topic, your annotations are likely to be less focused, and you will need to highlight and annotate again when your paper's direction is more firmly fixed in your mind.

WRITING ABOUT LITERATURE

Writing about literature—or about anything else, for that matter—is an idiosyncratic process during which many activities occur at once: As you write, you think of ideas; as you think of ideas, you clarify the focus of your essay; and as you clarify your focus, you reshape your paragraphs and sentences and refine your word choice. Even though this process sounds chaotic, it may be described as having three stages: *planning, drafting,* and *revising and editing.* Remember, however, that although for the sake of clarity we discuss these stages separately, they actually overlap.

PLANNING AN ESSAY

Considering Your Audience

Sometimes—for example, in a journal entry—you write primarily for yourself. At other times, however, you write for an **audience.** As you write an essay, you should consider the special requirements of that audience. Is your audience your classmates or your instructor? Can you assume your readers are familiar with your paper's topic and with any technical terms you will use, or will they need brief plot summaries or definitions of key terms? If your audience is your instructor, remember that he or she is a representative of a larger academic audience and therefore expects accurate information; standard English; correct grammar, mechanics, and spelling; logical arguments; and a certain degree of stylistic fluency. In addition, your instructor expects you to support your assertions with specific information, to express yourself clearly and explicitly, and to document your sources. In short, your instructor wants to see how well you think and whether you are able to arrange your ideas into a well-organized, coherent essay.

In addition to being a member of a general academic audience, your instructor is also a member of a particular community of scholars—in this case, those who study literature. By writing about literature, you engage in a dialogue with this community. For this reason, you should adhere to the specific *conventions*—procedures that by habitual use have become accepted practice—its members follow. Many of the conventions that apply specifically to writing about literature—matters of style, format, and the like—will be discussed in this book.

Understanding Your Purpose

In addition to considering your audience, you need to consider your **purpose** (or purposes) for writing. Sometimes you write with a single purpose in mind; at other times a single assignment or writing task may suggest more than one purpose. In general terms, you may write for any of the following reasons:

Writing to Respond When you write to *respond*, your goal is to discover and express your reactions to a work. To record your responses you engage in relatively informal, personal activities, such as brainstorming, listing, and journal writing (see pp. 22–23). As you write you explore your own ideas, forming and reforming your impressions of the work.

Writing to Interpret When you write to *interpret*, you explain a work's possible meanings. To do so, you may summarize, identify examples, or compare and contrast the work to other works or to your own experiences. Then, you may go on to analyze the work, studying each of its elements in turn, putting complex statements in your own words, defining difficult concepts, or placing ideas in context.

Writing to Evaluate When you write to *evaluate*, your purpose is to assess a work's literary merits. You may consider not only its aesthetic appeal, but also its ability to retain that appeal over time and across national or cultural boundaries. As you write, you use your own critical sense and the opinions of experts in the field to help you make judgments about the work.

Choosing a Topic

When you write an essay about literature, you develop an idea about a literary work or works—an analysis of the point of view of a story, a discussion of the theme of a poem, an examination of a character in a play, or a comparison between two works, for example. Before you begin your writing, you should make certain that you understand your assignment. Do you know how much time you have to complete your essay? Are you expected to rely on your own ideas, or are you able to consult journal articles in the library? Is your essay to focus on a specific work or on a particular element of literature? Do you have to write on an assigned topic, or are you free to choose a topic? About how long should your essay be? Do you understand exactly what the assignment is asking you to do?

Sometimes your assignment limits your options by telling you what you are to discuss:

- Write an essay in which you analyze Robert Frost's use of the color white in his poem "Design."
- Discuss Hawthorne's use of allegory in his short story "Young Goodman Brown."
- Write a short essay in which you explain Nora's actions at the end of Ibsen's *A Doll House*.

Sometimes, however, your instructor will give you no specific guidelines other than a paper's length and format. In such situations, where you must choose a topic on your own, you can find a topic by brainstorming or by writing journal entries. As you engage in these activities, however, keep in mind that you have many options for writing papers about literature. Some of these options are listed here.

- Compare two works of literature.
- Compare two characters or some attribute of those characters.
- Trace a common theme—jealousy, revenge, repression, coming of age—in several works.
- Consider how a common subject—war, love, nature—is treated in several works.
- Examine a single element in one or more works—for instance, plot, point of view, or figurative language.
- Focus on a single aspect of that element, such as the role of flashbacks, the effect of a shifting narrative perspective, or the use of metaphor.
- Apply a critical theory to a work of literature—for instance, apply a feminist perspective to Anne Sexton's "Cinderella."
- Examine connections between an issue treated in a work of literature—for instance, academic pressure in Janice Mirikitani's "Suicide Note"—and that same issue as it is treated in sociological or psychological journals or in the popular press.
- Examine some aspect of history or biography and consider its impact on a literary work—for instance, the influence of his World War I experiences on Wilfred Owen's poems.

- Explore a problem within a work and propose a possible solution—for example, what is the narrator's true reason for killing Porphyria in Robert Browning's poem "Porphyria's Lover"?

Any of the options above may lead you to an interesting topic. Remember, however, that you will still have to narrow the scope of your topic so that it fits within the limits of your assignment.

Finding Something to Say

Once you have a topic, you have to find something to say about it. The information that you collected when you highlighted and annotated will help you to formulate the statement that will be the central idea of your essay and lead you to ideas that can support that statement.

A number of strategies can help you to find supporting material:

- You can discuss ideas with others—friends, classmates, instructors, or parents, for example.
- You can ask questions.
- You can do research.
- You can **freewrite**—that is, keep writing on your topic for a given period of time without pausing to consider style, structure, or content.

Three other strategies—*brainstorming, keeping a journal,* and *listing*—are especially helpful.

Brainstorming When you **brainstorm,** you jot down ideas—single words, phrases, or sentences; statements or questions; quotations, paraphrases, summaries, or your own ideas—as they occur to you, moving as quickly as possible. Your starting point may be a general assignment, a particular work (or works) of literature, a specific topic, or even a thesis statement; in fact, you can brainstorm at any stage of the writing process, and you can repeat this activity as often as you like.

The brainstorming notes that follow were made by a student preparing to write a paper on the relationships between children and parents in four poems. She began by brainstorming about each poem in turn and went on to consider thematic relationships among the poems. These notes represent her preliminary reactions to one of the four poems she planned to study, Adrienne Rich's 1984 poem "A Woman Mourned by Daughters" (p. 42).

Brainstorming Notes

(Memory:) then and now
    Then: leaf, straw, dead insect (= light); ignored
    Now: swollen, puffed up, weight (= heavy); focus of attention.
        controls their movements.

*Kitchen = a "universe"
    Teaspoons, goblets, etc. = concrete representations of
mother;
        also = obligations, responsibilities (like plants and
father)
    → (weigh on them, keep
        them under her spell)
Milestones of past: weddings, being fed as children
"You breathe upon us now"
    PARADOX? (Dead, she breathes, has weight, fills house and sky. Alive, she was a dead insect, no one paid attention to her.)

Keeping a Journal You can use a journal to find ideas—and, later, to help you to find a topic or a thesis. In a **journal** you expand your marginal annotations and go on to record your responses to works you have read, note questions, explore emerging ideas, experiment with possible paper topics, try to paraphrase or summarize difficult concepts, or speculate about a work's ambiguities. A journal is the place to take chances, to try out ideas that may seem frivolous or irrelevant; here you can think on paper until connections become clear or ideas crystallize. You can also use your journal as a convenient place to collect your brainstorming notes and, later, your lists of related ideas.

As he prepared to write a paper analyzing the role of Jim, the "gentleman caller" in Tennessee Williams's play *The Glass Menagerie*, a student explored ideas in the following journal entry:

> When he tells Laura that being disappointed is not the same as being discouraged, and that he's disappointed but not discouraged, Jim reveals his role as a symbol of the power of newness and change—a "bulldozer" that will clear out whatever is in its path, even delicate people like Laura. But the fact that he is disappointed shows Jim's human side. He has run into problems since high school, and these problems have blocked his progress toward a successful future. Working at the warehouse, Jim needs Tom's friendship to remind him of what he used to be (and what he still can be?), and this shows his insecurity. He isn't as sure of himself as he seems to be.

This journal entry reflects the student's initial response to a character; it is personal and subjective. Even so, these preliminary explorations can eventually help him to decide on a specific direction for his essay.

Listing After you have actively read a work, you should have a good many underlinings and marginal notes. Some of this material will relate to your topic, and some will be irrelevant. **Listing** is the process of examining the notes you collected through brainstorming, keeping a journal, and annotating your text; deciding what material is pertinent; and arranging that material into categories so that you can determine a direction for your essay. As you prepare to list, review your information and consider the categories your notes suggest. Then, after writing down these categories, list specific information under each heading. As you list information, you will discover new ideas and new connections among ideas. Listing enables you to discover patterns: to see repeated images, similar characters, recurring words and phrases, and interrelated themes or ideas. Identifying these patterns helps you to decide which points to make in your paper and what information you will use to support these points. Remember that the lists you make do not yet reflect the order or emphasis of the ideas you will develop in your paper. As your ideas become more focused, you will add, delete, and rearrange material.

After reading Lorrie Moore's experimental short story "How to Talk to Your Mother (Notes)," a student arranged material from her annotations, brainstorming notes, and journal entries into the following lists of related details. Her topic was the relationship between the details of the narrator's personal life and the events of the larger world. This topic suggested categories under which she could arrange her material.

PERSONAL/COMMONPLACE
    Details of day-to-day life
        Laundromat
        Apple crisp
        Dishwasher
        Meals
        Party
        Funeral
    Babies
        Abortions
        Kids on public transportation
        Stretch marks
        Doll ("the Sue")
        Brother's children
WORLD
    Songs
        "You'll Never Walk Alone"
        "Oklahoma!"
        "Three Little Fishies"
        "Shoofly Pie"
    Historical Events
        Dead Sea Scrolls discovered
        Elections
        Germany invades Poland
        Bicentennial
        Grandma Moses dies
        Kennedy is shot

<u>Scientific/Medical Events</u>
   Polyurethane heart
   Temporary artificial heart
   Moon landing

Deciding on a Thesis

After completing your listing, you should try to express the direction of your thinking in a tentative **thesis**—a statement, often expressed in a single sentence, that the rest of your essay supports. This idea, which you will develop as you write, should emerge out of your highlighting, annotations, brainstorming notes, journal entries, and lists of related points. (In many cases, in fact, you will decide on a tentative thesis at an earlier stage of the writing process.)

An effective thesis tells readers what your essay will discuss and how you will approach your material. Consequently, it should be precisely worded, making its point clear to your readers. It should contain no vague words or inexact diction that will make it difficult for readers to follow your discussion. Although the statement "The use of sound in Tennyson's poem 'The Eagle' is interesting" is accurate, it does not convey any clear idea to your readers because the words *sound* and *interesting* are not specific enough. An effective thesis might be "Unity in 'The Eagle' is achieved by Tennyson's use of alliteration, assonance, and rhyme throughout the poem." In addition to being specific, your thesis should give your readers an accurate sense of the scope and direction of your essay. It should not make promises that you do not intend to fulfill or contain extraneous details that might confuse your readers. If, for example, you are going to write a paper about the dominant image in a poem, your thesis should not imply that you will focus on setting or tone.

Remember that as you organize your ideas and as you write, you will probably modify and sharpen your tentative thesis. Sometimes you will even begin your essay with one idea about a work and end it with an entirely different idea. If this happens, be sure to revise your support paragraphs so that they are consistent with your changes and so that the points you include support your new thesis. If you find that your thoughts about your topic are changing, remember that this is how the writing process works. As you write you will discover new ideas, and your essay will be stronger as a result.

Preparing an Outline

Once you have decided on a tentative thesis and have some idea of how you will support it, you can begin to plan your essay's structure. Quite often, an outline can help you to shape your essay. Not all writers outline, but many do at some point in the writing process because it helps them to clarify their ideas and the relationship of these ideas to one another. Realizing, however, that they will discover many new ideas as they write, even these writers seldom use a detailed formal outline, preferring a scratch outline that lists just the major points they plan to make.

A **scratch outline,** perhaps the most useful kind of outline for a short paper, is an informal list of the main points you will discuss in your essay in the order in which they will be introduced. As its name implies, a scratch outline is rough, lacking the detail and the degree of organization of a more formal outline. The main purpose of a scratch outline is to give you a sense of the shape and order of your paper and thus enable you to begin writing. A student writing a short essay on American poet Edwin Arlington Robinson's use of irony in his 1910 poem "Miniver Cheevy" (p. 361) used the following scratch outline as a guide:

```
SPEAKER'S ATTITUDE
    Ironic
    Cynical
    Critical
USE OF DICTION
    Formal
    Detached
USE OF ALLUSIONS
    Thebes
    Camelot
    Priam
    Medici
USE OF REPETITION
    "Miniver"
    "thought"
    repetitious rhyme
```

Once this outline was complete, the student was ready to write a first draft.

DRAFTING

Your first draft is not a finished product but a preliminary version of your paper, something to react to and revise. Still, before you begin to write, you should be familiar with one of the most common ways of arranging information: thesis and support. In a **thesis and support** paper you present your thesis in your introduction, support your thesis in the body paragraphs of your essay, and restate your thesis or summarize your points in your conclusion. Knowing this basic method of organizing information will not only help you to write your first draft, but also help you with the revision that you do later.

Before you draft your paper, you should review the material you have collected to support your thesis.

First, make sure that you have collected enough information to support your thesis. The judgments you make are only as convincing as the evidence you present to support them. As you read and took notes, you collected examples from the work or works about which

REVISING AND EDITING

As soon as you begin to draft your essay, you begin the process of revision. Before you are satisfied with your essay, you will probably write several drafts, each more closely focused and more coherent than the previous one.

Strategies for Revision

Two strategies can help you to revise your drafts: *peer review* and a *dialogue with your instructor*.

Peer review is a process in which students assess each other's work. This activity may be carried out in informal sessions, during which one student comments on another's draft, or it may be a formal process in which a student responds to specific questions on a form supplied by the instructor. In either case, one student's reaction can help another student develop a draft. Peer review can be carried out on any draft, and questions can focus on style, essay structure, or any other issue.

A **dialogue with your instructor**—in conference or in writing—can give you a sense of how to proceed with your revision. Establishing such an oral or written dialogue can help you learn how to respond critically to your own writing, and your reactions to your instructor's comments on any draft can help you to clarify your essay's goals. (If your instructor is not available, you may be able to schedule a conference at a writing center, if your college has such a facility.) Using your own responses as well as those of your classmates and your instructor, you can write drafts that are increasingly more consistent with these goals.

The Revision Process

As you move through successive drafts, the task of revising your essay about literature will be easier if you follow a systematic process. As you read and react to your essay, assess the effectiveness of the larger elements—thesis and support, for instance—and proceed to examine increasingly smaller details.

Thesis First, reconsider your thesis. Is it carefully and precisely worded? Does it provide a realistic idea of what your essay will cover? Does it make a point that is worth supporting? It is not enough, for instance, to base an essay about literature on a vague thesis like one of the following:

Vague: Many important reasons exist to explain why Margot Macomber's shooting of her husband was probably intentional.

Vague: Dickens's characters are a lot like those of Addison and Steele.

To give focus and direction to your essay a thesis statement must be more pointed and more specific, as the following revisions are:

you are writing—summaries, paraphrases, or quoted lines of narrative, verse, or dialogue—to back up your assertions. Just how many of these examples you need to use in your draft depends on the nature of your thesis and how skeptical you believe your audience to be. In general, the more inclusive your thesis, the more material you need to support it. For example, if you were supporting the rather narrow thesis that the dialogue of a certain character in the second scene of a play was wooden or awkward, only a few examples would be enough. However, if you wanted to support the inclusive thesis that Nora and Torvald Helmer in Henrik Ibsen's 1879 play *A Doll House* are trapped in their roles, you would need to present quite a number of examples.

Second, see if the work includes any examples that contradict your thesis. Before you can establish your thesis with a high degree of certainty, you should look for examples that contradict it. For example, if you plan to support the thesis that in *A Doll House* Ibsen makes a strong case for the rights of women, you should look for counterexamples. Can you find subtle hints in the play that suggest women should remain locked in their traditional roles and continue to defer to their fathers and husbands?

Finally, consider whether you need to use literary criticism to help you support your thesis. You could strengthen the thesis that *A Doll House* challenged contemporary attitudes about marriage by including the fact that when the play first opened, Ibsen was convinced by an apprehensive theater manager to write another ending. In the new ending, Ibsen had Nora decide, after she stopped briefly to look in at her sleeping children, that she could not leave her family. In some cases, information from another source can lead you to change your thesis. For example, after reading *A Doll House,* you could decide that Ibsen's purpose was to make a strong case for the rights of women. In class, however, you might learn that Ibsen repeatedly said that his play was about the rights of all human beings, not just women. This information could lead you to a thesis that suggests Torvald is just as trapped in his role as Nora is in hers. Naturally, Ibsen's interpretation of his work does not invalidate your first judgment, but it does suggest another conclusion that is worth investigating.

After you have carefully evaluated your supporting material, you can begin drafting your essay, using your scratch outline as your guide. Your goal is to get your ideas down on paper, so you should write quickly. Once you have a draft, you will be able to examine the connections among ideas and to evaluate preliminary versions of your paragraphs and sentences. Do not worry about constructing the "perfect" introduction and conclusion. Many writers, knowing that their ideas will change as they write, postpone writing these paragraphs until a later draft, preferring instead to begin with just their tentative thesis. Your first draft is naturally going to be rough and will probably not achieve the clarity of thought that you want; still, it enables you to see the ideas that you have outlined begin to take shape.

Revised: Although Hemingway's text states that Margot Macomber "shot at the buffalo," a careful analysis of her relationship with her husband suggests that in fact she intended to kill him.

Revised: With their extremely familiar, almost caricature-like physical and moral traits, many of Charles Dickens's minor characters reveal a debt to the "characters" created by the seventeenth-century essayists Joseph Addison and Richard Steele for the newspaper The Spectator.

Supporting Ideas Next, assess the appropriateness of your **supporting ideas** and consider whether you present enough support for your thesis. Make sure that you have supported all points with specific, concrete examples from the work or works you are discussing, briefly summarizing key events, quoting dialogue or description, describing characters or settings, or paraphrasing key ideas. Make certain, however, that your own ideas control the essay and that you have not substituted plot summary for analysis and interpretation. Your goal is to draw a conclusion about one or more works and to support that conclusion with pertinent details. If a plot detail supports a point you wish to make, include a *brief* summary of the event or series of events, showing its relevance by explicitly connecting the summary to the point you are making. For example:

At the end of "Counterparts," when Farrington returns home after a day of frustration and abuse at work, his reaction is to strike out at his son Tom. This act shows that while he and his son are similarly victimized, Farrington is also the counterpart of his tyrannical boss.

Introduction The **introduction** of an essay about literature should specifically identify the works to be discussed and indicate the emphasis of the paper to follow. Depending on your paper's topic, you may want to provide some historical background or biographical information or to discuss the work in relation to other, similar works. Like all introductions, the one you write for an essay about literature should create interest in your topic and include a clear statement of the essay's thesis. The following introduction, while more than adequate for a first draft, is in need of revision:

Revenge, which is defined as "the chance to retaliate, get satisfaction, take vengeance, or inflict damage or injury in return for an injury, insult, etc.," is a major component in many of the stories we have read. The stories that will be discussed here deal with a variety of ways to seek revenge. In my essay, I will show some of these differences.

Although the student clearly identifies her paper's topic, she does not specify the works she will discuss or indicate the particular point she will make about revenge. Her tired opening strategy, a dictionary definition, is not likely to arouse interest in her topic, and her announcement of her intention in the last sentence is intrusive and unnecessary. The following revision is much more effective:

> In Edgar Allan Poe's "The Cask of Amontillado" Montresor vows revenge on Fortunato for an unspecified "insult"; in Ring Lardner's "Haircut" Paul, a young retarded man, gets even with a cruel practical joker who has taunted him for years. Both of these stories present characters who seek revenge, and both stories end in murder. However, the murderers' motivations are presented very differently. In "Haircut" the unreliable narrator is unaware of the significance of many events, and his ignorance helps to create sympathy for the murderer. In "The Cask of Amontillado," where the untrustworthy narrator is the murderer himself, Montresor's inability to offer a convincing motive turns the reader against him.

Conclusion In your conclusion you restate your thesis or sum up your essay's main points and also make a graceful exit. The concluding paragraph below represents an acceptable effort for a first draft, but it communicates little:

> Although the characters of Montresor and Paul were created by different authors at different times, they do have similar motives and goals. However, they are portrayed very differently.

One possible revision echoes the introductory paragraph, incorporating a brief quotation from one of the stories.

> In fact, then, what is significant is not whether or not each murderer's acts are justified, but rather how each murderer, and each victim, is portrayed by the narrator. Montresor—driven by a thirst to avenge "a thousand injuries" as well as a final insult—is shown to be sadistic and unrepentent; in "Haircut" it is Jim, the victim, whose sadism and lack of remorse are revealed to the reader.

Topic Sentences When you have revised your introduction and conclusion, you should begin to focus on your body paragraphs. In particular, be sure you have communicated the direction of your ideas, and the precise relationships of ideas to one another, with clearly worded **topic sentences,** statements that present the main ideas of your paragraphs.

Be especially careful to avoid abstractions and vague generalities in topic sentences.

<u>Vague:</u>   One similarity revolves around the dominance of the men by women. (*What exactly is the similarity?*)

<u>Revised:</u>   In both stories, a man is dominated by a woman.

<u>Vague:</u>   There is one reason for the fact that Jay Gatsby remains a mystery. (*What is the reason?*)

<u>Revised:</u>   Because <u>The Great Gatsby</u> is narrated by the outsider <u>Nick Carraway</u>, Jay Gatsby himself remains a mystery.

When revising the key topic sentences that are intended to move readers from one point (or section of your paper) to another, be sure that the relationship between the ideas they link is clear.

<u>Relationship between ideas unclear:</u>   Now the poem's imagery will be discussed.

<u>Revised:</u>   Another reason for the poem's effectiveness is its unusual imagery.

<u>Relationship between ideas unclear:</u>   The sheriff's wife is another interesting character.

<u>Revised:</u>   Like her friend Mrs. Hale, the sheriff's wife also has mixed feelings about what Mrs. Wright has done.

Sentences and Words   After reviewing your paper's topic sentences, turn your attention to **transitions,** particularly the words and phrases that link sentences. Be sure that every needed transitional element has been supplied, and that each word or phrase you have selected conveys an accurate relationship (sequence, contradiction, and so on) between ideas. When you are satisfied with the clarity and appropriateness of your paper's transitions, move on to stylistic considerations such as diction and sentence variety.

Next, focus on the special stylistic conventions that govern essays about works of literature. For instance, use present tense verbs when discussing literary works (Jake Barnes *is* a major character in Ernest Hemingway's novel *The Sun Also Rises*). Use past tense verbs only when discussing historical events (Stephen Crane's *The Red Badge of Courage* deals with a battle that *took* place during the American Civil War), presenting biographical data (Samuel Taylor Coleridge *was* a close friend of William Wordsworth's), or referring to events that took place before the time of the work's main action (Hamlet's father *was* murdered by Claudius, his mother's new husband). In addition, eliminate subjective expressions, such as *I think, in my opinion, I believe, it seems to me,* and *I feel.* These phrases weaken your argument by suggesting that its ideas are "only" opinions and have no objective validity.

Source Material and Documentation Make certain that all references to sources are integrated smoothly and documented appropriately (see Appendix A, Documenting Sources).

- Acknowledge all sources, including the work or works under discussion, using the documentation style of the Modern Language Association (MLA).
- Combine paraphrases, summaries, and quotations with your own interpretations, weaving quotations smoothly into your paper. Introduce the words or ideas of others with a phrase that identifies their source, and end with appropriate parenthetical documentation.
- Use quotations *only* when something vital would be lost if you did not reproduce the author's exact words.
- Integrate quotations shorter than four lines smoothly into your paper. Make sure that you set off quotations with quotation marks.
- Set off quotations of more than four lines by indenting ten spaces from the margin. Double space, and do not use quotation marks. If you are quoting a single paragraph, do not indent the first line.
- Use the correct reference formats for fiction, poetry, and drama. When citing a part of a short story or novel, supply the page number (143); for a poem, give the line numbers (3–5); for a play, include the act, scene, and line numbers (II.ii.17–22).

Editing

Once you have finished revising, edit your paper to make certain that grammar, punctuation, spelling, and mechanics are correct. As you edit, pay particular attention to the mechanical conventions of literary essays. For instance, titles of short works and titles of parts of long works—short stories, short poems, and magazine or journal articles—should be in quotation marks ("A Rose for Emily"); titles of long works—books, long poems, plays, and newspapers and journals, for example—should be underlined or set in italics (*Invisible Man;* the *Washington Post*).

In addition, refer to authors of literary works by their full names in your first reference to them and by their last names in subsequent references. Never refer to them by their first names, and never use titles that indicate marital status (*Willa Cather* or *Cather,* never Willa or Miss Cather). Also, make sure you have used literary terms accurately. For example, be careful to avoid confusing **narrator** or **speaker** with author; feelings or opinions expressed by a narrator or character do not necessarily represent those of the author. Do not say, "In the poem 'Patterns' Amy Lowell expresses her anger" when you mean that the **persona**—the speaker in the poem, who may or may not be the poet—expresses anger.

When your editing is complete, give your essay a descriptive title; before you retype or reprint it, make sure that its format conforms to your instructor's requirements.

CHAPTER 3

UNDERSTANDING POETRY

NIKKI GIOVANNI
(1945–   )

Poetry
(1975)

    poetry is motion graceful
    as a fawn
    gentle as a teardrop
    strong like the eye
5 finding peace in a crowded room
    we poets tend to think
    our words are golden
    though emotion speaks too
    loudly to be defined
10 by silence

    sometimes after midnight or just before
    the dawn
    we sit typewriter in hand
    pulling loneliness around us
15 forgetting our lovers or children
    who are sleeping
    ignoring the weary wariness
    of our own logic
    to compose a poem

20   no one understands it
    it never says "love me" for poets are
    beyond love
    it never says "accept me" for poems seek not
    acceptance but controversy
25 it only says "i am" and therefore
    i concede that you are too

                a poem is pure energy
                horizontally contained
                between the mind
       30   of the poet and the ear of the reader
                if it does not sing discard the ear
                for poetry is song
                if it does not delight discard
                the heart for poetry is joy
       35   if it does not inform then close
                off the brain for it is dead
                if it cannot heed the insistent message
                that life is precious

                which is all we poets
       40   wrapped in our loneliness
                are trying to say

ARCHIBALD MACLEISH
(1892–1982)

Ars Poetica[1]
(1926)

A poem should be palpable and mute
As a globed fruit,

Dumb
As old medallions to the thumb,

5 Silent as the sleeve-worn stone
Of casement ledges where the moss has grown—

A poem should be wordless
As the flight of birds.

A poem should be motionless in time
10 As the moon climbs,

Leaving, as the moon releases
Twig by twig the night-entangled trees,

---

[1] Art of Poetry.

Leaving, as the moon behind the winter leaves,
Memory by memory the mind—

15 A poem should be motionless in time
As the moon climbs.

A poem should be equal to:
Not true.

For all the history of grief
20 An empty doorway and a maple leaf.

For love
The leaning grasses and two lights above the sea—

A poem should not mean
But be.

MARIANNE MOORE
(1887–1972)

Poetry
(1921)

I, too, dislike it: there are things that are important beyond all this
    fiddle.
Reading it, however, with a perfect contempt for it, one discovers
    in it
after all, a place for the genuine.

    Hands that can grasp, eyes
5   that can dilate, hair that can rise
        if it must, these things are important not because a

high-sounding interpretation can be put upon them but because they are
    useful. When they become so derivative as to become unintelligible,
    the same thing may be said for all of us, that we
10   do not admire what
    we cannot understand: the bat
      holding on upside down or in quest of something to
eat, elephants pushing, a wild horse taking a roll, a tireless wolf under
    a tree, the immovable critic twitching his skin like a horse that
        feels a

15   flea, the base-
       ball fan, the statistician—
           nor is it valid
               to discriminate against "business documents and

   school-books";[1] all these phenomena are important. One must make a
20   distinction
       however: when dragged into prominence by half poets, the result is
           not poetry,
       nor till the poets among us can be
           "literalists of
25   the imagination"[2]—above
               insolence and triviality and can present

   for inspection, "imaginary gardens with real toads in them," shall
       we have
   it. In the meantime, if you demand on the one hand,
   the raw material of poetry in
30   all its rawness and
       that which is on the other hand
               genuine, you are interested in poetry.

DEFINING POETRY

Throughout history and across various national and cultural boundaries, poetry has held an important place. In ancient China and Japan, for example, poetry was prized above all else, and no individual was considered educated who could not write a good poem. One story tells of a samurai warrior who, when defeated, asked for a pen and paper. Thinking that he wanted to write a will before being executed, his captor granted his wish. Instead of writing a will, however, the warrior wrote a farewell poem which so impressed his captor that he immediately released him.

---

[1] Moore quotes the *Diaries of Tolstoy* (New York, 1917): "Where the boundary between prose and poetry lies, I shall never be able to understand. . . . Poetry is verse; prose is not verse. Or else poetry is everything with the exception of business documents and school books."

[2] A reference (given by Moore) to W. B. Yeats's "William Blake and His Illustrations" (in *Ideas of Good and Evil*, 1903): "The limitation of his view was from the very intensity of his vision; he was a too literal realist of the imagination as others are of nature; and because he believed that the figures seen by the mind's eye, when exhalted by inspiration, were 'external existences,' symbols of divine essences, he hated every grace of style that might obscure their liniments."

To the ancient Greeks and Romans, poetry was the medium of spiritual and philosophical expression. Epics such as *The Iliad* and *The Aeneid* are written in verse, and so are dramas such as *Oedipus the King* and *Antigone*. Passages of the Bible, the Koran, and the Hindu holy books are also written in poetry. Today, throughout the world, poetry continues to delight and to inspire. For many people, in many places, poetry is the language of the emotions, the medium of expression they use when they speak from the heart.

But what exactly *is* poetry? Do all poets—and all readers—mean the same thing when they speak about poetry? Is a poem "pure energy / horizontally contained / between the mind / of the poet and the ear of the reader" as Nikki Giovanni describes it? Or is a poem, as Archibald MacLeish says, "Dumb," "Silent," "wordless," and "motionless in time"? Or is it simply what Marianne Moore calls "all this fiddle"?

Despite the longstanding place of poetry in our lives, many people—including poets themselves—have difficulty deciding just what poetry is. One way of defining poetry is to say that it uses language to condense experience into an intensely concentrated package, with each sound, each word, each image, and each line carrying tremendous weight. But beyond this, it is difficult to pin down what makes a particular arrangement of words or lines a poem. Part of the problem is that poetry has many guises. A poem may be short or long, accessible or obscure; it may express a mood or tell a story; it may be set on the page in a familiar poetic form—a sonnet, a couplet, a haiku—or follow no conventional pattern; it may or may not have a regular, identifiable meter or a rhyme scheme; it may depend heavily on elaborate imagery, figures of speech, irony, complex allusions or symbols, or repeated sounds—or it may use none of these poetic conventions.

To further complicate the issue, different readers, different poets, different generations of readers and poets, and different cultures may have different expectations about poetry. Readers respond to words differently and see different relationships among ideas; their responses may influence their ideas about whether a work is a poem or not. Poets have different purposes, belong to different critical schools, and represent different eras and cultures. As a result, they have different assumptions about poetry, and these conflicting assumptions raise questions. Must poetry be written to delight or inspire, or can a poem have a political or social message? And must this message be conveyed subtly, embellished with imaginatively used sounds and words, or can it be explicit and straightforward? These questions, which have been debated by literary critics as well as by poets for many years, have no easy answers—and perhaps no answers at all. A haiku—short, rich in imagery, adhering to a rigid formal structure—is certainly poetry, and so is a political poem like Wole Soyinka's "Telephone Conversation" (p. 6). To some Western readers, however, a haiku might seem too plain and understated to be poetic, and Soyinka's poem might seem to be a political tract masquerading as poetry. Still, most readers would agree that the following lines qualify as poetry.

WILLIAM SHAKESPEARE
(1564–1616)

That Time of Year Thou Mayst in Me Behold
(1609)

That time of year thou mayst in me behold
When yellow leaves, or none, or few, do hang
Upon those boughs which shake against the cold,
Bare ruined choirs, where late the sweet birds sang.
5 In me thou see'st the twilight of such day
As after sunset fadeth in the west,
Which by and by black night doth take away,
Death's second self that seals up all in rest.
In me thou see'st the glowing of such fire,
10 That on the ashes of his youth doth lie,
As the deathbed whereon it must expire,
Consumed with that which it was nourished by.
This thou perceiv'st, which makes thy love more strong,
To love that well which thou must leave ere long.

This poem possesses many of the characteristics that Western readers have come to associate with poetry. For instance, its lines have a regular pattern of rhyme and meter that identifies it as a **sonnet.** The poem also includes a complex network of related imagery and figurative language that compares the lost youth of the aging speaker to the sunset and to autumn. Finally, the pair of rhyming lines at the end of the poem states a familiar poetic theme: The lovers' knowledge that they must eventually die makes their love stronger.

Even though the next poem is quite different from the sonnet above, most readers would probably agree that it, too, is a poem.

LOUIS ZUKOFSKY
(1904–1978)

I Walk in the Old Street
(1944)

I walk in the old street
to hear the beloved songs
afresh
this spring night.

5 Like the leaves—my loves wake—
not to be the same
or look tireless to the stars
and a ripped doorbell.

Unlike Shakespeare's sonnet, Zukofsky's poem does not have a regular metrical pattern or rhyme scheme. Its diction is more conversational than poetic, and one of its images—a "ripped doorbell"—stands in stark contrast to the other, more conventionally "poetic" images. Nevertheless, the poem's subject—love—is a traditional one, and it echoes some of the sentiments of the Shakespeare sonnet. Finally, the poem's division into stanzas and its use of imaginative comparisons ("Like the leaves—my loves wake—") are unmistakably poetic.

Although the two preceding works can easily be classified as poems, readers might have trouble with the following lines.

E. E. CUMMINGS
(1894–1962)

l(a
(1923)

l(a

le
af
fa

5 ll

s)
one
l

iness

Unlike the other poems, "l(a" does not at first seem to have any of the characteristics normally associated with poetry. It has no meter, rhyme, or imagery. It has no repeated sounds, no figures of speech, no symbols. It cannot even be read aloud because its "lines" are made up of fragments of words. In spite of its odd appearance, however, "l(a" does present an idea that is poetic. Reconstructed, the words that Cummings broke apart are

"l (a leaf falls) one l iness."

Thus the poem expresses a conventional poetic theme: the loneliness and isolation of the individual. At the same time, by breaking words into bits and pieces, Cummings emphasizes the possibilities of language and suggests the need to break out of customary ways of using words to define experience.

It is true that most poems, particularly those divided into stanzas, look like poems, and it is also true that poems tend to use compressed language. Beyond this, however, what makes a poem a poem is more a matter of degree than a question of whether or not it conforms to a strict set of rules. A poem is likely to use *more* imagery, figurative language, rhyme, and so on than a prose piece—but, then again, it may not.

A NOTE ON READING POETRY

Some readers say they do not like poetry because they find it obscure or intimidating. One reason some people have difficulty reading poetry is that it frequently presents information in subtle (and therefore potentially confusing) ways; it does not immediately "get to the point" as journalistic articles or business letters do. One could argue, however, that by concentrating experience, poetry actually "gets to the point" in ways—and to degrees—that other kinds of writing do not. Even so, some readers see poetry as an alien form. They have the misconception that poetry must be filled with obscure allusions, complex metrical schemes, and flowery diction. Others feel excluded from what they see as its secret language and mysterious structure, viewing poetry as something that must be deciphered. Certainly, understanding poetry often requires close reading, hard work, and concentration. Because it is compressed, poetry often omits exposition and explanation; consequently, readers must be willing to take the time to interpret ideas and to supply missing connections. Many readers are simply not motivated to dig deeply for what they perceive to be uncertain rewards. But not all poems are difficult, and even those that are often are well worth the effort.

RECOGNIZING KINDS OF POETRY

Almost all poetry can be assigned to one of two categories: *narrative* poems, which recount a story, and *lyric* poems (generally shorter than narrative poems), which communicate a speaker's mood, feelings, or state of mind.

Narrative Poetry

Although any brief poem that tells a story, such as Edwin Arlington Robinson's "Richard Cory" (p. 364), or even a popular song like Bruce Springsteen's "My Hometown" (p. 380) may be considered a narrative poem, the two most familiar forms of narrative poetry are the *epic* and the *ballad*.

Epic poems recount the accomplishments of heroic figures, typically including settings of sweeping scale, superhuman feats, and the participation of gods and supernatural beings. The language of epic poems is elevated and frequently elaborate. Epics span many cultures—from Homer's *Odyssey* (Greek) to *Beowulf* (Anglo-Saxon) to *The Epic of Gilgamesh* (Babylonian). In ancient times, epics were handed down through an oral tradition; more recently, poets have written literary epics, such as John Milton's *Paradise Lost* and Nobel Prize–winning poet Derek Walcott's 1990 *Omeros,* which follow many of the same conventions.

The **ballad** is another type of narrative poetry with roots in an oral tradition. Originally intended to be sung, a ballad uses repeated words and phrases, including a refrain, to advance its story. Some—but not all—ballads use the **ballad stanza** (p. 216). For examples of traditional ballads in this text, see "Bonny Barbara Allen" (p. 274), "Sir Patrick Spence" (p. 275), and "Western Wind" (p. 277). Dudley Randall's "Ballad of Birmingham" (p. 102) and Gwendolyn Brooks's "The Ballad of Chocolate Mabbie" (p. 405) are examples of modern ballads.

Lyric Poetry

Like narrative poems, lyric poems take various forms.

An **elegy** is a poem in which a poet mourns the death of a specific person, as in Robert Hayden's "Homage to the Empress of the Blues" (p. 323), about the singer Bessie Smith. Other examples of this type of elegy include Edna St. Vincent Millay's "Elegy before Death" (p. 134) and A. E. Housman's "To an Athlete Dying Young" (p. 329). Sometimes, however, an elegy's subject is more general. Thomas Gray's "Elegy Written in a Country Churchyard" (p. 317), for example, mourns the inevitable death of all people.

An **ode** is a long lyric poem, formal and serious in style, tone, and subject matter. An ode typically has a fairly complex stanzaic pattern, such as the **terza rima** used by Percy Bysshe Shelley in "Ode to the West Wind" (p. 368). Other odes in this text include John Keats's "Ode to a Nightingale" (p. 335) and "Ode on a Grecian Urn" (p. 333).

An **aubade** is a poem about morning, usually celebrating the coming of dawn. An example is Philip Larkin's "Aubade" (p. 339).

A **meditation** is a lyric poem that focuses on a physical object, using this object as a vehicle for considering larger issues. Edmund Waller's "Go, Lovely Rose" (p. 391) is a meditation.

A **pastoral**—for example, Christopher Marlowe's "The Passionate Shepherd to His Love" (p. 344)—is a lyric poem that celebrates the simple, idyllic pleasures of country life.

Finally, a **dramatic monologue** is a poem whose speaker addresses one or more unseen listeners, revealing much more than he or she intends. Robert Browning's "My Last Duchess" (p. 78) and "Porphyria's Lover" (p. 93) and Alfred, Lord Tennyson's "Ulysses" (p. 387) are three dramatic monologues that appear in this text.

DISCOVERING THEMES IN POETRY

A poem can be about anything. For example, a poet can contemplate a flower, remember a parent, declare undying love, speculate about the mysteries of the universe, retell a classical myth, express a fear of death, argue for social justice, offer a definition of poetry, or relive the horrors of war.

Although no subject is really inappropriate for poetic treatment, certain conventional subjects recur frequently. Poets often write about love, nature, death, family, the folly of human desires, and the inevitability of growing old. They explore the concept of mutability, or change; the **carpe diem** theme ("life is brief, so let us seize the day"); and the idea of a lost, irrecoverable past. They write political and social protest, and they write satire. Within these broad categories, however, lie many possibilities. Poems "about nature," for instance, may praise the beauty of nature, assert the superiority of its simplest creatures over humans, consider its evanescence, or mourn its destruction. Similarly, poems "about death" may examine the difficulty of facing one's own mortality, eulogize a friend, assert the need for the acceptance of life's cycles, or cry out against death's inevitability.

A poem's **theme,** then, is more than its general subject matter. It includes the ideas the poet explores, the concerns the poem examines. More specifically, a poem's theme is its main point or idea.

In order to discover the theme of a poem, readers look at its form, its voice, its language, its images, its allusions, its sound—all of its individual elements. Together, these elements convey the ideas that are important in the poem. Of course, a poem may not communicate the same meaning to every reader. Different readers bring different backgrounds, attitudes, and experiences to a poem, and therefore they see different things and give weight to different things.

The following poem is rich enough in language and content to suggest a variety of different interpretations.

ADRIENNE RICH
(1929-   )

A Woman Mourned by Daughters
(1984)

>   Now, not a tear begun,
>   we sit here in your kitchen,
>   spent, you see, already.
>   You are swollen till you strain
> 5 this house and the whole sky.
>   You, whom we so often

succeeded in ignoring!
You are puffed up in death
like a corpse pulled from the sea;
10 we groan beneath your weight.
And yet you were a leaf,
a straw blown on the bed,
you had long since become
crisp as a dead insect.
15 What is it, if not you,
that settles on us now
like satins you pulled down
over our bridal heads?
What rises in our throats
20 like food you prodded in?
Nothing could be enough.
You breathe upon us now
through solid assertions
of yourself: teaspoons, goblets,
25 seas of carpet, a forest
of old plants to be watered,
an old man in an adjoining
room to be touched and fed.
And all this universe
30 dares us to lay a finger
anywhere, save exactly
as you would wish it done.

In the most general terms "A Woman Mourned by Daughters" is about the speaker's mother. More specifically, it explores a number of different ideas: the passing of time; the relationships between mother and daughters, father and daughters, husband and wife; the power of memory. Its central theme, however, might be expressed as a **paradox:** "After death, a person may be more present than she was when she was alive."

Many different elements in the poem suggest this interpretation. The poem's speaker directly addresses her mother. Her voice is searching, questioning, and the unusually unpoetic diction ("You, whom we so often / succeeded in ignoring") and metrical irregularities give the poem a halting, uncertain quality. The poem's words, images, and figurative language establish the central idea: Alive, the mother was light as a leaf or straw or a dead insect; dead, she seems "swollen" and "puffed up," and the daughters feel crushed by her weight. The concrete details of her life—"teaspoons, goblets, / seas of carpet . . ."—weigh on her survivors and keep them under her spell. In her kitchen, her memory is alive; in death, she has tremendous power over her daughters.

Like most complex poems, this one supports several alternate readings as well as the interpretation above. Some readers will focus on the negative language used to describe the mother; others might emphasize the images of domesticity; still others might concentrate on the role of the absent sisters and the almost-absent father. Any of these focuses can lead to a redefinition of the poem's theme.

The following poem is also about a parent, yet it explores different ideas.

RAYMOND CARVER
(1938–1988)

Photograph of My Father in His Twenty-Second Year
(1983)

> *October.* Here in this dank, unfamiliar kitchen
> I study my father's embarrassed young man's face.
> Sheepish grin, he holds in one hand a string
> of spiny yellow perch, in the other
> 5 a bottle of Carlsbad beer.
>
> In jeans and denim shirt, he leans
> against the front fender of a 1934 Ford.
> He would like to pose bluff and hearty for his posterity,
> wear his old hat cocked over his ear.
> 10 All his life my father wanted to be bold.
>
> But the eyes give him away, and the hands
> that limply offer the string of dead perch
> and the bottle of beer. Father, I love you,
> yet how can I say thank you, I who can't hold my liquor either,
> 15 and don't even know the places to fish?

Like Rich's speaker, Carver's is also in the family kitchen. Studying a picture of his father, this speaker sees through the photograph's facade. Instead of seeing the "bold," "bluff and hearty" young man his father wanted to be, he sees him as he was: "embarrassed" and "sheepish," with limp hands. In the last three lines of the poem, the speaker addresses his father directly, drawing an analogy between his father's shortcomings and his own. This frank acknowledgment of his own vulnerability and the explicit comparison between father and son suggest that the poem's central theme has more to do with the speaker than with his father—perhaps with the ambivalent nature of his love for this man who has passed on to him his own faults and failings. It is clear that the poem has something to say about the link between parent and child—something specific and, perhaps, something universal.

The poem that appears below also looks back on a parent, but here the adult speaker assumes a child's point of view.

JUDITH ORTIZ COFER
(1952–   )

My Father in the Navy: A Childhood Memory
(1982)

Stiff and immaculate
in the white cloth of his uniform
and a round cap on his head like a halo,
he was an apparition on leave from a shadow-world
5 and only flesh and blood when he rose from below
the waterline where he kept watch over the engines
and dials making sure the ship parted the waters
on a straight course.
Mother, brother and I kept vigil
10 on the nights and dawns of his arrivals,
watching the corner beyond the neon sign of a quasar
for the flash of white our father like an angel
heralding a new day.
His homecomings were the verses
15 we composed over the years making up
the siren's song that kept him coming back
from the bellies of iron whales
and into our nights
like the evening prayer.

Even as an adult the speaker seems still not to know her father, whom she remembers as "stiff and immaculate," dressed in white, "an apparition on leave from a shadow-world." She remembers him as being "like an angel," wearing his cap "like a halo." Lines 14–16, alluding to Odysseus (the hero of Homer's *The Odyssey*), give the father a mythical quality, characterizing him as a long-missing, long-awaited wanderer. The reference to the "siren's song" in line 16, also an allusion to *The Odyssey,* suggests the adult speaker's realization that the father is drawn back—perhaps against his will—to the family. Together, the poem's tone and images convey the child's view of the father as elusive and unreal—an impression the adult speaker neither confirms nor corrects. Perhaps, then, the poem suggests that the speaker is still struggling to understand her father's complex role in her life; perhaps, too, it suggests the universal difficulty of a child's trying to understand a parent.

EXERCISE: DISCOVERING THEMES IN POETRY

The seven poems on the pages that follow share a common subject matter—each is about the speaker's parent—yet each explores different ideas. Read each poem, keeping the following questions in mind.

1. What is the speaker's attitude toward his or her parent?
2. Which words and images suggest positive associations? Which help to create a negative impression?
3. How does the poem's sound contribute to the impression of the parent it conveys?
4. How would you characterize the poem's tone? For example, is the poem sentimental, humorous, angry, resentful, or regretful?
5. What themes are explored in the poem? What do you think is the poem's central theme?
6. What does the poem say about the parent? What does it reveal about the speaker?

THEODORE ROETHKE
(1908–1963)

My Papa's Waltz
(1948)

The whiskey on your breath
Could make a small boy dizzy;
But I hung on like death:
Such waltzing was not easy.

5 We romped until the pans
Slid from the kitchen shelf;
My mother's countenance
Could not unfrown itself.

The hand that held my wrist
10 Was battered on one knuckle;
At every step you missed
My right ear scraped a buckle.

You beat time on my head
With a palm caked hard by dirt,
15 Then waltzed me off to bed
Still clinging to your shirt.

DYLAN THOMAS
(1914–1953)

Do Not Go Gentle into That Good Night[1]
(1952)

Do not go gentle into that good night,
Old age should burn and rave at close of day;
Rage, rage against the dying of the light.

Though wise men at their end know dark is right,
5 Because their words had forked no lightning they
Do not go gentle into that good night.

Good men, the last wave by, crying how bright
Their frail deeds might have danced in a green bay,
Rage, rage against the dying of the light.

10 Wild men who caught and sang the sun in flight,
And learn, too late, they grieved it on its way,
Do not go gentle into that good night.

Grave men, near death, who see with blinding sight
Blind eyes could blaze like meteors and be gay,
15 Rage, rage against the dying of the light.

And you, my father, there on the sad height,
Curse, bless, me now with your fierce tears, I pray,
Do not go gentle into that good night.
Rage, rage against the dying of the light.

SIMON J. ORTIZ
(1941–   )

My Father's Song
(1976)

Wanting to say things,
I miss my father tonight.
His voice, the slight catch,
the depth from his thin chest,

[1] This poem was written during the last illness of the poet's father, D. J. Thomas.

5 the tremble of emotion
in something he has just said
to his son, his song:

We planted corn one Spring at Acu—
we planted several times
10 but this one particular time
I remember the soft damp sand
in my hand.

My father had stopped at one point
to show me an overturned furrow;
15 the plowshare had unearthed
the burrow nest of a mouse
in the soft moist sand.

Very gently, he scooped tiny pink animals
into the palm of his hand
20 and told me to touch them.
We took them to the edge
of the field and put them in the shade
of a sand moist clod.

I remember the very softness
25 of cool and warm sand and tiny alive mice
and my father saying things.

COLLEEN J. McELROY
(1935–   )

My Father's Wars
(1984)

Once he followed simple rules
of casual strength,
summoned violence with the flick
of combat ribbon or hash mark;
5 now he forces a pulse into treasonous muscles
and commands soap opera villains.
He is camped in a world regimented
by glowing tubes,
his olive-black skin begging for the fire
10 of unlimited color.

In towns where he can follow
the orders of silence,
gunfights are replayed
in thirty-minute intervals
15 familiar as his stiff right arm
or the steel brace scaffolding his leg.

By midday the room is filled
with game shows and private eyes hurling
questions against all those who swear
20 their innocence;
his wife is in full retreat
and jumps when he answers in half-formed words
of single grunts deadly as shrapnel.
He need not remind her
25 he is always the hero;
the palms of his hands
are muddy with old battle lines.
He has fallen
heir to brutal days where he moves
30 battalions of enemies;
his mornings are shattered with harsh echoes
of their electronic voices.

Here he is on neutral ground
and need not struggle to capture words
35 he can no longer force his brain to master;
he plans his roster
and does not attend to his wife's
rapid-fire review of the neighbor's behavior.
He recalls too clearly the demarcation of blacks,
40 of Buffalo Soldier and 93rd Division.
By late afternoon he is seen rigidly
polishing his car in broad one-arm swipes,
its side windows and bumpers emblazoned
with stickers: US ARMY RETIRED REGULAR

LUCILLE CLIFTON
(1936–   )

My Mama Moved among the Days
(1969)

My Mama moved among the days
like a dreamwalker in a field;
seemed like what she touched was hers
seemed like what touched her couldn't hold,
5 she got us almost through the high grass
then seemed like she turned around and ran
right back in
right back on in

ROBERT HAYDEN
(1913–1980)

Those Winter Sundays
(1962)

Sundays too my father got up early
and put his clothes on in the blueblack cold,
then with cracked hands that ached
from labor in the weekday weather made
5 banked fires blaze. No one ever thanked him.

I'd wake and hear the cold splintering, breaking.
When the rooms were warm, he'd call,
and slowly I would rise and dress,
fearing the chronic angers of that house,

10 Speaking indifferently to him,
who had driven out the cold
and polished my good shoes as well.
What did I know, what did I know
of love's austere and lonely offices?

SEAMUS HEANEY
(1939–   )

Digging
(1966)

Between my finger and my thumb
The squat pen rests; snug as a gun.

Under my window, a clean rasping sound
When the spade sinks into gravelly ground:
5 My father, digging. I look down

Till his straining rump among the flowerbeds
Bends low, comes up twenty years away
Stooping in rhythm through potato drills
Where he was digging.

10 The coarse boot nestled on the lug, the shaft
Against the inside knee was levered firmly.
He rooted out tall tops, buried the bright edge deep
To scatter new potatoes that we picked
Loving their cool hardness in our hands.
15 By God, the old man could handle a spade.
Just like his old man.

My grandfather cut more turf in a day
Than any other man on Toner's bog.
Once I carried him milk in a bottle
20 Corked sloppily with paper. He straightened up
To drink it, then fell to right away

Nicking and slicing neatly, heaving sods
Over his shoulder, going down and down
For the good turf. Digging.

25 The cold smell of potato mould, the squelch and slap
Of soggy peat, the curt cuts of an edge
Through living roots awaken in my head.
But I've no spade to follow men like them.

Between my finger and my thumb
30 The squat pen rests.
I'll dig with it.

CHAPTER 4

READING AND WRITING ABOUT POETRY

READING POETRY

Sometimes readers approach poetry purely for pleasure. At other times, however, reading a poem is the first step toward writing about it—and, through writing, toward learning more about it. The following guidelines, which focus on issues discussed elsewhere in this section, may help direct your approach and enrich your reading of a poem.

- Rephrase the poem in your own words. What does your paraphrase reveal about the poem's subject and central concerns? What is lost or gained in your paraphrase of the poem?
- Consider the poem's **voice.** Who is the poem's persona or speaker? How would you characterize the poem's tone? Is the poem ironic? (See Chapter 5.)
- Study the poem's **diction** and look up unfamiliar words in a dictionary. How does word choice affect your reaction to the poem? What do the connotations of words reveal about the poem? What level of diction is used? Is dialect used? How does the word order contribute to your reading of the poem? (See Chapter 6.)
- Examine the poem's **imagery.** What kind of imagery dominates? What specific images are used? Is a pattern of imagery present? How does use of imagery enrich the poem? (See Chapter 7.)
- Identify the poem's **figures of speech.** Does the poet use metaphor? Simile? Personification? Hyperbole? Understatement? Metonymy or synecdoche? Apostrophe? How do figures of speech affect your reading of the poem? (See Chapter 8.)
- Listen to the **sound** of the poem. Are rhythm and meter regular or irregular? How do rhythm and meter reinforce the poem's central concerns? Does the poem use alliteration? Assonance? Rhyme? How do these elements enhance the poem? (See Chapter 9.)
- Look at the poem's **form.** Is the poem written in closed or open form? Is the poem constructed as a sonnet? A sestina? A villanelle? An epigram? A haiku? Is the poem an example of

concrete poetry? How does the poem's form reinforce its ideas? (See Chapter 10.)
- Consider the poem's use of **symbol, allegory, allusion,** or **myth.** Does the poem make use of symbols? Allusions? How do symbols or allusions support its theme? Is the poem an allegory? Does the poem retell or interpret a myth? (See Chapter 11.)
- Identify the poem's **theme.** What central theme or themes does the poem explore? How are the themes expressed? (See Chapter 3.)

ACTIVE READING

When you approach a poem that you plan to write about, you engage in active reading just as you would if you were reading a short story or a play. When you finish recording your reactions to the poem, you focus on a topic, develop ideas that will help you to explore that topic, decide on a thesis, prepare an outline, and draft and revise an essay.

Catherine Whittaker, a student in an introduction to literature course, was asked to write a three- to five-page essay comparing any *two* of the seven poems about parents that appear in the exercise in Chapter 3 (pp. 46–51). Her instructor told the class that the essay should reflect students' own reactions to the poem, not the opinions of literary critics. Catherine chose to write her essay about Robert Hayden's "Those Winter Sundays" and Seamus Heaney's "Digging." As she planned and wrote her paper, she was guided by the process described in Chapter 2, Reading and Writing about Literature.

Previewing

Catherine Whittaker began her work by previewing each poem and then reading it more closely to see which ones she wanted to write about. She knew she wanted to study two poems that had an affectionate, straightforward tone, so she began by eliminating those she considered obscure or difficult and those whose portrait of the speaker's parent did not seem sympathetic.

Previewing helped Catherine to narrow down her choices. As she looked through "Those Winter Sundays," she was drawn immediately to words in the opening lines ("Sundays too . . ."; "blueblack cold"). She had the same reaction to "The squat pen rests; snug as a gun" in line 2 of "Digging." In each case, the words made Catherine want to examine the poem further. She noticed too that both poems were divided into stanzas of varying lengths and that both used a first-person voice to write about a father. Keeping these features in mind, Catherine began a close reading of each poem.

Highlighting and Annotating

As Catherine read and reread "Those Winter Sundays" and "Digging," she recorded her comments and questions. The highlighted and annotated poems appear on page 54.

ROBERT HAYDEN
(1913–1980)

Those Winter Sundays
(1962)

Sundays too my father got up early
and put his clothes on in the blueblack cold,
then with cracked hands that ached
from labor in the weekday weather made
5 banked fires blaze. No one ever thanked him.

I'd wake and hear the cold splintering, breaking.
When the rooms were warm, he'd call,
and slowly I would rise and dress,
fearing the chronic angers of that house,

10 Speaking indifferently to him,
who had driven out the cold
and polished my good shoes as well.
What did I know, what did I know
of love's austere and lonely offices?

SEAMUS HEANEY
(1939–   )

Digging
(1966)

Between my finger and my thumb
The squat pen rests; snug as a gun.

Under my window, a clean rasping sound
When the spade sinks into gravelly ground:
5 My father, digging. I look down

Till his straining rump among the flowerbeds
Bends low, comes up twenty years away
Stooping in rhythm through potato drills
Where he was digging.

10 The coarse boot nestled on the lug, the shaft
Against the inside knee was levered firmly.

He rooted out tall tops, buried the bright edge deep
To scatter new potatoes that <u>we picked</u>   *Was it a family task?*
Loving their cool hardness in <u>our hands</u>.

15 By God, the old man could handle a spade. } *Two generations could "handle a spade" can the poet dig?*
Just like his old man.

My grandfather cut more turf in a day
Than any other man on Toner's bog.   *Was the poet a young child at the time?*
Once I carried him milk in a bottle
20 Corked <u>sloppily with paper</u>. He straightened up
To drink it, then <u>fell to right away</u>   — *The grandfather was a hard worker*

Nicking and slicing <u>neatly, heaving sods</u>   *Almost like an art of digging?*
Over his shoulder, <u>going down and down</u>
For the good turf. Digging.

25 The cold smell of potato mould, the squelch and slap
Of soggy peat, the curt cuts of an edge   *What does it make the poet remember?*
Through living roots <u>awaken in my head</u>.
But I've no spade to follow <u>men like them</u>. *What are "men like them" like?*

Same as first 2 lines
Between my finger and my thumb
30 The <u>squat pen</u> rests. — *Why is this repeated again?*
I'll <u>dig with it</u>. — *Dig for what?*

Catherine found both poems' language appealing, and she believed her highlighting and annotating had produced some valuable results. For example, she noticed some parallels between the two poems: Both focus on the past, both portray fathers as hard workers, and neither mentions a mother.

WRITING ABOUT POETRY

PLANNING AN ESSAY

Catherine was far from finding a specific topic for her paper, but her work did suggest some interesting possibilities. She was especially intrigued by the way both poems depict fathers as actively engaged in physical tasks.

Choosing a Topic

One idea Catherine thought she might want to write about in her paper was the significance of the speakers' attitudes toward their fathers: Although both see their fathers as hardworking men, the speaker in "Those Winter Sundays" has mixed feelings about his father's devotion to his family, while the speaker in "Digging" is more appreciative. Catherine explored this idea in her journal.

Journal Entries

"Those Winter Sundays"

Why did the father get up early every morning? One could imagine that he had a large family and had little money. There is no mention of a mother. Images are created of the utter coldness and a "chronic anger" of the house. The father not only made fires to warm the house but also polished his child's (or children's) shoes—maybe for church. And yet, the child seems not to care or appreciate the father's efforts. Is he too young to say thank you, or are there other problems in the house for which the child blames the father?

"Digging"

In the poem, the poet seems to be contemplating the subject about which to write when the sounds of digging capture his attention. He remembers the steady, artful rhythm of his father's digging of the potatoes and how they (probably the poet, and his brothers and sisters) picked out the cool potatoes. His memories appear to be entirely appreciative of his father's and grandfather's hard work and skill. He does, however, feel regret that he is not like these dedicated men. He cannot use a shovel but hopes to use his pen in order to write and make his own contributions as a writer.

When Catherine reread her journal entries, she felt she had moved closer to a specific topic for her paper. The more she reviewed the poems, the more confident she felt exploring their similar views of the fathers' roles and their contrasting attitudes toward these fathers. Now Catherine needed to generate a list of specific similarities and differences between the two poems before she could write a draft of her paper.

Finding Something to Say

Brainstorming   Catherine returned to the highlighted and annotated poems in order to compile the following brainstorming notes.

Brainstorming Notes

DISSIMILARITIES

"Those Winter Sundays"
— there are family problems
— the child acts ambiguously toward his father
— there is sympathy felt for the father
— atmosphere of tension

"Digging"
— only happy memories are involved
— the child admires his father
— only happy family relations
— atmosphere of happiness and togetherness

SIMILARITIES
— the fathers are hard workers
— the fathers appear to love their children
— similar time—impression that the events happened years ago
— children, now grown, appreciate their fathers' dedication
— children, now grown, are inspired by their fathers' determination

After finishing her brainstorming, Catherine reviewed her notes carefully. As connections between the two poems came into focus, she was able to decide on a thesis and on a tentative order in which to present her ideas.

Deciding on a Thesis

The more Catherine thought about the two poems, the more she focused on their similarities. She expressed a possible main idea for her paper in the following thesis statement.

Tentative Thesis Statement

Robert Hayden's "Those Winter Sundays" and "Digging" by Seamus Heaney are poems that were inspired by fathers and composed as tributes to fathers. Although their family backgrounds are different, the now-grown poets realize the determination and dedication of their fathers and are subsequently empassioned in their writings.

Preparing an Outline

Before preparing a scratch outline, Catherine reviewed her notes to identify the specific ideas she wanted to address in her first draft. Then she arranged those ideas in a logical order.

Scratch Outline: "Those Winter Sundays" and "Digging"

"Those Winter Sundays"
<u>Poet reflects back on childhood</u>
—father's hard work
—his misunderstanding and lack of appreciation for everything his father did

<u>Family setting in childhood</u>
—tension in the house
—no mother mentioned in the poem

<u>Poet's realization of father's love and dedication</u>

"Digging"
<u>Poet reminisces</u>
—father's skill and hard work
—grandfather's steady heaving of sods
—children's participation and acceptance

<u>Happiness of the family</u>

<u>The desire for the poet to continue the tradition</u>

DRAFTING

With a thesis statement and scratch outline to guide her, Catherine wrote the following first draft of her essay. Her instructor's comments appear in the margins and at the end of the paper.

A Comparison of Two Poems about Fathers:
First Draft

Robert Hayden's "Those Winter Sundays" and "Digging" by Seamus Heaney are poems that are inspired by fathers and composed as tributes to their fathers. Although their family backgrounds may be different, the now-grown (poets) realize the determination and dedication of their fathers and are consequently empassioned in their writings. *[careful - you're confusing poet and speaker]*

In "Those Winter Sundays," Hayden reflects back on his childhood. He remembers the many Sundays when his father got up early to start the fires so as to make the house warm for his children's awakening. The poet pictures his father's hands made rough by his weekday work. These same hands not only made the fires on Sunday but also polished his son's good shoes, in preparation, no doubt, for church. *[good detail but quotations would be helpful]*

Hayden also quite clearly remembers that his father was never thanked for his work. The reader imagines that the father had many children and may have been poor. There were inner tensions in the house and, quite noticeably, there is no mention of a mother.

Looking back, the poet now realizes the dedication and austere care with which his father took care of the family. As a child, he never thanked his father, but now, as an adult, the poet seems to appreciate the simple kindness of his father.

In a similar sense, Seamus Heaney writes "Digging" as a tribute to his father and grandfather. *[Here too quotations from the poem would strengthen your discussion]*

He also reminisces about his father and remembers with clarity the skill with which his father dug the potatoes. The grandfather, too, is remembered, as is his technique for neatly heaving sods.

There is an atmosphere of happiness with this poem. With the children helping the father harvest the potatoes, a sense of family togetherness is created. The reader feels that this family is a hard-working, but nevertheless, happy one.

As the poet reminisces about his childhood, he realizes that, unlike his father and grandfather, he will never be a master of shovelling or a person using physical strength to earn a living. He wishes to be like his father before him, desiring to accomplish and contribute. However, for the poet, any "digging" to be done will be by his pen, in the form of literature.

To conclude, the fathers in these poets' pasts inspire them to write. An appreciation and admiration for their fathers' dedication is achieved only after the children mature into adults. It is then that the fathers' impact on their children's lives is realized for its true importance.

Good start! When you revise, focus on the following:
- *Edit use of "poet" and "speaker" carefully. You cannot assume that these poems reflect the poets' own lives or attitudes toward their fathers.*
- *Add more specific references to the poems, particularly quotations.*
- *Consider adding brief references to other poems about parents.*
- *Consider rearranging your material into a point-by-point comparison, which will make the specific points of similarity and difference clearer.*

Let's discuss this draft at a conference.

First Draft: Commentary

After submitting her first draft, Catherine met with her instructor for a pre-revision conference. Together, they reviewed not only her first draft, but also her annotations, journal entries, brainstorming notes, and scratch outline. During the meeting, her instructor elaborated on his marginal comments and, building on ideas Catherine herself had discovered, helped her develop a plan for revision.

Catherine's instructor liked her approach to the poems, and he agreed that their similarities were worth exploring in detail. He thought, however, that her references to the poems' language and ideas needed to be much more specific, and that her current pattern of organization—discussing "Those Winter Sundays" first and then moving on to consider "Digging"—made the specific similarities between the two poems difficult to see.

Because the class had studied other poems in which speakers try to resolve their ambivalent feeling toward their parents, Catherine's instructor also suggested that she briefly discuss these poems to provide a wider context for her ideas. Finally, he explained the difference between the perspective of the poet and that of the **speaker,** a persona the poet creates, reminding her to edit carefully with this distinction in mind.

As she reexamined her ideas in light of her discussion with her instructor, Catherine looked again at both the annotated poems and her brainstorming notes. She then recorded her thoughts about her progress in her journal.

Journal Entry

After reviewing the poems again and talking to Professor Jackson, I discovered some additional points that I want to include in my final draft. The connection between the poet's pen and the shovel is evident in "Digging," as is the cold and the tensions in the house in "Those Winter Sundays." The tones of the two poems should also be discussed. Specifically, I think that the poet's choice of "austere" in "Those Winter Sundays" has significance and must be included. In my next draft, I'll expand my first draft—hopefully, without reading into the poems too much. I also need to reorganize my ideas so parallels between the two poems will be clearer.

Because this journal entry suggested a new arrangement of ideas within her essay, Catherine prepared a new scratch outline to guide her revision.

Scratch Outline: Second Draft

Reflections on their fathers
   Both Poems
      —fathers' dedication and hard work

Family Similarities and Differences
   "Digging"
      —loving and caring

   "Those Winter Sundays"
      —family problems (tone of the poem)

Lessons learned from Father
   "Digging"
      —inspiration (symbolism of pen and shovel)
      —realization of father's inner strength

   "Those Winter Sundays"
      —realization of father's inner strength
      —"austere" caring (images of cold)

Brief discussion of other poems about fathers

After once again reviewing all the material she had accumulated, Catherine prepared a second draft.

A Comparison of Two Poems about Fathers:
Second Draft

Robert Hayden's "Those Winter Sundays" and Seamus Heaney's "Digging" are two literary pieces that are tributes to their fathers. The inspiration and admiration wrought from the dedication of the fathers is an element evident in each poem. Although the nature of the two family relationships may differ, the common thread of the love of fathers for their children weaves through each poem.

Reflections on one's childhood can bring assorted memories to light. Presumably, Hayden and Heaney are now adults and reminisce on their childhood with a mature sense of enlightenment not found in childhood. Both poets describe their fathers' hard work and dedication to their families. Hayden remembers that even after working hard all week, his father would get up early on Sunday to warm the house in preparation for his children's rising. The poet vividly portrays his father's hands, describing "cracked hands that ached from labor in the weekday weather" (3–4). And yet, these same hands not only built the fires that drove out the cold but also polished his children's good shoes.

In a similar way, Heaney reminisces about his father's and grandfather's digging of soil and sod, elaborating on their skill and dedication to their task.

The fathers in these poems appear to be the hardest of workers, laborers who sought to support their families. Not only did they have a dedication to their work, but they also cared about and undoubtedly loved their children. Looking back, Hayden realizes that, although his childhood may not have been perfect nor his family life entirely without problems, his father loved him. Heaney's depiction of the potato picking makes us imagine a loving family led by a father and grandfather who worked together and included the children in both work and celebration. Heaney grows to become a man who has nothing but respect for his father and grandfather, wishing to emulate them and somehow follow their greatness.

Although similarities exist between the sons and fathers in the poems, the family life differs between the two. Perhaps it is the tone of the poems that best typifies the family atmosphere. The tone of "Digging" is wholesome, earthy, natural, and happy, emphasizing the healthy and caring nature of the poet's childhood. In reminiscing, Heaney seems to have no negative memories concerning his father or family. In contrast, the tone of Hayden's poem is very much like the coldness of the Sunday mornings. Even though the father warmed the house, the "chronic angers of that house" (9) did not leave with the cold. The poet, as a child, seems full of resentment toward the father, no doubt blaming him for the family problems. (Curiously, it is the father and not a mother that polishes the children's good shoes. Was there no mother?) The reader senses that the father-son communication evident in Heaney's family is missing in Hayden's.

There are many other poets who have written about their fathers. Simon J. Ortiz in "My Father's Song" writes a touching tribute to his father, who taught him to respect and care for the lives of animals and to appreciate earthly wonders. In other poems, such as Theodore Roethke's "My Papa's Waltz" and Colleen J. McElroy's "My Father's Wars," the fathers are depicted as imperfect, vulnerable people who try to cope with life as well as possible.

"Digging" and "Those Winter Sundays" are poems written from the inspirations of sons, admiring and appreciating their fathers. Childhood memories act not only as images of the past but also as aids for the poets' self-realization and enlightenment. Even after childhood, the fathers' influence over their sons is evident; only now do the poets appreciate its true importance.

Second Draft: Commentary

When she reread her second draft, Catherine thought she had accomplished some of what she had set out to do: She had, for example, added specific details and rearranged her discussion. However, she still was not satisfied with the depth of her analysis of the poem's language and tone (she had not, for example, considered the importance of the word *austere* or examined the significance of Heaney's equation of spade and pen). In addition, she realized she was still confusing poet and speaker, as her instructor had pointed out in his written comments on her first draft. She also thought that the material in paragraph 5 about other poems, although interesting, was distracting, so she decided to relocate it. She also planned to edit and proofread carefully as she prepared her final draft.

Wittaker 1

Catherine Wittaker
Professor Jackson
English 102
5 March 1993

Digging for Memories

Robert Hayden's "Those Winter Sundays" and Seamus Heaney's "Digging" are two literary pieces that are tributes to the speakers' fathers. Although the depiction of the families, as well as the tones of the two poems, differs, the common thread of the love of fathers for their children is woven through each poem.

Many other poets have written about children and their fathers. Simon J. Ortiz in "My Father's Song" (p. 47) writes a touching tribute to a father who taught the speaker to respect and care for the lives of animals and to appreciate earthly wonders. In other poems, such as Theodore Roethke's "My Papa's Waltz" (p. 46) and Colleen J. McElroy's "My Father's Wars," (p. 48) the fathers are depicted as imperfect, vulnerable people who try to cope with life as well as possible.

As all these poems reveal, reflections on childhood can bring assorted memories to light, as they do for Hayden's and Heaney's speakers. Now adults, they reminisce about their childhoods with a mature sense of enlightenment not found in childhood. Both speakers describe their fathers' hard work and dedication to their families. Hayden's speaker remembers that even after working hard all week, his father would get up early on Sunday to warm the house in preparation for his children's

Thesis

¶ 5 from second draft has been relocated. References to poems in Chapter 11 of this text include complete authors' names and titles.

Speaker and author are clearly distinguished.

rising. The speaker vividly portrays his father's hands, describing "cracked hands that ached from labor in the weekday weather" (3-4). And yet, these same hands not only built the fires that drove out the cold, but also polished his children's good shoes. In a similar way, Heaney's speaker reminisces about his father's and grandfather's digging of soil and sod, elaborating on their skill and their dedication to their task.

Parenthetical references cite line numbers.

The fathers in these poems appear to be the hardest of workers, laborers who sought to support their families. Not only were they dedicated to their work, but they also seem to have cared about and to have loved their children. Looking back, Hayden's speaker realizes that, although his childhood may not have been perfect and his family life was not entirely without problems, his father loved him. Heaney's depiction of the potato picking makes us imagine a loving family led by a father and grandfather who worked together and included the children in both work and celebration. Heaney's speaker grows to become a man who has nothing but respect for his father and grandfather, wishing to emulate them and somehow fill their shoes.

Although similarities exist between the sons and fathers in the poems, the family life the two poems depict is very different. Perhaps it is the tone of the poems that best reveals the family atmosphere. The tone of "Digging" is wholesome, earthy, natural and happy, emphasizing the healthy and caring nature of the speaker's childhood. In reminiscing, Heaney's speaker seems to have no negative memories

Whittaker 3

concerning his father or family. In contrast, the tone of Hayden's poem is very much like the coldness of the Sunday mornings. Even though the father warmed the house, the "chronic angers of that house" (9) did not leave with the cold. The speaker, as a child, seems full of resentment toward the father, no doubt blaming him for the family problems. The reader senses that the father-son communication evident in Heaney's poem is missing in Hayden's.

In spite of their differences, the reader cannot go away from either poem without the impression that both speakers learned important lessons from their fathers. Both fathers had a great amount of inner strength and dedication to their families. As the years pass, Hayden's speaker now realizes the depth of his father's devotion to his family. He uses the description of the "blueblack cold" (2) that was splintered and broken by the fires lovingly prepared by his father to suggest the strength and compassion with which his father tried to keep his family free from harm and tension. The cold suggests the tensions of the family which the father is determined to force out of the house through his "austere and lonely offices" (14).

In Seamus Heaney's poem, the father and grandfather also had a profound impact on the young speaker. As the memories come pouring back, the speaker's admiration for the men who came before him forces him to reflect on his own life and work. He realizes that he will never have the proficiency to do the physical labor of his relatives: "I've no spade

Topic sentence stresses paper's emphasis on similarities.

to follow men like them" (28). However, just as the shovel was the tool of his father and grandfather, the pen will be the tool with which the speaker will work. The shovel suggests the hard work, effort, and determination of the men who came before him, while the pen is the literary equivalent of the shovel. Heaney's speaker has been inspired by his father and grandfather and hopes to accomplish with a pen in the world of literature what they accomplished with a shovel on the land.

Conclusion   "Digging" and "Those Winter Sundays" are poems written from the perspective of sons, admiring and appreciating their fathers. Childhood memories act not only as images of the past but also as aids for the speakers' self-realization and enlightenment. Even after childhood, the fathers' influence over their sons is evident; only now, however, do the speakers appreciate its true importance.

Final Draft: Commentary

As she revised further, Catherine expanded her analysis, looking more closely at the language and tone of both poems. To support and clarify her points, she added more direct quotations from "Those Winter Sundays" and "Digging," taking care to reproduce words and punctuation marks accurately and to cite line numbers in parentheses after each quotation. She also moved her discussion of other poems to paragraph 2, where it provides a smooth transition from her introduction to her discussion of Hayden and Heaney. Her final response to the poems is more fully developed and more convincing than her earlier drafts were. The added material places additional stress on her paper's main idea: The two poems, despite their differences, share some fundamental similarities.

CHAPTER 5

VOICE

EMILY DICKINSON
(1830–1886)

I'm Nobody! Who are you?
(1891)

I'm Nobody! Who are you?
Are you—Nobody—Too?
Then there's a pair of us?
Don't tell! they'd advertise—you know!

5 How dreary—to be—Somebody!
How public—like a Frog—
To tell one's name—the livelong June—
To an admiring Bog!

THE PERSON IN THE POEM

In fiction, the author's word choice—including clichés, idioms, verbal idiosyncrasies, and the like—enables readers to form a mental impression of the narrator and to decide whether the voice that tells the story is sophisticated or unsophisticated, trustworthy or untrustworthy, innocent or experienced. Like fiction, poetry depends on a **speaker** who describes events, feelings, and ideas to readers. Finding out as much as possible about this speaker can help readers to interpret the poem. For example, the speaker in Emily Dickinson's "I'm Nobody! Who are you?" seems at once shy and playful. The first stanza of the poem suggests that the speaker is a private person, perhaps with little self-esteem. As the poem continues, however, the voice emerges as almost defiant. In a sense the speaker's two voices represent two ways of relating to the world. The first voice expresses the private self—internal, isolated, and revealed through poetry; the second reveals the public self—external, self-centered, and inevitably superficial. Far from being defeated by shyness, the speaker claims to have chosen her status as "Nobody."

One question readers might ask about "I'm Nobody! Who are you?" is how close the speaker's voice is to the poet's. Readers who conclude that the poem is about the poet's public and private responsibilities may be tempted to see the speaker and the poet as one. But this is not necessarily the case. Like the narrator of a short story, the speaker of a poem is a **persona** or mask that the poet assumes within the poem. Some readers mistakenly think that the speaker is always the poet and that the ideas expressed by the speaker are the poet's. Granted, in some poems little distance exists between the poet and the speaker, but only a thorough understanding of the poet's life and work can confirm such a relationship. Without hard evidence to support a link between speaker and poet, readers should not assume they are one and the same.

In most cases the speaker is quite different from the poet. And even when the speaker's voice conveys the attitude of the poet, it may do so indirectly. In "The Chimney Sweeper" (p. 280), for example, William Blake assumes the voice of a child to criticize the system of child labor that existed in eighteenth-century England. Even though the child speaker does not understand the conditions that cause his misery, readers sense the poet's attitude as the trusting speaker describes the conditions under which he works. The poet's indignation is especially apparent in the biting irony of the last line, in which the victimized speaker innocently assures readers that if all people do their duty, "they need not fear harm."

Sometimes, as in a work of fiction, the poem's speaker is anonymous: The speaker uses the third person and remains outside the poem. In this case—as in William Carlos Williams's "Red Wheelbarrow" (p. 140), for instance—the first-person voice is absent. At other times, the speaker has a set identity—a king, a beggar, a highwayman, a sheriff, a husband, a wife, a rich man, a chimney sweep, a child, a mythical figure, an explorer, a teacher, a faithless lover, a saint, or even a flower, an animal, or a clod of earth. Whatever the case, the speaker is not necessarily the poet, but a creation that the poet uses to convey his or her ideas. (For this reason a group of poems by a single poet can have very different voices.) Notice in the following poem how the poet assumes the mask of a fictional character.

LOUISE GLÜCK
(1943–   )

Gretel in Darkness
(1971)

This is the world we wanted. All who would have seen us dead
Are dead. I hear the witch's cry
Break in the moonlight through a sheet of sugar: God rewards.
Her tongue shrivels into gas. . . .

                                        Now, far from women's arms
 And memory of women, in our father's hut
 We sleep, are never hungry.
 Why do I not forget?
 My father bars the door, bars harm
 From this house, and it is years.

 No one remembers. Even you, my brother.
 Summer afternoons you look at me as though you meant
 To leave, as though it never happened. But I killed for you.
 I see armed firs, the spires of that gleaming kiln come back, come back—

 Nights I turn to you to hold me but you are not there.
 Am I alone? Spies
 Hiss in the stillness, Hansel we are there still, and it is real, real,
 That black forest, and the fire in earnest.

The speaker in this poem is Gretel from the fairy tale "Hansel and Gretel," commenting on her life in the years after her encounter with the witch in the forest. Speaking to her brother, Gretel observes that they now live in the world they wanted. They live with their father in his hut, and the witch and the wicked stepmother are dead. Even so, the memory of the events in the forest haunt Gretel and make it impossible for her to live "happily ever after." The "armed firs," the "gleaming kiln," and "the black forest" break through the "sheet of sugar" that her life has become.

By assuming the persona of Gretel, Louise Glück can convey some interesting and complex ideas. On one level Gretel represents any person who has lived through a traumatic experience. Memories of the event keep breaking through into the present, frustrating her attempts to reestablish her belief in the goodness of the world. The voice we hear is sad, alone, and frightened: "Nights I turn to you to hold me," she says, "but you are not there." Although the murder Gretel committed for her brother was justified, it seems to haunt her. "No one remembers," laments Gretel, not even her brother. At some level she realizes that by killing the witch she has killed a part of herself, perhaps the part of women that men fear and transform into witches and wicked stepmothers. The world that is left after the killing is the father's and the brother's, not hers, and she is now alone in a dark world haunted by the memories of the black forest. In this sense Gretel—"Now, far from women's arms / And memory of women"—may be the symbolic voice of all victimized women who, because of men, act against their own best interests—and regret it.

Various elements in a poem can help you to discover information about its speaker. The title can shed light on the speaker and sometimes give insight into the speaker's context or purpose, as Glück's title does.

Word choice can also provide information about the speaker. Notice in the following poem, for example, how Spanish words help to define the poem's frame of reference and to characterize the speaker.

LEONARD ADAMÉ
(1947–   )

My Grandmother Would Rock Quietly and Hum
(1973)

    in her house
    she would rock quietly and hum
    until her swelled hands
    calmed

5 in summer
    she wore thick stockings
    sweaters
    and grey braids

    (when "el cheque"[1] came
10 we went to Payless
    and I laughed greedily
    when given a quarter)

    mornings,
    sunlight barely lit
15 the kitchen
    and where
    there were shadows
    it was not cold

    she quietly rolled
20 flour tortillas—
    the "papas"[2]
    cracking in hot lard
    would wake me

    she had lost her teeth
25 and when we ate
    she had bread
    soaked in "café"[3]

---

[1] The check.

[2] Potatoes.

[3] Coffee.

always her eyes
were clear
30 and she could see
as I cannot yet see—
through her eyes
she gave me herself

she would sit
35 and talk
of her girlhood—
of things strange to me:
   México
   epidemics
40   relatives shot
   her father's hopes
   of this country—
how they sank
with cement dust
45 to his insides

now
when I go
to the old house
the worn spots
50 by the stove
echo of her shuffling
and
México
still hangs in her
55 fading
calendar pictures

In this poem the speaker is an adult recalling childhood memories of his grandmother. Spanish words—*el cheque, tortillas, papas,* and *café*—indicate that the speaker is of Hispanic descent. His easy use of English, his comment that talk of Mexico is strange to him, and his observation that he cannot yet see through his grandmother's eyes suggest, however, that he is not in touch with his ethnic identity. At one level, the grandmother evokes nostalgic memories of the speaker's youth. At another level, as a living symbol of his ties with Mexico, she connects him to the ethnic culture he is trying to recover. The poem ends on an ambivalent note: Even though the speaker is able to return to "the old house," the pictures of Mexico are fading, perhaps suggesting the speaker's assimilation into mainstream American culture.

    Direct statements by the speaker can also help to establish his or her identity. Notice in the poem that follows how the first line of each stanza establishes the identity of the speaker.

LANGSTON HUGHES
(1902–1967)

Negro
(1926)

    I am a Negro:
        Black as the night is black,
        Black like the depths of my Africa.

    I've been a slave:
5   Caesar told me to keep his door-steps clean.
        I brushed the boots of Washington.

    I've been a worker:
        Under my hand the pyramids arose.
        I made mortar for the Woolworth Building.

10 I've been a singer:
        All the way from Africa to Georgia
        I carried my sorrow songs.
        I made ragtime.

    I've been a victim:
15   The Belgians cut off my hands in the Congo.
        They lynch me still in Mississippi.

    I am a Negro:
        Black as the night is black,
        Black like the depths of my Africa.

Here the speaker explicitly identifies himself as "a Negro" and assumes the various roles African Americans have historically played in Western society—slave, worker, singer, and victim. By so doing, he gives voice to his nameless ancestors who, by being forced to serve others, were deprived of their identities. By presenting not just their suffering, but also their accomplishments, the speaker asserts his pride in being black. The speaker also implies that the suffering of African Americans has been caused by economic exploitation: Roman and Egyptian imperialism, Belgian colonialism, and American capitalism all used black labor to help build their societies. In this context the speaker's implied warning is clear: Except for the United States, all the societies that have persecuted blacks have declined, and long after these empires have fallen, black people still endure.

    In each of the preceding poems, the speaker is alone. The following poem, a **dramatic monologue,** presents a more complex situation in which the poet adopts a voice and creates a complete dramatic scene. The speaker is developed as a character whose distinctive temperament is revealed through his own words as he addresses a silent listener.

ROBERT BROWNING
(1812–1889)

My Last Duchess
(1842)

Ferrara

That's my last Duchess painted on the wall,
Looking as if she were alive. I call
That piece a wonder, now: Frà Pandolf's[1] hands
Worked busily a day, and there she stands.
5 Will't please you sit and look at her? I said
"Frà Pandolf" by design, for never read
Strangers like you that pictured countenance,
The depth and passion of its earnest glance,
But to myself they turned (since none puts by
10 The curtain I have drawn for you, but I)
And seemed as they would ask me, if they durst,
How such a glance came there; so, not the first
Are you to turn and ask thus. Sir, 'twas not
Her husband's presence only, called that spot
15 Of joy into the Duchess' cheek: perhaps
Frà Pandolf chanced to say "Her mantle laps
Over my lady's wrist too much," or "Paint
Must never hope to reproduce the faint
Half-flush that dies along her throat": such stuff
20 Was courtesy, she thought, and cause enough
For calling up that spot of joy. She had
A heart—how shall I say?—too soon made glad,
Too easily impressed; she liked whate'er
She looked on, and her looks went everywhere.
25 Sir, 'twas all one! My favor at her breast,
The dropping of the daylight in the West,
The bough of cherries some officious fool
Broke in the orchard for her, the white mule
She rode with round the terrace—all and each
30 Would draw from her alike the approving speech,
Or blush, at least. She thanked men—good! but thanked
Somehow—I know not how—as if she ranked

---

[1] "Brother" Pandolf, a fictive painter.

>   My gift of a nine-hundred-years-old name
>   With anybody's gift. Who'd stoop to blame
>   35 This sort of trifling? Even had you skill
>   In speech—(which I have not)—to make your will
>   Quite clear to such an one, and say, "Just this
>   Or that in you disgusts me; here you miss,
>   Or there exceed the mark"—and if she let
>   40 Herself be lessoned so, nor plainly set
>   Her wits to yours, forsooth, and made excuse
>   —E'en then would be some stooping; and I choose
>   Never to stoop. Oh sir, she smiled, no doubt,
>   Whene'er I passed her; but who passed without
>   45 Much the same smile? This grew; I gave commands;
>   Then all smiles stopped together. There she stands
>   As if alive. Will't please you rise? We'll meet
>   The company below, then. I repeat,
>   The Count your master's known munificence
>   50 Is ample warrant that no just pretense
>   Of mine for dowry will be disallowed;
>   Though his fair daughter's self, as I avowed
>   At starting, is my object. Nay, we'll go
>   Together down, sir. Notice Neptune,[2] though,
>   55 Taming a sea horse, thought a rarity,
>   Which Claus of Innsbruck[3] cast in bronze for me!

The Duke referred to in the poem is most likely Alfonso II, Duke of Ferrara, Italy, whose young wife, Lucrezia, died in 1561 after only three years of marriage. Shortly after her death, the Duke began negotiations to marry again. The poem opens with the Duke showing a portrait of his late wife to an emissary of an unnamed Count who is there to arrange a marriage between the Duke and the Count's daughter. The Duke remarks that the artist, Frà Pandolf, has caught a certain look upon the Duchess's face. This look aroused the jealousy of the Duke, who thought that it should have been for him alone. According to the Duke, the Duchess's crime was to have a heart "too soon made glad," "Too easily impressed." Eventually the Duke could stand the situation no longer; after he "gave commands," the smiles "stopped together."

Much of what readers learn about the Duke's state of mind comes from what is implied by his words. As he discusses the painting, the Duke unintentionally reveals himself to be obsessively possessive and jealous, referring to "*my* last Duchess," "*my* favor at her breast," and "*my* gift of a nine-hundred-years-old name." He keeps the picture of his late wife well

---

[2] God of the sea.

[3] An imaginary—or unidentified—sculptor. The Count of Tyrol's capital was at Innsbrück, Austria.

hidden behind a curtain that no one draws except him. His interest in the picture has little to do with the memory of his wife, however. In death the Duchess has become just what the Duke always wanted her to be: a private ornament that reflects his good taste.

The listener plays a subtle but important role in the poem. The emissary's presence establishes the dramatic situation that reveals the character of the Duke. The real purpose of the Duke's story is to tell the emissary exactly what he expects from his prospective bride and to explain the financial settlement he wants from her father. In so doing, the Duke conveys only the information that he wants the emissary to take back to his master, the Count. Although he appears vain and superficial, the Duke is actually extraordinarily shrewd. Throughout the poem he turns the conversation to his own ends and gains the advantage through flattery and false modesty. Notice, for example, that he claims he has little skill in speaking when actually he is cleverly manipulating the conversation. The success of the poem lies in the poet's ability to develop the voice of this complex character, who combines the superficial elegance and the shocking cruelty that, for Browning, typify the Italian Renaissance.

POEMS FOR FURTHER READING: THE PERSON IN THE POEM

LESLIE MARMON SILKO
(1948–)

Where Mountain Lion Lay Down with Deer
(1973)

I climb the black rock mountain
  stepping from day to day
                silently.
I smell the wind for my ancestors
5   pale blue leaves
   crushed wild mountain smell.
Returning
  up the gray stone cliff
  where I descended
10   a thousand years ago.
Returning to faded black stone.
  where mountain lion lay down with deer.
It is better to stay up here
              watching wind's reflection
15   in tall yellow flowers.

The old ones who remember me are gone
          the old songs are all forgotten
and the story of my birth.
How I danced in snow-frost moonlight
20   distant stars to the end of the Earth,
How I swam away
                in freezing mountain water
                    narrow mossy canyon tumbling down
                         out of the mountain
25   out of the deep canyon stone
                down
                    the memory
                         spilling out
                              into the world.

READING AND REACTING

1. Who does the speaker's voice represent in line 4? In line 9? Can you explain this shift?
2. From where is the speaker returning? What is the speaker trying to recover?
3. **JOURNAL ENTRY:** The poet is a Native American. How important is it for you to know this information about her? In what way does information about the poet's identity affect your reactions to the speaker of the poem?

JANICE MIRIKITANI
(1942–   )

Suicide Note
(1987)

. . An Asian American college student was reported to
have jumped to her death from her dormitory window. Her
body was found two days later under a deep cover of snow.
Her suicide note contained an apology to her
parents for having received less than a perfect
four point grade average. . .

How many notes written. . .
ink smeared like birdprints in snow.

    not good enough   not pretty enough   not smart enough
dear mother and father.
5 I apologize
for disappointing you.
I've worked very hard,
    not good enough
harder, perhaps to please you.
10 If only I were a son, shoulders broad
as the sunset threading through pine,
I would see the light in my mother's
eyes, or the golden pride reflected
in my father's dream
15 of my wide, male hands worthy of work
and comfort.
I would swagger through life
muscled and bold and assured,
drawing praises to me
20 like currents in the bed of wind, virile
with confidence.
    not good enough   not strong enough   not good enough

I apologize.
Tasks do not come easily.
25 Each failure, a glacier.
Each disapproval, a bootprint.
Each disappointment,
ice above my river.
So I have worked hard.
30   not good enough
My sacrifice I will drop
bone by bone, perched
on the ledge of my womanhood,
fragile as wings.
35   not strong enough
It is snowing steadily
surely not good weather
for flying—this sparrow
sillied and dizzied by the wind
40 on the edge.
    not smart enough
I make this ledge my altar
to offer penance.
This air will not hold me,

45 the snow burdens my crippled wings,
my tears drop like bitter cloth
softly into the gutter below.
    not good enough   not strong enough   not smart enough
        Choices thin as shaved
50   ice. Notes shredded
        drift like snow
on my broken body,
covers me like whispers
of sorries
55 sorries.
Perhaps when they find me
they will bury
my bird bones beneath
a sturdy pine
60 and scatter my feathers like
unspoken song
over this white and cold and silent
breast of earth.

READING AND REACTING

1. This poem presents a suicide note that is also an apology. Why does the speaker feel she must apologize?
2. What attitude does the speaker convey toward her parents? What emotions do you think she feels toward them?
3. **JOURNAL ENTRY:** Is the college student who speaks in this poem a stranger to you? Or is her voice in any way like that of students you know?

THE TONE OF THE POEM

Not only does a poem have a speaker, but it also has a **tone** which conveys the speaker's attitude toward his or her subject and audience. In speech, stressing a syllable in a sentence can modify or color a statement, drastically affecting the meaning of a sentence. For example, the statement "Of course you would want to go to that restaurant" seems relatively straightforward. Changing the emphasis to "Of course *you* would want to go to *that* restaurant" suggests sarcasm or criticism. However, conveying a particular tone to readers is a challenge to poets because readers rarely hear their spoken voices. Instead, poets indicate tone by using techniques such as rhyme, meter, word choice, sentence structure, figures of speech, and imagery.

The range of tones is wide. For example, a speaker in a poem may be joyful, sad, playful, serious, comic, intimate, formal, relaxed, condescending, or ironic. Consider how the tone of the following poem conveys the speaker's attitude.

ROBERT FROST
(1874–1963)

Fire and Ice
(1923)

>   Some say the world will end in fire,
>   Some say in ice.
>   From what I've tasted of desire
>   I hold with those who favor fire.
> 5 But if it had to perish twice,
>   I think I know enough of hate
>   To say that for destruction ice
>   Is also great
>   And would suffice.

The speaker uses word choice, rhyme, and understatement to comment on the human condition. He implies that although hate is destructive, so too is indifference and that the end of the world can come as a result of either. The distinctive tone of the poem is created in a number of ways. First, colloquialisms like "I've" and "great" give the poem an informal tone. In addition, the conciseness and the simple, regular meter and rhyme suggest an **epigram**—a short poem that makes a pointed comment in an unusually clear, and often witty, manner. This pointedness is consistent with the poem's glib, unemotional tone, as is the last line's wry understatement that ice "would suffice." Finally, the contrast between the poem's serious message and its informal style and offhand tone is consistent with the speaker's detached, almost smug, manner.

Sentence structure can also shed light on the speaker's tone. Consider the following poem, in which a speaker makes a comment about war.

THOMAS HARDY
(1840–1928)

The Man He Killed
(1902)

"Had he and I but met
By some old ancient inn,
We should have sat us down to wet
Right many a nipperkin![1]

5   "But ranged as infantry,
And staring face to face,
I shot at him as he at me,
And killed him in his place.

"I shot him dead because—
10   Because he was my foe,
Just so: my foe of course he was;
That's clear enough; although

"He thought he'd 'list, perhaps,
Off-hand-like—just as I—
15 Was out of work—had sold his traps—
No other reason why.

"Yes; quaint and curious war is!
You shoot a fellow down
You'd treat if met where any bar is,
20   Or help to half-a-crown."

The speaker of this poem is a soldier who tells his story about World War I in the first person. Quotation marks indicate that the speaker is engaged in conversation—perhaps in a pub. The speaker's colloquial dialect indicates that he is probably of the English working class. For him the object of war is simple: Kill or be killed. To Hardy, the speaker seems to represent all men who are thrust into a war without understanding its underlying economic or ideological causes. In this sense the speaker and his enemy are both victims of forces beyond their comprehension or control.

    The sentence structure of the poem helps to convey the attitude of the speaker toward his subject. In the first two stanzas of the poem, sentences are smooth and unbroken. The third and fourth stanzas,

---

[1] A small container of liquor.

however, use broken syntax to reflect the narrator's disturbed state of mind as he tells about the man he killed. The smooth sentence structure in the last stanza, the attempt to trivialize the incident ("Yes; quaint and curious war is!"), and the poem's singsong meter and regular rhyme scheme (*met/wet, inn/nipperkin*) suggest that the speaker is trying to regain his composure by trivializing the incident.

Longer poems frequently combine more than one tone to reflect the changing moods of the speaker. In the next poem, for example, the speaker's tone changes abruptly at the end.

AMY LOWELL
(1874–1925)

Patterns
(1915)

I walk down the garden paths,
And all the daffodils
Are blowing, and the bright blue squills.
I walk down the patterned garden-paths
5 In my stiff, brocaded gown.
With my powdered hair and jewelled fan,
I too am a rare
Pattern. As I wander down
The garden paths.

10 My dress is richly figured,
And the train
Makes a pink and silver stain
On the gravel, and the thrift
Of the borders.
15 Just a plate of current fashion
Tripping by in high-heeled, ribboned shoes.
Not a softness anywhere about me,
Only whalebone[1] and brocade.
And I sink on a seat in the shade
20 Of a lime tree. For my passion
Wars against the stiff brocade.
The daffodils and squills
Flutter in the breeze
As they please.
25 And I weep;
For the lime-tree is in blossom
And one small flower has dropped upon my bosom.

---

[1] Used in making corsets.

And the plashing of waterdrops
In the marble fountain
30 Comes down the garden-paths.
The dripping never stops.
Underneath my stiffened gown
Is the softness of a woman bathing in a marble basin,
A basin in the midst of hedges grown
35 So thick, she cannot see her lover hiding,
But she guesses he is near,
And the sliding of the water
Seems the stroking of a dear
Hand upon her.
40 What is Summer in a fine brocaded gown!
I should like to see it lying in a heap upon the ground.
All the pink and silver crumpled up on the ground.

I would be the pink and silver as I ran along the paths,
And he would stumble after,
45 Bewildered by my laughter.
I should see the sun flashing from his sword-hilt and buckles
   on his shoes.
I would choose
To lead him in a maze along the patterned paths,
A bright and laughing maze for my heavy-booted lover.
50 Till he caught me in the shade,
And the buttons of his waistcoat bruised my body as he clasped me,
Aching, melting, unafraid.
With the shadows of the leaves and the sundrops,
And the plopping of the waterdrops,
55 All about us in the open afternoon—
I am very like to swoon
With the weight of this brocade,
For the sun sifts through the shade.

Underneath the fallen blossom
60 In my bosom,
Is a letter I have hid.
It was brought to me this morning by a rider from the Duke.
Madam, we regret to inform you that Lord Hartwell
Died in action Thursday se'nnight.[2]
65 As I read it in the white, morning sunlight,
The letters squirmed like snakes.
"Any answer, Madam," said my footman.
"No," I told him.
"See that the messenger takes some refreshment.

[2] "Seven night," or a week ago Thursday.

70 No, no answer."
And I walked into the garden,
Up and down the patterned paths,
In my stiff, correct brocade.
The blue and yellow flowers stood up proudly in the sun,
75 Each one.
I stood upright too,
Held rigid to the pattern
By the stiffness of my gown.
Up and down I walked.
80 Up and down.

In a month he would have been my husband.
In a month, here, underneath this lime,
We would have broken the pattern;
He for me, and I for him,
85 He as Colonel, I as Lady,
On this shady seat.
He had a whim
That sunlight carried blessing.
And I answered, "It shall be as you have said."
90 Now he is dead.

In Summer and in Winter I shall walk
Up and down
The patterned garden-paths
In my stiff, brocaded gown.
95 The squills and daffodils
Will give place to pillared roses, and to asters, and to snow.
I shall go
Up and down,
In my gown.
100 Gorgeously arrayed,
Boned and stayed.
And the softness of my body will be guarded from embrace
By each button, hook, and lace.
For the man who should loose me is dead,
105 Fighting with the Duke in Flanders,[3]
In a pattern called a war.
Christ! What are patterns for?

The speaker begins by describing herself walking down garden paths. She wears a stiff brocaded gown, has powdered hair, and carries a jewelled

---

[3] Region in northwestern Europe, including part of northern France and western Belgium. Flanders was the site of a historic World War I battle.

fan. By her own admission she is "a plate of current fashion." Although her tone seems controlled, she is preoccupied by sensual thoughts. Beneath her "stiffened gown" is the "softness of a woman bathing in a marble basin," and the "sliding of the water" in a fountain reminds the speaker of the stroking of her lover's hand. She imagines herself shedding her brocaded gown and running with her lover along the maze of "patterned paths." The sensuality of the speaker's thoughts stands in marked contrast to the images of stiffness and control that dominate the poem; her passion "wars against the stiff brocade." She is also full of repressed rage. After all, she knows that her lover has been killed, and she realizes the meaninglessness of the patterns and the rituals of her life, patterns to which she has conformed, just as her lover has by going to war and doing what he was supposed to do. Her tone is a combination of barely contained anger and frustration. In the last line of the poem, when the speaker finally lets out her rage, the tone changes abruptly.

POEMS FOR FURTHER READING: TONE

SIMON J. ORTIZ
(1941–   )

Speaking
(1977)

I take him outside
under the trees,
have him stand on the ground.
We listen to the crickets,
5 cicadas, million years old sound.
Ants come by us.
I tell them,
"This is he, my son.
This boy is looking at you.
10 I am speaking for him."

The crickets, cicadas,
the ants, the millions of years
are watching us,
hearing us.
15 My son murmurs infant words,
speaking, small laughter
bubbles from him.
Tree leaves tremble.
They listen to this boy
20 speaking for me.

READING AND REACTING

1. How would you characterize the speaker's tone? Is it consistent throughout? Explain.
2. What is the speaker's attitude toward his son's baby talk? Why does the speaker describe his son as murmuring "infant words"?
3. What do you think the speaker means when he says, "the millions of years / are watching us"? What does this comment suggest about the speaker?
4. **JOURNAL ENTRY:** The first stanza ends with the father speaking for his infant son, and the last stanza ends with the son speaking for the father. How does this shift help you to understand the poem?

WILLIAM WORDSWORTH
(1770–1850)

The World Is Too Much with Us
(1807)

    The world is too much with us; late and soon,
    Getting and spending, we lay waste our powers;
    Little we see in Nature that is ours;
    We have given our hearts away, a sordid boon!
5 This Sea that bares her bosom to the moon;
    The winds that will be howling at all hours,
    And are up-gathered now like sleeping flowers;
    For this, for everything, we are out of tune;
    It moves us not. Great God! I'd rather be
10 A Pagan suckled in a creed outworn;
    So might I, standing on this pleasant lea,
    Have glimpses that would make me less forlorn;
    Have sight of Proteus[1] rising from the sea;
    Or hear old Triton[2] blow his wreathèd horn.

READING AND REACTING

1. What is the speaker's attitude toward the contemporary world? What is the cause of the condition he complains about?

---

[1] Sometimes said to be Poseidon's son, this Greek sea god had the ability to change shapes at will and to tell the future.

[2] The trumpeter of the sea, this sea god is usually pictured blowing on a conch shell. Triton was the son of Poseidon, ruler of the sea.

2. This poem is a **sonnet**, a highly structured traditional form. How do the rhyme scheme and the regular meter establish the poem's tone?

3. **JOURNAL ENTRY:** Imagine you are a modern-day environmentalist, labor organizer, or corporate executive. How would you react to the sentiments expressed in this poem?

SYLVIA PLATH
(1932–1963)

Morning Song
(1962)

Love set you going like a fat gold watch.
The midwife slapped your footsoles, and your bald cry
Took its place among the elements.

Our voices echo, magnifying your arrival. New statue.
5 In a drafty museum, your nakedness
Shadows our safety. We stand round blankly as walls.

I'm no more your mother
Than the cloud that distills a mirror to reflect its own slow
Effacement at the wind's hand.

10 All night your moth-breath
Flickers among the flat pink roses. I wake to listen:
A far sea moves in my ear.

One cry, and I stumble from bed, cow-heavy and floral
In my Victorian nightgown.
15 Your mouth opens clean as a cat's. The window square
Whitens and swallows its dull stars. And now you try
Your handful of notes;
The clear vowels rise like balloons.

READING AND REACTING

1. Who is the speaker? To whom is she speaking? What does the poem reveal about her?

2. What is the poem's subject? What attitudes about her subject does the poet probably expect the reader to have?

3. How is the tone of the first stanza different from that of the third? What does this difference show about the speaker's assumptions about motherhood?

ROBERT HERRICK
(1591–1674)

To the Virgins, to Make Much of Time
(1648)

Gather ye rosebuds while ye may,
    Old Time is still a-flying;
And this same flower that smiles today,
    Tomorrow will be dying.

5 The glorious lamp of heaven, the sun,
    The higher he's a-getting,
The sooner will his race be run,
    And nearer he's to setting.

That age is best which is the first,
10   When youth and blood are warmer;
But being spent, the worse, and worst
    Times still succeed the former.

Then be not coy, but use your time,
    And while ye may, go marry;
15 For having lost but once your prime,
    You may forever tarry.

READING AND REACTING

1. How would you characterize the speaker? Whom is the speaker addressing? Does he expect his listeners to share his views?
2. The speaker develops the poem almost like an argument. What is the speaker's main point? How does he support it?
3. What effect does the use of rhyme in the poem have on its tone?
4. **JOURNAL ENTRY:** Whose side are you on—the speaker's or those he addresses?

A SPECIAL CASE OF TONE: IRONY

Just as in fiction and drama, **irony** in poetry occurs when a discrepancy exists between two levels of meaning or experience. Consider the tone of the following lines by Stephen Crane:

Do not weep, maiden, for war is kind.
Because your lover threw wild hands toward the sky
And the afrightened steed ran on alone,
Do not weep.
War is kind.

How can war be "kind"? Isn't war exactly the opposite of "kind"? Surely the speaker does not intend his words to be taken literally. Thus, by making this statement, the speaker actually conveys the opposite idea: War is a cruel and mindless exercise of violence.

Skillfully used, irony is a powerful way of making a comment about a situation or of manipulating a reader's emotions. Implicit in irony is the writer's assumption that readers will not be misled by the literal meaning of a statement. In order for irony to work, readers must recognize the disparity between what is said and what is meant, or between what a character or speaker thinks is occurring and what readers know to be happening.

One kind of irony that appears in poetry is **dramatic irony,** which occurs when a character or speaker believes one thing and readers realize something else. In the following poem the poet uses a deranged speaker to tell a story that is filled with irony.

ROBERT BROWNING
(1812–1889)

Porphyria's Lover
(1836)

The rain set early in to-night,
    The sullen wind was soon awake,
It tore the elm-tops down for spite,
    And did its worst to vex the lake:
5   I listened with heart fit to break.
When glided in Porphyria; straight
    She shut the cold out and the storm,
And kneeled and made the cheerless grate
    Blaze up, and all the cottage warm;
10   Which done, she rose, and from her form
Withdrew the dripping cloak and shawl,
    And laid her soiled gloves by, untied
Her hat and let the damp hair fall,
    And, last, she sat down by my side
15   And called me. When no voice replied,
She put my arm about her waist,
    And made her smooth white shoulder bare,
And all her yellow hair displaced,

And, stooping, made my cheek lie there,
20   And spread, o'er all, her yellow hair,
    Murmuring how she loved me—she
        Too weak, for all her heart's endeavour,
    To set its struggling passion free
        From pride, and vainer ties dissever,
25   And give herself to me for ever.
    But passion sometimes would prevail,
        Nor could to-night's gay feast restrain
    A sudden thought of one so pale
        For love of her, and all in vain:
30   So, she was come through wind and rain.
    Be sure I looked up at her eyes
        Happy and proud; at last I knew
    Porphyria worshipped me; surprise
        Made my heart swell, and still it grew
35   While I debated what to do.
    That moment she was mine, mine, fair,
        Perfectly pure and good: I found
    A thing to do, and all her hair
        In one long yellow string I wound
40   Three times her little throat around,
    And strangled her. No pain felt she;
        I am quite sure she felt no pain.
    As a shut bud that holds a bee,
        I warily oped her lids: again
45   Laughed the blue eyes without a stain.
    And I untightened next the tress
        About her neck; her cheek once more
    Blushed bright beneath my burning kiss:
        I propped her head up as before,
50   Only, this time my shoulder bore
    Her head, which droops upon it still:
        The smiling rosy little head,
    So glad it has its utmost will,
        That all it scorned at once is fled,
55   And I, its love, am gained instead!
    Porphyria's love: she guessed not how
        Her darling one wish would be heard.
    And thus we sit together now,
        And all night long we have not stirred,
60   And yet God has not said a word!

Like Browning's "My Last Duchess" (p. 78) this poem is a **dramatic monologue.** The speaker presents his story in a straightforward manner, seemingly unaware of the horror of his tale. In fact, much of the effect of this poem comes from the speaker's telling his tale of murder in a flat, unemotional tone.

The irony of the poem and of its title gradually becomes apparent as the monologue progresses. Porphyria comes to the speaker through wind and rain and, after making a fire, takes off her dripping cloak and soiled gloves. At first the speaker fears that Porphyria is too weak to free herself from pride and vanity to love him. As he looks in her eyes, however, he comes to believe that she worships him. To preserve the perfection of Porphyria's love, the speaker strangles her with her own hair. He assures listeners, "I am quite sure she felt no pain." Like many of Browning's narrators, the speaker in this poem exhibits a selfish and perverse need to possess another person totally. The moment the speaker realizes that Porphyria loves him, he feels compelled to kill her and keep her his forever. According to him, she is at this point "mine, mine, fair, / Perfectly pure and good." In an attempt to justify his actions, the speaker reveals himself to be a deluded psychopathic killer. He believes that by murdering Porphyria he actually fulfills "Her darling one wish"—to preserve the purity of her love forever.

Another kind of irony is **situational irony,** which occurs when the situation itself conflicts with the readers' expectations. For example, in "Porphyria's Lover" the meeting of two lovers results not in joy and passion but in murder. Notice in the next poem too how the situation creates irony.

PERCY BYSSHE SHELLEY
(1792–1822)

Ozymandias
(1818)

    I met a traveler from an antique land
    Who said: Two vast and trunkless legs of stone
    Stand in the desert. Near them, on the sand,
    Half sunk, a shattered visage lies, whose frown,
5 And wrinkled lip, and sneer of cold command,
    Tell that its sculptor well those passions read
    Which yet survive, stamped on these lifeless things,
    The hand that mocked them, and the heart that fed;
    And on the pedestal these words appear:
10 "My name is Ozymandias,[1] king of kings:
    Look on my works, ye Mighty, and despair!"
    Nothing beside remains. Round the decay
    Of that colossal wreck, boundless and bare
    The lone and level sands stretch far away.

---

[1] The Greek name for Ramses II, ruler of Egypt in the thirteenth century B.C.

The speaker tells a tale about a colossal statue that lies shattered in the desert. Its head lies separated from the trunk, and the face has a wrinkled lip and a "sneer of cold command." On the pedestal of the monument are words exhorting all those who pass to "Look on my works, ye Mighty, and despair!" The situational irony of the poem has its source in the contrast between the "colossal wreck" and the boastful inscription on its base. To the speaker, Ozymandias stands for the vanity of those who mistakenly think they can withstand the ravages of time.

Perhaps the most common kind of irony found in poetry is **verbal irony,** which is created when words say one thing but mean another, often the opposite. When verbal irony is particularly biting, it is called **sarcasm**—for example, Stephen Crane's use of the word *kind* in his antiwar poem "War Is Kind." In speech verbal irony is easy to detect through the speaker's change in tone or emphasis. In writing, when these signals are absent, the situation becomes more difficult. Poets must depend on the context of a remark or on the contrast between a word and other images in the poem to create irony.

Consider how verbal irony is established in the following poem.

ARIEL DORFMAN
(1942–   )

Hope
(1988)

translated by Edith Grossman with the author

My son has been
missing
since May 8
of last year.

5   They took him
just for a few hours
they said
just for some routine
questioning.

10 After the car left,
the car with no license plate,
we couldn't

find out

anything else
15 about him.

But now things have changed.
We heard from a compañero
who just got out
that five months later
20 they were torturing him
in Villa Grimaldi,
at the end of September
they were questioning him
in the red house
25 that belonged to the Grimaldis.

They say they recognized
his voice his screams
they say.

Somebody tell me frankly
30 what times are these
what kind of world
what country?
What I'm asking is
how can it be
35 that a father's
joy
a mother's
joy
is knowing
40 that they
that they are still
torturing
their son?
Which means
45 that he was alive
five months later
and our greatest
hope
will be to find out
50 next year
that they're still torturing him
eight months later

and he may   might   could
still be alive.

Although it is not necessary to know the background of the poet to appreciate this poem, it does help to know that Ariel Dorfman is a native of Chile. After the assassination of Salvador Allende, Chile's elected socialist president, in September 1973, the civilian government was replaced by a military dictatorship. Civil rights were suspended, and activists, students, and members of opposition parties were arrested and frequently detained indefinitely, sometimes simply disappearing. The irony of this poem originates in the discrepancy between the way the word *hope* is used in the poem and the way it is usually used. For most people, hope has positive associations, but in the poem it takes on new meaning. This irony is not lost on the speaker.

POEMS FOR FURTHER READING: IRONY

W. H. AUDEN
(1907–1973)

The Unknown Citizen
(1939)

*(To JS/07/M/378
This Marble Monument Is Erected by the State)*

He was found by the Bureau of Statistics to be
One against whom there was no official complaint,
And all the reports on his conduct agree
That, in the modern sense of an old-fashioned word, he was a saint,
5 For in everything he did he served the Greater Community.
Except for the War till the day he retired
He worked in a factory and never got fired,
But satisfied his employers, Fudge Motors Inc.
Yet he wasn't a scab or odd in his views,
10 For his Union reports that he paid his dues,
(Our report on his Union shows it was sound)
And our Social Psychology workers found
That he was popular with his mates and liked a drink.
The Press are convinced that he bought a paper every day
15 And that his reactions to advertisements were normal in every way.
Policies taken out in his name prove that he was fully insured,
And his Health-card shows he was once in hospital but left it cured.
Both Producers Research and High-Grade Living declare
He was fully sensible to the advantages of the Installment Plan
20 And had everything necessary to the Modern Man,
A phonograph, a radio, a car and a frigidaire.
Our researchers into Public Opinion are content
That he held the proper opinions for the time of year;
When there was peace, he was for peace; when there was war, he went.
25 He was married and added five children to the population,

Which our Eugenist[1] says was the right number for a parent of his generation,
And our teachers report that he never interfered with their education.
Was he free? Was he happy? The question is absurd:
Had anything been wrong, we should certainly have heard.

READING AND REACTING

1. The unknown citizen represents modern citizens, who, according to the poem, are programmed like machines. How does the title help to establish the tone of the poem? How does the inscription on the monument help to establish the tone?
2. Who is the speaker? What is his attitude toward the unknown citizen? Does his attitude differ from the poet's? How can you tell?
3. What kinds of irony are present in the poem? Identify several examples.
4. **JOURNAL ENTRY:** This poem was written in 1939. Write a journal entry in which you discuss how well it has held up. Does its criticism apply to contemporary society, or does it seem dated?

ANNE SEXTON
(1928–1974)

Cinderella
(1970)

You always read about it:
the plumber with twelve children
who wins the Irish Sweepstakes.
From toilets to riches.
₅ That story.

Or the nursemaid,
some luscious sweet from Denmark
who captures the oldest son's heart.
From diapers to Dior.[1]
₁₀ That story.

---

[1] One who studies the science of human improvement, especially through genetic control.

[1] Fashion designer Christian Dior.

Or a milkman who serves the wealthy,
eggs, cream, butter, yogurt, milk,
the white truck like an ambulance
who goes into real estate
15 and makes a pile.
From homogenized to martinis at lunch.

Or the charwoman
who is on the bus when it cracks up
and collects enough from the insurance.
20 From mops to Bonwit Teller.[2]
That story.

Once
the wife of a rich man was on her deathbed
and she said to her daughter Cinderella:
25 Be devout. Be good. Then I will smile
down from heaven in the seam of a cloud.
The man took another wife who had
two daughters, pretty enough
but with hearts like blackjacks.
30 Cinderella was their maid.
She slept on the sooty hearth each night
and walked around looking like Al Jolson.[3]
Her father brought presents home from town,
jewels and gowns for the other women
35 but the twig of a tree for Cinderella.
She planted that twig on her mother's grave
and it grew to a tree where a white dove sat.
Whenever she wished for anything the dove
would drop it like an egg upon the ground.
40 The bird is important, my dears, so heed him.

Next came the ball, as you all know.
It was a marriage market.
The prince was looking for a wife.
All but Cinderella were preparing
45 and gussying up for the big event.
Cinderella begged to go too.
Her stepmother threw a dish of lentils
into the cinders and said: Pick them
up in an hour and you shall go.

[2] Exclusive department store.

[3] Al Jolson (Asa Yoelson; 1886–1950)—American singer and songwriter, famous for his "black-face" minstrel performances.

50 The white dove brought all his friends;
all the warm wings of the fatherland came,
and picked up the lentils in a jiffy.
No, Cinderella, said the stepmother,
you have no clothes and cannot dance.
55 That's the way with stepmothers.

Cinderella went to the tree at the grave
and cried forth like a gospel singer:
Mama! Mama! My turtledove,
send me to the prince's ball!
60 The bird dropped down a golden dress
and delicate little gold slippers.
Rather a large package for a simple bird.
So she went. Which is no surprise.
Her stepmother and sisters didn't
65 recognize her without her cinder face
and the prince took her hand on the spot
and danced with no other the whole day.

As nightfall came she thought she'd better
get home. The prince walked her home
70 and she disappeared into the pigeon house
and although the prince took an axe and broke
it open she was gone. Back to her cinders.
These events repeated themselves for three days.
However on the third day the prince
75 covered the palace steps with cobbler's wax
and Cinderella's gold shoe stuck upon it.
Now he would find whom the shoe fit
and find his strange dancing girl for keeps.
He went to their house and the two sisters
80 were delighted because they had lovely feet.
The eldest went into a room to try the slipper on
but her big toe got in the way so she simply
sliced it off and put on the slipper.
The prince rode away with her until the white dove
85 told him to look at the blood pouring forth.
That is the way with amputations.
They don't just heal up like a wish.
The other sister cut off her heel
but the blood told as blood will.
90 The prince was getting tired.
He began to feel like a shoe salesman.
But he gave it one last try.
This time Cinderella fit into the shoe
like a love letter into its envelope.

> 95 At the wedding ceremony
> the two sisters came to curry favor
> and the white dove pecked their eyes out.
> Two hollow spots were left
> like soup spoons.
>
> 100 Cinderella and the prince
> lived, they say, happily ever after,
> like two dolls in a museum case
> never bothered by diapers or dust,
> never arguing over the timing of an egg,
> 105 never telling the same story twice,
> never getting a middle-aged spread,
> their darling smiles pasted on for eternity
> Regular Bobbsey Twins.[4]
> That story.

READING AND REACTING

1. The first twenty-one lines of the poem act as a prelude. How does this prelude help to establish the speaker's ironic tone?
2. At times the speaker talks directly to readers. What effect do these asides have? Would the poem be more effective without them?
3. Throughout the poem, the speaker mixes contemporary colloquial expressions with the conventional diction of the fairy tale. How does the juxtaposition of these different kinds of diction create irony?
4. **JOURNAL ENTRY:** What details of the fairy tale does Sexton change in her poem? Why do you think she makes these changes?

DUDLEY RANDALL
(1914–   )

Ballad of Birmingham
(1969)

(On the bombing of a Church in Birmingham, Alabama, 1963)

> "Mother dear, may I go downtown
> Instead of out to play,
> And march the streets of Birmingham
> In a Freedom March today?"

---

[4] The two sets of twins—Nan and Bert, Flossie and Freddie—in a popular series of early twentieth-century children's books. They led an idealized, problem-free life.

5 "No, baby, no, you may not go,
For the dogs are fierce and wild,
And clubs and hoses, guns and jails
Aren't good for a little child."

"But, mother, I won't be alone.
10 Other children will go with me,
And march the streets of Birmingham
To make our country free."

"No, baby, no, you may not go,
For I fear those guns will fire.
15 But you may go to church instead
And sing in the children's choir."

She has combed and brushed her night-dark hair,
And bathed rose petal sweet,
And drawn white gloves on her small brown hands,
20 And white shoes on her feet.

The mother smiled to know her child
Was in the sacred place,
But that smile was the last smile
To come upon her face.

25 For when she heard the explosion,
Her eyes grew wet and wild.
She raced through the streets of Birmingham
Calling for her child.

She clawed through bits of glass and brick,
30 Then lifted out a shoe.
"O, here's the shoe my baby wore,
But, baby, where are you?"

READING AND REACTING

1. Who are the two speakers in the poem? How do their attitudes differ? How do these attitudes affect the tone of the poem?
2. What kinds of irony are present in the poem? Give examples of each kind you identify.
3. This poem is a **ballad,** a form of poetry written to be sung or recited. Ballads typically repeat words and phrases and have regular meter and rhyme. What is the effect of the regular rhyme, repeated words, and sing-song meter on the poem's tone?
4. **JOURNAL ENTRY:** This poem was written in response to the 1963 bombing of the 16th Street Baptist Church in Birmingham,

Alabama, a bombing that killed four children. How does this historical information help you to appreciate the irony of the poem?

Checklist for Writing about Voice

The Person in the Poem

- Who is the speaker in the poem?
- How close is the voice of the speaker to the voice of the poet?
- Does the speaker use the first or third person?
- Is the speaker anonymous, or does he or she have a set identity?
- In what way does the persona help the poet to convey his or her ideas?
- Does the title give information about the speaker?
- In what way do word choice and other uses of language provide information about the speaker?
- Does the speaker make any direct statements that help you to establish his or her identity or character?
- Does the speaker address anyone? How can you tell? Does the presence of a listener affect the speaker? Do the listener's reactions provide information about the state of mind and character of the speaker?

Tone

- What is the speaker's attitude toward his or her subject?
- In what way do word choice, rhyme, meter, sentence structure, figures of speech, and imagery help to convey the attitude of the speaker?
- Is the tone of the poem consistent? How do shifts in tone reflect the changing moods or attitudes of the speaker?
- Does any dramatic irony exist in the poem? Are there any examples of situational irony?
- Does verbal irony appear in the poem?

WRITING SUGGESTIONS: VOICE

1. Write an essay in which you compare your attitude toward your cultural identity with that of the speaker in "My Grandmother Would Rock Quietly and Hum" (p. 75).
2. Compare the women's voices in "Cinderella" (p. 99) and "Gretel in Darkness" (p. 73). In what way are their attitudes toward men similar? In what way are they different?

3. The theme of Herrick's poem "To the Virgins, to Make Much of Time" (p. 92) is known as **carpe diem** or "seize the day." Read Andrew Marvell's "To His Coy Mistress" (p. 175), which has the same theme, and compare its tone with that of "To the Virgins, to Make Much of Time."

4. Read the following poem by Emily Dickinson, and compare her speaker's use of the word *hope* with Ariel Dorfman's (p. 96).

"Hope" is the thing with feathers—
That perches in the soul—
And sings the tune without the words—
And never stops—at all—

And sweetest—in the Gale—is heard—
And sore must be the storm—
That could abash the little Bird—
That kept so many warm—

I've heard it in the chillest land—
And on the strangest Sea—
Yet, never, in Extremity,
It asked a crumb—of Me.

5. Because the speaker and the poet are not necessarily the same, poems by the same author can have different voices. Compare the voices of "Morning Song" (p. 91) and "Daddy" (p. 170), both by Sylvia Plath.

CHAPTER 6

WORD CHOICE, WORD ORDER

SIPHO SEPAMLA
(1932–)

Words, Words, Words*

We don't speak of tribal wars anymore
we say simple faction fights
there are no tribes around here
only nations
5 it makes sense you see
'cause from there
one moves to multinational
it makes sense you get me
'cause from there
10 one gets one's homeland
which is a reasonable idea
'cause from there
one can dabble with independence
which deserves warm applause
15 —the bloodless revolution

we are talking of words
words tossed around as if
denied location by the wind
we mean those words some spit
20 others grab
dress them up for the occasion
fling them on the lap of an audience
we are talking of those words
that stalk our lives like policemen
25 words no dictionary can embrace
words that change sooner than seasons
we mean words

---

* Publication date is not available.

that spell out our lives
words, words, words
30 for there's a kind of poetic licence
doing the rounds in these parts

Words identify and name, characterize and distinguish, compare and contrast. Words describe, limit, and embellish; words locate and measure. Without words, there cannot be a poem. Even though words may be elusive and uncertain and changeable, "tossed around as if / denied location by the wind" and "can change sooner than seasons," they still can "stalk our lives like policemen." In poetry, as in love and politics, words matter.

Beyond the quantitative—how many words, how many letters and syllables—is the much more important quality of words: Which are chosen, and why? Why are certain words placed next to others? What does a word suggest in a particular context? How are the words arranged? What exactly constitutes the right word?

WORD CHOICE

In poetry, even more than in fiction or drama, words tend to become the focus—sometimes even the true subject—of the work. For this reason, the choice of one word over another can be crucial to a poem's impact. A poem does much more than relate feelings or experiences. It suggests, through words, the significance of these feelings and experiences. Because poems are brief, they must compress many ideas into a few lines; poets know how much weight each individual word carries, and so they choose with great care, often selecting words that imply more than they state.

Poets may choose a word because of its sound. For instance, it may echo another word's sound, and such repetition may place emphasis on both words; it may rhyme with another word and therefore be needed to preserve the poem's rhyme scheme; or, it may have a certain combination of stressed and unstressed syllables needed to maintain the poem's metrical pattern. Occasionally, poets may even choose a word because of how it looks on the page. More often, they will select a word because it is part of a pattern of related words that helps to convey the poem's ideas.

At the same time, poets may choose words for their degree of abstraction or concreteness, specificity or generality. An *abstract* word refers to an intangible idea, condition, or quality, something that cannot be perceived by the senses—love, patriotism, and so on. A *concrete* word denotes an item that is a perceivable, tangible entity—for example, a kiss or a flag. *Specific* words denote particular items; *general* words refer to an entire class or group of items. As the following example illustrates, whether a word is specific or general is relative; its degree of specificity or generality depends on its relationship to other words.

> Poem → closed form poem → sonnet → seventeenth-century sonnet → Elizabethan sonnet → sonnet by Shakespeare → "My Mistress' Eyes Are Nothing Like the Sun"

Sometimes a poet wants a precise word, one that is specific and concrete. At other times, however, a poet might prefer general or abstract language, which may allow for more subtlety—or even for intentional ambiguity.

Finally, a word may be chosen for its **connotation**—what it suggests. Every word has one or more **denotations**—what it signifies without emotional associations, judgments, or opinions. The word *family*, for example, denotes "a group of related things or people." Connotation is a more complex matter, however, for a single word may have many different associations. In general terms, a word may have a connotation that is positive, neutral, or negative. Thus *family* may have a positive connotation when it describes a group of loving relatives, a neutral connotation when it describes a biological category, and an ironically negative connotation when it describes an organized crime family. Beyond this distinction, *family*, like any other word, may have a variety of emotional and social associations, suggesting loyalty, warmth, home, security, or duty. In fact, many words have somewhat different meanings in different contexts. To help guide their word choice, poets consider what a particular word may suggest to readers as well as what it denotes.

In the poem that follows the poet chooses words for their sounds, their relationships to other words, and their connotations, creating a poem in which diction subtly and effectively reinforces theme.

WALT WHITMAN
(1819–1892)

When I Heard the Learn'd Astronomer
(1865)

When I heard the learn'd astronomer,
When the proofs, the figures, were ranged in columns before me,
When I was shown the charts and diagrams, to add, divide, and measure them,
5 When I sitting heard the astronomer where he lectured with much applause in the lecture-room,
How soon unaccountable I became tired and sick,
Till rising and gliding out I wander'd off by myself,
In the mystical moist night-air, and from time to time,
10 Look'd up in perfect silence at the stars.

This poem might be paraphrased as follows: "When I grew restless listening to an astronomy lecture, I went outside, where I found I learned more just by looking at the stars than I had learned inside." But the paraphrase is neither as rich nor as complex as the poem. Through careful use of diction, Whitman establishes a dichotomy that supports the poem's central theme about the relative merits of two ways of learning.

The poem may be divided into two groups of four lines. The first four lines, unified by the repetition of "When," introduce the astronomer and his tools: "proofs," "figures," and "charts and diagrams" to be added, divided, and measured. In this section of the poem, the speaker is passive: He sits and listens ("I heard"; "I was shown"; "I sitting heard"). The repetition of "When" reinforces the dry monotony of the lecture. In the next four lines, the choice of words signals the change in the speaker's actions and reactions. The confined lecture hall is replaced by "the mystical moist night-air"; the dry lecture and automatic applause give way to "perfect silence"; instead of sitting passively the speaker becomes active (he rises, glides, wanders); instead of listening, he looks. The mood of the first half of the poem is restrained: The language is concrete and physical, and the speaker is studying, receiving information from a "learn'd" authority. The rest of the poem, celebrating intuitive knowledge and feelings, is more abstract, freer. Throughout the poem, the lecture hall contrasts sharply with the natural world outside its walls.

After considering the poem as a whole, readers should not find it hard to understand why the poet selected certain words. Whitman's use of "lectured" in line 4 rather than a more neutral word like "spoke" is appropriate both because of its suggestion of formality and distance and because it echoes "lecture-room" in the same line. The word "sick" in line 5 is striking because it connotes physical as well as emotional distress, more effectively conveying the extent of the speaker's discomfort than "bored" or "restless" would. "Rising" and "gliding" (6) are used rather than "standing" and "walking out" both because of the way their stressed vowel sounds echo each other (and echo "time to time" in the next line) and because of their connotation of dreaminess, which is consistent with "wander'd" (6) and "mystical" (7). The word "moist" (7) is chosen not only because its consonant sounds echo the *m* and *st* sounds in "mystical," but also because they contrast with the dry, airless lecture hall. Finally, line 8's "perfect silence" is a better choice than a reasonable substitute like "complete silence" or "total silence," which suggest the degree of the silence but not its quality.

In the next poem, too, the poet pays careful attention to word choice.

WILLIAM STAFFORD
(1914–   )

For the Grave of Daniel Boone
(1957)

The farther he went the farther home grew.
Kentucky became another room;
the mansion arched over the Mississippi;
flowers were spread all over the floor.
5 He traced ahead a deepening home,
and better, with goldenrod:

Leaving the snakeskin of place after place,
going on—after the trees
the grass, a bird flying after a song.
10 Rifle so level, sighting so well
his picture freezes down to now,
a story-picture for children.

They go over the velvet falls
into the tapestry of his time,
15 heirs to the landscape, feeling no jar:
it is like evening; they are the quail
surrounding his fire, coming in for the kill;
their little feet move sacred sand.

Children, we live in a barbwire time
20 but like to follow the old hands back—
the ring in the light, the knuckle, the palm,
all the way to Daniel Boone,
hunting our own kind of deepening home.
From the land that was his I heft this rock.

25 Here on his grave I put it down.

A number of words in "For the Grave of Daniel Boone" are noteworthy for their multiple denotations and connotations. In the first stanza, for example, "home" is not the concrete *house* but rather an abstract state, a dynamic concept that grows and deepens, encompassing states and rivers while becoming paradoxically more and more elusive. In literal terms, Boone's "home" at the poem's end is a narrow, confined space: his grave. In a wider sense, his home is the United States, particularly the natural landscape he explored. Thus the word "home" comes to have a variety of associations to readers beyond its denotative meaning: It suggests both the infinite possibilities beyond the frontier and the realities of civilization's walls and fences.

The word "snakeskin" denotes "the skin of a snake"; its most immediate connotations are smoothness and slipperiness. In this poem, however, the snakeskin signifies more, for it is Daniel Boone who is "leaving the snakeskin of place after place." Like a snake, Boone belongs to the natural world—and, like a snake, he wanders from place to place, shedding his skin as he goes. Thus the word "snakeskin," with its suggestion of rebirth and its links to nature, passing time, and the inevitability of change, is consistent with the image of Boone as both a man of nature and a restless wanderer, "a bird flying after a song."

In the poem's third stanza, both "velvet falls" and "tapestry of time" seem at first to have been selected solely for their pleasing repetition of sounds ("velvet falls"; "tapestry of time"). But both of these phrases also support the poem's theme. Alive, Boone was in constant movement; he was also larger than life. Now he has been reduced; "his picture freezes down to . . . / a story-picture for children" (11–12), and he is as static and inorganic as velvet or tapestry—no longer dynamic, like "falls" and "time."

The word "barbwire" (in line 19's phrase "barbwire time") is another word whose multiple meanings enrich the poem's theme. In the simplest terms "barbwire" denotes a metal fencing material. In light of the poem's concern with space and distance, "barbwire" (with its connotations of sharpness, danger, and confinement) may be seen as the antithesis of Boone's free or peaceful wilderness, evoking images of prisons and concentration camps and reinforcing the poem's central dichotomy between past freedom and present restriction.

The phrase "old hands" (20) also has multiple meanings in the context of the poem. On one level, the hands could belong to an elderly person holding a storybook; on another level, "old hands" could refer to those with considerable life experience—like Boone, who was an "old hand" at scouting. On still another level, given the poem's concern with time, "old hands" could suggest the hands of a clock.

For what it says literally and for what its words suggest, "For the Grave of Daniel Boone" communicates a good deal about the speaker's identification with Daniel Boone and with the nation he called home. Boone's horizons, his concept of "home," expanded as he wandered. Now, when he is frozen in time and space, a character in a child's picture book, a body in a grave, we are still "hunting our own kind of deepening home," but our horizons, like Boone's, have narrowed in this "barbwire time."

POEMS FOR FURTHER READING: WORD CHOICE

RUSSELL ENDO
(1956–   )

Susumu, My Name
(1988)

You are entitled to overhear
Susumu, my name, means
   "progress" in Japanese,
The progress of prosperity
5   and of good fortune.
The dust that seeped through
   makeshift barracks in Arizona[1]
Whet my parents' taste for the
   American Dream.
10 But my luck shall have to be
   different
I want my wheels to skim like
   the blades of the wind
Across all ruts.
15 I want my wheels to spin so fast
   That we stand still.
Are you with me?
Then may we whisper in the
   summer breeze
20 Susumu.

READING AND REACTING

1. Why does Endo use "overhear" in line 1? What connotations does this word have? What other words might he have substituted?
2. What is Endo's purpose in using the Japanese word "Susumu" as well as its English translation?

---

[1] Camps where Japanese Americans were confined during World War II.

ADRIENNE RICH
(1929–   )

Living in Sin
(1955)

She had thought the studio would keep itself,
no dust upon the furniture of love.
Half heresy, to wish the taps less vocal,
the panes relieved of grime. A plate of pears,
5 a piano with a Persian shawl, a cat
stalking the picturesque amusing mouse
had risen at his urging.
Not that at five each separate stair would writhe
under the milkman's tramp; that morning light
10 so coldly would delineate the scraps
of last night's cheese and three sepulchral bottles;
that on the kitchen shelf among the saucers
a pair of beetle-eyes would fix her own—
envoy from some black village in the mouldings . . .
15 Meanwhile, he, with a yawn,
sounded a dozen notes upon the keyboard,
declared it out of tune, shrugged at the mirror,
rubbed at his beard, went out for cigarettes;
while she, jeered by the minor demons,
20 pulled back the sheets and made the bed and found
a towel to dust the table-top,
and let the coffee-pot boil over on the stove.
By evening she was back in love again,
though not so wholly but throughout the night
25 she woke sometimes to feel the daylight coming
like a relentless milkman up the stairs.

READING AND REACTING

1. How might the poem's impact change if each of these words were deleted: "Persian" (5); "picturesque" (6); "sepulchral" (11); "minor" (19); "sometimes" (25)?

2. What words in the poem have strongly negative connotations? What do these words suggest about the relationship the poem describes?

3. This poem, about a woman in love, uses curiously few words conventionally associated with love poems. Instead, many of its words denote the everyday routine of housekeeping. Give examples of such words. Why do you think they are used?

4. JOURNAL ENTRY: What connotations does the title have? What other phrases have similar denotative meanings? How do their connotations differ? Why do you think Rich chose the title she did?

KARL SHAPIRO
(1913–   )

Auto Wreck
(1941)

    Its quick soft silver bell beating, beating,
    And down the dark one ruby flare
    Pulsing out red light like an artery,
    The ambulance at top speed floating down
5 Past beacons and illuminated clocks
    Wings in a heavy curve, dips down,
    And brakes speed, entering the crowd.
    The doors leap open, emptying light;
    Stretchers are laid out, the mangled lifted
10 And stowed into the little hospital.
    Then the bell, breaking the hush, tolls once,
    And the ambulance with its terrible cargo
    Rocking, slightly rocking, moves away,
    As the doors, an afterthought, are closed.

15 We are deranged, walking among the cops
    Who sweep glass and are large and composed.
    One is still making notes under the light.
    One with a bucket douches ponds of blood
    Into the street and gutter.
20 One hangs lanterns on the wrecks that cling,
    Empty husks of locusts, to iron poles.

    Our throats were tight as tourniquets,
    Our feet were bound with splints, but now,
    Like convalescents intimate and gauche,
25 We speak through sickly smiles and warn
    With the stubborn saw of common sense,
    The grim joke and the banal resolution.
    The traffic moves around with care,
    But we remain, touching a wound
30 That opens to our richest horror.
    Already old, the question Who shall die?
    Becomes unspoken Who is innocent?

For death in war is done by hands;
Suicide has cause and stillbirth, logic;
35 And cancer, simple as a flower, blooms.
But this invites the occult mind,
Cancels our physics with a sneer,
And spatters all we knew of denouement
Across the expedient and wicked stones.

READING AND REACTING

1. Comment on the verbs used in this poem. In what sense are they appropriate for a poem about an automobile accident?
2. Why is each of these words particularly startling or vivid in the context of the poem: "little" (10); "terrible" (12); "ponds" (18); "occult" (36); "wicked" (39)?
3. Comment on the logic of the pairing of these words: "large and composed" (16); "intimate and gauche" (24). What effect do you think the poet is trying to create?
4. **JOURNAL ENTRY:** How accurately do you think this poem conveys the experience of viewing an auto accident? Explain.

E. E. CUMMINGS
(1894–1962)

in Just—[1]
(1923)

in Just—
spring   when the world is mud—
luscious the little
lame balloonman
5 whistles   far   and wee

and eddieandbill come
running from marbles and
piracies and it's
spring

10 when the world is puddle-wonderful

---

[1] Also known as "Chansons Innocentes I."

    the queer
    old balloonman whistles
    far   and   wee
    and bettyandisbel come dancing

15 from hop-scotch and jump-rope and

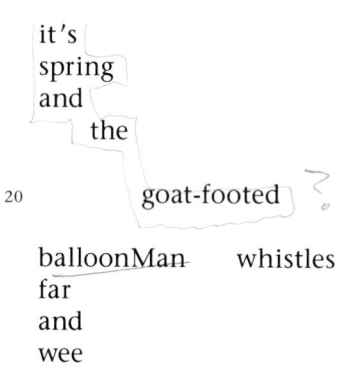

    it's
    spring
    and
       the

20   goat-footed

    balloonMan   whistles
    far
    and
    wee

READING AND REACTING

1. In this poem Cummings coins a number of words that he uses to modify other words. Identify these coinages, and explain their function in the poem. What other, more conventional, words could be used in their place?
2. What do you think Cummings means by "far and wee" in lines 5, 13, and 22–24? Why does he arrange the three words in a different way each time he uses them?

THEODORE ROETHKE
(1908–1963)

I Knew a Woman
(1958)

    I knew a woman, lovely in her bones,
    When small birds sighed, she would sigh back at them;
    Ah, when she moved, she moved more ways than one:
    The shapes a bright container can contain!
5 Of her choice virtues only gods should speak,
    Or English poets who grew up on Greek
    (I'd have them sing in chorus, cheek to cheek).

How well her wishes went! She stroked my chin,
She taught me Turn, and Counter-turn, and Stand;
10 She taught me Touch, that undulant white skin;
I nibbled meekly from her proffered hand;
She was the sickle; I, poor I, the rake,
Coming behind her for her pretty sake
(But what prodigious mowing we did make).

15 Love likes a gander, and adores a goose:
Her full lips pursed, the errant note to seize;
She played it quick, she played it light and loose;
My eyes, they dazzled at her flowing knees;
Her several parts could keep a pure repose,
20 Or one hip quiver with a mobile nose
(She moved in circles, and those circles moved).

Let seed be grass, and grass turn into hay:
I'm martyr to a motion not my own;
What's freedom for? To know eternity.
25 I swear she cast a shadow white as stone.
But who would count eternity in days?
These old bones live to learn her wanton ways:
(I measure time by how a body sways).

READING AND REACTING

1. Many of the words in Roethke's poem have double meanings—for example, "gander" and "goose" in line 15. Identify other words that have more than one meaning, and consider the function these multiple meanings serve.

2. The poem's language contains many surprises; often the word we expect is not the one we get. For example, "container" in line 4 is not a conventional means of describing a women. What other words are used in unusual ways? What does Roethke achieve through this technique?

3. Is there a difference between the denotation or connotation of the word "bones" in the phrases "lovely in her bones" (1) and "These old bones" (27)? Explain.

4. **JOURNAL ENTRY:** How does this poem differ from your idea of what a love poem should be?

EXERCISE: REVISIONS AND WORD CHOICE

Writing a poem can be hard work, typically requiring many revisions. In writing drafts of a poem, a poet moves closer and closer to what he or she considers to be "the right words." The exercise that follows asks you to focus on one poet's decisions.

Read Robert Frost's "In White" and a later version of the poem, called "Design," and answer the following questions.

1. What is suggested by the title "Design" that is not suggested by the title "In White"? Does each title suit the poem it introduces? Explain.
2. The word "white" is used several times in each poem; each poem also includes words that rhyme with "white" and other words that indicate color or relative shades of light and darkness. Do Frost's revisions change the significance of the color white? Explain.
3. What does the word "design" denote? What connotations does it have? Does it suggest the same thing in both versions of the poem?
4. Study the poem's last two lines. How can you explain the changes the poet made, particularly in the use of the word "design"?
5. What other changes in word choice did Frost make as he revised? What reasons might he have had for each change?
6. Do you think any words or phrases in "Design" should be restored to their original equivalents? Should any word be changed? Explain.

ROBERT FROST
(1874–1963)

In White
(1912)

A dented spider like a snowdrop white
On a white Heal-all, holding up a moth
Like a white piece of lifeless satin cloth—
Saw ever curious eye so strange a sight?

5 Portent in little, assorted death and blight
Like the ingredients of a witches' broth?
The beady spider, the flower like a froth,
And the moth carried like a paper kite.

What had that flower to do with being white,
10 The blue Brunella every child's delight?

What brought the kindred spider to that height?
(Make we no thesis of the miller's plight.)
What but design of darkness and of night?
Design, design! Do I use the word aright?

Design
(1936)

I found a dimpled spider, fat and white,
On a white heal-all, holding up a moth
Like a white piece of rigid satin cloth—
Assorted characters of death and blight
5 Mixed ready to begin the morning right,
Like the ingredients of a witches' broth—
A snow-drop spider, a flower like a froth,
And dead wings carried like a paper kite.

What had that flower to do with being white,
10 The wayside blue and innocent heal-all?
What brought the kindred spider to that height,
Then steered the white moth thither in the night?
What but design of darkness to appall?—
If design govern in a thing so small.

LEVELS OF DICTION

Like other writers, poets employ various levels of diction to convey their ideas. The diction of a poem may be formal or informal or fall anywhere in between, depending on the identity of the speaker and the speaker's attitude toward the reader and toward his or her subject. At one extreme, highly informal poems can be full of jargon, regionalisms, and slang. At the other extreme, very formal poems can be far removed in style and vocabulary from everyday speech. Many poems, of course, use language that falls somewhere between formal and informal diction. Still, to understand the range of poets' options, it is helpful to identify and contrast the two extremes of formal and informal diction.

FORMAL DICTION

Formal diction typically uses a learned vocabulary and grammatically correct forms. In general, formal diction does not include colloquialisms such as contractions and shortened word forms (*phone* for *telephone*). As the following poem illustrates, a speaker who uses formal diction can sound aloof and impersonal, even if he or she uses first-person pronouns.

MARGARET ATWOOD
(1939–)

The City Planners
(1966)

    Cruising these residential Sunday
streets in dry August sunlight:
what offends us is
the sanities:
5 the houses in pedantic rows, the planted
sanitary trees, assert
levelness of surface like a rebuke
to the dent in our car door.
No shouting here, or
10 shatter of glass; nothing more abrupt
than the rational whine of a power mower
cutting a straight swath in the discouraged grass.

But though the driveways neatly
sidestep hysteria
15 by being even, the roofs all display
the same slant of avoidance to the hot sky,
certain things:
the smell of spilled oil a faint

sickness lingering in the garages,
20 a splash of paint on brick surprising as a bruise,
a plastic hose poised in a vicious
coil; even the too-fixed stare of the wide windows

give momentary access to
the landscape behind or under
25 the future cracks in the plaster

when the houses, capsized, will slide
obliquely into the clay seas, gradual as glaciers
that right now nobody notices.

That is where the City Planners
30 with the insane faces of political conspirators
are scattered over unsurveyed
territories, concealed from each other,
each in his own private blizzard;

guessing directions, they sketch
35 transitory lines rigid as wooden borders
on a wall in the white vanishing air

tracing the panic of suburb
order in a bland madness of snows.

Atwood's speaker is clearly concerned about the poem's subject, but rather than use *I,* she uses the first-person plural (*us*) to maintain some distance and give the impression of avoiding emotional involvement. Although phrases such as "sickness lingering in the garages" and "insane faces of political conspirators" do express the speaker's disapproval, the use of formal words—"pedantic"; "rebuke"; "display"; "poised"; "obliquely"; "conspirators"; "transitory"—helps her to maintain her distance. The speaker herself, as well as her attack on the misguided city planners, gains credibility through her balanced tone and through the use of language that is as "professional" as theirs, with no slang, nonstandard diction, or colloquialisms. The combination of formal vocabulary, correct grammar, and controlled tone makes the speaker's appeal seem reasonable.

INFORMAL DICTION

Informal diction is the language closest to everyday conversation. It includes colloquialisms—contractions, shortened word forms, and the like—and it may also include slang, regional expressions, and even nonstandard words.

In the poem that follows the speaker uses informal diction to highlight the contrast between James Baca, a law student speaking to the graduating class of his old high school, and Joey Martinez, a graduating senior.

JIM SAGEL
(1947–)

Baca Grande[1]
(1982)

Una vaca se topó con un ratón y le dice:
"Tú- ¿tan chiquito y con bigote?" Y le responde el ratón:
"Y tú tan grandota- ¿y sin brassiere?"[2]

---

[1] *Baca* is both an incorrect spelling of the Spanish word "vaca" (cow) and the last name of one of the poem's characters. *Grande* means "large."

[2] A cow ran into a rat and said: " You—so small and with a moustache?" The rat responded: "And you—so big and without a bra?"

It was nearly a miracle
James Baca remembered anyone at all
from the old hometown gang
having been two years at Yale
5   no less
and halfway through law school
at the University of California at Irvine

They hardly recognized him either
in his three-piece grey business suit
10 and surfer-swirl haircut
with just the menacing hint
of a tightly trimmed Zapata moustache
            for cultural balance
and relevance

15 He had come to deliver the keynote address
to the graduating class of 80
at his old alma mater
and show off his well-trained lips
which laboriously parted
20   each Kennedyish "R"
and drilled the first person pronoun
through the microphone
like an oil bit
with the slick, elegantly honed phrases
25 that slid so smoothly
off his meticulously bleached
            tongue
He talked Big Bucks
with astronautish fervor and if he
30   the former bootstrapless James A. Baca
could dazzle the ass
off the universe
then even you
            yes you

35 Joey Martinez toying with your yellow
            tassle
and staring dumbly into space
could emulate Mr. Baca someday
            possibly
40 well
there was of course
such a thing
as being an outrageously successful
gas station attendant too

<pre>
45   let us never forget
    it doesn't really matter what you do
    so long as you excel
            James said
    never believing a word
50 of it
    for he had already risen
            as high as they go

    Wasn't nobody else
    from this deprived environment
55 who'd ever jumped
            straight out of college
    into the Governor's office
    and maybe one day
    he'd sit in that big chair
60   himself
    and when he did
    he'd forget this damned town
    and all the petty little people
    in it
65 once and for all

    That much he promised himself
</pre>

"Baca Grande" uses a casual, conversational style and many elements of informal diction. The poem uses numerous colloquialisms, including contractions; conversational placeholders, such as "no less" and "well"; shortened word forms, such as "gas station"; slang terms, such as "Big Bucks"; whimsical coinages ("Kennedyish," "astronautish," "bootstrapless"); nonstandard grammatical constructions, such as "Wasn't nobody else"; and even profanity. The level of language is perfectly appropriate for Joey Martinez and the rest of his class—suspicious, streetwise, and unimpressed by Baca's "three-piece grey business suit" and "surfer-swirl haircut." In fact, the informal diction is a key element in the poem, expressing the gap between the slick James Baca, with "his well-trained lips / which laboriously parted / each Kennedyish 'R'" and his audience, with their unpretentious, forthright speech. In this sense "Baca Grande" is as much a linguistic comment as a social one.

POEMS FOR FURTHER READING: LEVELS OF DICTION

BARBARA L. GREENBERG
(1932–   )

The Faithful Wife
(1978)

But if I *were* to have a lover, it would be someone
who could take nothing from you. I would, in conscience,
not dishonor you. He and I would eat at Howard Johnson's

which you and I do not enjoy. With him I would go
5 fishing because it is not your sport. He would wear blue
which is your worst color; he would have none of your virtues.

Not strong, not proud, not just, not provident, my lover
would blame me for his heart's distress, which you would never
think to do. He and I would drink too much and weep together

10 and I would bruise his face as I would not bruise your face
even in my dreams. Yes I would dance with him, but to a music
you and I would never choose to hear, and in a place

where you and I would never wish to be. He and I would speak
Spanish, which is not your tongue, and we would take
15 long walks in fields of burdock, to which you are allergic.

We would make love only in the morning. It would be
altogether different. I would know him with my other body,
the one that you have never asked to see.

READING AND REACTING

1. In what respect does this poem sound like everyday speech? What colloquial elements usually present in conversation are absent here?
2. The speaker seems to be addressing her husband. What words or phrases in the poem sound out of place given the identities of the participants in the conversation?
3. **JOURNAL ENTRY:** How do you interpret the poem's title? In what sense is it ironic? In what sense is it not?

RICHARD WILBUR
(1921–)

For the Student Strikers
(1970)

Go talk with those who are rumored to be unlike you,
And whom, it is said, you are so unlike.
Stand on the stoops of their houses and tell them why
You are out on strike.

5 It is not yet time for the rock, the bullet, the blunt
Slogan that fuddles the mind toward force.
Let the new sound in our streets be the patient sound
Of your discourse.

Doors will be shut in your faces, I do not doubt.
10 Yet here or there, it may be, there will start,
Much as the lights blink on in a block at evening,
Changes of heart.

They are your houses; the people are not unlike you;
Talk with them, then, and let it be done
15 Even for the grey wife of your nightmare sheriff
And the guardsman's son.

READING AND REACTING

1. Is this poem's diction primarily formal or informal? List the words that helped you to reach your conclusion.
2. What elements in the poem besides its vocabulary might lead you to characterize it as formal or informal?
3. **JOURNAL ENTRY:** This poem is an *exhortation,* a form of discourse intended to incite or encourage listeners to take action. Given the speaker's audience and subject matter, is its somewhat lofty level of diction appropriate? Explain.

CHARLES BUKOWSKI
(1920–   )

Dog Fight
(1984)

he draws up against my rear bumper in the fast lane,
I can see his head in the rear view mirror, his eyes
are blue and he sucks upon a dead cigar.
I pull over. he passes, then slows. I don't like
5 this.
I pull back into the fast lane, engage myself upon
his rear bumper. we are as a team passing through
Compton.
I turn the radio on and light a cigarette.
10 he ups it 5 mph, I do likewise. we are as a team
entering Inglewood.
he pulls out of the fast lane and I drive past.
then I slow. when I check the rear view he is
upon my bumper again.
15 he has almost made me miss my turnoff at Century.
I hit the blinker and fire across 3 lanes of
traffic, just make the off-ramp . . .
blazing past the front of an inflammable tanker.
blue eyes comes down from behind the tanker and
20 we veer down the ramp in separate lanes to the signal
and we sit there side by side, not looking at each
other.
I am caught behind an empty school bus as he idles
behind a Mercedes.
25 the signal switches and he is gone. I cut to the
inner lane behind him, then I see that the parking
lane is open and I flash by inside of him and the
Mercedes, turn up the radio, make the green as the
Mercedes and blue eyes run the yellow into the red.
30 they make it as I power it and switch back ahead of
them in their lane in order to miss a parked vegetable
truck.
now we are running 1-2-3, not a cop in sight, we are
moving through a 1980 California July
35 we are driving with skillful nonchalance
we are moving in perfect anger

we are as a team
approaching LAX:[1]
1-2-3
40   2-3-1
3-2-1.

READING AND REACTING

1. "Dog Fight" describes a car race from the emotionally charged perspective of a driver. Given this persona, comment on the appropriateness of the level of diction of the following words: "likewise" (10); "upon" (14); "nonchalance" (35); "perfect" (36).

2. Many of the words in the poem are **jargon**—specialized language associated with a particular trade or profession. In this case, Bukowski uses automotive terms and the action words and phrases that typically describe driving maneuvers. Would you characterize these words as formal, informal, or neither? Explain.

3. **JOURNAL ENTRY:** What colloquialisms are present in the poem? Could non-colloquial expressions be substituted for any of them? How would such substitutions change your response to the poem?

DIALECT

Dialect denotes a particular regional variety of language, which may differ from the most widely used standard spoken or written language in its pronunciation, its grammar, or its vocabulary. (It differs from *slang*, which tends to be associated with groups determined by age or special interest rather than region. In addition, slang is initially calculated to call attention to itself and its user, whereas dialect is not.) Dialect is generally used in poetry to convey the sense of an authentic, unedited voice. Because it is associated with a particular region, dialect can also create a sense of place.

The poem that follows is told in the voice of a rural mountain woman.

FAYE KICKNOSWAY
(1939–   )

Gracie
(1986)

I mean, I'm a no shoes hillbilly an' home
is deeper in the map than Kentucky or Tennessee an'
all I been raised to do is walk the chicken

---

[1] Los Angeles International Airport.

yard, spillin' grain from ma's
5 apron, maybe once a week wear a bonnet
into town. I have red hair an' white skin;

men lean on their elbows lookin' at me. Ma's
voice tells me, "Don't breathe so deep," an'
the preacher says how happy I'll be when I'm dead. Skin
10 touchin' skin is evil. I'm to keep inside the chicken
yard, no eye's to see beneath my bonnet.
Farm boys suck their cheeks an' call, "Come home

with me, I'll give you your own chicken
yard an' take you proudly once a week to town." Home
15 ain't enough. As I spill grain from ma's
apron, I see city streets hung with lights an'
a dark room with a window lookin' on the bonnet
of the sky. Voices stroke at my skin

through its walls. When the grain's gone from ma's
20 apron, I hang it on its hook by her bonnet.
I figure to be my own fare North an' leave home.
My legs are crossed under a counter. I smell chicken
fry. A man leans on his elbows; his eyes drink my skin.
In a dark room, my dress undoes my body an'

25 I lie with him. His hot mouth comes home
on mine. I expect to hear the preacher's or ma's
voice yellin' at me, but the only voices in the wall's
        skin
are strange an' soft. I have beer an' chicken
30 for breakfast. All day I wear his body like a bonnet.
My stockins are run. The streets are hung with lights an'
he sleeps. I stand by the window an'
look into the night's skin, fancy home an' the chicken
yard, ma's apron an' my head cool in its bonnet.

"Gracie" juxtaposes nonstandard grammatical forms such as "I been," "ain't," and "My stockins are run" with rich, understated figurative language such as "the bonnet / of the sky" and "Voices stroke at my skin." The speaker uses contractions; shortened word forms ("ma"); colloquialisms, such as "I mean," "a no shoes hillbilly," "deep" (for "deeply"), and "I figure"; and regionalisms, such as "chicken fry" and "I . . . fancy." Apostrophes indicate conversational pronunciation in words such as "an'," "touchin'," and "lookin'." The natural, colorful diction accurately reveals Gracie's complexity, and the apparent guilelessness of the dialect imparts a sense of authenticity and directness to the speaker's voice.

POEMS FOR FURTHER READING: DIALECT

ROBERT BURNS
(1759–1796)

John Anderson My Jo, John
(1790)

John Anderson my jo,[1] John,
    When we were first acquent,[2]
Your locks were like the raven,
    Your bonny brow was brent;[3]
5 But now your brow is beld,[4] John,
    Your locks are like the snaw;
But blessings on your frosty pow,[5]
    John Anderson my jo.

John Anderson my jo, John,
10   We clamb the hill thegither;
And mony a canty[6] day, John,
    We've had wi' ane anither:
Now we maun[7] totter down, John,
    And hand in hand we'll go,
15 And sleep together at the foot,
    John Anderson my jo.

READING AND REACTING

1. Reread the definition of dialect on page 127. In what respects does Burns's poem conform to this definition?
2. What particular words and phrases indicate that the speaker is speaking a Scots dialect? What effect does the use of dialect have on your perception of the speaker?
3. **JOURNAL ENTRY:** "Translate" the poem into modern colloquial English.

[1] Dear.
[2] Acquainted.
[3] Unwrinkled.
[4] Bald.
[5] Head.
[6] Happy.
[7] Must.

GWENDOLYN BROOKS
(1917–   )

We Real Cool
(1960)

The Pool Players.
Seven at the Golden Shovel.

We real cool. We
Left School. We

Lurk late. We
Strike straight. We
5 Sing sin. We
Thin gin. We

Jazz June. We
Die soon.

READING AND REACTING

1. This poem is written in an urban dialect. What elements identify its diction as dialect rather than simply informal?
2. How does the use of dialect affect your reaction to the poem?

WORD ORDER

The order in which words are arranged in a poem can be just as important as the choice of words. Because English nearly always requires a subject-verb-object arrangement, with adjectives preceding the nouns they modify, any departures from this order are immediately noticeable. Poets can use readers' expectations about word order to their advantage. Syntax can be natural, or it can be manipulated, with words intentionally placed out of conventional order. A poet may place emphasis on a word by locating it first or last in a line, or by placing it in a stressed position in the line. If its placement departs from conventional sequence, the word will have even greater emphasis. Choosing a particular word order can cause two related—or startlingly unrelated—words to fall in adjacent or parallel positions, calling attention to the similarity—or the difference—between them. Unconventional syntax can also serve a poem's rhyme or meter or highlight sound correspondences that might otherwise not be noticeable. Finally, haphazard syntax throughout a poem can reveal a speaker's mood—for example, giving a playful quality to a poem or suggesting a speaker's disoriented state.

In the poem that follows, the placement of many words departs from conventional English syntax.

EDMUND SPENSER
(1552–1599)

One Day I Wrote Her Name upon the Strand
(1595)

One day I wrote her name upon the strand,[1]
But came the waves and washed it away:
Again I wrote it with a second hand,
But came the tide and made my pains his prey.
5 "Vain man," said she, "that doest in vain assay,
A mortal thing so to immortalize,
For I myself shall like to this decay,
And eek[2] my name be wiped out likewise."
"Not so," quod[3] I, "let baser things devise,
10 To die in dust, but you shall live by fame:
My verse your virtues rare shall eternize,
And in the heavens write your glorious name.
Where whenas death shall all the world subdue,
Our love shall live, and later life renew."

"One Day I Wrote Her Name upon the Strand," a sonnet, has a fixed metrical pattern and rhyme scheme. To accommodate certain rhyming words that must fall at the ends of lines, the poet sometimes moves words out of their conventional order, as the following comparisons illustrate.

Conventional Word Order

"'Vain man,' she said, that doest *assay in vain.*"

"My verse shall *eternize your rare virtues.*"

Inverted Sequence

"'Vain man,' said she, that doest *in vain assay.*" ("Assay" appears at end of line 5, to rhyme with line 7's "decay.")

"My verse *your virtues rare shall eternize.*" ("Eternize" appears at end of line 11 to rhyme with line 9's "devise.")

[1] Beach.

[2] Also, indeed.

[3] Said.

132 Word Choice, Word Order

Conventional Word Order	**Inverted Sequence**
"Where whenas death shall *subdue all the world,* / Our love shall live, and *later renew life.*"	"Where whenas death shall *all the world subdue,* / Our love shall live, and *later life renew.*" (Rhyming words "subdue" and "renew" are placed at ends of lines.)

Because the metrical pattern of a poem may be used to stress certain words, words are occasionally moved out of order to insure that they fall on a stressed syllable. The following comparison illustrates this technique.

Conventional Word Order	**Inverted Sequence**
"But *the waves came* and washed it away."	"But *came the waves* and washed it away." (stress in line 2 falls on "waves" rather than on "the.")

As the comparisons show, Spenser's adjustments in syntax are motivated in part by a desire to preserve the sonnet's rhyme and meter.

The following poem does more than simply invert words: It presents an intentionally disordered syntax.

E. E. CUMMINGS
(1894–1962)

anyone lived in a pretty how town
(1940)

anyone lived in a pretty how town
(with up so floating many bells down)
spring summer autumn winter
he sang his didn't he danced his did.

5 Women and men (both little and small)
cared for anyone not at all
they sowed their isn't they reaped their same
sun moon stars rain

children guessed (but only a few
10 and down they forgot as up they grew
autumn winter spring summer)
that noone loved him more by more

when by now and tree by leaf
she laughed his joy she cried his grief

15 bird by snow and stir by still
anyone's any was all to her

someones married their everyones
laughed their cryings and did their dance
(sleep wake hope and then) they
20 said their nevers they slept their dream

stars rain sun moon
(and only the snow can begin to explain
how children are apt to forget to remember
with up so floating many bells down)

25 one day anyone died i guess
(and noone stooped to kiss his face)
busy folk buried them side by side
little by little and was by was

all by all and deep by deep
30 and more by more they dream their sleep
noone and anyone earth by april
wish by spirit and if by yes.

Women and men (both dong and ding)
summer autumn winter spring
35 reaped their sowing and went their came
sun moon stars rain

At times Cummings, like Spenser, manipulates syntax in response to the demands of rhyme and meter—for example, in line 10. But Cummings goes much further: He uses unpredictable syntax as part of a scheme that encompasses other unusual elements of the poem, such as its unexpected departures from the musical metrical pattern (for example, in line 3 and line 8) and from the rhyme scheme (for example, in lines 3 and 4), and its use of parts of speech in unfamiliar contexts. Together, these techniques create a playful quality. The refreshing disorder of the syntax (for instance, in lines 1–2, line 10, and line 24) adds to the poem's striking effect.

POEMS FOR FURTHER READING: WORD ORDER

EDNA ST. VINCENT MILLAY
(1892–1950)

Elegy before Death
(1921)

There will be rose and rhododendron
    When you are dead and under ground;
Still will be heard from white syringas
    Heavy with bees, a sunny sound;

5 Still will the tamaracks be raining
    After the rain has ceased, and still
Will there be robins in the stubble,
    Grey sheep upon the warm green hill.

Spring will not ail nor autumn falter;
10   Nothing will know that you are gone,—
Saving alone some sullen plough-land
    None but yourself sets foot upon;

Saving the may-weed and the pig-weed
    Nothing will know that you are dead,—
15 These, and perhaps a useless wagon
    Standing beside some tumbled shed.

Oh, there will pass with your great passing
    Little of beauty not your own,—
Only the light from common water,
20   Only the grace from simple stone!

READING AND REACTING

1. Reword the poem using conventional syntax. What words and phrases in the poem appear out of expected order?
2. How do the poem's meter and rhyme scheme require the poet to depart from conventional syntax?
3. What words and phrases are emphasized by departures from conventional word order? In what ways does this emphasis strengthen the poem?

W. H. AUDEN
(1907–1973)

Look, Stranger
(1936)

Look, stranger, at this island now
The leaping light for your delight discovers,
Stand stable here
And silent be,
5 That through the channels of the ear
May wander like a river
The swaying sound of the sea.

Here at the small field's ending pause
Where the chalk wall falls to the foam, and its tall ledges
10 Oppose the pluck
And knock of the tide,
And the shingle scrambles after the suck-
ing surf, and the gull lodges
A moment on its sheer side.

15 Far off like floating seeds the ships
Diverge on urgent voluntary errands:
And the full view
Indeed may enter
And move in memory as now these clouds do,
20 That pass the harbor mirror
And all the summer through the water saunter.

READING AND REACTING

1. "Look, Stranger" is very dependent on **alliteration,** as in "leaping light" (2) and "Stand stable here / And silent be" (3–4). In addition to a regular rhyme scheme, the poem includes internal rhymes such as "light . . . delight" (2) and imperfect rhymes such as "harbor mirror" (20) and "wander . . . river" (6). How might this strong emphasis on sound have affected the poet's decisions about syntax? Be specific.

2. Do any words gain added emphasis by virtue of their unexpected position? Which ones? Why is this emphasis important to the poem as a whole?

Checklist for Writing about Word Choice and Word Order

Word Choice

- What words are of central importance in the poem?
- What is the denotative meaning of each of these key words?
- Why is each word chosen instead of a synonym? (For example, is the word chosen for its sound? Its connotation? Its relationship to other words in the poem? Its contribution to the poem's metrical pattern?)
- What other words could be effectively used in place of words now in the poem?
- How would substitutions change the poem's meaning?
- Which key words have neutral connotations? Which have negative connotations? Which have positive connotations? Beyond its literal meaning, what does each word suggest?
- Are any words repeated? Why?
- What is the poem's general level of diction?
- Why is this level of diction used? Is it effective?
- Does the poem mix different levels of diction? To what end?
- Does the poem use dialect? For what purpose?

Word Order

- Is the poem's syntax straightforward, or are words arranged in unexpected order?
- What phrases represent departures from conventional syntax?
- What is the purpose of the unusual syntax? (For example, is it necessary to preserve the poem's meter or rhyme scheme? To highlight particular sound correspondences? To place emphasis on a particular word or phrase? To reflect the speaker's mood?)
- How would the poem's impact be changed if conventional syntax were used?

WRITING SUGGESTIONS: WORD CHOICE, WORD ORDER

1. Reread the two poems in this chapter by E. E. Cummings: "in Just—" (p. 115) and "anyone lived in a pretty how town" (p. 132). If you like, you may also read one or two additional poems in this text by Cummings. To what extent do you believe Cummings chooses words for their sound? For their appearance on the page? Explain.

2. The tone of "We Real Cool" (p. 130) is flat and unemotional; its subject matter, however, is serious. Expand this concise poem into an

essay or story that uses more detailed, more emotional language to communicate the speaker's hopeless situation.

3. Reread "Gracie" (p. 127) and choose another poem in the text whose speaker is a woman. Compare the two speakers' levels of diction and choice of words. What does their speech reveal about their lives?

4. Reread "For the Grave of Daniel Boone" (p. 110) alongside either Andrew Suknaski's "The Bitter Word" (p. 386) or Delmore Schwartz's "The True-Blue American" (p. 262). What does each poem's choice of words reveal about the speaker's attitude toward his subject?

5. Compare the choice of words and the level of diction in Margaret Atwood's "The City Planners" (p. 120) and William Blake's "London" (p. 282). Pay particular attention to each poem's use of language to express social or political criticism.

CHAPTER 7

IMAGERY

JANE FLANDERS
(1940–)

Cloud Painter
(1984)

Suggested by the life and art of John Constable[1]

At first, as you know, the sky is incidental—
a drape, a backdrop for trees and steeples.
Here an oak clutches a rock (already he works outdoors),
a wall buckles but does not break,
5   water pearls through a lock, a haywain[2] trembles.

The pleasures of landscape are endless. What we see
around us should be enough.
Horizons are typically high and far away.

Still, clouds let us drift and remember. He is, after all,
10   a miller's son, used to trying
to read the future in the sky, seeing instead
ships, horses, instruments of flight.
Is that his mother's wash flapping on the line?
His schoolbook, smudged, illegible?

15   In this period the sky becomes significant.
Cloud forms are technically correct—mares' tails,
sheep-in-the-meadow, thunderheads.
You can almost tell which scenes have been interrupted
by summer showers.

20   Now his young wife dies.
His landscapes achieve belated success.

---

[1] John Constable (1776–1837)—British painter noted for his landscapes.

[2] An open horse-drawn wagon for carrying hay.

138

He is invited to join the Academy. I forget
whether he accepts or not.

Because poetry—and, for that matter, all literature—is concerned with expanding the perception of readers, poets devote a good deal of attention to appealing to the senses. In "Cloud Painter," for example, Flanders uses small details, such as the mother's wash on the line and the smudged schoolbook, to enable readers to visualize a particular scene in John Constable's early work. Clouds are described so readers can easily picture them—"mares' tails, / sheep-in-the-meadow, thunderheads." "Cloud Painter" is not just about the work of John Constable; it is also about the poet's ability to call up images in the minds of readers. To achieve her end, the poet uses **imagery,** language that evokes a physical sensation produced by one of the five senses—sight, hearing, taste, touch, or smell.

Although the effect can be quite complex, the way images work is simple. When you read the word *red,* your memory of the various red things that you have seen or heard about determines your visualization of the image. In addition, the word *red* may have emotional associations, or **connotations,** that define your response. A red sunset, for example, can have a positive connotation or a negative one depending on whether it is associated with a pleasurable experience or with air pollution. By choosing an image carefully, poets can not only help to create pictures in a reader's mind, but also suggest a great number of imaginative associations. These

John Constable. *Landscape, Noon, The Haywain.* 1821. Oil on canvas, 130.5 × 185.5 cm. London, National Gallery.

140 *Imagery*

associations help poets to establish the **atmosphere** or **mood** of the poem. The falling snow in "Stopping by Woods on a Snowy Evening" (p. 315), for example, creates a quiet, almost mystical mood.

Readers come to a poem with their own individual sets of experiences, so an image in a poem will not always suggest the same thing to all readers. In "Cloud Painter," for example, the poet presents the image of an oak clutching a rock in a painting. Although most readers will probably see a picture that is consistent with the one the poet sees, no two images will be identical. Every reader will have his or her own mental image of a particular tree clinging to a rock; some will be remembered experiences, while others will be imaginative creations. Some readers may even be familiar enough with the work of the painter John Constable to visualize a particular tree clinging to a particular rock in one of his paintings.

By conveying what the poet sees and experiences, images enable readers to participate in the poet's mental processes. Through this interaction between reader and poet, readers' minds are opened and enriched by perceptions and associations different from—and possibly more profound than—their own.

One advantage of images is their extreme economy. Just a few words enable poets to evoke specific emotions in readers and to approximate the experience the poet wishes to create. Consider in the following poem how just a few visual images create a picture.

WILLIAM CARLOS WILLIAMS
(1883–1963)

Red Wheelbarrow
(1923)

so much depends
upon

a red wheel
barrow

5   glazed with rain
water

beside the white
chickens

What is immediately apparent is the verbal economy of this poem. The poet does not tell readers what the barnyard smells like or what sounds the animals make. In fact, he does not even paint a detailed picture of the scene. How large is the wheelbarrow? What is it made of? How many chickens are in the barnyard? Without answering these questions, the poet uses the minimum number of words to suggest a scene upon which, he says, "so much depends."

The poem asks readers to pause for a moment and to consider the uniqueness and mystery of everyday objects. To the poet even the simplest scene can suggest beauty and harmony. Acting as a focal point for the poet's attention, the red wheelbarrow establishes a momentary connection between the poet and his world. Like a still-life painting, the wheelbarrow beside the white chickens gives order to a world that is full of seemingly unrelated objects. By asserting the importance of the objects in the poem, the poet suggests that our ability to perceive the objects of this world gives our lives meaning and that our ability to convey our perceptions to others is central to our lives as well as to art.

Another advantage of images is that they enable poets to move beyond certain limitations of language. In fact, images present abstract ideas that would be difficult or almost impossible to convey in any other way. Just one look at a dictionary will illustrate that concepts such as *beauty* and *mystery* are so general that they are difficult to define, let alone discuss in original terms. By choosing an image or series of images that embodies ideas such as these, however, poets can effectively and persuasively make their feelings known. Consider, for example, the following poem.

EZRA POUND
(1885–1972)

In a Station of the Metro
(1916)

The apparition of these faces in the crowd;
Petals on a wet, black bough.

What is the prose equivalent of this poem? It is almost impossible to paraphrase the poem because the facts it communicates are less important than the feelings associated with these facts. The poem's title indicates that the first line is meant to suggest a group of people standing in a station of the Paris subway. The scene, however, is identified not as a clear picture but as an apparition, suggesting that it is somehow unexpected or even dreamlike. In contrast with the image of the subway platform is the association of the people's faces with petals on the dark limb of a tree. The subway platform—dark, cold, wet, subterranean (associated with baseness, death, and hell)—is juxtaposed with white flowers—delicate, pale, radiant, lovely (associated with the ideal, life, and heaven). The effect of this contrast is startling. Notice, however, that the poet does not state the poem's main idea explicitly. The images, presented without comment, bear the entire weight of the poem.

Although images can be strikingly pictorial, they can also appeal to the senses of hearing, smell, taste, and touch. The following poem uses not only visual images but also images of sound and taste.

GARY SNYDER
(1930–   )

Some Good Things to Be Said for the Iron Age
(1970)

> A ringing tire iron
>   dropped on the pavement
> Whang of a saw
> brusht on limbs
> 5 the taste
>   of rust

The poem presents two aural images that are quite commonplace: the ringing of a tire iron and the sound of a saw. Both images gain power, however, through their visual isolation in the poem. Together they produce a harsh and jarring chord that creates a vague sense of uneasiness in the reader. This poem does more than present sensory images, though. It also conveys the speaker's interpretations of the images he presents. The last two lines of the poem imply not only that the time in which we live is base and mundane (an age of iron), but also that it is declining into an age of rust. This idea is reinforced by the repeated consonant sounds in *taste* and *rust* that make readers hold the final image of the poem on their tongues. The title of the poem ironically sums up the situation by suggesting that compared to the age that is approaching, the age of iron may indeed be "good." Thus, in the mind of the poet, ordinary events gain added significance, and images that spring from everyday experience become sources of enlightenment and insight.

In shorter poems, such as most of those discussed above, one or two images may serve as focal points. Longer poems, however, introduce patterns of imagery, groups of related images that create a more complex tapestry of sensory impressions. Notice in the following poem how several images join to create a painful tableau.

SUZANNE E. BERGER
(1944–   )

The Meal
(1984)

They have washed their faces until they are pale,
their homework is beautifully complete.
They wait for the adults to lean towards each other.
The hands of the children are oval
5 and smooth as pine-nuts.

The girls have braided and rebraided their hair,
and tied ribbons without a single mistake.
The boy has put away his coin collection.
They are waiting for the mother to straighten her lipstick,
10 and for the father to speak.

They gather around the table, carefully
as constellations waiting to be named.
Their minds shift and ready, like dunes.
It is so quiet, all waiting stars and dunes.

15 Their forks move across their plates without scraping,
they wait for the milk and the gravy
at the table with its forgotten spices.
They are waiting for a happiness to lift their eyes,
like sudden light flaring in the trees outside.

20 The white miles of the meal continue,
the figures still travel across a screen:
the father carving the Sunday roast,
her mouth uneven as a torn hibiscus,
their braids still gleaming in the silence.

This poem contains patterns of imagery that evoke silence, order, and emptiness. It begins with the image of faces washed "until they are pale" and goes on to describe the children's oval hands as being "smooth as pine-nuts." Forks move across plates "without scraping," and the table hints at the memory of "forgotten spices." Despite what is implied by the title of the poem, these children are actually emotionally starved. The attentive, well-scrubbed children sit at a table where, neither eating nor speaking, they wait for "the milk and the gravy" and for happiness that never comes. The "white miles of the meal" seem to go on forever, reinforcing the sterility and emptiness of the ritual.

Suggesting a lack of sensation or feeling, a kind of paralysis, the poem's images challenge conventional assumptions about the family.

Much visual imagery is **static,** freezing the moment to give it the timeless quality of painting or sculpture. "The Meal" presents just such a tableau, and so do "Red Wheelbarrow" (p. 140) and "In a Station of the Metro" (p. 141). Some imagery, however, is **kinetic;** that is, it attempts to show motion or change.

WILLIAM CARLOS WILLIAMS
(1883–1963)

The Great Figure
(1938)

Among the rain
and lights
I saw the figure 5
in gold
5 on a red
firetruck
moving
tense
unheeded
10 to gong clangs
siren howls
and wheels rumbling
through the dark city.

Speaking about this poem in his autobiography, Williams says that while walking in New York, he heard the sound of a fire engine. As he turned the corner, he saw a golden figure 5 on a red background speed by. The impression was so forceful that he immediately jotted down a poem about it. In the poem Williams attempts to recreate the sensation the figure 5 made as it moved into his consciousness. Notice that he presents the image as if it were a picture taken by a camera with a high-speed shutter. Readers are asked to see the speeding engine with the number 5 caught in tense focus by the camera. Notice too that the poet presents images in the order in which he perceived them: first the 5 and then the image of the red fire truck howling and clanging into the darkness. In this sense, "The Great Figure" is an equivalent of the speaker's experience, using images of sight, sound, and movement to evoke that experience in readers. The American painter Charles Demuth was fascinated by the kinetic quality of the poem. Working closely with his friend Williams, he attempted to capture the stop-action feature of the poem in a painting.

Charles Demuth (1883–1935) *The Figure 5, In Gold*. Oil on composition board, h. 36, w. 29¾ in. The Metropolitan Museum of Art, The Alfred Steiglitz Collection, 1949. (49.59.1) All rights reserved, The Metropolitan Museum of Art.

A special use of imagery called **synaesthesia** occurs when one type of sense is described in a way that is appropriate for another—for instance, when a sound is described with color. When people say they are feeling *blue* or describe music as *hot,* they are using synaesthesia. The poet John Keats uses this technique in the following lines from "Ode to a Nightingale" (p. 335):

> O, for a draught of vintage! that hath been
>   Cool'd a long age in the deep-delvéd earth,
>   Tasting of Flora and the country green,
>   Dance and Provençal song, and sunburnt mirth!

In this passage the speaker describes the taste of wine in terms of images that appeal to a variety of senses: flowers, the country green, dance, song, and sun.

POEMS FOR FURTHER READING: IMAGERY

DENNIS BRUTUS
(1924–   )

On the Island[1]
(1973)

I

Cement-grey floors and walls
cement-grey days
cement-grey time
and a grey susurration
5 as of seas breaking
winds blowing
and rains drizzling.

A barred existence
so that one did not need to look
10 at doors or windows
to know that they were sundered by bars
and one locked in a grey gelid stream
of unmoving time.

II

When the rain came
15 it came in a quick moving squall
moving across the island
murmuring from afar
then drumming on the roof
then marching fading away.

20 And sometimes one mistook
the weary tramp of feet
as the men came shuffling from the quarry
white-dust-filmed and shambling
for the rain
25 that came and drummed and marched away.

---

[1] "The Island" refers to Robben Island, located off Cape Town, South Africa. It is a prison for black political prisoners. The island has become a poignant symbol of repression and apartheid in South African poetry, highlighting themes of isolation, separation, and exile.

III

It was not quite envy
nor impatience
nor irritation
but a mixture of feelings
30 one felt
for the aloof deep-green dreaming firs
that poised in the island air
withdrawn, composed and still.

IV

On Saturday afternoons we were embalmed in time
35 like specimen moths pressed under glass;
we were immobile in the sunlit afternoon
waiting;
Visiting time:
until suddenly like a book snapped shut
40 all possibilities vanished as zero hour passed
and we knew another week would have to pass.

READING AND REACTING

1. What is the central theme of the poem? In what ways do the images reinforce this theme?
2. Most of the images in this poem are visual. What other kinds of images are present? What do they add?
3. **JOURNAL ENTRY:** Each of the poem's four separate sections is characterized by a different pattern of imagery. How do the images differ from section to section? *Why* do you think they are different?

MICHELLE CLIFF
(1946–   )

A Visit to the Secret Annex[1]
(1979)

What kinds of times are these, when
A talk about trees is almost a crime
Because it implies a silence about so many
*   horrors?*

            Bertolt Brecht, "For Those Born Later"

---

[1] An apartment in Amsterdam where Anne Frank and her family hid to avoid being sent to a concentration camp during World War II.

I was born later
not into this world.
The trees were not the same
The horrors not exact—but similar

5 I walk along the *Prinsengracht*[2]—a late-spring afternoon
a visitor—cooled by the air from the canals.

I sight my destination—pass it by
Return on the heels of a group of schoolchildren.

The stairs stretch up
10 into perpendicular flights
I begin my climb.

I had not expected my feelings to be so. . . . What?
(Then why did I turn around?)

Cold sweat pours out of my head and through the cloth of my
15 burgundy shirt. The back of my shirt sticks flat. I can feel it
darkening.

(By now I have learned to fight
pretending I am not touched.)

Here in these narrow, empty rooms
20 (Why do I say "empty"? The place is filled with other people—
silent people reading the legends and walking back and forth—
past the ornamental toilet—baroque, green scrolls curl around
two birds with tails entwined on the bowl. Delft? I wonder.)

Here in these rooms alone I am terrified of tears (and what
25 follows? shame? embarrassment?) and feel an onslaught
coming if I give in.

I lock my eyes. Sweat pours out instead   tidal   salt.
Redirected by my bitten lips and tongue from the pinpoints at
the corners of my eyes to the entire surface of my body. My
30 skin.

Yes, my girl. I say this to myself. (Because part of me is a girl
and part of me is a woman speaking to her.) Here is the heroine
you once had and wondered about.

The girl you loved.

[2] The street where the secret annex was located.

I meet her suspended in this place. At thirteen, fourteen, fifteen.
At four or so a Montessori student. A baby held by an elegant
mother.

Would I have changed places
were that the only choice?

I glance at the two walls where she fixed her pinups.
Norma Shearer, Deanna Durbin, Ginger Rogers—lips reddened
wildly from the rotogravure.[3]
There are pictures of the "little princesses"[4]—Elizabeth and
Margaret Rose.
Another picture showing roses. In the foreground of a country
house. Her dream house? Didn't we all have dream houses?

The *Westerkerk*[5] next-door strikes four. A window is open wide
onto a huge flowering chestnut in the garden of the church.

I turn to the tree. Breathe in its blossoms. Watch its fat leaves
move against a bright-blue sky.

I do not know how to calculate the ages of trees. (I have
studied closely how to calculate the ages of churches.)

I remember the childhood advice about the rings in a tree's
insides. But I can't slice the tree open. Just to tell if it's forty or
so.

I hold a conversation with myself about trees.
To see if she might have had a living tree as a companion—
even a tree in a churchyard—instead of one cut from colored
paper.

Still, she would have only sensed the tree, had the tree been
there.

Still, she might have listened for the hard drop of the fruit in fall,
while her father tracked the advance of the allies on his little
map. Imagined gathering the chestnuts and roasting them at
the side of a canal busy with barges and small family boats.

But she would never have seen her tree—the windows of the
hiding place were always shaded, covered with paper or

[3] A section of the newspaper produced by a special printing process.
[4] Princess Elizabeth, now Queen Elizabeth II, and her sister, Princess Margaret.
[5] A church with a clock tower that could be seen from the attic window.

painted blue.
To keep their existences secret   safe.

70 Had she cracked the pane to peek as her tree flowered, or shed
its fruit or leaves, she would have been killed.
Sooner.

Ah . . . the congregations of the *Westerkerk,* not knowing a group
of Jews hovered above them, above their chestnut tree.
75 Thinking they were *Judenrein.*[6]

READING AND REACTING

1. What do the recurring images of trees contribute to the poem?
2. Give examples of nonvisual images that occur in the poem—for example, the sound of the clock striking. Is there a pattern of nonvisual imagery in this poem?
3. What determines the order in which the details of the poem are presented?
4. **JOURNAL ENTRY:** Do you react to the scene described in the poem with as much anger and sadness as the speaker does? Can you think of a contemporary scene that would elicit a similar response from you?

---

[6] German for free or "clean" of Jews.

ERIC CHOCK
(1950–   )

Chinese Fireworks Banned in Hawaii
(1989)

for Uncle Wongie, 1987

Almost midnight, and the aunties[1]
are wiping the dinner dishes
back to their shelves,
cousins eat jook[2] from the huge vat
5 in the kitchen, and small fingers

---

[1] Older Chinese women.

[2] A thick soup made of various foods including rice.

help to mix the clicking ocean
of mah jong[3] tiles, so the uncles can play
through another round of seasons.
And you put down your whiskey
10 and go outside to find your long bamboo pole
so Uncle Al can help you tie on
a ten foot string of good luck,
red as the raw fish we want
on our plates every New Year's.
15 As you hang this fish over the railing
Uncle Al walks down the steps
and with his cigarette lighter
ignites it and jumps out of the way.
You lean back and jam the pole
20 into the bottom of your guts,
waving it across the sky,
whipping sparks of light from its tail,
your face in a laughing Buddha smile
as you trace your name in the stars
25 the way we teach our kids to do
with their sparklers.
This is the family picture
that never gets taken, everyone
drawn from dishes and food and games
30 and frozen at the sound
of 10,000 wishes filling our bodies
and sparkling our eyes.
You play the fish till its head explodes
into a silence that echoes,
35 scattering red scales to remind us of spirits
that live with us in Hawaii.
Then, as we clap and cheer,
the collected smoke of our consciousness
floats over Honolulu, as it has
40 each year for the last century.
But tonight, as we leave,
Ghislaine stuffs her styrofoam tea cup
full of red paper from the ground.
This is going to be history, she says.
45 Let's take some home.

---

[3] A game played with small tiles, often for long hours and sometimes for points or money.

READING AND REACTING

1. Red is a color that signifies good luck to the Chinese. Does it signify anything special to you? In what ways does the color red contribute to the mood of the poem?
2. Quite often a poet provides just enough information to enable readers to create a mental picture based on their own experience. What details does this poet expect readers to fill in for themselves? Given the subject matter of the poem, is the poet justified in assuming readers will be able to supply the missing details?
3. What comments does this poem make about being Chinese? About being Chinese in Hawaii?
4. **JOURNAL ENTRY:** What images would you assemble for a poem about your own "family picture / that never gets taken"?

MATSUO BASHO
(1644?–1694)

translated by Geoffrey Bownas and Anthony Thwaite

Four Haiku*

Spring:
A hill without a name
Veiled in morning mist.

The beginning of autumn:
Sea and emerald paddy
Both the same green.

The winds of autumn
Blow: yet still green
The chestnut husks.

A flash of lightning:
Into the gloom
Goes the heron's cry.

READING AND REACTING

1. A **haiku** is a three-line poem, a Japanese form that traditionally had seventeen syllables. Haiku are admired for their extreme

---

* Publication date is not available.

economy and their striking images. What are the central images in each of the haiku above? Do these images convey the speaker's emotions? Explain.

2. In another poem Basho says that art begins with "The depths of the country / and a rice-planting song." What do you think he means? In what way do the poems above exemplify this idea?

3. Does the brevity of these poems increase or decrease the impact of their images?

CAROLYN KIZER
(1925–   )

After Basho
(1984)

Tentatively, you
slip onstage this evening,
pallid, famous moon.

READING AND REACTING

1. What is the meaning of the word "after" in the title? What does the title tell readers about the writer's purpose?

2. What visual picture does the poem suggest? What mood does the poem's central image create?

3. What is the impact of "tentatively" in the first line and "famous" in the last line? How do the connotations of these words affect the image of the moon?

RICHARD WILBUR
(1921–   )

Sleepless at Crown Point
(1973)

All night, this headland
Lunges into the rumpling
Capework of the wind.

READING AND REACTING

1. What scene is the speaker describing?
2. What is the significance of the title?
3. How do the words "lunges" and "capework" help to establish the poem's central image?

JEAN TOOMER
(1894–1967)

Reapers
(1923)

Black reapers with the sound of steel on stones
Are sharpening scythes. I see them place the hones
In their hip-pockets as a thing that's done,
And start their silent swinging, one by one.
5 Black horses drive a mower through the weeds,
And there, a field rat, startled, squealing bleeds,
His belly close to ground. I see the blade,
Blood-stained, continue cutting weeds and shade.

READING AND REACTING

1. What determines the order in which the speaker arranges the images of the poem? At what point does he comment on these images?
2. The first four lines of the poem seem to suggest that the people are working contentedly. What image contradicts this impression? How does it do so?
3. What ideas are traditionally associated with the image of the reaper? The scythe? The harvest? (You may want to consult a reference work, such as *A Dictionary of Symbols* by J. E. Cirlot, in your college library.) In what way does the speaker rely on these associations to help him convey his ideas?

WILFRED OWEN
(1893–1918)

Dulce et Decorum Est[1]
(1920)

Bent double, like old beggars under sacks,
Knock-kneed, coughing like hags, we cursed through sludge,
Till on the haunting flares we turned our backs
And towards our distant rest began to trudge.
5 Men marched asleep. Many had lost their boots
But limped on, blood-shod. All went lame; all blind;
Drunk with fatigue; deaf even to the hoots
Of tired, outstripped Five-Nines[2] that dropped behind.

Gas! Gas! Quick, boys!—An ecstasy of fumbling,
10 Fitting the clumsy helmets just in time;
But someone still was yelling out and stumbling
And flound'ring like a man in fire or lime . . .
Dim, through the misty panes and thick green light,
As under a green sea, I saw him drowning.
15 In all my dreams, before my helpless sight,
He plunges at me, guttering, choking, drowning.

If in some smothering dreams you too could pace
Behind the wagon that we flung him in,
And watch the white eyes writhing in his face,
20 His hanging face, like a devil's sick of sin;
If you could hear, at every jolt, the blood
Come gargling from the froth-corrupted lungs,
Obscene as cancer, bitter as the cud
Of vile, incurable sores on innocent tongues,—
25 My friend, you would not tell with such high zest
To children ardent for some desperate glory,
The old Lie: Dulce et decorum est
Pro patria mori.

READING AND REACTING

1. Who is the speaker in this poem? What is his attitude toward his subject?

---

[1] The title and last lines are from Horace, Odes III, ii: "Sweet and fitting it is to die for one's country."

[2] Shells that explode on impact and release poison gas.

2. What patterns of imagery are present in the poem? To what senses do the images appeal?
3. In what ways do the images reinforce the central theme of the poem?
4. **JOURNAL ENTRY:** Does the knowledge that Owen died in World War I change your reaction to the poem, or are the poem's images compelling enough to eliminate the need for biographical footnotes?

Checklist for Writing about Imagery

- Do the images in the poem appeal to the sense of sight, touch, hearing, smell, or taste?
- Does the poem depend on a single image or a combination of images?
- Does the poem depend on a pattern of related imagery?
- What details make the images memorable?
- What mood do the images create?
- Do the images define or exemplify abstract concepts?
- Are the images static or kinetic? Are there any examples of synaesthesia?
- How do the poem's images help to convey its theme?
- How effective are the images? In what way do the images enhance your enjoyment of the poem?

WRITING SUGGESTIONS: IMAGERY

1. How are short poems such as "Some Good Things to Be Said for the Iron Age" (p. 142) and "In a Station of the Metro" (p. 141) like and unlike haiku?
2. Reread "Cloud Painter" (p. 138) and read "The Great Figure" (p. 144) and "Musée des Beaux Arts" (p. 270). Try to find a reproduction of the paintings to which one of the poems refers. Then, write a paper in which you draw some conclusions about the differences between artistic and poetic images.
3. Analyze the role of imagery in the depiction of the parent/child relationships in "The Meal" (p. 143), "My Papa's Waltz" (p. 46), and "Daddy" (p. 170). How does each poem's imagery convey the nature of the relationship it describes?
4. Write an essay in which you discuss the color imagery in "On the Island" (p. 146), "Chinese Fireworks Banned in Hawaii" (p. 150),

and "In a Station of the Metro" (p. 141). In what way does color reinforce the themes of the poems?

5. Sometimes, as in "A Visit to the Secret Annex" and "On the Island," imagery can be used to make a comment about the society in which a scene takes place. Choose two poems in which imagery functions in this way—"For the Union Dead" (p. 342), "Jury Selection" (p. 240), "The *Chicago Defender* Sends a Man to Little Rock" (p. 408), or "Composed upon Westminster Bridge" (p. 396), for example—and discuss how images contribute to each poem's social statement.

CHAPTER 8

FIGURES OF SPEECH

WILLIAM SHAKESPEARE
(1564–1616)

Shall I Compare Thee to a Summer's Day?
(1609)

    Shall I compare thee to a summer's day?
    Thou art more lovely and more temperate.
    Rough winds do shake the darling buds of May,
    And summer's lease hath all too short a date.
5 Sometime too hot the eye of heaven shines,
    And often is his gold complexion dimmed;
    And every fair from fair sometimes declines,
    By chance, or nature's changing course, untrimmed.
    But thy eternal summer shall not fade,
10 Nor lose possession of that fair thou ow'st;[1]
    Nor shall death brag thou wand'rest in his shade,
    When in eternal lines to time thou grow'st.
        So long as men can breathe or eyes can see,
        So long lives this, and this gives life to thee.

Although figurative language is used in all kinds of writing, poets in particular recognize the power of figures of speech to take readers beyond the literal meaning of a word. For this reason, **figures of speech**—expressions that suggest more than their literal meanings—are more prominent in poetry than in other kinds of writing. For example, the sonnet by Shakespeare that opens this chapter compares a loved one to a summer's day in order to make the point that, unlike the fleeting summer, the loved one will—within the poem—remain forever young. But this sonnet goes beyond the obvious equation (loved one = summer's day); Shakespeare's assertion that his loved one will live forever in his poem actually says more about his own talent and reputation (and about his skillful use of figurative language) than about his loved one's beauty.

---

[1] Beauty you possess.

SIMILE, METAPHOR, AND PERSONIFICATION

When William Wordsworth opens a poem with "I wandered lonely as a cloud" (p. 396), he conveys a good deal more than he would if he just said "I wandered, lonely." By comparing himself in his loneliness to a cloud, he suggests that like the cloud he is a part of nature, and that he too is drifting, passive, blown by winds, and lacking will or substance. With figures of speech such as these, poets suggest a wide spectrum of feelings and associations in very few words. The phrase "I wandered lonely as a cloud" is a **simile,** a comparison between two unlike items that includes *like* or *as*. When an imaginative comparison between two unlike things does not include *like* or *as*—that is, when it says "a is b" rather than "a is like b"—it is a **metaphor.**

Accordingly, when the speaker in Adrienne Rich's "Living in Sin" (p. 113) speaks of "daylight coming / like a relentless milkman up the stairs," she is using a strikingly original simile to suggest that daylight brings not the conventional associations of promise and awakening, but rather a stale routine that is greeted without enthusiasm. This idea is consistent with the rest of the poem, which is a grim account of an unhappy relationship. However, when the speaker in Audre Lorde's poem says "Rooming houses are old women" (p. 162), she uses a metaphor, equating two elements to stress their common associations with emptiness, transience, and hopelessness. In addition, by identifying rooming houses as old women, Lorde is using a special kind of comparison called **personification**—attributing human traits and characteristics to an inanimate idea or object.

Sometimes, as in Wordsworth's "I wandered lonely as a cloud," a single simile or metaphor can be appreciated for what it communicates on its own. At other times, a simile or metaphor is one of several related figurative comparisons that work together to communicate a poem's meaning. In still other cases, a single *extended simile* or *extended metaphor* is developed throughout a poem. The following poem presents a series of related figurative comparisons. Together, they suggest the depth of the problem the poem explores in a manner that each individual comparison could not do alone.

LANGSTON HUGHES
(1902–1967)

Dream Deferred
(1951)

What happens to a dream deferred?

Does it dry up
like a raisin in the sun?

        Or fester like a sore—
5   And then run?
        Does it stink like rotten meat?
        Or crust and sugar over—
        like a syrupy sweet?

        Maybe it just sags
10   like a heavy load.

        Or does it explode?

The dream to which Hughes alludes in his 1951 poem is the dream of racial equality. By extension, it is also the American Dream—or any important unrealized dream. His speaker offers six tentative answers to the question posed in the poem's first line, and five of the six are presented as similes. As the poem unfolds, the speaker considers different alternatives: The dream can shrivel up and die, fester, decay, crust over—or just sag under the weight of the burden those who hold the dream must carry. In each case, the speaker makes an abstract entity—a dream—into a concrete item—a raisin in the sun, a sore, rotten meat, syrupy candy, a heavy load. The final line of the poem, italicized for emphasis, gains power less from what it says than for what it leaves unsaid. Unlike the other alternatives explored in the poem, *"Or does it explode?"* is not presented as a simile. Nevertheless, because of the pattern of figurative language the poem has established, readers supply the other, unspoken half of the comparison: ". . . like a bomb."

    Throughout the next poem the poet develops a single extended simile.

LAWRENCE FERLINGHETTI
(1919–   )

Constantly Risking Absurdity
(1958)

    Constantly risking absurdity
                    and death
        whenever he performs
                above the heads
5   of his audience
    the poet like an acrobat
              climbs on rime
                    to a high wire of his own making
    and balancing on eyebeams
10   above a sea of faces
        paces his way

                              to the other side of day
            performing entrechats
                              and sleight-of-foot tricks
15 and other high theatrics
                              and all without mistaking
                  any thing
                         for what it may not be

            For he's the super realist
20   who must perforce perceive
                  taut truth
                         before the taking of each stance or step
      in his supposed advance
                         toward that still higher perch
25 where Beauty stands and waits
                  with gravity
                         to start her death-defying leap

      And he
            a little charleychaplin man
30   who may or may not catch
      her fair eternal form
                  spreadeagled in the empty air
      of existence

Ferlinghetti draws an extended comparison between a poet and an acrobat, characterizing the poet as a kind of all-purpose circus performer, at once swinging recklessly on a trapeze and balancing carefully on a tightrope. The simile is introduced in line 6 ("The poet like an acrobat"), and the poem follows the poet/acrobat through fanciful gymnastics, always in some sense referring to both poet and acrobat. What the poem suggests is that the poet, like an acrobat, works hard at his craft but manages to make it all look easy. Something of an exhibitionist, the poet is innovative and creative, taking impossible chances yet also building on traditional skills in his quest for truth and beauty. Moreover, like an acrobat, the poet is balanced "on eyebeams / above a sea of faces," for he too depends on audience reaction to help him keep his performance focused. The poet may be "the super realist," but he also has plenty of playful tricks up his sleeve: "*entrechats* / and sleight-of-foot tricks / and other high theatrics," including puns ("above the heads / of his audience"), unexpected rhyme ("climbs on rime"), alliteration ("taut truth"), coinages ("a little charleychaplin man"), and all the other linguistic acrobatics available to creators of poems. (In fact, the poem's layout on the page suggests the acrobatics it describes.) Like these tricks, the poem's central simile is a whimsical one, perhaps suggesting that Ferlinghetti is poking fun at poets who take their craft too seriously. In any case, the simile helps him to illustrate the acrobatic possibilities of language in a fresh and original manner.

The following poem develops an extended metaphor that equates inanimate objects with human beings.

AUDRE LORDE
(1934–1992)

Rooming Houses Are Old Women
(1968)

Rooming houses are old women
rocking dark windows into their whens
waiting incomplete circles
rocking
5   rent office to stoop to
community bathrooms to gas rings and
under-bed boxes of once useful garbage
city issued with a twice monthly check
and the young men next door
10 with their loud midnight parties
and fishy rings left in the bathtub
no longer arouse them
from midnight to mealtime no stops inbetween
light breaking to pass through jumbled up windows
15 and who was it who married the widow that Buzzie's son messed with?

To Welfare and insult form the slow shuffle
from dayswork to shopping bags
heavy with leftovers
Rooming houses
20 are old women waiting
searching
through darkening windows
the end or beginning of agony
old women seen through half-ajar doors
25 hoping
they are not waiting
but being
the entrance to somewhere
unknown and desired
30 but not new.

So closely does Lorde equate rooming houses and women in this poem that at times it is difficult to tell which of the two is actually the poem's subject. Despite the poem's assertion, rooming houses are *not* old women; however, they are *comparable to* the old women who live there, for their walls enclose a lifetime of disappointments as well as the physical detritus of life. Like old women, rooming houses are in decline, rocking away their remaining years. Like the houses they inhabit, these women's boundaries are fixed—"rent office to stoop to / community bathrooms to gas rings"— and their hopes and expectations are few. They are surrounded by other people's loud parties, but their own lives have been reduced to a "slow shuffle" to nowhere, a hopeless, frightened—and perhaps pointless— "waiting / searching." Over time, the women and the places in which they live have become one. By using an unexpected comparison between two seemingly unrelated entities, the poem illuminates both the essence of the rooming houses and the essence of their elderly occupants.

POEMS FOR FURTHER READING: SIMILE, METAPHOR, AND PERSONIFICATION

ROBERT BURNS
(1759–1796)

Oh, My Love Is Like a Red, Red Rose
(1796)

    Oh, my love is like a red, red rose
        That's newly sprung in June;
    My love is like the melody
        That's sweetly played in tune.

5 So fair art thou, my bonny lass,
        So deep in love am I;
    And I will love thee still, my dear,
        Till a' the seas gang[1] dry.

    Till a' the seas gang dry, my dear,
10   And the rocks melt wi' the sun;
    And I will love thee still, my dear,
        While the sands o' life shall run.

    And fare thee weel, my only love!
        And fare thee weel awhile!
15 And I will come again, my love
        Though it were ten thousand mile.

---

[1] Go.

READING AND REACTING

1. Why does the speaker compare his love to a rose? What other simile is used in the poem? For what purpose is it used?
2. Where does the speaker seem to exaggerate the extent of his love? Why does he exaggerate? Does this exaggeration weaken the effectiveness of his similes? Explain.
3. What determines the placement of the similes at the beginning of the poem? What would be the effect of moving them to the end?

JOHN UPDIKE
(1932–   )

Ex-Basketball Player
(1958)

Pearl Avenue runs past the high-school lot,
Bends with the trolley tracks, and stops, cut off
Before it has a chance to go two blocks,
At Colonel McComsky Plaza. Berth's Garage
5 Is on the corner facing west, and there,
Most days, you'll find Flick Webb, who helps Berth out.

Flick stands tall among the idiot pumps—
Five on a side, the old bubble-head style,
Their rubber elbows hanging loose and low.
10 One's nostrils are two S's, and his eyes
An E and O. And one is squat, without
A head at all—more of a football type.

Once Flick played for the high-school team, the Wizards.
He was good: in fact, the best. In '46
15 He bucketed three hundred ninety points,
A county record still. The ball loved Flick.
I saw him rack up thirty-eight or forty
In one home game. His hands were like wild birds.

He never learned a trade, he just sells gas,
20 Checks oil, and changes flats. Once in while,
As a gag, he dribbles an inner tube,
But most of us remember anyway.
His hands are fine and nervous on the lug wrench.
It makes no difference to the lug wrench, though.

25 Off work, he hangs around Mae's luncheonette.
Grease-gray and kind of coiled, he plays pinball,
Smokes those thin cigars, nurses lemon phosphates.
Flick seldom says a word to Mae, just nods
Beyond her face toward bright applauding tiers
30 Of Necco Wafers, Nibs, and Juju Beads.

READING AND REACTING

1. Explain the use of personification in the second stanza and in the poem's last two lines. What two elements make up each figurative comparison? How are the two elements in each pair alike?
2. What kind of figure of speech is each of the following: "His hands were like wild birds" (18); "Grease-gray and kind of coiled" (26)? What other figures of speech can you identify in the poem?
3. **JOURNAL ENTRY:** How do the poem's descriptions and figures of speech convey the narrator's attitude toward Flick Webb? Do you think Flick himself shares the narrator's assessment? Explain.

ADRIENNE RICH
(1929–)

The Roofwalker
(1961)

for Denise

Over the half-finished houses
night comes. The builders
stand on the roof. It is
quiet after the hammers,
5 the pulleys hang slack.
Giants, the roofwalkers,
on a listing deck, the wave
of darkness about to break
on their heads. The sky
10 is a torn sail where figures
pass magnified, shadows
on a burning deck.

I feel like them up there:
exposed, larger than life,
15 and due to break my neck.

                    Was it worth while to lay—
                    with infinite exertion—
                    a roof I can't live under?
                    —All those blueprints,
20   closings of gaps,
                    measurings, calculations?
                    A life I didn't choose
                    chose me: even
                    my tools are the wrong ones
25   for what I have to do.
                    I'm naked, ignorant,
                    a naked man fleeing
                    across the roofs
                    who could with a shade of difference
30   be sitting in the lamplight
                    against the cream wallpaper
                    reading—not with indifference—
                    about a naked man
                    fleeing across the roofs.

READING AND REACTING

1. Is the speaker's comparison of herself with a roofwalker a metaphor or a simile? Explain. Is this comparison a valid one? What characteristics does the speaker share with the roofwalkers?
2. What other comparisons are made in the poem? Are these comparisons metaphors or similes? Explain.
3. **JOURNAL ENTRY:** Do you think the speaker is examining her personal life or her professional life? Why?

RANDALL JARRELL
(1914–1965)

The Death of the Ball Turret Gunner
(1945)

From my mother's sleep I fell into the State
And I hunched in its belly till my wet fur froze.
Six miles from earth, loosed from its dream of life,
I woke to black flak and the nightmare fighters.
5 When I died they washed me out of the turret with a hose.

READING AND REACTING

1. Who is the speaker? To what does he compare himself in the poem's first two lines? What words establish this comparison?
2. Contrast the speaker's actual identity with the one he creates for himself in lines 1–2. What elements of his actual situation do you think lead him to characterize himself as he does in lines 1–2?
3. **JOURNAL ENTRY:** Both this poem and "Dulce et Decorum Est" (p. 155) use figurative language to describe the horrors of war. Which poem has a greater impact on you? How does the figurative language contribute to this impact?

MARGE PIERCY
(1934–   )

The Secretary Chant
(1973)

My hips are a desk.
From my ears hang
chains of paper clips.
Rubber bands form my hair.
5 My breasts are wells of mimeograph ink.
My feet bear casters.
Buzz. Click.
My head is a badly organized file.
My head is a switchboard
10 where crossed lines crackle.
Press my fingers
and in my eyes appear
credit and debit.
Zing. Tinkle.
15 My navel is a reject button.
From my mouth issue canceled reams.
Swollen, heavy, rectangular
I am about to be delivered
of a baby
20 Xerox machine.
File me under W
because I wonce
was
a woman.

READING AND REACTING

1. Examine each of the poem's figures of speech. Do they all make reasonable comparisons, or are some far-fetched or hard to visualize? Explain the relationship between the secretary and each item with which she is compared.

2. **JOURNAL ENTRY:** The speaker's frequent use of metaphor rather than simile (as in line 1's "My hips are a desk") creates a distorted physical image of the secretary. Does this image undermine, or even trivialize, the poem's point, or does it strengthen the poem? Explain.

JOHN DONNE
(1572–1631)

A Valediction: Forbidding Mourning
(1611)

As virtuous men pass mildly away,
    And whisper to their souls to go,
Whilst some of their sad friends do say
    The breath goes now, and some say no:

5 So let us melt, and make no noise,
    No tear-floods, nor sigh-tempests move;
'Twere profanation of our joys
    To tell the laity[1] our love.

Moving of th' earth brings harms and fears;
10   Men reckon what it did and meant;
But trepidation of the spheres,
    Though greater far, is innocent.

Dull sublunary lovers' love
    (Whose soul is sense) cannot admit
15 Absence, because it doth remove
    Those things which elemented it.

But we, by a love so much refined
    That ourselves know not what it is,

---

[1] Here, "common people."

>   Inter-assurèd of the mind,
> 20   Care less, eyes, lips, and hands to miss.
>
>   Our two souls, therefore, which are one,
>   Though I must go, endure not yet
>   A breach, but an expansiòn,
>   Like gold to airy thinness beat.
>
> 25 If they be two, they are two so
>   As stiff twin compasses are two:
>   Thy soul, the fixed foot, makes no show
>   To move, but doth, if th' other do.
>
>   And though it in the center sit,
> 30   Yet when the other far doth roam,
>   It leans and harkens after it,
>   And grows erect as that comes home.
>
>   Such wilt thou be to me, who must,
>   Like th' other foot, obliquely run;
> 35 Thy firmness makes my circle just,[2]
>   And makes me end where I begun.

READING AND REACTING

1. Beginning with line 25 the poem develops an extended metaphor, called a *conceit*, which compares the speaker and his loved one to "twin compasses" (26), attached and yet separate. Why is the compass an especially apt metaphor? What qualities of the compass does the poet emphasize?

2. Earlier, the poem uses other figures of speech to characterize both the lovers' union and their separation. To what other events does the speaker compare his separation from his loved one? To what other elements does he compare their attachment?

3. **JOURNAL ENTRY:** Does the poem's use of figurative language strike you as reasonable or exaggerated? Explain.

HYPERBOLE AND UNDERSTATEMENT

Two additional kinds of figurative language, hyperbole and understatement, also give poets the opportunity to suggest meaning beyond the literal level of language.

[2] Perfect.

Hyperbole is intentional exaggeration—saying more than is actually meant. In the poem "Oh, My Love Is Like a Red, Red Rose" (p. 163), when the speaker says that he will love his lady until all the seas go dry, he is using hyperbole. **Understatement** is just the opposite—saying less than is meant. When the speaker in the poem "Fire and Ice" (p. 84), weighing two equally grim alternatives for the end of the world, says that "for destruction ice / Is also great / And would suffice," he is using understatement. In both cases, poets rely on their readers' understanding that their words are not to be taken literally.

By using hyperbole poets can attract readers' attention—for example, with exaggerated anger or graphic images of horror. But poets use hyperbole to ridicule and satirize as well as to inflame and shock. With understatement, poets can convey powerful emotions subtly, without unnecessary artifice or embellishment, allowing the ideas to speak for themselves.

The emotionally charged poem that follows uses hyperbole to attract attention, conveying anger and bitterness that seem almost beyond the power of words.

SYLVIA PLATH
(1932–1963)

Daddy
(1965)

You do not do, you do not do
Any more, black shoe
In which I have lived like a foot
For thirty years, poor and white,
5 Barely daring to breathe or Achoo.

Daddy, I have had to kill you.
You died before I had time—
Marble-heavy, a bag full of God,
Ghastly statue with one grey toe
10 Big as a Frisco seal

And a head in the freakish Atlantic
Where it pours bean green over blue
In the waters off beautiful Nauset.
I used to pray to recover you.
15 Ach, du.[1]

---

[1] Ah, you.

In the German tongue, in the Polish town[2]
Scraped flat by the roller
Of wars, wars, wars.
But the name of the town is common.
20 My Polack friend

Says there are a dozen or two.
So I never could tell where you
Put your foot, your root,
I never could talk to you.
25 The tongue stuck in my jaw.

It stuck in a barb wire snare.
Ich, ich, ich, ich,[3]
I could hardly speak.
I thought every German was you.
30 And the language obscene

An engine, an engine
Chuffing me off like a Jew.
A Jew to Dachau, Auschwitz, Belsen.[4]
I began to talk like a Jew.
35 I think I may well be a Jew.

The snows of the Tyrol, the clear beer of Vienna
Are not very pure or true.
With my gypsy ancestress and my weird luck
And my Taroc pack and my Taroc pack
40 I may be a bit of a Jew.

I have always been scared of *you*,
With your Luftwaffe,[5] your gobbledygoo.
And your neat moustache
And your Aryan eye, bright blue.
45 Panzer[6]-man, panzer-man, O You—

Not God but a swastika
So black no sky could squeak through.
Every woman adores a Fascist,

---

[2] Grabôw, where Plath's father was born.

[3] I, I, I, I.

[4] Nazi concentration camps.

[5] The German air force.

[6] Protected by armor. The Panzer division was the German armored division.

The boot in the face, the brute
50 Brute heart of a brute like you.

You stand at the blackboard, daddy,
In the picture I have of you,
A cleft in your chin instead of your foot
But no less a devil for that, no not
55 Any less the black man who

Bit my pretty red heart in two.
I was ten when they buried you.
At twenty I tried to die
And get back, back, back to you.
60 I thought even the bones would do.

But they pulled me out of the sack,
And they stuck me together with glue.
And then I knew what to do.
I made a model of you,
65 A man in black with a Meinkampf[7] look

And a love of the rack and the screw.
And I said I do, I do.
So daddy, I'm finally through.
The black telephone's off at the root,
70 The voices just can't worm through.

If I've killed one man, I've killed two—
The vampire who said he was you
And drank my blood for a year,
Seven years, if you want to know.
75 Daddy, you can lie back now.

There's a stake in your fat black heart
And the villagers never liked you.
They are dancing and stamping on you.
They always *knew* it was you.
80 Daddy, daddy, you bastard, I'm through.

In her anger and frustration the speaker sees herself as a helpless victim—a foot entrapped in a shoe, a Jew in a concentration camp—of her father's (and, later, her husband's) absolute tyranny. Thus her hated father is characterized as a "black shoe," "a bag full of God," a "ghastly statue," and, eventually, a Nazi, a torturer, the devil, a vampire. The

---

[7] *Mein Kampf* (My Struggle) is Adolf Hitler's autobiography.

poem "Daddy" is widely accepted by scholars as autobiographical, and the fact that Plath's own father was actually neither a Nazi nor a sadist (nor, obviously, the devil or a vampire) makes it clear that the figurative comparisons in the poem are wildly exaggerated. Even so, they may convey the poet's true feelings toward her father—and, perhaps, toward the patriarchal society in which she lived. Plath uses hyperbole as the medium through which to communicate these emotions to readers who she knows cannot possibly feel the way she does. Her purpose, therefore, is not just to shock but also to enlighten, to persuade, and perhaps even to empower her readers. Throughout the poem, the inflammatory language is set in ironic opposition to the childish, affectionate term "Daddy"—most strikingly in the last line's choked out "Daddy, daddy, you bastard, I'm through." The result of the exaggerated rhetoric is a poem that is vivid and shocking. And, while some might believe that Plath's almost wild exaggeration undermines the poem's impact, others would argue that the powerful figurative language is necessary to convey the extent of the speaker's rage and enhance the poem's impact.

Like "Daddy," the next poem presents a situation whose emotional impact is devastating. In this case, however, the poet does not use emotional language; instead, he uses understatement, presenting the events without embellishment.

DAVID HUDDLE
(1942–   )

Holes Commence Falling
(1979)

    The lead & zinc company
    owned the mineral rights
    to the whole town anyway,
    and after drilling holes
5 for 3 or 4 years,
    they finally found the right
    place and sunk a mine shaft.
    We were proud
    of all that digging,
10 even though nobody from
    town got hired. They
    were going to dig right
    under New River and hook up
    with the mine at Austinville.
15 Then people's wells
    started drying up just like
    somebody'd shut off a faucet,

and holes commenced falling,
big chunks of people's yards
20 would drop 5 or 6 feet,
houses would shift and crack.
Now and then the company'd
pay out a little money
in damages; they got a truck
25 to haul water and sell it
to the people whose wells
had dried up, but most
everybody agreed the
situation wasn't
30 serious.

Although "Holes Commence Falling" relates a tragic sequence of events, the tone of the poem is matter-of-fact and the language is understated. Certainly the speaker could have overdramatized the events, using inflated rhetoric to denounce big business and to predict disastrous events for the future. At the very least, he could have colored the events with realistic emotions, assigning blame to the lead and zinc company with justifiable anger. Instead, the speaker is so restrained, so offhand, so passive that readers must supply the missing emotions themselves—realizing, for example, that when the speaker concludes "everybody agreed the / situation wasn't / serious," he means just the opposite.

Throughout the poem, unpleasant events are recounted without comment and without emotion. As it proceeds, the poem traces the high and low points in the town's fortunes, but for every hope ("We were proud / of all that digging") there is a disappointment ("even though nobody from / town got hired"). The lead and zinc company offers some compensation for the damage it does, but it is never enough. The present tense verb of the poem's title indicates that the problems the town faces—wells drying up, yards dropping, houses shifting and cracking—are regular occurrences. Eventually, readers come to see that what is not said, what lurks just below the surface—anger, powerlessness, resentment, hopelessness—is the poem's real subject. The speaker's laconic speech and tired tone seem to suggest an attitude of resignation, but the obvious contrast between the understated tone and the seriousness of the problem creates a sense of irony that makes the speaker's real attitude toward the lead and zinc company clear.

POEMS FOR FURTHER READING: HYPERBOLE AND UNDERSTATEMENT

ANNE BRADSTREET
(1612?–1672)

To My Dear and Loving Husband
(1678)

If ever two were one, then surely we.
If ever man were lov'd by wife, then thee;
If ever wife was happy in a man,
Compare with me ye women if you can.
5 I prize thy love more than whole Mines of gold,
Or all the riches that the East doth hold.
My love is such that Rivers cannot quench,
Nor ought but love from thee, give recompence.
Thy love is such I can no way repay,
10 The heavens reward thee manifold I pray.
Then while we live, in love lets so persever,
That when we live no more, we may live ever.

READING AND REACTING

1. Review the claims the poem's speaker makes about her husband in lines 5–8. Are such exaggerated declarations of love necessary, or would the rest of the poem be sufficient to convey the extent of her devotion to her husband?
2. **JOURNAL ENTRY:** Compare this poem's declarations of love to those of Robert Burns's speaker in "Oh, My Love Is Like a Red, Red Rose" (p. 163). Which speaker do you believe is more convincing? Why?

ANDREW MARVELL
(1621–1678)

To His Coy Mistress
(1681)

Had we but world enough and time,
This coyness, lady, were no crime.
We would sit down and think which way
To walk, and pass our long love's day.

     5 Thou by the Indian Ganges' side
       Should'st rubies find; I by the tide
       Of Humber[1] would complain. I would
       Love you ten years before the Flood,
       And you should, if you please, refuse
   10 Till the conversion of the Jews.
       My vegetable love should grow
       Vaster than empires, and more slow.
       An hundred years should go to praise
       Thine eyes, and on thy forehead gaze,
   15 Two hundred to adore each breast,
       But thirty thousand to the rest.
       An age at least to every part,
       And the last age should show your heart.
       For, lady, you deserve this state,
   20 Nor would I love at lower rate.
          But at my back I always hear
       Time's wingèd chariot hurrying near,
       And yonder all before us lie
       Deserts of vast eternity.
   25 Thy beauty shall no more be found,
       Nor in thy marble vault shall sound
       My echoing song; then worms shall try
       That long preserved virginity,
       And your quaint honor turn to dust,
   30 And into ashes all my lust.
       The grave's a fine and private place,
       But none, I think, do there embrace.
          Now therefore, while the youthful hue
       Sits on thy skin like morning glew[2]
   35 And while thy willing soul transpires
       At every pore with instant fires,
       Now let us sport us while we may;
       And now, like amorous birds of prey,
       Rather at once our time devour
   40 Than languish in his slow-chapped[3] power.
       Let us roll all our strength and all
       Our sweetness up into one ball
       And tear our pleasures with rough strife
       Thorough the iron gates of life.
   45 Thus, though we cannot make our sun
       Stand still, yet we will make him run.

---

[1] An estuary in the east coast of England.

[2] Dew.

[3] Slowly crushing.

READING AND REACTING

1. In this poem Marvell's speaker sets out to convince a reluctant woman to become his lover. In order to make his case more convincing, he uses hyperbole, exaggerating time periods, sizes, spaces, and the possible fate of the woman should she refuse him. Identify as many examples of hyperbole as you can.
2. The tone of "To His Coy Mistress" is more whimsical than serious. Given this tone, what is the purpose of Marvell's use of hyperbole?

ROBERT FROST
(1874–1963)

"Out, Out—"
(1916)

    The buzz saw snarled and rattled in the yard
    And made dust and dropped stove-length sticks of wood,
    Sweet-scented stuff when the breeze drew across it.
    And from there those that lifted eyes could count
5 Five mountain ranges one behind the other
    Under the sunset far into Vermont.
    And the saw snarled and rattled, snarled and rattled,
    As it ran light, or had to bear a load.
    And nothing happened: day was all but done.
10 Call it a day, I wish they might have said
    To please the boy by giving him the half hour
    That a boy counts so much when saved from work.
    His sister stood beside them in her apron
    To tell them 'Supper.' At the word, the saw,
15 As if to prove saws knew what supper meant,
    Leaped out at the boy's hand, or seemed to leap—
    He must have given the hand. However it was,
    Neither refused the meeting. But the hand!
    The boy's first outcry was a rueful laugh,
20 As he swung toward them holding up the hand
    Half in appeal, but half as if to keep
    The life from spilling. Then the boy saw all—
    Since he was old enough to know, big boy
    Doing a man's work, though a child at heart—
25 He saw all spoiled. 'Don't let him cut my hand off—
    The doctor, when he comes. Don't let him, sister!'
    So. But the hand was gone already.

>   The doctor put him in the dark of ether.
>   He lay and puffed his lips out with his breath.
>   30 And then—the watcher at his pulse took fright.
>   No one believed. They listened at his heart.
>   Little—less—nothing!—and that ended it.
>   No more to build on there. And they, since they
>   Were not the one dead, turned to their affairs.

READING AND REACTING

1. The poem's title is an **allusion** to a passage in Shakespeare's *Macbeth* (V.v.23–28) which attacks the brevity and meaninglessness of life in very emotional terms:

   >   "Out, out brief candle!
   > Life's but a walking shadow, a poor player,
   > That struts and frets his hour upon the stage
   > And then is heard no more. It is a tale
   > Told by an idiot, full of sound and fury,
   > Signifying nothing."

   What idea do you think Frost wants to convey through the title "*Out, Out—*"?

2. Explain why each of the following qualifies as understatement:

   "Neither refused the meeting." (18)

   "He saw all spoiled." (25)

   "So." (27)

   ". . . that ended it." (32)

   "No more to build on there." (33)

   Can you identify any other examples of understatement in the poem?

3. **JOURNAL ENTRY:** Do you think the poem's impact is strengthened or weakened by its understated tone? Explain.

DONALD HALL
(1928–   )

My Son, My Executioner
(1955)

> My son, my executioner,
>   I take you in my arms,

Quiet and small and just astir,
And whom my body warms.

5 Sweet death, small son, our instrument
Of immortality,
Your cries and hungers document
Our bodily decay.

We twenty-five and twenty-two,
10   Who seemed to live forever,
Observe enduring life in you
And start to die together.

READING AND REACTING

1. Because the speaker is a young man holding his newborn son in his arms, the equation in line 1 comes as a shock. What is Hall's purpose in opening with such a startling statement?
2. In what sense is the comparison between baby and executioner a valid one? Could you argue that, given their underlying similarities, Hall is *not* using hyperbole? Explain.

MARGARET ATWOOD
(1939–   )

You Fit into Me
(1971)

you fit into me
like a hook into an eye

a fish hook
an open eye

READING AND REACTING

1. What connotations does Atwood expect readers to associate with the phrase "you fit into me"? What does the speaker seem at first to mean by "like a hook into an eye" in line 2?
2. The speaker's shift to the brutal suggestions of lines 3 and 4 is calculated to shock readers. Does the use of hyperbole here have another purpose in the context of the poem? Explain.

METONYMY AND SYNECDOCHE

Metonymy and synecdoche are two related figures of speech. **Metonymy** is the substitution of the name of one thing for the name of another thing that most readers associate with the first—for example, using *hired gun* to mean "paid assassin" or using *suits* for "business executives." A specific kind of metonymy, called **synecdoche**, involves the substitution of a part for the whole (for example, using *bread*—as in "Give us this day our daily bread"—to mean "food") or the whole for a part (for example, saying "You can take the boy out of Brooklyn, but you can't take Brooklyn [meaning its distinctive traits] out of the boy"). Instead of describing something by saying it is like something else (as in simile) or by equating it with something else (as in metaphor), writers can characterize something by using a term that evokes the item or concept. The following poem illustrates the use of synecdoche.

RICHARD LOVELACE
(1618–1658)

To Lucasta
Going to the Wars
(1649)

    Tell me not, Sweet, I am unkind
        That from the nunnery
    Of thy chaste breast and quiet mind,
        To war and arms I fly.

5 True, a new mistress now I chase,
        The first foe in the field;
    And with a stronger faith embrace
        A sword, a horse, a shield.

    Yet this inconstancy is such
10   As you too shall adore;
    I could not love thee, Dear, so much,
        Loved I not Honor more.

In this poem the use of synecdoche allows the poet to condense a number of complex ideas into a very few words. In line 3, when he says that he is flying from his loved one's "chaste breast and quiet mind," the speaker is using "breast" and "mind" to stand for all his loved one's physical and intellectual attributes. In line 8, when he says that he is embracing "A sword, a horse, a shield," he is using these three items to represent all the trappings of war—and, in fact, to represent war itself.

POEM FOR FURTHER READING: METONYMY AND SYNECDOCHE

DYLAN THOMAS
(1914–1953)

The Hand That Signed the Paper
(1936)

The hand that signed the paper felled a city;
Five sovereign fingers taxed the breath,
Doubled the globe of dead and halved a country;
These five kings did a king to death.

5 The mighty hand leads to a sloping shoulder,
The finger joints are cramped with chalk;
A goose's quill has put an end to murder
That put an end to talk.

The hand that signed the treaty bred a fever,
10 And famine grew, and locusts came;
Great is the hand that holds dominion over
Man by a scribbled name.

The five kings count the dead but do not soften
The crusted wound nor stroke the brow;
15 A hand rules pity as a hand rules heaven;
Hands have no tears to flow.

READING AND REACTING

1. When the speaker uses the word "hand" in the expression "the hand that signed the paper," to what larger entity is he really referring?
2. What purpose does the substitution of "hand" for a larger entity serve in the poem?
3. Does "hand" stand for the same thing throughout the poem, or does its meaning change? Explain.

APOSTROPHE

With **apostrophe**, a speaker addresses his or her poem to an absent person or thing—for example, a historical or literary figure or even an inanimate object or an abstract concept.

In the following poem, for example, the speaker uses apostrophe when she addresses Vincent Van Gogh.

SONIA SANCHEZ
(1934–   )

On Passing thru Morgantown, Pa.
(1984)

    i saw you
    vincent van
    gogh perched
    on those pennsylvania
5 cornfields communing
    amid secret black
    bird societies. yes.
    i'm sure that was
    you exploding your
10 fantastic delirium
    while in the
    distance
    red indian
    hills beckoned.

Expecting her readers to be aware that Van Gogh is a Dutch postimpressionist painter known for his mental instability as well as for his art, Sanchez is able to give added meaning to a phrase such as "fantastic delirium" as well as to the poem's visual images. The speaker sees Van Gogh perched like a black bird on a fence, and at the same time she also sees what he sees. Like Van Gogh, then, the speaker sees the Pennsylvania cornfields as both a natural landscape and an "exploding" work of art.

POEMS FOR FURTHER READING: APOSTROPHE

ALLEN GINSBERG
(1926–   )

A Supermarket in California
(1956)

What thoughts I have of you tonight, Walt Whitman,[1] for I walked down the sidestreets under the trees with a headache self-conscious looking at the full moon.
   In my hungry fatigue, and shopping for images, I went into the neon fruit supermarket, dreaming of your enumerations!
   What peaches and what penumbras! Whole families shopping at night! Aisles full of husbands! Wives in the avocados, babies in the tomatoes!—and you, Garcia Lorca,[2] what were you doing down by the watermelons?

   I saw you, Walt Whitman, childless, lonely old grubber, poking among the meats in the refrigerator and eyeing the grocery boys.[3]
   I heard you asking questions of each: Who killed the pork chops? What price bananas? Are you my Angel?
   I wandered in and out of the brilliant stacks of cans following you, and followed in my imagination by the store detective.
   We strode down the open corridors together in our solitary fancy tasting artichokes, possessing every frozen delicacy, and never passing the cashier.

   Where are we going, Walt Whitman? The doors close in an hour. Which way does your beard point tonight?
   (I touch your book[4] and dream of our odyssey in the supermarket and feel absurd.)
   Will we walk all night through solitary streets? The trees add shade to shade, lights out in the houses, we'll both be lonely.

---

[1] Walt Whitman (1819–1892)—American poet. Whitman's poems frequently praise the commonplace and often contain lengthy "enumerations."

[2] Federico García Lorca (1899–1936)—Spanish poet and dramatist.

[3] Whitman's sexual orientation is the subject of much debate. Ginsberg is suggesting here that Whitman was homosexual.

[4] *Leaves of Grass.*

25   Will we stroll dreaming of the lost America of love past blue automobiles in driveways, home to our silent cottage?

    Ah, dear father, graybeard, lonely old courage-teacher, what America did you have when Charon[5] quit poling his ferry and you got out on a smoking bank and stood watching the boat disappear on the black waters
30 of Lethe?[6]

READING AND REACTING

1. In this poem Ginsberg's speaker addresses Walt Whitman, a nineteenth-century American poet. What attitude does the speaker seem to have toward Whitman?
2. Is this poem serious, or is it supposed to be read as a playful experiment? How can you tell?
3. **JOURNAL ENTRY:** Read the excerpt from Walt Whitman's "Song of Myself" on page 393. In what way does your reading of this excerpt help you to understand Ginsberg's purpose in having his speaker address Whitman?

WALT WHITMAN
(1819–1892)

A Noiseless Patient Spider
(1881)

    A noiseless patient spider,
    I mark'd where on a little promontory it stood isolated,
    Mark'd how to explore the vacant vast surrounding,
    It launch'd forth filament, filament, filament, out of itself,
5 Ever unreeling them, ever tirelessly speeding them.

    And you O my soul where you stand,
    Surrounded, detached, in measureless oceans of space,
    Ceaselessly musing, venturing, throwing, seeking the spheres to connect them,
    Till the bridge you will need be form'd, till the ductile anchor hold,
10 Till the gossamer thread you fling catch somewhere, O my soul.

---

[5] In Greek mythology, the ferryman who transported the souls of the dead across the Styx and Acheron rivers to the underworld.

[6] The mythological underworld river whose waters caused the dead to forget their former lives.

READING AND REACTING

1. This poem has at its center a figurative comparison between the soul and a spider. In what respects are the two comparable?
2. Where in the poem does the poet use apostrophe? What does its presence contribute to the poem? Would the poem be as effective without its use of apostrophe? Explain.

Checklist for Writing about Figures of Speech

- Are any figures of speech present in the poem? Identify each example of simile, metaphor, personification, hyperbole, understatement, metonymy, synecdoche, and apostrophe.
- What two elements are being compared in each use of simile, metaphor, and personification? Is the comparison justified? What characteristics do the two items being compared share?
- How do figurative comparisons contribute to the impact of the poem as a whole?
- Does the poet use hyperbole? Why? For example, is it used to move or to shock readers, or is its use intended to produce a humorous or satirical effect?
- Does the poet use understatement? For what purpose? Would more straightforward language be more effective?
- In metonymy and synecdoche, what item is being substituted for another? What purpose does the substitution serve?
- If the poem includes apostrophe, whom or what does the speaker address? What is accomplished through the use of apostrophe?

WRITING SUGGESTIONS: FIGURES OF SPEECH

1. Various figures of speech are often used to portray characters in a poem. Choose two or three poems that focus on a single character—for example, "Ex-Basketball Player" (p. 164), "Richard Cory" (p. 364), or "Gracie" (p. 127)—and explain how figures of speech are used to characterize the poem's central figure.
2. Write an essay in which you discuss the different ways poets use figures of speech to examine the nature of poetry. What kinds of figures of speech do poets use to describe their craft? (You might consider the three poems about poetry that open Chapter 1.)
3. Write an essay in which you compare Adrienne Rich's "The Roofwalker" (p. 165) with Lawrence Ferlinghetti's "Constantly

Risking Absurdity" (p. 160). Pay particular attention to the similarities between Ferlinghetti's identification of the poet with an acrobat and Rich's identification of her speaker with a roofwalker.

4. Look through the Poems for Further Reading section, and find a poem that uses either hyperbole or understatement. Write a paper in which you examine the use of hyperbole or understatement in the poem.

5. What figures of speech do various poets use to examine a particular subject—for example, love, nature, war, or death? Choose two poems that share a common subject (such as Linda Hogan's "Heritage" on p. 323 and Barry Spacks's "Finding a Yiddish Paper on the Riverside Line" on p. 379), and write a paper in which you draw some general conclusions about the relative effectiveness of the poems' use of figurative language to examine that subject.

CHAPTER 9

SOUND

WALT WHITMAN
(1819–1892)

Had I the Choice*

Had I the choice to tally greatest bards,
To limn[1] their portraits, stately, beautiful, and emulate at will,
Homer with all his wars and warriors—Hector, Achilles, Ajax,
Or Shakespeare's woe-entangled Hamlet, Lear, Othello—Tennyson's fair ladies,
5 Meter or wit the best, or choice conceit to wield in perfect rhyme, delight of singers;
These, these, O sea, all these I'd gladly barter,
Would you the undulation of one wave, its trick to me transfer,
Or breathe one breath of yours upon my verse,
And leave its odor there.

RHYTHM

Rhythm—the regular recurrence of sounds—is at the heart of all natural phenomena: the beating of a heart, the lapping of waves against the shore, the croaking of frogs on a summer's night, the whisper of wheat swaying in the wind. In fact, even mechanical phenomena, such as the movement of rush-hour traffic through a city's streets, have a kind of rhythm. Poetry, which explores these phenomena, often tries to reflect the same rhythms. Walt Whitman makes this point in "Had I the Choice" when he says that he would gladly trade the "perfect rhyme" of Shakespeare for the ability to transfer "the undulation of one wave" to verse.

Effective public speakers frequently repeat certain key words and phrases to create a rhythm. In his speech "I Have a Dream," for example,

---

* Publication date is not available.

[1] To describe, depict.

Martin Luther King, Jr., repeats the phrase "I have a dream" to create a cadence that ties the final section of the speech together:

> "I have a dream that one day this nation will rise up. . . . I have a dream that one day on the red hills of Georgia. . . . I have a dream that the state of Mississippi. . . ."

Poets, too, enhance rhythm by using repeated words and phrases. Consider the use of repetition in the following poem.

GWENDOLYN BROOKS
(1917–   )

Sadie and Maud
(1945)

Maud went to college.
Sadie stayed at home.
Sadie scraped life
With a fine-tooth comb.

5 She didn't leave a tangle in.
Her comb found every strand.
Sadie was one of the livingest chits
In all the land.

Sadie bore two babies
10 Under her maiden name.
Maud and Ma and Papa
Nearly died of shame.

When Sadie said her last so-long
Her girls struck out from home.
15 (Sadie had left as heritage
Her fine-tooth comb.)

Maud, who went to college,
Is a thin brown mouse.
She is living all alone
20 In this old house.

Much of the force of the poem comes from its balanced structure and regular rhyme and meter, underscored by the repeated words "Sadie" and "Maud," which shift the focus from one person to the other and back again ("Maud went to college / Sadie stayed home"). The poem's singsong rhythm recalls the chants children recite when jumping rope.

This evocation of carefree childhood ironically contrasts with the adult realities that both Sadie and Maud face as they grow up: Sadie stays at home, leads a fast life, and has two children "under her maiden name"; Maud goes to college and ends up "a thin brown mouse." The speaker implies that the alternatives Sadie and Maud represent are both undesirable. Although Sadie "scraped life / with a fine-tooth comb," she dies young and leaves nothing to her girls but her desire to experience life. Maud, who graduated from college, shuts out life and cuts herself off from her roots.

The distribution of words among the lines of a poem—and even the appearance of words on a printed page—can also affect rhythm. These techniques are used in **open form** poetry (Chapter 10), which dispenses with traditional patterns of versification. In the following excerpt from a poem by E. E. Cummings, for example, an unusual arrangement of words forces readers first to slow down and then to speed up, creating a rhythm that emphasizes a key phrase—"The / lily":

> the moon is hiding
> in her hair.
> The
> lily
> of heaven
> full of all dreams,
> draws down.

Poetic rhythm—the repetition of stresses and pauses—is an essential element in poetry. Rhythm helps to convey a poem's mood and, in combination with other poetic elements, conveys the poet's emphasis and communicates the poem's meaning. Although rhythm can be affected by the regular repetition of words and phrases or by the arrangement of words into lines, poetic rhythm is largely created by **meter**, the pattern of stressed and unstressed syllables that governs a poem's lines.

METER

A **stress** (or accent) occurs when one syllable is given more emphasis than another, unstressed, syllable; fór · ceps, bá · sic, il · lú · sion, ma · lár · i · a. In a poem, even one-syllable words can be stressed to create a particular effect. For example, in Elizabeth Barrett Browning's line "How do I love thee? Let me count the ways," the metrical pattern that places stress on "love" creates one meaning; stressing "I" would create another.

Scansion is the process of analyzing patterns of strong and weak stresses within a line. The most common method of poetic notation involves indicating stressed syllables with a ∕ and unstressed syllables with a ⌣. Although scansion gives readers the "beat" of the poem, it only approximates the sound of spoken language, which contains an infinite variety of stresses. By providing a graphic representation of the stressed and unstressed syllables of a poem, scansion aids understanding, but it is no substitute for reading the poem aloud and experimenting with various degrees and patterns of emphasis.

The basic unit of meter is a **foot**—a group of syllables with a fixed pattern of stressed and unstressed syllables. The following chart illustrates the most common types of feet that occur in English and American verse.

Foot	Stress Pattern	Example
Iamb	⏑ /	They pace | in sleek | chi val|ric cer|tain ty (Adrienne Rich)
Trochee	/ ⏑	Thóu, when | thou re|turn'st, wilt | tell me. (John Donne)
Anapest	⏑ ⏑ /	With a hey, | and a ho, | and a hey | nonino (William Shakespeare)
Dactyl	/ ⏑ ⏑	Constantly | risking ab|surdity (Lawrence Ferlinghetti)

Iambic and *anapestic* meters are called *rising meters* because they progress from unstressed to stressed syllables. *Trochaic* and *dactylic* meters are known as *falling meters* because they move from stressed to unstressed syllables.

The following types of metrical feet, less common than those above, are used for emphasis or to provide variety rather than to create the dominant meter of a line.

Spondee	/ /	Pomp, pride | and circumstance of glorious war! (William Shakespeare)
Pyrrhic	⏑ ⏑	A horse! a horse! My king|dom for | a horse! (William Shakespeare)

A line of poetry has **meter** when the feet form a definite, rhythmic pattern. Each line is measured by the number of feet it contains.

monometer one foot   **pentameter** five feet
dimeter two feet   **hexameter** six feet
trimeter three feet   **heptameter** seven feet
tetrameter four feet   **octameter** eight feet

The metrical pattern of a line of verse gets its name from the combination of the name of the foot it contains with the name that describes the length of the line. For example, the most common foot in English poetry is the **iamb**, most often occurring in lines of three or five feet.

Eight hun|dred of | the brave   *Iambic trimeter*
(William Cowper)

O, how | much more | doth
beau|ty beau|teous seem   *Iambic pentameter*
(William Shakespeare)

Because **iambic pentameter** is so well suited to the rhythms of English speech, writers frequently use it in plays and poems. Shakespeare's plays, for example, are written in unrhymed lines of iambic pentameter called **blank verse**.

Many other metrical combinations are also possible; a few are suggested below.

Like a | high-born | maiden   *Trochaic trimeter*
(Percy Bysshe Shelley)

The As|syr|ian came down |
like the wolf | on the fold   *Anapestic tetrameter*
(Lord Byron)

Maid en most | beau ti ful |
mother most | boun ti ful, | la   *Dactylic hexameter*
dy of | lands, (A. C.
Swinburne)

The yel|low fog | that rubs | its
back | upon | the win | *Iambic heptameter*
dow-panes (T. S. Eliot)

Scansion can be an extremely technical process, and when students are bogged down with anapests and dactyls, they can easily forget that poetic meter is not an end in itself. Meter should be appropriate for the ideas expressed by the poem, and it should help to create a suitable tone. A light skipping rhythm, for example, would be inappropriate for an **elegy**, and a heavy, slow rhythm would surely be out of place in an **epigram** or a limerick. The following poem illustrates the different types of metrical feet.

SAMUEL TAYLOR COLERIDGE
(1772–1834)

Metrical Feet
(1806)

Lesson for a Boy

Trochee trips from long to short;
From long to long in solemn sort
Slow Spondee stalks; strong foot! yet ill able
Ever to come up with Dactyl trisyllable.
5 Iambics march from short to long—
With a leap and a bound the swift Anapests throng;
One syllable long, with one short at each side,
Amphibrachys hastes with a stately stride—
First and last being long, middle short, Amphimacer
10 Strikes his thundering hoofs like a proud high-bred Racer.
If Derwent[1] be innocent, steady, and wise,
And delight in the things of earth, water, and skies;
Tender warmth at his heart, with these meters to show it,
With sound sense in his brains, may make Derwent a poet—
15 May crown him with fame, and must win him the love
Of his father on earth and his Father above.
        My dear, dear child!
Could you stand upon Skiddaw,[2] you would not from its whole ridge
See a man who so loves you as your fond S. T. COLERIDGE.

Each line of Coleridge's poem illustrates the qualities of the particular metrical foot he describes. Thus Coleridge makes the point that different meters enable poets to achieve different effects.

---

[1] Coleridge's son.

[2] A mountain in the Lake District of England.

Even poems with regular meter may contain individual lines that depart from the dominant metrical pattern. Poets frequently vary the number of feet in a line to relieve monotony or to accommodate the demands of meaning or emphasis. One way to vary the meter of a poem is to use lines composed of varying numbers of metrical feet. Consider in the following poem how the poet uses iambic lines of varying lengths.

EMILY DICKINSON
(1830–1886)

I Like to See It Lap the Miles
(1891)

I like to see it lap the Miles—
And lick the Valleys up—
And stop to feed itself at Tanks—
And then—prodigious step

5 Around a Pile of Mountains—
And supercilious peer
In Shanties—by the sides of Roads—
And then a Quarry pare

To fit its Ribs
10 And crawl between
Complaining all the while
In horrid—hooting stanza—
Then chase itself down Hill—

And neigh like Boanerges[1]—
15 Then—punctual as a Star
Stop—docile and omnipotent
At its own stable door—

The poem is a single sentence that, except for some short pauses, stretches unbroken from beginning to end. Iambic lines of varying lengths actually suggest the movements of the train that the poet describes. Iambic tetrameter lines, such as the first, give readers a sense of the train's steady, rhythmic movement across a flat landscape, and shorter lines ("To fit its Ribs / And crawl between") suggest its slowing motion. Beginning with two iambic dimeter lines and progressing to iambic trimeter lines, the third

---

[1] A vociferous preacher and orator. Also, the name, meaning "son of thunder," Jesus gave to apostles John and James because of their fiery zeal.

stanza increases in speed just like the train that is racing downhill "In horrid—hooting stanza—."

A poet can also vary the meter of a poem by using more than one type of metrical foot. Any variation in a metrical pattern—substituting a trochee for an iamb, for instance—immediately calls attention to itself. Poets are aware of this fact and use it to their own advantage. For example, in line 16 of "I Like to See It Lap the Miles," the poet departs from iambic meter by placing unexpected stress on the first word, *stop*. By emphasizing this word, the poet brings the flow of the poem to an abrupt halt, suggesting the jolt riders experience when a train comes to a stop. In the following segment from "The Rime of the Ancient Mariner," Samuel Taylor Coleridge also departs from his poem's dominant iambic meter.

> The ship | was cheered, | the har|bor cleared,
> Merri|ly did | we drop
> Below | the kirk, | below | the hill,
> Below | the light|house top.

Although these lines are arranged in iambic tetrameter, the poet uses a trochee in the second line, breaking the meter in order to accommodate the natural pronunciation of "merrily" as well as to place stress on the word.

Another way of varying the meter is to introduce a rhythmical pause known as a **caesura**—a Latin word meaning "a cutting"—within a line. When scanning a poem, you indicate a caesura with this mark: ‖. Unless a line is extremely short, it probably will contain a caesura. Most commonly the pause occurs near the middle of a line:

> How do I love thee? ‖ Let me count the ways.
> *Elizabeth Barrett Browning*

> Two loves I have ‖ of comfort and despair.
> *William Shakespeare*

A caesura can, however, occur at any point in the line:

> High on a throne of royal state, ‖ which far
> Outshone the wealth of Ormus ‖ and of Ind
> *John Milton*

In fact, more than one caesura can occur in a single line:

> 'Tis good. ‖ Go to the gate. ‖ Somebody knocks.
> *William Shakespeare*

As you can see from the preceding examples, the pauses in a line can have a definite effect on the line's rhythm. Notice, for example, the variations in the rhythm produced by the caesuras in the following lines of iambic pentameter:

> High on a throne of royal state, ‖ which far
> Outshone the wealth of Ormus ‖ and of Ind,
> Or where the gorgeous East ‖ with richest hand
> Showers on her kings ‖ barbaric pearl and gold,
> Satan exalted sat, ‖ by merit raised.
>
> *John Milton*

Although the end of a line may mark the end of a metrical unit, it does not always coincide with the end of a sentence. Poets may choose to indicate a pause at this point, or they may continue, without a break, to the next line. Lines that have distinct pauses at the end—usually signaled by punctuation—are called **end-stopped lines.** Lines that do not end with strong pauses are called **run-on lines.** (Sometimes literary scholars use the term **enjambment** to describe this type of line.) End-stopped lines can seem formal, or even forced, because their length is rigidly dictated by the poem's meter, rhythm, and rhyme scheme. In the following excerpt from John Keats's "La Belle Dame Sans Merci" (p. 331), for example, rhythm, meter, and rhyme dictate the pauses that occur at the ends of the lines:

> O, what can ail thee, knight-at-arms,
>   Alone and palely loitering?
> The sedge has withered from the lake,
>   And no birds sing.

In contrast to end-stopped lines, run-on lines seem more natural. Because their ending points are determined by the rhythms of speech and by the meaning and emphasis the poet wishes to convey rather than by meter and rhyme, run-on lines are suited to the open form of most modern poetry. In the following lines from the 1967 poem "We Have Come Home," by the Gambian poet Lenrie Peters, run-on lines give the poem a conversational tone:

> We have come home
> From the bloodless war
> With sunken hearts
> Our boots full of pride—
> From the true massacre of the soul
> When we have asked
> 'What does it cost
> To be loved and left alone?'

Rather than relying exclusively on end-stopped or run-on lines, poets often use a combination of the two to produce the effects they want. By varying the rhythm of the poem, they create a meter that suits their ideas. In the following lines from "Pot Roast" (p. 384) by Mark Strand, for example, the juxtaposition of end-stopped and run-on lines controls the rhythm:

> I gaze upon the roast,
> that is sliced and laid out
> on my plate
> and over it
> I spoon the juices
> of carrot and onion.
> And for once I do not regret
> the passage of time.

POEMS FOR FURTHER READING: RHYTHM AND METER

ADRIENNE RICH
(1929–   )

Aunt Jennifer's Tigers
(1951)

> Aunt Jennifer's tigers prance across a screen,
> Bright topaz denizens of a world of green.
> They do not fear the men beneath the tree;
> They pace in sleek chivalric certainty.
>
> 5 Aunt Jennifer's fingers fluttering through her wool
> Find even the ivory needle hard to pull.
> The massive weight of Uncle's wedding band
> Sits heavily upon Aunt Jennifer's hand.
>
> When Aunt is dead, her terrified hands will lie
> 10 Still ringed with ordeals she was mastered by.
> The tigers in the panel that she made
> Will go on prancing, proud and unafraid.

READING AND REACTING

1. What is the dominant metrical pattern of the poem? In what way does the meter enhance the ironic contrast the poem develops?
2. The lines in stanza 1 are end-stopped, those in stanza 2 are run-on, and those in stanza 3 combine the two techniques. What is achieved by this variation in rhythm?

3. What ideas does the poet emphasize by using caesuras in the first and fourth lines of the last stanza?

ETHERIDGE KNIGHT
(1931–1991)

For Malcolm,[1] A Year After
(1986)

Compose for Red a proper verse;
Adhere to foot and strict iamb;
Control the burst of angry words
Or they might boil and break the dam.
5 Or they might boil and overflow
And drench me, drown me, drive me mad.
So swear no oath, so shed no tear,
And sing no song blue Baptist sad.
Evoke no image, stir no flame,
10 And spin no yarn across the air.
Make empty anglo tea lace words—
Make them dead white and dry bone bare.

Compose a verse for Malcolm man,
And make it rime and make it prim.
15 The verse will die—as all men do—
But not the memory of him!
Death might come singing sweet like C,
Or knocking like the old folk say,
The moon and stars may pass away,
20 But not the anger of that day.

READING AND REACTING

1. Why do you think Knight chooses to write a "proper verse" in "strict iamb"? Do you think this meter is an appropriate choice?
2. What does Knight achieve by using end-stopped lines? What would be the effect of using run-on lines?
3. Where in the poem does Knight use caesuras? Why does he use this device in each instance?

---

[1] Malcolm X.

4. **JOURNAL ENTRY:** How would you describe the mood of the speaker? Is the meter of the poem consistent with his mood? Explain.

ALLITERATION AND ASSONANCE

Just as poetry depends on rhythm, it also depends on the sounds of individual words. An effect pleasing to the ear, such as "Did he who made the Lamb make thee?" from William Blake's "The Tyger" (p. 282), is called **euphony.** A jarring or discordant effect, such as "The vorpal blade went snicker-snack!" from Lewis Carroll's "Jabberwocky" (p. 210), is called **cacophony.**

One of the earliest, and perhaps the most primitive, methods of enhancing sound is **onomatopoeia,** which occurs when the sound of a word echoes its meaning, as it does in common words such as *bang, crash,* and *hiss.* Poets make broad application of this technique by using combinations of words that suggest a correspondence between sound and meaning. Notice how Edgar Allan Poe uses this device in the following segment from his poem "The Bells":

>   Yet the ear, it fully knows,
>   By the twanging
>   And the clanging,
>   How the danger ebbs and flows;
>   Yet the ear distinctly tells,
>   In the jangling
>   And the wrangling
>   How the danger sinks and swells
> By the sinking or the swelling in the anger of the bells—
>   Of the bells,—
>   Of the bells, bells, bells, bells. . . .

Poe's primary objective in this poem is to recreate the sound of ringing bells. Although he succeeds, the poem (113 lines long in its entirety) eventually becomes quite tedious. A more subtle use of onomatopoetic words appears in the following passage from *An Essay on Criticism* by Alexander Pope:

> Soft is the strain when Zephyr gently blows,
> And the smooth stream in smoother numbers flows;
> But when the loud surges lash the sounding shore,
> The hoarse, rough verse should like the torrent roar:
> When Ajax strives some rock's vast weight to throw,
> The line too Labors, and the words move slow.

After earlier admonishing readers that sound must echo sense, Pope uses onomatopoetic words such as *lash* and *roar* to convey the fury of the sea, and he uses repeated consonants to echo the sounds these words suggest. Notice, for example, how the *s* and *m* sounds suggest the gently blowing Zephyr and the flowing of the smooth stream and how the series of *r* sounds echoes the torrent's roar.

Alliteration—the repetition of consonant sounds in consecutive or neighboring words, usually at the beginning of words—is another device used to enhance sound in a poem. Both Poe ("sinks and swells") and Pope ("smooth stream") make use of alliteration in the preceding excerpts, and so does Alfred, Lord Tennyson in the following poem.

ALFRED, LORD TENNYSON
(1809–1892)

The Eagle
(1851)

He clasps the crag with crooked hands;
Close to the sun in lonely lands,
Ringed with the azure world, he stands.

The wrinkled sea beneath him crawls:
5 He watches from his mountain walls,
And like a thunderbolt he falls.

Repeated hard *c* sounds in the first two lines of the poem give the lines a harsh, flinty quality. These sounds strengthen the lines and, by echoing the sharp sound of the eagle's "crooked" hands holding fast to the rocky "crags," reinforce the meaning of the words. The *l* sounds in line 2 ("lonely lands") slow down the rhythm of the line and reflect the expansiveness and isolation of the world in which the eagle lives.

The following poem also uses alliteration to create special aural effects.

N. SCOTT MOMADAY
(1934–   )

Comparatives
(1976)

Sunlit sea,
the drift of fronds,
and banners
of bobbing boats—
5 the seaside

      upon the planks,
      the coil and
      crescent of flesh
      extending
10 just into death.

      Even so,
      in the distant,
      inland sea,
      a shadow runs,
15 radiant,
      rude in the rock:
      fossil fish,
      fissure of bone
      forever.
20 It is perhaps
      the same thing,
      an agony
      twice perceived.

      It is most like
25 wind on waves—
      mere commotion,
      mute and mean,
      perceptible—
      that is all.

Throughout the poem, Momaday uses alliteration to create a subtle effect. Repeated *s* sounds in line 1 echo the fluid motion of the sea, and in lines 3 and 4 *b* sounds suggest the bobbing of boats. In the second stanza, *r* sounds mirror the smooth movement of a shadow across a rock. And finally, in stanza 3, repeated *w* and *m* sounds suggest the wind blowing across the waves. Together, these sounds underscore the major theme of the poem: Nature, like the wind on the waves and a shadow on a rock, is something that can be perceived but never fully understood.

    Assonance—the repetition of the same or similar vowel sounds, especially in stressed syllables—can also enrich a poem. When it is used solely to produce aural effects, assonance can be distracting. Consider, for example, the monotony and clumsiness of the repeated vowel sounds in Tennyson's "Many a morning on the moorland did we hear the copses ring. . . ." When used more subtly, however, assonance can enhance the effectiveness of a poem. John Keats was aware of the possibilities of assonance when he wrote these lines from "Bright Star":

    The mo̅ving waters at their priest-like task
      Of pu̅re ablu̲tion round earth's human shores

Notice how the repeated vowel sounds suggest the liquid flow of the "moving waters." Certainly Keats could have used other words to describe the sea, but had he done so, he would have lost the beauty and aural reinforcement that assonance provides.

Assonance can also unify an entire poem. In the following poem, assonance emphasizes the thematic connections among words in order to unify the poem's ideas.

ROBERT HERRICK
(1591–1674)

Delight in Disorder
(1648)

> A sweet disorder in the dress
> Kindles in clothes a wantonness.
> A lawn[1] about the shoulders thrown
> Into a fine distractión;
> 5 An erring lace, which here and there
> Enthralls the crimson stomacher;[2]
> A cuff neglectful, and thereby
> Ribbons to flow confusedly;
> A winning wave, deserving note,
> 10 In the tempestuous petticoat;
> A careless shoestring, in whose tie
> I see a wild civility;
> Do more bewitch me than when art
> Is too precise in every part.

Repeated vowel sounds extend throughout this poem—for instance, "shoulders" and "thrown" in line 3; and "tie," "wild," and "precise" in lines 11, 12, and 14. Using alliteration as well as assonance, Herrick subtly connects certain words—"tempestuous petticoat," for example. By connecting these words, he calls attention to the pattern of imagery that helps to convey the poem's theme. Because these patterns occur with such regularity, it is difficult to dismiss them as chance. In the hands of a poet such as Herrick, they may be seen as deliberate strategies calculated to enhance the poem and to appeal to readers.

---

[1] A shawl made of fine fabric.
[2] A decorative covering for the breasts.

RHYME

In addition to alliteration and assonance, poets enhance the possibilities of sound with **rhyme**—the use of matching sounds in two or more words: "tight" and "might"; "born" and "horn"; "sleep" and "deep." For a rhyme to be **perfect,** final vowel and consonant sounds must be the same, as they are in each of the preceding examples. **Imperfect rhyme** (sometimes called *near rhyme, slant rhyme, approximate rhyme,* or *consonance*) occurs when the final consonant sounds in two words are the same but vowel sounds are different—"learn/barn," or "pads/lids," for example. William Stafford uses imperfect rhyme in "Traveling through the Dark" (p. 381) when he rhymes "road" with "dead." Finally, **eye rhyme** occurs when two words look alike but are pronounced differently—for example, "watch" and "catch."

Rhymes can be classified according to the position of the rhyming syllables in a line of verse. The most common type of rhyme is **end rhyme,** which occurs at the end of a line.

> Tyger! Tyger! burning <u>bright</u>
> In the forests of the <u>night</u>
>
> William Blake "The Tyger"

Internal rhyme occurs within a line.

> The Sun came up upon the left,
> Out of the <u>sea</u> came <u>he</u>!
> And he shone <u>bright</u> and on the <u>right</u>
> Went down into the sea.
>
> Samuel Taylor Coleridge "The Rime of the Ancient Mariner"

Beginning rhyme occurs at the beginning of a line.

> Red River, red river,
> <u>Slow</u> flow heat is silence
> <u>No</u> will is still as a river
> <u>Still</u>. Will heat move
>
> T. S. Eliot "Virginia"

Rhymes can also be classified according to their number of corresponding syllables. **Masculine rhyme** (also called **rising rhyme**) occurs when single syllables correspond ("can"/"ran"; "descend"/"contend"). **Feminine rhyme** (also called **double rhyme** or **falling rhyme**) occurs when two syllables, a stressed followed by an unstressed, correspond ("ocean"/"motion"; "leaping"/"sleeping").

Finally, **triple rhyme** occurs when three syllables correspond. Although not as common as the other two, triple rhyme is frequently used for humorous or satiric purposes, as in the following lines from the long poem *Don Juan* by Lord Byron:

> Sagest of women, even of widows, she
>   Resolved that Juan should be quite a paragon,
> And worthy of the noblest pedigree:
>   (His sire of Castile, his dam from Aragon).

In some cases, when it is overused or used in unexpected places, rhyme can create unusual and even comic effects. In the following poem, for example, humor is created by the incongruous connections established by rhymes such as "priest"/"beast" and "pajama"/"lllama."

OGDEN NASH
(1902–1971)

The Lama
(1931)

> The one-l lama
> He's a priest.
> The two-l llama,
> He's a beast.
> 5 And I will bet
> A silk pajama
> There isn't any
> Three-l lllama.

Rhyme can place emphasis on certain words, and it can establish a network of sounds that reinforces the relationship of ideas throughout a poem. It can also give an entire poem unity. The conventional way to see how a poem's rhyme scheme operates is to chart rhyming sounds that appear at the ends of lines. The sound that ends the first line is designated *a*, and all subsequent lines that end in that sound are also labeled *a*. The next sound to appear at the end of a line, and all other lines whose last sounds rhyme with it, are designated *b*, and so on. The lines of the poem that follows have been labeled in this manner to identify its rhyme scheme.

RICHARD WILBUR
(1921–   )

A Sketch
(1975)

Into the lower right   *a*
Square of the window frame   *b*
There came   *b*
      with scalloped flight   *a*

5 A goldfinch, lit upon   *c*
The dead branch of a pine,   *d*
Shining,   *d*
      and then was gone,   *c*

Tossed in a double arc   *e*
10 Upward into the thatched   *f*
And cross-hatched   *f*
      pine-needle dark.   *e*

Briefly, as fresh drafts stirred   *g*
The tree, he dulled and gleamed   *h*
15 And seemed   *h*
      more coal than bird,   *g*

Then, dodging down, returned   *i*
In a new light, his perch   *j*
A birch—   *j*
20   twig, where he burned   *i*

In the sun's broadside ray,   *k*
Some seed pinched in his bill.   *l*
Yet still   *l*
      he did not stay,   *k*

25 But into a leaf-choken pane,   *m*
Changeful as even in heaven,   *n*
Even   *n*
      in Saturn's reign,   *m*

Tunneled away and hid.   *o*
30 And then? But I cannot well   *p*
Tell you   *p*
      all that he did.   *o*

> It was like glancing at rough   *q*
> Sketches tacked on a wall,   *r*
> 35 And all   *r*
>   so less than enough   *q*
>
> Of gold on beaten wing,   *s*
> I could not choose that one   *t*
> Be done   *t*
> 40   as the finished thing.   *s*

The rhyme scheme of this poem (*abba, cddc,* etc.) is extremely regular, yet it is hardly noticeable until it is charted. This does not mean, however, that the rhyme is unimportant. On the contrary, the rhyme scheme reinforces the poem's meaning and binds lines into structural units, connecting the first and fourth as well as the second and third lines of each stanza. In stanza 1 "right" and "flight" draw lines 1 and 4 of the stanza together, enclosing "fame" and "came" in lines 2 and 3. The pattern begins again with the next stanza and continues throughout the rest of the poem. Like the elusive goldfinch the poet describes, the rhymes are difficult to follow with the eye. In this sense the rhyme reflects the central theme of the poem: the difficulty of capturing in words a reality which, like the goldfinch, is forever shifting.

Naturally, rhyme does not have to be subtle to enrich a poem. An obvious rhyme scheme can communicate meaning by forcing attention on a relationship between ideas that are not normally linked. Notice how Alexander Pope uses this technique in the following excerpt from *An Essay on Man:*

> Honour and shame from no condition rise;
> Act well your part, there all the honour lies.
> Fortune in men has some small diff'rence made,
> One flaunts in rags, one flutters in brocade;
> The cobbler aproned, and the parson gowned,
> The friar hooded, and the monarch crowned.
> "What differ more (you cry) than crown and cowl?"
> I'll tell you, friend; a wise man and a fool.
>
> You'll find, if once the monarch acts the monk,
> Or, cobbler-like, the parson will be drunk,
> Worth makes the man, and want of it, the fellow;
> The rest is all but leather or prunella.[1]
>   Stuck o'er with titles and hung round with strings,
> That thou mayest be by kings, or whores of kings.
> Boast the pure blood of an illustrious race,
> In quiet flow from Lucrece[2] to Lucrece;

---

[1] Heavy cloth the color of prunes.

[2] In Roman legend, she stabbed herself after being defiled by Sextus Tarquinius.

But by your fathers' worth if yours you rate,
Count me those only who were good and great.

The lines of this poem are written in **heroic couplets,** with a rhyme scheme of *aa, bb, cc, dd,* and so on. In heroic couplets, greater stress falls on the second line of the couplet, especially the last word of the line. Coming at the end of the line, this word receives double emphasis: It is strengthened both because of its position in the line and because it is rhymed with the last word of the couplet's first line. In some cases rhyme joins opposing ideas and in so doing reinforces an idea that runs through the entire passage—the contrast between the high and the low, the virtuous and the immoral. For example, "gowned" and "crowned" in lines 5 and 6 convey the opposite conditions of the parson and the monarch and exemplify the idea expressed in lines 3 and 4 that fortune, not virtue, determines the station of individuals. Throughout this passage, then, rhyme emphasizes key ideas and helps to convey the meaning of the poem.

POEMS FOR FURTHER READING: ALLITERATION, ASSONANCE, AND RHYME

ALICE WALKER
(1944–   )

Revolutionary Petunias
(1972)

Sammy Lou of Rue
sent to his reward
the exact creature who
murdered her husband,
5 using a cultivator's hoe
with verve and skill;
and laughed fit to kill
in disbelief
at the angry, militant
10 pictures of herself
the Sonneteers quickly drew:
not any of them people that
she knew.
A backwoods woman
15 her house was papered with
funeral home calendars and
faces appropriate for a Mississippi
Sunday School. She raised a George,

a Martha, a Jackie and a Kennedy. Also
20 a John Wesley Junior.[1]
"Always respect the word of God,"
she said on her way to she didn't
know where, except it would be by
electric chair, and she continued
25 "Don't yall forgit to *water*
my purple petunias."

READING AND REACTING

1. Although this poem has no definite rhyme scheme, it does contain some words that rhyme. Why do you think Walker uses rhyme where she does? What, if anything, do these rhymes add to the poem?
2. The first line contains an example of internal rhyme. Are there other examples?
3. **JOURNAL ENTRY:** What is the significance of Sammy Lou's last words? How do they help you interpret the poem's title?

GERARD MANLEY HOPKINS
(1844–1889)

Pied Beauty
(1918)

Glory be to God for dappled things—
  For skies of couple-color as a brinded[1] cow;
    For rose-moles all in stipple upon trout that swim;
Fresh-firecoal chestnut-falls; finches' wings;
5   Landscape plotted and pieced—fold, fallow, and plow;
    And áll trádes, their gear and tackle and trim.[2]

All things counter, original, spare, strange;
  Whatever is fickle, freckled (who knows how?)
    With swift, slow; sweet, sour; adazzle, dim;
10 He fathers-forth whose beauty is past change:
        Praise him.

---

[1] John Wesley (1730–1791), a British religious leader and the founder of Methodism.

---

[1] Brindled (streaked).

[2] Equipment.

READING AND REACTING

1. Identify examples of onomatopoeia, alliteration, assonance, imperfect rhyme, and perfect rhyme. Do you think all these techniques are necessary?
2. What is the central theme of this poem? In what way do the sounds of the poem convey this idea?
3. Identify examples of masculine rhymes and feminine rhymes.
4. **JOURNAL ENTRY:** Hopkins uses both pleasing and discordant sounds in the poem. How does his use of euphony and cacophony affect your reactions to the poem?

DENISE LEVERTOV
(1923–)

The Ache of Marriage
(1964)

The ache of marriage:

thigh and tongue, beloved,
are heavy with it,
it throbs in the teeth

5 We look for communion
and are turned away, beloved,
each and each

It is leviathan and we
in its belly[1]
10 looking for joy, some joy
not to be known outside it

two by two in the ark of
the ache of it.

READING AND REACTING

1. What words and phrases does Levertov repeat throughout the poem? Why?

---

[1] A reference to the biblical story of Jonah and the whale.

2. Identify repeated vowel and consonant sounds in the poem. What do these repeated vowel and consonant sounds contribute to the poem?
3. **JOURNAL ENTRY:** This poem has no end rhyme. Would the addition of end rhyme strengthen the poem?

WILLIAM SHAKESPEARE
(1564–1616)

Fear No More the Heat o' the Sun[1]
(c. 1610)

Fear no more the heat o' the sun,
    Nor the furious winter's rages;
Thou thy worldly task hast done,
    Home art gone, and ta'en thy wages:
5 Golden lads and girls all must,
As chimney-sweepers, come to dust.

Fear no more the frown o' the great;
    Thou art past the tyrant's stroke;
Care no more to clothe and eat;
10   To thee the reed is as the oak:
The scepter, learning, physic, must
All follow this, and come to dust.

Fear no more the lightning flash,
    Nor the all-dreaded thunder stone;[2]
15 Fear not slander, censure rash;
    Thou hast finished joy and moan:
All lovers young, all lovers must
Consign to thee, and come to dust.

No exorciser harm thee!
20 Nor no witchcraft charm thee!
Ghost unlaid forbear thee!
Nothing ill come near thee!
Quiet consummation have;
And renownéd be thy grave!

---

[1] Sung as a lament for Imogen in Shakespeare's play *Cymbeline* (IV. ii).
[2] Thunder was commonly believed to be caused by falling stones or meteorites.

READING AND REACTING

1. Chart the rhyme scheme of this poem. In what way does it reinforce the meaning of the poem?
2. What techniques other than rhyme does the poet use to create particular aural effects?
3. This poem was written as a **dirge**, a song of grief for someone who has died. In what way are the sounds of the poem appropriate for its purpose?

LEWIS CARROLL
(1832–1898)

Jabberwocky
(1871)

'Twas brillig, and the slithy toves
    Did gyre and gimble in the wabe:
All mimsy were the borogoves,
    And the mome raths outgrabe.

5 "Beware the Jabberwock, my son!
    The jaws that bite, the claws that catch!
Beware the Jubjub bird, and shun
    The frumious Bandersnatch!"

He took his vorpal sword in hand;
10   Long time the manxome foe he sought—
So rested he by the Tumtum tree
    And stood awhile in thought.

And, as in uffish thought he stood,
    The Jabberwock, with eyes of flame,
15 Came whiffling through the tulgey wood,
    And burbled as it came!

One, two! One, two! And through and through
    The vorpal blade went snicker-snack!
He left it dead, and with its head
20   He went galumphing back.

"And hast thou slain the Jabberwock?
    Come to my arms, my beamish boy!

O frabjous day! Callooh, Callay!"
He chortled in his joy.

25 'Twas brillig, and the slithy toves
Did gyre and gimble in the wabe:
All mimsy were the borogoves,
And the mome raths outgrabe.

READING AND REACTING

1. Even though the poem contains some nonsense words, it does tell a story. What is the story?
2. Many words in this poem may be unfamiliar to you. Are they actual words? Use a dictionary to check before you dismiss any. Do some words seem to have meaning in the context of the poem regardless of whether or not they appear in the dictionary? Explain.
3. **JOURNAL ENTRY:** This poem contains many examples of onomatopoeia. What ideas do the various words' sounds connote?

Checklist for Writing about Sound

Rhythm and Meter

- Does the poem contain repeated words and phrases? If so, how do they help to create rhythm?
- Does the poem have regular meter, or does the meter vary from line to line?
- In what ways does the meter contribute to the overall effect of the poem?
- Which lines of the poem contain caesuras? What effect do they have?
- Are the lines of the poem end-stopped, run-on, or a combination of the two? What effects are produced by the presence or absence of pauses at the ends of lines?

Alliteration, Assonance, and Rhyme

- Does the poem contain any examples of onomatopoeia?
- Are there any examples of alliteration or assonance?
- Does the poem have a regular rhyme scheme?
- Does the poem use internal rhyme? Beginning rhyme?
- Does the poem include examples of masculine, feminine, or triple rhyme?
- In what ways does rhyme provide unity?
- How does the rhyme reinforce the ideas in the poem?

WRITING SUGGESTIONS: SOUND

1. William Blake's "The Tyger" appeared in a collection entitled *Songs of Experience*. Compare this poem (p. 282) to "The Lamb" (p. 281), which appeared in a collection called *Songs of Innocence*. In what way are the speakers in these two poems relatively "innocent" or "experienced"? How does sound help to convey the attitude of the speakers in these two poems?

2. Write an essay in which you compare the themes of "Aunt Jennifer's Tigers" (p. 196) and "Revolutionary Petunias" (p. 206). In what ways does sound reinforce each poem's themes?

3. "The Faithful Wife" (p. 124) and "Sadie and Maud" (p. 188) deal with attitudes toward home and family. How does the presence or absence of rhyme in these poems communicate their ideas about this subject?

4. Robert Frost once said that writing poems that have no meter is like playing tennis without a net. What do you think he meant? Do you agree? After reading "Out, Out—" (p. 177), "Stopping By Woods on a Snowy Evening" (p. 315), or "The Road Not Taken" (p. 315), write an essay in which you assess Frost's use of meter.

5. Select two or three contemporary poems that have no end rhyme. Write an essay in which you discuss what these poets gained and lost by not using rhyme.

CHAPTER 10

FORM

JOHN KEATS
(1795–1821)

On the Sonnet
(1819)

If by dull rhymes our English must be chained,
And like Andromeda,[1] the sonnet sweet
Fettered, in spite of painéd loveliness,
Let us find, if we must be constrained,
5 Sandals more interwoven and complete
To fit the naked foot of Poesy:
Let us inspect the lyre, and weigh the stress
Of every chord, and see what may be gained
By ear industrious, and attention meet;
10 Misers of sound and syllable, no less
Than Midas[2] of his coinage, let us be
Jealous of dead leaves in the bay-wreath crown;
So, if we may not let the Muse be free,
She will be bound with garlands of her own.

The **form** of a literary work is its general organizing principle. **Poetic form** is described in terms of a particular work's rhyme, meter, and stanzaic pattern.

Until the twentieth century, most poetry was written in **closed form,** characterized by regular patterns of meter, rhyme, line length, and stanzaic divisions. Early poems that were passed down through the oral tradition—epics and ballads, for example—relied on regular form to increase their impact and to facilitate memorization. Even after poems were written down, poets tended to favor regular patterns. In fact, such regular form was, until relatively recently, what distinguished poetry from prose. Of course, strict adherence to such regular patterns sometimes produced

---

[1] In Greek mythology, Andromeda was chained to a rock to appease a sea monster.

[2] King Midas was granted his wish that all he touched would turn to gold.

poems that were, in John Keats's words, "chained" by "dull rhymes" and "fettered" by the rules governing a particular form. But rather than feeling "constrained" by form, many poets experimented with traditional forms—as well as with imagery, figures of speech, allusion, and other techniques—stretching convention to its limits.

In addition to experimenting within traditional forms, poets also experimented (as they continue to do) with new forms—forms governed by different metrical patterns, rhyme schemes, and arrangements of lines. As they sought new means of expression, poets turned to forms used by poets in other cultures, adapting them to the demands of their own languages. English and American poets, for example, adopted (and still use) early French forms, such as the villanelle and the sestina, and early Italian forms, such as the Petrarchan sonnet and terza rima. More recently, the nineteenth-century American poet Henry Wadsworth Longfellow studied Icelandic epics; the twentieth-century poet Ezra Pound studied the works of French troubadours; and Pound and other twentieth-century American poets, such as Richard Wright and Carolyn Kizer, were inspired by Japanese haiku.

Eventually, more and more poets moved away from closed form to experiment with **open form** poetry (sometimes called **free verse** or *vers libre*), varying line length, abandoning stanzaic divisions, breaking lines in unexpected places, and even abandoning any semblance of formal structure. In English, nineteenth-century poets—such as William Blake, Matthew Arnold, and, in particular, Walt Whitman—experimented with lines of irregular meter and length. (Well before this time, Asian poetry and certain Biblical passages in Hebrew had used a type of free verse.) In nineteenth-century France, Symbolist poets such as Baudelaire, Rimbaud, Verlaine, and Mallarmé also used free verse. Later, in the early twentieth century, a group of American poets including Ezra Pound, William Carlos Williams, and Amy Lowell, who were associated with a movement known as **imagism,** wrote poetry that dispensed with traditional principles of English versification, creating new rhythms and meters.

Although much contemporary English and American poetry is composed in open form, many poets also write in closed form—even in very traditional, highly structured patterns. Still, new forms, and new variations of old forms, are being created all the time. And, because contemporary poets do not feel bound by rules or restrictions about what constitutes "acceptable" poetic form, they are free to discover the form that best suits the poem's purpose, subject, language, and theme.

CLOSED FORM

A **closed form** poem looks symmetrical; it has an identifiable, repeated pattern, with lines of similar length arranged in groups of two, three, four, or more. Such poems also tend to rely on regular metrical patterns and rhyme schemes.

Despite the connotations of its name, however, closed form poetry does not have to be confining or conservative. Sometimes contemporary poets experiment by using characteristics of open form poetry (such as lines of varying length) within a closed form, or by moving back and forth within a single poem from open to closed to open form. Sometimes they (like their eighteenth-century counterparts) experiment with closed form by combining different stanzaic forms (stanzas of two and three lines, for example) within a single poem.

Even when poets work within a traditional form, such as a **sonnet,** they can still break new ground. For example, they can create a sonnet with an unexpected meter or rhyme scheme, add an extra line or even extra stanzas to a traditional sonnet form, combine two different traditional sonnet forms in a single poem, or write an abbreviated version of a lengthy form, such as a **sestina** or a **villanelle.** (See the section on Traditional Forms in this chapter for examples of such experiments.) Finally, poets always feel free to use traditional forms as building blocks, combining them in innovative ways to create new patterns and new forms.

Sometimes a pattern simply determines the meter of a poem's individual lines. Sometimes the pattern extends to the stanza level: Lines are arranged into groups of two, three, four, or more. At still other times, as in the case of certain traditional forms, a poetic pattern applies to an entire poem.

BLANK VERSE

A line of **blank verse** has ten syllables and a set pattern of five stressed and five unstressed syllables called **iambic pentameter.** Many passages from Shakespeare's plays, such as the following lines from *Hamlet* are written in blank verse:

> To sleep, perchance to dream, ay there's the rub,
> For in that sleep of death what dreams may come
> When we have shuffled off this mortal coil
> Must give us pause—there's the respect
> That makes calamity of so long life:

For a contemporary use of blank verse, see John Updike's "Ex-Basketball Player" (p. 164).

STANZA

A **stanza** is a group of two or more lines with the same metrical pattern—and often with a given rhyme scheme as well—separated by blank space from other such groups of lines. The stanza in poetry is like the paragraph in prose: It groups related thoughts into units.

A two-line stanza with rhyming lines of similar length and meter is called a **couplet.** The **heroic couplet,** first used by Chaucer and especially popular throughout the eighteenth century, consists of two rhymed lines of iambic pentameter, with a weak pause after the first line and a strong pause after the second. The following example, from Alexander Pope's *An Essay on Criticism,* is a heroic couplet:

> True ease in writing comes from art, not chance,
> As those move easiest who have learned to dance.

Contemporary poems composed of couplets include Maxine Kumin's "Morning Swim" (p. 338) and Barry Spacks's "Finding a Yiddish Paper on the Riverside Line" (p. 379).

A three-line stanza with lines of similar length and a set rhyme scheme is called a **tercet.** Percy Bysshe Shelley's "Ode to the West Wind" (p. 368) is built largely of tercets:

> O wild West Wind, thou breath of Autumn's being,
> Thou, from whose unseen presence the leaves dead
> Are driven, like ghosts from an enchanter fleeing,
>
> Yellow, and black, and pale, and hectic red,
> Pestilence-stricken multitudes: O Thou,
> Who chariotest to their dark wintry bed

Although in many tercets all three lines rhyme, "Ode to the West Wind" uses a special rhyme scheme, also used by Dante, called **terza rima.** This rhyme scheme (*aba, bcb, cdc, ded,* and so on) creates an interlocking series of stanzas: Line 2's *dead* looks ahead to the rhyming words *red* and *bed,* which close lines 4 and 6, and the pattern continues throughout the poem.

A four-line stanza with lines of similar length and a set rhyme scheme is called a **quatrain.** The quatrain, the most widely used and versatile unit in English and American poetry, is used by William Wordsworth in the following excerpt from "She Dwelt among the Untrodden Ways" (p. 397):

> A violet by a mossy stone
>   Half hidden from the eye!
> Fair as a star, when only one
>   Is shining in the sky.

Quatrains are frequently used by contemporary poets as well—for instance, in Theodore Roethke's "My Papa's Waltz" (p. 46), Adrienne Rich's "Aunt Jennifer's Tigers" (p. 196), and William Stafford's "Traveling through the Dark" (p. 381).

One special kind of quatrain, called the **ballad stanza,** alternates lines of eight and six syllables; typically, only the second and fourth lines rhyme. The following lines from "Sir Patrick Spence" (p. 275) illustrate the ballad stanza:

>   The king sits in Dumferling toune,
>   Drinking the blude-reid wine:
>   'O whar will I get guid sailor
>   To sail this schip of mine?'

Common measure, a four-line stanzaic pattern closely related to the ballad stanza, is used in hymns as well as in poetry. It differs from the ballad stanza in that its rhyme scheme is *abab* rather than *abcb*. In contemporary poetry this pattern appears in Donald Hall's "My Son, My Executioner" (p. 178).

Other stanzaic forms include **rhyme royal,** a seven-line stanza (*ababbcc*) set in iambic pentameter, used in Sir Thomas Wyatt's sixteenth-century poem "They Flee from Me That Sometimes Did Me Seke" as well as in Theodore Roethke's twentieth-century "I Knew a Woman" (p. 116); **ottava rima,** an eight-line stanza (*abababcc*) set in iambic pentameter; and the Spenserian stanza, a nine-line form (*ababbcbcc*) whose first eight lines are set in iambic pentameter and whose last line is in iambic hexameter. The Romantic poets John Keats and Percy Bysshe Shelley were among those who used this form. (See Chapter 9 for definitions and examples of various metrical patterns.)

TRADITIONAL FORMS

The Sonnet

Perhaps the most familiar kind of closed form poem written in English is the **sonnet,** a fourteen-line poem with a distinctive rhyme scheme and metrical pattern. The English or **Shakespearean sonnet,** which consists of fourteen lines divided into three quatrains and a concluding couplet, is written in iambic pentameter and follows the rhyme scheme *abab cdcd efef gg.* The **Petrarchan sonnet,** popularized in the fourteenth century by the Italian Francesco Petrarch, also consists of fourteen lines of iambic pentameter, but these lines are divided into an eight-line unit called an **octave** and a six-line unit (composed of two tercets) called a **sestet**. The rhyme scheme of the octave is *abba abba;* the rhyme scheme of the sestet is *cde cde.*

The conventional structures of these sonnet forms reflect the arrangement of ideas within a poem: In the Shakespearean sonnet the poet typically presents three "paragraphs" of related thoughts, introducing an idea in the first quatrain, developing it in the two remaining quatrains, and summing up in a succinct closing couplet. In the Petrarchan sonnet the octave introduces a problem that is resolved in the sestet. (Many Shakespearean sonnets also have a problem-solution structure.) Some sonnets vary the traditional patterns somewhat to suit the poem's language or ideas. For example, the rhyme scheme may depart from the pattern to avoid a forced rhyme or unnatural stress on a syllable, or the problem-solution break may not occur between octave and sestet.

The following poem follows the form of a traditional English sonnet.

WILLIAM SHAKESPEARE
(1564–1616)

When, in Disgrace with Fortune and Men's Eyes
(1609)

> When, in disgrace with Fortune and men's eyes,
> I all alone beweep my outcast state,
> And trouble deaf heaven with my bootless[1] cries,
> And look upon myself and curse my fate,
> 5 Wishing me like to one more rich in hope,
> Featured like him, like him with friends possessed,
> Desiring this man's art, and that man's scope,
> With what I most enjoy contented least,
> Yet in these thoughts myself almost despising,
> 10 Haply[2] I think on thee, and then my state,
> Like to the lark at break of day arising
> From sullen earth, sings hymns at heaven's gate;
>   For thy sweet love rememb'red such wealth brings
>   That then I scorn to change my state with kings.

This sonnet is written in iambic pentameter and has a conventional rhyme scheme: *abab* (eyes-state-cries-fate), *cdcd* (hope-possessed-scope-least), *efef* (despising-state-arising-gate), *gg* (brings-kings). In this poem, in which the speaker explains how thoughts of his loved one can rescue him from despair, each quatrain is unified by rhyme as well as by subject. In the first quatrain the speaker presents his problem: He is down on his luck and out of favor with his peers, isolated in self-pity and cursing his fate. In the second quatrain he develops this idea further: He is envious of others and dissatisfied with things that usually please him. In the third quatrain the focus shifts: Although the first two quatrains develop a dependent clause ("When. . . .") that introduces a problem, line 9 begins to present the resolution. In the third quatrain the speaker explains how, in the midst of his despair and self-hatred, he thinks of his loved one, and his spirits soar. The closing couplet sums up the mood transformation the poem describes and explains its significance: When the speaker realizes the emotional riches his loved one gives him, he is no longer envious of others.

[1] Futile.

[2] Luckily.

POEMS FOR FURTHER READING: THE SONNET

CLAUDE McKAY
(1890–1948)

The White City
(1922)

I will not toy with it nor bend an inch.
Deep in the secret chambers of my heart
I muse my life-long hate, and without flinch
I bear it nobly as I live my part.
5 My being would be a skeleton, a shell,
If this dark Passion that fills my every mood,
And makes my heaven in the white world's hell,
Did not forever feed me vital blood.
I see the mighty city through a mist—
10 The strident trains that speed the goaded mass,
The poles and spires and towers vapor-kissed,
The fortressed port through which the great ships pass,
The tides, the wharves, the dens I contemplate,
Are sweet like wanton loves because I hate.

READING AND REACTING

1. In what sense is the speaker's mood similar to that of the speaker in "When, in Disgrace with Fortune and Men's Eyes"? How is it different?
2. How is the speaker's description of the city in the third quatrain consistent with the emotions he expresses in lines 1–8?
3. The closing couplet of a Shakespearean sonnet traditionally sums up the sonnet's concerns. Is this true here? Explain.
4. **JOURNAL ENTRY:** Given the speaker's passionate anger at "the white world's hell" in which he lives, is the traditional, formal structure of the sonnet a logical choice? Explain.

JOHN KEATS
(1795–1821)

On First Looking into Chapman's Homer[1]
(1816)

> Much have I traveled in the realms of gold,
>   And many goodly states and kingdoms seen;
>   Round many western islands have I been
> Which bards in fealty to Apollo[2] hold.
> 5 Oft of one wide expanse had I been told
>   That deep-browed Homer ruled as his demesne,[3]
>   Yet did I never breathe its pure serene[4]
> Till I heard Chapman speak out loud and bold.
> Then felt I like some watcher of the skies
> 10   When a new planet swims into his ken;
> Or like stout Cortez[5] when with eagle eyes
>   He stared at the Pacific—and all his men
> Looked at each other with a wild surmise—
>   Silent, upon a peak in Darien.[6]

READING AND REACTING

1. Is this a Petrarchan or a Shakespearean sonnet? Explain.
2. The sestet's change of focus is introduced with the word "Then" in line 9. How does this word move readers from octave to sestet?
3. **JOURNAL ENTRY:** How does the mood of the sestet differ from the mood of the octave? How does the language differ?

---

[1] The translation of Homer by Elizabethan poet George Chapman.
[2] Greek god of light, truth, reason, male beauty; associated with music and poetry.
[3] Realm, domain.
[4] Air, atmosphere.
[5] It was Vasco de Balboa (not Hernando Cortez as Keats suggests) who first saw the Pacific Ocean, from "a peak in Darien," in Panama.
[6] Former name of the Isthmus of Panama.

GWENDOLYN BROOKS
(1917–   )

First Fight. Then Fiddle
(1949)

First fight. Then fiddle. Ply the slipping string
With feathery sorcery; muzzle the note
With hurting love; the music that they wrote
Bewilder, bewilder. Qualify to sing
5 Threadwise. Devise no salt, no hempen thing
For the dear instrument to bear. Devote
The bow to silks and honey. Be remote
A while from malice and from murdering.
But first to arms, to armor. Carry hate
10 In front of you and harmony behind.
Be deaf to music and to beauty blind.
Win war. Rise bloody, maybe not too late
For having first to civilize a space
Wherein to play your violin with grace.

READING AND REACTING

1. What is the subject of Brooks's poem? What does she mean by "fight" and "fiddle"?
2. What is the poem's rhyme scheme? Is it a Petrarchan or a Shakespearean sonnet?
3. Study the poem's capitalization and punctuation carefully. Why do you think Brooks chooses to end many of her sentences in mid-line?

The Sestina

The **sestina,** introduced in thirteenth-century France, is composed of six six-line stanzas and a three-line conclusion called an **envoi.** Although the sestina's pattern requires no end rhyme, it does require that each line end with one of six key words. The alternation of these six words in different positions—but always at the ends of lines—in each of the poem's six stanzas creates a rhythmic verbal pattern that unifies the poem.

ALBERTO ALVARO RIOS
(1952–   )

Nani
(1982)

Sitting at her table, she serves
the sopa de arroz[1] to me
instinctively, and I watch her,
the absolute mamá, and eat words
5 I might have had to say more
out of embarrassment. To speak,
now-foreign words I used to speak,
too, dribble down her mouth as she serves
me albóndigas.[2] No more
10 than a third are easy to me.
By the stove she does something with words
and looks at me only with her
back. I am full. I tell her
I taste the mint, and watch her speak
15 smiles at the stove. All my words
make her smile. Nani never serves
herself, she only watches me
with her skin, her hair. I ask for more.

I watch the mamá warming more
20 tortillas for me. I watch her
fingers in the flame for me.
Near her mouth, I see a wrinkle speak
of a man whose body serves
the ants like she serves me, then more words
25 from more wrinkles about children, words
about this and that, flowing more
easily from these other mouths. Each serves
as a tremendous string around her,
holding her together. They speak
30 nani was this and that to me
and I wonder just how much of me
will die with her, what were the words
I could have been, was. Her insides speak
through a hundred wrinkles, now, more

---

[1] Rice soup.
[2] Meatballs.

35 than she can bear, steel around her,
shouting, then, What is this thing she serves?

She asks me if I want more.
I own no words to stop her.
Even before I speak, she serves.

In many respects Rios's poem closely follows the form of the traditional sestina. For instance, it interweaves six key words—"serves," "me," "her," "words," "more," and "speak"—through six groups of six lines each, rearranging the order in which the words appear so that the first line of each group of six lines ends with the key word that closed the preceding group of lines. The poem repeats the key words in exactly the order prescribed: *abcdef, faebdc, cfdabe,* and so on. In addition, the sestina closes with a three-line envoi that includes all six of the poem's key words, three at the ends of lines and three within the lines. However, Rios departs from the sestina form by grouping his six sets of six lines not into six separate stanzas but rather into two eighteen-line stanzas.

The sestina form suits Rios's subject matter well. The focus of the poem, on the verbal and nonverbal interaction between the poem's "me" and "her," is reinforced by each of the related words. "Nani" is a poem about communication, and the key words return to probe this theme again and again. Throughout the poem these repeated words help to create a fluid, melodic, and tightly woven work.

POEM FOR FURTHER READING: THE SESTINA

ELIZABETH BISHOP
(1911–1979)

Sestina
(1965)

September rain falls on the house.
In the failing light, the old grandmother
sits in the kitchen with the child
beside the Little Marvel Stove,
5 reading the jokes from the almanac,
laughing and talking to hide her tears.

She thinks that her equinoctial tears
and the rain that beats on the roof of the house
were both foretold by the almanac,

10 but only known to a grandmother.
    The iron kettle sings on the stove.
    She cuts some bread and says to the child,

    It's time for tea now; but the child
    is watching the teakettle's small hard tears
15 dance like mad on the hot black stove,
    the way the rain must dance on the house.
    Tidying up, the old grandmother
    hangs up the clever almanac

    on its string. Birdlike, the almanac
20 hovers half open above the child,
    hovers above the old grandmother
    and her teacup full of dark brown tears.
    She shivers and says she thinks the house
    feels chilly, and puts more wood in the stove.

25 *It was to be,* says the Marvel Stove.
    It know what I know, says the almanac.
    With crayons the child draws a rigid house
    and a winding pathway. Then the child
    puts in a man with buttons like tears
30 and shows it proudly to the grandmother.

    But secretly, while the grandmother
    busies herself about the stove,
    the little moons fall down like tears
    from between the pages of the almanac
35 into the flower bed the child
    has carefully placed in the front of the house.

    Time to plant tears, says the almanac.
    The grandmother sings to the marvellous stove
    and the child draws another inscrutable house.

READING AND REACTING

1. Does the poet's need to end lines with certain key words strain the poem's syntax at any point? Explain.
2. Does this sestina use alliteration, assonance, or rhyme? Where? How do these techniques enhance the poem?
3. **JOURNAL ENTRY:** How are the six key words connected by the poem's theme?

The Villanelle

The **villanelle,** first introduced in France in the Middle Ages, is a nineteen-line poem composed of five tercets and a concluding quatrain; its rhyme scheme is *aba aba aba aba aba abaa.* Two different lines are systematically repeated in the poem: Line 1 appears again in lines 6, 12, and 18, and line 3 reappears as lines 9, 15, and 19. Thus each tercet concludes with an exact (or close) duplication of either line 1 or line 3, and the final quatrain concludes by repeating both line 1 and line 3.

THEODORE ROETHKE
(1908–1963)

The Waking
(1953)

I wake to sleep, and take my waking slow.
I feel my fate in what I cannot fear.
I learn by going where I have to go.

We think by feeling. What is there to know?
5 I hear my being dance from ear to ear.
I wake to sleep, and take my waking slow.

Of those so close beside me, which are you?
God bless the Ground! I shall walk softly there,
And learn by going where I have to go.

10 Light takes the Tree; but who can tell us how?
The lowly worm climbs up a winding stair;
I wake to sleep, and take my waking slow.

Great Nature has another thing to do
To you and me; so take the lively air,
15 And, lovely, learn by going where to go.

This shaking keeps me steady. I should know.
What falls away is always. And is near.
I wake to sleep, and take my waking slow.
I learn by going where I have to go.

"The Waking," like all villanelles, closely intertwines threads of sounds and words. The repeated lines and the very regular rhyme and meter give the poem a monotonous, almost hypnotic, rhythm. Not only does this poem use end rhyme and repetition of lines, but it also makes extensive use of alliteration (I feel my fate in what I cannot fear") and internal rhyme ("I hear my being dance from ear to ear"; "I wake to sleep and take my waking slow"). The result is a tightly constructed poem of overlapping sounds and images. (For another well-known example of a villanelle, see Dylan Thomas's "Do Not Go Gentle into That Good Night" (p. 47).

POEM FOR FURTHER READING: THE VILLANELLE

WILLIAM MEREDITH
(1919–   )

In Memory of Donald A. Stauffer
(1987)

Armed with an indiscriminate delight
His ghost left Oxford five summers ago,
Still on the sweet, obvious side of right.

How many friends and students talked all night
5 With this remarkable teacher? How many go
Still armed with his indiscriminate delight?

He liked, but often could not reach, the bright:
Young people sometimes prefer not to know
About the sweet or obvious sides of right.

10 But how all arrogance involves a slight
To knowledge, his humility would show
Them, and his indiscriminate delight

In what was true. This was why he could write
Commonplace books: his patience lingered so
15 Fondly on the sweet, obvious side of right.

What rare anthology of ghosts sits till first light
In the understanding air where he talks now,
Armed with his indiscriminate delight
There on the sweet and obvious side of right?

READING AND REACTING

1. Review the definition of *villanelle* and explain how Meredith's poem expands the possibilities of the traditional villanelle.
2. Try to make the changes you believe are necessary to make Meredith's poem absolutely consistent with the prescribed form of the villanelle. How do your changes change the poem?
3. **JOURNAL ENTRY:** What kinds of subjects do you think would be most appropriate for villanelles? Why? What subjects, if any, do you think would not be suitable? Explain.

The Epigram

Originally, an epigram was an inscription carved in stone on a monument or statue. As a literary form, an **epigram** is a very brief poem that makes a pointed, often sarcastic, comment in a surprising twist at the end. In a sense, it is a poem with a punch line. Although some epigrams rhyme, others do not. Many are only two lines long, but others are somewhat longer. What they have in common is their economy of language and their tone. One of the briefest of epigrams, written by Ogden Nash, appeared in *The New Yorker* magazine in 1931.

> The Bronx?
> No thonx.

In just four words, Nash manages to convey the unexpected, using rhyme and creative spelling to characterize a borough of New York City. The poem's two lines are perfectly balanced, making the contrast between the noncommittal tone of the first and the negative tone of the second quite striking.

POEMS FOR FURTHER READING: THE EPIGRAM

Read the two epigrams that follow and explain the point each one makes. Then evaluate each poem. What qualities do you conclude make an epigram effective?

SAMUEL TAYLOR COLERIDGE
(1772–1834)

What Is an Epigram?
(1802)

What is an epigram? a dwarfish whole,
Its body brevity, and wit its soul.

WILLIAM BLAKE
(1757–1827)

Her Whole Life Is an Epigram
(c. 1793–1811)

Her whole life is an epigram: smack, smooth & neatly penned,
Platted[1] quite neat to catch applause, with a sliding noose at the end.

Haiku

Like an epigram, a haiku compresses words into a very small package. Unlike an epigram, however, a haiku focuses not on the idea but on the image. The **haiku**, a traditional Japanese form, is a brief unrhymed poem that presents the essence of some aspect of nature, concentrating a vivid image in just three lines. Although in the strictest sense the haiku consists of seventeen syllables divided into lines of five, seven, and five syllables, respectively, not all poets conform to this rigid form.

The following poem is a translation of a classic Japanese haiku by Matsuo Basho:

Silent and still: then
Even sinking into the rocks,
The cicada's screech.

Notice that this poem conforms to the haiku's three-line structure and traditional subject matter, vividly depicting a natural scene without comment or analysis.

As the following poem illustrates, haiku in English is not always consistent with the traditional haiku in form or subject matter.

---

[1] Braided.

RICHARD BRAUTIGAN
(1935–1984)

Widow's Lament*

It's not quite cold enough
to go borrow some firewood
from the neighbors.

Brautigan's haiku adheres to the traditional pattern's number of lines and syllable count, and its central idea is expressed in very concentrated terms. The poem's focus, however, is not the natural world but human psychology. Moreover, without the title, the poem would be so ambiguous as to be meaningless. In this sense, the poet "cheats" the form, depending on the title's four syllables as well as on the seventeen of the poem itself to convey his ideas.

POEMS FOR FURTHER READING: HAIKU

RICHARD WRIGHT
(1908–1960)

Hokku Poems
(1960)

I am nobody
A red sinking autumn sun
Took my name away

Make up your mind snail!
5 You are half inside your house
And halfway out!

In the falling snow
A laughing boy holds out his palms
Until they are white

10 Keep straight down this block
Then turn right where you will find
A peach tree blooming

---

* Publication date is not available.

With a twitching nose
A dog reads a telegram
On a wet tree trunk

The spring lingers on
In the scent of a damp log
Rotting in the sun

Whose town did you leave
O wild and drowning spring rain
And where do you go?

The crow flew so fast
That he left his lonely caw
Behind in the fields

READING AND REACTING

1. The poems in this group of modern English haiku differ in several respects from the traditional Japanese form. Consider the form and subject matter of each haiku carefully, and explain how each is like and unlike a classic haiku.

2. **JOURNAL ENTRY:** Referring to the additional haiku poems in Chapter 7 as well as to those in this chapter, write a broad definition of haiku that applies to all of them.

OPEN FORM

An **open form** poem makes occasional use of rhyme and meter, but it has no familiar, easily identifiable pattern or design—that is, no conventional stanzaic divisions, no consistent metrical pattern, and no repeated rhyme scheme. Still, although open form poetry does lack a distinguishable pattern of meter, rhyme, or line length, it is not necessarily shapeless, untidy, or randomly ordered. All poems have form, and the form of a poem may be determined by factors such as the appearance of words on the printed page or pauses in natural speech as well as by conventional metrical patterns or rhyme schemes.

Open form poetry invites readers to participate in the creative process, to discover the relationship between form and meaning. Some modern poets believe that only open form offers them freedom to express their ideas or that the subject matter or mood of their poetry demands a relaxed, experimental approach to form. For example, when Lawrence Ferlinghetti portrays the poet as an acrobat who "climbs on rime" (p. 160), he constructs the poem in a way that is consistent with the poet/acrobat's willingness to take risks. Thus the poem's idiosyncratic form supports its ideas about the possibilities of poetry and the poet as experimenter.

Without a set structure, however, poets must create forms that suit their needs, and they must continue to shape and reshape the look of the poem on the page as they revise its words. Sometimes this absence of prescribed form presents a problem. More often open form represents a challenge, a way to experiment with fresh arrangements of words and new juxtapositions of ideas.

For poets such as Walt Whitman (see p. 235), Allen Ginsberg (see p. 183), and Carl Sandburg (see the poem that follows), open form provided an opportunity to experiment with meter and line length that could vary widely within a single poem.

CARL SANDBURG
(1878–1967)

Chicago
(1914)

    Hog Butcher for the World,
    Tool Maker, Stacker of Wheat,
    Player with Railroads and the Nation's Freight Handler;
    Stormy, husky, brawling,
5   City of the Big Shoulders:
They tell me you are wicked and I believe them, for I have seen
    your painted women under the gas lamps luring the farm boys.
And they tell me you are crooked and I answer: Yes, it is true I
    have seen the gunman kill and go free to kill again.
10 And they tell me you are brutal and my reply is: On the faces of
    women and children I have seen the marks of wanton hunger.
And having answered so I turn once more to those who sneer at this
    my city, and I give them back the sneer and say to them:
Come and show me another city with lifted head singing so proud
15   to be alive and coarse and strong and cunning.
Flinging magnetic curses amid the toil of piling job on job, here is a tall
    bold slugger set vivid against the little soft cities;
Fierce as a dog with tongue lapping for action, cunning as a savage
    pitted against the wilderness,
20   Bareheaded,
    Shoveling,
    Wrecking,
    Planning,
    Building, breaking, rebuilding,
25 Under the smoke, dust all over his mouth, laughing with white teeth,
Under the terrible burden of destiny laughing as a young man laughs,

Laughing even as an ignorant fighter laughs who has never lost a battle,
Bragging and laughing that under his wrist is the pulse, and under his ribs the heart of the people,
30   Laughing!
Laughing the stormy, husky, brawling laughter of Youth, half-naked, sweating, proud to be Hog Butcher, Tool Maker, Stacker of Wheat, Player with railroads and Freight Handler to the Nation.

Although "Chicago" does not wander all over the page, it represents a departure from traditional form. It uses capitalization and punctuation conventionally, and it generally (but not always) divides words into lines consistent with the natural divisions of phrases and sentences. However, the poem is not divided into stanzas, and its lines vary widely in length—from a single word isolated on a line to a line crowded with words—and follow no particular metrical pattern. Instead, its form is created through its pattern of alternating sections of long and short lines; through its repeated words and phrases ("They tell me" in lines 6–10, "under" in lines 25–26, and "laughing" in lines 25–31, for example); through alliteration (for instance, "slugger set vivid against the little soft cities" in line 17); and most of all through the piling up of words into catalogs in lines 1–5, 20–24, and 32–33.

In order to understand Sandburg's reasons for choosing such a form, we must consider the poem's subject matter and theme. "Chicago" celebrates the scope and power of a "stormy, husky, brawling" city, one that is exuberant and outgoing, not sedate and civilized. Chicago the city does not conform to anyone else's rules; it is, after all, "Bareheaded, / Shoveling, / Wrecking, / Planning, / Building, breaking," constantly active, in flux, on the move, "proud to be alive." "Fierce as a dog . . . cunning as a savage," the city is characterized as, among other things, a worker, a fighter, and a harborer of harlots and killers and hungry women and children. Such characterizations clearly demand a departure from the orderly confines of stanzaic form and measured rhyme and meter, a kind of form better suited to "the little soft cities" than to the "tall / bold slugger" that is Chicago.

Of course open form poetry does not have to look like Sandburg's prose poem. The next poem experiments with a different kind of open form.

LOUISE GLÜCK
(1943–   )

Life Is a Nice Place
(1966)

      Life is a nice place (They change
          the decorations
    every season; and the music,
      my dear, is just too
5   marvellous, they play you
anything from birds to Bach. And
     every day the Host
arranges for some clever sort
    of contest and they give
10   the most
fantastic prizes; I go absolutely
green. Of course, celebrities abound;
I've even seen Love waltzing around
   in amusing disguises.) to
15   visit. But
I wouldn't want to live there.

Glück's poem includes several end rhymes ("too"/"you"; "Host"/ "most"; "abound"/"around"). It also has a visible pattern on the page, broadening and narrowing with some regularity. Moreover, it has a clear syntactical structure, with one main sentence interrupted by parenthetical comments, and it uses capitalization and punctuation conventionally. The poem clearly has a form, but it is fresh and idiosyncratic, with neither stanzaic divisions nor repeated patterns of rhyme or meter to anchor it to tradition.

    The poem's unusual form suits both its subject and its sarcastic tone. It is divided into five sentences, but only the final sentence ends at the end of a line. Moreover, the first sentence ("Life is a nice place . . . to visit") begins in line 1 but does not conclude until the end of the poem. The long parenthetical intrusion, unusual in itself, keeps readers from seeing at first that the poem is a grim new twist on an old cliché: "Life is a nice place . . . / to visit. But / I wouldn't want to live there."

    The poem's first line is ironic, for the life the speaker chronicles is shallow, false, and ultimately meaningless. It is a cross between a stage set and a cocktail party, where love is elusive ("waltzing around / in amusing disguises") and nature is artificially recreated by piped-in music and painted backdrops. Although a traditional structure and regular rhyme and meter could, through their contrast with the subject matter, create ironic tension, Glück chooses an unconventional form that visually reinforces the empty cycles of the life the poem describes. Breaks in lines are not determined by conventional phrasing or punctuation but largely by the demands of form, which create unusual word groups such as "every season; and the music, is just too" and "fantastic prizes; I go absolutely." These odd juxtapositions suggest the random quality of the speaker's encounters and, perhaps, the unpredictability of her life.

The poem that follows, a rather extreme example of open form, looks almost as if it has spilled out of a box of words.

E. E. CUMMINGS
(1894–1962)

the sky was can dy
(1925)

>   the
>   sky
>   was
>   can dy lu
> 5   minous
>   edible
>   spry
>   pinks shy
>   lemons
> 10   greens   coo   l choc
>   olate
>   s.
>
>   un   der,
>   a   lo
> 15   co
>   mo
>   tive   s pout
>   ing
>   vi
> 20   o
>   lets

Cummings's poem, like many of his works, seems ready to fly off the page. Its irregular line length and unconventional capitalization, punctuation, and word divisions immediately draw readers' attention to its form. Despite these oddities, and despite the absence of orderly rhyme and meter, the poem does have its conventional elements. A closer examination reveals that the poem's theme—the beauty of the sky—is quite conventional; that the poem is divided, although somewhat crudely, into two sections; and that the poet does use some rhyme—"spry" and "shy," for example. However, Cummings's sky is described not in traditional terms, but rather as something "edible," not only in terms of color but of flavor as well. The breaks within words ("can dy lu / minous"; "coo l choc / olate / s" seem to expand each word's possibilities, visually stretching them to the limit, extending their taste and visual image over several lines and, in the case of the last two words, visually reinforcing the picture the words describe. In addition, the isolation of syllables exposes hidden rhyme, as in "lo / co / mo" and "lu" and "coo." By using open form, Cummings makes a clear statement about the capacity of a poem to move beyond the traditional boundaries set by words and lines.

POEMS FOR FURTHER READING: OPEN FORM

WALT WHITMAN
(1819–1892)

from Out of the Cradle Endlessly Rocking
(1881)

Out of the cradle endlessly rocking,
Out of the mocking-bird's throat, the musical shuttle,
Out of the Ninth-month[1] midnight,
Over the sterile sands and the fields beyond, where the child leaving his bed wander'd alone, bareheaded, barefoot,
5 Down from the shower'd halo,
Up from the mystic play of shadows twining and twisting as if they were alive,
Out from the patches of briers and blackberries,
From the memories of the bird that chanted to me,
From your memories sad brother, from the fitful risings and fallings I heard,
10 From under that yellow half-moon late-risen and swollen as if with tears,
From those beginning notes of yearning and love there in the mist,
From the thousand responses of my heart never to cease,
From the myriad thence-arous'd words,
From the word stronger and more delicious than any,
15 From such as now they start the scene revisiting,
As a flock, twittering, rising, or overhead passing,

---

[1] The Quaker designation for September. In context, an allusion to the human birth cycle.

Borne hither, ere all eludes me, hurriedly,
A man, yet by these tears a little boy again,
Throwing myself on the sand, confronting the waves,
20 I, chanter of pains and joys, uniter of here and hereafter,
Taking all hints to use them, but swiftly leaping beyond them,
A reminiscence sing

READING AND REACTING

1. This excerpt, the first twenty-two lines of a poem nearly two hundred lines long, has no regular metrical pattern or rhyme scheme. What elements give it form?
2. What factors account for the varying lengths of the poem's lines?
3. **JOURNAL ENTRY:** Compare this excerpt with the excerpt from Whitman's "Song of Myself" (p. 393). In what respects are the forms of the two poems similar?

DIANE WAKOSKI
(1937–)

Sleep
(1966)

    The mole
    lifting snouts—
    full of strained black dirt
            —his perfect tunnel
5   sculptured
            to fit
            the fat
            body. Sleep
    fits tight
10 —must keep bringing out.
    the fine grit
    to keep size
    for even one day.

READING AND REACTING

1. This poem's form seems to be in direct conflict with the logical divisions suggested by syntax and punctuation. For instance, the words in lines 4–9 are set between dashes, indicating a parenthetical comment, yet only lines 4–8 are visually aligned. Also, line 10

ends with a period, but lines 11–13 are clearly part of the same sentence as line 10. How might you explain the poet's decision to create such tension?

2. In what sense might the poem's discussion of the mole's constant search for the perfect size tunnel apply to the form of the poem?

3. **JOURNAL ENTRY:** Why did the poet place the words "Sleep / fits tight" (8–9) where she did? Could—or should—these words be relocated? If so, where might they be placed, and what changes in form or punctuation would the poet have to make?

ROBERT HAYDEN
(1913–   )

Monet's "Waterlilies"[1]
(1966)

(for Bill and Sonja)

Today as the news from Selma[2] and Saigon[3]
poisons the air like fallout,
    I come again to see
the serene great picture that I love.
Here space and time exist in light
the eye like the eye of faith believes.
    The seen, the known
dissolve in irridescence, become
illusive flesh of light
    that was not, was, forever is.

O light beheld as through refracting tears.
Here is the aura of that world
    each of us has lost.
Here is the shadow of its joy.

---

[1] Claude Monet (1840–1926), French impressionist painter. The poet's description of the painter's use of light in this particular painting is equally applicable to most of Monet's work.

[2] Selma, a city in central Alabama. In 1965 a peaceful demonstration in support of voting rights for blacks was brutally squelched by the Selma police. Two civil rights supporters were killed: one, minister James Reeb, was beaten to death on a town street; the other, homemaker Viola Liuzzo, was shot by Ku Klux Klansmen as she was driving along a highway.

[3] Saigon, the capital of the former South Vietnam, now known as Ho Chi Minh City. All news of the Vietnam War was cleared through Saigon by U.S. authorities.

READING AND REACTING

1. The speaker stands before Monet's "Waterlilies," where he takes temporary refuge from the turbulent world. Why does Hayden choose not to use the soothing rhythms and comforting shape of closed form to convey the serenity of the moment? Do you think he made the right choice?
2. Hayden indents lines 3, 7, 10, and 13. What purpose, if any, do these indentations serve?
3. Why is the poem divided into two sections?

WILLIAM CARLOS WILLIAMS
(1883–1963)

Spring and All
(1923)

By the road to the contagious hospital
under the surge of the blue
mottled clouds driven from the
northeast—a cold wind. Beyond, the
5 waste of broad, muddy fields
brown with dried weeds, standing and fallen

patches of standing water
the scattering of tall trees

All along the road the reddish
10 purplish, forked, upstanding, twiggy
stuff of bushes and small trees
with dead, brown leaves under them
leafless vines—

Lifeless in appearance, sluggish
15 dazed spring approaches—

They enter the new world naked,
cold, uncertain of all
save that they enter. All about them
the cold, familiar wind—

20 Now the grass, tomorrow
the stiff curl of wildcarrot leaf

>   One by one objects are defined—
>   It quickens: clarity, outline of leaf
>
>   But now the stark dignity of
> 25 entrance—Still, the profound change
>   has come upon them: rooted, they
>   grip down and begin to awaken

READING AND REACTING

1. What elements of traditional closed form are present in "Spring and All"? What elements are absent?
2. Why is the poem divided into sections? What does Williams accomplish by isolating two sets of two lines each (7–8; 14–15)?
3. "Spring and All" uses assonance, alliteration, and repetition. Give several examples of each technique, and explain the purpose of each usage in the context of the poem.
4. **JOURNAL ENTRY:** "Spring and All" includes only two periods. Elsewhere, where readers might expect to find end punctuation, the poet uses colons, dashes, or no punctuation at all. Why do you think the poet made these decisions about the use of punctuation?

LAWRENCE FERLINGHETTI
(1919–   )

Don't Let That Horse Eat That Violin
(1958)

>   Don't let that horse
>   eat that violin
>   cried Chagall's[1] mother
>   But he
> 5   kept right on
>   painting
>
>   And became famous
>
>   And kept on painting
>   The Horse With Violin In Mouth
>
> 10 And when he finally finished it
>   he jumped up upon the horse

---

[1] Marc Chagall (1887–1985), Russian-born painter and printmaker.

and rode away
waving the violin

And then with a low bow gave it
15 to the first naked nude he ran across

And there were no strings
attached

READING AND REACTING

1. In what respects is the poem's form appropriate for its language, tone, and subject matter?
2. What factors determine the arrangement of words in lines? Are the breaks between lines purely arbitrary, or is there some logic to the poet's word groupings?
3. **JOURNAL ENTRY:** Marc Chagall is an artist known for whimsical paintings in which people, animals, and even buildings seem to float in space. How does the form of Ferlinghetti's poem reflect the form of Chagall's work? (If possible, try to examine a reproduction of one of Chagall's paintings.)

LUCIA PERILLO
(1958–   )

Jury Selection
(1985)

If they only could have put that in the papers, how the winter
    light hangs thickly in those southern Massachusetts towns,
sucking orange at four P.M. from the last spasm of daylight, then
    glowing morbid and humming
5 with a sound barely audible—not human, more like some rasping
    harmonic twanged
from the animated hulk of machinery that somewhere keeps it
    all running: this town
where the fish have been abandoned for over a century, the old
10   men left
with just the memory of fish swimming in their bones, telling
    stories about the Azores
from their perch on rusted forty-gallon drums that have come to
    rest on the riprap
15 that's been brought in to seal the village from the sea. And what
    it would feel like to be a man

walking around smothering inside the fester of all that—you can
    almost understand why they did it,
raped that woman on the pool table at Big Dan's,[1] in the broad
    daylight of Bobby Darin singing Volare for a quarter
then Mack the Knife on the replay,
    . . . *cause old mackie's back in town* . . .
                                and the mown green felt
    smelling of wet wool and—yes, sweet jesus—even fish, their
    blood stirring with the sea.
You can almost understand why a woman might have needed it.
But before it gets too complicated, remember: we're supposed to
    work with only the available labels
to construct questions that will discern shades of meaning,
    measure culpability. Whether this woman
has a houseful of gray babies in dirty sleepers, which one's
    father has been named,
where it has happened before, who had drunk which kind of liquor
and how much. She says she only went into the tavern for a minute
to tug on the silver nozzles of the cigarette machine, but the thin
    curtains that line her bedroom windows
are clearly visible from the street. The whole town knows. Even
    some of these young men carry the blue nickels of her
    thumbprints on the back of their thighs, from this time,
but also the times before. Who whimpered, which ones came in her
and how often, which ones merely watched without speaking
    from the threshold.
The men were of a darker race, refusing to speak our language
    and moving their dark arms
in the ancestral motions of urging we only dimly remember,
    which still arouse us even in our embarrassment, through the
    electric current
of testimony. Whether a crime has been committed (because the
    woman has her Chesterfields, her change coins clenched &
    sweaty in her palm)
or not, their long-boned faces make this offense more
    palpable—the slick skin
and elegant hard moustaches recalling to us the brown eyes of our own
    lives, when in darkness
the vestiges of something we do not claim to know rise out from
    our bodies
and we seize it and do violence.

We all do violence.

---

[1] In March 1983, a twenty-two-year-old mother of two was brutally gang-raped on a pool table at Big Dan's Tavern in New Bedford, Massachusetts. The victim stated that bar patrons had cheered on her attackers. Two onlookers were acquitted; four men were convicted of aggravated rape.

Because the woman was as dark as any of the others,
60 with no green card and a name you won't find in the phone book.
What is on trial here is a thousand years of women plodding on
     thick legs, arms draped with string baskets,
towards some market in another continent, where boats pull into
     the waiting lips of shore
65 to meet these women and laud the correctness of their sexless
     march with fruit and cod and men come home
with the musk of Ecuadorian whores still riding on their loins.
In the end, the real trial takes place in words exchanged
in pissed-up alleyways between tight stone buildings, in words
70 that are to us guttural and pronounced with too much tongue.
In the end the jury forgives everything but the pool table.
And on the streets of town, in the late afternoon light,
mothers tear their dresses away from their stout provincial
     breasts, and carry placards, and weep,
75 and spit at no one in particular,
for the love of their sons,
not the love of their daughters.

READING AND REACTING

1. This poem comments on the gang rape of a woman in a bar in New Bedford, Massachusetts, a fishing town whose population includes a large number of people of Portuguese descent. What points is the speaker making about the crime and its aftermath?
2. Could you divide this poem into stanzas? If you did, where would you make the divisions? Why?
3. **JOURNAL ENTRY:** Given the speaker's many concerns—the crime, the victim, the townspeople, the position of men and women in contemporary society—and the complexity of her attitudes toward her subject, is the form of the poem appropriate? Explain.

CONCRETE POETRY

With roots in the ancient Greek *pattern poems* and the sixteenth- and seventeenth-century *emblem poems*, contemporary **concrete poetry** uses words—and, sometimes, different fonts, type sizes, and even colors of printing—to shape a picture on the page. The form of a concrete poem is not something that emerges from the poem's words and images, but something predetermined by the visual image the poet has decided to create. Although some concrete poems are little more than novelties, others—like the following poem—can be original and enlightening.

MAY SWENSON
(1919–   )

Women
(1970)

```
        Women                   Or they
     should be                should be
      pedestals              little horses
        moving              those wooden
5       pedestals              sweet
         moving              oldfashioned
        to the                 painted
         motions               rocking
         of men                horses

10      the gladdest things in the toyroom

           The              feelingly
           pegs             and then
          of their          unfeelingly
           ears             To be
15       so familiar        joyfully
         and dear           ridden
        to the trusting     rockingly
       fists             ridden until
       To be chafed      the restored

20 egos dismount and the legs stride away

        Immobile            willing
        sweetlipped         to be set
         sturdy             into motion
         and smiling        Women
25        women             should be
          should always     pedestals
           be waiting       to men
```

The curved shape of the poem immediately reinforces its title, and the arrangement of words on the page suggests a variety of visual directions readers might follow. The two columns seem at first to suggest two alternatives: "Women should be. . . ." / "Or they should be. . . ." A closer look, however, reveals that the poem's central figures of speech, such as woman as rocking horse and woman as pedestal, move back and forth between the two columns of images. This exchange of positions might suggest that the two possibilities are really just two ways of looking at one limited role. Thus the experimental form of the poem visually challenges the apparent complacency of its words, suggesting that women, like words, need not fall into traditional roles or satisfy conventional expectations.

POEMS FOR FURTHER READING: CONCRETE POETRY

GEORGE HERBERT
(1593–1633)

Easter Wings
(1633)

Lord, who createdst man in wealth and store,
Though foolishly he lost the same,
Decaying more and more
Till he became
Most poor;
With the
Oh, let me rise
As larks, harmoniously,
And sing this day thy victories;
Then shall the fall further the flight in me.

My tender age in sorrow did begin;
And still with sicknesses and shame
Thou didst so punish sin,
That I became
Most thin.
With thee
Let me combine,
And feel this day thy victory;
For if I imp my wing on thine,
Affliction shall advance the flight in me.

READING AND REACTING

1. In this example of an emblem poem, lines are arranged so that shape and language reinforce each other. Explain how this is accomplished. (For example, how does line length support the poem's images and ideas?)
2. This poem has a definite rhyme scheme. How would you describe it? What is the relationship between the rhyme scheme and the poem's visual divisions?

ROBERT HOLLANDER
(1933–   )

You Too? Me Too—Why Not? Soda Pop
(1968)

        I am
        look
        ing at
        the Co
        caCola
        bottle
        which is
        green wi
        th ridges
        just like
 c   c   c
 o   o   o
 l   l   l
 u   u   u
 m   m   m
 n   n   n
 s   s   s
and on itself it says

    COCA-COLA
    reg.u.s.pat.off.

exactly like an art pop
statue of that kind of
bottle but not so green
that the juice inside
gives other than the co
lor it has when I pour
it out in a clear glass
glass on this table top
(It's making me thirsty
all this winking and
beading of Hippocrene
please let me pause
drinking the fluid in)
ah! it is enticing how
each color is the same
brown in green bottle
brown in uplifted glass
making each utensil on
the table laid a brown
fork in a brown shade
making me long to watch
them harvesting the crop
which makes the deep-aged
rich brown wine of America
that is to say which makes
soda   pop

READING AND REACTING

1. **JOURNAL ENTRY:** Is this a poem, or is it just a clever novelty? Explain.

Checklist for Writing about Form

- Is the poem written in open or closed form? On what characteristics do you base your conclusion?
- Why did the poet choose open or closed form? For example, is the poem's form consistent with its subject matter, tone, or theme? Is it determined by the conventions of the era in which it was written?
- If the poem is arranged in closed form, does the pattern apply to single lines, groups of lines, or the entire poem? What factors determine the breaks between groups of lines?
- Is the poem a sonnet? A sestina? A villanelle? An epigram? A haiku? How do the traditional form's conventions suit the poem's language and theme? Is the poem consistent with the requirements of the form at all times, or does it break any new ground?
- If the poem is arranged in open form, what determines the breaks at the ends of lines?
- Are certain words or phrases isolated on lines? Why?
- How do elements such as assonance, alliteration, rhyme, and repetition of words give the poem form?
- What use does the poet make of punctuation and capitalization? Of white space on the page?
- Is the poem a concrete poem? How does the poet use the visual shape of the poem to convey meaning?

WRITING SUGGESTIONS: FORM

1. Reconsider the explanations of closed and open form in this chapter. Would you consider concrete poetry to be open or closed? Explain your position in a short essay, supporting your conclusion with specific references to the three concrete poems in this chapter.
2. Some poets—for example, Emily Dickinson and Robert Frost—write both open and closed form poems. Choose one open and one closed form poem by a single poet, and explain the poet's possible reasons for choosing each type of form. In your analysis of the two poems, defend the poet's choices if you can.

3. Are complex forms, such as the villanelle and the sestina, just exercises, or even merely opportunities for poets to show off their skills, or do the special demands of the forms add something valuable to the poem? To help you answer this question, read "Do Not Go Gentle into That Good Night" (p. 47), and analyze Dylan Thomas's use of the villanelle's structure to enhance his poem's theme. Or, study Elizabeth Bishop's "Sestina" (p. 223), and consider how her use of the sestina's form helps her to convey her theme.
4. The following open form poem is an alternate version of May Swenson's "Women" (p. 243). Read the two poems carefully, and write an essay in which you compare the two. What differences do you notice? Which do you think was written first? Why? Do the two poems make the same point? Which makes the point with less ambiguity? Which is more effective? Why?

Women Should Be Pedestals

Women should be pedestals
moving pedestals
moving to the motions of men
Or they should be little horses
5 those wooden sweet oldfashioned painted rocking horses
the gladdest things in the toyroom
The pegs of their ears so familiar and dear
to the trusting fists
To be chafed feelingly
10 and then unfeelingly
To be joyfully ridden
until the restored egos dismount and the legs stride away
Immobile sweetlipped sturdy and smiling
women should always be waiting
15 willing to be set into motion
Women should be pedestals to men

CHAPTER 11

SYMBOL, ALLEGORY, ALLUSION, MYTH

WILLIAM BLAKE
(1757–1827)

The Sick Rose
(1794)

O Rose thou art sick.
The invisible worm
That flies in the night,
In the howling storm:

5 Has found out thy bed
Of crimson joy:
And his dark secret love
Does thy life destroy.

SYMBOL

Like fiction and drama, poetry uses symbols as a kind of shorthand, as a subtle way of introducing a significant idea or attitude. A **symbol** is an idea or image that suggests something else—but not in the simple way that a dollar sign stands for money or a flag represents a country. A symbol is an image that transcends its literal, or denotative meaning, in complex ways by suggesting other items or ideas. For instance, if someone gives a rose to a loved one, it could simply be a sign of love. But in the William Blake poem "The Sick Rose," the rose has a range of contradictory and complementary meanings. For what does the rose stand? Beauty? Perfection? Passion? All of these ideas? Some of them? As this poem illustrates, the distinguishing characteristic of a symbol is that it refuses to be pinned down or easily defined.

Such ambiguity can be frustrating, but it is precisely this characteristic of a symbol that enables it to enrich a work and to give it additional layers of meaning. As Robert Frost has said, a symbol is a little thing that touches a larger thing. Notice in the following poem how the central symbol does just this.

ROBERT FROST
(1874–1963)

For Once, Then, Something
(1923)

    Others taunt me with having knelt at well-curbs
    Always wrong to the light, so never seeing
    Deeper down in the well than where the water
    Gives me back in a shining surface picture
5 Me myself in the summer heaven, godlike,
    Looking out of a wreath of fern and cloud puffs.
    Once, when trying with chin against a well-curb,
    I discerned, as I thought, beyond the picture,
    Through the picture, a something white, uncertain,
10 Something more of the depths—and then I lost it.
    Water came to rebuke the too clear water.
    One drop fell from a fern, and lo, a ripple
    Shook whatever it was lay there at bottom,
    Blurred it, blotted it out. What was that whiteness?
15 Truth? A pebble of quartz? For once, then, something.

The central symbol in this poem is the "something" that the speaker thinks he discerns at the bottom of a well. Traditionally the contemplation of a well suggests a search for truth. In this poem the speaker remarks that he always seems to look down the well at the wrong angle, so that all he can see is his own reflection—the surface, not the depths. Once the speaker thought he saw something "beyond the picture," something "white, uncertain," but the image remained indistinct, disappearing when a drop of water from a fern caused the water to ripple. The poem ends with the speaker questioning the significance of what he saw. Like a reader encountering a symbol, the speaker is left trying to come to terms with images that cannot be clearly perceived and suggestions that cannot be readily understood. In light of the elusive nature of truth, all the speaker can do is ask questions that have no definite answers.

    Literary symbols—those that appear in works of fiction, poetry, or drama—can be *conventional, universal,* or *private.* **Conventional symbols** are those recognized by people who share certain cultural and social assumptions. National flags, for example, evoke a general and agreed-upon response in most people of a particular country and, for better or for worse, American children perceive the golden arches of McDonald's as a symbol of food, fun, and happiness. **Universal symbols** are those likely to be recognized by people regardless of their culture. In 1890, the noted Scottish anthropologist Sir James George Frazer wrote the first version of his work *The Golden Bough,* in which he showed parallels between the rites and beliefs of early cultures and those of Christianity. Fascinated by Frazer's work, the psychologist Carl Jung sought to explain these similarities by formulating a theory of **archetypes,** which held that certain images or ideas reside in the subconscious of all people. According to Jung, archetypal, or universal, symbols include water, symbolizing rebirth; spring, symbolizing growth; and winter, symbolizing death.

Sometimes literary symbols can be obscure or highly idiosyncratic **private symbols.** The works of William Blake and W. B. Yeats, for example, combine symbols from a number of different cultural, theological, and philosophic sources to form complex networks of symbolic associations. To Blake, for example, the scientist Isaac Newton represents the tendency of scientists to quantify experience while ignoring the beauty and mystery of nature. Readers cannot begin to understand Blake's highly individualistic use of Newton as a symbol until they have read a number of his more challenging poems.

Most often, however, literary symbols in poems are not this obscure. In the following poem, for instance, the poet introduces a cross—a symbol that has familiar associations—but makes his own use of it.

JIM SIMMERMAN[*]

Child's Grave, Hale County, Alabama
(1983)

Someone drove a two-by-four
through the heart of this hard land
that even in a good year
will notch a plow blade worthless,
5 snap the head off a shovel,
or bow a stubborn back.
He'd have had to steal
the wood from a local mill
or steal, by starlight, across
10 his landlord's farm, to worry
a fencepost out of its well
and lug it the three miles home.
He'd have had to leave his wife
asleep on a corn shuck mat,
15 leave his broken brogans[1]
by the stove, to slip outside,
quiet as sin, with the child
bundled in a burlap sack.

---

[*] Birth date is not available.

[1] Sturdy, heavy work shoes, frequently ankle high.

What a thing to have to do
on a cold night in December,
1936, alone
but for a raspy wind
and the red, rock-ridden dirt
things come down to in the end.
Whoever it was pounded
this shabby half-cross
into the ground must have toiled
all night to root it so:
five feet buried with the child
for the foot of it that shows.
And as there are no words
carved here, it's likely that
the man was illiterate,
or addled with fatigue,
or wrenched simple-minded
by the one simple fact.
Or else the unscored lumber
driven deep into the land
and the hump of busted rock
spoke too plainly of his grief:
forty years layed by and still
there are no words for this.

Even in non-Christian cultures, the cross on a grave is a readily identifiable symbol of death and rebirth. In this poem, however, the cross is presented not just as a conventional Christian symbol, but also as a symbol of the tenant farmer's hard work and difficult life. In this sense the cross also suggests the poverty that helped bring about the death of the child and the social conditions that existed during the Depression. These associations take readers down through many layers of meaning, so that the cross may ultimately stand for the tenant farmer's whole life (the cross *he* has to bear), not just for the death of the child. By no means does this interpretation exhaust the possible symbolic significance of the cross in the poem. For example, the crude cross might also suggest the rage and grief of the individual who made it, or it might call to mind the poor who live and die in anonymity. Certainly the poet could have assigned a fixed meaning to the cross that marks the child's grave, but he chose instead, by suggesting various ideas through a single powerful symbol, to let readers arrive at their own conclusions.

How do you know when an idea or image is a symbol? At what point do you decide that a particular detail goes beyond the literal level and takes on symbolic significance? When, for example, is a rose more than a rose or a cross more than a cross? Frequently you can recognize a symbol by its prominence or repetition. In "Child's Grave, Hale County,

Alabama," for example, the cross is introduced in the first line of the poem and it is the focal point of the poem; in "The Sick Rose" the importance of the rose is emphasized by the title and reinforced throughout the poem.

It is not enough, however, to identify an image or idea that seems to suggest something else. Your decision that a particular item has some symbolic value must be supported by the details of the poem and make sense within the context of the ideas developed in the poem. Moreover, the symbol must suggest the poem's theme. Notice in the following poem how the image of the volcano leads readers to the poem's central theme.

EMILY DICKINSON
(1830–1886)

Volcanoes Be in Sicily
(1914)

Volcanoes be in Sicily
And South America
I judge from my Geography—
Volcanos nearer here
5   A Lava step at any time
Am I inclined to climb—
A Crater I may contemplate
Vesuvius at Home.

This poem opens with a statement of fact: Volcanoes are located in Sicily and South America. In lines 3 and 4, however, the speaker makes the improbable observation that volcanoes are located near where she is at the moment. Readers familiar with Dickinson know that she lived in Amherst, Massachusetts, a town with no volcanoes. This information leads readers to suspect they should not take the speaker's observation literally and that in the context of the poem volcanoes may have symbolic significance. But what do volcanoes suggest here? On the one hand, volcanoes represent the awesome creative power of nature; on the other hand, they suggest its destructiveness. The speaker's contemplation of the crater of Vesuvius—the volcano that buried Pompeii in A.D. 79—is therefore filled with contradictory associations. Since Dickinson was a recluse, volcanoes—active, destructive, unpredictable, and dangerous—may be seen as symbolic of everything she fears in the outside world and, perhaps, within herself. She has a voyeur's attraction to danger and power, but she is also afraid of them. For this reason she may feel safer contemplating Vesuvius at home—not experiencing exotic lands, but simply reading a geography book.

POEMS FOR FURTHER READING: SYMBOL

LANGSTON HUGHES
(1902–1967)

Island
(1951)

Wave of sorrow,
Do not drown me now:

I see the island
Still ahead somehow.

5 I see the island
And its sands are fair:

Wave of sorrow,
Take me there.

READING AND REACTING

1. Is the island a universal, conventional, or private symbol? Explain your answer.
2. Is the wave of sorrow a symbol?
3. **JOURNAL ENTRY:** Beyond its literary meaning, what might the island in this poem suggest? Consider several possibilities.

THEODORE ROETHKE
(1908–1963)

Night Crow
(1944)

When I saw that clumsy crow
Flap from a wasted tree,
Over the gulfs of dream
Flew a tremendous bird
5 Further and further away
Into a moonless black,
Deep in the brain, far back.

READING AND REACTING

1. What is the significance of the title? In what way does it help you to interpret the symbolic significance of the crow?
2. How is the "clumsy crow" different from the crow "Deep in the brain"? Are both these crows symbols?
3. **JOURNAL ENTRY:** It has been suggested that "Night Crow" is a commentary on the difference between reality and imagination. Does the poem's use of symbols support such an interpretation? Explain.

HOWARD NEMEROV
(1920–   )

The Goose Fish
(1955)

On the long shore, lit by the moon
To show them properly alone,
Two lovers suddenly embraced
So that their shadows were as one.
5 The ordinary night was graced
For them by the swift tide of blood
That silently they took at flood,
And for a little time they prized
    Themselves emparadised.

10 Then, as if shaken by stage-fright
Beneath the hard moon's bony light,
They stood together on the sand—
Embarrassed in each other's sight
But still conspiring hand in hand,
15 Until they saw, there underfoot,
As though the world had found them out,
The goose fish turning up, though dead,
    His hugely grinning head.

There in the china light he lay,
20 Most ancient and corrupt and grey
They hesitated at his smile.
Wondering what it seemed to say
To lovers who a little while
Before had thought to understand,
25 By violence upon the sand,

> The only way that could be known
> To make a world their own.
>
> It was a wide and moony grin
> Together peaceful and obscene;
> 30 They knew not what he would express,
> So finished a comedian
> He might mean failure or success,
> But took it for an emblem of
> Their sudden, new and guilty love
> 35 To be observed by, when they kissed,
>   That rigid optimist.
>
> So he became their patriarch,
> Dreadfully mild in the half-dark.
> His throat that the sand seemed to choke,
> 40 His picket teeth, these left their mark
> But never did explain the joke
> That so amused him, lying there
> While the moon went down to disappear
> Along the still and tilted track
> 45   That bears the zodiac.

READING AND REACTING

1. What is the mood of the poem before the goose fish appears? How does it change after he is introduced? Why does it change?
2. What details of the poem suggest that the goose fish has symbolic significance?
3. List three possible interpretations of the symbol of the goose fish. In what way does the rest of the poem support each of these interpretations?
4. In what way could the setting of this poem be considered symbolic?

ALLEGORY

Allegory is a form of narrative that takes abstract ideas; equates them with people, places, and things; and turns them into a story. Like symbolism, allegory uses things to suggest other things. Unlike symbols, however, allegorical elements do not have a range of possible meanings; on the contrary, they can always be assigned specific meanings. (Because writers use allegory to instruct, they gain nothing by hiding its significance.) These allegorical figures, each with a strict equivalent on a literal level, form a network that offers a political or moral lesson.

Quite often an allegory involves a journey or adventure, as in the case of Dante's *Divine Comedy*, which traces a journey through Hell, Purgatory, and Heaven. Within an allegory everything can have meaning: the road upon which the characters walk, the people they encounter, or the phrase that one of them repeats throughout the journey. Once you understand the **allegorical framework**—the allegory's system of correspondences—your main task is to see how the various details fit within this system. Some poems can be relatively straightforward, but others can be so complicated that it takes a great deal of time and effort to unlock their meaning. In the following poem the poet uses a journey as the central element in her allegory.

CHRISTINA ROSSETTI
(1830–1894)

Uphill
(1861)

Does the road wind uphill all the way?
    Yes, to the very end.
Will the day's journey take the whole long day?
    From morn to night, my friend.

5 But is there for the night a resting-place?
    A roof for when the slow dark hours begin.
May not the darkness hide it from my face?
    You cannot miss that inn.

Shall I meet other wayfarers at night?
10   Those who have gone before.
Then must I knock, or call when just in sight?
    They will not keep you standing at that door.

Shall I find comfort, travel-sore and weak?
    Of labor you shall find the sum.
15 Will there be beds for me and all who seek?
    Yea, beds for all who come.

"Uphill" uses a question and answer structure to describe a journey along an uphill road. Like the journey described in John Bunyan's seventeenth-century allegory *The Pilgrim's Progress,* this is a spiritual one that suggests a person's uphill journey through life. The day and night duration of the journey stands for life and death, and the inn at the end of the road stands for the grave, the final resting place.

POEM FOR FURTHER READING: ALLEGORY

ADRIENNE RICH
(1929–   )

Diving into the Wreck
(1973)

    First having read the book of myths,
    and loaded the camera,
    and checked the edge of the knife-blade,
    I put on
5 the body-armor of black rubber
    the absurd flippers
    the grave and awkward mask.
    I am having to do this
    not like Cousteau with his
10 assiduous team
    aboard the sun-flooded schooner
    but here alone.

    There is a ladder.
    The ladder is always there
15 hanging innocently
    close to the side of the schooner.
    We know what it is for,
    we who have used it.
    Otherwise
20 it's a piece of maritime floss
    some sundry equipment.

    I go down.
    Rung after rung and still
    the oxygen immerses me
25 the blue light
    the clear atoms
    of our human air.
    I go down.
    My flippers cripple me,
30 I crawl like an insect down the ladder
    and there is no one
    to tell me when the ocean
    will begin.

First the air is blue and then
it is bluer and then green and then
black I am blacking out and yet
my mask is powerful
it pumps my blood with power
the sea is another story
the sea is not a question of power
I have to learn alone
to turn my body without force
in the deep element.

And now: it is easy to forget
what I came for
among so many who have always
lived here
swaying their crenellated fans
between the reefs
and besides
you breathe differently down here.

I came to explore the wreck.
The words are purposes.
The words are maps.
I came to see the damage that was done
and the treasures that prevail.
I stroke the beam of my lamp
slowly along the flank
of something more permanent
than fish or weed

the thing I came for:
the wreck and not the story of the wreck
the thing itself and not the myth
the drowned face always staring
toward the sun
the evidence of damage
worn by salt and sway into this threadbare beauty
the ribs of the disaster
curving their assertion
among the tentative haunters.

This is the place.
And I am here, the mermaid whose dark hair
streams black, the merman in his armored body
We circle silently
about the wreck
we dive into the hold.
I am she: I am he

whose drowned face sleeps with open eyes
whose breasts still bear the stress
80 whose silver, copper, vermeil cargo lies
obscurely inside barrels
half-wedged and left to rot
we are the half-destroyed instruments
that once held to a course
85 the water-eaten log
the fouled compass

We are, I am, you are
by cowardice or courage
the one who finds our way
90 back to this scene
carrying a knife, a camera
a book of myths
in which
our names do not appear.

READING AND REACTING

1. At one level this poem is about a deep-sea diver's exploration of a wrecked ship. What details suggest that the poet wants you to see something more?
2. Explain the allegorical elements presented in the poem. What, for example, might the diver and the wreck represent?
3. Does the poem contain any symbols? How can you tell? What do they contribute to the allegory?
4. **JOURNAL ENTRY:** Explain what the speaker means in lines 62–63 when she says that she came for "the wreck and not the story of the wreck / the thing itself and not the myth." In what way does this remark suggest an allegorical interpretation of the poem?

ALLUSION

An **allusion** is a brief reference to a person, place, or event, historical or actual, that readers are expected to recognize. Like symbols and allegories, allusions deepen a work by introducing associations and attitudes from another context.

When poets use allusions, they assume that they and their readers share a common body of knowledge. If, when reading a poem, you come across a name with which you are not familiar, take the time to look it up in a dictionary or an encyclopedia. As you have probably realized by now, a large part of the meaning of a poem may depend on an unfamiliar reference.

260 Symbol, Allegory, Allusion, Myth

Although poets usually expect readers to recognize their references, some use allusions to exclude readers from their work. In his 1922 poem "The Waste Land," for example, T. S. Eliot makes allusions to historical events, ancient languages, and obscure literary works. (He even includes a set of notes to accompany his poem, but they do little more than complicate an already complicated text.) As you might expect, critical response to this poem was mixed, with some critics saying that it was a work of genius and others saying that it was pretentious.

Allusions can come from any source: history, the arts, other works of literature, the Bible, current events, or even the personal life of the poet. In the following poem, the Nigerian poet and playwright Wole Soyinka alludes to contemporary political figures.

WOLE SOYINKA
(1934–   )

Future Plans
(1972)

The meeting is called
To odium: Forgers, framers
Fabricators Inter-
national. Chairman,
5 A dark horse, a circus nag turned blinkered sprinter
Mach Three
We rate him—one for the Knife
Two for 'iavelli, Three—
Breaking speed
10 Of the truth barrier by a swooping detention decree

Projects in view:
Mao Tse Tung in league
With Chiang Kai. Nkrumah
Makes a secret
15 Pact with Verwood, sworn by Hastings Banda.
Proven: Arafat
In flagrante cum
Golda Meir. Castro drunk
With Richard Nixon
20 Contraceptives stacked beneath the papal bunk . . .
. . . and more to come

This poem is structured like an agenda for a meeting. From the moment it announces that a meeting has been called "To odium" (a pun on "to order"), it is clear that the poem will be a bitter political satire. Those in attendance are "Forgers, framers / Fabricators." Stanza 2 contains three allusions that shed light on the character of the chairman. The first is to Mack the Knife, a petty criminal in Bertolt Brecht and Kurt Weill's 1933 *Threepenny Opera*. The second is to Niccolò Machiavelli, whose 1532 book *The Prince* advocates the use of unscrupulous means to strengthen the State. The last is to the term *mach,* which denotes the speed of an airplane in relation to the speed of sound—mach one, two, three, and so on. Through these allusions the poem implies that the meeting's chairman has been chosen for his ability to engage in violence, to be ruthless, and to break the "truth barrier"—that is, to lie.

The rest of the poem alludes to individuals involved in global politics, specifically the politics of developing nations. Instead of fighting for the rights of the oppressed, however, these people consolidate their own political power by collaborating with those who oppose their positions. Thus Mao Tse-tung, the former communist leader of China, is in league with Chiang Kai-shek, his old Nationalist Chinese enemy; Yassir Arafat, the leader of the Palestine Liberation Organization, is linked with Golda Meir, the former prime minister of Israel; Kwame Nkrumah, the first president of Ghana, conspires with Hendrick Verwoerd, the former prime minister of South Africa, assassinated in 1966; and former President Richard Nixon gets drunk with Cuba's communist leader, Fidel Castro. These allusions suggest the essential meaninglessness of political alliances and the extreme disorder of world politics. The ideological juxtapositions show the underlying sameness and interchangeability of various political philosophies, none of which has the answer to the world's problems. Whether the poem is satirizing the United Nations and its idealistic agenda, criticizing the tendency of politics to make strange bedfellows, or showing how corrupt all politicians are, its allusions enable the poet to enlarge the frame of reference of the poem and thus to communicate his ideas effectively.

The following poem uses allusions to writers, as well as to a myth, to develop its theme.

WILLIAM MEREDITH
(1919–   )

Dreams of Suicide
(1980)

(in sorrowful memory of Ernest Hemingway,
Sylvia Plath, and John Berryman)

i

   I reach for the awkward shotgun not to disarm
   you, but to feel the metal horn,
   furred with the downy membrane of dream.
   More surely than the unicorn,
5 you are the mythical beast.

ii

Or I am sniffing an oven. On all fours
I am imitating a totemic animal
but she is not my totem or the totem
of my people, this is not my magic oven.

iii

10 If I hold you tight by the ankles,
still you fly upward from the iron railing.
Your father made these wings,
after he made his own, and now from beyond
he tells you *fly down*, in the voice
15 my own father might say *walk, boy*.

This poem is dedicated to the memory of three writers who committed suicide. In each stanza the speaker envisions in a dream the death of one of the writers. In the first stanza he dreams of Ernest Hemingway, who killed himself with a shotgun. The speaker grasps the metal horn of Hemingway's shotgun and transforms him into a mythical beast who, like a unicorn, represents the rare, unique talent of the artist. In the second stanza the speaker dreams of Sylvia Plath, who asphyxiated herself in a gas oven. He sees himself, like Plath, on his knees imitating an animal sniffing an oven. Finally, in the third stanza, the speaker dreams of John Berryman, who leaped to his death. Berryman is characterized as Icarus, a mythological figure who, along with his father Daedalus, fled Crete by building wings made of feathers and wax. Together they flew away, but, ignoring his father's warning, Icarus flew too close to the sun and, when the wax melted, fell to his death in the sea. Like Icarus, Berryman ignores the warning of his father and, like Daedalus, the speaker tries to stop Berryman. In this poem, then, the speaker uses allusions to make a point about the difficult lives of writers and, perhaps, to convey his own empathy for those who could not survive the struggle to reconcile art and life.

POEM FOR FURTHER READING: ALLUSION

DELMORE SCHWARTZ
(1913–1966)

The True-Blue American
(1959)

Jeremiah Dickson was a true-blue American,
For he was a little boy who understood America, for he felt that he must
Think about *everything;* because that's *all* there is to think about,

Knowing immediately the intimacy of truth and comedy,
5 Knowing intuitively how a sense of humor was a necessity
For one and for all who live in America. Thus, natively, and
Naturally when on an April Sunday in an ice cream parlor Jeremiah
Was requested to choose between a chocolate sundae and a banana split
He answered unhesitatingly, having no need to think of it
10 Being a true-blue American, determined to continue as he began:
Rejecting the either-or of Kierkegaard,[1] and many another European;
Refusing to accept alternatives, refusing to believe the choice of
    between;
Rejecting selection; denying dilemma; electing absolute affirmation:
    knowing
15   in his breast
            The infinite and the gold
            Of the endless frontier, the deathless West.
"Both: I will have them both!" declared this true-blue American
In Cambridge, Massachusetts, on an April Sunday, instructed
20   By the great department stores, by the Five-and-Ten,
Taught by Christmas, by the circus, by the vulgarity and the grandeur of
    Niagara Falls and the Grand Canyon,
Tutored by the grandeur, vulgarity, and infinite appetite gratified and
    Shining in the darkness, of the light
25 On Saturdays at the double bills of the moon pictures,
The consummation of the advertisements of the imagination of the light
Which is as it was—the infinite belief in infinite hope—of Columbus,
    Barnum, Edison, and Jeremiah Dickson.

READING AND REACTING

1. To what does the title of the poem refer? What does the title add to the poem?
2. Read a short article about Kierkegaard in a one-volume encyclopedia. Why does Schwartz allude to him in line 11?
3. Is the name Jeremiah Dickson an allusion? What is the significance of this name? What would be the effect of giving the "true-blue American" a more obviously ethnic name? A more common name?
4. What is the significance of the allusions to places in lines 19–22 and individuals in lines 27 and 28?
5. **JOURNAL ENTRY:** What does this poem say about patriotism? Do you share the speaker's sentiments?

---

[1] Sören Kierkegaard (1813–1855)—Danish philosopher who greatly influenced twentieth-century existentialism. *Either-Or* (1841) is one of his best known works.

MYTH

A **myth** is a narrative that embodies—and in some cases helps to explain—the religious, philosophical, moral, and political values of a culture. Using gods and supernatural beings, myths explain occurrences in the natural world. More generally, the term *myth* can also refer to private belief systems invented by individual poets as well as to any fully realized fictitious setting in which a literary work takes place, such as the myths of William Faulkner's Yoknapatawpha County or Lawrence Durrell's Alexandria. Contrary to popular usage, however, *myth* is not synonymous with *falsehood*. In the broadest sense, myths are stories—usually whole groups of stories—that can be true, partly true, or false and that express the deepest beliefs of a culture. According to this definition, then, *The Iliad* and *The Odyssey,* the Koran, and the Old and New Testaments can all be regarded as myths.

According to the mythologist Joseph Campbell, the appeal of myths is that they contain truths linking people together, whether they live today or lived 2,500 years ago. They do, after all, attempt to explain phenomena that human beings care about regardless of when and where they live. It is not surprising, then, that myths frequently contain archetypal images that cut across cultural and racial boundaries and touch us on a very deep and basic level. Thus when Orpheus descends into Hades to rescue his wife, Eurydice, he acts out the human desire to transcend the finality of death; and when Telemachus sets out in search of his father, Odysseus, he reminds readers that in a way we all are lost children searching for parents. When Icarus ignores his father and flies too near the sun and when Pandora cannot resist looking into a box that she has been told not to open, we are reminded of the basic weaknesses we all share.

When poets use myths in their works, they are actually making allusions. They expect readers to bring to the poem the cultural, emotional, and ethical context of the myths to which the poem alludes. At one time, when educated individuals studied the Greek and Latin classics as well as the Bible, poets could be reasonably sure that readers would recognize the mythic allusions they made. Because this is no longer the case, readers usually have to consult dictionaries, encyclopedias, or collections of myths, such as the *New Larousse Encyclopedia of Mythology* or *Bullfinch's Mythology,* to identify a mythological allusion. Without this background information, many readers are unable to understand the full significance of an allusion or its application within the poem. Although many of the references in this anthology are accompanied by notes, these notes may not provide all the detail that you will require to understand each mythological allusion and determine its significance within the poem. Occasionally you may have to look for answers beyond this text.

Sometimes a poet will allude to a myth in a title; sometimes references to various myths will appear throughout a poem; at other times, a poem will focus on a single myth. In each case, as in the following poem, the use of myth can help to communicate the poem's theme.

COUNTEE CULLEN
(1903–1946)

Yet Do I Marvel
(1925)

>I doubt not God is good, well-meaning, kind,
>And did He stoop to quibble could tell why
>The little buried mole continues blind,
>Why flesh that mirrors Him must some day die,
>5 Make plain the reason tortured Tantalus
>Is baited by the fickle fruit, declare
>If merely brute caprice dooms Sisyphus
>To struggle up a never-ending stair.
>Inscrutable His ways are, and immune
>10 To catechism by a mind too strewn
>With petty cares to slightly understand
>What awful brain compels His awful hand.
>Yet do I marvel at this curious thing:
>To make a poet black, and bid him sing!

The speaker in this poem begins by affirming his belief in the benevolence of God, but he then goes on to question why God engages in what appear to be capricious acts. As part of his catalog of questions, the speaker mentions Tantalus and Sisyphus, two figures from Greek mythology. Tantalus was a king who was admitted to the society of the gods. Because his behavior was so abominable, he was condemned to stand up to his chin in a pool of water over which hung a branch laden with fruit. When he got thirsty and tried to drink, the level of the water would drop, and when he got hungry and reached for fruit, it would move just out of his grasp. Thus Tantalus was doomed to be near what he most desired, but to remain forever unable to obtain it. Like Tantalus, Sisyphus was also condemned to Hades. For his disrespect to Zeus he was sentenced to endless toil. Every day, Sisyphus would push a gigantic boulder up a steep hill. As he neared the top, the boulder would slip down the hill, and he would have to begin again. Like Tantalus and Sisyphus, the speaker in the poem is forced to toil in vain. He wonders why a well-meaning God would "make a poet black and bid him sing" in a racist society that will not listen to his voice. Thus the poet's two allusions to Greek mythology enrich the poem by connecting the suffering of the speaker to a universal drama that has been acted out again and again.

POEMS FOR FURTHER READING: MYTH

JOSEPH BRODSKY
(1940–   )

The Star of the Nativity
(1988)

translated by Joseph Brodsky

In the cold season, in a locality accustomed to heat more than
to cold, to horizontality more than to a mountain,
a child was born in a cave in order to save the world;
it blew as only in deserts in winter it blows, athwart.

5 To him, all things seemed enormous: his mother's breast, the steam
out of the ox's nostrils, Caspar, Balthazar, Melchior—the team
of Magi, their presents heaped by the door, ajar.
He was but a dot, and a dot was the star.

Keenly, without blinking, though pallid, stray
10 clouds, upon a child in the manger, from far away—
from the depth of the Universe, from its opposite end—the star
was looking into the cave. And that was the Father's stare.

READING AND REACTING

1. To what does the title of the poem refer? Why does the title focus on the star and not on the child?
2. Consult an encyclopedia or a New Testament, and identify Caspar, Balthazar, and Melchior. In what way is the child contrasted with them?
3. The word "cold" is used twice in the first two lines of the poem. What is the significance of this repetition?
4. **JOURNAL ENTRY:** On what elements of the birth of Christ does the poet focus? What comment is he making about Christ? About people?

LOUISE ERDRICH
(1954–   )

Windigo
(1984)

For Angela

The Windigo is a flesh-eating, wintry demon with a man buried deep inside of it. In some Chippewa stories, a young girl vanquishes this monster by forcing boiling lard down its throat, thereby releasing the human at the core of ice.

You knew I was coming for you, little one,
when the kettle jumped into the fire.
Towels flapped on the hooks,
and the dog crept off, groaning,
5 to the deepest part of the woods.

In the hackles of dry brush a thin laughter started up.
Mother scolded the food warm and smooth in the pot
and called you to eat.
But I spoke in the cold trees:
10 *New one, I have come for you, child hide and lie still.*

The sumac pushed sour red cones through the air.
Copper burned in the raw wood.
You saw me drag toward you.
Oh touch me, I murmured, and licked the soles of your feet.
15 You dug your hands into my pale, melting fur.

I stole you off, a huge thing in my bristling armor.
Steam rolled from my wintry arms, each leaf shivered
from the bushes we passed
until they stood, naked, spread like the cleaned spines of fish.

20 Then your warm hands hummed over and shoveled themselves full
of the ice and the snow. I would darken and spill
all night running, until at last morning broke the cold earth
and I carried you home,
a river shaking in the sun.

READING AND REACTING

1. Do you think Erdrich can reasonably expect readers to be familiar with the Native American myth in the poem? Does her introduction provide enough information for those who are not?

2. Who is the speaker in the poem? How would you characterize the speaker? What advantage does Erdrich gain by assuming this persona?
3. What is the major theme of this poem? How does the myth of the Windigo express this theme?
4. **JOURNAL ENTRY:** How is the Windigo described in the introduction like and unlike the one portrayed in the poem?

WILLIAM BUTLER YEATS
(1865–1939)

Leda and the Swan
(1924)

A sudden blow: the great wings beating still
Above the staggering girl, her thighs caressed
By the dark webs, her nape caught in his bill,
He holds her helpless breast upon his breast.

5 How can those terrified vague fingers push
The feathered glory from her loosening thighs?
And how can body, laid in that white rush,
But feel the strange heart beating where it lies?

A shudder in the loins engenders there
10 The broken wall, the burning roof and tower
And Agamemnon dead.
                Being so caught up,
So mastered by the brute blood of the air,
Did she put on his knowledge with his power
Before the indifferent beak could let her drop?

READING AND REACTING

1. Look up the myth of Leda in an encyclopedia. What event is described in this poem? What is the mythological significance of the event?
2. How is Leda portrayed? Why is the swan described as a "feathered glory" (6)? Why in the poem's last line is Leda dropped by his "indifferent beak"?
3. Stanza 3 refers to the Trojan War, which was indirectly caused by the event described in the poem. In what way does the allusion to the Trojan War develop the theme of the poem?

4. Does the poem answer the questions asked in its last two lines? Explain.

DEREK WALCOTT[1]
(1930–)

Sea Grapes[2]
(1971)

That sail which leans on light,
tired of islands,
a schooner beating up the Caribbean

for home, could be Odysseus,
₅ home-bound on the Aegean;
that father and husband's

longing, under gnarled sour grapes, is
like the adulterer hearing Nausicaa's[3] name
in every gull's outcry.

₁₀ This brings nobody peace. The ancient war
between obsession and responsibility
will never finish and has been the same

for the sea-wanderer or the one on shore
now wriggling on his sandals to walk home,
₁₅ since Troy sighed its last flame,

and the blind giant's boulder heaved the trough
from whose ground-swell the great hexameters come
to the conclusions of exhausted surf.

The classics can console. But not enough.

READING AND REACTING

1. This poem includes many references to Homer's *The Odyssey*. Can a reader appreciate the poem without having read Homer?

---

[1] Winner of the 1992 Nobel Prize in literature.

[2] Small tropical trees found on sandy beaches.

[3] A young woman who befriended Odysseus.

2. In the context of the myth of Odysseus, what is the "ancient war / between obsession and responsibility" (10–11) to which the speaker refers? Does this conflict have a wider application in the context of the poem? Explain.

3. Consider the following lines from the poem: "and the blind giant's boulder heaved the trough / from whose ground-swell the great hexameters come / to the conclusions of exhausted surf" (16–18). In what sense does the blind giant's boulder create the great hexameters? In what way does the trough end up as exhausted surf?

4. **JOURNAL ENTRY:** Explain what the speaker means in the poem's last line when he says, "The classics can console. But not enough." Do you agree with him?

W. H. AUDEN
(1907–1973)

Musée des Beaux Arts
(1940)

About suffering they were never wrong,
The Old Masters: how well they understood
Its human position; how it takes place
While someone else is eating or opening a window or just walking
    dully along
5 How, when the aged are reverently, passionately waiting
For the miraculous birth, there always must be
Children who did not specially want it to happen, skating
On a pond at the edge of the wood:
They never forgot
10 That even the dreadful martyrdom must run its course
Anyhow in a corner, some untidy spot
Where the dogs go on with their doggy life and the torturer's horse
Scratches its innocent behind on a tree.
In Brueghel's *Icarus,* for instance: how everything turns away
15 Quite leisurely from the disaster; the ploughman may
Have heard the splash, the forsaken cry,
But for him it was not an important failure; the sun shone
As it had to on the white legs disappearing into the green
Water; and the expensive delicate ship that must have seen
20 Something amazing, a boy falling out of the sky,
Had somewhere to get to and sailed calmly on.

"The Fall of Icarus," by Brueghel. Photograph by Giraudon.

READING AND REACTING

1. Look at the painting that accompanies this poem. To what details in the painting does the poet allude?
2. Reread the summary of the myth of Icarus on p. 262. What does Auden's allusion to the myth contribute to the poem's meaning?
3. What point does the poet make with reference to the "Old Masters" (2)?
4. **JOURNAL ENTRY:** Does Brueghel's "Fall of Icarus" help you to understand the poem? How?

Checklist for Writing about Symbol, Allegory, Allusion, Myth

Symbol

- Are there any symbols in the poem? What leads you to believe they are symbols?
- Are these symbols conventional?
- Are they universal or archetypal?
- Does the work contain any private symbols?
- What is the literal meaning of the symbol in the context of the poem?

- Beyond its literal meaning, what else could the symbol suggest?
- How does your interpretation of the symbol enhance your understanding of the poem?

Allegory

- Are there any allegorical elements within the poem? How can you tell?
- What do the allegorical elements signify on a literal level?
- What lesson does the allegory illustrate?

Allusion

- Are there any allusions in the poem?
- Do you recognize the names, places, historical events, or literary works to which the poet alludes?
- What does each allusion add to the poem? In what way does each deepen the poem's meaning? Does any allusion interfere with your understanding or enjoyment of the poem?
- Would the poem be more effective without a particular allusion?

Myth

- What myths or mythological figures are alluded to?
- How does the poem use myth to convey its meaning?
- How faithful is the poem to the myth? Does the poet add material to the myth? Are any details from the original myth omitted? Is any information distorted? Why?

WRITING SUGGESTIONS: SYMBOL, ALLEGORY, ALLUSION, MYTH

1. Read "Aunt Jennifer's Tigers" (p. 196) and "Diving into the Wreck" (p. 257) by Adrienne Rich. Then write an essay in which you discuss the similarities and the differences in Rich's use of symbols in the two works.

2. Many popular songs make use of allusion. Choose one or two popular songs that you know well and analyze their use of allusion, paying particular attention to whether the allusions expand the impact and meaning of the song or create barriers to your understanding.

3. Read the Emily Dickinson poem "Because I Could Not Stop for Death" (p. 297), and then write an interpretation of the poem giving allegorical equivalents to the concrete objects in the poem.

4. What applications do the lessons of myth have for twentieth-century life? Choose two or three poems from the section on myth

and consider how myths can be used to make generalizations about our own lives. Explain.

5. Both Judith Ortiz Cofer's "My Father in the Navy: A Childhood Memory" (p. 45) and Derek Walcott's "Sea Grapes" (p. 269) allude to Homer's *The Odyssey*. Read a summary of this story in an encyclopedia or other reference book and write an essay in which you discuss how the authors' treatments of Homer's tale are alike and how they are different. What specific use does each poet make of the story?

POETRY

FOR FURTHER READING

ANNA AKHMATOVA
(1889–1966)

He Loved Three Things Alone
(1911)

He loved three things alone:
White peacocks, evensong,
Old maps of America.
He hated children crying,
5 And raspberry jam with his tea,
And womanish hysteria.
. . . And he had married me.

ANONYMOUS

Bonny Barbara Allan

(traditional Scottish ballad)

It was in and about the Martinmas[1] time,
   even the green leaves were afalling,
That Sir John Graeme, in the West Country,
   Fell in love with Barbara Allan.

5 He sent his men down through the town,
   To the place where she was dwelling;
"O haste and come to my master dear,
   Gin[2] ye be Barbara Allan."

---

[1] Saint Martin's Day, November 11.

[2] If.

O hooly,[3] hooly rose she up,
10   To the place where he was lying,
And when she drew the curtain by:
    "Young man, I think you're dying."

"O it's I'm sick, and very, very sick,
    And 'tis a' for Barbara Allan."—
15 "O the better for me ye's never be,
    Tho your heart's blood were aspilling.

"O dinna ye mind,[4] young man," said she,
    "When ye was in the tavern adrinking,
That ye made the health gae round and round,
20   And slighted Barbara Allan?"

He turned his face unto the wall,
    And death was with him dealing:
"Adieu, adieu, my dear friends all,
    And be kind to Barbara Allan."

25 And slowly, slowly raise she up,
    And slowly, slowly left him,
And sighing said she could not stay,
    Since death of life had reft him.

She had not gane a mile but twa,
30   When she heard the dead-bell ringing,
And every jow[5] that the dead-bell geid,
    It cried, "Woe to Barbara Allan!"

"O mother, mother, make my bed!
    O make it saft and narrow!
35 Since my love died for me today,
    I'll die for him tomorrow."

Sir Patrick Spence

(traditional Scottish ballad)

The king sits in Dumferling toune,
    Drinking the blude-reid wine:
"O whar will I get guid sailor
    To sail this schip of mine?"

---

[3] Slowly.

[4] Don't you remember.

[5] Stroke.

⁵ Up and spak an eldern knicht,
　　Sat at the kings richt kne:
"Sir Patrick Spence is the best sailor
　　That sails upon the se."

The king has written a braid letter,
¹⁰　　And signed it wi' his hand,
And sent it to Sir Patrick Spence,
　　Was walking on the sand.

The first line that Sir Patrick red,
　　A loud lauch lauchèd he;
¹⁵ The next line that Sir Patrick red,
　　The teir blinded his ee.

"O wha[1] is this has don this deid,
　　This ill deid don to me,
To send me out this time o' the yeir,
²⁰　　To sail upon the se!

"Mak haste, mak haste, my mirry men all,
　　Our guid schip sails the morne."
"O say na sae[2] my master deir,
　　For I feir a deadlie storme.

²⁵ "Late late yestreen I saw the new moone,
　　Wi' the auld moone in hir arme,
And I feir, I feir, my deir master,
　　That we will cum to harme."

O our Scots nobles wer richt laith[3]
³⁰　　To weet[4] their cork-heild schoone;[5]
Bot lang owre[6] a' the play wer playd,
　　Their hats they swam aboone.[7]
O lang, lang may their ladies sit,
　　Wi' their fans into their hand,
³⁵ Or ere they se Sir Patrick Spence
　　Cum sailing to the land.

---

[1] Who.

[2] Not so.

[3] Loath.

[4] Wet.

[5] Shoes.

[6] Before.

[7] Above.

O lang, lang may the ladies stand,
    Wi' their gold kems[8] in their hair,
Waiting for their ain[9] deir lords,
40   For they'll se thame na mair.

Haf owre,[10] haf owre to Aberdour,
    It's fiftie fadom deip,
And thair lies guid Sir Patrick Spence,
    Wi' the Scots lords at his feit.

Western Wind

(English lyric)

Western wind, when wilt thou blow,
The small rain down can rain?
Christ, if my love were in my arms,
And I in my bed again!

IMAMU AMIRI BARAKA [LEROI JONES]
(1934–   )

Watergate
(1974)

"Dead Crow" is an ol ugly
eagle
i know
run a "eagle
5 laundry"
wash
eagles
over & over
this eagle wash
10 hisself
like lady macbeth
blood mad & sterile
hooked teeth
pulled
15 out
in a flag costume
just stripes
no stars

---

[8] Combs.
[9] Own.
[10] Halfway over.

JOHN BERRYMAN
(1914–1972)

Dream Song #14
(1964)

Life, friends, is boring. We must not say so.
After all, the sky flashes, the great sea yearns,
we ourselves flash and yearn,
and moreover my mother told me as a boy
5 (repeatingly) "Ever to confess you're bored
means you have no

Inner Resources." I conclude now I have no
inner resources, because I am heavy bored.
Peoples bore me,
10 literature bores me, especially great literature,
Henry bores me, with his plights & gripes
as bad as achilles,

who loves people and valiant art, which bores me.
And the tranquil hills, & gin, look like a drag
15 and somehow a dog
has taken itself & its tail considerably away
into mountains or sea or sky, leaving
behind: me, wag.

ELIZABETH BISHOP
(1911–1979)

The Fish
(1946)

I caught a tremendous fish
and held him beside the boat
half out of water, with my hook
fast in a corner of his mouth.
5 He didn't fight.
He hadn't fought at all.
He hung a grunting weight,
battered and venerable
and homely. Here and there
10 his brown skin hung in strips

like ancient wallpaper,
and its pattern of darker brown
was like wallpaper:
shapes like full-blown roses
15 stained and lost through age.
He was speckled with barnacles,
fine rosettes of lime,
and infested
with tiny white sea-lice,
20 and underneath two or three
rags of green weed hung down.
While his gills were breathing in
the terrible oxygen
—the frightening gills,
25 fresh and crisp with blood,
that can cut so badly—
I thought of the coarse white flesh
packed in like feathers,
the big bones and the little bones,
30 the dramatic reds and blacks
of his shiny entrails,
and the pink swim-bladder
like a big peony.
I looked into his eyes
35 which were far larger than mine
but shallower, and yellowed,
the irises backed and packed
with tarnished tinfoil
seen through the lenses
40 of old scratched isinglass.
They shifted a little, but not
to return my stare.
—It was more like the tipping
of an object toward the light.
45 I admired his sullen face,
the mechanism of his jaw,
and then I saw
that from his lower lip
—if you could call it a lip—
50 grim, wet, and weaponlike,
hung five old pieces of fish-line,
or four and a wire leader
with the swivel still attached,
with all their five big hooks
55 grown firmly in his mouth.
A green line, frayed at the end
where he broke it, two heavier lines,
and a fine black thread

and crimped from the strain and snap
60 when it broke and he got away.
Like medals with their ribbons
frayed and wavering,
a five haired beard of wisdom
trailing from his aching jaw.
65 I stared and stared
and victory filled up
the little rented boat,
from the pool of bilge
where oil had spread a rainbow
70 around the rusted engine
to the bailer rusted orange,
the sun-cracked thwarts,
the oarlocks on their strings,
the gunnels—until everything
75 was rainbow, rainbow, rainbow!
And I let the fish go.

WILLIAM BLAKE
(1757–1827)

The Chimney Sweeper
(1789)

When my mother died I was very young,
And my father sold me while yet my tongue
Could scarcely cry "'weep! 'weep! 'weep! 'weep!"
So your chimneys I sweep, and in soot I sleep.

5 There's little Tom Dacre, who cried when his head,
That curled like a lamb's back, was shaved: so I said
"Hush, Tom! never mind it, for when your head's bare
You know that the soot cannot spoil your white hair."

And so he was quiet, and that very night,
10 As Tom was a-sleeping, he had such a sight!
That thousands of sweepers, Dick, Joe, Ned, and Jack,
Were all of them locked up in coffins of black.

And by came an Angel who had a bright key,
And he opened the coffins and set them all free;
15 Then down a green plain leaping, laughing, they run,
And wash in a river, and shine in the sun.

Then naked and white, all their bags left behind,
They rise upon clouds and sport in the wind;
And the Angel told Tom, if he'd be a good boy,
He'd have God for his father, and never want joy.

And so Tom awoke; and we rose in the dark,
And got with our bags and our brushes to work.
Though the morning was cold, Tom was happy and warm;
So if all do their duty they need not fear harm.

The Lamb
(1789)

Little Lamb, who made thee?
Dost thou know who made thee?
Gave thee life & bid thee feed,
By the stream & o'er the mead;
Gave thee clothing of delight,
Softest clothing wooly bright;
Gave thee such a tender voice,
Making all the vales rejoice!
Little Lamb who made thee?
Dost thou know who made thee?

Little Lamb I'll tell thee,
Little Lamb I'll tell thee!
He is callèd by thy name,
For he calls himself a Lamb:
He is meek & he is mild,
He became a little child:
I a child & thou a lamb,
We are callèd by his name.
Little Lamb God bless thee.
Little Lamb God bless thee.

London
(1794)

I wander through each chartered street,
Near where the chartered Thames does flow,
And mark in every face I meet
Marks of weakness, marks of woe.

5 In every cry of every man,
In every infant's cry of fear,
In every voice, in every ban,
The mind-forged manacles I hear.

How the chimney-sweeper's cry
10 Every black'ning church appalls;
And the hapless soldier's sigh
Runs in blood down palace walls.

But most through midnight streets I hear
How the youthful harlot's curse
15 Blasts the new born infant's tear,
And blights with plagues the marriage hearse.

The Tyger
(1794)

Tyger! Tyger! burning bright
In the forests of the night,
What immortal hand or eye
Could frame thy fearful symmetry?

5 In what distant deeps or skies
Burnt the fire of thine eyes?
On what wings dare he aspire?
What the hand dare seize the fire?

And what shoulder, and what art,
10 Could twist the sinews of thy heart?
And when thy heart began to beat,
What dread hand? and what dread feet?

What the hammer? what the chain?
In what furnace was thy brain?
15 What the anvil? what dread grasp
Dare its deadly terrors clasp?

When the stars threw down their spears,
And watered heaven with their tears,
Did he smile his work to see?
20 Did he who made the Lamb make thee?

Tyger! Tyger! burning bright
In the forests of the night,
What immortal hand or eye
Dare frame thy fearful symmetry?

ROBERT BLY
(1926–   )

Snowfall in the Afternoon
(1962)

1.

The grass is half-covered with snow.
It was the sort of snowfall that starts in late afternoon.
And now the little houses of the grass are growing dark.

2.

If I reached my hands down, near the earth,
5 I could take handfuls of darkness!
A darkness was always there, which we never noticed.

3.

As the snow grows heavier, the cornstalks fade further away,
And the barn moves nearer to the house.
The barn moves all alone in the growing storm.

4.

10 The barn is full of corn, and moving toward us now,
Like a hulk blown toward us in a storm at sea;
All the sailors on deck have been blind for many years.

LOUISE BOGAN
(1879–1970)

Women
(1923)

Women have no wilderness in them,
They are provident instead,
Content in the tight hot cell of their hearts
To eat dusty bread.

5 They do not see cattle cropping red winter grass,
They do not hear
Snow water going down under culverts
Shallow and clear.

They wait, when they should turn to journeys,
10 They stiffen, when they should bend.
They use against themselves that benevolence
To which no man is friend.

They cannot think of so many crops to a field
Or of clean wood cleft by an axe.
15 Their love is an eager meaninglessness
Too tense, or too lax.

They hear in every whisper that speaks to them
A shout and a cry.
As like as not, when they take life over their door-sills
20 They should let it go by.

ELIZABETH BARRETT BROWNING
(1806–1861)

How Do I Love Thee?
(1850)

How do I love thee? Let me count the ways.
I love thee to the depth and breadth and height
My soul can reach, when feeling out of sight
For the ends of being and ideal grace.
5 I love thee to the level of every day's
Most quiet need, by sun and candle-light.
I love thee freely, as men strive for right.
I love thee purely, as they turn from praise.
I love thee with the passion put to use
10 In my old griefs, and with my childhood's faith.
I love thee with a love I seemed to lose
With my lost saints. I love thee with the breath,
Smiles, tears, of all my life; and, if God choose,
I shall but love thee better after death.

CHRISTOPHER BUCKLEY
(1948–   )

Why I'm in Favor of a Nuclear Freeze
(1986)

Because we were 18 and still wonderful in our bodies,
because Harry's father owned a ranch and we had
nothing better to do one Saturday, we went hunting
doves among the high oaks and almost wholly quiet air . . .
5 Traipsing the hills and deer paths for an hour,
we were ready when the first ones swooped—
and we took them down in smoke much like the planes
in the war films of our regimented youth.
                                    Some were dead
10 and some knocked cold, and because he knew how
and I just couldn't, Harry went to each of them and,
with thumb and forefinger, almost tenderly, squeezed
the last air out of their slight necks.
                              Our jackets grew
15 heavy with birds and for a while we sat in the shade
thinking we were someone, talking a bit of girls—
who would "go", who wouldn't, how love would probably
always be beyond our reach . . . We even talked of the nuns
who terrified us with God and damnation. We both recalled
20 that first prize in art, the one pinned to the cork board
in front of class, was a sweet blond girl's drawing
of the fires and coals, the tortured souls of Purgatory.
Harry said he feared eternity until he was 17, and,
if he ever had kids, the last place they would go would be
25 a parochial school.
                    On our way to the car, having forgotten
which way the safety was off or on, I accidentally discharged
my borrowed 12 gauge, twice actually—one would have been Harry's
head if he were behind me, the other my foot, inches to the right.
30 We were almost back when something moved in the raw, dry grass,
and without thinking, and on the first twitch of two tall ears,
we together blew the ever-loving-Jesus out of a jack rabbit
until we couldn't tell fur from dust from blood . . .
                                              Harry has
35 a family, two children as lovely as any will ever be—
he hasn't hunted in years . . . and that once was enough for me.
Anymore, a good day offers a moment's praise for the lizards
daring the road I run along, or it offers a dusk in which
yellow meadow larks scrounge fields in the grey autumn light . . .
40 Harry and I are friends now almost 30 years, and the last time

we had dinner, I thought about that rabbit, not the doves
which we swore we would cook and eat, but that rabbit—
why the hell had we killed it so cold-heartedly? And I saw
that it was simply because we had the guns, because we could . . .

GEORGE GORDON, LORD BYRON
(1788–1824)

She Walks in Beauty
(1815)

1

She walks in beauty, like the night
   Of cloudless climes and starry skies;
And all that's best of dark and bright
   Meet in her aspect and her eyes:
5 Thus mellowed to that tender light
   Which heaven to gaudy day denies.

2

One shade the more, one ray the less,
   Had half impaired the nameless grace
Which waves in every raven tress,
10   Or softly lightens o'er her face;
Where thoughts serenely sweet express
   How pure, how dear their dwelling place.

3

And on that cheek, and o'er that brow,
   So soft, so calm, yet eloquent,
15 The smiles that win, the tints that glow,
   But tell of days in goodness spent,
A mind at peace with all below,
   A heart whose love is innocent!

THOMAS CAMPION
(1567–1620)

There Is a Garden in Her Face
(1617)

    There is a garden in her face
Where roses and white lilies grow;
    A heav'nly paradise is that place
Wherein all pleasant fruits do flow.
5   There cherries grow which none may buy
    Till "Cherry-ripe" themselves do cry.

    Those cherries fairly do enclose
Of orient pearl a double row,
    Which when her lovely laughter shows,
10 They look like rose-buds filled with snow;
    Yet them nor peer nor prince can buy,
    Till "Cherry-ripe" themselves do cry.

    Her eyes like angels watch them still;
Her brows like bended bows do stand,
15   Threat'ning with piercing frowns to kill
All that attempt, with eye or hand
    Those sacred cherries to come nigh
    Till "Cherry-ripe" themselves do cry.

RAYMOND CARVER
(1938–1988)

Gravy
(1988)

No other word will do. For that's what it was. Gravy.
Gravy these past ten years.
Alive, sober, working, loving and
being loved by a good woman. Eleven years
5 ago he was told he had six months to live
at the rate he was going. And he was going
nowhere but down. So he changed his ways
somehow. He quit drinking! And the rest?
After that it was *all* gravy, every minute

10 of it, up to and including when he was told about,
well, some things that were breaking down and
building up inside his head. "Don't weep for me,"
he said to his friends. "I'm a lucky man.
I've had ten years longer than I or anyone
15 expected. Pure gravy. And don't forget it."

GEOFFREY CHAUCER
(1343–1400)

from The Canterbury Tales
(1386–1387)

(General Prologue)

Whan that Aprill with his shoures soote[1]
The droghte of March[2] hath perced to the roote,
And bathed every veyne[3] in swich licour[4]
Of which vertu[5] engendred is the flour;
5 Whan Zephirus[6] eek with his sweete breeth
Inspired hath in every holt and heeth[7]
The tendre croppes,[8] and the yonge sonne[9]
Hath in the Ram his halfe cours yronne,[10]
And smale foweles maken melodye,
10 That slepen al the nyght with open eye—
So priketh hem nature in hir corages—
Thanne longen folk to goon on pilgrimages,
And palmeres[11] for to seken straunge strondes[12]

[1] Gentle showers.

[2] Dryness of March.

[3] Veins in the plants.

[4] Such liquid.

[5] Potency.

[6] The west wind; in classical mythology, husband of Flora, goddess of flowers, and father of Carpus, god of fruit.

[7] Woodland and plain.

[8] New foliage.

[9] Just beginning its annual journey after the vernal equinox. In Chaucer's time the English legal year began on March 25.

[10] The zodiacal house of Aries (the Ram) in Chaucer's time extended from March 12 to April 11.

[11] Professional pilgrims whose emblem was a palm frond.

[12] Lands.

To ferne halwes, kowthe[13] in sondry londes;
15 And specially from every shires ende
Of Engelond to Caunterbury they wende
The hooly blisful martir[14] for to seke
That hem hath holpen whan that they were seeke.[15]
Bifil that in that seson on a day
20 In Southwerk[16] at the Tabard[17] as I lay
Redy to wenden on my pilgrymage
To Caunterbury with ful devout corage,
At nyght was come into that hostelrye
Wel nyne and twenty in a compaignye
25 Of sondry folk, by aventure[18] yfalle
In felaweship, and pilgrimes were they alle,
That toward Caunterbury wolden ryde.
The chambres and the stables weren wyde,
And wel we weren esed atte beste.[19]
30 And shortly,[20] whan the sonne was to reste,
So hadde I spoken with hem everichon
That I was of hir felaweship anon,[21]
And made forward[22] erly for to ryse,
To take oure wey ther as I yow devyse.[23]
35   But nathelees, whil I have tyme and space,
Er that I ferther in this tale pace,
Me thynketh it acordaunt to resoun
To telle yow al the condicioun[24]
Of ech of hem, so as it semed me,
40 And whiche they weren, and of what degree,[25]
And eek in what array that they were inne,
And at a knyght than wol I first bigynne.

[13] Faraway saints (or shrines), known.

[14] Blessed St. Thomas à Becket, martyred in Canterbury Cathedral in 1170.

[15] Helped, sick.

[16] The borough south of London bridge.

[17] Inn identified by a sign shaped like a smock.

[18] Chance.

[19] Accommodated in the best manner.

[20] To be brief about it.

[21] Immediately.

[22] (We) made an agreement.

[23] (Will) relate.

[24] Circumstances.

[25] Status (rank).

JUDITH ORTIZ COFER
(1952–   )

Lessons of the Past
(1990)

For my daughter

I was born the year my father learned to march
    in step
with other men, to hit bull's eyes, to pose for
    sepia photos
in dress uniform outside Panamanian nightspots
    —pictures
he would send home to his pregnant teenage
    bride inscribed:
To my best girl.

My birth made her a madonna, a husbandless
    young woman
with a legitimate child, envied by all the tired
    women
of the pueblo as she strolled my carriage down
    dirt roads,
both of us dressed in fine clothes bought with
    army checks.

                  When he came home,
he bore gifts: silk pajamas from the orient for
    her; a pink
iron crib for me. People filled our house to wel-
    come him.
He played Elvis loud and sang along in his new
    English.
She sat on his lap and laughed at everything.

They roasted a suckling pig out on the patio.
    Later,
no one could explain how I had climbed over the
    iron bars
and into the fire. Hands lifted me up quickly,
    but not before
the tongues had licked my curls.

                  There is a picture of me
taken soon after: my hair clipped close to my
    head,
my eyes enormous—about to overflow with fear.
I look like a miniature of one of those women

in Paris after World War II, hair shorn,
being paraded down the streets in shame,
40 for having loved the enemy.

                        But then things changed,
and some nights he didn't come home. I remember
hearing her cry in the kitchen. I sat on the rock-
45   ing chair
waiting for my cocoa, learning how to count, *uno,*
   dos, tres,
cuatro, cinco, on my toes. So that when he came
   in,
50 smelling strong and sweet as sugarcane syrup,
I could surprise my *Papasito*—
who liked his girls smart, who didn't like
   crybabies—
with a new lesson, learned well.

SAMUEL TAYLOR COLERIDGE
(1772–1834)

Kubla Khan[1]
(1797–1798)

Or, a Vision in a Dream. A Fragment.

In Xanadu did Kubla Khan
A stately pleasure-dome decree:
Where Alph,[2] the sacred river, ran
Through caverns measureless to man
5   Down to a sunless sea.
So twice five miles of fertile ground
With walls and towers were girdled round;
And there were gardens bright with sinuous rills,
Where blossomed many an incense-bearing tree;
10 And here were forests ancient as the hills,
Enfolding sunny spots of greenery.

But oh! that deep romantic chasm which slanted
Down the green hill athwart a cedarn cover!

---

[1] Coleridge mythologizes the actual Kublai Khan, a thirteenth-century Mongol emperor, as well as the Chinese city of Xanadu.

[2] Probably derived from the Greek river Alpheus, whose waters, according to legend, rose from the Ionian Sea in Sicily as the fountain of Arethusa.

A savage place! as holy and enchanted
15 As e'er beneath a waning moon was haunted
By woman wailing for her demon-lover!
And from this chasm, with ceaseless turmoil seething,
As if this earth in fast thick pants were breathing,
A mighty fountain momently was forced:
20 Amid whose swift half-intermitted burst
Huge fragments vaulted like rebounding hail,
Or chaffy grain beneath the thresher's flail:
And 'mid these dancing rocks at once and ever
It flung up momently the sacred river.
25 Five miles meandering with a mazy motion
Through wood and dale the sacred river ran,
Then reached the caverns measureless to man,
And sank in tumult to a lifeless ocean:
And 'mid this tumult Kubla heard from far
30 Ancestral voices prophesying war!
    The shadow of the dome of pleasure
    Floated midway on the waves;
    Where was heard the mingled measure
    From the fountain and the caves.
35 It was a miracle of rare device,
A sunny pleasure-dome with caves of ice!

    A damsel with a dulcimer
    In a vision once I saw:
    It was an Abyssinian maid,
40   And on her dulcimer she played,
    Singing of Mount Abora.[3]
    Could I revive within me
    Her symphony and song,
    To such a deep delight 'twould win me,
45 That with music loud and long,
I would build that dome in air,
That sunny dome! those caves of ice!
And all who heard should see them there,
And all should cry, Beware! Beware!
50 His flashing eyes, his floating hair!
Weave a circle round him thrice,[4]
And close your eyes with holy dread,
For he on honey-dew hath fed,
And drunk the milk of Paradise.

---

[3] Some scholars see a reminiscence here of John Milton's *Paradise Lost IV*, 280–82: "where Abassin kings their issue guard / Mount Amara, though this by some supposed / True Paradise under the Ethiop Line."

[4] A magic ritual, to keep away intruding spirits.

HART CRANE
(1899-1932)

To Brooklyn Bridge
(1926)

How many dawns, chill from his rippling rest
The seagull's wings shall dip and pivot him,
Shedding white rings of tumult, building high
Over the chained bay waters Liberty—

5 Then, with inviolate curve, forsake our eyes
As apparitional as sails that cross
Some page of figures to be filed away;
—Till elevators drop us from our day . . .

I think of cinemas, panoramic sleights
10 With multitudes bent toward some flashing scene
Never disclosed, but hastened to again,
Foretold to other eyes on the same screen;

And Thee, across the harbor, silver-paced
As though the sun took step of thee, yet left
15 Some motion ever unspent in thy stride,—
Implicitly thy freedom staying thee!

Out of some subway scuttle, cell or loft
A bedlamite speeds to thy parapets,
Tilting there momently, shrill shirt ballooning,
20 A jest falls from the speechless caravan.

Down Wall, from girder into street noon leaks,
A rip-tooth of the sky's acetylene;
All afternoon the cloud-flown derricks turn . . .
Thy cables breathe the North Atlantic still.

25 And obscure as that heaven of the Jews,
Thy guerdon . . . Accolade thou dost bestow
Of anonymity time cannot raise:
Vibrant reprieve and pardon thou dost show.

O harp and altar, of the fury fused,
30 (How could mere toil align thy choiring strings!)
Terrific threshold of the prophet's pledge,
Prayer of pariah, and the lover's cry,—

Again the traffic lights that skim thy swift
Unfractioned idiom, immaculate sigh of stars,
35 Beading thy path—condense eternity:
And we have seen night lifted in thine arms.

Under thy shadow by the piers I waited;
Only in darkness is thy shadow clear.
The City's fiery parcels all undone,
40 Already snow submerges an iron year . . .

O Sleepless as the river under thee,
Vaulting the sea, the prairies' dreaming sod,
Unto us lowliest sometime sweep, descend
And of the curveship lend a myth to God.

VICTOR HERNÁNDEZ CRUZ
(1949–   )

Anonymous
(1982)

And if I lived in those olden times
With a funny name like Choicer or
Henry Howard, Earl of Surrey, what chimes!
I would spend my time in search of rhymes
5 Make sure the measurement termination surprise
In the court of kings snapping till woo sunrise
Plus always be using the words *alas* and *hath*
And not even knowing that that was my path
Just think on the Lower East Side of Manhattan
10 It would have been like living in satin
Alas! The projects hath not covered the river
Thou see-est vision to make thee quiver
Hath I been delivered to that "wildernesse"
So past
15 I would have been the last one in the
Dance to go
Taking note the minuet so slow
All admire my taste
Within thou *mambo* of much more haste.

COUNTEE CULLEN
(1903–1946)

For a Lady I Know
(1925)

She even thinks that up in heaven
  Her class lies late and snores,
While poor black cherubs rise at seven
  To do celestial chores.

E. E. CUMMINGS
(1894–1962)

Buffalo Bill's
(1923)

Buffalo Bill's
defunct
        who used to
        ride a watersmooth-silver
5   stallion
and break onetwothreefourfive pigeonsjustlikethat
                                                Jesus
he was a handsome man
                     and what i want to know is
10 how do you like your blueeyed boy
Mister Death

next to of course god america i
(1926)

"next to of course god america i
love you land of the pilgrims' and so forth oh
say can you see by the dawn's early my
country 'tis of centuries come and go
5 and are no more what of it we should worry
in every language even deafanddumb
thy sons acclaim your glorious name by gorry
by jingo by gee by gosh by gum

why talk of beauty what could be more beaut-
10 iful than these heroic happy dead
who rushed like lions to the roaring slaughter
they did not stop to think they died instead
then shall the voice of liberty be mute?"

He spoke. And drank rapidly a glass of water

JAMES DICKEY
(1923–   )

Adultery
(1966)

We have all been in rooms
We cannot die in, and they are odd places, and sad.
Often Indians are standing eagle-armed on hills

In the sunrise   open wide to the Great Spirit
5 Or gliding in canoes   or cattle are browsing on the walls
Far away   gazing down with the eyes of our children

Not far away   or there are men driving
The last railspike, which has turned
Gold in their hands. Gigantic forepleasure lives

10 Among such scenes, and we are alone with it
At last. There is always some weeping
Between us   and someone is always checking

A wrist watch by the bed to see how much
Longer we have left. Nothing can come
15 Of this   nothing can come

Of us: of me with my grim techniques
Or you who have sealed your womb
With a ring of convulsive rubber:

Although we come together,
20 Nothing will come of us. But we would not give
It up, for death is beaten

By praying Indians   by distant cows   historical
Hammers   by hazardous meetings that bridge
A continent. One could never die here

25 Never die   never die
While crying. My lover, my dear one
I will see you next week

When I'm in town. I will call you
If I can. Please get hold of   please don't
30 Oh God, Please don't any more I can't bear . . . Listen:
We have done it again   we are
Still living. Sit up and smile,
God bless you. Guilt is magical.

EMILY DICKINSON
(1830–1886)

Because I Could Not Stop for Death
(1863)

Because I could not stop for Death—
He kindly stopped for me—
The Carriage held but just Ourselves—
And Immortality.

5 We slowly drove—He knew no haste
And I had put away
My labor and my leisure too,
For His Civility—

We passed the School, where Children strove
10 At Recess—in the Ring—
We passed the Fields of Gazing Grain—
We passed the Setting Sun—
Or rather—He passed Us—
The Dews drew quivering and chill—

15 For only Gossamer, my Gown—
      My Tippet[1]—only Tulle—

      We paused before a House that seemed
      A Swelling of the Ground—
      The Roof was scarcely visible—
   20 The Cornice—in the Ground—

      Since then—'tis Centuries—and yet
      Feels shorter than the Day
      I first surmised the Horses' Heads
      Were toward Eternity—

I Heard a Fly Buzz—When I Died
(c. 1862)

   I heard a Fly buzz—when I died—
   The Stillness in the Room
   Was like the Stillness in the Air—
   Between the Heaves of Storm—

 5 The Eyes around—had wrung them dry—
   And Breaths were gathering firm
   For that last Onset—when the King
   Be witnessed—in the Room—

   I willed my Keepsakes—Signed away
10 What portion of me be
   Assignable—and then it was
   There interposed a Fly—

   With Blue—uncertain stumbling Buzz—
   Between the light—and me—
15 And then the Windows failed—and then
   I could not see to see—

I Taste a Liquor Never Brewed
(1861)

   I taste a liquor never brewed—
   From Tankards scooped in Pearl—
   Not all the Frankfort Berries[1]
   Yield such an Alcohol!

---

[1] Cape.

---

[1] This line is a variant reading for the usually accepted "Not all the Vats upon the Rhine." In both cases, the poet refers to German wine.

5 Inebriate of Air—am I—
And Debauchee of Dew—
Reeling—thro endless summer days—
From inns of Molten Blue—

When "Landlords" turn the drunken Bee
10 Out of the Foxglove's door—
When Butterflies—renounce their "drams"—
I shall but drink the more!

Till Seraphs swing their snowy Hats—
And Saints—to windows run—
15 To see the little Tippler
From Manzanilla[2] come!

The Soul Selects Her Own Society
(1862)

The Soul selects her own Society—
Then—shuts the Door—
To her divine Majority—
Present no more—

5 Unmoved—she notes the Chariots—pausing—
At her low Gate—
Unmoved—an Emperor be kneeling
Upon her Mat—

I've known her—from an ample nation—
10 Choose One—
Then—close the Valves of her attention—
Like Stone—

Wild Nights—Wild Nights!
(1890, c. 1861)

Wild Nights—Wild Nights!
Were I with thee
Wild Nights should be
Our luxury!

5 Futile—the Winds—
To a Heart in port—
Done with the Compass—
Done with the Chart!

---

[2] A pale Spanish sherry.

		Rowing in Eden—
10 Ah, the Sea!
		Might I but moor—Tonight—
		In Thee!

JOHN DONNE
(1572–1631)

Batter My Heart, Three-Personed God
(c. 1610)

Batter my heart, three-personed God, for You
As yet but knock, breathe, shine, and seek to mend.
That I may rise and stand, o'erthrow me, and bend
Your force to break, blow, burn, and make me new.
5 I, like an usurped town to another due,
Labor to admit You, but Oh! to no end.
Reason, Your viceroy in me, me should defend,
But is captived, and proves weak or untrue.
Yet dearly I love You, and would be lovèd fain,
10 But am betrothed unto Your enemy;
Divorce me, untie or break that knot again;
Take me to You, imprison me, for I,
Except You enthrall me, never shall be free,
Nor ever chaste, except You ravish me.

Death Be Not Proud
(c. 1610)

Death be not proud, though some have callèd thee
Mighty and dreadful, for thou art not so;
For those whom thou think'st thou dost overthrow
Die not, poor death, nor yet canst thou kill me.
5 From rest and sleep, which but thy pictures be,
Much pleasure, then from thee much more must flow,
And soonest our best men with thee do go,
Rest of their bones, and soul's delivery.
Thou art slave to fate, chance, kings, and desperate men,
10 And dost with poison, war, and sickness dwell,
And poppy, or charms can make us sleep as well,
And better than thy stroke; why swell'st thou then?
One short sleep past, we wake eternally,
And death shall be no more; death, thou shalt die.

Song
(1633)

Go and catch a falling star,
    Get with child a mandrake root,[1]
Tell me where all past years are,
    Or who cleft the Devil's foot,
5 Teach me to hear mermaids singing,
    Or to keep off envy's stinging,
        And find
        What wind
Serves to advance an honest mind.

10 If thou be'st borne to strange sights,
    Things invisible to see,
Ride ten thousand days and nights,
    Till age snow white hairs on thee,
Thou, when thou return'st, wilt tell me
15   All strange wonders that befell thee,
        And swear
        Nowhere
Lives a woman true, and fair.

If thou findst one, let me know,
20   Such a pilgrimage were sweet—
Yet do not, I would not go,
    Though at next door we might meet;
Though she were true, when you met her,
    And last, till you write your letter,
25   Yet she
        Will be
False, ere I come, to two, or three.

RITA DOVE
(1952–   )

The Satisfaction Coal Company
(1986)

1.

What to do with a day.
Leaf through *Jet*. Watch T.V.
Freezing on the porch

---

[1] The mandrake root (or mandragora), which is forked and resembles the lower part of the human body, was thought to be an aphrodisiac.

but he goes anyhow, snow too high
5 for a walk, the ice treacherous.
Inside, the gas heater takes care of itself;
he doesn't even notice being warm.

Everyone says he looks great.
Across the street a drunk stands smiling
10 at something carved in a tree.
The new neighbor with the floating hips
scoots out to get the mail
and waves once, brightly,
storm door clipping her heel on the way in.

2.

15 Twice a week he had taken the bus down Glendale hill
to the corner of Market. Slipped through
the alley by the canal and let himself in.
Started to sweep
with terrible care, like a woman
20 brushing shine into her hair,
same motion, same lullaby.
No curtains—the cop on the beat
stopped outside once in the hour
to swing his billy club and glare.

25 It was better on Saturdays
when the children came along:
he mopped while they emptied
ashtrays, clang of glass on metal
then a dry scutter. Next they counted
30 nailheads studding the leather cushions.
Thirty-four! they shouted,
that was the year and
they found it mighty amusing.

But during the week he noticed more—
35 lights when they gushed or dimmed
at the Portage Hotel, the 10:32
picking up speed past the B & O switchyard,
floorboards trembling and the explosive
kachook kachook kachook kachook
40 and the oiled rails ticking underneath.

3.

They were poor then but everyone had been poor.
He hadn't minded the sweeping,

just the thought of it—like now
when people ask him what he's thinking
45 and he says *I'm listening.*

Those nights walking home alone,
the bucket of coal scraps banging his knee,
he'd hear a roaring furnace
with its dry, familiar heat. Now the nights
50 take care of themselves—as for the days,
there is the canary's sweet curdled song,
the wino smiling through his dribble.
Past the hill, past the gorge
choked with wild sumac in summer,
55 the corner has been upgraded.
Still, he'd like to go down there someday
to stand for a while, and get warm.

MICHAEL DRAYTON
(1563–1631)

Since There's No Help
(1619)

Since there's no help, come let us kiss and part;
Nay, I have done, you get no more of me,
And I am glad, yea, glad with all my heart
That thus so cleanly I myself can free;
5 Shake hands for ever, cancel all our vows,
And when we meet at any time again,
Be it not seen in either of our brows
That we one jot of former love retain.
Now at the last gasp of Love's latest breath,
10 When, his pulse failing, Passion speechless lies,
When Faith is kneeling by his bed of death,
And Innocence is closing up his eyes,
    Now if thou wouldst, when all have given him over,
    From death to life thou mightst him yet recover.

PAUL LAURENCE DUNBAR
(1872–1906)

We Wear the Mask
(1913)

We wear the mask that grins and lies,
It hides our cheeks and shades our eyes—
This debt we pay to human guile;
With torn and bleeding hearts we smile,
And mouth with myriad subtleties.

Why should the world be over-wise,
In counting all our tears and sighs?
Nay, let them only see us, while
    We wear the mask.

We smile, but, O great Christ, our cries
To thee from tortured souls arise.
We sing, but oh the clay is vile
Beneath our feet, and long the mile;
But let the world dream otherwise,
    We wear the mask!

T. S. ELIOT
(1888–1965)

Journey of the Magi[1]
(1927)

"A cold coming we had of it,
Just the worst time of the year
For a journey, and such a long journey:
The ways deep and the weather sharp,
The very dead of winter."[2]
And the camels galled, sore-footed, refractory,

---

[1] In the poem, one of the three wise men who ventured east to pay tribute to the infant Jesus (see Matthew 12:1–12) recalls the experience.

[2] The five quoted lines are adapted from a passage in a 1622 Christmas Day sermon by Bishop Lancelot Andrewes.

Lying down in the melting snow.
There were times we regretted
The summer palaces on slopes, the terraces,
10 And the silken girls bringing sherbet.
Then the camel men cursing and grumbling
And running away, and wanting their liquor and women,
And the night-fires going out, and the lack of shelters,
And the cities hostile and the towns unfriendly
15 And the villages dirty and charging high prices:
A hard time we had of it.
At the end we preferred to travel all night,
Sleeping in snatches,
With the voices singing in our ears, saying
20 That this was all folly.

Then at dawn we came down to a temperate valley,
Wet, below the snow line, smelling of vegetation;
With a running stream and a water-mill beating the darkness,
And three trees[3] on the low sky,
25 And an old white horse[4] galloped away in the meadow.
Then we came to a tavern with vine-leaves over the lintel,
Six hands at an open door dicing for pieces of silver,[5]
And feet kicking the empty wine-skins.
But there was no information, and so we continued
30 And arrived at evening, not a moment too soon
Finding the place; it was (you may say) satisfactory.
All this was a long time ago, I remember,
And I would do it again, but set down
This set down
35 This: were we led all that way for
Birth or Death? There was a Birth, certainly,
We had evidence and no doubt. I had seen birth and death,
But had thought they were different; this Birth was
Hard and bitter agony for us, like Death, our death.
40 We returned to our places, these Kingdoms,
But no longer at ease here, in the old dispensation,
With an alien people clutching their gods.
I should be glad of another death.

---

[3] Refers to the three crosses at Calvary (see Luke 23:32–33).

[4] Refers to the white horse of the conquering Christ in Revelation 19:11–16.

[5] Echoes the soldiers dicing for Christ's garments, as well as his betrayal by Judas.

The Love Song of J. Alfred Prufrock
(1917)

S'io credessi che mia risposta fosse
A persona che mai tornasse al mondo,
Questa fiamma staria senza piu scosse.
Ma perciocche giammai di questo fondo
Non torno vivo alcun, s'i'odo il vero,
Senza tema d'infamia ti rispondo.[1]

Let us go then, you and I,
When the evening is spread out against the sky
Like a patient etherized upon a table;
Let us go, through certain half-deserted streets,
5 The muttering retreats
Of restless nights in one-night cheap hotels
And sawdust restaurants with oyster-shells:
Streets that follow like a tedious argument
Of insidious intent
10 To lead you to an overwhelming question . . .
Oh, do not ask, "What is it?"
Let us go and make our visit.

In the room the women come and go
Talking of Michelangelo.

15 The yellow fog that rubs its back upon the window-panes,
The yellow smoke that rubs its muzzle on the window-panes
Licked its tongue into the corners of the evening,
Lingered upon the pools that stand in drains,
Let fall upon its back the soot that falls from chimneys,
20 Slipped by the terrace, made a sudden leap,
And seeing that it was a soft October night,
Curled once about the house, and fell asleep.

And indeed there will be time
For the yellow smoke that slides along the street,
25 Rubbing its back upon the window-panes;
There will be time, there will be time
To prepare a face to meet the faces that you meet;

---

[1] The epigraph is from Dante's *Inferno*, Canto XXVII. In response to the poet's question about his identity, Guido da Montefelto, who for his sin of fraud must spend eternity wrapped in flames, replies: "If I thought that I was speaking to someone who could go back to the world, this flame would shake me no more. But since from this place nobody ever returns alive, if what I hear is true, I answer you without fear of infamy."

There will be time to murder and create,
And time for all the works and days[2] of hands
30 That lift and drop a question on your plate;
Time for you and time for me,
And time yet for a hundred indecisions,
And for a hundred visions and revisions,
Before the taking of a toast and tea.

35 In the room the women come and go
Talking of Michelangelo.

And indeed there will be time
To wonder, "Do I dare?" and, "Do I dare?"
Time to turn back and descend the stair,
40 With a bald spot in the middle of my hair—
(They will say: "How his hair is growing thin!")
My morning coat, my collar mounting firmly to the chin,
My necktie rich and modest, but asserted by a simple pin—
(They will say: "But how his arms and legs are thin!")
45 Do I dare
Disturb the universe?
In a minute there is time
For decisions and revisions which a minute will reverse.

For I have known them all already, known them all:—
50 Have known the evenings, mornings, afternoons,
I have measured out my life with coffee spoons;
I know the voices dying with a dying fall[3]
Beneath the music from a farther room.
　　So how should I presume?

55 And I have known the eyes already, known them all—
The eyes that fix you in a formulated phrase,
And when I am formulated, sprawling on a pin,
When I am pinned and wriggling on the wall,
Then how should I begin
60 To spit out all the butt-ends of my days and ways?
　　And how should I presume?

And I have known the arms already, known them all—
Arms that are braceleted and white and bare

---

[2] "Works and Days" is the title of a work by the eighth-century Greek Hesiod, whose poem celebrates farm work.

[3] Allusion to Orsino's speech in *Twelfth Night* (I, i), "That strain again! It had a dying fall."

(But in the lamplight, downed with light brown hair!)
65 Is it perfume from a dress
That makes me so digress?
Arms that lie along a table, or wrap about a shawl.
    And should I then presume?
    And how should I begin? . . .

70 Shall I say, I have gone at dusk through narrow streets
And watched the smoke that rises from the pipes
Of lonely men in shirt-sleeves, leaning out of windows? . . .

I should have been a pair of ragged claws
Scuttling across the floors of silent seas.

75 And the afternoon, the evening, sleeps so peacefully!
Smoothed by long fingers,
Asleep . . . tired . . . or it malingers,
Stretched on the floor, here beside you and me.
Should I, after tea and cakes and ices,
80 Have the strength to force the moment to its crisis?
But though I have wept and fasted, wept and prayed,
Though I have seen my head (grown slightly bald) brought in upon
    a platter,[4]
I am no prophet—and here's no great matter;
I have seen the moment of my greatness flicker,
85 And I have seen the eternal Footman[5] hold my coat, and snicker,
And in short, I was afraid.

And would it have been worth it, after all,
After the cups, the marmalade, the tea,
Among the porcelain, among some talk of you and me,
90 Would it have been worth while,
To have bitten off the matter with a smile,
To have squeezed the universe into a ball
To roll it toward some overwhelming question,
To say: "I am Lazarus,[6] come from the dead,
95 Come back to tell you all, I shall tell you all"—
If one, settling a pillow by her head,
    Should say: "That is not what I meant at all.
    That is not it, at all."

---

[4] Like John the Baptist, who was beheaded by King Herod (see Matthew 14:3–11).

[5] Perhaps death, or fate.

[6] Lazarus was raised from the dead by Christ (see John 11:1–44).

And would it have been worth it, after all,
100 Would it have been worth while,
After the sunsets and the dooryards and the sprinkled streets,
After the novels, after the teacups, after the skirts that trail along
    the floor—
And this, and so much more?—
It is impossible to say just what I mean!
105 But as if a magic lantern threw the nerves in patterns on a screen:
Would it have been worth while
If one, settling a pillow or throwing off a shawl,
And turning toward the window, should say:
    "That is not it at all,
110   That is not what I meant, at all."

                    . . .

No! I am not Prince Hamlet, nor was meant to be;
Am an attendant lord, one that will do
To swell a progress,[7] start a scene or two,
Advise the prince; no doubt, an easy tool,
115 Deferential, glad to be of use,
Politic, cautious, and meticulous;
Full of high sentence,[8] but a bit obtuse;
At times, indeed, almost ridiculous—
Almost, at times, the Fool.

120 I grow old . . . I grow old . . .
I shall wear the bottoms of my trousers rolled.

Shall I part my hair behind? Do I dare to eat a peach?
I shall wear white flannel trousers, and walk upon the beach.
I have heard the mermaids singing, each to each.

125 I do not think that they will sing to me.

I have seen them riding seaward on the waves
Combing the white hair of the waves blown back
When the wind blows the water white and black.

We have lingered in the chambers of the sea
130 By sea-girls wreathed with seaweed red and brown
Till human voices wake us, and we drown.

---

[7] Here, in the Elizabethan sense of a royal journey.

[8] Opinions.

JAMES A. EMANUEL
(1921–)

Emmett Till[1]
(1968)

I hear a whistling
Through the water.
Little Emmett
Won't be still.
5 He keeps floating
Round the darkness,
Edging through
The silent chill.
Tell me, please,
10 That bedtime story
Of the fairy
River Boy
Who swims forever,
Deep in treasures,
15 Necklaced in
A coral toy.

LOUISE ERDRICH
(1954–)

Dear John Wayne
(1984)

August and the drive-in picture is packed.
We lounge on the hood of the Pontiac
surrounded by the slow-burning spirals they sell
at the window, to vanquish the hordes of mosquitoes.
5 Nothing works. They break through the smoke-screen for blood.

Always the look-out spots the Indians first,
spread north to south, barring progress.
The Sioux, or Cheyenne, or some bunch

---

[1] Emmett Till, a fourteen-year-old black youth from Chicago, was visiting relatives in Mississippi in 1955 when he made what he thought was an innocent remark to a white woman. Several days later his body was found in the river with a heavy cotton gin fan tied around his neck with barbed wire.

in spectacular columns, arranged like SAC missiles,
10 their feathers bristling in the meaningful sunset.

The drum breaks. There will be no parlance.
Only the arrows whining, a death-cloud of nerves
swarming down on the settlers
who die beautifully, tumbling like dust weeds
15 into the history that brought us all here
together: this wide screen beneath the sign of the bear.

The sky fills, acres of blue squint and eye
that the crowd cheers. His face moves over us,
a thick cloud of vengeance, pitted
20 like the land that was once flesh. Each rut,
each scar makes a promise: *It is
not over, this fight, not as long as you resist.*

Everything we see belongs to us.
A few laughing Indians fall over the hood
25 slipping in the hot spilled butter.
*The eye sees a lot, John, but the heart is so blind.
How will you know what you own?*
He smiles, a horizon of teeth
the credits reel over, and then the white fields
30 again blowing in the true-to-life dark.
The dark films over everything.
We get into the car
scratching our mosquito bites, speechless and small
as people are when the movie is done.
35 We are back in ourselves.

How can we help but keep hearing his voice,
the flip side of the sound-track, still playing:
*Come on, boys, we've got them
where we want them, drunk, running.*
40 *They will give us what we want, what we need:
The heart is a strange wood inside of everything
we see, burning, doubling, splitting out of its skin.*

ROBERT FRANCIS
(1901–   )

Pitcher
(1953)

His art is eccentricity, his aim
How not to hit the mark he seems to aim at,

His passion how to avoid the obvious,
His technique how to vary the avoidance.

5 The others throw to be comprehended. He
Throws to be a moment misunderstood.

Yet not too much. Not errant, arrant, wild,
But every seeming aberration willed.

Not to, yet still, still to communicate
10 Making the batter understand too late.

ROBERT FROST
(1874–1963)

Acquainted with the Night
(1928)

I have been one acquainted with the night.
I have walked out in rain—and back in rain.
I have outwalked the furthest city light.

I have looked down the saddest city lane.
5 I have passed by the watchman on his beat
And dropped my eyes, unwilling to explain.

I have stood still and stopped the sound of feet
When far away an interrupted cry
Came over houses from another street,

10 But not to call me back or say good-by;
And further still at an unearthly height,
One luminary clock against the sky

Proclaimed the time was neither wrong nor right.
I have been one acquainted with the night.

Birches
(1915)

When I see birches bend to left and right
Across the lines of straighter darker trees,
I like to think some boy's been swinging them.

But swinging doesn't bend them down to stay
5 As ice-storms do. Often you must have seen them
Loaded with ice a sunny winter morning
After a rain. They click upon themselves
As the breeze rises, and turn many-colored
As the stir cracks and crazes their enamel.
10 Soon the sun's warmth makes them shed crystal shells
Shattering and avalanching on the snow-crust—
Such heaps of broken glass to sweep away
You'd think the inner dome of heaven had fallen.
They are dragged to the withered bracken by the load,
15 And they seem not to break; though once they are bowed
So low for long, they never right themselves:
You may see their trunks arching in the woods
Years afterwards, trailing their leaves on the ground
Like girls on hands and knees that throw their hair
20 Before them over their heads to dry in the sun.
But I was going to say when Truth broke in
With all her matter-of-fact about the ice-storm
I should prefer to have some boy bend them
As he went out and in to fetch the cows—
25 Some boy too far from town to learn baseball,
Whose only play was what he found himself,
Summer or winter, and could play alone.
One by one he subdued his father's trees
By riding them down over and over again
30 Until he took the stiffness out of them,
And not one but hung limp, not one was left
For him to conquer. He learned all there was
To learn about not launching out too soon
And so not carrying the tree away
35 Clear to the ground. He always kept his poise
To the top branches, climbing carefully
With the same pains you use to fill a cup
Up to the brim, and even above the brim.
Then he flung outward, feet first, with a swish,
40 Kicking his way down through the air to the ground.
So was I once myself a swinger of birches.
And so I dream of going back to be.
It's when I'm weary of considerations,
And life is too much like a pathless wood
45 Where your face burns and tickles with the cobwebs
Broken across it, and one eye is weeping
From a twig's having lashed across it open.
I'd like to get away from earth awhile
And then come back to it and begin over.
50 May no fate willfully misunderstand me

And half grant what I wish and snatch me away
Not to return. Earth's the right place for love:
I don't know where it's likely to go better.
I'd like to go by climbing a birch tree,
55 And climb black branches up a snow-white trunk
Toward Heaven, till the tree could bear no more,
But dipped its top and set me down again.
That would be good both going and coming back.
One could do worse than be a swinger of birches.

Mending Wall
(1914)

Something there is that doesn't love a wall,
That sends the frozen-ground-swell under it,
And spills the upper boulders in the sun;
And makes gaps even two can pass abreast.
5 The work of hunters is another thing:
I have come after them and made repair
Where they have left not one stone on a stone,
But they would have the rabbit out of hiding,
To please the yelping dogs. The gaps I mean,
10 No one has seen them made or heard them made,
But at spring mending-time we find them there.
I let my neighbor know beyond the hill;
And on a day we meet to walk the line
And set the wall between us once again.
15 We keep the wall between us as we go.
To each the boulders that have fallen to each.
And some are loaves and some so nearly balls
We have to use a spell to make them balance:
"Stay where you are until our backs are turned!"
20 We wear our fingers rough with handling them.
Oh, just another kind of outdoor game,
One on a side. It comes to little more:
There where it is we do not need the wall:
He is all pine and I am apple orchard.
25 My apple trees will never get across
And eat the cones under his pines, I tell him.
He only says, "Good fences make good neighbors."
Spring is the mischief in me, and I wonder
If I could put a notion in his head:
30 "*Why* do they make good neighbors? Isn't it
Where there are cows? But here there are no cows.
Before I built a wall I'd ask to know
What I was walling in or walling out,
And to whom I was like to give offense.

35 Something there is that doesn't love a wall,
That wants it down." I could say "Elves" to him,
But it's not elves exactly, and I'd rather
He said it for himself. I see him there
Bringing a stone grasped firmly by the top
40 In each hand, like an old-stone savage armed.
He moves in darkness as it seems to me,
Not of woods only and the shade of trees.
He will not go behind his father's saying,
And he likes having thought of it so well
45 He says again, "Good fences make good neighbors."

The Road Not Taken
(1915)

Two roads diverged in a yellow wood,
And sorry I could not travel both
And be one traveler, long I stood
And looked down one as far as I could
5 To where it bent in the undergrowth;

Then took the other, as just as fair,
And having perhaps the better claim,
Because it was grassy and wanted wear;
Though as for that the passing there
10 Had worn them really about the same,

And both that morning equally lay
In leaves no step had trodden black.
Oh, I kept the first for another day!
Yet knowing how way leads on to way,
15 I doubted if I should ever come back.

I shall be telling this with a sigh
Somewhere ages and ages hence:
Two roads diverged in a wood, and I—
I took the one less traveled by,
20 And that has made all the difference.

Stopping by Woods on a Snowy Evening
(1923)

Whose woods these are I think I know.
His house is in the village though;
He will not see me stopping here
To watch his woods fill up with snow.

5 My little horse must think it queer
To stop without a farmhouse near
Between the woods and frozen lake
The darkest evening of the year.

He gives his harness bells a shake
10 To ask if there is some mistake.
The only other sound's the sweep
Of easy wind and downy flake.

The woods are lovely, dark and deep,
But I have promises to keep,
15 And miles to go before I sleep,
And miles to go before I sleep.

NIKKI GIOVANNI
(1943–   )

Nikki-Rosa
(1968)

childhood remembrances are always a drag
if you're Black
you always remember things like living in Woodlawn[1]
with no inside toilet
5 and if you become famous or something
they never talk about how happy you were to have your mother
all to yourself and
how good the water felt when you got your bath from one of those
big tubs that folk in chicago barbecue in
10 and somehow when you talk about home
it never gets across how much you
understood their feelings
as the whole family attended meetings about Hollydale
and even though you remember
15 your biographers never understand
your father's pain as he sells his stock
and another dream goes
and though you're poor it isn't poverty that
concerns you
20 and though they fought a lot

---

[1] A predominantly black suburb of Cincinnati, Ohio.

it isn't your father's drinking that makes any difference
but only that everybody is together and you
and your sister have happy birthdays and very good christmasses
and I really hope no white person ever has cause to write about me
25 because they never understand Black love is Black wealth and they'll
probably talk about my hard childhood and never understand that
all the while I was quite happy

THOMAS GRAY
(1716–1771)

Elegy Written in a Country Churchyard
(1753)

    The curfew tolls the knell of parting day,
        The lowing herd wind slowly o'er the lea,
    The plowman homeward plods his weary way,
        And leaves the world to darkness and to me.

5 Now fades the glimmering landscape on the sight,
        And all the air a solemn stillness holds,
    Save where the beetle wheels his droning flight,
        And drowsy tinklings lull the distant folds;

    Save that from yonder ivy-mantled tower
10   The moping owl does to the moon complain
    Of such, as wand'ring near her secret bower,
        Molest her ancient solitary reign.

    Beneath those rugged elms, that yew tree's shade,
        Where heaves the turf in many a mold'ring heap,
15 Each in his narrow cell forever laid,
        The rude[1] forefathers of the hamlet sleep.

    The breezy call of incense-breathing morn,
        The swallow twitt'ring from the straw-built shed,
    The cock's shrill clarion, or the echoing horn[2]
20   No more shall rouse them from their lowly bed.

    For them no more the blazing hearth shall burn,
        Or busy housewife ply her evening care;

---

[1] Simple.

[2] Of the fox-hunters.

No children run to lisp their sire's return,
    Or climb his knees the envied kiss to share.

25 Oft did the harvest to their sickle yield,
    Their furrow oft the stubborn glebe[3] has broke;
How jocund did they drive their team afield!
    How bowed the woods beneath their sturdy stroke!

Let not Ambition mock their useful toil,
30   Their homely joys, and destiny obscure;
Nor Grandeur hear with a disdainful smile
    The short and simple annals of the poor.

The boast of heraldry[4] the pomp of pow'r,
    And all that beauty, all that wealth e'er gave,
35 Awaits alike th' inevitable hour.
    The paths of glory lead but to the grave.

Nor you, ye proud, impute to these the fault,
    If Mem'ry o'er their tomb no trophies raise,
Where through the long-drawn aisle and fretted[5] vault
40   The pealing anthem swells the note of praise.

Can storied urn or animated bust
    Back to its mansion call the fleeting breath?
Can Honor's voice provoke the silent dust,
    Or Flatt'ry soothe the dull cold ear of Death?

45 Perhaps in this neglected spot is laid
    Some heart once pregnant with celestial fire;
Hands that the rod of empire might have swayed,
    Or waked to ecstasy the living lyre.

But knowledge to their eyes her ample page
50   Rich with the spoils of time did ne'er unroll;
Chill Penury[6] repressed their noble rage,
    And froze the genial current of the soul.

Full many a gem of purest ray serene,
    The dark unfathomed caves of ocean bear:

---

[3] Sod.

[4] Nobility.

[5] Inlaid with designs.

[6] Poverty.

55 Full many a flower is born to blush unseen,
      And waste its sweetness on the desert air.

Some village Hampden,[7] that with dauntless breast
      The little tyrant of his field withstood;
Some mute inglorious Milton[8] here may rest,
60   Some Cromwell,[9] guiltless of his country's blood.

Th' applause of list'ning senates to command,
      The threats of pain and ruin to despise,
To scatter plenty o'er a smiling land,
      And read their hist'ry in a nation's eyes,

65 Their lot forbade; nor circumscribed alone
      Their growing virtues, but their crimes confined;
Forbade to wade through slaughter to a throne,
      And shut the gates of mercy on mankind,

The struggling pangs of conscious truth to hide,
70   To quench the blushes of ingenuous[10] shame,
Or heap the shrine of Luxury and Pride
      With incense kindled at the Muse's[11] flame.

Far from the madding[12] crowd's ignoble strife,
      Their sober wishes never learned to stray;
75 Along the cool sequestered vale of life
      They kept the noiseless tenor of their way.

Yet ev'n these bones from insult to protect
      Some frail memorial still erected nigh,

---

[7] John Hampden (1594–1643), English statesman, cousin of Oliver Cromwell and popular hero of the parliamentarians after his arrest by Charles I in 1642, helped begin the civil war.

[8] John Milton (1608–1674), British poet.

[9] Oliver Cromwell (1599–1658), English statesman, Lord Protector of England (1653–1658). Cromwell first attempted to reconcile differences among Charles I, Parliament, and the army; following the king's defeat in 1648, Cromwell subjugated the Irish and invaded Scotland to defeat Charles II. He established the Protectorate (1653) but ultimately failed to find constitutional grounds for his rule. Despite his genius and forceful character, Cromwell was forced by the necessities of governing to commit many acts that can only be described as cruel and intolerant.

[10] Innocent.

[11] In Greek mythology, any of the nine daughters of Mnemosyne and Zeus, each of whom presided over a different art or science.

[12] Frenzied.

With uncouth rhymes and shapeless sculpture decked,
    Implores the passing tribute of a sigh.

Their name, their years, spelt by th' unlettered Muse,
    The place of fame and elegy supply:
And many a holy text around she strews,
    That teach the rustic moralist to die.

For who to dumb Forgetfulness a prey,
    This pleasing anxious being e'er resigned,
Left the warm precincts of the cheerful day,
    Nor cast one longing ling'ring look behind?

On some fond breast the parting soul relies,
    Some pious drops the closing eye requires;
Ev'n from the tomb the voice of Nature cries,
    Ev'n in our ashes live their wonted fires.

For thee, who mindful of th' unhonored dead
    Dost in these lines their artless tale relate;
If chance[13] by lonely contemplation led,
    Some kindred spirit shall inquire thy fate,

Haply[14] some hoary-headed swain[15] may say,
    "Oft have we seen him at the peep of dawn
Brushing with hasty steps the dews away
    To meet the sun upon the upland lawn.

"There at the foot of yonder nodding beech
    That wreathes its old fantastic roots so high,
His listless length at noontide would he stretch,
    And pore upon the brook that babbles by.

"Hard by yon wood, now smiling as in scorn,
    Mutt'ring his wayward fancies he would rove,
Now drooping, woeful wan, like one forlorn,
    Or crazed with care, or crossed in hopeless love.

"One morn I missed him, on the customed hill,
    Along the heath and near his fav'rite tree;
Another came; not yet beside the rill,[16]
    Nor up the lawn, nor at the wood was he;

---

[13] If by chance.

[14] Perhaps.

[15] Gray-haired shepherd.

[16] Brook.

"The next with dirges due in sad array
        Slow through the churchway path we saw him borne.
115 Approach and read (for thou canst read) the lay,[17]
        Graved on the stone beneath yon aged thorn."

The Epitaph

Here rests his head upon the lap of Earth
        A youth to Fortune and to Fame unknown.
Fair Science[18] *frowned not on his humble birth,*
120   *And Melancholy marked him for her own.*

Large was his bounty, and his soul sincere,
        Heav'n did a recompense as largely send:
He gave to Mis'ry all he had, a tear,
        He gained from Heav'n ('twas all he wished) a friend.

125 *No farther seek his merits to disclose,*
        Or draw his frailties from their dread abode,
(There they alike in trembling hope repose),
        The bosom of His Father and his God.

THOMAS HARDY
(1840–1928)

Channel Firing
(1914)

That night your great guns, unawares,
Shook all our coffins[1] as we lay,
And broke the chancel window-squares,
We thought it was the Judgment Day

5 And sat upright. While drearisome
Arose the howl of wakened hounds:
The mouse let fall the altar-crumb,
The worms drew back into the mounds,

---

[17] Song, poem.

[18] Knowledge.

---

[1] For centuries, it has been the practice in England to bury people under the flooring or in the basements of churches.

The glebe[2] cow drooled. Till God called, "No;
It's gunnery practice out at sea
Just as before you went below;
The world is as it used to be:

"All nations striving strong to make
Red war yet redder. Mad as hatters
They do no more for Christés sake
Than you who are helpless in such matters.

"That this is not the judgment hour
For some of them's a blessed thing,
For if it were they'd have to scour
Hell's floor for so much threatening. . . .

"Ha, ha. It will be warmer when
I blow the trumpet (if indeed
I ever do; for you are men,
And rest eternal sorely need)."

So down we lay again. "I wonder,
Will the world ever saner be,"
Said one, "than when He sent us under
In our indifferent century!"

And many a skeleton shook his head.
"Instead of preaching forty year,"
My neighbor Parson Thirdly said,
"I wish I had stuck to pipes and beer."

Again the guns disturbed the hour,
Roaring their readiness to avenge,
As far inland as Stourton Tower.[3]
And Camelot,[4] and starlit Stonehenge.[5]

---

[2] A small field.

[3] Erected in the eighteenth century in Wiltshire, England, to commemorate King Alfred the Great's defeat of the Danes in 878.

[4] Legendary site of King Arthur's court.

[5] A group of stones on Salisbury Plain, believed by many, including Hardy, to be the site of ancient druidic rituals.

ROBERT HAYDEN
(1913–   )

Homage to the Empress of the Blues[1]
(1966)

Because there was a man somewhere in a candystripe silk shirt,
gracile and dangerous as a jaguar and because a woman moaned
for him in sixty-watt gloom and mourned him Faithless Love
Twotiming Love Oh Love Oh Careless Aggravating Love,

5   She came out on the stage in yards of pearls, emerging like
    a favorite scenic view, flashed her golden smile and sang.

Because grey laths began somewhere to show from underneath
torn hurdygurdy lithographs of dollfaced heaven;
and because there were those who feared alarming fists of snow
10 on the door and those who feared the riot-squad of statistics,

    She came out on the stage in ostrich feathers, beaded satin,
    and shone that smile on us and sang.

LINDA HOGAN
(1947–   )

Heritage
(1979)

From my mother, the antique mirror
where I watch my face take on her lines.
She left me the smell of baking bread
to warm fine hairs in my nostrils,
5 she left the large white breasts that weigh down
my body.

From my father I take his brown eyes,
the plague of locusts that leveled our crops,
they flew in formation like buzzards.

10 From my uncle the whittled wood
that rattles like bones

---

[1] An epitaph for Bessie Smith, American jazz singer, 1894–1937.

and is white
and smells like all our old houses
that are no longer there. He was the man
15 who sang old chants to me, the words
my father was told not to remember.

From my grandfather who never spoke
I learned to fear silence.
I learned to kill a snake
20 when you're begging for rain.

And grandmother, blue-eyed woman
whose skin was brown,
she used snuff.
When her coffee can full of black saliva
25 spilled on me
it was like the brown cloud of grasshoppers
that leveled her fields.
It was the brown stain
that covered my white shirt,
30 my whiteness a shame.
That sweet black liquid like the food
she chewed up and spit into my father's mouth
when he was an infant.
It was the brown earth of Oklahoma
35 stained with oil
She said tobacco would purge your body of poisons.
It has more medicine than stones and knives
against your enemies.

That tobacco is the dark night that covers me.
40 She said it is wise to eat the flesh of deer
so you will be swift and travel over many miles.
She told me how our tribe has always followed a stick
that pointed west
that pointed east.
45 From my family I have learned the secrets
of never having a home.

GARRETT KAORU HONGO
(1951–   )

The Hongo Store
29 Miles Volcano
Hilo, Hawaii
(1982)

From a Photograph

My parents felt those rumblings
Coming deep from the earth's belly,
Thudding like the bell of the Buddhist Church.
Tremors in the ground swayed the bathinette
5 Where I lay squalling in soapy water.

My mother carried me around the house,
Back through the orchids, ferns, and plumeria
Of that greenhouse world behind the store,
And jumped between gas pumps into the car.

10 My father gave it the gun
And said, "Be quiet," as he searched
The frequencies, flipping for the right station
(The radio squealing more loudly than I could cry).

And then even the echoes stopped—
15 The only sound the Edsel's grinding
And the bark and crackle of radio news
Saying stay home or go to church.

"Dees time she no blow!"
My father said, driving back
20 Over the red ash covering the road.
"I worried she went go for broke already!"

So in this print the size of a matchbook,
The dark skinny man, shirtless and grinning,
A toothpick in the corner of his smile,
25 Lifts a naked baby above his head—
Behind him the plate glass of the store only cracked.

GERARD MANLEY HOPKINS
(1844–1889)

God's Grandeur
(1877)

    The world is charged with the grandeur of God.
        It will flame out, like shining from shook foil;
        It gathers to a greatness, like the ooze of oil
    Crushed. Why do men then now not reck his rod?
5   Generations have trod, have trod, have trod;
        And all is seared with trade; bleared, smeared with toil;
        And wears man's smudge and shares man's smell: the soil
    Is bare now, nor can foot feel, being shod.
    And for all this, nature is never spent;
10   There lives the dearest freshness deep down things;
    And though the last lights off the black West went
        Oh, morning, at the brown brink eastward, springs—
    Because the Holy Ghost over the bent
        World broods with warm breast and with ah! bright wings.

The Windhover[1]
(1877)

To Christ Our Lord

    I caught this morning morning's minion,[2] kingdom of daylight's
        dauphin, dapple-dawn-drawn Falcon, in his riding
        Of the rolling level underneath him steady air, and striding
    High there, how he rung upon the rein[3] of a wimpling[4] wing
5   In his ecstasy! then off, off forth on swing,
        As a skate's heel sweeps smooth on a bow-bend: the hurl and gliding
        Rebuffed the big wind. My heart in hiding
    Stirred for a bird,—the achieve of, the mastery of the thing!
    Brute beauty and valor and act, oh, air, pride, plume, here
10   Buckle! and the fire that breaks from thee then, a billion
    Times told lovelier, more dangerous, O my chevalier!

---

[1] The kestrel, a European falcon, so called for its ability to hover in the air with its head to the wind.

[2] Favorite.

[3] A horse is "rung upon the rein" when it circles at the end of a long rein held by the trainer.

[4] Rippling.

No wonder of it: shéer plód, makes plow down sillion[5]
Shine, and blue-bleak embers, ah my dear,
Fall, gall themselves, and gash gold-vermilion.

A. E. HOUSMAN
(1859–1936)

Terence, This Is Stupid Stuff
(1896)

"Terence,[1] this is stupid stuff:
You eat your victuals fast enough;
There can't be much amiss, 'tis clear,
To see the rate you drink your beer.
5 But oh, good Lord, the verse you make,
It gives a chap the belly-ache.
The cow, the old cow, she is dead;
It sleeps well, the horned head:
We poor lads, 'tis our turn now
10 To hear such tunes as killed the cow.
Pretty friendship 'tis to rhyme
Your friends to death before their time
Moping melancholy mad:
Come, pipe a tune to dance to, lad."

15   Why, if 'tis dancing you would be,
There's brisker pipes than poetry.
Say, for what were hop-yards meant,
Or why was Burton built on Trent?
Oh many a peer of England brews
20 Livelier liquor than the Muse,[2]
And malt does more than Milton can
To justify God's ways to man.[3]

---

[5] The ridge between two furrows.

---

[1] The original title of Housman's *A Shropshire Lad* was *The Poems of Terence Hearsay*. Terence was a Roman poet, author of satiric comedies; here, Terence is used as the poet's name for himself.

[2] The lines here compare the Muses, mythological figures who inspire artists, with the products of the breweries of Burton-on-Trent. (Many of the brewery owners were named "peers of England"—that is, dukes, earls, viscounts, barons, or marquis.)

[3] Alludes to Milton's promise in *Paradise Lost* (I:17–26) to "justify the ways of God to men."

Ale, man, ale's the stuff to drink
For fellows whom it hurts to think:
25 Look into the pewter pot
To see the world as the world's not.
And faith, 'tis pleasant till 'tis past:
The mischief is that 'twill not last.
Oh I have been to Ludlow[4] fair
30 And left my necktie God knows where,
And carried half-way home, or near,
Pints and quarts of Ludlow beer:
Then the world seemed none so bad,
And I myself a sterling lad;
35 And down in lovely muck I've lain,
Happy till I woke again.
Then I saw the morning sky:
Heigho, the tale was all a lie;
The world, it was the old world yet,
40 I was I, my things were wet,
And nothing now remained to do
But begin the game anew.

Therefore, since the world has still
Much good, but much less good than ill,
45 And while the sun and moon endure
Luck's a chance, but trouble's sure,
I'd face it as a wise man would,
And train for ill and not for good.
'Tis true, the stuff I bring for sale
50 Is not so brisk a brew as ale:
Out of a stem that scored the hand
I wrung it in a weary land.
But take it: if the smack is sour,
The better for the embittered hour;
55 It should do good to heart and head
When your soul is in my soul's stead;
And I will friend you, if I may,
In the dark and cloudy day.

There was a king reigned in the East:
60 There, when kings will sit to feast,
They get their fill before they think
With poisoned meat and poisoned drink.
He gathered all that springs to birth
From the many-venomed earth;

---

[4] A Shropshire town.

⁶⁵ First a little, thence to more,
He sampled all her killing store;
And easy, smiling, seasoned sound,
Sate the king when healths went round.
They put arsenic in his meat
⁷⁰ And stared aghast to watch him eat;
They poured strychnine in his cup
And shook to see him drink it up:
They shook, they stared as white's their shirt:
Them it was their poison hurt.
⁷⁵ —I tell the tale that I heard told.
Mithridates, he died old.[5]

To an Athlete Dying Young
(1896)

The time you won your town the race
We chaired you through the market-place;
Man and boy stood cheering by,
And home we brought you shoulder-high.

⁵ Today, the road all runners come,
Shoulder-high we bring you home,
And set you at your threshold down,
Townsman of a stiller town.

Smart lad, to slip betimes away
¹⁰ From fields where glory does not stay,
And early though the laurel grows
It withers quicker than the rose.

Eyes the shady night has shut
Cannot see the record cut,
¹⁵ And silence sounds no worse than cheers
After earth has stopped the ears.

Now you will not swell the rout
Of lads that wore their honors out,
Runners whom renown outran
²⁰ And the name died before the man.

So set, before its echoes fade,
The fleet foot on the sill of shade,

---

[5] Mithridates VI, a pre-Christian king of Pontus, supposedly took small doses of poison daily to make him immune.

        And hold to the low lintel up
        The still-defended challenge-cup.

25 And round that early-laureled head
    Will flock to gaze the strengthless dead,
    And find unwithered on its curls
    The garland briefer than a girl's.

BEN JONSON
(1573?–1637)

On My First Son
(1603)

    Farewell, thou child of my right hand,[1] and joy.
    My sin was too much hope of thee, loved boy;
    Seven years thou wert lent to me, and I thee pay,
    Exacted by thy fate, on the just day.[2]
5 Oh, could I lose all father now. For why
    Will man lament the state he should envỳ?—
    To have so soon 'scaped world's and flesh's rage,
    And, if no other misery, yet age.
    Rest in soft peace, and asked, say, "Here doth lie
10 Ben Jonson his best piece of poetry,"
    For whose sake henceforth all his vows be such
    As what he loves may never like[3] too much.

To Celia
(1616)

    Drink to me only with thine eyes,
        And I will pledge with mine;
    Or leave a kiss but in the cup,
        And I'll not ask for wine.
5 The thirst that from the soul doth rise
        Doth ask a drink divine;
    But might I of Jove's nectar sup,
        I would not change for thine.

---

[1] Translation of the Hebrew name of Benjamin, Jonson's son.

[2] The very day.

[3] Thrive.

I sent thee late a rosy wreath,
10   Not so much honoring thee
As giving it a hope that there
    It could not withered be.
But thou thereon didst only breathe,
    And sent'st it back to me;
15 Since when it grows, and smells, I swear,
    Not of itself but thee.

DONALD JUSTICE
(1925–   )

On the Death of Friends in Childhood
(1960)

We shall not ever meet them bearded in heaven,
Nor sunning themselves among the bald of hell;
If anywhere, in the deserted schoolyard at twilight,
Forming a ring, perhaps, or joining hands
5 In games whose very names we have forgotten.
Come, memory, let us seek them there in the shadows.

JOHN KEATS
(1795–1821)

La Belle Dame Sans Merci:[1] A Ballad
(1819, 1820)

1

O what can ail thee, knight at arms,
    Alone and palely loitering?
The sedge has wither'd from the lake,
    And no birds sing.

---

[1] The title, which means "The Lovely Lady Without Pity," was taken from a medieval poem by Alain Chartier.

2

    O what can ail thee, knight at arms,
        So haggard and so woe-begone?
    The squirrel's granary is full,
        And the harvest's done.

3

    I see a lily on thy brow
        With anguish moist and fever dew,
    And on thy cheeks a fading rose
        Fast withereth too.

4

    I met a lady in the meads,
        Full beautiful, a fairy's child;
    Her hair was long, her foot was light,
        And her eyes were wild.

5

    I made a garland for her head,
        And bracelets too, and fragrant zone;[2]
    She look'd at me as she did love,
        And made sweet moan.

6

    I set her on my pacing steed,
        And nothing else saw all day long,
    For sidelong would she bend, and sing
        A fairy's song.

7

    She found me roots of relish sweet,
        And honey wild, and manna dew,
    And sure in language strange she said—
        I love thee true.

8

    She took me to her elfin grot,[3]
        And there she wept, and sigh'd full sore,
    And there I shut her wild wild eyes
        With kisses four.

[2] Belt.
[3] Grotto.

9

And there she lullèd me asleep,
    And there I dream'd—Ah! woe betide!
The latest[4] dream I ever dream'd
    On the cold hill's side.

10

I saw pale kings, and princes too,
    Pale warriors, death pale were they all;
They cried—"La belle dame sans merci
    Hath thee in thrall!"

11

I saw their starv'd lips in the gloam[5]
    With horrid warning gapèd wide,
And I awoke and found me here
    On the cold hill's side.

12

And this is why I sojourn here,
    Alone and palely loitering,
Though the sedge is wither'd from the lake,
    And no birds sing.

Ode on a Grecian Urn[1]
(1819, 1820)

1

Thou still unravish'd bride of quietness,
    Thou foster-child of silence and slow time,
Sylvan[2] historian, who canst thus express
A flowery tale more sweetly than our rhyme:
What leaf-fring'd legend haunts about thy shape
    Of deities or mortals, or of both,

---

[4] Last.

[5] Twilight.

---

[1] Though many urns similar to the one Keats describes actually exist, the subject of the poem is purely imaginary.

[2] Pertaining to woods or forests.

In Tempe[3] or the dales of Arcady?[4]
What men or gods are these? What maidens loth?
What mad pursuit? What struggle to escape?
10   What pipes and timbrels? What wild ecstasy?

2

Heard melodies are sweet, but those unheard
 Are sweeter; therefore, ye soft pipes, play on;
Not to the sensual ear, but, more endear'd,
 Pipe to the spirit ditties of no tone:
15 Fair youth, beneath the trees, thou canst not leave
 Thy song, nor ever can those trees be bare;
  Bold lover, never, never canst thou kiss,
Though winning near the goal—yet, do not grieve;
 She cannot fade, though thou hast not thy bliss,
20 For ever wilt thou love, and she be fair!

3

Ah, happy, happy boughs! that cannot shed
 Your leaves, nor ever bid the spring adieu;
And, happy melodist, unwearied,
 For ever piping songs for ever new;
25 More happy love! more happy, happy love!
 For ever warm and still to be enjoy'd,
  For ever panting, and for ever young;
All breathing human passion far above,
 That leaves a heart high-sorrowful and cloy'd,
30 A burning forehead, and a parching tongue.

4

Who are these coming to the sacrifice?
 To what green altar, O mysterious priest,
Lead'st thou that heifer lowing at the skies,
 And all her silken flanks with garlands drest?
35 What little town by river or sea shore,
 Or mountain-built with peaceful citadel,
  Is emptied of this folk, this pious morn?
And, little town, thy streets for evermore
 Will silent be; and not a soul to tell
40 Why thou art desolate, can e'er return.

---

[3] A beautiful valley in Greece.

[4] The valleys of Arcadia, a mountainous region on the Greek peninsula. Like Tempe, they represent a rustic pastoral ideal.

5

O Attic[5] shape! Fair attitude! with brede[6]
    Of marble men and maidens overwrought,[7]
With forest branches and the trodden weed;
    Thou, silent form, dost tease us out of thought
45 As doth eternity: Cold Pastoral!
    When old age shall this generation waste,
        Thou shalt remain, in midst of other woe
Than ours, a friend to man, to whom thou say'st,
"Beauty is truth, truth beauty,"—that is all
50   Ye know on earth, and all ye need to know.

Ode to a Nightingale
(1819)

1

My heart aches, and a drowsy numbness pains
    My sense, as though of hemlock I had drunk,
Or emptied some dull opiate to the drains
    One minute past, and Lethe-wards[1] had sunk:
5 Tis not through envy of thy happy lot,
    But being too happy in thine happiness,—
        That thou, light-winged Dryad[2] of the trees,
        In some melodious plot
Of beechen green, and shadows numberless,
10   Singest of summer in full-throated ease.

2

O, for a draught of vintage! that hath been
    Cool'd a long age in the deep-delved earth,
Tasting of Flora[3] and the country green,
    Dance, and Provençal song,[4] and sunburnt mirth!
15 O for a beaker full of the warm South,

---

[5] Characteristic of Athens or Athenians.

[6] Braid.

[7] Elaborately ornamented.

---

[1] Toward Lethe, the river in Hades whose waters cause forgetfulness.

[2] In Greek mythology, a tree spirit, a wood nymph.

[3] Roman goddess of flowers; also, the flowers themselves.

[4] Provence, in southern France, was famous in medieval times for its troubadors, who wrote and performed love songs.

        Full of the true, the blushful Hippocrene,[5]
            With beaded bubbles winking at the brim,
            And purple-stained mouth;
    That I might drink, and leave the world unseen,
20   And with thee fade away into the forest dim:

3

Fade far away, dissolve, and quite forget
    What thou among the leaves hast never known,
The weariness, the fever, and the fret
    Here, where men sit and hear each other groan;
25 Where palsy shakes a few, sad, last gray hairs,
    Where youth grows pale, and spectre-thin, and dies;
        Where but to think is to be full of sorrow
            And leaden-eyed despairs,
    Where Beauty cannot keep her lustrous eyes,
30   Or new Love pine at them beyond to-morrow.

4

Away! away! for I will fly to thee,
    Not charioted by Bacchus[6] and his pards,
But on the viewless wings of Poesy,
    Though the dull brain perplexes and regards:
35 Already with thee! tender is the night,
    And haply the Queen-Moon is on her throne,
        Cluster'd around by all her starry Fays;[7]
            But here there is no light,
    Save what from heaven is with the breezes blown
40   Through verdurous glooms and winding mossy ways.

5

I cannot see what flowers are at my feet,
    Nor what soft incense hangs upon the boughs,
But, in embalmed[8] darkness, guess each sweet
    Wherewith the seasonable month endows
45 The grass, the thicket, and the fruit-tree wild;
    White hawthorn, and the pastoral eglantine;[9]
        Fast fading violets cover'd up in leaves;
            And mid-May's eldest child,

---

[5] Fountain of the Muses on Mt. Helicon; a source of poetic inspiration.

[6] Greek god of wine.

[7] Fairies.

[8] Perfumed.

[9] Sweetbrier, or honeysuckle.

          The coming musk-rose, full of dewy wine,
50   The murmurous haunt of flies on summer eves.

6

Darkling[10] I listen; and, for many a time
      I have been half in love with easeful Death,
Call'd him soft names in many a mused[11] rhyme,
      To take into the air my quiet breath;
55 Now more than ever seems it rich to die,
      To cease upon the midnight with no pain,
          While thou art pouring forth thy soul abroad
              In such an ecstasy!
   Still wouldst thou sing, and I have ears in vain—
60   To thy high requiem become a sod.

7

Thou wast not born for death, immortal Bird!
      No hungry generations tread thee down;
The voice I hear this passing night was heard
      In ancient days by emperor and clown:
65 Perhaps the self-same song that found a path
      Through the sad heart of Ruth,[12] when, sick for home,
          She stood in tears amid the alien corn;[13]
              The same that oft-times hath
   Charm'd magic casements, opening on the foam
70   Of perilous seas, in faery lands forlorn.

8

Forlorn! the very word is like a bell
      To toll me back from thee to my sole self!
Adieu! the fancy[14] cannot cheat so well
      As she is fam'd to do, deceiving elf.
75 Adieu! adieu! thy plaintive anthem[15] fades
      Past the near meadows, over the still stream,
          Up the hill-side; and now 'tis buried deep
              In the next valley-glades:

---

[10] In the dark.

[11] Meditated.

[12] The widow of Mahlon in the biblical Book of Ruth. She is sad and homesick because she left her home with her mother-in-law to go to Bethlehem. While there she married Boaz, a rich landowner. She was the great-grandmother of King David.

[13] Wheat.

[14] Imagination. Compare "the viewless wings of Poesy," line 33.

[15] Hymn.

Was it a vision, or a waking dream?
Fled is that music:—Do I wake or sleep?

When I Have Fears
(1818)

When I have fears that I may cease to be
   Before my pen has gleaned my teeming brain,
Before high-pilèd books, in charact'ry,[1]
   Hold like rich garners the full-ripened grain;
When I behold, upon the night's starred face,
   Huge cloudy symbols of a high romance,
And think that I may never live to trace
   Their shadows, with the magic hand of chance;
And when I feel, fair creature of an hour,
   That I shall never look upon thee more,
Never have relish in the faery power
   Of unreflecting love!—then on the shore
Of the wide world I stand alone, and think
Till Love and Fame to nothingness do sink.

MAXINE KUMIN
(1925–   )

Morning Swim
(1965)

Into my empty head there come
a cotton beach, a dock wherefrom

I set out, oily and nude
through mist, in chilly solitude.

There was no line, no roof or floor
to tell the water from the air.

Night fog thick as terry cloth
closed me in its fuzzy growth.

I hung my bathrobe on two pegs.
I took the lake between my legs.

[1] Print.

Invaded and invader, I
went overhand on that flat sky.

Fish twitched beneath me, quick and tame.
In their green zone they sang my name

15 and in the rhythm of the swim
I hummed a two-four-time slow hymn.

I hummed *Abide with Me*. The beat
rose in the fine thrash of my feet,

rose in the bubbles I put out
20 slantwise, trailing through my mouth.

My bones drank water; water fell
through all my doors. I was the well

that fed the lake that met my sea
in which I sang *Abide with Me*.

PHILIP LARKIN
(1922–1985)

Aubade
(1977)

    I work all day, and get half-drunk at night.
Waking at four to soundless dark, I stare.
In time the curtain-edges will grow light.
Till then I see what's really always there:
5 Unresting death, a whole day nearer now,
Making all thought impossible but how
And where and when I shall myself die.
Arid interrogation: yet the dread
Of dying, and being dead,
10 Flashes afresh to hold and horrify.

    The mind blanks at the glare. Not in remorse
—The good not done, the love not given, time
Torn off unused—nor wretchedly because
An only life can take so long to climb
15 Clear of its wrong beginnings, and may never;
But at the total emptiness for ever,
The sure extinction that we travel to

And shall be lost in always. Not to be here,
Not to be anywhere,
20 And soon; nothing more terrible, nothing more true.

This is a special way of being afraid
No trick dispels. Religion used to try,
That vast moth-eaten musical brocade
Created to pretend we never die,
25 And specious stuff that says *No rational being
Can fear a thing it will not feel,* not seeing
That this is what we fear—no sight, no sound,
No touch or taste or smell, nothing to think with,
Nothing to love or link with,
30 The anaesthetic from which none come round.

And so it stays just on the edge of vision,
A small unfocused blur, a standing chill
That slows each impulse down to indecision.
Most things may never happen: this one will,
35 And realization of it rages out
In furnace-fear when we are caught without
People or drink. Courage is no good:
It means not scaring others. Being brave
Lets no one off the grave.
40 Death is no different whined at than withstood.

Slowly light strengthens, and the room takes shape.
It stands plain as a wardrobe, what we know,
Have always known, know that we can't escape,
Yet can't accept. One side will have to go.
45 Meanwhile telephones crouch, getting ready to ring
In locked-up offices, and all the uncaring
Intricate rented world begins to rouse.
The sky is white as clay, with no sun.
Work has to be done.
50 Postmen like doctors go from house to house.

DENISE LEVERTOV
(1923–   )

What Were They Like?
(1966)

1) Did the people of Viet Nam
    use lanterns of stone?

2) Did they hold ceremonies
      to reverence the opening of buds?
   3) Were they inclined to rippling laughter?
   4) Did they use bone and ivory,
      jade and silver, for ornament?
   5) Had they an epic poem?
   6) Did they distinguish between speech and singing?

   1) Sir, their light hearts turned to stone.
      It is not remembered whether in gardens
      stone lanterns illumined pleasant ways.
   2) Perhaps they gathered once to delight in blossom,
      but after the children were killed
      there were no more buds.
   3) Sir, laughter is bitter to the burned mouth.
   4) A dream ago, perhaps. Ornament is for joy.
      All the bones were charred.
   5) It is not remembered. Remember,
      most were peasants; their life
      was in rice and bamboo.
      When peaceful clouds were reflected in the paddies
      and the water buffalo stepped surely along terraces,
      maybe fathers told their sons old tales.
      When bombs smashed the mirrors
      there was time only to scream.
   6) There is an echo yet, it is said,
      of their speech which was like a song.
      It is reported their singing resembled
      the flight of moths in moonlight.
      Who can say? It is silent now.

STEPHEN SHU-NING LIU
(1930–   )

My Father's Martial Art
(1982)

When he came home Mother said he looked
like a monk and stank of green fungus.
At the fireside he told us about life
at the monastery: his rock pillow,
his cold bath, his steel-bar lifting
and his wood-chopping. He didn't see
a woman for three winters, on Mountain O Mei.

"My Master was both light and heavy.
He skipped over treetops like a squirrel.
10 Once he stood on a chair, one foot tied
to a rope. We four pulled; we couldn't
move him a bit. His kicks could split
a cedar's trunk."

I saw Father break into a pumpkin
15 with his fingers. I saw him drop a hawk
with bamboo arrows. He rose before dawn, filled
our backyard with a harsh sound *hah, hah, hah*:
there was his Black Dragon Sweep, his Crane Stand,
his Mantis Walk, his Tiger Leap, his Cobra Coil . . .
20 Infrequently he taught me tricks and made me
fight the best of all the village boys.

From a busy street I brood over high cliffs
on O Mei, where my father and his Master sit:
shadows spread across their faces as the smog
25 between us deepens into a funeral pyre.
But don't retreat into night, my father.
Come down from the cliffs. Come
with a single Black Dragon Sweep and hush
this oncoming traffic with your *hah, hah, hah.*

ROBERT LOWELL
(1917–1977)

For the Union Dead
(1959)

*"Relinquunt omnia
servare rem publicam."*[1]

The old South Boston Aquarium stands
in a Sahara of snow now. Its broken windows are boarded.
The bronze weathervane cod has lost half its scales.
The airy tanks are dry.

---

[1] "They gave up everything to preserve the Republic." A monument in Boston Common bears a similar form of this quotation. Designed by Augustus Saint-Gaudens, the monument is dedicated to Colonel Robert Gould Shaw and the African-American troops he commanded during a Civil War battle at Fort Wagner, South Carolina, on July 18, 1863.

Once my nose crawled like a snail on the glass;
my hand tingled
to burst the bubbles
drifting from the noses of the cowed, compliant fish.

My hand draws back. I often sigh still
for the dark downward and vegetating kingdom
of the fish and reptile. One morning last March,
I pressed against the new barbed and galvanized

fence on the Boston Common. Behind their cage,
yellow dinosaur steamshovels were grunting
as they cropped up tons of mush and grass
to gouge their underworld garage.

Parking spaces luxuriate like civic
sandpiles in the heart of Boston.
A girdle of orange, Puritan-pumpkin colored girders
braces the tingling Statehouse,

shaking over the excavations, as it faces Colonel Shaw
and his bell-cheeked Negro infantry
on St. Gauden's shaking Civil War relief,
propped by a plank splint against the garage's earthquake.

Two months after marching through Boston,
half the regiment was dead;
at the dedication,
William James[2] could almost hear the bronze Negroes breathe.

Their monument sticks like a fishbone
in the city's throat.
Its Colonel is as lean
as a compass-needle.

He has an angry wrenlike vigilance,
a greyhound's gentle tautness;
he seems to wince at pleasure,
and suffocate for privacy.

He is out of bounds now. He rejoices in man's lovely,
peculiar power to choose life and death—
when he leads his black soldiers to death,
he cannot bend his back.

[2] Harvard psychologist and philosopher (1842–1910).

On a thousand small town New England greens,
the old white churches hold their air
of sparse, sincere rebellion; frayed flags
quilt the graveyards of the Grand Army of the Republic.

45 The stone statues of the abstract Union Soldier
grow slimmer and younger each year—
wasp-waisted, they doze over muskets
and muse through their sideburns . . .

Shaw's father wanted no monument
50 except the ditch,
where his son's body was thrown
and lost with his "niggers."

The ditch is nearer.
There are no statues for the last war here;
55 on Boylston Street, a commercial photograph
shows Hiroshima boiling

ever a Mosler Safe,[3] the "Rock of Ages"
that survived the blast. Space is nearer.
When I crouch to my television set,
60 the drained faces of Negro school-children rise like balloons.

Colonel Shaw
is riding on his bubble,
he waits
for the blessed break.

65 The Aquarium is gone. Everywhere,
giant finned cars nose forward like fish;
a savage servility
slides by on grease.

CHRISTOPHER MARLOWE
(1564–1593)

The Passionate Shepherd to His Love
(1600)

Come live with me and be my love,
And we will all the pleasures prove

---

[3] A brand of safe known for being especially strong.

That valleys, groves, hills, and fields,
Woods, or steepy mountain yields.

5 And we will sit upon the rocks,
Seeing the shepherds feed their flocks
By shallow rivers, to whose falls
Melodious birds sing madrigals.

And I will make thee beds of roses
10 And a thousand fragrant posies,
A cap of flowers and a kirtle[1]
Embroidered all with leaves of myrtle;

A gown made of the finest wool
Which from our pretty lambs we pull;
15 Fair-linèd slippers for the cold,
With buckles of the purest gold;

A belt of straw and ivy buds,
With coral clasps and amber studs.
And if these pleasures may thee move,
20 Come live with me and be my love.

The shepherds' swains shall dance and sing
For thy delight each May morning.
If these delights thy mind may move,
Then live with me and be my love.

CLAUDE McKAY
(1890–1948)

If We Must Die
(1922)

If we must die, let it not be like hogs
Hunted and penned in an inglorious spot,
While round us bark the mad and hungry dogs,
Making their mock at our accursed lot.
5 If we must die, O let us nobly die,
So that our precious blood may not be shed
In vain; then even the monsters we defy
Shall be constrained to honor us though dead!

---

[1] Skirt.

O kinsmen! we must meet the common foe!
10 Though far outnumbered let us show us brave,
And for their thousand blows deal one deathblow!
What though before us lies the open grave?
Like men we'll face the murderous, cowardly pack,
Pressed to the wall, dying, but fighting back!

EDNA ST. VINCENT MILLAY
(1892–1950)

What Lips My Lips Have Kissed
(1923)

What lips my lips have kissed, and where, and why,
I have forgotten, and what arms have lain
Under my head till morning; but the rain
Is full of ghosts tonight, that tap and sigh
5 Upon the glass and listen for reply,
And in my heart there stirs a quiet pain
For unremembered lads that not again
Will turn to me at midnight with a cry.
Thus in the winter stands the lonely tree,
10 Nor knows what birds have vanished one by one,
Yet knows its boughs more silent than before:
I cannot say what loves have come and gone,
I only know that summer sang in me
A little while, that in me sings no more.

JOHN MILTON
(1608–1674)

When I Consider How My Light Is Spent[1]
(1655?)

When I consider how my light is spent,
   Ere half my days in this dark world and wide,

---

[1] A meditation on his blindness.

      And that one talent[2] which is death to hide
      Lodged with me useless, though my soul more bent
5 To serve therewith my Maker, and present
      My true account, lest He returning chide;
      "Doth God exact day-labor, light denied?"
I fondly[3] ask. But Patience, to prevent
That murmur, soon replies, "God doth not need
10   Either man's work or His own gifts. Who best
      Bear His mild yoke, they serve Him best. His state
Is kingly: thousands at His bidding speed,
      And post o'er land and ocean without rest;
      They also serve who only stand and wait."

JANICE MIRIKITANI
(1942–   )

Breaking Silence
(1981)

After forty years of silence about the experience of Japanese Americans in World War II concentration camps, my mother testified before the Commission on Wartime Relocation and Internment of Japanese American Civilians in 1981.

(Quoted excerpts from my mother's testimony, modified with her permission)

For my mother

There are miracles that happen
she said.
From the silences
in the glass caves of our ears,
5 from the crippled tongue,
from the mute, wet eyelash,
testimonies waiting like winter.
    We were told
that silence was better
10 golden like our skin,
    useful like
go quietly,

---

[2] See Jesus' parable of the talents in Matthew 25:14–30.

[3] Foolishly.

            easier like
don't make waves,
15   expedient like
horsestalls and deserts.

                    "Mr. Commissioner. . .
                    . . . the U.S. Army Signal Corps confiscated
                    our property. . . it was subjected to
20   vandalism and ravage. All improvements
                    we had made before our incarceration
                    was stolen or destroyed. . .
                    I was coerced into signing documents
                    giving you authority to take. . . "
25   to take
                    to take.

My mother,
soft as tallow,
words peeling from her
30 like slivers of yellow flame.
Her testimony,
a vat of boiling water
surging through the coldest
bluest vein.
35   She had come to her land
as shovel, hoe and sickle searing
reed and rock and dead brush
labored to sinew the ground
to soften gardens pregnant with seed
40 awaiting each silent morning
birthing
fields of flowers,
mustard greens and tomatoes
throbbing like the sea.
45   And then
All was hushed for announcements:
        "Take only what you can carry. . . "
We were made to believe our faces
betrayed us.
50 Our bodies were loud
with yellow screaming flesh
needing to be silenced
behind barbed wire.

                    "Mr. Commissioner. . .
55   . . . it seems we were singled out
                    from others who were under suspicion.

Our neighbors were of German and
Italian descent, some of whom were
not citizens. . . It seems we were
singled out. . . "

She had worn her work
like lemon leaves,
shining in her sweat,
driven by her dreams that honed
the blade of her plow.
The land she built
like hope
grew quietly
irises, roses, sweet peas
opening, opening.
    And then
all was hushed for announcements:
    ". . . to be incarcerated for your own good"
The sounds of her work
bolted in barracks. . .
silenced.

Mr. Commissioner. . .
So when you tell me I must limit
testimony,
when you tell me my time is up,
I tell you this:
Pride has kept my lips
pinned by nails
my rage coffined.
But I exhume my past
to claim this time.
My youth is buried in Rohwer,[1]
Obachan's ghost visits Amache Gate.[1]
My niece haunts Tule Lake.[1]
Words are better than tears,
so I spill them.
I kill this,
the silence. . .

There are miracles that happen
she said,
and everything is made visible.
    We see the cracks and fissures in our soil:
We speak of suicides and intimacies,

---

[1] During World War II, Japanese-Americans were interned at these places.

of longings lush like wet furrows,
100 of oceans bearing us toward imagined riches,
of burning humiliations and
crimes by the government.
Of self hate and of love that breaks
through silences.
105   We are lightning and justice.
    Our souls become transparent like glass
revealing tears for war-dead sons
red ashes of Hiroshima
jagged wounds from barbed wire.
110   We must recognize ourselves at last.
    We are a rainforest of color
and noise.
    We hear everything.
    We are unafraid.

115   Our language is beautiful.

N. SCOTT MOMADAY
(1934–   )

Earth and I Gave You Turquoise
(1975)

Earth and I gave you turquoise
    when you walked singing
We lived laughing in my house
    and told old stories
5 You grew ill when the owl cried
We will meet on Black Mountain

I will bring you corn for planting
    and we will make fire
Children will come to your breast
10   You will heal my heart
I speak your name many times
The wild cane remembers you

My young brother's house is filled
    I go there to sing
15 We have not spoken of you
    but our songs are sad
When the Moon Woman goes to you
    I will follow her white way

Tonight they dance near Chinle
20   by the seven elms
There your loom whispered beauty
    They will eat mutton
and drink coffee till morning
You and I will not be there

25 I saw a crow by Red Rock
        standing on one leg
    It was the black of your hair
        The years are heavy
    I will ride the swiftest horse
30 You will hear the drumming of hooves

PAT MORA
(1942–   )

Elena
(1984)

My Spanish isn't enough.
I remember how I'd smile
listening to my little ones,
understanding every word they'd say,
5 their jokes, their songs, their plots.
        Vamos a pedirle dulces a mamá. Vamos.
But that was in Mexico.
Now my children go to American high schools.
They speak English. At night they sit around
10 the kitchen table, laugh with one another.
I stand by the stove and feel dumb, alone.
I bought a book to learn English.
My husband frowned, drank more beer.
My oldest said, "*Mamá,* he doesn't want you
15 to be smarter than he is." I'm forty,
embarrassed at mispronouncing words,
embarrassed at the laughter of my children,
the grocer, the mailman. Sometimes I take
my English book and lock myself in the bathroom,
20 say the thick words softly,
for if I stop trying, I will be deaf
when my children need my help.

HOWARD NEMEROV
(1920–   )

The Air Force Museum at Dayton
(1984)

Under the barrel roof in solemn gloom
The weapons, instruments, and winged shapes,
The pictured dead in period costume,
Illustrate as in summary time-lapse

5 Photography the planetary race
That in the span of old men still around
Arose from Kitty Hawk to sky to space,
Cooped up as if it never left the ground.

After the pterodactyl and the Wright
10 Brothers every kite carries a gun
As it was meant to do, for right and might
Are properly understood by everyone.

Destructive powers, and speeds still unforeseen
But half a life ago, stand passive here,
15 Contraptions that have landed on the Moon
Or cancelled cities in a single flare.

When anything's over, it turns into art,
Religion, history; what's come to pass
Bows down the mind and presses upon the heart:
20 The ancient bombsight here enshrined in glass

Is the relic left us of a robot saint
With a passion for accuracy, who long ago
Saw towns as targets miniature and quaint,
Townsfolk invisible that far below.

PABLO NERUDA
(1904–1973)

The United Fruit Co.[1]
(1950)

translated by Robert Bly

When the trumpet sounded, it was
all prepared on the earth,
and Jehovah parceled out the earth
to Coca-Cola, Inc., Anaconda,
5 Ford Motors, and other entities:
The Fruit Company, Inc.
reserved for itself the most succulent,
the central coast of my own land,
the delicate waist of America.
10 It rechristened its territories
as the "Banana Republics"
and over the sleeping dead,
over the restless heroes
who brought about the greatness,
15 the liberty and the flags,
it established the comic opera:
abolished the independencies,
presented crowns of Caesar,
unsheathed envy, attracted
20 the dictatorship of the flies,
Trujillo flies, Tacho flies,
Carias flies, Martinez flies,
Ubico flies,[2] damp flies
of modest blood and marmalade,
25 drunken flies who zoom
over the ordinary graves,
circus flies, wise flies
well trained in tyranny.

Among the bloodthirsty flies
30 the Fruit Company lands its ships,
taking off the coffee and the fruit;

---

[1] Incorporated in New Jersey in 1899 by Andrew Preston and Minor C. Keith, United Fruit became the major force in growing, transporting, and merchandising Latin American produce, especially bananas. The company is also notorious for its involvement in politics and is a symbol for many of "Yankee" imperialism and oppression.

[2] Trujillo, Tacho, Carias, Martinez, and Ubico are all political dictators.

the treasure of our submerged
territories flows as though
on plates into the ships.

35 Meanwhile Indians are falling
into the sugared chasms
of the harbors, wrapped
for burial in the mist of the dawn:
a body rolls, a thing
40 that has no name, a fallen cipher,
a cluster of dead fruit
thrown down on the dump.

HILTON OBENZINGER
(1947–   )

Yes, We Have No Bananas[1]
(1980)

"*Yes, we have no bananas.*"
That's what they sang as my father clung
to the rails of the steam ship
pale from the depths of steerage.
5 *Ellis Island has no bananas?*
No bananas in this, the Goldeneh Medina?[2]

In Lublin he wanders through the woods
with his friends to picnic.
Pounced upon by thugs—"*Jews!*
10 *Out of our woods, you dirty Jews!*"—
they were chased back towards the ghetto
until he grabs some acorns, fires
them back, cracks some heads:
"*I'll teach you to beat on Jews!*"

15 "*Yes, we have no bananas*"
was what they sang
on the Lower East Side.
"*Apple pie & coffee*" was all the English he knew.

---

[1] American song by Frank Silver and Irving Kohn, published in 1923.

[2] Golden city or land of plenty.

   "Apple pie & coffee," he said
₂₀ & others they laugh, these Americans,
   they call him a *"greenhorn,"*
   & they sing *"Yes,*
   we have no bananas,"
   as he wanders the garment district
₂₅ looking for work,
   eating apple pie & coffee
   day after day in the automat.

SHARON OLDS
(1942–)

The One Girl at the Boys Party
(1983)

  When I take my girl to the swimming party
  I set her down among the boys. They tower and
  bristle, she stands there smooth and sleek,
  her math scores unfolding in the air around her.
₅ They will strip to their suits, her body hard and
  indivisible as a prime number,
  they'll plunge in the deep end, she'll subtract
  her height from ten feet, divide it into
  hundreds of gallons of water, the numbers
₁₀ bouncing in her mind like molecules of chlorine
  in the bright blue pool. When they climb out,
  her ponytail will hang its pencil lead
  down her back, her narrow silk suit
  with hamburgers and french fries printed on it
₁₅ will glisten in the brilliant air, and they will
  see her sweet face, solemn and
  sealed, a factor of one, and she will
  see their eyes, two each,
  their legs, two each, and the curves of their sexes,
₂₀ one each, and in her head she'll be doing her
  wild multiplying, as the drops
  sparkle and fall to the power of a thousand from her body.

LINDA PASTAN
(1932–   )

Ethics
(1980)

In ethics class so many years ago
our teacher asked this question every fall:
if there were a fire in a museum
which would you save, a Rembrandt painting
or an old woman who hadn't many
years left anyhow? Restless on hard chairs
caring little for pictures or old age
we'd opt one year for life, the next for art
and always half-heartedly. Sometimes
the woman borrowed my grandmother's face
leaving her usual kitchen to wander
some drafty, half imagined museum.
One year, feeling clever, I replied
why not let the woman decide herself?
Linda, the teacher would report, eschews
the burdens of responsibility.
This fall in a real museum I stand
before a real Rembrandt, old woman,
or nearly so, myself. The colors
within this frame are darker than autumn,
darker even than winter—the browns of earth,
though earth's most radiant elements burn
through the canvas. I know now that woman
and painting and season are almost one
and all beyond saving by children.

BORIS PASTERNAK
(1890–1960)

In Everything I Want to Get
(1974)

*Un livre est un grand cimetière où sur la plupart des tombes
on ne peut plus lire les noms effacés.*[1]

Marcel Proust

---

[1] A book is a big cemetery where most of the names on the tombstones are now effaced and unreadable.

In everything I want to get
to the real essence.
In work, in search for the way,
in the heart's turmoil.

5 To the essence of past days,
to their causes,
to the basis, to the roots,
to the core.

All the time catching the thread
10 of fates, of events,
to live, think, feel, love,
to make discoveries.

O if only I could,
even in part,
15 I would write eight lines,
about the properties of passion.

About lawlessness, about sins,
races, chases,
hurried surprises,
20 elbows and palms.

SYLVIA PLATH
(1932–1963)

Metaphors
(1960)

I'm a riddle in nine syllables,
An elephant, a ponderous house,
A melon strolling on two tendrils.
O red fruit, ivory, fine timbers!
5 This loaf's big with its yeasty rising.
Money's new-minted in this fat purse.
I'm a means, a stage, a cow in calf.
I've eaten a bag of green apples,
Boarded the train there's no getting off.

EZRA POUND
(1885–1972)

The River-Merchant's Wife: A Letter[1]
(1915)

While my hair was still cut straight across my forehead
I played about the front gate, pulling flowers.
You came by on bamboo stilts, playing horse,
You walked about my seat, playing with blue plums.
5 And we went on living in the village of Chokan:[2]
Two small people, without dislike or suspicion.
At fourteen I married My Lord you.
I never laughed, being bashful.
Lowering my head, I looked at the wall.
10 Called to, a thousand times, I never looked back.

At fifteen I stopped scowling,
I desired my dust to be mingled with yours
Forever and forever and forever.
Why should I climb the lookout?
15 At sixteen you departed,
You went into far Ku-to-yen,[3] by the river of swirling eddies,
And you have been gone five months.
The monkeys make sorrowful noise overhead.

You dragged your feet when you went out.
20 By the gate now, the moss is grown, the different mosses,
Too deep to clear them away!
The leaves fall early this autumn, in wind.
The paired butterflies are already yellow with August
Over the grass in the West garden;
25 They hurt me. I grow older.
If you are coming down through the narrows of the river Kiang,[4]
Please let me know beforehand,
And I will come out to meet you
      As far as Cho-fu-sa.[5]

---

[1] This is one of the many translations Pound made of Chinese poems. The poem is a free translation of Li Po's (701–762) "Two Letters from Chang-Kan."

[2] Chang-Kan.

[3] An island in the river Ch'ū-t'ang.

[4] The Japanese name for the river Ch'ū-t'ang (see note 3). Pound's translations are based on commentaries derived from Japanese scholars; therefore, he usually uses Japanese instead of Chinese names.

[5] A beach several hundred miles upstream of Nanking.

SIR WALTER RALEIGH
(1552?–1618)

The Nymph's Reply to the Shepherd
(1589?)

    If all the world and love were young,
    And truth in every shepherd's tongue,
    These pretty pleasures might me move
    To live with thee and be thy love.

5 Time drives the flocks from field to fold,
    When rivers rage and rocks grow cold;
    And Philomel[1] becometh dumb;
    The rest complains of cares to come.

    The flowers do fade, and wanton fields
10 To wayward winter reckoning yields:
    A honey tongue, a heart of gall,
    Is fancy's spring, but sorrow's fall.

    Thy gowns, thy shoes, thy beds of roses,
    Thy cap, thy kirtle, and thy posies
15 Soon break, soon wither, soon forgotten,
    In folly ripe, in reason rotten.

    Thy belt of straw and ivy buds,
    Thy coral clasps and amber studs,
    All these in me no means can move
20 To come to thee and be thy love.

    But could youth last, and love still breed,
    Had joys no date, nor age no need,
    Then these delights my mind might move
    To live with thee and be thy love.

JOHN CROWE RANSOM
(1888–1974)

Bells for John Whiteside's Daughter
(1924)

    There was such speed in her little body,
    And such lightness in her footfall,

---

[1] The nightingale.

It is no wonder her brown study
Astonishes us all.

5 Her wars were bruited in our high window.
We looked among orchard trees and beyond,
Where she took arms against her shadow,
Or harried unto the pond

The lazy geese, like a snow cloud
10 Dripping their snow on the green grass,
Tricking and stopping, sleepy and proud,
Who cried in goose, Alas,

For the tireless heart within the little
Lady with rod that made them rise
15 From their noon apple-dreams, and scuttle
Goose-fashion under the skies!

But now go the bells, and we are ready;
In one house we are sternly stopped
To say we are vexed at her brown study,
20 Lying so primly propped.

HENRY REED
(1914–   )

Naming of Parts
(1946)

Today we have naming of parts. Yesterday,
We had daily cleaning. And tomorrow morning,
We shall have what to do after firing. But today,
Today we have naming of parts. Japonica[1]
5 Glistens like coral in all of the neighboring gardens,
    And today we have naming of parts.

This is the lower sling swivel. And this
Is the upper sling swivel, whose use you will see,
When you are given your slings. And this is the piling swivel,
10 Which in your case you have not got. The branches

---

[1] A shrub having waxy flowers in a variety of colors.

Hold in the gardens their silent, eloquent gestures,
　　Which in our case we have not got.

This is the safety-catch, which is always released
With an easy flick of the thumb. And please do not let me
15 See anyone using his finger. You can do it quite easy
If you have any strength in your thumb. The blossoms
Are fragile and motionless, never letting anyone see
　　Any of them using their finger.

And this you can see is the bolt. The purpose of this
20 Is to open the breech, as you see. We can slide it
Rapidly backwards and forwards: we call this
Easing the spring. And rapidly backwards and forwards
The early bees are assaulting and fumbling the flowers:
　　They call it easing the Spring.

25 They call it easing the Spring: it is perfectly easy
If you have any strength in your thumb: like the bolt,
And the breech, and the cocking-piece, and the point of balance,
Which in our case we have not got; and the almond-blossom
Silent in all of the gardens and the bees going backwards and forwards,
30　　For today we have the naming of parts.

EDWIN ARLINGTON ROBINSON
(1869–1935)

Miniver Cheevy
(1910)

Miniver Cheevy, child of scorn,
　　Grew lean while he assailed the seasons;
He wept that he was ever born,
　　And he had reasons.

5 Miniver loved the days of old
　　When swords were bright and steeds were prancing;
The vision of a warrior bold
　　Would set him dancing.

Miniver sighed for what was not,
10　　And dreamed, and rested from his labors;

> He dreamed of Thebes[1] and Camelot,[2]
> > And Priam's[3] neighbors.
>
> Miniver mourned the ripe renown
> > That made so many a name so fragrant;
> 15 He mourned Romance, now on the town,
> > And Art, a vagrant.
>
> Miniver loved the Medici,[4]
> > Albeit he had never seen one;
> He would have sinned incessantly
> 20   Could he have been one.
>
> Miniver cursed the commonplace
> > And eyed a khaki suit with loathing;
> He missed the medieval grace
> > Of iron clothing.
>
> 25 Miniver scorned the gold he sought,
> > But sore annoyed was he without it;
> Miniver thought, and thought, and thought,
> > And thought about it.
>
> Miniver Cheevy, born too late,
> 30   Scratched his head and kept on thinking;
> Miniver coughed, and called it fate,
> > And kept on drinking.

Mr. Flood's Party
(1921)

> Old Eben Flood, climbing alone one night
> Over the hill between the town below
> And the forsaken upland hermitage
> That held as much as he should ever know
> 5 On earth again of home, paused warily.
> The road was his with not a native near;
> And Eben, having leisure, said aloud,
> For no man else in Tilbury Town to hear:

---

[1] The setting of many Greek legends, including that of Oedipus.

[2] The legendary site of King Arthur's court.

[3] Priam was the last King of Troy; his "neighbors" included Helen, Aeneas, and Hector.

[4] Rulers of Florence, Italy, from the fifteenth through the eighteenth centuries. During the Renaissance, Lorenzo de Medici was a renowned patron of the arts.

"Well, Mr. Flood, we have the harvest moon
10 Again, and we may not have many more;
The bird is on the wing, the poet[1] says,
And you and I have said it here before.
Drink to the bird." He raised up to the light
The jug that he had gone so far to fill,
15 And answered huskily: "Well, Mr. Flood,
Since you propose it, I believe I will."

Alone, as if enduring to the end
A valiant armor of scarred hopes outworn,
He stood there in the middle of the road
20 Like Roland's ghost winding a silent horn.[2]
Below him, in the town among the trees,
Where friends of other days had honored him,
A phantom salutation of the dead
Rang thinly till old Eben's eyes were dim.

25 Then, as a mother lays her sleeping child
Down tenderly, fearing it may awake,
He set the jug down slowly at his feet
With trembling care, knowing that most things break;
And only when assured that on firm earth
30 It stood, as the uncertain lives of men
Assuredly did not, he paced away,
And with his hand extended paused again:

"Well, Mr. Flood, we have not met like this
In a long time; and many a change has come
35 To both of us, I fear, since last it was
We had a drop together. Welcome home!"
Convivially returning with himself,
Again he raised the jug up to the light;
And with an acquiescent quaver said:
40 "Well, Mr. Flood, if you insist, I might.

"Only a very little, Mr. Flood—
For auld lang syne. No more, sir; that will do."
So, for the time, apparently it did,
And Eben evidently thought so too;
45 For soon amid the silver loneliness
Of night he lifted up his voice and sang,

---

[1] Edward FitzGerald.

[2] In the *Chanson de Roland,* a medieval French romance, Roland and his soldiers are trapped and killed at a mountain pass; Roland waits until the last minute before his death to sound his horn to signal for help from his emperor, Charlemagne.

Secure, with only two moons listening,
Until the whole harmonious landscape rang—

"For auld lang syne." The weary throat gave out,
50 The last word wavered; and the song being done,
He raised again the jug regretfully
And shook his head, and was again alone.
There was not much that was ahead of him,
And there was nothing in the town below—
55 Where strangers would have shut the many doors
That many friends had opened long ago.

Richard Cory
(1897)

Whenever Richard Cory went down town,
We people on the pavement looked at him:
He was a gentleman from sole to crown,
Clean favored, and imperially slim.

5 And he was always quietly arrayed,
And he was always human when he talked;
But still he fluttered pulses when he said,
"Good-morning," and he glittered when he walked.

And he was rich—yes, richer than a king—
10 And admirably schooled in every grace:
In fine, we thought that he was everything
To make us wish that we were in his place.

So on we worked, and waited for the light,
And went without the meat, and cursed the bread;
15 And Richard Cory, one calm summer night,
Went home and put a bullet through his head.

THEODORE ROETHKE
(1908–1963)

Child on Top of a Greenhouse
(1942)

The wind billowing out the seat of my britches,
My feet crackling splinters of glass and dried putty,
The half-grown chrysanthemums staring up like accusers,

Up through the streaked glass, flashing with sunlight,
5 A few white clouds all rushing eastward,
A line of elms plunging and tossing like horses,
And everyone, everyone pointing up and shouting!

SONIA SANCHEZ
(1934–   )

right on: white america
(1970)

    this country might have
been a pio
   neer land
once.
5   but.   there ain't
no mo
    indians   blowing
custer's[1] mind
        with a different
10 image of america.
            this country
might have
      needed shoot/
outs/ daily/
15   once.
         but. there ain't
no mo real/ white/   allamerican
         bad/guys.
just.
20 u & me.
      blk/ and un/armed.
this country might have
been a pion
     eer land.   once.
25   and it still is.
check out
    the falling
gun/shells   on our blk/tomorrows.

---

[1] General George Armstrong Custer (1839–1876) was killed by Sioux in his "last stand" at the Little Bighorn in Montana.

CARL SANDBURG
(1878–1967)

Fog
(1916)

>The fog comes
>on little cat feet.
>It sits looking
>over harbor and city
>5 on silent haunches
>and then moves on.

MONGONE WALLY SEROTE
(1944–   )

For Don M.—Banned
(1982)

>it is a dry white season
>dark leaves don't last, their brief lives dry out
>and with a broken heart they dive down gently headed for earth,
>not even bleeding.
>5 it is a dry white season brother,
>only the trees know the pain as they still stand erect
>dry like steel, their branches dry like wire,
>indeed, it is a dry white season
>but seasons come to pass.

WILLIAM SHAKESPEARE
(1564–1616)

Let Me Not to the Marriage of True Minds
(1609)

>Let me not to the marriage of true minds
>Admit impediments.[1] Love is not love

---

[1] A reference to "The Order of Solemnization of Matrimony" in the Anglican Book of Common Prayer: "I require that if either of you know any impediments why ye may not be lawfully joined together in Matrimony, ye do now confess it."

Which alters when it alteration finds,
Or bends with the remover to remove:
5 Oh, no! it is an ever-fixéd mark,
That looks on tempests and is never shaken;
It is the star to every wandering bark,
Whose worth's unknown, although his height[2] be taken.
Love's not Time's fool,[3] though rosy lips and cheeks
10 Within his bending sickle's compass come;
Love alters not with his brief hours and weeks,
But bears it out even to the edge of doom.[4]
If this be error and upon me proved,
I never writ, nor no man ever loved.

My Mistress' Eyes Are Nothing Like the Sun
(1609)

My mistress' eyes are nothing like the sun;
Coral is far more red than her lips' red;
If snow be white, why then her breasts are dun;
If hairs be wires, black wires grow on her head.
5 I have seen roses damasked red and white,
But no such roses see I in her cheeks;
And in some perfumes is there more delight
Than in the breath that from my mistress reeks.
I love to hear her speak, yet well I know
10 That music hath a far more pleasing sound;
I grant I never saw a goddess go:
My mistress, when she walks, treads on the ground.
    And yet, by heaven, I think my love as rare
    As any she, belied with false compare.

Not Marble, Nor the Gilded Monuments
(1609)

Not marble, nor the gilded monuments
Of princes, shall outlive this powerful rhyme;
But you shall shine more bright in these contents
Than unswept stone, besmeared with sluttish time.
5 When wasteful war shall statues overturn,
And broils root out the work of masonry,

---

[2] Although the altitude of a star may be measured, its worth is unknowable.

[3] That is, mocked by Time.

[4] Doomsday.

Nor Mars[1] his sword nor war's quick fire shall burn
The living record of your memory.
'Gainst death and all-oblivious enmity
Shall you pace forth; your praise shall still find room
Even in the eyes of all posterity
That wear this world out to the ending doom.
So, till the judgment that yourself arise,
You live in this, and dwell in lovers' eyes.

PERCY BYSSHE SHELLEY
(1792–1822)

Ode to the West Wind
(1820)

I

O wild West Wind, thou breath of Autumn's being,
Thou, from whose unseen presence the leaves dead
Are driven, like ghosts from an enchanter fleeing,

Yellow, and black, and pale, and hectic[1] red,
Pestilence-stricken multitudes: O Thou,
Who chariotest to their dark wintry bed

The winged seeds, where they lie cold and low,
Each like a corpse within its grave, until
Thine azure sister of the Spring[2] shall blow

Her clarion o'er the dreaming earth, and fill
(Driving sweet buds like flocks to feed in air)
With living hues and odours plain and hill:

Wild Spirit, which art moving everywhere;
Destroyer and Preserver; hear, O hear!

---

[1] God of War.

---

[1] Reference to a tubercular fever that produces flushed cheeks.

[2] The west wind of the spring.

II

15 Thou on whose stream, mid the steep sky's commotion,
Loose clouds like Earth's decaying leaves are shed,
Shook from the tangled boughs of Heaven and Ocean,

Angels of rain and lightning: there are spread
On the blue surface of thine aery surge,
20 Like the bright hair uplifted from the head

Of some fierce Maenad,[3] even from the dim verge
Of the horizon to the zenith's height,
The locks of the approaching storm. Thou Dirge

Of the dying year, to which this closing night
25 Will be the dome of a vast sepulchre,
Vaulted with all thy congregated might

Of vapours, from whose solid atmosphere
Black rain and fire and hail will burst: O hear!

III

Thou who didst waken from his summer dreams
30 The blue Mediterranean, where he lay,
Lulled by the coil of his crystalline streams,

Beside a pumice isle in Baiae's bay,[4]
And saw in sleep old palaces and towers
Quivering within the wave's intenser day,

35 All overgrown with azure moss and flowers
So sweet, the sense faints picturing them! Thou
For whose path the Atlantic's level powers

Cleave themselves into chasms, while far below
The sea-blooms and the oozy woods which wear
40 The sapless foliage of the ocean, know

Thy voice, and suddenly grow grey with fear,
And tremble and despoil themselves: O hear!

---

[3] A female votary who danced wildly in ceremonies for Dionysus (or Bacchus), Greek god of wine and vegetation, who according to legend died in the fall and was reborn in the spring.

[4] A bay in the Mediterranean Sea, west of Naples. It was known for the opulent villas built by Roman emperors along its shores.

IV

If I were a dead leaf thou mightest bear;
If I were a swift cloud to fly with thee;
A wave to pant beneath thy power, and share

The impulse of thy strength, only less free
Than thou, O Uncontrollable! If even
I were as in my boyhood, and could be

The comrade of thy wanderings over Heaven,
As then, when to outstrip thy skiey speed
Scarce seemed a vision; I would ne'er have striven

As thus with thee in prayer in my sore need,
Oh! lift me as a wave, a leaf, a cloud!
I fall upon thorns of life! I bleed!

A heavy weight of hours has chained and bowed
One too like thee: tameless, and swift, and proud.

V

Make me thy lyre,[5] even as the forest is:
What if my leaves are falling like its own!
The tumult of thy mighty harmonies

Will take from both a deep, autumnal tone,
Sweet though in sadness. Be thou, Spirit fierce,
My spirit! Be thou me, impetuous one!

Drive my dead thoughts over the universe
Like withered leaves to quicken a new birth!
And, by the incantation of this verse,

Scatter, as from an unextinguished hearth
Ashes and sparks, my words among mankind!
Be through my lips to unawakened Earth

The trumpet of a prophecy! O Wind,
If Winter comes, can Spring be far behind?

---

[5] An Aeolian harp, a stringed instrument that produces musical sounds when exposed to the wind.

SIR PHILIP SIDNEY
(1554–1586)

Astrophel and Stella
(1591)

    Who will in fairest book of Nature know,
    How Virtue may best lodged in beauty be,
    Let him but learn of Love to read in thee,
    Stella, those fair lines, which true goodness show.
5 There shall he find all vices' overthrow,
    Not by rude force, but sweetest sovereignty
    Of reason, from whose light those night birds fly;
    That inward sun in thine eyes shineth so.
    And not content to be Perfection's heir
10 Thyself, dost strive all minds that way to move,
    Who mark in thee what is in thee most fair.
    So while thy beauty draws the heart to love,
    As fast thy Virtue bends that love to good:
    "But ah," desire still cries, "give me some food."

CHARLES SIMIC
(1938–   )

Birthday Star Atlas
(1986)

    Wildest dream, Miss Emily,
    Then the coldly dawning suspicion—
    Always at the loss—come day
    Large black birds overtaking men who sleep in ditches.

5 A whiff of winter in the air. Sovereign blue,
    Blue that stands for intellectual clarity
    Over a street deserted except for a far off dog,
    A police car, a light at the vanishing point

    For the children to solve on the blackboard today—
10 Blind children at the school you and I know about.
    Their gray nightgowns creased by the north wind;
    Their fingernails bitten from time immemorial.

We're in a long line outside a dead letter office.
We're dustmice under a conjugal bed carved with exotic fishes and
    monkeys.
15 We're in a slow drifting coalbarge huddled around the television set
Which has a wire coat-hanger for an antenna.

A quick view (by satellite) of the polar regions
Maternally tucked in for the long night.
Then some sort of interference—parallel lines
20 Like the ivory-boned needles of your grandmother knitting our fates
    together.

All things ambiguous and lovely in their ambiguity,
Like the nebulae in my new star atlas—
Pale ovals where the ancestral portraits have been taken down.
The gods with their goatees and their faint smiles

25 In company of their bombshell spouses,
Naked and statuesque as if entering a death camp.
They smile, too, stroke the Triton wrapped around the mantle clock
When they are not showing the whites of their eyes in theatrical ecstasy.

Nostalgias for the theological vaudeville.
30 A false springtime cleverly painted on cardboard
For the couple in the last row to sigh over
While holding hands which unknown to them

Flutter like bird-shaped scissors . . .
Emily, the birthday atlas!
35 I kept turning its pages awed
And delighted by the size of the unimaginable;

The great nowhere, the everlasting nothing—
Pure and serene doggedness
For the hell of it—and love,
40 Our nightly stroll the color of silence and time.

BORIS SLUTSKY*

How Did They Kill My Grandmother?
translated by Elaine Feinstein

How did they kill my grandmother?
I'll tell you how they killed her.
One morning a tank rolled up to
a building where
5 the hundred and fifty Jews of our town who,
weightless
        from a year's starvation,
and white
        with the knowledge of death,
10 were gathered holding their bundles.
And the German polizei[1] were
herding the old people briskly;
and their tin mugs clanked as
the young men led them away
15   far away.

But my small grandmother
my seventy-year-old grandmother
began to curse and
scream at the Germans;
20 shouting that I was a soldier.
She yelled at them: My grandson
is off at the front fighting!
Don't you dare
touch me!
25 Listen, you
        can hear our guns!

Even as she went off, my grandmother
cried abuse,
        starting all over again
30 with her curses.
From every window then
Ivanovnas and Andreyevnas
Sidorovnas and Petrovnas
sobbed: You tell them, Polina
35 Matveyevna, keep it up!

---

* Birth date of author and publication date of poem are not available.

[1] Police.

They all yelled together:
"What can we do against
this enemy, the Hun?"
Which was why the Germans chose
40 to kill her inside the town.

A bullet struck her hair
and kicked her grey plait down.
My grandmother fell to the ground.
That is how she died there.

STEVIE SMITH
(1902–1971)

Not Waving But Drowning
(1957)

Nobody heard him, the dead man,
But still he lay moaning:
I was much further out than you thought
And not waving but drowning.

5 Poor chap, he always loved larking
And now he's dead
It must have been too cold for him his heart gave way,
They said.

Oh, no no no, it was too cold always
10 (Still the dead one lay moaning)
I was much too far out all my life
And not waving but drowning.

CATHY SONG
(1955–   )

Lost Sister
(1983)

1

In China,
even the peasants
named their first daughters

Jade—
the stone that in the far fields
could moisten the dry season,
could make men move mountains
for the healing green of the inner hills
glistening like slices of winter melon.

And the daughters were grateful:
they never left home.
To move freely was a luxury
stolen from them at birth.
Instead, they gathered patience,
learning to walk in shoes
the size of teacups,[1]
without breaking—
the arc of their movements
as dormant as the rooted willow,
as redundant as the farmyard hens.
But they traveled far
in surviving,
learning to stretch the family rice,
to quiet the demons,
the noisy stomachs.

2

There is a sister
across the ocean,
who relinquished her name,
diluting jade green
with the blue of the Pacific.
Rising with a tide of locusts,
she swarmed with others
to inundate another shore.
In America,
there are many roads
and women can stride along with men.

But in another wilderness,
the possibilities,
the loneliness,
can strangulate like jungle vines.
The meager provisions and sentiments
of once belonging—

---

[1] A reference to the practice of binding young girls' feet so that they remain small. This practice, which crippled women, was common in China until the communist revolution.

fermented roots, Mah-Jongg[2] tiles and firecrackers—
set but a flimsy household
45 in a forest of nightless cities.
A giant snake rattles above,
spewing black clouds into your kitchen.
Dough-faced landlords
slip in and out of your keyholes,
50 making claims you don't understand,
tapping into your communication systems
of laundry lines and restaurant chains.

You find you need China:
your one fragile identification,
55 a jade link
handcuffed to your wrist.
You remember your mother
who walked for centuries,
footless—
60 and like her,
you have left no footprints,
but only because
there is an ocean in between,
the unremitting space of your rebellion.

GARY SOTO
(1952–   )

Black Hair
(1985)

At eight I was brilliant with my body.
In July, that ring of heat
We all jumped through, I sat in the bleachers
Of Romain Playground, in the lengthening
5 Shade that rose from our dirty feet.
The game before us was more than baseball.
It was a figure—Hector Moreno
Quick and hard with turned muscles,
His crouch the one I assumed before an altar
10 Of worn baseball cards, in my room.

---

[2] Or mahjong, an ancient Chinese game played with dice and tiles.

I came here because I was Mexican, a stick
Of brown light in love with those
Who could do it—the triple and hard slide,
The gloves eating balls into double plays.
15 What could I do with 50 pounds, my shyness,
My black torch of hair, about to go out?
Father was dead, his face no longer
Hanging over the table or our sleep,
And mother was the terror of mouths
20 Twisting hurt by butter knives.

In the bleachers I was brilliant with my body,
Waving players in and stomping my feet,
Growing sweaty in the presence of white shirts.
I chewed sunflower seeds. I drank water
25 And bit my arm through the late innings.
When Hector lined balls into deep
Center, in my mind I rounded the bases
With him, my face flared, my hair lifting
Beautifully, because we were coming home
30 To the arms of brown people.

History
(1977)

Grandma lit the stove.
Morning sunlight
Lengthened in spears
Across the linoleum floor.
5 Wrapped in a shawl,
Her eyes small
With sleep.
She sliced papas,[1]
Pounded chiles
10 With a stone
Brought from Guadalajara.[2]
                              After
Grandpa left for work,
She hosed down
15 The walk her sons paved
And in the shade
Of a chinaberry,
Unearthed her

---

[1] Potatoes.

[2] A city in Mexico.

Secret cigar box
20 Of bright coins
And bills, counted them
In English,
Then in Spanish,
And buried them elsewhere.
25 Later, back
From the market,
Where no one saw her,
She pulled out
Pepper and beet, spines
30 Of asparagus
From her blouse,
Tiny chocolates
From under a paisley bandana,
And smiled.

35 That was the '50s,
And Grandma in her '50s,
A face streaked
From cutting grapes
And boxing plums.
40 I remember her insides
Were washed of tapeworm,
Her arms swelled into knobs
Of small growths—
Her second son
45 Dropped from a ladder
And was dust.
And yet I do not know
The sorrows
That sent her praying
50 In the dark of a closet,
The tear that fell
At night
When she touched
Loose skin
55 Of belly and breasts.
I do not know why
Her face shines
Or what goes beyond this shine,
Only the stories
60 That pulled her
From Taxco[3] to San Joaquin,

---

[3] A city in Mexico.

Delano to Westside,[4]
The places
In which we all begin.

BARRY SPACKS
(1931–   )

Finding a Yiddish[1] Paper on the Riverside Line
(1978)

Again I hold these holy letters,
Never learned. Dark candelabras.

Once they glowed in the yellow light
Through the chicken smell of Friday night,[2]

5 My father in his peach-stained shirt
Scrubbing off twelve hours' dirt

While I drew my name on misted glass.
Now trim suburban houses pass

And on my lap the headlines loom
10 Like strangers in the living room.

STEPHEN SPENDER
(1909–   )

An Elementary School Classroom in a Slum
(1939)

Far far from gusty waves, these children's faces.
Like rootless weeds the torn hair round their paleness.

---

[4] Places in California.

[1] Yiddish, a language derived from High German and spoken by Eastern European Jews, is written in Hebrew characters.

[2] The Jewish Sabbath begins at sundown on Friday. Chicken is traditionally served at the Sabbath meal.

The tall girl with her weighed-down head. The paper-seeming boy with
    rat's eyes. The stunted unlucky heir
5 Of twisted bones, reciting a father's gnarled disease,
His lesson from his desk. At back of the dim class,
One unnoted, sweet and young: his eyes live in a dream
Of squirrels' game, in tree room, other than this.

On sour cream walls, donations. Shakespeare's head
10 Cloudless at dawn, civilized dome riding all cities.
Belled, flowery, Tyrolese valley. Open-handed map
Awarding the world its world. And yet, for these
Children, these windows, not this world, are world,
Where all their future's painted with a fog,
15 A narrow street sealed in with a lead sky,
Far far from rivers, capes, and stars of words.

Surely Shakespeare is wicked, the map a bad example
With ships and sun and love tempting them to steal—
For lives that slyly turn in their cramped holes
20 From fog to endless night? On their slag heap, these children
Wear skins peeped through by bones and spectacles of steel
With mended glass, like bottle bits on stones.
All of their time and space are foggy slum
So blot their maps with slums as big as doom.

25 Unless, governor, teacher, inspector, visitor,
This map becomes their window and these windows
That open on their lives like crouching tombs
Break, O break open, till they break the town
And show the children to the fields and all their world
30 Azure on their sands, to let their tongues
Run naked into books, the white and green leaves open
The history theirs whose language is the sun.

BRUCE SPRINGSTEEN
(1949–   )

My Hometown
(1984)

I was eight years old and running with a dime in my hand
Into the bus stop to pick up a paper for my old man
I'd sit on his lap in that big old Buick and steer as we drove through
    town

He'd tousle my hair and say son take a good look around
5 This is your hometown
This is your hometown
This is your hometown
This is your hometown

In '65 tension was running high at my high school
10 There was a lot of fights between the black and white
There was nothing you could do
Two cars at a light on a Saturday night in the back seat there was a gun
Words were passed in a shotgun blast
Troubled times had come to my hometown
15 My hometown
My hometown
My hometown

Now Main Street's whitewashed windows and vacant stores
Seems like there ain't nobody wants to come down here no more
20 They're closing down the textile mill across the railroad tracks
Foreman says these jobs are going boys and they ain't coming back to
    your hometown
Your hometown
Your hometown
Your hometown

25 Last night me and Kate we laid in bed talking about getting out
Packing up our bags maybe heading south
I'm thirty-five we got a boy of our own now
Last night I sat him up behind the wheel and said son take a good look
    around this is your hometown

WILLIAM STAFFORD
(1914–   )

Traveling through the Dark
(1962)

Traveling through the dark I found a deer
dead on the edge of the Wilson River road.
It is usually best to roll them into the canyon:
that road is narrow; to swerve might make more dead.

5 By glow of the tail-light I stumbled back of the car
and stood by the heap, a doe, a recent killing;

she had stiffened already, almost cold.
I dragged her off; she was large in the belly.

My fingers touching her side brought me the reason—
10 her side was warm; her fawn lay there waiting,
alive, still, never to be born.
Beside that mountain road I hesitated.

The car aimed ahead its lowered parking lights;
under the hood purred the steady engine.
15 I stood in the glare of the warm exhaust turning red;
around our group I could hear the wilderness listen.

I thought hard for us all—my only swerving—
then pushed her over the edge into the river.

DONA STEIN
(1935–   )

Putting Mother By
(1977)

We are in her kitchen;
we have one enormous
pot and all the spices
are together.

5 We are too tiny and take
so long to sterilize
the jar; finally, more
water is boiling, waiting.
We don't have to call,
10 she hears and comes
into her kitchen.

We lift her over the pot;
she slips into the water
without a murmur.
15 She does not try to get out.

Later, we stand on tiptoes
and watch her inside
the Mason jar floating
in liquid by bay leaves
20 and flakes of pepper.

Dill weed floats like
a pine tree around her hair.

We look at each other, we
press our noses against
25 the jar and see she is more
surprised than anything else.

Carefully we carry her down
into the cellar; we store
her next to the peaches and plums;
30 we have her now.

WALLACE STEVENS
(1879–1955)

Anecdote of the Jar
(1923)

I placed a jar in Tennessee,
And round it was, upon a hill.
It made the slovenly wilderness
Surround that hill.

5 The wilderness rose up to it,
And sprawled around, no longer wild.
The jar was round upon the ground
And tall and of a port in air.

It took dominion everywhere.
10 The jar was gray and bare.
It did not give of bird or bush,
Like nothing else in Tennessee.

Disillusionment of Ten O'clock
(1923)

The houses are haunted
By white night-gowns.
None are green,
Or purple with green rings,
5 Or green with yellow rings,
Or yellow with blue rings.
None of them are strange,

With socks of lace
And beaded ceintures.[1]
10 People are not going
To dream of baboons and periwinkles.
Only, here and there, an old sailor,
Drunk and asleep in his boots,
Catches tigers
15 In red weather.

The Emperor of Ice-Cream
(1923)

Call the roller of big cigars,
The muscular one, and bid him whip
In kitchen cups concupiscent curds.
Let the wenches dawdle in such dress
5 As they are used to wear, and let the boys
Bring flowers in last month's newspapers.
Let be be finale of seem.
The only emperor is the emperor of ice-cream.

Take from the dresser of deal,[1]
10 Lacking the three glass knobs, that sheet
On which she embroidered fantails[2] once
And spread it so as to cover her face.
If her horny feet protrude, they come
To show how cold she is, and dumb.
15 Let the lamp affix its beam.
The only emperor is the emperor of ice-cream.

MARK STRAND
(1934–)

Pot Roast
(1978)

I gaze upon the roast,
that is sliced and laid out

---

[1] Girdles, or belts, around the waist.

---

[1] Fir or pine wood.

[2] According to Stevens, "the word fantails does not mean fans, but fantail pigeons."

on my plate
and over it
I spoon the juices
of carrot and onion.
And for once I do not regret
the passage of time.

I sit by a window
that looks
on the soot-stained brick of buildings
and do not care that I see
no living thing—not a bird,
not a branch in bloom,
not a soul moving
in the rooms
behind the dark panes.
These days when there is little
to love or to praise
one could do worse
than yield
to the power of food.
So I bend
to inhale
the steam that rises
from my plate, and I think
of the first time
I tasted a roast
like this.
It was years ago
in Seabright,
Nova Scotia;
my mother leaned
over my dish and filled it
and when I finished
filled it again.
I remember the gravy,
its odor of garlic and celery,
and sopping it up
with pieces of bread.

And now
I taste it again.
The meat of memory.
The meat of no change.
I raise my fork in praise,
and I eat.

ANDREW SUKNASKI
(1942–   )

The Bitter Word
(1976)

from fort walsh
colonel irvine brings the bitter word
to sitting bull at wood mountain
makes clear the government welcomes the teton—
5 yet they must not expect provisions
or food from canada

sitting bull proudly replies:
when did i ever ask you for provisions?
before i beg
10 *i will cut willows for my young men to use*
while killing mice to survive

in the spring of 1881
sitting bull gathers his remaining 1200 sioux
and treks to fort qu'appelle to make
15 the final request for a reservation—
inspector sam steele tells them
the great white mother wishes them to return
to their own country
(a rather curious view of a people
20 whose meaning of country changes with
the migrations of tatanka)[1]
steele politely refuses the request
and supplies enough provisions for the return
to wood mountain

25 death by summer is certain
while irvine makes sure
provisions and seed never arrive
seeing the migrating game
sitting bull knew the tatanka
30 would never return
though his people dreamed of white tatanka rising
from the subterranean meadows others fled to
(hideous shrieks of red river carts grating in
their ears)

---

[1] A Lakota-Nakota (Sioux) word meaning "god-animal" and referring here to the buffalo.

35 he must have sensed the hunger to follow
which was exactly what the authorities hoped for
on both sides of the border

ALFRED, LORD TENNYSON
(1809–1892)

Ulysses[1]
(1833)

It little profits that an idle king,
By this still hearth, among these barren crags,
Matched with an agèd wife, I mete and dole
Unequal laws unto a savage race
5 That hoard, and sleep, and feed, and know not me.
I cannot rest from travel; I will drink
Life to the lees. All times I have enjoyed
Greatly, have suffered greatly, both with those
That loved me, and alone; on shore, and when
10 Through scudding drifts the rainy Hyades[2]
Vexed the dim sea. I am become a name;
For always roaming with a hungry heart
Much have I seen and known—cities of men
And manners, climates, councils, governments,
15 Myself not least, but honored of them all—
And drunk delight of battle with my peers,
Far on the ringing plains of windy Troy.[3]
I am a part of all that I have met;
Yet all experience is an arch wherethrough
20 Gleams that untraveled world whose margin fades
Forever and forever when I move.

---

[1] A legendary Greek king of Ithaca and hero of Homer's *Odyssey*, Ulysses (or Odysseus) is noted for his daring and cunning. After his many adventures—including encounters with the Cyclops, the cannibalistic Laestrygones, and the enchantress Circe—Ulysses returned home to his faithful wife, Penelope. Tennyson portrays an older Ulysses pondering his situation.

[2] A group of stars whose rising was supposedly followed by rain, and hence stormy seas.

[3] An ancient city in Asia Minor. According to legend, Paris, King of Troy, abducted Helen, initiating the famed Trojan war, in which numerous Greek heroes, including Ulysses, fought.

How dull it is to pause, to make an end,
To rust unburnished, not to shine in use!
As though to breathe were life! Life piled on life
Were all too little, and of one to me
Little remains; but every hour is saved
From that eternal silence, something more,
A bringer of new things; and vile it were
For some three suns to store and hoard myself,
And this grey spirit yearning in desire
To follow knowledge like a sinking star,
Beyond the utmost bound of human thought.
    This is my son, mine own Telemachus,
To whom I leave the scepter and the isle—
Well-loved of me, discerning to fulfill
This labor, by slow prudence to make mild
A rugged people, and through soft degrees
Subdue them to the useful and the good.
Most blameless is he, centered in the sphere
Of common duties, decent not to fail
In offices of tenderness, and pay
Meet adoration to my household gods,
When I am gone. He works his work, I mine.
    There lies the port; the vessel puffs her sail;
There gloom the dark, broad seas. My mariners,
Souls that have toiled, and wrought, and thought with me—
That ever with a frolic welcome took
The thunder and the sunshine, and opposed
Free hearts, free foreheads—you and I are old;
Old age hath yet his honor and his toil.
Death closes all; but something ere the end,
Some work of noble note, may yet be done,
Not unbecoming men that strove with Gods.
The lights begin to twinkle from the rocks;
The long day wanes; the low moon climbs; the deep
Moans round with many voices. Come, my friends,
'Tis not too late to seek a newer world.
Push off, and sitting well in order smite
The sounding furrows; for my purpose holds
To sail beyond the sunset, and the baths
Of all the western stars, until I die.
It may be that the gulfs will wash us down;
It may be we shall touch the Happy Isles,[4]
And see the great Achilles,[5] whom we knew.

---

[4] Elysium, or Paradise, believed to be in the far western ocean.

[5] Famed Greek hero of the Trojan War.

⁶⁵ Though much is taken, much abides; and though
We are not now that strength which in old days
Moved earth and heaven, that which we are, we are—
One equal temper of heroic hearts,
Made weak by time and fate, but strong in will
⁷⁰ To strive, to seek, to find, and not to yield.

DYLAN THOMAS
(1914–1953)

Fern Hill
(1946)

Now as I was young and easy under the apple boughs
About the lilting house and happy as the grass was green,
    The night above the dingle[1] starry,
      Time let me hail and climb
⁵   Golden in the heydays of his eyes,
And honored among wagons I was prince of the apple towns
And once below a time I lordly had the trees and leaves
      Trail with daisies and barley
    Down the rivers of the windfall light.

¹⁰ And as I was green and carefree, famous among the barns
About the happy yard and singing as the farm was home,
    In the sun that is young once only,
      Time let me play and be
    Golden in the mercy of his means,
¹⁵ And green and golden I was huntsman and herdsman, the calves
Sang to my horn, the foxes on the hills barked clear and cold,
      And the sabbath rang slowly
    In the pebbles of the holy streams.

All the sun long it was running, it was lovely, the hay
²⁰ Fields high as the house, the tunes from the chimneys, it was air
    And playing, lovely and watery
      And fire green as grass.
    And nightly under the simple stars
As I rode to sleep the owls were bearing the farm away,
²⁵ All the moon long I heard, blessed among stables, the nightjars

---

[1] Wooded valley.

                    Flying with the ricks, and the horses
                        Flashing into the dark.

    And then to awake, and the farm, like a wanderer white
    With the dew, come back, the cock on his shoulder: it was all
            Shining, it was Adam and maiden,
                The sky gathered again
            And the sun grew round that very day.
    So it must have been after the birth of the simple light
    In the first, spinning place, the spellbound horses walking warm
            Out of the whinnying green stable
                On to the fields of praise.

    And honored among foxes and pheasants by the gay house
    Under the new made clouds and happy as the heart was long,
            In the sun born over and over,
                I ran my heedless ways,
            My wishes raced through the house high hay
    And nothing I cared, at my sky blue trades, that time allows
    In all his tuneful turning so few and such morning songs
            Before the children green and golden
                Follow him out of grace,

    Nothing I cared, in the lamb white days, that time would take me
    Up to the swallow thronged loft by the shadow of my hand,
            In the moon that is always rising,
                Nor that riding to sleep
            I should hear him fly with the high fields
    And wake to the farm forever fled from the childless land.
    Oh as I was young and easy in the mercy of his means,
            Time held me green and dying
        Though I sang in my chains like the sea.

MARGARET WALKER
(1915-   )

Lineage
(1942)

        My grandmothers were strong.
        They followed plows and bent to toil.
        They moved through fields sowing seed.
        They touched earth and grain grew.

They were full of sturdiness and singing.
My grandmothers were strong.

My grandmothers are full of memories
Smelling of soap and onions and wet clay
With veins rolling roughly over quick hands
They have many clean words to say.
My grandmothers were strong.
Why am I not as they?

EDMUND WALLER
(1606–1687)

Go, Lovely Rose
(1645)

    Go, lovely rose,
Tell her that wastes her time and me
    That now she knows,
When I resemble her to thee,
How sweet and fair she seems to be.

    Tell her that's young
And shuns to have her graces spied,
    That hadst thou sprung
In deserts where no men abide,
Thou must have uncommended died.

    Small is the worth
Of beauty from the light retired:
    Bid her come forth,
Suffer herself to be desired,
And not blush so to be admired.

    Then die, that she
The common fate of all things rare
    May read in thee,
How small a part of time they share
That are so wondrous sweet and fair.

TOM WAYMAN
(1945–)

Wayman in Quebec
(1977)

It began simply enough, as an invitation
for Wayman to spend a few days at a lake
in the Laurentians, but as soon as Wayman's car
crossed over the bridge at Hull, what's this?
5 the trees along the highway suddenly became
"les arbres" and a house
"une maison" and Wayman was relieved to see
the familiar face of Colonel Sanders
revolving reassuringly, but, wait,
10 below his customary goatee, the Colonel was now selling
"les poulets frits à la Kentucky"

Wayman felt he should be able
after all those high-school tests he had endured
to inquire politely as to where he was going:
15 "Bonjour. Où est la direction à Chénéville?"
or something like that, but his heart sank
at the last moment, and all he could stutter out
was "Chénéville? Chénéville?" *Keep going the way you're headed*
a calm voice comforted him. *Turn left at the next set of lights.*

20 So he was off through the traffic again
or maybe he was "parmi les autos" or that might be
"les voitures d'occasion" as the signs had it.
Anyway, driving along with "la rivière" gleaming away
behind the riverside farms, that is, "les fermes"
25 all this time Wayman was considering
How do you say Wayman *in Quebec?* and also
What am I doing here?

PHYLLIS WHEATLEY
(1754–1784)

On Being Brought from Africa to America
(1773)

'Twas mercy brought me from my *Pagan* land,
Taught my benighted soul to understand

That there's a God, that there's a *Saviour* too:
Once I redemption neither sought nor knew.
5 Some view our sable race with scornful eye,
"Their colour is a diabolic die."
Remember, *Christians, Negroes,* black as *Cain,*
May be refin'd, and join th' angelic train.

WALT WHITMAN
(1819–1892)

Cavalry Crossing a Ford
(1865)

A line in long array where they wind betwixt green islands,
They take a serpentine course, their arms flash in the sun—hark to the musical clank,
Behold the silvery river, in it the splashing horses loitering stop to drink,
Behold the brown-faced men, each group, each person a picture, the negligent rest on the saddles,
5 Some emerge on the opposite bank, others are just entering the ford—while,
Scarlet and blue and snowy white,
The guidon flags flutter gayly in the wind.

from Song of Myself
(1855)

1

I celebrate myself, and sing myself,
And what I assume you shall assume,
For every atom belonging to me as good belongs to you.

I loafe and invite my soul,
5 I lean and loafe at my ease observing a spear of summer grass.

My tongue, every atom of my blood, form'd from this soil, this air,
Born here of parents born here from parents the same, and their parents the same,
I, now thirty-seven years old in perfect health begin,
Hoping to cease not till death.

10 Creeds and schools in abeyance,
Retiring back a while sufficed at what they are, but never forgotten,

I harbor for good or bad, I permit to speak at every hazard,
Nature without check with original energy.

2

Houses and rooms are full of perfumes, the shelves are crowded with perfumes,
15 I breathe the fragrance myself and know it and like it,
The distillation would intoxicate me also, but I shall not let it.

The atmosphere is not a perfume, it has no taste of the distillation, it is odorless,
It is for my mouth forever, I am in love with it,
I will go to the bank by the wood and become undisguised and naked,
20 I am mad for it to be in contact with me.

The smoke of my own breath,
Echoes, ripples, buzz'd whispers, love-root, silk-thread, crotch and vine,
My respiration and inspiration, the beating of my heart, the passing of blood and air through my lungs,
The sniff of green leaves and dry leaves, and of the shore and dark-color'd sea-rocks, and of hay in the barn,
25 The sound of the belch'd words of my voice loos'd to the eddies of the wind,
A few light kisses, a few embraces, a reaching around of arms,
The play of shine and shade on the trees as the supple boughs wag,
The delight alone or in the rush of the streets, or along the fields and hill-sides,
The feeling of health, the full-noon trill, the song of me rising from bed and meeting the sun.

30 Have you reckon'd a thousand acres much? have you reckon'd the earth much?
Have you practis'd so long to learn to read?
Have you felt so proud to get at the meaning of poems?

Stop this day and night with me and you shall possess the origin of all poems,
You shall possess the good of the earth and sun, (there are millions of suns left,)
35 You shall no longer take things at second or third hand, nor look through the eyes of the dead, nor feed on the spectres in books,
You shall not look through my eyes either, nor take things from me,
You shall listen to all sides and filter them from your self.

RICHARD WILBUR
(1921–   )

Museum Piece
(1950)

The good gray guardians of art
Patrol the halls on spongy shoes,
Impartially protective, though
Perhaps suspicious of Toulouse.[1]

5 Here dozes one against the wall,
Disposed upon a funeral chair.
A Degas[2] dancer pirouettes
Upon the parting of his hair.

See how she spins! The grace is there,
10 But strain as well is plain to see.
Degas loved the two together:
Beauty joined to energy.

Edgar Degas purchased once
A fine El Greco,[3] which he kept
15 Against the wall beside his bed
To hang his pants on while he slept.

WILLIAM CARLOS WILLIAMS
(1883–1963)

This Is Just to Say
(1938)

I have eaten
the plums
that were in
the icebox

---

[1] Henri de Toulouse-Lautrec (1864–1901)—French artist, famous for his paintings of Parisian café life, prostitutes, and popular entertainers.

[2] Edgar Degas (1834–1871)—French painter and sculptor, noted for his many studies of ballet dancers.

[3] El Greco (Domenikos Theotokopoulos; 1541–1614)—Greek-born painter who worked mainly in Spain.

     5 and which
       you were probably
       saving
       for breakfast

       Forgive me
    10 they were delicious
       so sweet
       and so cold

WILLIAM WORDSWORTH
(1770–1850)

Composed upon Westminster Bridge
(1807)

Earth has not anything to show more fair:
Dull would he be of soul who could pass by
A sight so touching in its majesty:
This City now doth, like a garment, wear
5 The beauty of the morning; silent, bare,
Ships, towers, domes, theatres, and temples lie
Open unto the fields, and to the sky;
All bright and glittering in the smokeless air.
Never did sun more beautifully steep
10 In his first splendor, valley, rock, or hill;
Ne'er saw I, never felt, a calm so deep!
The river glideth at his own sweet will:
Dear God! the very houses seem asleep;
And all that mighty heart is lying still!

I Wandered Lonely as a Cloud
(1807)

I wandered lonely as a cloud
    That floats on high o'er vales and hills,
When all at once I saw a crowd,
    A host, of golden daffodils,
5 Beside the lake, beneath the trees,
Fluttering and dancing in the breeze.

Continuous as the stars that shine
    And twinkle on the milky way,

They stretched in never-ending line
10   Along the margin of a bay:
Ten thousand saw I at a glance,
Tossing their heads in sprightly dance.

The waves beside them danced; but they
    Out-did the sparkling waves in glee;
15 A poet could not but be gay,
    In such a jocund company;
I gazed—and gazed—but little thought
What wealth the show to me had brought:

For oft, when on my couch I lie
20   In vacant or in pensive mood,
They flash upon that inward eye
    Which is the bliss of solitude;
And then my heart with pleasure fills,
And dances with the daffodils.

She Dwelt among the Untrodden Ways
(1800)

She dwelt among the untrodden ways
    Beside the springs of Dove,[1]
A Maid whom there were none to praise
    And very few to love:
5 A violet by a mossy stone
    Half hidden from the eye!
—Fair as a star, when only one
    Is shining in the sky.

JAMES WRIGHT
(1927–1980)

A Blessing
(1961)

Just off the highway to Rochester, Minnesota,
Twilight bounds softly forth on the grass.
And the eyes of those two Indian ponies

---

[1] River in the Lake District of England.

Darken with kindness.
5 They have come gladly out of the willows
To welcome my friend and me.
We step over the barbed wire into the pasture
Where they have been grazing all day, alone.
They ripple tensely, they can hardly contain their happiness
10 That we have come.
They bow shyly as wet swans. They love each other.
There is no loneliness like theirs.
At home once more,
They begin munching the young tufts of spring in the darkness.
15 I would like to hold the slenderer one in my arms,
For she has walked over to me
And nuzzled my left hand.
She is black and white,
Her mane falls wild on her forehead,
20 And the light breeze moves me to caress her long ear
That is delicate as the skin over a girl's wrist.
Suddenly I realize
That if I stepped out of my body I would break
Into blossom.

WILLIAM BUTLER YEATS
(1865–1939)

Crazy Jane Talks with the Bishop
(1933)

I met the Bishop on the road
And much said he and I.
"Those breasts are flat and fallen now,
Those veins must soon be dry;
5 Live in a heavenly mansion,
Not in some foul sty."

"Fair and foul are near of kin,
And fair needs foul," I cried.
"My friends are gone, but that's a truth
10 Nor grave nor bed denied,
Learned in bodily lowliness
And in the heart's pride.

"A woman can be proud and stiff
When on love intent;

15 But Love has pitched his mansion in
   The place of excrement;
   For nothing can be sole or whole
   That has not been rent."

An Irish Airman Foresees His Death
(1919)

I know that I shall meet my fate
Somewhere among the clouds above;
Those that I fight I do not hate,
Those that I guard I do not love;
5 My country is Kiltartan Cross
My countrymen Kiltartan's poor,
No likely end could bring them loss
Or leave them happier than before.
Now law, nor duty bade me fight,
10 Nor public men, nor cheering crowds,
A lonely impulse of delight
Drove to this tumult in the clouds;
I balanced all, brought all to mind,
The years to come seemed waste of breath,
15 A waste of breath the years behind
In balance with this life, this death.

The Lake Isle of Innisfree
(1892)

I will arise and go now, and go to Innisfree,[1]
And a small cabin build there, of clay and wattles[2] made:
Nine bean-rows will I have there, a hive for the honey-bee,
And live alone in the bee-loud glade.

5 And I shall have some peace there, for peace comes dropping slow,
Dropping from the veils of the morning to where the cricket sings;
There midnight's all a glimmer, and noon a purple glow,
And evening full of the linnet's wings.
I will arise and go now, for always night and day
10 I hear lake water lapping with low sounds by the shore;
While I stand on the roadway, or on the pavements grey,
I hear it in the deep heart's core.

---

[1] An island in Lough (Lake) Gill, County Sligo, in Ireland.

[2] Stakes interwoven with twigs or branches, used for walls and roofing.

Sailing to Byzantium
(1927)

That is no country for old men. The young
In one another's arms, birds in the trees
—Those dying generations—at their song,
The salmon-falls, the mackerel-crowded seas,
5 Fish, flesh, or fowl, commend all summer long
Whatever is begotten, born, and dies.
Caught in that sensual music all neglect
Monuments of unaging intellect.

An aged man is but a paltry thing,
10 A tattered coat upon a stick, unless
Soul clap its hands and sing, and louder sing
For every tatter in its mortal dress,
Nor is there singing school but studying
Monuments of its own magnificence;
15 And therefore I have sailed the seas and come
To the holy city of Byzantium.

O sages standing in God's holy fire
As in the gold mosaic of a wall,
Come from the holy fire, perne in a gyre,
20 And be the singing-masters of my soul.
Consume my heart away; sick with desire
And fastened to a dying animal
It knows not what it is; and gather me
Into the artifice of eternity.

25 Once out of nature I shall never take
My bodily form from any natural thing,
But such a form as Grecian goldsmiths make
Of hammered gold and gold enameling
To keep a drowsy Emperor awake;
30 Or set upon a golden bough to sing
To lords and ladies of Byzantium
Of what is past, or passing, or to come.

The Second Coming[1]
(1921)

Turning and turning in the widening gyre[2]
The falcon cannot hear the falconer;
Things fall apart; the center cannot hold;
Mere anarchy is loosed upon the world,
5 The blood-dimmed tide is loosed, and everywhere
The ceremony of innocence is drowned;
The best lack all conviction, while the worst
Are full of passionate intensity.[3]

Surely some revelation is at hand;
10 Surely the Second Coming is at hand;
The Second Coming! Hardly are those words out
When a vast image out of *Spiritus Mundi*[4]
Troubles my sight: somewhere in sands of the desert
A shape with lion body and the head of a man,
15 A gaze blank and pitiless as the sun,
Is moving its slow thighs, while all about it
Reel shadows of the indignant desert birds.
The darkness drops again; but now I know
That twenty centuries[5] of stony sleep
20 Were vexed to nightmare by a rocking cradle,
And what rough beast, its hour come round at last,
Slouches towards Bethlehem to be born?

---

[1] The Second Coming usually refers to the return of Christ. Yeats theorized cycles of history, much like the turning of a wheel. Here he offers a poetic comment on his view of the dissolution of civilization at the end of one such cycle.

[2] Spiral.

[3] Lines 4–8 refer to the Russian Revolution (1917).

[4] The Spirit of the World. Yeats believed all souls to be connected by a "Great Memory."

[5] The centuries since the birth of Christ.

YEVGENY YEVTUSHENKO
(1933–)

Lies
(1962)

Telling lies to the young is wrong.
Proving to them that lies are true is wrong.
Telling them that God's in his heaven
and all's well with the world is wrong.
5 The young know what you mean. The young are people.
Tell them the difficulties can't be counted,
and let them see not only what will be
but see with clarity these present times.
Say obstacles exist they must encounter
10 sorrow happens, hardship happens.
The hell with it. Who never knew
the price of happiness will not be happy.
Forgive no error you recognize,
it will repeat itself, increase,
15 and afterwards our pupils
will not forgive in us what we forgave.

POETRY CASEBOOK

This casebook contains ten poems by Gwendolyn Brooks, a collection of source materials,[1] and a student paper offering insights into various aspects of Brooks's work.

Poems

- from *A Street in Bronzeville* (1945)
    "The Ballad of Chocolate Mabbie"
    "A Song in the Front Yard"
- from *Annie Allen* (1949)
    "People Who Have No Children Can Be Hard"
    "What Shall I Give My Children?"
- from *The Bean Eaters* (1960)
    "The Bean Eaters"
    "The *Chicago Defender* Sends a Man to Little Rock"
- from *In the Mecca* (1968)
    "The Blackstone Rangers"
    "The Ballad of Rudolph Reed"
- from *The World of Gwendolyn Brooks* (1971)
    "Medgar Evers"
- from *To Disembark* (1981)
    "The Boy Died in My Alley"

(Other poems by Brooks included elsewhere in this text are "Sadie and Maud," from *A Street in Bronzeville* (p. 188); "First Fight. Then Fiddle," from *Annie Allen* (p. 221); and "We Real Cool," from *The Bean Eaters* (p. 130).)

Source Materials

- Brooks, Gwendolyn. "An Interview with Myself." *Triquarterly* 60 (1984): 405–10. An interview with Gwendolyn Brooks, conducted

---

[1] Note that the articles in this casebook do not use current MLA documentation style. See Appendix A for new MLA format.

by the poet herself, in which she discusses her background and her ideas about poetry in general and the role of African-American poets in particular.

- Brooks, Gwendolyn. *Report from Part One.* Detroit: Broadside Press, 1972. A section of an article in which Brooks discusses her African-American identity.
- Baker, Houston, A., Jr. "The Achievement of Gwendolyn Brooks." *A Life Distilled: Gwendolyn Brooks, Her Poetry and Fiction.* Ed. Maria K. Mootry and Gary Smith. Urbana: U of Illinois P, 1987. 21–29. A discussion of Brooks's use of traditional forms to explore the African-American experience.
- Stavros, George. "An Interview with Gwendolyn Brooks." *Contemporary Literature* 11.1 (Winter 1970): 1–20. Excerpts from an interview with the poet conducted in 1969.
- Smith, Gary. "Gwendolyn Brooks's 'Children of the Poor,' Metaphysical Poetry and the Inconditions of Love." *A Life Distilled: Gwendolyn Brooks, Her Poetry and Fiction.* Ed. Maria K. Mootry and Gary Smith. Urbana: U of Illinois P, 1987. 165–76. An article that examines Gwendolyn Brooks's use of the sonnet form.
- Mootry, Maria K. "'Chocolate Mabbie' and 'Pearl May Lee': Gwendolyn Brooks and the Ballad Tradition." *CLA Journal* 30.3 (March 1987): 278–93. An excerpt from an article about Gwendolyn Brooks's use of ballad themes and techniques as well as new variations on the ballad tradition.
- Smith, Gary. "Gwendolyn Brooks's *A Street in Bronzeville,* the Harlem Renaissance and the Mythologies of Black Women." *American Women Poets.* Ed. Harold Bloom. New York: Chelsea, 1986. 86–89. Excerpts from a critical article about the relationship between Brooks's poetry and the poetry of the Harlem Renaissance.

After reading the poems and the accompanying critical articles that follow them, carefully consider the questions at the end of the casebook (p. 452). Then, decide on a topic for a three- to five-page essay on the work of Gwendolyn Brooks. For guidelines on evaluating literary criticism, see p. 13; for guidelines on using source materials, see p. 461. Make sure your paper follows the conventions for documenting sources outlined in Appendix A.

A complete student paper, "Racial Consciousness in 'The Ballad of Rudolph Reed,'" which uses sources in this casebook, begins on p. 454.

GWENDOLYN BROOKS (1917–) was, in 1950, the first African American to win a Pulitzer Prize (for her second book of poems, *Annie Allen*). Born in Topeka, Kansas, Brooks was raised in a section of Chicago called "Bronzeville," which provided the setting for her first published poetry collection, *A Street in Bronzeville* (1945). She remembers "a sparkly childhood with two fine parents" who encouraged their daughter to love music and poetry. When Brooks was barely twenty years old, her mother gave her poems to Langston Hughes and James Weldon Johnson, two of the most distinguished writers of the Harlem Renaissance. They both became Brooks's literary and personal mentors. Brooks, who ran poetry workshops for radical black activists during the late 1960s, continues to be deeply involved in the intellectual and artistic development of the young people around her. She is also the poet laureate of Illinois. Beyond the collections cited in the casebook, Brooks is known for her volumes *Riot* (1969), *Family Pictures* (1970), *Aloneness* (1971), *Aurora* (1972), *Beckonings* (1975), *Primer for Blacks* (1980), *Black Love* (1982), *Mayor Harold Washington* and *Chicago, The I Will City* (1983), and *The Near Johannesburg Boy, and Other Poems* (1987). Collected works include *Selected Poems* (1963), *The World of Gwendolyn Brooks* (1971), and *Blacks* (1987). She also published a novel, *Maud Martha* (1953), and *Report from Part One: An Autobiography* (1972).

From her earliest work, Brooks showed a remarkable ability to blend elements of traditional and modernist poetry with the language and rhythms of African-American life. Yet whether the voice is cool and restrained (as in "People Who Have No Children Can Be Hard") or ironically colloquial (as in "We Real Cool"), Brooks's poems are dense, complex, and often surprising explorations that provide the deepest rewards to her readers.

The Ballad of Chocolate Mabbie
(1945)

It was Mabbie without the grammar school gates.
And Mabbie was all of seven.
And Mabbie was cut from a chocolate bar.
And Mabbie thought life was heaven.

Photo by Bill Tague.

5 The grammar school gates were the pearly gates,
For Willie Boone went to school.
When she sat by him in history class
Was only her eyes were cool.

It was Mabbie without the grammar school gates
10 Waiting for Willie Boone.
Half hour after the closing bell!
He would surely be coming soon.

Oh, warm is the waiting for joys, my dears!
And it cannot be too long.
15 Oh, pity the little poor chocolate lips
That carry the bubble of song!

Out came the saucily bold Willie Boone.
It was woe for our Mabbie now.
He wore like a jewel a lemon-hued lynx
20 With sand-waves loving her brow.

It was Mabbie alone by the grammar school gates.
Yet chocolate companions had she:
Mabbie on Mabbie with hush in the heart.
Mabbie on Mabbie to be.

A Song in the Front Yard
(1945)

I've stayed in the front yard all my life.
I want a peek at the back
Where it's rough and untended and hungry weed grows.
A girl gets sick of a rose.

5 I want to go in the back yard now
And maybe down the alley,
To where the charity children play.
I want a good time today.

They do some wonderful things.
10 They have some wonderful fun.
My mother sneers, but I say it's fine
How they don't have to go in at quarter to nine.

My mother, she tells me that Johnnie Mae
Will grow up to be a bad woman.
15 That George'll be taken to Jail soon or late
(On account of last winter he sold our back gate).

But I say it's fine. Honest, I do.
And I'd like to be a bad woman, too,
And wear the brave stockings of night-black lace
20 And strut down the streets with paint on my face.

People Who Have No Children Can Be Hard
(1949)

People who have no children can be hard:
Attain a mail of ice and insolence:
Need not pause in the fire, and in no sense
Hesitate in the hurricane to guard.
5 And when wide world is bitten and bewarred
They perish purely, waving their spirits hence
Without a trace of grace or of offense
To laugh or fail, diffident, wonder-starred.
While through a throttling dark we others hear
10 The little lifting helplessness, the queer
Whimper-whine; whose unridiculous
Lost softness softly makes a trap for us.
And makes a curse. And makes a sugar of
The malocclusions, the inconditions of love.

What Shall I Give My Children?
(1949)

What shall I give my children? who are poor,
Who are adjudged the leastwise of the land,
Who are my sweetest lepers, who demand
No velvet and no velvety velour;
5 But who have begged me for a brisk contour,
Crying that they are quasi, contraband
Because unfinished, graven by a hand
Less than angelic, admirable or sure.
My hand is stuffed with mode, design, device.
10 But I lack access to my proper stone.
And plenitude of plan shall not suffice
Nor grief nor love shall be enough alone
To ratify my little halves who bear
Across an autumn freezing everywhere.

The Bean Eaters
(1960)

They eat beans mostly, this old yellow pair.
Dinner is a casual affair.

Plain chipware on a plain and creaking wood,
Tin flatware.
5 Two who are Mostly Good.
Two who have lived their day,
But keep on putting on their clothes
And putting things away.

And remembering . . .
10 Remembering, with twinklings and twinges,
As they lean over the beans in their rented back room that
    is full of beads and receipts and dolls and cloths,
    tobacco crumbs, vases and fringes.

The *Chicago Defender*[1] Sends a Man to Little Rock
(1960)

Fall, 1957[2]

In Little Rock the people bear
Babes, and comb and part their hair
And watch the want ads, put repair
To roof and latch. While wheat toast burns
5 A woman waters multiferns.

Time upholds or overturns
The many, tight, and small concerns.

In Little Rock the people sing
Sunday hymns like anything,
10 Through Sunday pomp and polishing.

And after testament and tunes,
Some soften Sunday afternoons
With lemon tea and Lorna Doones.

I forecast
15 And I believe
Come Christmas Little Rock will cleave
To Christmas tree and trifle, weave,
From laugh and tinsel, texture fast.

---

[1] A weekly newspaper for African-American readers.

[2] When black students first entered the high school in Little Rock, Arkansas, in 1957, the city erupted in race riots protesting desegregation.

In Little Rock is baseball; Barcarolle.[3]
20 That hotness in July . . . the uniformed figures raw and implacable
And not intellectual,
Batting the hotness or clawing the suffering dust.
The Open Air Concert, on the special twilight green. . . .
When Beethoven is brutal or whispers to lady-like air.
25 Blanket-sitters are solemn, as Johann troubles to lean
To tell them what to mean. . . .

There is love, too, in Little Rock. Soft women softly
Opening themselves in kindness,
Or, pitying one's blindness,
30 Awaiting one's pleasure
In azure
Glory with anguished rose at the root. . . .
To wash away old semi-discomfitures.
They re-teach purple and unsullen blue.
35 The wispy soils go. And uncertain
Half-havings have they clarified to sures.

In Little Rock they know
Not answering the telephone is a way of rejecting life,
That it is our business to be bothered, is our business
40 To cherish bores or boredom, be polite
To lies and love and many-faceted fuzziness.
I scratch my head, massage the hate-I-had.
I blink across my prim and pencilled pad.
The saga I was sent for is not down.
45 Because there is a puzzle in this town.
The biggest News I do not dare
Telegraph to the Editor's chair:
"They are like people everywhere."

The angry Editor would reply
50 In hundred harryings of Why.

And true, they are hurling spittle, rock,
Garbage and fruit in Little Rock.
And I saw coiling storm a-writhe
On bright madonnas. And a scythe
55 Of men harassing brownish girls.
(The bows and barrettes in the curls
And braids declined away from joy.)

---

[3] A Venetian gondolier's song, or one suggesting the rhythm of rowing.

I saw a bleeding brownish boy. . . .

The lariat lynch-wish I deplored.

60 The loveliest lynchee was our Lord.

The Blackstone Rangers[1]
(1968)

I

AS SEEN BY DISCIPLES

There they are.
Thirty at the corner.
Black, raw, ready.
Sores in the city
5 that do not want to heal.

II

THE LEADERS

Jeff. Gene. Geronimo. And Bop.
They cancel, cure and curry.
Hardly the dupes of the downtown thing
the cold bonbon,
10 the rhinestone thing. And hardly
in a hurry.
Hardly Belafonte, King,
Black Jesus, Stokely, Malcolm X or Rap.
Bungled trophies.
15 Their country is a Nation on no map.

Jeff, Gene, Geronimo and Bop
in the passionate noon,
in bewitching night
are the detailed men, the copious men.
20 They curry, cure,
they cancel, cancelled images whose Concerts
are not divine, vivacious; the different tins
are intense last entries; pagan argument;
translations of the night.

25 The Blackstone bitter bureaus
(bureaucracy is footloose) edit, fuse
unfashionable damnations and descent;

---

[1] A Chicago street gang.

and exulting, monstrous hand on monstrous hand,
construct, strangely, a monstrous pearl or grace.

III

Gang Girls

A RANGERETTE

30 Gang Girls are sweet exotics.
Mary Ann
uses the nutrients of her orient,
but sometimes sighs for Cities of blue and jewel
beyond her Ranger rim of Cottage Grove.
35 (Bowery Boys, Disciples, Whip-Birds will
dissolve no margins, stop no savory sanctities.)

Mary is
a rose in a whiskey glass.

Mary's
40 Februaries shudder and are gone. Aprils
fret frankly, lilac hurries on.
Summer is a hard irregular ridge.
October looks away.
And that's the Year!
45   Save for her bugle-love.
Save for the bleat of not-obese devotion.
Save for Somebody Terribly Dying, under
the philanthropy of robins. Save for her Ranger
bringing
50 an amount of rainbow in a string-drawn bag.
"Where did you get the diamond?" Do not ask:
but swallow, straight, the spirals of his flask
and assist him at your zipper; pet his lips
and help him clutch you.

55 Love's another departure.
Will there be any arrivals, confirmations?
Will there be gleaming?

Mary, the Shakedancer's child
from the rooming-flat, pants carefully, peers at
60 her laboring lover. . . .
          Mary! Mary Ann!
Settle for sandwiches! settle for stocking caps!
for sudden blood, aborted carnival,
the props and niceties of non-loneliness—
65 the rhymes of Leaning.

The Ballad of Rudolph Reed
(1960)

Rudolph Reed was oaken.
His wife was oaken too.
And his two girls and his good little man
Oakened as they grew.

5 "I am not hungry for berries.
I am not hungry for bread.
But hungry hungry for a house
Where at night a man in bed

"May never hear the plaster
10 Stir as if in pain.
May never hear the roaches
Falling like fat rain.

"Where never wife and children need
Go blinking through the gloom.
15 Where every room of many rooms
Will be full of room.

"Oh my home may have its east or west
Or north or south behind it.
All I know is I shall know it,
20 And fight for it when I find it."

It was in a street of bitter white
That he made his application.
For Rudolph Reed was oakener
Than others in the nation.

25 The agent's steep and steady stare
Corroded to a grin.
*Why, you black old, tough old hell of a man,
Move your family in!*

Nary a grin grinned Rudolph Reed,
30 Nary a curse cursed he,
But moved in his House. With his dark little wife,
And his dark little children three.

A neighbor would *look*, with a yawning eye
That squeezed into a slit.
35 But the Rudolph Reeds and the children three
Were too joyous to notice it.

For were they not firm in a home of their own
With windows everywhere
And a beautiful banistered stair
40 And a front yard for flowers and a back yard for grass?

The first night, a rock, big as two fists.
The second, a rock big as three.
But nary a curse cursed Rudolph Reed.
(Though oaken as man could be.)

45 The third night, a silvery ring of glass.
Patience ached to endure.
But he looked, and lo! small Mabel's blood
Was staining her gaze so pure.

Then up did rise our Rudolph Reed
50 And pressed the hand of his wife,
And went to the door with a thirty-four
And a beastly butcher knife.

He ran like a mad thing into the night.
And the words in his mouth were stinking.
55 By the time he had hurt his first white man
He was no longer thinking.

By the time he had hurt his fourth white man
Rudolph Reed was dead.
His neighbors gathered and kicked his corpse.
60 "Nigger—" his neighbors said.

Small Mabel whimpered all night long,
For calling herself the cause.
Her oak-eyed mother did no thing
But change the bloody gauze.

Medgar Evers[1]
(1964)

For Charles Evers[2]

The man whose height his fear improved he
arranged to fear no further. The raw
intoxicated time was time for better birth or a final death.

---

[1] African-American civil rights leader who was shot and killed by a sniper in 1963.

[2] Medgar Evers's brother.

Old styles, old tempos, all the engagement of
the day—the sedate, the regulated fray—
the antique light, the Moral rose, old gusts,
tight whistlings from the past, the mothballs
in the Love at last our man forswore.

Medgar Evers annoyed confetti and assorted
brands of businessmen's eyes.

The shows came down: to maxims and surprise.
And palsy.

Roaring no rapt arise-ye to the dead, he
leaned across tomorrow. People said that
he was holding clean globes in his hands.

The Boy Died in My Alley
(1981)

Without my having known.
Policeman said, next morning,
"Apparently died Alone."
"You heard a shot?" Policeman said.
Shots I hear and Shots I hear.
I never see the dead.

The Shot that killed him yes I heard
as I heard the Thousand shots before;
careening tinnily down the nights
across my years and arteries.

Policeman pounded on my door.
"Who is it?" "POLICE!" Policeman yelled.
"A Boy was dying in your alley.
A Boy is dead, and in your alley.
And have you known this Boy before?"

I have known this Boy before.
I have known this Boy before, who
ornaments my alley.
I never saw his face at all.
I never saw his futurefall.
But I have known this Boy.

I have always heard him deal with death.
I have always heard the shout, the volley.

I have closed my heart-ears late and early.
25 And I have killed him ever.

I joined the Wild and killed him
with knowledgeable unknowing.
I saw where he was going.
I saw him Crossed. And seeing,
30 I did not take him down.

He cried not only "Father!"
but "Mother!
Sister!
Brother."
35 The cry climbed up the alley.
It went up to the wind.
It hung upon the heaven
for a long
stretch-strain of Moment.

40 The red floor of my alley
is a special speech to me.

An Interview with Myself

Gwendolyn Brooks

QUESTION: Why are you interviewing yourself?

GB: Because I know the facts and nuances.

Q: Describe your "background."

GB: Nothing Strange. No child abuse, no prostitution, no Mafia membership. A sparkly childhood, with two fine parents and one brother, in a plain but warmly enclosing two-storey gray house (we always rented the top floor). Our house, regularly painted by my father (sometimes with the help of his friend Berry Thompson), had a back yard and a front yard, both pleasant with hedges and shrubs and trees and flowers. My father recited fascinating poetry, and sang to us jolly or haunting songs. My favorite was "Asleep in the Deep": "Many brave hearts are asleep in the deep, so beware—be-e-e-e WARE"; his voice went down sincerely, down and down and down; suddenly the living room was a theater. My mother sang, too, and played the piano almost every day. She loved music. Classical, popular, spiritual, *all* music. She wrote music; she had gone to a class to study harmony. My parents and my brother and I observed all the holidays. We made much of the Table. It entertained, variously, turkey and pumpkin pie, fruitcake and mince pie,

"Easter ham," birthday-cake creations. My brother and my mother and I (not my father) enjoyed family and church picnics, went to Riverview, Sunday School, the Regal Theatre and the Metropolitan and Harmony theaters, neighborhood parties, the Field Museum. . . . Our life was family-oriented, so we did a lot of family visiting. Aunt Ella and Uncle Ernest, Aunt Gertie and Uncle Paul lived in Chicago (all near each other now, out in Lincoln Cemetery), so we saw them frequently; but there were also aunts, uncles and cousins in Milwaukee, Topeka, and Kalamazoo, so in the summer, sometimes, we would get on a train and go visit those folks. We children enjoyed those visits so—enjoyed watching, deciphering! We enjoyed our schooltimes, too. As soon as we were old enough, my mother got us library cards; and there were many books in the house, including the Harvard Classics. Our parents were intelligent and courageous; they subscribed to duty, decency, dignity, industry—*kindness.*

Q: Why is your name, almost always, followed by the phrase "Pulitzer Prize"?

GB: Because I was the first black to be given a Pulitzer of any kind. That was in 1950, for my second book of poetry, *Annie Allen.* Thirty-three years later, another black woman has received a Pulitzer, this time for a novel, *The Color Purple* (multitalented Alice Walker). Several estimable black males won the prize in those intervening years—starting with the remarkable *Ebony* photographer, Moneta Sleet Jr. (In 1971 *Ebony* sent the two of us to Montgomery, Alabama, to work up a feature on "After-the-Storm" Montgomery. We would dash into the street; I would seize and question anyone who looked storyful, while amiable Moneta photographed away. One of the most enjoyable adventures of my life; I've always thanked Senior Editor Herb Nipson for choosing me to share that trip with Moneta.)

Q: You promised a nice little Pulitzer story.

GB: Here is a nice little Pulitzer story, one of many Pulitzer stories I'll tell you later. On Pulitzer announcement day, this past spring, I heard Alice's award mentioned on radio, minutes before I was to address an audience at the University of Missouri in Kansas City. I announced this Happening—mentioning the strange thirty-three-year gap—and asked the audience to celebrate with applause. The audience applauded. And some of the audience tsk-tsked appropriately: because, you see, in those thirty-three years black women writers had not been idle. We had Paule Marshall. We had Mari Evans. We had Margaret Walker, Toni Cade Bambara, Audre Lorde, Lucille Clifton, Toni Morrison, Ai, Dolores Kendrick, Sonia Sanchez. Many others. Talented women. Writers of poetry *and* prose, strikingly effective *and* interesting *and* English-nourishing *and* blackness-preserving. When you really think of thirty-three years stretching between myself in

1950 and Alice in 1983, you have to gasp.

Q: Talk about the late sixties.

GB: Speaking of nourishment—my nourishment of nourishments was in the years 1967 to 1972. As I've said of those years, the "new" black ideal italicized black identity, solidarity, self-possession, self-address. Furthermore, the *essential* black ideal vitally acknowledged African roots. Came Oscar Brown Jr.'s variety show, "Opportunity, Please Knock." I met many of the Blackstone Rangers comprising, chiefly, that cast. They liked me and respected me. I started a poetry workshop for interested Rangers, college students, teen organizers. Later I paid Walter Bradford, a young organizer-friend of Oscar's, to run a one-year workshop for Rangers only. It was highly successful. My original group stayed with me several years. Eventually, many of them got teaching jobs here and there, across the country.

Among them, I had two good *Sons of the Revolution*. That's irony. We had no Revolution. We had a healthy rebellion. These "Sons," Walter Bradford and Don L. (Haki) Lee, taught me a little of what I needed to know about The Great World around me. I found myself reading, with profit, the books Haki recommended: such books as Fanon's *The Wretched of the Earth*, Lundberg's *The Rich and the Super-Rich*, DuBois' *The Souls of Black Folk*, Zora Neale Hurston's novels. We talked, we walked, we read our work in taverns and churches and jail. I invited writers like James Baldwin and John O. Killens to my house to meet them, to exchange views with them. At such parties, and at our own regular meetings, and at our street festivals, the air was hot, heavy with logic, illogic, zeal, construction. What years those were—years of hot-breathing hope, clean planning, and sizable black cross-reference and reliance. OF COURSE I know those years couldn't and shouldn't "return"! The flaws have been witnessed and cataloged, with great energy (and inventiveness). I needn't repeat. Much is gone and forgotten, the good and the not-good. But there's something under-river; pride surviving, pride and self-respect surviving, however wobbly or wondering.

Well, those young people adopted and instructed me. They put me on The Wall of Respect! (Forty-third and Langley.)

The theme poem of that Blacktime's essence was Haki's "New Integrationist":

> I
> seek
> integration
> of
> negroes
> with
> Black
> people

Q: Talk about the Poet Laureate Awards.

GB: When I was made Poet Laureate of Illinois, following Carl Sandburg's death, I wanted to substantiate the honor with assistance to the young. I spend about $2,000 each spring on a competition that involves at least twenty high-school and elementary-school awards, and a ceremony—for many years now—at the University of Chicago, with presentations, recitations. The Chicago newspapers have been cooperative, giving my young poets a forum every year.

Q: Do you feel you've had your share of honors?

GB: Indeed! There's even the Gwendolyn Brooks Junior High School at 147th and Wallace (Harvey), and the Gwendolyn Brooks Cultural Center at Western Illinois University.

Q: Have you written fiction?

GB: Short stories and novellas I am not proud of. And a novel, *Maud Martha,* published by Harper & Row. *Maud Martha* is a lovely little novel about a lovely little person, wrestling with the threads of her milieu. Of course this "lovely little person" was the essence of myself, or aspects of myself tied with as neat a ribbon as my innocence could manage. The novel is very funny, very often!—and not at all disappointing, even *though* my heroine was never raped, did not become a lady of the evening, did not enter the world of welfare mothers (I admire Diahann Carroll's underrated movie "Claudine"), did not murder the woman who stepped on her toe in the bus. I said in my autobiographical novel "an autobiographical novel is a better testament, a better thermometer, than a memoir can be. For who, in presenting a 'factual' account, is going to tell the absolute, the horrifying or exquisite, the incredible Truth?" An autobiographical novel is allowing. There's fact-meat in the soup, among the chunks of fancy: but, generally, definite identification will be difficult. . . . Much that happened to Maudie has not happened to me; and she is a nicer and a better-coordinated creature than I am. I can say that lots in the "story" was taken out of my own life and twisted, highlighted or dimmed, dressed up or down.

Q: What is a poet? What is poetry?

GB: There are hundreds of definitions. A poet is one who distils experience—strains experience. A poet looks—sees. Poets oblige themselves to see. Poetry is siren, prose is survey. I keep telling children: "Poetry comes out of life. What happened to you yesterday and last week and six years ago and ten minutes ago and what you *surmise* may happen tomorrow is poetry-in-the-rough. Strain it—distil—work the magic of carefully-chosen *words* upon it—and there's poetry."

Q: What is the meaning of T.H.E.M.?

GB: "Trying Hard to Express Myself." I organized the eighteen teenagers on my block into a forum. T.H.E.M. was their choice of a name. They met at my house, flopped on the floor when chairage was exhausted, discussed numbers of things: school, sex, drugs, politics—Africa. One of them tired of discussions on Africa this, Africa that. She judged, "We're never going there. We're going *no*where. We're folks who have nothing at all to do with Africa." So I sent her to Ghana, with another girl from our "club," and my daughter as chaperone. Couldn't have had a better chaperone! My daughter Nora Blakely writes prose and poetry, has taught in elementary school and at Roosevelt University, dances and teaches dancing, choreographs. On the way, my voyagers had a few days in London and in Paris. I wanted to help extend the horizons of these young people, and they met with me for about four years. During that time I gave them scholarships, took them to black plays and movies, bought books and educational magazines for them, brought "career people" to speak to them— writers, a senator, a photographer, an editor, an actress. They were not shy in the presence of these "career people": they challenged, corrected, extended. (These youngsters were also "watch-workers," who kept a collective eye on the block and reported disturbances to the police.) Our best-enjoyed nourishment, however, was the unrestricted exhilaration of "mere" communication.

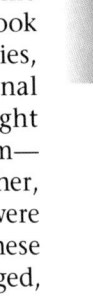

from **Report from Part One**

Gwendolyn Brooks

Until 1967 my own blackness did not confront me with a shrill spelling of itself. I knew that I was what most people were calling "a Negro;" I called myself that, although always the word fell awkwardly on a poet's ear; I had never liked the sound of it (Caucasian has an ugly sound, too, while the name Indian is beautiful to look at and to hear.) *And* I knew that people of my coloration and distinctive history had been bolted to trees and sliced or burned or shredded; knocked to the back of the line; provided with separate toilets, schools, neighborhoods: denied, when possible, voting rights: hounded, hooted at, or shunned, or patronizingly patted (often the patting-hand was, I knew, surreptitiously wiped after the Kindness, so that unspeakable contamination might be avoided.) America's social climate, it seemed, was trying to tell me something. It was trying to tell me something Websterian. Yet, although almost secretly, I had always felt that to be black was good. Sometimes, there would be an approximate whisper around me: *others* felt, it seemed, that to be black was good. The translation would have been something like "Hey— being black is *fun.*" Or something like "Hey—our folks have got stuff to be proud of!" Or something like "Hey—since we are so good why aren't we treated like the other 'Americans?'"

Suddenly there was New Black to meet. In the spring of 1967 I met some of it at the Fisk University Writers' Conference in Nashville.

Coming from white white white South Dakota State College I arrived in Nashville, Tennessee, to give one more "reading." But blood-boiling surprise was in store for me. First, I was aware of a general energy, an electricity, in look, walk, speech, *gesture* of the young blackness I saw all about me. I had been "loved" at South Dakota State College. Here, I was coldly Respected. Here, the heroes included the novelist-director, John Killens, editors David Llorens, and Hoyt Fuller, playwright Ron Milner, historians John Henrik Clarke and Lerone Bennett (and even poor Lerone was taken to task, by irate members of a no-nonsense young audience, for affiliating himself with *Ebony Magazine*, considered at that time a traitor for allowing skin-bleach advertisements in its pages, and for over-featuring light-skinned women). Imamu Amiri Baraka, then "LeRoi Jones," was expected. He arrived in the middle of my own offering, and when I called attention to his presence there was jubilee in Jubilee Hall.

All that day and night, Margaret Danner Cunningham—another Old Girl, another coldly Respected old Has-been—and an almost hysterical Gwendolyn B. walked about in amazement, listening, looking, learning. *What was going on!*

In my cartoon basket I keep a cartoon of a stout, dowager-hatted, dowager-furred Helen Hokinson woman. She is on parade in the world. She is a sign-carrier in the wild world. Her sign says "Will someone please tell me what is going on?" Well, although I cannot give a full-blooded answer to that potent question, I have been supplied—the sources are plural—with helpful materials: hints, friendly *and* inimical clues, approximations, statistics, "proofs" of one kind and another; from these I am trying to weave the coat that I shall wear. In 1967's Nashville, however, the somewhat dotty expression in the eyes of the cartoon-woman, the *agapeness,* were certainly mine. I was in some inscrutable and uncomfortable wonderland. I didn't know what to make of what surrounded me, of what with hot sureness began almost immediately to invade me. *I* had never been, before, in the general presence of such insouciance, such live firmness, such confident vigor, such determination to mold or carve something DEFINITE.

Up against the wall, white man! was the substance of the Baraka shout, at the evening reading he shared with fierce Ron Milner among intoxicating drumbeats, heady incense and organic underhumming. Up against the wall! And a pensive (until that moment) white man of thirty or thirty-three abruptly shot himself into the heavy air, screaming "Yeah! *Yeah!* Up against the wall, Brother! KILL 'EM ALL! KILL 'EM ALL!"

I thought that was interesting.

There is indeed a new black today. He is different from any the world has known. He's a tall-walker. Almost firm. By many of his own *brothers* he is not understood. And he is understood by *no* white. Not the wise white; not the Schooled white; not the Kind white. Your *least* pre-requisite toward an understanding of the new black is an exceptional Doctorate which can be conferred only upon those with the proper properties of bitter birth and intrinsic sorrow. I know this is infuriating, especially to those professional Negro-understanders, some of them so *very* kind, with special portfolio, special savvy. But I cannot say anything other, because nothing other is the truth.

I—who have "gone the gamut" from an almost angry rejection of my dark skin by some of my brain-washed brothers and sisters to a surprised queenhood in the new black sun—am qualified to enter at least the kindergarten of new consciousness now. New consciousness and trudge-toward-progress.

I have hopes for myself.

The Achievement of Gwendolyn Brooks

Houston A. Baker, Jr.

> A writer writes out of his own family background, out of his own immediate community, during his formative period. And he writes out of his own talent and his own individual vision. Now if he doesn't, if he tries to get away from that by bending it to some ideological line, then he is depriving the group of its uniqueness. What we need is individuals. If the white society has tried to do anything to us, it has tried to keep us from being individuals.[1]
>
> —*Ralph Ellison*

Gwendolyn Brooks, like W. E. B. Du Bois, seems caught between two worlds. And both she and Du Bois manifest the duality of their lives in their literary works; Du Bois wrote in a beautiful, impressionistic style set off by quotations from the world's literary masters. Brooks writes tense, complex, rhythmic verse that contains the metaphysical complexities of John Donne and the word magic of Apollinaire, Eliot, and Pound. The high style of both authors, however, is often used to explicate the condition of black Americans trapped behind a veil that separates them from the white world. What one seems to have is white style and black content—two warring ideals in one dark body.

This apparent dichotomy has produced a confusing situation for Gwendolyn Brooks. The world of white arts and letters has pointed to her with pride; it has bestowed kudos and a Pulitzer Prize. The world of black arts and letters has looked on with mixed emotion, and pride has been only one part of the mixture. There have also been troubling questions about the poet's essential "blackness," her dedication to the melioration of the black Americans' social conditions. The real duality appears when we realize that Gwendolyn Brooks—although praised and awarded—does not appear on the syllabi of most American literature courses, and her name seldom appears in the annual scholarly bibliographies of the academic world. It would seem she is a black writer after all, *not* an American writer. Yet when one listens to the voice of today's black-revolutionary consciousness, one often hears that Brooks's early poetry fits the white, middle-class patterns that Imamu Baraka has seen as characteristic of "Negro literature."[2]

When one turns to her canon, one finds that she has abided the questions of both camps. Etheridge Knight has perfectly captured her enduring quality in the following lines:

> O courier on pegasus, O Daughter of Parnassus
> O Splendid woman of the purple stitch.
> When beaten and blue, despairingly we sink
> Within obfuscating mire,
> O, cradle in your bosom us, hum your lullabies
> And soothe our souls with kisses of verse
> That stir us on to search for light.
> O Mother of the world. Effulgent lover of the Sun!
> For ever speak the truth.[3]

She has the Parnassian inspiration and the earth-mother characteristics noted by the poet; her strength has come from a dedication to truth. The truth that concerns her does not amount to a facile realism or a heavy naturalism, although "realism" is the word that comes to mind when one reads a number of poems in *A Street in Bronzeville* (1945).

Poems, or segments, such as "kitchenette building," "a song in the front yard," and "the vacant lot," all support the view that the writer was intent on a realistic, even a naturalistic, portrayal of the life of lower-echelon urban dwellers:

> We are things of dry hours and the involuntary plan,
> Grayed in, and gray. "Dream" makes a giddy sound, not strong
> Like "rent," "feeding a wife," "satisfying a man."[4]

> My mother, she tells me that Johnnie Mae
> Will grow up to be a bad woman.
> That George'll be taken to Jail soon or late
> (On account of last winter he sold our back gate.)
> (*WGB*, p. 12)

> And with seeing the squat fat daughter
> Letting in the men
> When majesty has gone for the day—
> And letting them out again.
> (*WGB*, p. 25)

These passages reinforce the designation of Brooks as a realist, and poems such as "The Sundays of Satin-Legs Smith," "We Real Cool," "A Lovely Love," and the volume *Annie Allen* can be added to the list. If she had insisted on a strict realism and nothing more, she could perhaps be written off as a limited poet. But she is no mere chronicler of the condition of the black American poor. Even her most vividly descriptive verses contain an element that removes them from the realm of a cramped realism. All of her characters have both ratiocinative and imaginative capabilities; they have the ability to reason, dream, muse, and remember. This ability distinguishes them from the naturalistic literary victim caught in an environmental maze. From the realm of "raw and unadorned life," Satin-Legs Smith creates his own world of bright colors, splendid attire, and soft loves in the midst of a cheap hotel's odor and decay. The heroine of "The Anniad" conjures up a dream world, covers it in silver plate, populates it with an imaginary prince, and shores up magnificent fragments against the ruins of war. And Jessie Mitchell's mother seeks refuge from envy and death in a golden past:

> She revived for the moment settled and dried-up triumphs,
> Forced perfume into old petals, pulled up the droop,
> Refueled
> Triumphant long-exhaled breaths.
> Her exquisite yellow youth. . . .
>
> (*WGB*, p. 329)

Gwendolyn Brooks's characters, in short, are infinitely human because at the core of their existence is the imaginative intellect.

Given the vision of such characters, it is impossible to agree with David Littlejohn, who wishes to view them as simplistic mouthpieces for the poet's sensibility;[5] moreover, it is not surprising that the characters' concerns transcend the ghetto life of many black Americans. They reflect the joy of childhood, the burdens and contentment of motherhood, the distortions of the war-torn psyche, the horror of blood-guiltiness, and the pains of the anti-hero confronted with a heroic ideal. Brooks's protagonists, personae, and speakers, in short, capture all of life's complexities, particularly the complexity of an industrialized age characterized by swift change, depersonalization, and war.

In "Gay Chaps at the Bar," the poet shows her concern for a theme that has had a great influence on twentieth-century British and American art. In one section, "my dreams, my works, must wait till after hell," she employs the food metaphors characteristic of her writing to express the incompleteness that accompanies war:

> I hold my honey and I store my bread
> In little jars and cabinets of my will.
> I label clearly, and each latch and lid
> I bid, Be firm till I return from hell.
> I am very hungry. I am incomplete.
>
> (*WGB*, p. 50)

In another section, "piano after war," she captures the mental anguish occasioned by war. The rejuvenation the speaker has felt in the "golden rose" music feeding his "old hungers" suddenly ends:

> But suddenly, across my climbing fever
> Of proud delight—a multiplying cry.
> A cry of bitter dead men who will never
> Attend a gentle maker of musical joy.
> Then my thawed eye will go again to ice.
> And stone will shove the softness from my face.
>
> (*WGB*, p. 52)

In "The Anniad" and the "Appendix to the Anniad," the poet deals once again with the chaos of arms: War destroys marriage, stifles fertility, and turns men to creatures of "untranslatable ice." Her work, therefore, joins the mainstream of twentieth-century poetry in its treatment of the terrors of war, and her message comes to us through, as I have mentioned, the imaginative intellect of characters who evoke sympathy and identification.

War, however, is not the only theme that allies Gwendolyn Brooks with the mainstream. One finds telling and ironical speculation in "the preacher: ruminates behind the sermon":

> Perhaps—who knows?—He tires
>   of looking down.
> Those eyes are never lifted. Never
>   straight.
> Perhaps sometimes He tires of
>   being great
> In solitude. Without a hand to
>   hold.
>
> (*WGB*, p. 15)

In "Strong Men, Riding Horses," we have a Prufrockian portrait of the anti-hero. After his confrontation with the ideals of a Western film, the persona comments:

> I am not like that. I pay rent, am
>   addled
> By illegible landlords, run, if
>   robbers call.
>
> What mannerisms I present,
>   employ,
> Are camouflage, and what my
>   mouths remark
> To word-wall off that broadness of
>   the dark

> Is pitiful.
> I am not brave at all.
>
> (*WGB*, p. 313)

In "Mrs. Small," one has a picture of the "Mr. Zeros" (or Willie Lomans) of a complex century, and in "A Bronzeville Mother Loiters in Mississippi. Meanwhile a Mississippi Mother Burns Bacon," we have an evocation of the blood-guiltiness of the white psyche in an age of dying colonialism. Brooks presents these themes with skill because she has the ability to endow each figure with a unique, individualizing vision of the world.

If they were considered in isolation, however, the characters and concerns of the verse would not mark the poet as an outstanding writer. Great poetry demands word magic, a sense of the infinite possibilities of language. In this technical realm Brooks is superb. Her ability to dislocate and mold language into complex patterns of meaning can be observed in her earliest poems and in her latest volumes—*In The Mecca* (1968), *Riot* (1969), and *Family Pictures* (1970). The first lines of "The Sundays of Satin-Legs Smith" are illustrative:

> INAMORATAS, with an approbation,
> Bestowed his title. Blessed his
>   inclination.
>
> He wakes, unwinds, elaborately:
>   a cat
> Tawny, reluctant, royal. He is fat
> And fine this morning. Definite.
>   Reimbursed.
>
> (*WGB*, p. 26)

The handling of polysyllabics is not in the least strained, and the movement is so graceful that one scarcely notices the rhymed couplets. Time and again this word magic is at work, and the poet's varying rhyme schemes lend a subtle resonance that is not found in the same abundance in the works of other acknowledged American writers. It is important to qualify this judgment, however, for while Brooks employs polysyllabics and forces words into striking combinations, she preserves colloquial rhythms. Repeatedly one is confronted by a realistic voice—not unlike that in Robert Frost's poetry—that carries one along the dim corridors of the human psyche or down the rancid halls of a decaying tenement. Brooks's colloquial narrative voice, however, is more prone to complex juxtapositions than Frost's, as a stanza from "The Anniad" illustrates:

> Doomer, though, crescendo-comes
> Prophesying hecatombs.
> Surrealist and cynical.
> Garrulous and guttural.
> Spits upon the silver leaves.
> Denigrates the dainty eves
> Dear dexterity achieves.
>
> (WGB, pp. 85–86)

This surely differs from Frost's stanzas, and the difference resides in the poet's obvious joy in words. She fuses the most elaborate words into contexts that allow them to speak naturally or to sing beautifully her meaning.

Brooks is not indebted to Frost alone for technical influences; she also acknowledges her admiration for Langston Hughes. Although a number of her themes and techniques set her work in the twentieth-century mainstream, there are those that place it firmly in the black American literary tradition. One of her most effective techniques is a sharp, black, comic irony that is closely akin to the scorn Hughes directed at the ways of white folks throughout his life. When added to her other skills, this irony proves formidable. "The Lovers of the Poor" is unsparing in its portrayal of ineffectual, middle-age, elitist philanthropy:

> Their guild is giving money to
>   the poor.
> The worthy poor. The very very
>   worthy
> And beautiful poor. Perhaps just
>   not too swarthy?
> Perhaps just not too dirty nor too
>   dim
> Nor—passionate. In truth, what
>   they could wish
> Is—something less than derelict
>   or dull.
> Not staunch enough to stab,
>   though, gaze for gaze!
> God shield them sharply from the
>   beggar-bold!
>
> (WGB, p. 334)

Hughes could not have hoped for better. And the same vitriol is directed at whites who seek the bizarre and exotic by "slumming" among blacks in "I love those little booths at Benvenuti's":

> But how shall they tell people
>   they have been
> Out Bronzeville way? For all the
>   nickels in
> Have not bought savagery or
>   defined a "folk."
> The colored people will not
>   "clown."

The colored people arrive, sit
    firmly down,
Eat their Express Spaghetti, their
    T-bone steak,
Handling their steel and crockery
    with no clatter,
Laugh punily, rise, go firmly out
    of the door.

(WGB, p. 111)

The poet's chiding, however, is not always in the derisive mode. She often turns an irony of loving kindness on black Americans. "We Real Cool" would fit easily into the canon of Hughes or Sterling Brown:

We real cool. We
Left School. We

Lurk late. We
Strike straight. We

Sing sin. We
Thin gin. We

Jazz June. We
Die soon.

(WGB, p. 315)

The irony is patent, but the poet's sympathy and admiration for the folk are no less obvious (the bold relief of "We," for example). A sympathetic irony in dealing with the folk has characterized some of the most outstanding works in the black American literary tradition, from Paul Laurence Dunbar's "Jimsella" and the novels of Claude McKay to Ralph Ellison's *Invisible Man* and the work of recent writers such as George Cain and Louise Meriwether. All manifest a concern with the black man living in the "promised land" of the American city, and Brooks's *A Street in Bronzeville, Annie Allen,* "The Bean Eaters," and "Bronzeville Woman in a Red Hat" likewise reveal the employment of kindly laughter to veil the tears of a desperate situation. In her autobiography, *Report from Part One,* she attests to having been in the situation and to having felt its deeper pulsations: "I lived on 63rd Street [in Chicago] . . . and there was a good deal of life in the raw all about me. You might feel that this would be disturbing, but it was not. It contributed to my writing progress. I wrote about what I saw and heard in the street."[6]

Finally, there are the poems of protest. A segregated military establishment comes under attack in both "The Negro Hero" and "the white troops had their orders but the Negroes looked like men." The ignominies of lynching are exposed in "A Bronzeville Mother Loiters in Mississippi. Meanwhile, a Mississippi Mother Burns Bacon." And in poems like "Riders to the Blood-red Wrath" and "The Second Sermon on the Warpland," Brooks expresses the philosophy of militant resistance that has characterized the black American literary tradition from the day a black slave first sang of Pharaoh's army. The poet, in short, has spoken forcefully against the indignities suffered by black Americans in a racialistic society. Having undertaken a somewhat thorough revaluation of her role as a black poet in an era of transition, she has stated and proved her loyalty to the task of creating a new consciousness in her culture. Her shift from a major white publishing firm to an independent black one (Broadside

Press) for her autobiography is an indication of her commitment to the cause of black institution-building that has been championed by a number of today's black artists. One might, however, take issue with her recent statement that she was "ignorant" until enlightened by the black activities and concerns of the 1960s. Although she is currently serving as one of the most engaged artistic guides for a culture, she is more justly described as a herald than as an uninformed convert. She has mediated the dichotomy that left Paul Laurence Dunbar (whose *Complete Poems* she read at an early age) a torn and agonized man. Of course, she had the example of Dunbar, the Harlem Renaissance writers, and others to build upon, but at times even superior talents have been incapable of employing the accomplishments of the past for their own ends. Unlike the turn-of-the-century poet and a number of Renaissance writers, Brooks has often excelled the surrounding white framework, and she has been able to see clearly beyond it to the strengths and beauties of her own unique cultural tradition.

Gwendolyn Brooks represents a singular achievement. Beset by a double consciousness, she has kept herself from being torn asunder by crafting poems that equal the best in the black and white American literary traditions. Her characters are believable, her themes manifold, and her technique superb. The critic (whether black or white) who comes to her work seeking only support for his ideology will be disappointed for, as Etheridge Knight pointed out, she has ever spoken the truth. And truth, one likes to feel, always lies beyond the boundaries of any one ideology. Perhaps Brooks's most significant achievement is her endorsement of this point of view. From her hand and fertile imagination have come volumes that transcend the dogma on either side of the American veil. In their transcendence, they are fitting representatives of an "Effulgent lover of the Sun!"

Notes

[1] Ralph Ellison and James Alan McPherson, "Indivisible Man," *The Atlantic* 226 (Dec. 1970): p. 60.

[2] Imamu Amiri Baraka (LeRoi Jones), "The Myth of a 'Negro Literature,'" *Home: Social Essays* (New York: William Morrow, 1966), pp. 105–15.

[3] Etheridge Knight, "To Gwendolyn Brooks," *Poems from Prison* (Detroit: Broadside Press, 1968), p. 30.

[4] Gwendolyn Brooks, "kitchenette building," *The World of Gwendolyn Brooks* (New York: Harper & Row, 1971), p. 4.

[5] David Littlejohn, *Black on White: A Critical Survey of Writings by American Negroes* (New York: Viking Press, 1969), pp. 89–94.

[6] Gwendolyn Brooks, *Report from Part One* (Detroit: Broadside Press, 1972), p. 133.

An Interview with Gwendolyn Brooks

George Stavros

Q. There is a quality of pathos about all of your characters and compassion in your treatment of them. Many of them make a pitiful attempt to be what they cannot be.

A. Some of them. Not all of them; some of them are very much interested in just the general events of their own lives.

Q. Let me suggest one of the frequently anthologized poems, "A Song in the Front Yard," about a girl who "gets sick of a rose" and decides she'd like to leave the comfort and pleasure of the front yard to see what life would be like in the back.

A. Or out in the alley, where the charity children play, based on my own resentment when I was a little girl, having to come inside the front gate after nine—oh, earlier than that in my case.

Q. Isn't there a yearning to get away in many such portraits?

A. I wouldn't attach any heavy significance to that particular poem, because that was the lightest kind of a little poem.

Q. How about a poem like "Sadie and Maud," a little lyric, I think in quatrains, contrasting Maud, who turns out to be a lonely brown "mouse," and Sadie, who "scraped life/With a fine tooth comb"?

A. Those are imaginary characters, purely imaginary.

. . .

Q. How about the seven pool players in the poem "We Real Cool"?

A. They have no pretensions to any glamor. They are supposedly dropouts, or at least they're in the poolroom when they should possibly be in school, since they're probably young enough, or at least those I saw were when I looked in a poolroom, and they . . . . First of all, let me tell you how that's supposed to be said, because there's a reason why I set it out as I did. These are people who are essentially saying, "Kilroy is here. We are." But they're a little uncertain of the strength of their identity. [Reads:]

> We real cool. We
> Left school. We
>
> Lurk late. We
> Strike straight. We
>
> Sing sin. We
> Thin gin. We
>
> Jazz June. We
> Die soon.

The "We"—you're supposed to stop after the "We" and think about their validity, and of course there's no way for you to tell whether it should be said softly or not, I suppose, but I say it rather softly because I want to represent their basic uncertainty, which they don't bother to question every day, of course.

Q. Are you saying that the form of this poem, then, was determined by the colloquial rhythm you were trying to catch?

A. No, determined by my feeling about these boys, these young men.

Q. These short lines, then, are your own invention at this point? You don't have any literary model in mind; you're not thinking of Eliot or Pound or anybody in particular. . . ?

A. My gosh, no! I don't even admire Pound, but I do like, for instance, Eliot's "Prufrock" and *The Waste Land,* "Portrait of a Lady," and some others of those earlier poems. But nothing of the sort ever entered my mind. When I start writing a poem, I don't think about models or about what anybody else in the world has done.

. . .

Q. How do you feel about that climate in regard to what the black writer is doing now? Do you think his task is becoming easier, more difficult, more important?

A. I think it is the task or job or responsibility or pleasure or pride of any writer to respond to his climate. You write about what is in the world. I think I would be silly, and so would LeRoi Jones, to sit down now under the trees and write about the Victorian age, unless there's some special reference we could make to what's going on now.

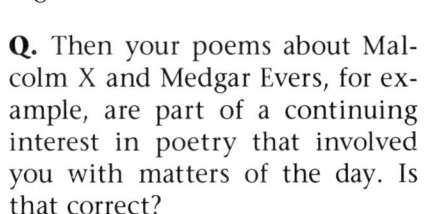

Q. Then your poems about Malcolm X and Medgar Evers, for example, are part of a continuing interest in poetry that involved you with matters of the day. Is that correct?

A. No, I didn't involve myself with Medgar Evers' assassination—I merely reacted to it, and I described what he had done, the effects he had had on the assaulting elements of his society, and I ended, most beautifully, I thought: "People said that / he was holding clean globes in his hands."

Q. What did you mean when you said he had departed from "Old styles, old tempos, all the engagement of / the day—the sedate, the regulated fray . . . "?

A. [Reads:] ". . . the antique light, the Moral rose, old gusts, / tight whistlings from the past, the mothballs / in the Love at last our man forswore." He just up and decided he wasn't going to have anything else to do with the stale traditions of the past and the hindrances and restrictions that American response to horrors had been concerned with.

Q. In other words, an impatience with injustice and continuing oppression.

A. Yes, he decided he would just "have none" of it anymore and would do something about righting things for his people.

Gwendolyn Brooks's "Children of the Poor," Metaphysical Poetry and the Inconditions of Love

Gary Smith

> It is not a permanent necessity that poets should be interested in philosophy, or in any other subject. We can only say that it appears likely that poets in our civilization, as it exists at present, must be *difficult*. Our civilization comprehends great variety and complexity, and this variety and complexity, playing upon a refined sensibility, must produce various and complex results. The poet must become more and more comprehensive, more allusive, more indirect, in order to force, to dislocate if necessary, language into his meaning.
>
> —T. S. Eliot, The Metaphysical Poets[1]

Despite Gwendolyn Brooks's recent protest that the sonnet is irrelevant to her artistic goal of blackening English,[2] she is arguably one of America's finest sonneteers. Throughout the early phases of her writing career, before her association with the Black Arts Movement of the 1960s, she repeatedly turned to the sonnet to express her dual commitment to socially relevant and well-crafted poetry. Moreover, she was able to sustain these two often contradictory purposes without creating polemical verse or writing in an art for art's sake mode. Her success in achieving both commitment and craftsmanship is underscored by the many awards she has received for her poetry—especially her sonnets. Her initial public recognition as a sonneteer came in the form of the Eunice Tietjens Award (1944) for "Gay Chaps at the Bar"; this poem along with nine others form the antiwar sonnet cycle that concludes her first published volume, *A Street in Bronzeville* (1945). Her second volume, *Annie Allen* (1949), for which she won a Pulitzer Prize (1950), contains no less than eight sonnets. And in her third volume, *The Bean Eaters* (1960), Brooks includes two of her most critically acclaimed sonnets, "A Lovely Love" and "The Egg Boiler."

In part, Brooks's attraction to the sonnet might be traced to the influence of the New Negro poets, her immediate literary predecessors during the Harlem Renaissance, had upon her work. From these poets, Brooks learned that the four-hundred-year-old and largely genteel sonnet form could be used as a devastating instrument of social protest and that the inherent tensions in the sonnet's syllogistic structure could be used to argue against racism and social injustice. She also knew that the sonnet form had been mastered by most of the major poets writing in the English language.

For example, Claude McKay and Countee Cullen, two of the leading sonneteers among the New Negro poets, primarily used the English romantic poets as models for their sonnets. In two of their most famous sonnets, "If We Must Die" and "From the Dark Tower," the poets freely adapted the Romantic themes and literary styles of Keats, Wordsworth, and Shelley.[3] Their poems, written in iambic pentameter with exact rhymes, are models of traditional Shakespearean and Petrarchan sonnets. However, both poets were obviously immune to the modernist rebellion against romantic lyricism, pastoral imagery, and traditional versification that was underway when their poems were written. Nonetheless, their sonnets indirectly address the paradoxical questions of racism and socioeconomic injustice in America. The metaphorical language of McKay's sonnets—"hogs," "dogs," "monsters," and "kinsmen,"—has inspired any number of outcries against oppression and injustice; whereas the "Dark Tower" of Cullen's sonnet describes any place of forced labor and captivity. The two sonnets are not only timeless in their social protest but also noticeably colorless.

While the New Negro poets demonstrated to Brooks that race was incidental to the tradition of well-crafted and universal poetry, two other individuals had decisive influences upon her distinctly modern poetic voice. The first was the distinguished poet and statesman, James Weldon Johnson; the second was Inez Stark, the Chicago socialite and reader for *Poetry* magazine. In his brief but incisive commentary on several poems Brooks sent him, Johnson wrote: "You have an unquestionable talent and feeling for poetry. Continue to write—at the same time, study carefully the work of the best modern poets—not to imitate them, but to help cultivate the highest possible standard of self-criticism."[4] The immediate effect of Johnson's advice was to provide a "standard" for Brooks's poetry other than the one she found in the New Negro poetry. To her substantial reading list that already included Milton, Spenser, Donne, and Shakespeare, Brooks added Frost, Eliot, Cummings, and Pound.[5]

Stark complemented Johnson's theoretical advice with practical criticism of Brooks's poetry. In the poetry workshop she organized for a group of aspiring poets on Chicago's Southside, Stark gave Brooks lessons in traditional versification as well as modernist poetics. Her classroom texts included Robert Hillyer's *First Principles of Verse* as well as *Poetry,* the magazine that featured many of the modernist poets. As the following quotation indicates, Stark translated into plain, outspoken English the very essence of modernist poetics:

> All you need in this poem are the last four lines. . . . You must be careful not to list the obvious things. They, in these days (wartime) are more than ever a weakening influence on the strengths we need. Use them only to illustrate boredom and inanity.
> I don't understand too well what it's all about but it has three FINE lines.
> Dig at this until you have us see all the skeleton and no fat.
> (Report, pp. 66–67, emphasis in the original)

The criticism Stark offered Brooks emphasizes imagistic compression, ironic understatement, and temporal and spatial dislocations. These characteristics, of course, were radical departures from the romantic and generally discursive styles of McKay and Cullen.

Johnson and Stark's stylistic advice provides a partial explanation for Brooks's difficulty as a modern poet. Her best work comprehends not only the protest tradition of the New Negro poetry, but also the traditional and contemporary styles of European and American poetry. To be sure, it is the precise juggling of these various and complex traditions that contributes to the metaphysical quality of her verse. Like John Donne, the seventeenth-century metaphysical poet, Brooks creates a depth and range of feeling in her poetry that often overshadows her commonplace subject matter; she also displays a metaphysical wit that features startling and incongruent figures of speech; and she uses poetic diction that is a mixture of formal and colloquial speech.[6]

Donne's *Holy Sonnet XIV*[7] offers a striking example of the difficulties associated with metaphysical poetry. Its octave summarizes the persona's paradoxical religious feelings:

> Batter my heart, three-personed God; for you
> As yet but knock, breathe, shine, and seek to mend;
> That I may rise and stand, o'erthrow me, and bend
> Your force, to break, blow, burn, and make me new.
> I, like an usurped town, to another due,
> Labor to admit You, but Oh, to no end!
> Reason, Your viceroy in me, me should defend,
> But is captivated, and proves weak or untrue.

The speaker literally implores God to save him from the inner forces that threaten to destroy his religious faith. His heart-felt desperation is dramatized by the plosives that accompany his penitential outburst: "break," "blow," and "burn." However, the ninth line, with its volta, begins the turn toward a partial resolution of the persona's ordeal:

> Yet dearly I love You and would be loved fain,
> But am betrothed unto Your enemy:
> Divorce me, untie or break that knot again
> Take me to You, imprison me, for I,
> Except You enthrall me, never shall be free,
> Nor ever chaste, except You ravish me.

In a voice less strident than the one that controls the poem, the persona finally resolves his predicament with a simple declaration of love: "Yet dearly I love You."

The initial difficulty one experiences while reading the sonnet is structural. Donne has altered the conventional Petrarchan rhyme pattern by adding a Shakespearean couplet to the final quatrain. Within the sonnet, this structural change creates two voltas: at the end of the second and third quatrains; whereas, in the conventional Petrarchan sonnet, the volta usually occurs at the first point, and in the Shakespearean sonnet, it is withheld until the penultimate line. On one level, one doubling of the volta thwarts the reader's expectation for an early resolution of the persona's paradoxical dilemma; on another level, it lessens the dramatic distance between the opening conceit, "Batter my heart, three-personed God," and the final one, "Except you enthrall me, never shall be free."

This structural complexity is compounded by the sonnet's metaphorical language. In the initial quatrain, God is prefigured as an artisan capable of transforming the persona, who imagines himself a misshapen vessel. But rather than draw this metaphorical analogy to a point of conclusion, the second quatrain introduces another conceit: The speaker is a beleaguered town and God a liberating force. And in the final quatrain, the speaker equates God to a lover. Of course, this triunal metaphor, vessel-town-woman, lends itself to a multitude of interpretations, none of which totally answers the sonnet's paradoxical question: How can the persona's fractured religious faith be restored by a three-personed God? One possible answer—that the speaker's love negotiates the logical gaps between the three different conceits—is plausible on an emotional or metaphysical level but not a rational one.

The final complexity within the sonnet is Donne's poetic diction. In the opening lines, he takes his words from the metal arts: "batter," "knock," "shine," and "mend"; whereas in the second quatrain, he turns to the military: "usurped town," "viceroy," "defend," and "captived." Finally, he utilizes the diction of love and courtship: "betrothed," "enthrall," "chaste," and "ravish." These disparate choices are intended, in part, to startle the reader into an awareness of the subliminal relationships between words and ideas. They reinforce the complex and paradoxical nature of Donne's religious faith. But more important, the words, like the sonnet's structure and metaphorical conceits, characterize Donne's metaphysical sensibility.

Brooks's sonnet sequence, *The Children of the Poor*,[8] contains many of the same stylistic difficulties one finds in Donne's *Holy Sonnets*, but it also presents a distinct departure from many of his themes. While Brooks consistently experiments with the sonnet's syllogistic structure, she does not always adhere to the theme of resolution. Her sonnets do not attempt to resolve their paradoxical dilemmas as much as they graphically display a mind that alternately associates and disassociates itself from the dilemmas. Like Donne, Brooks also entertains questions of religious faith in her sonnets, yet she rejects religion as a viable means of resolving complex social problems. Finally, as in Donne's *Holy Sonnets*, love plays a decisive role in Brooks's sonnets, but she is most adept at describing its absence. Indeed, her overriding theme, "the inconditions of love," examines the sociopsychological forces in modern society that deny love.

The Children of the Poor consists of five sonnets. As protest sonnets, they address the question of socioeconomic injustice. Brooks's thematic focus is upon the most vulnerable members of society—black children. Throughout *The Children of the Poor,* Brooks manipulates form to underscore her theme. In each sonnet, she uses a mixture of both Petrarchan and Shakespearean forms. While the octave conforms to the Petrarchan rhyme pattern, *abba* and *abba,* the sestet offers a series of complex variations on the Shakespearean rhyme pattern: *efef* and *gg.* This diversity reinforces the complexity of the emotional responses to the paradoxical questions within each sonnet. Furthermore, the multiple couplets that Brooks employs in the sestet—especially in the first three sonnets—thwart the expected resolution of the sonnets' dilemmas; instead they heighten the sense of the mother's frustration and her inability to provide meaningful answers to her children.

In the first sonnet, for example, the Petrarchan rhyme pattern of the octave underscores the ordered yet constrained lives of childless people:

> People who have no children can be hard:
> Attain a mail of ice and insolence:
> Need not pause in the fire, and in no sense
> Hesitate in the hurricane to guard.
> And when wide world is bitten and bewarred
> They perish purely, waving their spirits hence
> Without a trace of grace or of offense
> To laugh or fail, diffident, wonder-starred.

Here, the world of childless people is characterized as essentially callous and ingrown. Without children, they are indifferent to human and natural disasters, "pause in the fire," and "hesitate in the hurricane," as well as to their own lives, "they perish purely." The world of people with children, however, is marked ironically by self-containing contradictions:

> While through a throttling dark we others hear
> The little lifting helplessness, the queer
> Whimper-whine; whose unridiculous
> Lost softness softly makes a trap for us.
> And makes a curse. And makes a sugar of
> The malocclusions, the inconditions of love.
>
> (*WGB,* p. 99)

In this sestet, Brooks uses multiple couplets to reinforce the mother's feeling of enclosure. As opposed to a "mail of ice," parents are entrapped by the emotional needs of their children. The multiple couplets also thwart an expected resolution to the sonnet's implied, paradoxical question: Is human life more fulfilling with or without children? Rather than offering a possible answer, the couplets present a series of oxymorons:

soft trap, soft curse, and sugary malocclusions. These oxymorons become the metaphorical equivalents for the inconditions of love.

In the second sonnet, ingenious and incongruent figures of speech also reinforce the anti-love theme. The mother begins by comparing her children with lepers; this conceit is raised to a level of abstraction when she further compares them with "contraband"; and, finally, in the last quatrain, the speaker employs the mythological conceit of the alchemist's stone:[9]

> What shall I give my children?
>   who are poor,
> Who are adjudged the leastwise
>   of the land,
> Who are my sweetest lepers, who
>   demand
> No velvet and no velvety velour;
> But who have begged me for a
>   brisk contour,
> Crying that they are quasi,
>   contraband
> Because unfinished, graven by a
>   hand
> Less than angelic, admirable or
>   sure,
> My hand is stuffed with mode,
>   design, device.
> But I lack access to my proper
>   stone.
> And plenitude of plan shall not
>   suffice
> Nor grief nor love shall be enough
>   alone
> To ratify my little halves who
>   bear
> Across an autumn freezing
>   everywhere.
>   (WGB, p. 100)

At first reading, these heterogeneous metaphors startle the reader into a more acute awareness of the complex social problems of poverty; the disjunction, however, creates certain historical parallels that add to the richness of the mother's emotional stress in response to her paradoxical question: "What shall I give my children? who are poor?" Indeed, the movement of metaphors is from simple abstractions, "leastwise" and "poor," to Biblical and historical referents, "lepers" and "contraband,"[10] and finally to mythology, "proper stone." These figures of speech obviously avoid a concrete description of poverty and help distance the persona from her painful dilemma. Psychologically, her children are not simply shoeless and malnourished; they are freely associated with other outcasts in the Bible and in Afro-American history. The mother's awareness is further underscored by the descriptive terms she uses for her children, "sweetest lepers" and "little halves." These euphemisms connote a tacit acceptance of the judgment of her children as social undesirables. More important, they suggest the mother's "sweet" refusal to counter the social images of her children or, perhaps, to accept them as mirror images of herself. Thus, the sonnet's paradoxical question precipitates not an unequivocal defense of human love apart from poverty, but rather a dramatization of the mother's inner conflicts: how poverty has weakened the emotional underpinnings of her love.

Brooks's use of both colloquial and literary poetic diction plays a part in dramatizing the psychological problems of love and poverty. The octave of the third sonnet is particularly suggestive of this mixture of two poetic dictions:

> And shall I prime my children, pray, to pray?
> Mites, come invade most frugal vestibules
> Spectered with crusts of penitents' renewals
> And all hysterics arrogant for a day.
> Instruct yourselves here is no devil to pay.
> Children, confine your lights in jellied rules;
> Resemble graves; be metaphysical mules;
> Learn Lord will not distort nor leave the fray.
>
> (*WGB*, p. 101)

In the first line, the sonnet's paradoxical question contains an implied answer. The word "prime" is an elliptical expression that implies teaching at a primary level; when combined with the other two accented words in the line, "pray, to pray," it becomes an alliterative but sarcastic answer to the question. In the second line, "mites" is both a reference to insect pests and a diminutive qualifier for "children" as well as an ingenious reference to the small boxes used for special, Sunday school offerings. These connotations coalesce in the phrase, "invade most frugal vestibules," the nearly empty anteroom of the church where the children have come to pray.

In the third line, "spectered" connotes the mysterious, ghostly nature of Christian mythology, while "crusts of penitents' renewals" suggests bits of the sacramental wafer as well as the more domestic image of a nearly empty food closet. Moreover, in keeping with the mother's pessimism about religious belief, "all hysterics" infers an emotional catharsis that, "for a day," accompanies the children's intense religious worship.

While the word choices in the initial quatrain are allusively literary, those in the second are colloquial. The mother sarcastically admonishes her children, "instruct yourselves here is no devil to pay" and "confine your lights in jellied rules." The word "lights" signifies both religious enlightenment and self-knowledge, but ironically the mother instructs her children to confine their self-knowledge in the "jellied rules" of their religious training. This spiritual food, like the earlier "crust," does not, however, respond to the basic need of the poor children for nourishment. Without food, the children will "resemble graves." Finally, in a striking example of Brooks's use of colloquial and literary diction, the mother commands her children, "be metaphysical mules." She encourages her children to accept religion's meager offerings, and as the final two lines of the sonnet suggest, the mother will apply a "bandage" on their eyes to conceal their spiritual impoverishment.

While the first three sonnets dramatize the emotional paralysis and pessimism of a mother whose love has been undermined by poverty, the fourth sonnet presents a radical shift in tone and viewpoint. The poetic diction is more forceful and less encumbered by allusive figures of speech. Its perspective omits the dichotomies that characterize the mother's ambivalence in the earlier sonnets; its point of view is the collective, second person plural, "you." Its deliberate, self-assertive tone suggests someone who is actively engaged in the life struggles of her children:

> First fight. Then fiddle. Ply the slipping string
> With feathery sorcery; muzzle the note
> With hurting love; the music that they wrote
> Bewitch, bewilder. Qualify to sing
> Threadwise. Devise no salt, no hempen thing
> For the dear instrument to bear. Devote
> The bow to silks and honey. Be remote
> A while from malice and from murdering.
> But first to arms, to armor. Carry hate
> In front of you and harmony behind.
> Be deaf to music and to beauty blind.
> Win war. Rise bloody, maybe not too late
> For having first to civilize a space
> Wherein to play your violin with grace.
>   (*WGB*, p. 102)

The spondee, "First fight. Then fiddle," interrupts the regular iambic pentameter of the initial line. As plosives and imperatives, they underscore an emotional commitment to militant action as a response to the sonnet's implied, paradoxical question: How can the ideals of art—beauty and truth—be reconciled with the demands for socioeconomic justice?

This commitment is also conveyed in the sonnet's form and imagery. The octave, for example, argues that music-making and the discipline it involves have certain sociopsychological virtues: "Ply the slipping string," "muzzle the note," "Qualify to sing," and "Devote the bow to silks and honey." However, the sestet, with its volta in the ninth line, defiantly argues that militant action is necessary "to civilize a space / Wherein to play your violin with grace." Unlike the incongruent and heterogeneous figures of speech in the earlier sonnets, the images are neatly divided between militancy and music: "Carry hate in front of you and harmony behind."

The introspective and elegaic tone of the initial three sonnets returns in the final poem. As a protest sonnet, its paradoxical question, how can the poor—who have lived marginal lives—accept death, is perhaps a response to the previous sonnet's exhortation to militant social action.[11] The mother's commitment to socioeconomic justice for her children is still firm:

> When my dears die, the festival-colored brightness
> That is their motion and mild repartee
> Enchanted, a macabre mockery
> Charming the rainbow radiance into tightness
> And into a remarkable politeness
> That is not kind and does not want to be,
> May not they in the crisp encounter see

> Something to recognize and read as rightness?
> I say they may, so granitely discreet,
> The little crooked questionings inbound,
> Concede themselves on most familiar ground,
> Cold an old predicament of the breath:
> Adroit, the shapely prefaces complete,
> Accept the university of death.
>
> (*WGB*, p. 103)

In the octave, the euphemism, "dears die," replaces the earlier oxymoron, "sweetest lepers," as a descriptive term for the mother's children. The alliterative and playful word choices, "motion and mild" and "rainbow radiance," also help create an optimistic and enchanting tone in the poem. Furthermore, death becomes another euphemism, "crisp encounter."

The sestet, then, with its volta, "I say they may," answers the paradoxical question in the affirmative. The poverty and "crooked questionings" that characterize the children's lives have prepared them to accept death as a natural consequence of living. But by placing a couplet after the volta, Brooks thwarts our expectation for a stoic resolution of the sonnet. The last three lines further imply that death will actually begin life, because its "university" will provide answers that have eluded the mother. Death is a universal that ignores matters of race and class.

In retrospect, *The Children of the Poor* demonstrates Brooks's success in writing poetry that is both socially conscious and intricately crafted. Her sonnets belong to the modernist tradition in that they contain the variety, complexity, indirection, and dislocation T. S. Eliot suggests are the hallmarks of poets in our civilization. Nonetheless, she subscribes to the New Negro's faith in art as an instrument for social change. Like Cullen and McKay, her protest sonnets avoid specific mention of race as a social issue inextricably tied to poverty; moreover, as illustrated by the abrupt tonal shifts between the third and fourth sonnets, she often vacillates between overt militancy and painful introspection. Finally, if Brooks has abandoned the sonnet form as a means of addressing the socioeconomic concerns of blacks in her latest poetry, she remains committed to art as a means of negotiating racial differences. And in this sense, her commitment to art remains, by implication, a commitment to human life.

Notes

[1] T. S. Eliot, "The Metaphysical Poets," in *Selected Essays* (New York: Harcourt, Brace, 1950), p. 248.

[2] See Martha H. Brown, "Interview with Gwendolyn Brooks," *The Great Lakes Review* 6 (Summer 1979): 55.

[3] See Blyden Jackson and Louis D. Rubin, Jr., *Black Poetry in America: Two Essays in Historical Interpretation* (Baton Rouge: Louisiana State University Press, 1974), pp. 46–47.

[4] Gwendolyn Brooks, *Report from Part One* (Detroit: Broadside Press, 1972), p. 202. Hereinafter cited in the text as *Report*.

[5] See George Stavros, "An Interview with Gwendolyn Brooks," *Contemporary Literature* II (Winter 1970): 10.

[6] See Herbert J. C. Grierson, *Metaphysical Lyrics and Poems of the Seventeenth Century* (New York: Oxford University Press, 1959), pp. xiii–xxviii.

[7] For an interesting discussion of John Donne's *Holy Sonnets,* especially "Sonnet XIV," see *John Donne's Poetry,* ed. A. L. Clements (New York: W. W. Norton, 1966), pp. 246-59.

[8] Gwendolyn Brooks, *The World of Gwendolyn Brooks* (New York: Harper & Row, 1971), pp. 99–103. Hereinafter cited in the text as *WGB.*

[9] See R. Baxter Miller, "'Does Man Love Art?': The Humanistic Aesthetic of Gwendolyn Brooks," in *Black American Literature and Humanism,* ed. R. Baxter Miller (Lexington: University Press of Kentucky, 1981), pp. 104-6.

[10] Besides the usual meaning of goods forbidden by law, "contraband" was also used during the Civil War to identify slaves who fled to, or were smuggled behind, the Union lines or remained in territory captured by the Union Army.

[11] See Harry B. Shaw, *Gwendolyn Brooks* (Boston: Twayne Publishers, 1980), pp. 114-15.

"Chocolate Mabbie" and "Pearl May Lee": Gwendolyn Brooks and the Ballad Tradition

Maria K. Mootry

Among the five major volumes of Gwendolyn Brooks' poetry, one of the notably recurring poetic forms is the ballad. From "The Ballad of Chocolate Mabbie," in her first volume, to "The Ballad of Edie Barrow" in her last major book,[1] Brooks shows a continued interest in this popular or folk art form. Brooks' attraction to ballads is not unique. In their revolt against the artifice, formalism, and abstraction of eighteenth-century classicist poetry, romantic poets like Coleridge and Wordsworth often turned to folk ballads for subjects and techniques. They liked the fact that the ballad, as a folk form, focused on the outcasts of society, including abandoned mothers, prisoners, and beggars. At the same time, they valued the ballad's language and structure because it seemed to avoid the pretensions of eighteenth-century classicist poetry. In his famous preface to the second edition of *Lyrical Ballads,* Wordsworth maintains that the language of all poetry, like the language of the ballad, should be neutral, simple, and essentially the same as everyday speech. Coleridge and Wordsworth, however, aimed merely to *imitate* the ballad form in order to demonstrate the value of their new theory of poetics. Brooks' use of the ballad reflects a similar desire to recover a simpler, more direct, poetic form; it also reflects her belief that the poet should "vivify the commonplace."[2]

However, Brooks goes beyond the mere imitation of ballad themes and techniques to create more varied and complex structures. The result is that while on one level her ballads are simple and direct, on another level they are deeply ironic and complex, both in theme and technique. Thus through her use of ballads, Brooks meets the demands of two ostensibly disparate audiences: the "art for art's sake" audience with its emphasis on the poem as its own excuse for being and the "common" audience who looks for familiar structures and social or moral messages.[3] In the process, Brooks recovers the ballad tradition by using its themes and techniques; she reinvigorates that tradition by infusing it with new themes and variations; and finally, she critiques the tradition by using parodic techniques. The overall effect, however, is the revelation of contemporary, often unpleasant, truths about Afro-American and American society.

In this essay, observations of Brooks' use of the Western folk ballad tradition in her poetry will be based on the analysis of the [poem] "The Ballad of Chocolate Mabbie" (*WGB*, p. 14), which appeared in her first volume, *A Street in Bronzeville* (1945). This poem was selected not only because it is a literary ballad but because, as its title suggests, it is Brooksian in its emphasis on a "woman-identified" vision.[4] Gordon Hall Gerould, in his study of the European folk ballad, notes that "the sorrows peculiar to women serve the ballad poets . . . for some of their most poignant moments."[5] Brooks continues this thematic aspect of the European folk ballad tradition, often infusing into her own literary ballads the complex use of additional folk elements from the Afro-American spirituals and blues (sacred and secular) traditions. Before analyzing the poems, however, it may be useful to review briefly the major folk ballad conventions.

I. The Ballad Tradition

The original popular (or folk) ballad is anonymous, transmitted by oral tradition, and tells a story, often about events well known to is audience. Whatever affects the thoughts and emotions of a community may become the subject of a ballad, but the most frequent themes are unfaithful lovers, shocking murders, mysterious happenings, and political oppression. For example, the latter theme is expressed in the English ballads of Robin Hood, who defended the rights of the common people against the predatory rich. Perhaps because the story is usually well known to the audience, the ballad poet tends to present his narrative in a series of dramatically striking episodes. The audience is left to fill out the complete narrative since characterization is brief, transitions are abrupt, and action is often developed through dialogue.

The language of folk ballads is usually simple in diction and meter. However, because many ballads have been handed down from generation to generation, the diction often ranges from the Scottish or Anglo-Saxon vernacular to archaisms reflecting past poetic oral conventions or everyday usage. Inversions of syntactical structures are also common, perhaps to maintain earlier narrative conventions. Regarding stanzaic form, the typical folk ballad uses the ballad stanza, an *abcb* four-line stanza with alternating four-stress and three-stress lines. However, even where the ballad stanza is not employed, there tends to be the use of refrains and repetition of phrases or parallel phrasing. Often a refrain is repeated with only a slight change, creating what is called an incremental refrain.

Although many ballads begin *in medias res,* just as frequently the ballad employs stock opening phrases to establish its narrative structure. In any event, because of its elliptical episodic structure, colors, actions, and even dialogue are often metonymic and multifunctional. Finally, ballads often also close with some kind of summary stanza. This final stanza often continues the incremental nature of ballad repetition, as well as the simplicity with which tragic situations are presented.

These are some of the major features of the Western European folk ballad. Of course, there are many variations and exceptions to these rules, but for the purpose of this essay, these core conventions may serve as a guide in assessing how Brooks uses the folk ballad tradition and how she departs from it in two of her most powerful literary ballads.

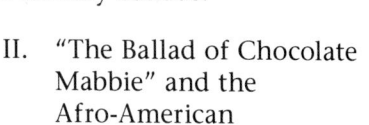

II. "The Ballad of Chocolate Mabbie" and the Afro-American Sacred Tradition

In "The Ballad of Chocolate Mabbie," Brooks deals with the pathos of intraracial discrimination, one of her recurring themes. Seven-year-old Mabbie falls in love with her classmate, Willie Boone, moons over him in history class, and waits for him outside the grammar school gates. In an epiphanic scene, Mabbie's erstwhile "lover" appears insouciantly in the company of a light-skinned, long-haired beauty. At the poem's conclusion, Mabbie is left to "chocolate companions" and to her own resources.

In "The Ballad of Chocolate Mabbie," Brooks uses many of the European ballad conventions mentioned above. For instance, the poem begins with an opening phrase which establishes its narrative character: "*It was* Mabbie without the grammar school gates. . . . " The use of the connective "and" reinforces both the poem's plot structure and its apparent simplicity. An almost childlike progression of sentences makes up this first stanza:

> *It was Mabbie* without the grammar school gates.
> *And* Mabbie was all of seven.
> *And* Mabbie was cut from a chocolate bar.
> *And* Mabbie thought life was heaven. (*WGB*, p. 14; emphasis mine)

Repetition appears in the phrasing "It was Mabbie . . . / And Mabbie was . . . / And Mabbie thought . . . ." This parallel repetition recurs in the third stanza, which repeats the opening line: "It was Mabbie without the grammar school gates." The repetition becomes incremental with the closing stanza, where the opening line is again repeated with the meaningful change of one word, "without," to the word "alone," i.e., "It was Mabbie *without* the grammar school gates" (first stanza) becomes "It was Mabbie *alone* by the grammar school gates" (sixth and last stanza—emphasis mine).

Archaic or somewhat outdated usages appear unobstrusively in "Chocolate Mabbie." The word "without" in the poem's first line is clearly archaic; and certain words have an archaic aura, e.g., "saucily," "woe," and "lemon-*hued*" in the fifth stanza. To this suggestion of the old ballad tradition, Brooks juxtaposes modern vernacular language, particularly in the key phrase, "cut from a chocolate bar." Also noteworthy is Brook's use of predominantly Anglo-Saxon words. Often monosyllabic, often with hard consonants, and often used alliteratively, these words with Anglo-Saxon roots create a harsh if vigorous tone and reinforce Brooks' debt to the European (English) folk tradition. Examples of these key words occurring in "Chocolate Mabbie" include "without," "gates," "seven," "cut," "thought," "heaven," "school," "cool," "soon," "brow," and "alone." Also, the preponderance of "to be" verbs and pronouns reflects an Anglo-Saxon linguistic base. One of the few interpolations of an Afro-American vernacular phrasing in the poem occurs in the fourth line of the second stanza where Brooks describes Mabbie's ardor for Willie: "Was only her eyes were cool" is at once a balladic inversion and a Black English construction. The very absence of sustained Black English in the poem accentuates this line, which interestingly anticipates the masterful title of one of Brooks' most famous poems, "We Real Cool."

Turning to its stanzaic form, "Chocolate Mabbie," like the traditional ballad, uses the *abcb* rhyme scheme with rhythmic alternating four-stress and three-stress lines. For instance, the first stanza of the poem scans as follows:

> It was, Mabbie without the
>   grammar school gates.
> And Mabbie was all of seven.
> And Mabbie was cut from a
>   chocolate bar.
> And Mabbie thought life was
>   heaven.

Further balladic elements include the repetition of phrases and the use of parallelisms mentioned above, particularly the incrementally juxtaposed line which opens the first and last stanzas:

> It was Mabbie *without* the
>   grammar school gates.

> It was Mabbie *alone* by the
> grammar school gates.

Balladic epithets also appear in such phrases as "the pearly gates," "bold Willie Boone," "lemon-hued lynx" and "sand-waves." Yet while these epithets merely *adorn* the traditional ballad, in "Chocolate Mabbie" they become hyperbolic, a mockery within a mock-tragedy. "Bold Willie Boone" and his "lemon-hued lynx" are inflated references to school children which infuse "Chocolate Mabbie" with a satiric tone. The foreshadowing voice of the narrator deepens the sense of satire when describing Mabbie's school gate vigil in the fourth stanza:

> Oh, warm is the waiting for joys,
>   my dears,
> And it cannot be too long.
> Oh, pity the little poor chocolate
>   lips
> That carry the bubble of song!

If exaggerated language in "Chocolate Mabbie" mocks the ballad tradition when it is applied to these prepubescent ordinary characters, the poem's understated plot similarly burlesques another major ballad feature, the episodic, sensationalist plot. While the plot of "Chocolate Mabbie" is "cinematic" in that it offers a montage-like series of images, in actuality the story is minimal. The reader observes a love-sick Mabbie outside the gates, observes Mabbie in the history class, and observes Mabbie desolately watching Willie leave with his "lemon-hued lynx." These everyday "events" in "Chocolate Mabbie" pale before the far more shocking events of such traditional ballads as "Sir Patrick Spence," in which a heroic sailor is involuntarily sent to his death, or "Child-Waters," where a young woman's consuming love ends in an illegitimate baby and public humiliation.

In spite of her occasional parodic stance, Brooks adds to the traditional ballad conventions a theme that is at once universal and particularized. "Chocolate Mabbie," at its core, is a poem about unrequited love. To the theme of unrequited love is added the theme of intraracial discrimination within the black community. As Arthur P. Davis has noted, this is a recurring issue in Brooks' poetry.[6] When this theme is linked to the theme of a female child's developing identity within the black community, it may not be sensationalist, but it does take on the power of a harsh revelation. The result, ultimately, is that "Chocolate Mabbie" is not only about the loss of love, but even more so, it is about the loss of innocence.

It is in addressing the theme of "innocence versus experience" that Brooks further modifies her use of the European ballad tradition by drawing on subjects and themes common to the Afro-American sacred folk tradition. The opening lines of "Chocolate Mabbie" express Mabbie's delusions of love in quasi-religious terms. To Mabbie, who "thought life was heaven," the grammar school gates have become "the pearly gates."

References to "pearly gates" recur frequently in Afro-American spirituals, usually when linked to the theme of the Second Coming. This messianic theme and its attendant imagery are parodically and mockingly reconstructed in the third stanza, where Mabbie's hopes for Willie's attention are expressed in the final line: "He would surely be coming soon." Thus, in another hyperbolic strategy, Mabbie is shown as having made a religion of love. Yet, from another perspective, the folk spirituals or sacred tradition is not so much mocked as used as an analogue of secular dilemma. In a further analogy to the biblical tradition, Mabbie, like Adam and Eve, is banished from her prelapsarian state. Thus if the imagery suggests apocalyptic visions, it also looks backward to the Fall. Mabbie's "guilt" is a moot point because she, like all humans, is original sin personified, being "graven by a hand less than angelic."[7] However, the implications are twofold. Brooks is not only speaking of original sin in a Calvinistic sense, but primarily of the social "sin" of being born black and female. In addressing this theme of loss of innocence, Brooks resorts neither to a sense of predestined fate nor to the romantic transcendence of ideal black womanhood so common to her predecessors during the Harlem Renaissance. Rather, the bitterness of Mabbie's rejection by Willie and the collapse of Mabbie's naive worldview is balanced by the implied possibility of the reconstruction of self in society. Mabbie must learn to use her personal resources, to cherish her "chocolate companions" and not to waste her personal resources, to cherish her "chocolate companions" and not to waste her time brooding over male "betrayal." As Brooks advised in her autobiography,

> [b]lack women must remember . . . [t]hat her [sic] personhood precedes her femalehood, that, sweet as sex may be, she cannot endlessly brood on Black man's blondes, blues and blunders. She is a person in the world—with wrongs to right, stupidities to outwit, *with* her man when possible, on her own when not. . . . Therefore she must, in the midst of tragedy and hatred and neglect . . . mightily enjoy the readily available: sunshine and pets and children and conversation and games and travel (tiny or large) and books and walks and chocolate cake. . . .

By infusing satire and parody into "Chocolate Mabbie" Brooks establishes the poem's distance from the simple folk ballad tradition. Despite the ballad conventions and sacred imagery, the poem has a mocking quality, which gives it a complex cutting edge and reinforces its ideas. The childlike syntax of the opening stanza goes beyond balladic simplicity to a primerlike quality. It is as if an elementary school child is adding sentence to sentence with no sense of subordination. This simplicity underscores the fact that on one level Brooks is writing about "puppy-love" and humorously focusing on a transitory childish crush and its inevitable demise. Yet, in the final stanza the narrator loses her sardonic tone. Thus the reader is reminded that if this is, from one perspective, childish subject matter, ultimately it is a serious poetic statement about the dilemma of growing up black and female in America.[8]

. . .

In conclusion, Brooks' use of folk traditions varies considerably. At times, it is straightforward, at other times parodic; and often it is a complex mixture of both. Further analysis of her use of the traditions of ballads, blues, and spirituals needs to be made before any full understanding of her art can be achieved. The relationship between the blues tradition and the ballad tradition, for instance, needs further exploration. At this point, based on [a powerful example,] it can be argued that Brooks turned to folk forms—ballad, blues, and spirituals—not out of any sentimental attachment to a given tradition but to deepen her poetic structure. While, on the surface, these folk elements make her poetry more accessible to the reader, a closer examination reveals insinuations and refinements of technique that augment the complexity so characteristic of her work. In so doing, Brooks has met her own criteria expressed in this early statement for an effective black poet:

> The Negro poet's most urgent duty, at present, is to polish his technique, his way of presenting his truths and his beauties, that these may be more insinuating, and therefore, more overwhelming.[9]

Notes

[1] Unless noted differently, all citations of primary texts refer to Gwendolyn Brooks, *The World of Gwendolyn Brooks* (New York: Harper, 1971), hereafter cited with pagination in the text as *WGB*. This omnibus includes *A Street in Bronzeville* (1945), *Annie Allen* (1949), *Maud Martha* (1953), *The Bean Eaters* (1960), and *In the Mecca* (1968).

[2] Remarks made during a reading in Carbondale, Illinois, at the Newman Center in October 1980.

[3] For Brooks' conscious attempt to weld craft to "humanity," see Frank Harriot, "The Life of a Pulitzer Poet," *Negro Digest,* August 1950, pp. 14–16.

[4] See Bethel's essay, "'This Infinity of Conscious Pain': Zora Neale Hurston and the Black Female Literary Tradition," from *All the Women Are White; All the Blacks are Men, But Some of Us Are Brave: Black Women's Studies,* ed. Gloria T. Hull, Patricia Bill Scott, and Barbara Smith (Old Westbury, New York: The Feminist Press, 1982), pp. 176–88. Bethel, p. 180.

[5] Gordon Hall Gerould, *The Ballad of Tradition* (Oxford: Clarendon, 1932), p. 48; hereafter cited in the text as Gerould. I am heavily indebted to Gerould for my discussion of the European ballad tradition.

[6] Arthur P. Davis, "The Black-and-Tan Motif in the Poetry of Gwendolyn Brooks," *CLA Journal,* 6, No. 2 (December 1962), pp. 90–97.

[7] See Brooks' Sonnet #2 from "The Children of the Poor" sequence in which the mother complains that her children are "sweetest lepers" because "graven by a hand less than angelic, admirable or sure" (*WGB,* p. 100).

[8] Gwendolyn Brooks, *Report from Part One: An Autobiography* (Detroit: Broadside Press, 1972), p. 204.

[9] Gwendolyn Brooks, "Poets Who Are Negroes," *Phylon,* 2 (December 1950), p. 312.

Gwendolyn Brooks's *A Street in Bronzeville,* the Harlem Renaissance and the Mythologies of Black Women

Gary Smith

When Gwendolyn Brooks published her first collection of poetry *A Street in Bronzeville* (1945) with Harper and Brothers, she already enjoyed a substantial reputation in the literary circles of Chicago. Nearly a decade earlier, her mother, Keziah Brooks, had arranged meetings between her daughter and James Weldon Johnson and Langston Hughes, two of the most distinguished Black writers of America's Harlem Renaissance. Determined to mold Gwendolyn into a *lady Paul Laurence Dunbar,* Mrs. Brooks proffered poems for the famous writers to read. While Johnson's advice to the young poet was abrupt, eventually he exerted an incisive influence on her later work. In a letter and a marginal note included on the returned poems, addressed to her on 30 August 1937, Johnson praised Brooks's obvious talent and pointed her in the direction of Modernist poetry:

> My dear Miss Brooks: I have read the poems you sent me last. Of them I especially liked *Reunion* and *Myself. Reunion* is very good, and *Myself* is good. You should, by all means, continue you[r] study and work. I shall always be glad to give you any assistance that I can. Sincerely yours. James Weldon Johnson.
>
> Dear Miss Brooks—You have an unquestionable talent and feeling for poetry. Continue to write—at the same time, study carefully the work of the best modern poets—not to imitate them, but to help cultivate the highest possible standards of self-criticism. Sincerely, James Weldon Johnson.

Of course, the irony in Johnson's advice, addressed as it is to the future *lady* Dunbar, is that he actually began his own career by conspicuously imitating Dunbar's dialect poems, *Lyrics of a Lowly Life;* yet he encourages Brooks to study the work of the "best Modern poets." He was, perhaps, reacting to the latent elements of modernism already found in her poetry; but the effect was to turn Brooks momentarily away from the Black aesthetic of Hughes's *Weary Blues* (1926) and Countee Cullen's *Color* (1925) toward the Modernist aesthetics of T. S. Eliot, Ezra Pound, and e. e. cummings. It is interesting to note, however, that, even though Johnson's second letter admonishes Brooks to study the Modernist poets, he cautions her "not to imitate them," but to read them with the intent of cultivating the "highest possible standards of self-criticism." Flattered by the older poet's attention and advice, Brooks embarked upon a serious attempt to absorb as much Modernist poetry as she could carry from the public library.

If Johnson played the part of literary mentor, Brooks's relationship with Hughes was more personal, warmer, and longer lasting. She was already on familiar terms with *Weary Blues,* so their first meeting was particularly inspirational. Brooks showed Hughes a packet of her poems, and he praised her talent and encouraged her to continue to write. Years later, after Brooks's reputation was firmly established by a Pulitzer Prize for *Annie Allen* (1949), her relationship with Hughes blossomed into mutual admiration. Hughes dedicated his collection of short stories, *Something in Common* (1963), to her. While Hughes's poetic style had an immeasurable influence on Brooks's poetry, she also respected his personal values and lifestyle. As she noted in her autobiography [*Report*], Hughes was her idol:

Langston Hughes! The words and deeds of Langston Hughes were rooted in kindness, and in pride. His point of departure was always a clear pride in his race. Race pride may be craft, art, or a music that combines the best of jazz and hymn. Langston frolicked and chanted to the measure of his own race-reverence.

He was an easy man. You could rest in his company. No one possessed a more serious understanding of life's immensities. No one was firmer in recognition of the horrors man imposes upon man, in hardy insistence on reckonings. But when those who knew him remember him the memory inevitably will include laughter of an unusually warm and tender kind. The wise man, he knew, will take some juice out of this one life that is his gift.

Mightily did he use the street. He found its multiple heart, its tastes, smells, alarms, formulas, flowers, garbage and convulsions. He brought them all to his tabletop. He crushed them to a writing paste. He himself became the pen.

In other words, while Johnson encouraged Brooks to find "standards for self-criticism" in Modernism, Hughes underscored the value of cultivating the ground upon which she stood. In Hughes, in both the poet and man, Brooks found standards for living: he was a model of witty candor and friendly unpretentiousness and, most importantly, a literary success. Hughes convinced Brooks that a Black poet need not travel outside the realm of his own experiences to create a poetic vision and write successful poetry. Unlike the Modernist Eliot who gathered much of his poetic material from the drawingrooms and salons of London, Hughes found his material in the coldwater flats and backstreets of Harlem. And Brooks, as is self-evident in nearly all her poetry, learned Hughes's example by heart.

II

The critical reception of *A Street in Bronzeville* contained, in embryo, many of the central issues in the scholarly debate that continues to engage Brooks's poetry. As in the following quotation from *The New York Times Book Review*, most reviewers were able to recognize Brooks's versatility and craft as a poet:

> If the idiom is colloquial, the language is universal. Brooks commands both the colloquial and more austere rhythms. She can vary manner and tone. In form, she demonstrates a wide range: quatrains, free verse, ballads, and sonnets—all appropriately controlled. The longer line suits her better than the short, but she is not verbose. In some of the sonnets, she uses an abruptness of address that is highly individual.

Yet, while noting her stylistic successes, not many critics fully understood her achievement in her first book. This difficulty was not only characteristic of critics who examined the formal aspects of prosody in her work, but also of critics who addressed themselves to the social realism in her poetry. Moreover, what Brooks gained at the hands of critics who focused on her technique, she lost to critics who chose to emphasize the exotic, Negro features of the book, as the following quote illustrates:

> *A Street in Bronzeville* ranges from blues ballads and funeral chants to verse in high humor. With both clarity and insight, it mirrors the impressions of life in an urban Negro community. The best poem is "The Sundays of Satin-Legs Smith," a poignant and hour-by-hour page out of a zoot-suiter's life. A subtle change of pace proves Brooks' facility in a variety of poetic forms.

The poems in *A Street in Bronzeville* actually served notice that Brooks had learned her craft well enough to combine successfully themes and styles from both the Harlem Renaissance and Modernist poetry. She even achieves some of her more interesting effects in the book by parodying the two traditions. She juggles the pessimism of Modernist poetry with the general optimism of the Harlem Renaissance. Three of her more notable achievements, "kitchenette building," "the mother," and "Sundays of Satin-Legs Smith," are parodic challenges to T. S. Eliot's dispirited anti-hero J. Alfred Prufrock. "[K]itchenette building" begins with Eliot-like emphasis on the dry infertility of modern life: "We are things of dry hours and the involuntary plan." The poem concludes with the humored optimism that "Since Number 5 is out of the bathroom / we think of lukewarm water, we hope to get in it." Another example is the alienated, seemingly disaffected narrator of "the mother" who laments the loss of her children but with the resurgent, hopeful voice that closes the poem: "Believe me, I loved you all." Finally a comparison could be made between the elaborate, self-assertive manner with which Satin-legs Smith dresses himself for his largely purposeless Sunday outing and the tentative efforts of his counterpart, J. Alfred Prufrock.

Because of the affinities *A Street in Bronzeville* shares with Modernist poetry and the Harlem Renaissance, Brooks was initiated not only into the vanguard of American literature, but also into what had been the inner circle of Harlem writers. Two of the Renaissance's leading poets, Claude McKay and Countee Cullen, addressed letters to her to mark the publication of *A Street in Bronzeville*. McKay welcomed her into a dubious but potentially rewarding career:

> I want to congratulate you again on the publication of 'A Street in Bronzeville' [sic] and welcome you among the band of hard working poets who do have something to say. It is a pretty rough road we have to travel, but I suppose much compensation is derived from the joy of being able to sing. Yours sincerely, Claude McKay. (October 10, 1945.)

Cullen pinpointed her dual place in American literature:

> I have just finished reading, 'A Street in Bronzeville' [sic] and want you to know that I enjoyed it thoroughly. There can be no doubt that you are a poet, a good one, with every indication of becoming a better. I am glad to be able to say 'welcome' to you to that too small group of Negro poets, and to the larger group of American ones. No one can deny you your place there. (August 24, 1945.)

The immediate interest in these letters is how both poets touch upon the nerve ends of the critical debate that surrounded *A Street in Bronzeville*. For McKay, while Brooks has "something to say," she can also "sing"; and for Cullen, she belongs not only to the minority of Negro poets, but also to the majority of American ones. Nonetheless, the critical question for both poets might well have been Brooks's relationship to the Harlem Renaissance. What had she absorbed of the important tenets of the Black aesthetic as expressed during the New Negro Movement? And how had she addressed herself, as a poet, to the literary movement's assertion of the folk and African culture, and its promotion of the arts as the agent to define racial integrity and to fuse racial harmony?

Aside from its historical importance, the Harlem Renaissance—as a literary movement—is rather difficult to define. There is, for example, no fixed or generally agreed upon date or event that serves as a point of origin for the movement. One might easily assign this date to the publication of McKay's poems *Harlem Shadows* (1922), Alaine Locke's anthology *The New Negro* (1925), or Cullen's anthology *Caroling Dusk* (1927). Likewise, the general description of the movement as a Harlem Renaissance is often questioned, since most of the major writers, with the notable exceptions of Hughes and Cullen, actually did not live and work in Harlem. Finally, many of the themes and literary conventions defy definition in terms of what was and what was not a New Negro poet. Nonetheless, there was a common ground of purpose and meaning in the works of the individual writers that permits a broad definition of the spirit and intent of the Harlem Renaissance. Indeed, the New Negro poets expressed a deep pride in being Black; they found reasons for this pride in ethnic identity and heritage; and they shared a common faith in the fine arts as a means of defining and reinforcing racial pride. But in the literal expression of these artistic impulses, the poets were either romantics or realists and, quite often within a single poem, both. The realistic impulse, as defined best in the poems of McKay's *Harlem Shadows,* was a sober reflection upon Blacks as second class citizens, segregated from the mainstream of American socioeconomic life, and largely unable to realize the wealth and opportunity that America promised. The romantic impulse, on the other hand, as defined in the poems of Sterling Brown's *Southern Road* (1932), often found these unrealized dreams in the collective strength and will of the folk masses. In comparing the poems in *A Street in Bronzeville* with various poems from the Renaissance, it becomes apparent that Brooks agrees, for the most part, with their prescriptions for the New Negro. Yet the unique contributions she brings to bear upon this tradition are extensive: 1) the biting ironies of intraracial discrimination, 2) the devaluation of love in heterosexual relationships between Blacks, and 3) the primacy of suffering in the lives of poor Black women.

III

The first clue that *A Street in Bronzeville* was, at the time of its publication, unlike any other book of poems by a Black American is its insistent emphasis on demystifying romantic love between Black men and women.

. . .

In *A Street in Bronzeville,* this romantic impulse for idealizing the Black woman runs headlong into the biting ironies of intraracial discrimination. In poem after poem in *A Street in Bronzeville,* within the well-observed caste lines of skin color, the consequences of dark pigmentation are revealed in drastic terms. One of the more popular of these poems, "The Ballad of Chocolate Mabbie," explores the tragic ordeal of Mabbie, the Black female heroine, who is victimized by her dark skin and her "saucily bold" lover, Willie Boone:

> It was Mabbie without the
>   grammar school gates.
> And Mabbie was all of seven.
> And Mabbie was cut from a
>   chocolate bar.

And Mabbie thought life was heaven.

Mabbie's life, of course, is one of unrelieved monotony; her social contacts are limited to those who, like her, are dark skinned, rather than "lemon-hued" or light skinned. But as Brooks makes clear, the larger tragedy of Mabbie's life is the human potential that is squandered:

> Oh, warm is the waiting for joys, my dears!
> And it cannot be too long.
> O, pity the little poor chocolate lips
> That carry the bubble of song!

. . .

For Brooks, unlike the Renaissance poets, the victimization of poor Black women becomes not simply a minor chord but a predominant theme of *A Street in Bronzeville*. Few, if any, of her female characters are able to free themselves from the web of poverty and racism that threatens to strangle their lives. The Black heroine in "obituary for a living lady" was "decently wild / As a child," but as a victim of society's hypocritical, puritan standards, she

> fell in love with a man who didn't know
> That even if she wouldn't let him touch her breasts she
> was still worth his hours.

In another example of the complex life-choices confronting Brooks's women, the two sisters of "Sadie and Maud" must choose between death-in-life and life-in-death. Maud, who went to college, becomes a "thin brown mouse," presumably resigned to spinsterhood, "living all alone / In this old house," while Sadie who "scraped life / With a fine-tooth comb" bears two illegitimate children and dies, leaving as a heritage for her children her "fine-tooth comb." What is noticeable in the lives of these Black women is a mutual identity that is inextricably linked with race and poverty.

. . .

Brooks's relationship with the Harlem Renaissance poets, as *A Street in Bronzeville* ably demonstrates, was hardly imitative. As one of the important links with the Black poetic tradition of the 1920s and 1930s, she enlarged the element of realism that was an important part of the Renaissance worldview. Although her poetry is often conditioned by the optimism that was also a legacy of the period, Brooks rejects outright their romantic prescriptions for the lives of Black women. And in this regard, she serves as a vital link with the Black Arts Movement of the 1960s that, while it witnessed the flowering of Black women as poets and social activists as well as the rise of Black feminist aesthetics in the 1970s, brought about a curious revival of romanticism in the Renaissance mode.

However, since the publication of *A Street in Bronzeville*, Brooks has not eschewed the traditional roles and values of Black women in American society; on the contrary, in her subsequent works, *Annie Allen* (1949), *The Bean Eaters* (1960), and *In the Mecca* (1968), she has been remarkably consistent in identifying the root cause of intraracial problems with the Black community as white racism and its pervasive socioeconomic effects. Furthermore, as one of the chief voices of the Black Arts Movement, she has developed a social vision, in such works as *Riot* (1969), *Family Pictures* (1970), and *Beckonings* (1975), that describes Black women and men as equally integral parts of the struggle for social and economic justice.

QUESTIONS

1. Consider the voice in Brooks's poetry. Is a consistent, recognizable voice present throughout, or does the voice of the speaker vary from poem to poem?
2. Study Brooks's comments about her own work. Do you believe her assessments and explanations are always accurate, or do you question her conclusions at times?
3. Do Brooks's poems apply only to the lives of African Americans, or do they also have relevance to the lives of other Americans—or to the lives of people in other countries? That is, to what degree are her themes universal, and to what degree are they race or culture specific?
4. Gwendolyn Brooks does not focus on conventional poetic subjects such as love, nature, or death. Could you argue that these subjects are nevertheless present in many of her poems?
5. Brooks is essentially a formalist poet, relying on traditional forms with regular rhyme, meter, and stanzaic divisions—for example, the ballad and the sonnet. Are such traditional forms appropriate for her subject matter?
6. What patterns of imagery and figurative language recur in Brooks's poems?
7. Consider the effects of Brooks's use of caesura in her sonnets. What do these stops in mid-line contribute to the poems?
8. What is the significance of the religious references in Brooks's poetry—for example, at the end of "The *Chicago Defender* Sends a Man to Little Rock"?
9. What is Brooks's motive in using regular—at times singsong—meter and rhyme in poems with serious subjects, such as "The Ballad of Rudolph Reed" (p. 412) and "Sadie and Maud" (p. 188)? Does the poem's sound undercut or enhance its meaning in such cases?

10. What other poets might you compare with Brooks? Why are they comparable?
11. To what degree are Brooks's poems concerned with women's issues—or even with feminism? Are such themes central to her poetry, merely incidental, or nonexistent?
12. Many of Brooks's most recent poems focus explicitly on social issues. For example, "Jane Addams," an unpublished 1989 poem, is about the woman who founded the first settlement house in the United States, and a 1987 poem, "Thinking of Elizabeth Steinberg," focuses on a six-year-old victim of child abuse. How do the poems in this casebook address issues of social justice?

Adam Goren
Professor West
Literature 201
8 April 1993

Racial Consciousness in
"The Ballad of Rudolph Reed"

According to Gwendolyn Brooks, she did not come to terms with the implications of being a black writer until 1967. At that time she was forced to confront the fact that although she was accepted by the white world of letters, she was regarded as irrelevant by militant blacks (Brooks, Report 419). Certainly much in Brooks's poetry shows she is a poet who values the themes and forms of the traditional Western literary canon. She writes poetry that reflects universal human concerns; she writes in traditional poetic forms, such as the sonnet and the ballad; and she uses white writers as models (Baker 421). Even so, the body of Brooks's works -- including many poems written before 1967 -- illustrates that race has always been a major concern (Baker 421). Her 1960 poem "The Ballad of Rudolph Reed," typical of her early poetry, illustrates how Brooks uses a conventional poetic form -- the ballad -- to treat an unconventional poetic subject: racial intolerance.

In "The Ballad of Rudolph Reed," Gwendolyn Brooks tells of an African-American family's encounter with racial violence when they move into a white neighborhood. The strength of

Rudolph Reed, the protagonist of the poem, and his family is clearly evoked with the use of the word <u>oaken</u> in the first stanza of the poem:

> Rudolph Reed was oaken.
> His wife was oaken too.
> And his two good girls and his good little man
> Oakened as they grew. (1-4)

Reed and his family move to the white neighborhood to escape the deplorable conditions of their former home. According to Reed, he is hungry for the peace and security that most white people take for granted. All he wants is a house in which he "May never hear the roaches / Falling like fat rain" and "Where never wife and children need / Go blinking through the gloom" (11-14). In other words, Reed, like other Americans, is taking the United States government at its word and trying to claim a piece of the American dream for himself and his family.

The traditional meter and the simple, direct language of the ballad are well suited to communicating Reed's hope and determination. Like Robin Hood, a subject of many English ballads, Reed confronts political oppression and fights for the rights of the common person (Mootry 439). Brooks's use of traditional ballad rhyme scheme and meter suggests a link between Reed's quest and the subjects of other romantic ballads. This evocation of an idealized romantic past stands in direct contrast, however, to the contemporary racial brutality that exists outside Reed's new house. "[T]oo joyous to notice it" (412), the family is oblivious to the racism that will destroy their short-lived happiness.

Soon after the family moves into its new house, neighbors begin throwing rocks through the windows. Reed withstands these assaults for three nights until his child is injured by a piece of broken glass. Grabbing a gun and a butcher knife, he runs out to defend his house:

> He ran like a mad thing into the night.
> And the words in his mouth were stinking.
> By the time he had hurt his first white man
> He was no longer thinking.
> By the time he had hurt his fourth white man
> Rudolph Reed was dead. (53-58)

One of the ironies of the poem is that Reed, who is repeatedly described as <u>oaken</u>, is unable to endure the rocks and insults of his white neighbors. Throughout the poem the word <u>oaken</u> is repeated like a ballad refrain. Reed and his wife are <u>oaken</u>; his children <u>oaken</u> as they grow; and Reed is <u>oakener</u> than others. Traditionally, the oak tree is known for its strength. The oak, however, is unable to bend and, as a result, it can be uprooted in a storm. The duality of this image embodies the dilemma facing African Americans in 1960. On the one hand, they had to be strong to survive the kind of racial brutality described in the poem. On the other hand, being too strong made it likely that they, like Reed, would confront the white power structure and be broken by it. "The Ballad of Rudolph Reed" offers no way out of this dilemma;

indeed, it suggests that as long as the racial situation in the United States remains polarized, men and women, like Reed and his wife, will be oppressed and even killed.

    The ballad structure that so easily communicates the hopeful mood of the first part of the poem is also able to convey the brutality of the final part of the poem. The quaintness of the ballad's old-fashioned language - - "nary a curse" - - (30) and inverted sentence structure - - "Then up did rise our Rudolph Reed" - - (49), by evoking an earlier, more innocent time, emphasizes the fundamental irony of Reed's predicament: He is attacked simply for wanting to improve his life. Obviously, the American Dream, as well as all it implies, was not meant to include African Americans. Running like "a mad thing into the night" (53), Reed seems like a character in a "B" movie or a nightmare. In this case, however, the situation as well as the brutality is all too real: "His neighbors gathered and kicked his corpse. / 'Nigger - - ' his neighbors said" (59-60).

    By the last stanza, violence, grief, and resignation have replaced the hope and determination expressed at the beginning of the poem. All that remains of Reed and his dream is the image of a mother comforting her wounded child:

> Small Mabel whimpered all night long
> For calling herself the cause.
> Her oak-eyed mother did no thing
> But change her bloody gauze. (61-64)

Despite its bitterness, the poem does offer some comfort. Reed's wife remains "oak-eyed" (63) -- that is, strong -- and both she and her daughter survive the attack. The implication is that they will continue the struggle and possibly triumph over those who killed Reed.

"The Ballad of Rudolph Reed" was written in 1960, well before Brooks says she understood the implications of being a black writer in America. Despite Brooks's assertions to the contrary, the themes she explores in this poem are similar to those she explores in many poems written after 1967 (Smith 430). Brooks's impatience with the white power structure and her anger about the oppression of African Americans -- ideas apparent in "Medgar Evers" and "A Boy Died in My Alley" -- clearly dominate "The Ballad of Rudolph Reed." Using the ballad to express her ideas, Brooks combines her mastery of traditional forms with her need to create a poetry that is relevant to African Americans. Houston A. Baker, Jr., perhaps best sums up her achievement when he says that throughout her career Brooks has created works "that equal the best in the black and white American literary traditions" (Baker 427).

Works Cited

Baker, Houston, A., Jr. "The Achievement of Gwendolyn Brooks." Kirszner and Mandell. 421.

Brooks, Gwendolyn. from "<u>Report from Part One</u>." Kirszner and Mandell. 419.

---. "The Ballad of Rudolph Reed." Kirszner and Mandell. 412 .

Kirszner, Laurie G., and Stephen R. Mandell, eds. <u>Literature: Reading, Reacting, Writing.</u> 2nd. ed. Fort Worth: Harcourt, 1994.

Mootry, Maria K. "'Chocolate Mabbie' and 'Pearl May Lee': Gwendolyn Brooks and the Ballad Tradition." Kirszner and Mandell. 439.

Smith, Gary. "Gwendolyn Brooks's 'Children of the Poor,' Metaphysical Poetry and the Inconditions of Love." Kirszner and Mandell. 430.

APPENDIX A

DOCUMENTING SOURCES

Documentation is the acknowledgment that information you use to support ideas in a paper comes from an outside source. In general you should give credit to your sources whenever you quote, paraphrase, summarize, or in any other way incorporate the ideas of others into your work. Not to do so—on purpose or by accident—is to commit **plagiarism,** to appropriate the intellectual property of others. By following accepted standards of documentation, you not only help avoid plagiarism, but also show your readers that you write with care and precision. In addition, you enable them to distinguish your ideas from those of your sources and, if they wish, to consult the sources you cite.

Not all ideas from your sources need to be documented. You can assume that certain ideas—facts from encyclopedias, textbooks, newspapers, magazines, and dictionaries, or even from television and radio—are common knowledge. Even if the information is new to you, it need not be documented as long as it is generally available and you do not use the exact wording of your source. Information that is in dispute or that is the original contribution of a particular person, however, *must* be documented. You need not, for example, document the fact that Arthur Miller's *Death of a Salesman* was first performed in 1949 or that it won a Pulitzer Prize for drama. (You could find this information in any current encyclopedia.) You would, however, have to document a critic's interpretation of a performance or a scholar's analysis of an early draft of the play.

Students of literature use the documentation style recommended by the Modern Language Association of America (MLA), a professional organization of more than 25,000 teachers and students of English and other languages. This method of documentation, the one that you should use any time you write a literature paper, has three parts: *parenthetical references in the text, a list of works cited,* and *explanatory notes.*

PARENTHETICAL REFERENCES IN THE TEXT

MLA documentation uses references inserted in parentheses within the text that refer to a list of works cited at the end of the paper. A typical **parenthetical reference** consists of the author's last name and a page number.

> Gwendolyn Brooks uses the sonnet form to create poems that have a wide social and aesthetic range (Williams 972).

If you use more than one source by the same author, include a shortened title in the parenthetical reference. In the following entry, "Brooks's Way" is a shortened form of the complete title of the article "Gwendolyn Brooks's Way with the Sonnet."

> Brooks not only knows Shakespeare, Spenser, and Milton, she also knows the full range of African-American poetry (Williams, "Brooks's Way" 972).

If the author's name or the title of the work is included in the text, only a page reference is necessary.

> According to Gladys Margaret Williams in "Gwendolyn Brooks's Way with the Sonnet," Brooks combines a sensitivity to poetic forms with a depth of emotion appropriate for her subject matter (972–73).

Keep in mind that you punctuate parenthetical references differently with paraphrases and summaries, direct quotations run in with the text, and quotations of more than four lines.

With paraphrases and summaries

Place the parenthetical documentation one space after the last word of the sentence and before the final punctuation:

> In her works Brooks combines the pessimism of Modernist poetry with the optimism of the Harlem Renaissance (Smith 978).

With direct quotations run in with the text

Place the parenthetical documentation one space after the quotation marks and before the final punctuation:

> According to Gary Smith, Brooks's <u>A Street in Bronzeville</u> "conveys the primacy of suffering in the lives of poor Black women" (980).

According to Gary Smith, the poems in <u>A Street in Bronzeville,</u> "served notice that Brooks had learned her craft . . . ." (978).

Along with Thompson we must ask, "Why did it take so long for critics to acknowledge that Gwendolyn Brooks is an important voice in twentieth-century American poetry" (123)?

With quotations set off from the text

Omit the quotation marks and place the parenthetical documentation two spaces after the final punctuation.

> For Gary Smith, the identity of Brooks's African-American women is inextricably linked with their sense of race and poverty:
>> For Brooks, unlike the Renaissance poets, the victimization of poor Black women becomes not simply a minor chord but a predominant theme of <u>A Street in Bronzeville</u>. Few, if any, of her female characters are able to free themselves from a web of poverty that threatens to strangle their lives. (980)

[Note that quotations of more than four lines are indented ten spaces from the margin and are not enclosed within quotation marks.]

SAMPLE REFERENCES

The following formats are used for the parenthetical references required in papers about literature.

An entire work

August Wilson's play <u>Fences</u> treats many themes frequently expressed in modern drama.

[When citing an entire work, include the name of the author in the text instead of in a parenthetical reference.]

A work by two or three authors

> Myths cut across boundaries and cultural spheres and reappear in strikingly similar forms from country to country (Feldman and Richardson 124).

> The effect of a work of literature depends on the audience's predispositions that derive from membership in various social groups (Hovland, Janis, and Kelley 87).

A work by more than three authors

> Hawthorne's short stories frequently use a combination of allegorical and symbolic methods (Guerin et al. 91).

[The abbreviation *et al.* is Latin for "and others."]

A work in an anthology

> In his essay "Flat and Round Characters" E. M. Forster distinguishes between one-dimensional characters and those that are well developed (Stevick 223–31).

[This note cites the anthology, edited by Stevick, in which Forster's essay appears.]

A work with volume and page numbers

> In 1961 one of Albee's plays, <u>The Zoo Story,</u> was finally performed in America (Eagleton 2:17).

An indirect source

> Wagner observed that myth and history stood before him "with opposing claims" (qtd. in Winkler 10).

[The abbreviation *qtd. in* (quoted in) indicates that the quoted material was not taken from the original source.]

A play or poem with numbered lines

> "Give thy thoughts no tongue," says Polonius, "Nor any unproportioned thought his act" (I.iii.59–60).

[The parentheses contain the act, scene, and line numbers, separated by periods.]

> "I muse my life-long hate, and without flinch / I bear it nobly as I live my part," says Claude McKay in his bitterly ironic poem "The White City" (3–4).

[Notice that a slash {/} is used to separate lines of poetry run in with the text. The parenthetical reference cites the lines quoted.]

THE LIST OF WORKS CITED

Parenthetical references refer to a **list of works cited** that includes all the sources used in your paper. (If your list includes all the works consulted, whether you cite them or not, use the title *Works Consulted.*) Begin the works cited list on a new page, continuing the page numbers of the paper. For example, if the text of the paper ends on page 6, the works cited section will begin on page 7.

Arrange entries alphabetically, according to the last name of each author (or the first word of the title if the author is unknown). Articles—*a, an,* and *the*—at the beginning of a title are not considered first words. Thus *A Handbook of Critical Approaches to Literature* would be alphabetized under *H.* In order to conserve space, publishers' names are abbreviated—for example, *Harcourt* for Harcourt Brace College Publishers. Double-space the entire works cited list between and within entries. Begin each entry at the left margin, and indent subsequent lines five spaces. The entry itself generally has three divisions—author, title, and publishing information—separated by a period and two spaces.

A book by a single author

> Kingston, Maxine Hong. The Woman Warrior: Memoirs of a Girlhood among Ghosts. New York: Knopf, 1976.

A book by two or three authors

> Feldman, Burton, and Robert D. Richardson. The Rise of Modern Mythology. Bloomington: Indiana UP, 1972.

[Notice that only the *first* author's name is in reverse order.]

A book by more than three authors

> Guerin, Wilfred, et al., eds. A Handbook of Critical Approaches to Literature. New York: Harper, 1979.

Two or more works by the same author

> Novoa, Juan-Bruce. Chicano Authors: Inquiry by Interview. Austin, U of Texas P, 1980.
>
> ---. "Themes in Rudolfo Anaya's Work." Address given at New Mexico State University. Las Cruces, 11 Apr. 1987.

[List two or more works by the same author in alphabetical order by title. Use three hyphens followed by a period to take the place of the author's name in second and subsequent entries.]

An edited book

> Oosthuizen, Ann, ed. Sometimes When it Rains: Writings by South African Women. New York: Pandora, 1987.

A book with a volume number

> Eagleton, T. Allston. A History of the New York Stage. Vol. 2. Englewood Cliffs: Prentice, 1987. 3 vols.

[All three volumes have the same title.]

> Durant, Will, and Ariel Durant. The Age of Napoleon: A History of European Civilization from 1789 to 1815. New York: Simon, 1975. Vol. 11 of The Story of Civilization. 11 vols.

[Each volume has a different title.]

A short story in an anthology

> Salinas, Marta. "The Scholarship Jacket." Nosotros: Latina Literature Today. Ed. Maria del Carmen Boza, Beverly Silva, and Carmen Valle. Binghamton: Bilingual Press, 1986. 68–70.

[Place the inclusive page numbers two spaces after the year of publication.]

A poem in an anthology

> Simmerman, Jim. "Child's Grave, Hale County, Alabama." The Pushcart Prize, X: Best of the Small

Presses. Ed. Bill Henderson. New York: Penguin, 1986. 198-99.

A play in an anthology

Hughes, Langston. Mother and Child. Black Drama Anthology. Ed. Woodie King and Ron Miller. New York: NAL, 1986. 399-406.

An article in an anthology

Forster, E. M. "Flat and Round Characters." The Theory of the Novel. Ed. Philip Stevick. New York: Free, 1980. 223-31.

More than one article from the same anthology

If you are using more than one selection from an anthology, cite the entire anthology. In addition, list the individual selections separately (in alphabetical order according to the author's last name) without including the anthology title or any publication information. Cite only the author, title, anthology editor's last name, and the inclusive page numbers on which the selection appears.

Kirszner, Laurie G., and Stephen R. Mandell, eds. Literature: Reading, Reacting, Writing. 2nd ed. Fort Worth: Harcourt, 1994.

Rich, Adrienne. "Diving into the Wreck." Kirszner and Mandell. 811-813.

A translation

Carpentier, Alejo. Reasons of State. Trans. Francis Partridge. New York: Norton, 1976.

An article in a journal

LeGuin, Ursula K. "American Science Fiction and the Other." Science Fiction Studies 2 (1975): 208-10.

An article in a magazine

Milosz, Czeslaw. "A Lecture." The New Yorker 22 June 1992: 32.

"Solzhenitsyn: An Artist Becomes an Exile." *Time* 25 Feb. 1974: 34+.

[34+ indicates that the article appears on pages that are not consecutive; in this case the article begins on page 34 and then continues on page 37. An unsigned article is entered by title on the works cited list.]

An article in a daily newspaper

Oates, Joyce Carol. "When Characters from the Page Are Made Flesh on the Screen." *New York Times* 23 March 1986, sec. 2:1+.

An encyclopedia article

"Dance Theatre of Harlem." *Encyclopaedia Britannica: Micropaedia.* 1985 ed.

[You do not need to include publication information for well-known reference books.]

Grimstead, David. "Fuller, Margaret Sarah." *Encyclopedia of American Biography.* Ed. John A. Garraty. New York: Harper, 1974.

[Include publication information when citing reference books that are not well known.]

An interview

Brooks, Gwendolyn. "Interview." *Triquarterly* 60 (1984): 74–92.

A lecture or address

Novoa, Juan-Bruce. "Themes in Rudolfo Anaya's Work." Address given at New Mexico State University. Las Cruces, 11 Apr. 1987.

EXPLANATORY NOTES

You can use explanatory notes, indicated by a superscript (a raised number) in the text, to cite several sources at once or to provide commentary or explanations that do not fit smoothly into your paper. The full text of these notes appears on the first numbered page following the last page of the paper. (If your paper has no explanatory notes, the works cited page follows the last page of the paper.) Like works cited entries, explanatory notes are double spaced within and between entries. However, the first line of each explanatory note is indented five spaces, with subsequent lines flush with the left-hand margin.

TO CITE SEVERAL SOURCES

In the paper

Surprising as it may seem, there have been many attempts to define literature.[1]

In the note

[1]Arnold 72; Eagleton 1-2; Howe 43-44; and Abrams 232-34.

FOR EXPLANATIONS

In the paper

In recent years gothic novels have achieved great popularity.[3]

In the note

[3]Gothic novels, works written in imitation of medieval romances, originally relied on supernatural occurrences. They flourished in the late eighteenth and early nineteenth centuries.

SAMPLE LITERATURE PAPER WITH MLA DOCUMENTATION

The following research paper, written for an introduction to literature course, follows MLA documentation format.

Jennifer Flemming

Professor Jussawalla

English 3112

12 May 1993

Rudolfo Anaya's <u>Bless Me, Ultima</u>:
A Microcosmic Representation of Chicano Literature

    Chicano authors have sometimes been called "noble savages," and they have been denied credit and recognition in the fields of literature and culture. Some scholars and teachers consider Chicano literature as "newly emerged" from recent political developments and therefore lacking in maturity and universal appeal, although others have traced its growth and development in the Southwest since the 16th century. The fact that most Chicano literature is based on social protest and is associated with political events also elicits less than positive responses from literary critics. The political nature of the literature causes it to be viewed as not quite legitimate. However, Chicano literature is neither "newly emerged" and thus lacking in maturity nor merely reflective of recent sociopolitical movements. On the contrary, Chicano literature not only records the Mexican-American experience in the American Southwest but also demonstrates the universality of that experience. Rudolfo Anaya's <u>Bless Me, Ultima</u>, which records the Mexican-American experience while describing the emotions universal to most ten-year-old boys, exemplifies the dual role of the best Chicano literature.

Flemming 2

Paredes and Paredes's definition of Chicano literature ties it to the Chicano's key role in the cultural development of the American Southwest:

> People like to record their experiences; Mexican-Americans have been no exception. They have had much to write about. Their lives have sometimes been stormy and often tragic, but always vital and intriguing. It is hardly surprising that Mexican-Americans have literary talents, for they are heirs to the European civilization of Spain and the Indian civilizations of Mexico, both of which produced great poets and storytellers. Furthermore, they have also been in contact with the history and literature of the United States. . . . (1)

This connection of the development of the literature with the locale is made by Luis Leal in his article "Mexican American Literature: A Historical Perspective" when he notes that Chicano literature had its origin when the Southwest was settled by the inhabitants of Mexico during colonial times (22). He emphasizes that the literature originated both from the contact of the colonial Mexicans with the Native Americans and from the contact with the Anglo culture that was moving westward. In fact, many of the themes of Chicano literature emphasize the coming in contact of two vastly different cultures. This is particularly true of Anaya's Bless Me, Ultima, which also reflects the universal emotions and feelings generated as a result of the clash of cultures.

Flemming 3

A recording of the experience of the Southwest is found in Anaya's Bless Me, Ultima, which ultimately develops universal themes of initiation and maturation (Novoa, "Themes"). In his novel about a young boy, Antonio, who moves from innocent adolescence to the ambiguous and morally corrupt adult world, the author expresses his culture's indigenous beliefs, myths, and legends.

Antonio's father tells him of the coming of the Spanish colonizers to the Valley, their contact with the American Indian culture which Ultima—an older grandmother figure—exemplifies, and the changes brought about in the village and the town by the coming of the Tejanos (Texans of Mexican descent). Yet the theme is universal, transcending the boundaries of his village. The events that result from the clash between the old and the new could take place anywhere in the world because they deal with religious hatred and with the conflicts between different ways of life.

The novel relates the story of a young boy and his friendship with a curandera (charlatan) named Ultima who comes to live with Antonio and his family. The arrival of Ultima has an enormous impact on him because he feels a kinship with her. For instance, through Ultima, Antonio—now nicknamed Tony—comes in contact with the local Indian religions. Ultima teaches him about herbs and shares with him her knowledge of their special magical properties. She also introduces Antonio to Narcisso, the Indian who teaches him the myth of the Golden

Flemming 4

Carp: "The people who killed the carp of the river . . . were punished by being turned into fish themselves. After that happened many years later, a new people came to live in this valley" (Anaya 110). This myth encapsulates the history of the Indian people, the Hispanic colonizers, and the Anglo settlers of New Mexico. Tony sees the reflection of the myth in his day-to-day life. The Indians and the Hispanics of the valley are gradually replaced by the "new people," the Anglos. This stirs in him deep love for his land, his people, and his lifestyle.

But at school he is teased for believing in these myths. His classmates, who have already laughed at his lunch of tortillas and his inability to speak English, taunt him about Ultima. Calling her a <u>bruja</u> (witch) they say, "Hey, Tony, can you make the ball disappear?" "Hey, Tony, do some magic" (Anaya 102). Tony suffers the angst of a ten-year-old taunted by these voices. He begins to suffer doubts about his identity and the rightness of his beliefs.

At the end of the book, when Ultima is killed by the townspeople for being a witch, Antonio falls to his knees to pray for her and in facing her death reaches his maturation. He knows what is right for him: "I praised the beauty of the Golden Carp" (Anaya 244).

Anaya has said, "When people ask me where my roots are, I look down at my feet. . . . They are here, in New Mexico, in the Southwest" (Novoa, <u>Chicano Authors</u> 185). The author's message is clear and undeniable: one must go back to one's roots, despite the conflicting pull of Americanization. It is this

Flemming 5

same message of faith and hope that Ultima, on her deathbed, gives to Antonio: Learn to accept life's experiences and feel the strength of who you are. In the character of Ultima, however, Anaya has created a symbol of beauty, harmony, understanding, and the power of goodness that transcends the limits of time and space and religious beliefs.

From the above examples it can be seen that Anaya is capable of producing Chicano literature that has universal appeal and themes. Anaya's novel records the Mexican-American experience of the Southwest while creating characters and portraying emotions of universal appeal. The social protest against Americanization is secondary to the treatment of myth and emotions.

Chicano literature cannot be considered just a by-product of the recent struggle for civil rights. This is not to minimize or deny the effects of the Chicano political movement and the new sense of awareness and direction that it has sparked (which includes the proliferation of Chicano literary texts). Although Chicano literature may appear to emphasize social protest and criticism of the dominant Anglo culture, or seem to be introspectively searching for self-definition, it will not be found lacking in universal appeal (Leal, Decade 42).

Flemming 6

Works Cited

Anaya, Rudolfo. Bless Me, Ultima. Berkeley: Tonatiuh, 1972.

Leal, Luis, et al. A Decade of Chicano Literature. Santa Barbara: La Causa, 1982.

---. "Mexican American Literature: A Historical Perspective." Modern Chicano Writers. Ed. Joseph Sommers and Tomas Ybarra-Fausto. Englewood Cliffs: Prentice, 1979. 18-40.

Novoa, Juan-Bruce. Chicano Authors: Inquiry by Interview. Austin: U of Texas P, 1980.

---. "Themes in Rudolfo Anaya's Work." Address given at New Mexico State University. Las Cruces, 11 Apr. 1987.

Paredes, Americo and Raymond Paredes. Mexican-American Authors. Boston: Houghton, 1973.

APPENDIX B

LITERARY HISTORY: ARISTOTLE TO THE TWENTIETH CENTURY

The standard literary *canon* (the works of authors commonly read and taught) has been, until very recently, mainly male, white, upper class, and European—with some American influence. The canon readers have been exposed to determines their understanding of what constitutes good literature. Most readers are not aware that the fiction, drama, and poetry now designated as "classics" represent a series of choices about literary worth made over a long period of time. During the past twenty-five years or so, many challenges to the traditional canon have been made. To understand both the development of the traditional canon and the challenges to that canon, it is important to understand the history of Western literary criticism.

BEGINNINGS: THE GREEKS AND ROMANS (c. 450 B.C.–A.D. 400)

The Western tradition begins with the Greeks. In the *Republic* Plato (427–347 B.C.) described the ideal state as well as the role of philosophers and poets. His pupil, Aristotle (384–322 B.C.), was by far the most significant classical influence on Europeans of the Middle Ages and the Renaissance. Even today drama critics and students pay careful attention to the theories presented in Aristotle's *Poetics* about how literature imitates life, how an audience responds with pity and fear to a tragedy, and how a well-written play is constructed.

The Romans contributed works on what would now be called "loftiness of style" (*On the Sublime*, Longinus, first century A.D.) and a treatise on the art of poetry (*Ars Poetica*, Horace, 65–8 B.C.). These writers were typically more interested in the craft of poetry—in how one might construct a poem that would have a pleasing effect on a reader—than in the power of the poet. In contrast to the Greek philosophical approach, Roman literary criticism was more like a practical handbook.

THE MIDDLE AGES (c. A.D. 400–1500)

After the fall of the West Roman Empire in the fifth century A.D., Christianity became the unifying force of Western culture. The literature of the European Middle Ages was for the most part didactic and exemplary. It was intended to demonstrate moral virtue in the hopes that people would follow the behavior patterns it praised. Much literature of this period took the form of morality and mystery plays, both of which had religious themes. Worldly art was discouraged because the clergy who kept learning alive during these hard times felt that the role of literature was to instruct people in the way to lead a virtuous life. Significant departures from moralistic literature appeared in the French romances, which depicted adventures undertaken in the cause of love, and in Chaucer's *Canterbury Tales*, which drew on English, French, and Italian sources. These served as an antidote to the traditional cautionary plays and tales. It is not surprising, given the strong moral purpose of most literature of the Middle Ages, that literary criticism was not a priority of the intellectual life of the period.

THE RENAISSANCE (c. 1500–1660)

During the fourteenth and fifteenth centuries, Europe emerged from the church-centered Middle Ages with a rebirth (*renaissance* is French for "rebirth") of learning. Renewed access to Greek and Roman writers led Renaissance humanists to a broad interest in intellectual considerations. Sir Philip Sidney's (1554–1586) *The Defense of Poesy* (c. 1580) is usually considered the most important work of literary criticism from this period. In his *Defense* Sidney argues that poetry must serve not simply to give pleasure, but also to contribute positively to the life of society. Unlike the writers of medieval allegories, however, Sidney believed that literature could—and should—have a moral impact without being didactic or prescriptive. Despite Sidney's contributions, Aristotle continued to be the undisputed arbiter of critical questions, although his role was complicated by the emergence of William Shakespeare (1564–1616) as a dramatist of exceptional talent.

Shakespeare's work posed a problem because many critics realized that he was a fine playwright despite his frequent disregard for Aristotle's rules governing well-constructed plays. As a result, a concern of criticism up to the eighteenth century became the reconciling of Aristotle's standards with the challenges of contemporary playwriting.

THE ENLIGHTENMENT (1660–1798)

Samuel Johnson (1709–1784), who devoted much of the preface of his edition of Shakespeare's plays to the question of the bard's departures from Aristotle's rules, was a major critical figure of the Enlightenment, a period of neoclassicism characterized by a revitalized interest in the values and ideas of the classical world, particularly of the Romans. Along with Johnson, poets John Dryden (1631–1700) and Alexander Pope (1688–1744), as well as philosopher Edmund Burke (1729–1797), compared contemporary practice with the ideals of their Roman forebears.

Burke, for instance, took on the subject of Longinus's *On the Sublime* in his own treatise, *The Origin of Our Ideas of the Sublime and the Beautiful* (1757). Eighteenth-century critics stressed the value of reason and what they called "common sense." Their architectural style, familiar to us in buildings like the Capitol building in Washington, D.C., provides a visual example of what they sought in literature: clarity, symmetry, discipline. They demanded that a play or poem be tightly constructed and favored the heroic couplet (two lines of rhymed iambic pentameter) as the perfect building block with which to construct didactic poems such as Pope's famous *Essay on Criticism* (1711), a scathing statement of neoclassical literary principles.

Thomas Paine's *Common Sense: Addressed to the Inhabitants of America* (1776) inspired his fellow Americans to revolution, and his *Rights of Man* (1791, 1792) made a stirring case for freedom as the right of every individual. The literature of the American Revolutionary Age, when Paine, Thomas Jefferson, Alexander Hamilton, Philip Freneau, and Joel Barlow were writing, reflected the patriotic concerns of the infant democracy.

THE ROMANTIC PERIOD (1798–1837)

Perhaps as an inevitable counterreaction to the Enlightenment came the Romantics. They believed that poetry was *not* an objective construction like a building with a precise and unchanging meaning but, instead, a subjective creation whose meaning depends on the poet's emotional state and a reader's personal response. Romantic poet William Blake (1757–1827) illustrated the conflict between romanticism and neoclassicism through his ardent dislike of the criticism of Enlightenment artist Joshua Reynolds. In his notes on Reynolds's views, Blake observed that the emphasis on materialism and on physical evidence (empiricism) impoverishes art. Blake believed that the neoclassicists denied both imagination and subjective experience their preeminent role in the creative process. He felt that the artist must begin from the most concrete and minute sensory experience in order to reach the truth. Unlike most eighteenth-century writers, Blake and his fellow Romantics believed in the importance of the individual example rather than the general principle.

Like Blake, Samuel Taylor Coleridge (1772–1834) and William Wordsworth (1770–1850) placed value on the mysterious and on the significance of the common person's experience. Wordsworth in particular stressed the importance of concrete, simple language and offered, in his preface to the second edition of *Lyrical Ballads* (1800), a definition of poetry that has since become famous. A poem, Wordsworth says, should originate in "the spontaneous overflow of powerful feelings" whose energy comes from "emotion recollected in tranquility." George Gordon, Lord Byron (1788–1824), who himself lived a flamboyant life of publicly expressed powerful emotions, created in his poetry the melancholy

Romantic hero, defiant and haunted by secret guilt. Percy Bysshe Shelley (1792–1822) makes perhaps the greatest claims for the poet's power and obligation to society in "A Defense of Poetry" (1821), where he argues that the "great instrument of moral good is the imagination."

The difference in attitude between neoclassicists and Romantics can also be seen through a comparison of the Shakespearean criticism of Samuel Johnson and Samuel Taylor Coleridge. In his *Preface to Shakespeare* (1765) Johnson argues that Shakespeare's faults include being much more concerned with pleasing an audience than with teaching it morals; he observes that often virtue is not rewarded, nor wickedness suitably punished. Additionally, Johnson notes, Shakespeare's diction is too elevated, and he lets the characters in the tragedies talk too much without advancing the action.

Coleridge, on the other hand, sees in the tragic character of Hamlet the prototype of the Romantic hero and argues in his lecture "Shakespeare's Judgment Equal to his Genius" (1836) that Shakespeare knew exactly what he was doing in describing how people actually behave rather than how they ought to behave.

John Keats (1795–1821), another Romantic poet, continued Coleridge's defense of Shakespeare. Keats believed that Shakespeare's intensity, particularly evident in the tragedies, moved his work onto another level altogether, where such judgments become irrelevant and the work itself takes on life through its relationship with "beauty and truth" rather than with teaching proper patterns of behavior.

The Romantics in general, both in Britain and in the United States, made claims for the poet as particularly close to God and nature. The American philosopher Ralph Waldo Emerson (1803–1882) thought nature offered to the poet a mystical symbolism, while Henry David Thoreau (1817–1862) extolled the view that man should live close to nature and follow his personal conscience, rather than the dictates of society. Mary Shelley (1797–1851) and Edgar Allan Poe (1809–1849) were influential in another strand of romanticism: the macabre, melancholy, and mysterious.

THE VICTORIAN PERIOD (1837–1901)

The literary problem facing the post-Romantic generation of critics was the familiar one of dealing with a world where sublime isolation and communing with nature were less and less possible, even as ideals. During the Victorian era rapid industrialization, poverty, population growth, and mass transportation contributed to a general sense that the world was changing rapidly, and people had difficulty coping with these changes. In England critics like poet Matthew Arnold (1822–1888) argued that literature could help anchor people to their world and that literary criticism, as an occupation, should be a "disinterested endeavor" whose responsibility was to minister to a modern society that had lost its faith in other things, particularly religion. Although Arnold differed in many ways from the Romantics, he too believed in the ability of poetry to help us live productive, satisfying lives.

Just before the turn of the nineteenth century, the pendulum swung back from the Arnoldian view that poetry has moral utility—and that the best of it is serious and elevating—to the view that art should exist for its own sake. The dichotomy seen by the Romantics between intellect and feeling became in the 1890s the split between art and the domain of science. Oscar Wilde (1854–1900), Stéphane Mallarmé (1842–1898), and Charles Baudelaire (1821–1867) all dealt with this dichotomy by retreating altogether to the world of art and denying connection with anything else. These members of the symbolist movement valued suggestion, private symbols, and evocative references in their poetry. They attempted to connect their writing with a spiritual world they believed existed but knew was not accessible by the rational methods of science.

Charles Darwin (1809–1882) popularized a biological theory of natural selection in his landmark *Origin of Species* (1859), and his theories influenced novels and poetry of the latter part of the century. Those who believed natural selection contradicted the Bible were outraged, and others interpreted his theories as evidence of latent bestiality in humans. The certainty that mankind was the center of the universe was undermined, as was the conviction that the universe had been intelligently planned for a good purpose.

American writers of the late nineteenth century, including William Dean Howells and Henry James, were noted for realism; others, including naturalists Frank Norris and Theodore Dreiser, explored the idea of individuals being at the mercy of their instinctual drives and of external sociological forces.

THE MODERN PERIOD (1901–Present)

In the next major attempt to demonstrate some objective significance to poetry, T. S. Eliot (1888–1965) argued against the lingering Romantic idea that a poem is the original child of a poet's inspiration. Instead, he proposed in "Tradition and the Individual Talent" (1917) that the poem supersedes the poet, who is merely the agent of its creation. Eliot argues that Wordsworth is wrong to put the poet in the central role of life-experiencer and recreator. According to Eliot, the poem itself will join the tradition, and it will be up to the *critic* to make sense of that tradition. To continue with the example of Shakespeare, Eliot's analysis of *Hamlet* focuses neither on the character of Hamlet and his personal agony (as did the Romantics) nor on the moral tone of the play (as did the neoclassicists), but rather on the story of Hamlet as treated by dramatists before Shakespeare. Eliot concludes that the problems with Shakespeare's play come about because he cannot successfully incorporate the early source materials with his own desire to write a play about the effect of Gertrude's guilt on her son. Thus Eliot judges Shakespeare within a literary and historical tradition rather than within a moral or personal context.

The twentieth century has produced many important critics and theoreticians of literature who built upon the legacy of the past, though some only to the extent that they attempt to contradict earlier approaches. The dominant critical views, which are discussed more fully in Appendix C, can be divided into three groupings: formal, those concerned with the structure or form of texts (formalism, structuralism, deconstruction); social, those concerned with texts in relation to social contexts (new historicism, feminism, Marxism); and personal, those concerned with the interaction of the individual (author or reader) and texts (reader-response criticism, psychoanalytic criticism).

Each of these theoretical approaches can be traced to precursors in the writings of authors in the early part of the twentieth century or before. Mary Wollstonecraft's *A Vindication of the Rights of Women* (1792), for example, was an early forerunner of feminism. Virginia Woolf wrote a number of essays, including *A Room of One's Own* (1929), on the effects upon women of the patriarchal Western society. She pointed out deeply entrenched attitudes and beliefs of male-oriented society that hindered women in the pursuit of realizing their creative possibilities.

Formalism, which acquired prominence in English and American criticism in the middle part of the century, actually began in the early part of the century in Moscow and Petrograd, and was initially a term used in a negative fashion because the techniques focused on patterns and devices in a work of literature and ignored the subject matter. Soon, however, formalism's logical appeal took hold, and it was advocated by Victor Shklovsky, Boris Eichenbaum, and Roman Jakobson in the 1920s.

The roots of psychoanalytic criticism can be traced to the psychological criticism of the early nineteenth century. Thomas Carlyle suggested in 1827 that the best criticism of the day was psychological, deriving meaning from a poem by analyzing the mental state and personality structure of the author.

Marxist criticism is based on the writings of Karl Marx and Friedrich Engels; they borrowed their key term *ideology* from French philosophers of the late eighteenth century who used it to label the study of how sense perceptions develop into concepts. And the term Marxism itself was used in the same period to mean a rigidly held set of political ideas. Marx and Engels adapted and changed the terms, investing them with new meaning that built upon meanings already present in the culture.

Though many literary theorists since Aristotle have stressed the importance of structure, the roots of structuralist criticism can be traced more directly to Russian formalists and French anthropologist Claude Levi-Strauss (1908–   ), who posited that all cultural phenomena have an underlying structural system. Deconstruction both reacts against the tenets of structuralism and builds upon the theories of German philosophers Friedrich Nietzsche (1844–1900) and Martin Heidegger

(1889–1976), who questioned the validity and verifiability of "truth," "knowledge," and other basic philosophical concepts.

Reader-response criticism is a late-twentieth-century approach, beginning in the 1960s, which focuses on the reader and the reader's process and experience, rather than on the text or the text and its historical context. And new historicism is an even more recent mode of literary study, beginning in the 1980s, that reacts to formalism, structuralism, and deconstruction, arguing that the historical context is an integral part of a literary work and that the text cannot be considered in isolation.

The theoretical positions and techniques of each of these approaches to the study of literature are considered in some detail in Appendix C.

APPENDIX C

TWENTIETH-CENTURY LITERARY THEORIES

As you become aware of various schools of literary criticism and read essays applying their principles, you see new ways to think about fiction, poetry, and drama. Just as you value the opinions of your peers and your professors, you will also find that the ideas of literary critics can enrich your own reactions and evaluations of literature. Keep in mind that no single literary theory offers the "right" way of approaching what you read; no single critic provides the definitive analysis of any short story, poem, or play. As you become aware of the richly varied possibilities of twentieth-century criticism, you will begin to recognize new possibilities, ask new questions, and discover new complexities in the works you read.

FORMALISM

Formalism stresses the importance of literary form in determining the meaning of a work. Each piece of literature is considered by itself, in isolation. Formalist scholars consider biographical, historical, and social questions to be irrelevant to the real meaning of a play, short story, novel, or poem. For example, a formalist would see the relationship between Adam and Eve in *Paradise Lost* as entirely unrelated to Milton's own marital concerns, and theological themes in the same work would be viewed as entirely separate from Milton's deep involvement with the Puritan religious and political cause in seventeenth-century England. Milton's intentions and readers' responses to the famous epic poem would also be regarded by formalists as irrelevant. Instead, formalists ask an interpreter to read the text closely, paying attention to organization and structure, to verbal nuances (suggested by connotation and figurative language), and to multiple meanings (often created through the writer's use of paradox and irony). The formalist critic tries to reconcile the tensions and oppositions inherent in the text in order to develop a unified reading.

The formalist movement in English language criticism began in England with I. A. Richards's *Practical Criticism* (1929). To explain and introduce his theory, Richards asked students to interpret famous poems without telling them the poet's names. Of course this strategy encouraged close reading of the text rather than reliance on a poet's reputation, biographical data, or historical context. The American formalist movement, called *new criticism,* was made popular largely by college instructors who realized that formalist criticism provided a useful way for students to work along with an instructor in interpreting a literary work rather than passively listening to a lecture on biographical, literary, and historical influences. In fact, the new critical theorists Cleanth Brooks and Robert Penn Warren put together a series of textbooks (*Understanding Poetry, Understanding Fiction,* and *Understanding Drama,* first published in the late 1930s) used in colleges for years. After the 1950s, many new critics began to reevaluate their theories and to broaden their approaches. Although few scholars currently maintain a strictly formalist approach, nearly every critical movement of this century, including feminist, Marxist, psychoanalytic, structuralist, and deconstructionist criticism, owes a debt to the close reading techniques introduced by the formalists.

A FORMALIST READING: KATE CHOPIN'S "THE STORM"

A formalist critic reading Chopin's "The Storm," might well begin by noting the story's three distinctive sections. What relationship do the sections bear to one another? What do we learn from the word choice, the figures of speech, and the symbols in these sections? And, most important, how do these considerations lead readers to a unified view of the story?

In the first section of "The Storm," the reader meets Bobinôt and his son Bibi. The description of the approaching clouds as "sombre," "sinister," and "sullen" suggests an atmosphere of foreboding, yet the initial alliteration of these words also introduces a poetic tone. The conversation between father and son in the final part of this section contrasts, yet does not conflict, with the rather formal language of the introduction. Both Bobinôt and Bibi speak in Cajun dialect, suggesting their humble origins, yet their words have a rhythm that echoes the poetic notes struck in the description of the storm. As the section closes, Bobinôt, thinking of his wife, Calixta, at home, buys a can of the shrimp he knows she likes and holds the treasure "stolidly," ironically suggesting the protection he cannot offer his wife in his separation from her during the coming storm.

The long second section brings the reader to the story's central action. Calixta, as she watches the rain, sees her former lover, Alcée, riding up to seek shelter. Just as in the first section, the language of the narrator is somewhat formal and always poetic, filled with sensuous diction and images. For instance, we see Calixta "unfasten[ing] her white sacque at the throat" and, later, Alcée envisions her lips "as red and moist as pomegranate seed." Again, paralleling the first section, the conversation of the characters is carried on in dialect, suggesting their lack of sophistication and their connection to the powerful natural forces that surround them. The lovemaking that follows, then, seems both natural and poetic. There is nothing sordid about this interlude and, as the final sections of the story suggest through their rather ordinary, matter-of-fact language, nothing has been harmed by Calixta and Alcée's yielding to passion.

In Section 3, Bobinôt brings home the shrimp, symbol of his love for Calixta, and, although we recognize the tension between Bobinôt's shy, gentle approach and Alcée's passion, the reader can accept the final sentence as literal rather than ironic. The "storms" (both the rain and the storm of passion) have passed, and no one has been hurt. The threat suggested in the opening sentences has been diffused; both the power and the danger evoked by the poetic diction of the first two sections have disappeared, to be replaced entirely by the rhythms of daily life and speech.

For Further Reading: Formalism
Brooks, Cleanth. *The Well Wrought Urn.* 1947.
Empson, William. *Seven Types of Ambiguity.* 1930.
Stallman, Robert W. *Critiques and Essays in Criticism. 1920–1948.* 1949.
Wellek, René. *A History of Modern Criticism. Vol. 6.* 1986.
Wimsatt, W. K. *The Verbal Icon.* 1954.

READER-RESPONSE CRITICISM

Reader-response criticism suggests a critical view that opposes formalism, seeing the reader's interaction with the text as central to interpretation. Unlike formalists, reader-response critics do not believe that a work of literature exists as a separate, closed entity. Instead, they consider the reader's contribution to the text as essential. A poem, short story, novel, or play is not a solid fabric, but rather a series of threads separated by gaps that readers must fill in, drawing on their own experiences and knowledge.

As we read realistic fiction (where the world of the text closely resembles what we call reality), we may not notice that we are contributing our interpretation. As we read one sentence and then the next, we develop expectations; and, in realistic stories, these expectations are generally met. Nevertheless, nearly every reader supplies personal meanings and observations, making each reader's experience unique and distinctive from every other reader's experience with the same work. For example, imagine Shakespeare's *Romeo and Juliet* as it might be read by a fourteen-year-old high school student and by her father. The young woman, whose age is the same as Juliet's, is almost certain to identify closely with the female protagonist and to "read" Lord Capulet, Juliet's father, as overbearing and rigid. The young reader's father, however, may be drawn to the poignant passage where Capulet talks with a prospective suitor, urging that he wait while Juliet has time to enjoy her youth. Capulet describes the loss of his other children and calls Juliet "the hopeful lady of my earth." While the young woman reading this line may interpret it as yet another indication of Capulet's possessiveness, her father may see it as a sign of love and even generosity. The twentieth-century father may "read" Capulet as a man willing to risk offending a friend in order to keep his daughter safe from the rigors of early marriage (and early childbearing). Whose interpretation is correct? Reader-response theorists would say that both readings are entirely possible and, therefore, equally "right."

The differing interpretations produced by different readers can be seen as simply the effect of the different personalities (and personal histories) involved in constructing meaning from the same series of clues. Not only does the reader "create" the work of literature, in large part, but the literature itself may work on the reader as he or she reads, altering the reader's experience, and thus the reader's interpretation. For example, the father reading *Romeo and Juliet* may alter his sympathetic view of Capulet as he continues through the play and observes the old Lord's later, angry exchanges with Juliet.

Reader-response theorists believe in the importance of recursive reading—that is, reading and rereading with the idea that no interpretation is carved in stone. A second or third interaction with the text may well produce a new interpretation. This changing view is particularly likely when the rereading takes place significantly later than the initial reading. For example, if the young woman just described reread *Romeo and Juliet* when she was middle-aged and herself the mother of teenage children, her reaction to Capulet would quite likely be different from her reaction when she read the work at age fourteen.

In one particular application of reader-response theory, the idea of developing readings is applied to the general reading public rather than to individual readers. *Reception theory,* as proposed by Hans Robert Jauss ("Literary History as a Challenge to Literary Theory" in *New Literary History,"* Vol. 2. 1970–71), suggests that each new generation reads the same works of literature differently. Because each age of readers has experienced different historical events, read different books, and been aware of different critical theories, each generation will view the same works very differently from its predecessors. Certainly a quick look back at the summary of literary history in Appendix B will support the credibility of this idea. Consider, for example, the changing views toward Shakespeare from the seventeenth to the twentieth centuries.

Reader-response criticism has received serious attention since the 1960s, with Norman Holland's *The Dynamics of Literary Response* (1968) formulating the theory. The German critic Wolfgang Iser (*The Implied Reader,* 1974) argued that in order to be an effective reader, one must be familiar with the conventions and "codes" of writing. This, then, is one reason for studying literature in a classroom, not to produce only approved interpretations, but to develop strategies and information that will make sense of a text. Stanley Fish, an American critic, goes even further, arguing that there may not be any "objective" text at all (*Is There a Text in This Class?,* 1980). Fish says that no two readers read the same book, though readers can be trained to have relatively similar responses to a text if they have had relatively similar experiences. For instance, if readers have gone to college and taken an introduction to literature course, where they have learned to respond to the various elements of literature such as character, theme, irony, and figurative language, they are likely to have similar responses to a text.

READER-RESPONSE READINGS: KATE CHOPIN'S "THE STORM"

To demonstrate possible reader-response readings, we can look at the same story previously considered from a formalist perspective. (Of course, if several formalist critics read the story, they too would each write a somewhat different interpretation.)

Written by a 25-Year-Old Man; Has Studied American Literature: In Kate Chopin's "The Storm," attention must be paid to the two adult male characters, Bobinôt and Alcée. Usually in a love triangle situation one man is portrayed more sympathetically than the other. But Chopin provides us with a dilemma. Alcée is not merely the cavalier seducer; he genuinely cares for Calixta. Neither is he the brooding hero. There is nothing gruff or angry about Alcée, and he returns to his family home with no apparent harm done following the passionate interlude. On the other hand, Bobinôt is not a cruel or abusive husband. We can see no clear reason for Calixta's affair except for her desire to fulfill a sexual longing for Alcée.

Written by an 18-Year-Old Man; First-Year Literature Course: Bibi doesn't seem to be a very important character in the story, but we should pay attention to him as a reflection of his father. At the beginning of the story, Bibi worries about his mother and he expresses his concern to his father. Bobinôt tries to reassure his son, but he gets up and buys a treat for Calixta as much to comfort himself as to get something for her. Then Bibi sits with his father, and it seems as if he has transferred all his worries to Bobinôt. In the third section of the story, after Calixta and Alcée have had their love affair, Bibi and Bobinôt come home. They both seem like children, worried about how Calixta will react. She, of course, is nice to them because she feels so guilty. At the end of Section 3, both father and son are happy and enjoying themselves. You can't help but feel great sympathy for them both because they are so loving and simple and because they have been betrayed by Calixta, who has not behaved the way a loving mother and wife should.

Written by a 45-Year-Old Woman; Has Studied Kate Chopin's Life and Work: A decade after the controversial novel *The Awakening* was published in 1899, one critic protested, "To think of Kate Chopin, who once contented herself with mild yarns about genteel Creole life . . . blowing us a hot blast like that!" (qtd. in Gilbert and Gubar 981).

This literary observer was shocked, as one might expect from an early-twentieth-century reader, by Chopin's frank picture of sexual relations, and particularly of the sexual feelings of the novel's heroine. One cannot help but wonder, however, whether the scandalized reader was really widely acquainted with Chopin.

Certainly he could not have read "The Storm." This short story is surprising for many reasons, but primarily because it shows a woman who is neither evil nor doomed enjoying, even glorying in, her sexuality. Calixta is presented as a good wife and loving mother, concerned about her husband and son who are away from home during the storm. Yet her connection to Bobinôt and Bibi does not keep her from passionately enjoying her interlude with Alcée. She goes to his arms unhesitatingly, with no false modesty or guilt (feigned or real) to hold her back. Somehow, this scenario does not seem to fit the definition of "a mild yarn about genteel Creole life."

For Further Reading: Reader-Response Criticism
Bleich, David. *Subjective Criticism.* 1978.
Iser, Wolfgang. *The Act of Reading: A Theory of Aesthetic Response.* 1978.
Rosenblatt, Louise. *The Reader, the Text, the Poem.* 1978.
Sulleiman, Susan, and Inge Crosman, eds. *The Reader in the Text.* 1980.
Tomkins, Jane P., ed. *Reader-Response Criticism.* 1980.

SOCIOLOGICAL CRITICISM

Like reader-response criticism, **sociological criticism** takes issue with formalism. Sociological theorists maintain that the literary work cannot be separated from the social context in which it was created. Literature reflects society and derives its essential existence and significance from the social situations to which it responds. Sociological critics speculate about why a particular work might have been written and explore the ways in which it reacts to a specific situation.

For instance, a sociological literary scholar might note with interest that Shakespeare's history plays about Richard II, Henry IV, and Henry V deal with the consequences of uncertain royal succession and usurpation. These dramas were written during the final reigning years of Queen Elizabeth I, a monarch who had not produced an heir and refused to designate one. Although the plays cited were set considerably before Elizabeth's time, a sociological critic might conclude that they reflect the English concern about the threat of monarchic chaos should Elizabeth die with no clear line of succession.

In the twentieth century two strong arms of sociological criticism have emerged as dominant: feminist criticism and Marxist criticism. They are particularly forceful theories because most of their practitioners have a strong commitment to these ideologies, which they apply as they read literature. Feminism and Marxism share a concern with segments of society that have been underrepresented and often ignored. These views are, of course, supported by modern critical theories such as the reader-response idea of gaps in the text that must be filled in through the reader's own experience and knowledge. In addition, the techniques of New Criticism (in particular, close reading of the text), psychoanalysis, and structuralism have allowed sociological critics to focus on what had been overlooked or skewed in traditional readings and to analyze how the experience of marginal and minority groups has been represented in literature.

FEMINIST CRITICISM

Feminist criticism began as a defined approach to literature in the late 1960s, although throughout the nineteenth century, women such as the Brontë sisters, George Eliot (Mary Ann Evans), Elizabeth Barrett Browning, and Christina Rossetti struggled for the right to be taken as seriously as their male counterparts. In addition, in 1929 Virginia Woolf, an experimental novelist and literary critic, published *A Room of One's Own*, a collection of essays describing the difficulties that women writers faced and defining a tradition of literature written by women.

Modern feminist criticism began with works such as Mary Ellman's *Thinking About Women* (1968), which focuses on the negative female stereotypes in books authored by men and points out alternative feminine characteristics suggested by women authors. Another pioneering feminist work was Kate Millet's *Sexual Politics* (1969), which analyzes the societal mechanisms that perpetuate male domination of women. Since that time feminist writings, though not unified in one theory or methodology, have appeared in ever growing numbers. Some feminist critics have adapted psychoanalytic, Marxist, or other post-structuralist theories, and others have broken new ground. In general, feminist critics take the view that our culture—and by extension our literature—is primarily patriarchal (controlled by males).

What is at issue is not anatomical sex, but gender. As Simone de Beauvoir explained, a person is not born feminine, as our society defines it, but rather becomes so because of cultural conditioning. According to feminist critics, paternalist Western culture has defined the feminine as "other" to the male, as passive and emotional in opposition to the masculine as dominating and rational.

Feminist critics claim that paternalist cultural stereotypes pervade works of literature in the canon. Feminists point out that, until very recently, the *canon* (the accepted body of significant literary works) has consisted of works almost exclusively written by males and has focused on male experiences. Female characters, when they do appear, are often subordinate to male characters. A female reader of these works must either identify with the male protagonist or accept a marginalized role.

One response of feminist critics is to reread works in the traditional canon. As Judith Fetterley explains in *The Resisting Reader* (1978), the reader "revisions" the text, focusing on the covert sexual bias in a literary work. For example, a feminist scholar might study Shakespeare's *Macbeth*, looking closely at the role played by Lady Macbeth and arguing that she was not, in fact, simply a cold-hearted villain. Instead, a feminist might see her as a victim of the circumstances of her time: Women were not permitted to follow their own ambitions but were relegated to supporting roles, living their lives through achievements of their husbands and sons.

A second focus of feminist scholars has been the redefinition of the canon. By seeking out, analyzing, and evaluating little-known works by women, feminist scholars have rediscovered women writers who were ignored or shunned by the reading public and by critics of their own times. Thus writers such as Kate Chopin (whose short story "The Storm" has been discussed above) and Charlotte Perkins Gilman (see "The Yellow Wall-Paper," p. 159), who wrote during the late nineteenth and early twentieth centuries, are now recognized as worthy of study and consideration.

A FEMINIST READING: TILLIE OLSEN'S "I STAND HERE IRONING"

To approach Tillie Olsen's "I Stand Here Ironing," feminist scholars might focus on the episodes in the story where the narrator describes her relationships and encounters with men.

> Some readings of Tillie Olsen's "I Stand Here Ironing" suggest that the narrator makes choices which doom her older daughter to a life of misunderstood confusion. If we look at the narrator's relationships with the men in her life, however, we can see that she herself is the story's main victim.
>
> At nineteen she is a mother, abandoned by her husband who leaves her a note saying that he "could no longer endure sharing want" with his wife and infant daughter. This is the first desertion we hear about in the narrator's life, and although she agonizingly describes her painful decisions and the mistakes she makes with Emily, we cannot help but recognize that she is the one who stays and tries to make things right. Her actions contrast sharply with those of her husband, who runs away, implying that his wife and daughter are burdens too great for him to bear.
>
> The second abandonment is more subtle than the first but no less devastating. After the narrator has remarried, she is once again left alone to cope with a growing family while Bill goes off to war. True, this desertion comes for a "noble" purpose and is probably not voluntary, but Emily's mother must, nevertheless, seek one of the low-paying jobs available to women to supplement her allotment checks. This time she is again forced to leave her children because her husband must serve the needs of the male-dominated military establishment.
>
> The narrator is alone at crucial points in Emily's life and must turn away from her daughter simply in order to survive. Although she has been brought up in a world that teaches women to depend on men, she

learns she is ultimately alone. Although the desertions she endures are not always intentional, she must bear the brunt of circumstances that are not her choice but are, rather, foisted on her by the patriarchal society in which she lives.

For Further Reading: Feminist Criticism

Benstock, Shari, ed. *Feminist Issues in Literary Scholarship*. 1987.
Eagleton, Mary, ed. *Feminist Issues in Literary Theory: A Reader*. 1986.
Gilbert, Sandra, and Susan Gubar. *The Madwoman in the Attic*. 1979.
———, eds. *The Norton Anthology of Literature by Women*. 1985.
Jacobus, Mary. *Reading Woman: Essays in Feminist Criticism*. 1986.
Miller, Nancy, K., ed. *The Poetics of Gender*. 1986.
Showalter, Elaine. *A Literature of Their Own*. 1977.
———. *Sisters Choice: Tradition and Change in American Women's Writing*. 1991.

MARXIST CRITICISM

Scholars influenced by Marxist criticism base their readings of literature on the social and economic theories of Karl Marx (*Das Kapital*, 1867–94) and his colleague and coauthor Friedrich Engels (*The Communist Manifesto*, 1884). Marx and Engels believed that the dominant capitalist middle class would eventually be challenged and overthrown by the working class. In the meantime, however, middle-class capitalists exploit the working class, who produce excess products and profits yet do not share in the benefits of their labor. Marx and Engels further regarded all parts of the society in which they lived—religious, legal, educational, governmental—as tainted by what they saw as the corrupt values of middle-class capitalists.

Marxist critics apply these views to their readings of poetry, fiction, and drama. They attempt to analyze the literary works of any historical era as products of the ideology, or network of concepts, that supports the interests of the cultural elite and suppresses those of the working class. Some Marxist critics see all Western literature as distorted by the privileged views of the elite class, but most believe that at least some creative writers reject the distorted views of their society and instead see clearly the wrongs to which working class people have been subjected. For example, George Lukacs, a Hungarian Marxist critic, proposed that great works of literature create their own worlds, which reflect life with clarity. These great works, though not written by Marxists, can be studied for their revealing examples of class conflict and other Marxist concerns. A Marxist critic would certainly look with favor on Charles Dickens, who in nearly every novel pointed out inequities in the political, legal, and educational establishments of his time. Those who remember Oliver Twist's pitiful plea for "more" workhouse porridge (refused by evil Mr. Bumble, who skims money from funds intended to feed the impoverished inmates) cannot help but see fertile ground for the Marxist critic, who would certainly applaud Dickens's scathing criticism of Victorian social and economic inequality.

Although Marxist criticism developed in the 1920s and 1930s in Germany and the Soviet Union, British and American Marxism has received greatest attention since 1960 with works such as Raymond Williams's *Culture and Society, 1780–1950* (1960) and Terry Eagleton's *Criticism and Ideology* (1976).

A MARXIST READING: TILLIE OLSEN'S "I STAND HERE IRONING"

The Marxist theorist reading Tillie Olsen's "I Stand Here Ironing" might concentrate on the episodes demonstrating how both the narrator's and Emily's fates have been directly affected by the capitalist society in which they lived.

Tillie Olsen's "I Stand Here Ironing" stands as a powerful indictment of the capitalist system. The narrator and her daughter Emily are repeatedly exploited and defeated by the pressures of the economic system in which they live.

The narrator's first child, Emily, is born into the world of the 1930s depression—an economic disaster brought on by the excesses and greed of Wall Street. When the young mother is deserted by her husband, there are no government programs in place to help her. She says it was the "pre-relief, pre-WPA world of the depression" that forced her away from her child and into "a job hashing at night." Although she is willing to work, she is paid so poorly that she must finally send Emily to live with her husband's family. Raising the money to bring Emily back takes a long time, and after this incident Emily's health, both physical and emotional, is precarious.

After Emily's episode with the measles, we get a hard look at what the few social programs that existed were like. The child is sent—at the urging of a government social worker—to a convalescent home. The narrator notes bitterly, "They still send children to that place. I see pictures on the society page of sleek young women planning affairs to raise money for it, or dancing at the affairs, or decorating Easter eggs or filling Christmas stockings for the children." The privileged class basks in the artificial glow of their charity work for the poor, yet the newspapers never show pictures of the hospitalized children who are kept isolated from anyone they loved and forced to eat "runny eggs . . . or mush with lumps." Here again the mother is separated from her daughter by a system that discriminates against the poor. Because the family cannot afford private treatment, Emily is forced to undergo treatment in a public institution that not only denies her any contact with her family, but also cruelly forbids her to save the letters she receives from home. Normal family relationships are severely disrupted by an uncaring economic structure that offers the poor only grudging and punitive aid.

It is clear that the division between mother and daughter is initiated and exacerbated by the social conditions in which they live. Because they are poor, they are separated at crucial times and, therefore, never get to know each other fully. Thus neither can truly understand the ordeals the other has been forced to endure.

For Further Reading: Marxist Criticism

Bullock, Chris, and David Peck, eds. *Guide to Marxist Literary Criticism.* 1980.
Eagleton, Terry. *Marxism and Literary Criticism.* 1976.
Jameson, Fredric. *Marxism and Form.* 1971.
Strelka, Joseph P., ed., *Literary Criticism and Sociology.* 1973.
Williams, Raymond. *Marxism and Literature.* 1977.

NEW HISTORICISM

New historicist critics focus on a text in relation to the historical and cultural contexts of the period in which it was created and periods in which it was critically evaluated. These contexts are not considered simply as "background" to a text but as integral parts of a text. History itself is not an entity composed of objective fact; rather, like literature, history is interpreted and reinterpreted depending on the power structure of a society.

Louis Althusser, for example, suggests that ideology intrudes in the discourse of an era, positioning readers in a way that "subjects" them to the interests of the ruling establishment. Michel Foucault reflects that the discourse of an era defines the nature of "truth" and what behaviors are acceptable, sane, or criminal. "Truth," for Foucault, is produced by interaction of power and the systems in which the power flows, and it changes as society changes. Mikhail Bakhtin suggests that all discourse is dialogic, meaning that any discourse contains within it many independent and sometimes conflicting voices.

Literature, in new historical criticism, is not "trans-historical"; that is, it does not exist outside time and place and cannot be interpreted without reference to the era in which it was written. Criticism likewise cannot be evaluated without reference to the time and place in which it was written. A fallacy of much criticism, according to new historicists, is to consider a literary text as an organic whole, ignoring the diversity of conflicting voices in a text or in the cultural context in which a text is embedded. Indeed, Stephen Greenblatt prefers the term "cultural poetics" to new historicism because it acknowledges the integral role literature and art play in the culture of any era of history. Works of art and literature, according to Greenblatt, actively foster subversive elements or voices but somehow "contain" those forces in ways that defuse challenges to existing culture.

New historicists also point out that readers, like texts, are influenced and shaped by the cultural context of their eras. A thoroughly objective "reading" of a text is, then, impossible. All readers to some degree "appropriate" a text. Acknowledging this problem, some new historicists present their criticism of texts as "negotiations" between past and present contexts. Thus criticism of a particular work of literature would involve both the cultural contexts of the era in which the text was written and the critic's present cultural context; and the critic would acknowledge how the latter context influences the interpretation of the former.

Beginning in the early 1970s, feminist critics adopted some new historicist positions, focusing on male-female power conflicts. And critics interested in multicultural texts stressed the role of the dominant white culture in suppressing or marginalizing the texts of non-whites. Marxist critics, including Raymond Williams, have adopted the term "cultural materialism" in discussing their mode of new historicism, which focuses on the political significance of a literary text.

A NEW HISTORICIST READING: "THE YELLOW WALL-PAPER"

A new historicist scholar might write an essay about "The Yellow Wall-Paper" as an illustration of the destructive effects of the patriarchical culture of the late nineteenth century upon women. This reading would be vastly different from that of most nineteenth-century critics who interpreted the story as a harrowing case study of female mental illness. Even earlier twentieth century readings have considered the narrator's mental illness caused by her individual psychological problems. New historicist critics might focus on the social conventions of the time, which produced conflicting discourses that drove the narrator to madness.

The female narrator of "The Yellow Wall-Paper," who is writing in her private journal (which is the text of the short story), explains that her husband, a physician, has diagnosed her as having a "temporary nervous depression—a slight hysterical tendency." She says she should believe such a "physician of high standing" and cooperate with his treatment, which is to confine her to a room in an isolated country estate and compel her to rest and have no visitors and not to write. The "cure" is intended to reduce her nervousness, she further explains. But as the story unfolds, the narrator relates that she suspects the treatment will not cure her because it leaves her alone with her thoughts without even her writing to occupy her mind. Her husband's "cure" forces her into a passive role and eliminates any possibility of asserting her own personality. However, she guiltily suggests that her own lack of confidence in her husband's diagnosis may be what is preventing her cure.

The text of "The Yellow Wall-Paper" can, then, be divided into at least two conflicting discourses: 1) the husband, who speaks with the authority of a highly respected physician and a husband, two positions reinforced by the patriarchical culture of the time; and 2) the narrator, whose own hesitant personal female voice contradicts the masculine voice or discourse but undermines itself because it keeps reminding her that women should obey their husbands and physicians.

A third discourse underlies the two dominant ones—that of the gothic horror tale, a popular genre of the late nineteenth century. The narrator in "The Yellow Wall-Paper" is isolated against her will in a room with barred windows in an almost deserted palatial country mansion she describes as "the most beautiful place"; she is at the mercy of her captor, in this case her husband; she is not sure whether she is hallucinating and thinks the mansion may be haunted; she does not know whom to trust, not being sure whether her husband really wants to "cure" her or to punish her for expressing her rebellion.

The narrator learns to hide her awareness of the conflicting discourses. She avoids mentioning her thoughts and fears about her illness or her fancies about the house being haunted, and she hides her writing. She speaks reasonably and in "a very quiet voice." But this inability to speak freely to anyone is a kind of torture, and alone in her room with the barred windows, she takes up discourse with the wallpaper. At first she describes it as "one of those sprawling flamboyant patterns committing every artistic sin." But she is fascinated by the pattern, which has been distorted by mildew and by portions that have been torn away. The narrator begins to strip off the wallpaper to free a woman she thinks is trapped inside; and, eventually, she visualizes herself as that woman, trapped, yet freed by the destruction of the wallpaper. The narrator retreats, or escapes into madness, driven there by the multiple discourses she cannot resolve.

For Further Reading: New Historicist Criticism

Geertz, Clifford. "Thick Description: Toward an Interpretive Theory of Culture," in *The Interpretation of Cultures*. 1973.
Greenblatt, Stephen, ed. *Representing the English Renaissance*. 1988.
Rabinov, Paul, ed. *The Foucault Reader*. 1986.
Veeser, H. Aram, ed. *The New Historicism*. 1989.

PSYCHOANALYTIC CRITICISM

Psychoanalytic criticism focuses on a work of literature as an expression in fictional form of the inner workings of the human mind. The premises and procedures used in psychoanalytic criticism were developed by Sigmund Freud (1846–1939), though some critics disagree strongly with his conclusions and their therapeutic and literary applications. Feminists, for example, take issue with Freud's notion that women are inherently masochistic. Some of the major points of Freud's theories depend on the idea that much of what is most significant to us does not take place in our conscious life. Freud believed that we have been forced (mostly by the rigors of having to live in harmony with other people) to repress much of our experience and many of our desires in order to coexist peacefully with others.

Some of this repressed experience Freud saw as available to us through dreams and other unconscious structures. He believed that literature could often be interpreted as the reflection of our unconscious life. Freud himself was among the first psychoanalytic critics, often using the techniques developed for interpreting dreams to interpret literature. Among other analyses, he wrote an insightful study of Dostoevsky's *The Brothers Karamazov* as well as brief commentaries on several of Shakespeare's plays, including *A Midsummer Night's Dream, Macbeth, King Lear,* and *Hamlet*. The latter study may have inspired a classic of psychoanalytic criticism: Ernest Jones's *Hamlet and Oedipus* (1949), in which Jones explains Hamlet's strange reluctance to act against his Uncle Claudius as resulting from Hamlet's unresolved longings for his mother and subsequent drive to eliminate his father. Since Hamlet's own father is dead, Jones argues that Claudius becomes, in the young man's subconscious mind, a father substitute. Hamlet, then, cannot make up his mind to kill his uncle because he does not see a simple case of revenge (for Claudius's murder of his father) but rather a complex web that includes incestuous desire for his own mother (now wed to Claudius). Jones continues his analysis to include the suggestion that Shakespeare himself experienced such a conflict and reflected his own Oedipal feelings in *Hamlet*.

A French psychoanalyst, Jacques Lacan (1901–1981), combined Freudian theories with structuralist literary theories to argue that the essential alienating experience of the human psyche is the acquisition of language. Lacan believes that once you can name yourself and distinguish yourself from others, you have entered the difficult social world that requires you to repress your instincts. Like Lacan, who modified and adapted psychoanalytic criticism to connect it to structuralism, many twentieth-century literary scholars, including Marxists and feminists, have found useful approaches in psychoanalytic literary theory (see, for example, Mary Jacobus's *Reading Woman: Essays in Feminist Criticism,* 1986).

PSYCHOANALYTIC TERMS

To fully appreciate psychoanalytic criticism, you should understand the following terms:

- *id*—The part of the mind that determines sexual drives and other unconscious compulsions that urge individuals to unthinking gratification.
- *ego*—Conscious mind that strives to deal with the demands of the id and to balance its needs with messages from the superego.
- *superego*—Part of the unconscious that seeks to repress the demands of the id and to prevent gratification of basic physical appetites. The superego, then, is a sort of censor that represents the prohibitions of society, religion, family beliefs, and so on.

- *condensation*—A process that takes place in dreams (and in literature) when several elements from the repressed unconscious are linked together to form a new, yet disguised, whole.
- *symbolism*—Use of representative objects to stand for forbidden (often sexual) objects. This process takes place in dreams and in literature. For instance, a pole, knife, or gun may stand for the penis.
- *displacement*—Substitution of a socially acceptable desire for a desire that is not acceptable. Again, this process may take place in dreams or in literature. For example, a woman who experiences sexual desires for her son may instead dream of caressing a neighbor who has the same first name as (or who looks like) her son.
- *Oedipus complex*—Repressed desire of a son to unite sexually with his mother and kill his father. According to Freud, all young boys go through this stage, but most resolve these conflicts before puberty.
- *projection*—Defense mechanism in which people mistakenly see in others antisocial impulses they fail to recognize in themselves.

A PSYCHOANALYTIC READING: EDGAR ALLAN POE'S "THE CASK OF AMONTILLADO"

Since Edgar Allan Poe died in 1849, six years before Freud was born, Poe could not possibly have known Freud's work. Nevertheless, psychoanalytic critics argue that the principles discovered by Freud and those who followed were always inherent in human nature. Therefore, it is perfectly plausible to use modern psychiatric terms when analyzing a work that was written before their invention.

Montresor, the protagonist of Poe's "The Cask of Amontillado," has long fascinated readers who have puzzled over his motives for the story's climactic action when he imprisons his rival, Fortunato, and leaves him to die. Montresor claims that Fortunato has insulted him and has dealt him a "thousand injuries." Yet when we meet Fortunato, although he appears something of a pompous fool, none of his actions—or even his comments—seems powerful enough to motivate Montresor's thirst for revenge.

If, however, we consider a defense mechanism, first named "projection" and described by Sigmund Freud, we gain a clearer picture of Montresor. Those who employ projection are often people who experience antisocial impulses yet are not conscious of these impulses. It seems highly likely that Fortunato has not persecuted Montresor; rather, Montresor himself has experienced the impulse to act in a hostile manner toward Fortunato. We know, for instance, that Fortunato belongs to the exclusive order of masons because he gives Montresor the secret masonic sign. Montresor's failure to recognize the sign shows that he is only a mason in the grimmest literal sense. Montresor clearly resents Fortunato's high standing and projects onto Fortunato all of his own hostility toward those who (he thinks) have more or know more than he does. Thus he imagines that Fortunato's main business in life is to persecute and insult him.

Montresor's obsessive behavior further indicates his pathology. He plans Fortunato's punishment with the cunning one might ordinarily reserve for a major battle, cleverly figuring out a way to keep his servants from the house and to lure the ironically named Fortunato to his death. Each step of the revenge is carefully plotted. This is no sudden crime of passion, but rather the diabolically anticipated act of a deeply disturbed mind.

If we understand Montresor's need to take all of the hatred and anger that is inside himself and to rid himself of those socially unacceptable emotions by projecting them on to someone else, then we can see how he rationalizes as deserved revenge a crime that seems otherwise nearly unmotivated. By killing Fortunato, Montresor symbolically kills the evil in himself. It is interesting to note that the final lines of the story support this reading. Montresor observes that "for half of a century no mortal has disturbed" the bones. In other words, these unacceptable emotions have not again been aroused. His last words, a Latin phrase from the mass for the dead meaning "rest in peace," suggest that only through his heinous crime has he found release from the torment of his own hatred.

For Further Reading: Psychoanalytic Criticism

Freud, Sigmund. *The Interpretation of Dreams.* 1900.
Gardner, Shirley N., ed. *The (M)other Tongue: Essays in Feminist Psychoanalytic Interpretation.* 1985.
Kris, Ernst. *Psychoanalytic Explorations in Art.* 1952.
Nelson, Benjamin, ed. *Sigmund Freud on Creativity and the Unconscious.* 1958.
Wright, Elizabeth. *Psychoanalytic Criticism: Theory in Practice.* 1984.

STRUCTURALISM

Structuralism is a literary movement with roots in linguistics and anthropology that concentrates on literature as a system of signs which have no inherent meaning except in their agreed-upon or conventional relation to one another. Structuralism is usually described by its proponents not as a new way to interpret literary works, but rather as a way to understand how works of literature come to have meaning for us. Because structuralism developed from linguistic theory, some structuralists use linguistic approaches to literature. That is, they talk about literary texts using terms employed by linguists (such as *morpheme* and *phoneme*) as they study the nature of language. Many structuralists, however, use the linguistic model as an analogy. To understand the analogy, then, you need to know a bit of linguistic theory.

The French linguist Ferdinand de Saussure (*Course in General Linguistics,* 1915) suggested that the relationship between an object and the name we use to designate it is purely arbitrary. What, for example, makes "C-A-T" signify a small, furry animal with pointed ears and whiskers? It is only our learned expectation that makes us associate "cat" with the family feline pet. Had we grown up in France, we would make the same association with *chat,* or in Mexico with *gato.* Therefore, the words we use to designate objects (linguists call these words *signs*) make sense only within the large context of our entire language system and would not be understood as meaningful by someone who did not know that language system. Further, Saussure pointed out, signs become truly useful only when we use them to designate difference. For instance, "cat" becomes useful when we want to differentiate a small furry animal that meows from a small furry animal that barks. Saussure was interested in how language, as a structure of conventions, worked. He asked intriguing questions about the underlying rules that allowed this made-up structure of signs to work, and his pioneering study caught the interest of scholars in many fields.

Many literary scholars saw linguistic structuralism as analogous to the study of literary works. Literary structuralism leads readers to think of poems, short stories, novels, and dramas not as self-contained and individual entities that have some kind of inherent meaning, but rather as part of a larger literary system. In order to fully appreciate and analyze the work, the reader must understand the system within which it operates. Like linguistic structuralism, literary structuralism focuses on the importance of difference. We must, for example, understand the difference between the structure of poetry and the structure of prose before we can make sense of a sentence like this:

> so much depends
> upon
> a red wheel
> barrow
>
> (from William Carlos Williams, "Red Wheelbarrow," p. 694)

Readers unacquainted with the conventions of poetry would find these lines meaningless and confusing, although if they knew the conventions of prose they would readily understand this sentence:

> So much depends upon a red wheelbarrow.

The way we interpret any group of "signs," then, depends on how they are structured and on the way we understand the system that governs their structure.

Structuralists believe that literature is basically artificial because although it uses the same "signs" as our everyday language, which has as its purpose giving information, the purpose of literature is *not* primarily to relay data. For example, a poem like Dylan Thomas's "Do Not Go Gentle into That Good Night" (p. 601) is written in the linguistic form of a series of commands, yet the poem goes much further than that. Its meaning is created not only by our understanding the lines as a series of commands, but also by our recognition of the poetic form, the rhyming conventions, and the figures of speech Thomas uses. We can only fully discuss the poem within the larger context of our literary knowledge.

A STRUCTURALIST READING: WILLIAM FAULKNER'S "BARN BURNING"

A structuralist reading tries to bring to light some of the assumptions about language and form that we are likely to take for granted. Looking at the opening paragraph of Faulkner's "Barn Burning," a structuralist critic might first look at an interpretation that reads the passage as a stream of Sarty's thoughts. The structuralist critic might then consider the assumptions a reader would have to make to see what Faulkner has written as the thoughts of an illiterate child. Next, the structuralist might look at evidence to suggest the language in this section operates outside the system of language that would be available to Sarty and that, therefore, "Barn Burning" opens not with a simple recounting of the main character's thoughts but rather with something far more complex.

The opening paragraph of William Faulkner's "Barn Burning" is often read as an excursion into the mind of Sarty, the story's young protagonist. When we read the passage closely, however, we note that a supposedly simple consciousness is represented in a highly complex way. For Sarty—uneducated and illiterate—the "scarlet devils" and "silver curve of fish" on the labels of food tins serve as direct signs appealing to his hunger. It is unlikely, however, that Sarty could consciously understand what he sees and express it as metaphor. We cannot, then, read this opening passage as a recounting of the thoughts that pass through Sarty's mind. Instead, these complex sentences and images offer possibilities that reach far outside the limits of Sarty's linguistic system.

Because our own knowledge is wider than Sarty's, the visual images the narrator describes take on meanings for us that are unavailable to the young boy. For example, like Sarty, we know that the "scarlet devils" stand for preserved ham. Yet the devils also carry another possible connotation. They may indicate evil and thus serve to emphasize the despair and grief Sarty feels are ever-present. So, then, we are given images that flash through the mind of an illiterate young boy, apparently intended to suggest his poverty and ignorance (he cannot read the words on the labels), yet we are led to see a highly complicated set of meanings. When we encounter later in the passage Sarty's articulated thought, "our enemy . . . ourn! mine and hisn both! . . . ," his down-to-earth dialect shows clearly the sharp distinction between the system of language the narrator uses to describe Sarty's view of the store shelves and the system of language Sarty uses to describe what he sees and feels.

For Further Reading: Structuralism

Barthes, Roland. *Critical Essays.* 1964.
Culler, Jonathan. *Structuralist Poetics.* 1975.
Hawkes, Terence. *Structuralism and Semiotics.* 1977.
Pettit, Philip. *The Concept of Structuralism: A Critical Analysis.* 1975.
Scholes, Robert. *Structuralism in Literature: An Introduction.* 1974.

DECONSTRUCTION

Deconstruction is a literary movement developed from structuralism. It argues that every text contains within it some ingredient undermining its purported system of meaning. In other words, the structure that seems to hold the text together is unstable because it depends on the conclusions of a particular ideology (for instance, the idea that women are inferior to men or that peasants are content with their lowly position in life), conclusions that are not really as natural or inevitable as the text may pretend. The practice of finding the point at which the text falls apart because of these internal inconsistencies is called deconstruction.

Deconstructive theorists share with formalists and structuralists a concern for the work itself rather than for biographical, historical, or ideological influences. Like formalists, deconstructionists focus on possibilities for multiple meanings within texts. However, while formalists seek to explain paradox by discovering tensions and ironies that can lead to a unified reading, deconstructionists insist on the primacy of multiple possibilities. Any given text is capable of yielding many divergent readings, all of which are equally valid and yet all of which may in some way undermine and oppose one another.

Like structuralists, deconstructionists see literary texts as part of larger systems of discourse. A key structuralist technique is identifying opposites in an attempt to show the structure of language used in a work. Having identified the opposites, the structuralist rests the case. Deconstructionists, however, go further. Jacques Derrida, a French philosopher, noticed that these oppositions do not simply reflect linguistic structures but are the linguistic response to the way people deal with their beliefs (their ideologies). For instance, if you believe strongly that democracy is the best possible form of government, you tend to lump other forms of government into the category of nondemocracies. If a government is nondemocratic, that—not its other distinguishing characteristics—would be significant to you. This typical ideological response operates in all kinds of areas of belief, even ones we are not aware of. Deconstructionists contend that texts tend to give away their ideological basis by means of this opposition.

Derrida called this distinction between "A" and "Not-A" (rather than "A" and "B") *différance,* a word he coined to suggest a concept represented by the French verb *différer,* which has two meanings: "to be different" and "to defer." (Note that in Derrida's new term an "a" is substituted for an "e"—a distinction that can be seen in writing, but not heard in speaking.) When a deconstructionist uncovers *différance* through careful examination of a text, he or she also finds an (often unwitting) ideological bias. Deconstructionists argue that the reader must transcend such ideological biases and must instead acknowledge contradictory possibilities as equally worthy of consideration. No one meaning can or should be designated as correct.

Deconstruction, then, is not really a system of criticism (and, in fact, deconstructionists resist being labeled as a school of criticism). Rather, deconstruction offers a way to take apart a literary text and thereby reveal its separate layers. Deconstructionists often focus on the metaphorical nature of language, claiming that all language is basically metaphoric because the sign we use to designate any given object or action stands apart from the object itself. In fact, deconstructionists believe that all writing is essentially literary and metaphorical because language, by its very nature, can only *stand for* what we call reality or truth; it cannot *be* reality or truth.

A major contribution of deconstructive critics lies in their playful approach to language and to literary criticism. They refuse to accept as absolute any one way of reading poetry, fiction, or drama, and they guard against what they see as the fixed conclusions and arbitrary operating assumptions of many schools of criticism.

A DECONSTRUCTIONIST READING: FLANNERY O'CONNOR'S "A GOOD MAN IS HARD TO FIND

A deconstructionist reading of Flannery O'Connor's "A Good Man is Hard to Find" might challenge the essentially religious interpretations the author offered of her own stories in essays and letters. A deconstructionist critic might argue that the author's reading of the story is no more valid than anyone else's, and that the story can just as legitimately be read as an investigation of the functions of irony in language.

Flannery O'Connor has explained that the grotesque and violent aspects of her stories are intended to shock the reader into recognizing the inhospitable nature of the world and thereby the universal human need for divine grace. The last sentence of "A Good Man is Hard to Find" is spoken by The Misfit, who has just murdered a family of travelers: "It's no real pleasure in life."

However, the language of O'Connor's stories is extremely ironic. That is, her narrators and characters often say one thing but mean another. So it is possible that their statements are not empirically true but are representations of a persona or elements of a story they have created using language.

The Grandmother, for example, lives almost entirely in fictions—newspaper clippings, stories for the grandchildren, her belief that The Misfit is a good man. On the other hand, The Misfit is more literal than the Grandmother in his perception of reality. He knows, for example, whether the car has turned over once or twice. But he too is posing, at first as the tough guy who rejects religious and societal norms by saying, "It's nothing for you to do but enjoy the few minutes you got left the best way you can—by killing somebody or burning down his house or doing some other meanness to him. No pleasure but meanness." Finally, he poses as the pessimist—or, according to O'Connor's reading, the Christian—who claims, "It's no real pleasure in life." The contradictions in The Misfit's language make it impossible to tell which of these façades is "real."

For Further Reading: Deconstruction

Abrams, M. H. "Rationality and the Imagination in Cultural History." *Critical Inquiry* 2 (1976): 447–64. (Abrams claims deconstructionists are parasites who depend on other critics to come up with interpretations that can be deconstructed.)

Arac, Jonathan, Wlad Godzich, and Wallace Martin, eds. *The Yale Critics: Deconstruction in America*. 1983.

Berman, Art. *From the New Criticism to Deconstruction*. 1988.

Culler, Jonathan. *On Deconstruction: Theory and Criticism After Structuralism*. 1982.

Jefferson, Ann. "Structuralism and Post-Structuralism." *Modern Literary Theory: A Comparative Introduction*. 1982.

Johnson, Barbara. *The Critical Difference: Essays in the Contemporary Rhetoric of Reading*. 1980.

Leitsch, Vincent B. *Deconstructive Theory and Practice*. 1982.

Miller, J. Hillis. "The Critic as Host." In *Deconstruction and Criticism*. Ed. Harold Bloom, et al. 1979. (response to Abrams article above)

Norris, Christopher. *Deconstruction: Theory and Practice*. 1982.

GLOSSARY OF LITERARY TERMS

Alexandrine Iambic hexameter, a common form in French poetry but relatively rare in English poetry.

Allegorical figure or framework See **Allegory**.

Allegory Story with two parallel and consistent levels of meaning, one literal and one figurative, in which the figurative level offers a moral or political lesson; Edmund Spenser's *The Faerie Queen* and Nathaniel Hawthorne's "Young Goodman Brown" are examples of allegory. An **allegorical figure** has only one meaning (for instance, it may represent good or evil), as opposed to a **symbol**, which may suggest a complex network of meanings. An **allegorical framework** is the system of ideas that conveys the allegory's message.

Alliteration Repetition of initial sounds in a series of words, as in Blake's "The Chimney Sweeper": "So your chimneys I sweep, and in soot I sleep." Alliteration may be reinforced by repeated sounds within and at the ends of words.

Allusion Reference, often to literature, history, mythology, or the Bible, that is unacknowledged in the text but that the author expects a reader to recognize. An example of allusion in a title is Charles Baxter's "Gryphon" (a mythical beast). Some modern writers, notably T.S. Eliot and James Joyce, use allusions drawn from their private reading, expecting few readers to understand them.

Ambiguity Intentional device in which authors evoke a number of possible meanings of a word or grammatical structure by leaving unclear which meaning they intend.

Anapest See **Meter**.

Apostrophe Figure of speech in which an absent character or a personified force or object is addressed directly, as if it were present or could comprehend: "O Rose, thou art sick!"

Archetype Image or symbol that is so common or significant to a culture that it seems to have a universal importance. The psychologist Carl Jung felt that because archetypes are an inherent part of psyches, we recognize them subconsciously when we encounter them and therefore give them a greater meaning than they would otherwise possess. Many archetypes appear in classical myths (for example, a journey to the underworld).

Assonance Repetition of vowel sounds in a series of words: "creep three feet."

Aubade Poem about morning, usually celebrating the dawn—for example, Philip Larkin's "Aubade."

Ballad Narrative poem, rooted in an oral tradition, usually arranged in quatrains rhyming *abcb* and containing a refrain.

Ballad stanza See **Stanza**.

Beginning rhyme See **Rhyme**.

Blank verse Lines of unrhymed iambic pentameter in no particular stanzaic form. Because iambic pentameter resembles the rhythms of ordinary English speech, blank verse is often unobtrusive; for instance, Shakespeare's noble characters usually use it, though they may seem to us at first reading to be speaking in prose. See **Meter**.

Cacophony Harsh or unpleasant spoken sound created by clashing consonants: "squawking chipmunks."

Caesura Strong or long pause in the middle of a poetic line, created by punctuation or by the sense of the poem, as in Yeats's "Leda and the Swan": "And Agamemnon dead. Being so caught up. . . ."

Carpe diem Literally, "seize the day"; the philosophy that gave its name to a kind of seventeenth-century poetry arguing that one should enjoy life today before it passes one by, as seen in Herrick's "To the Virgins, to Make Much of Time."

Characterization Way in which writers develop their characters and reveal those characters' traits to readers.

Classicism Attitude toward art that values symmetry, clarity, discipline, and objectivity. Neoclassicism, such as that practiced in eighteenth-century Europe, appreciated those qualities as found in Greek and Roman art and culture; Alexander Pope's poetry follows neoclassical principles.

Closed form Type of poetic structure that has a recognizable rhyme scheme, meter, or stanzaic pattern.

Common measure See **Stanza**.

Conceit Extended or complicated metaphor, common in the Renaissance, that is impressive largely because it shows off an author's power to manipulate and sustain a striking comparison between two dissimilar items; John Donne's use of the compass metaphor in "A Valediction: Forbidding Mourning" is an example.

Concrete poem Poem whose typographical appearance on the page reenforces its theme, as with George Herbert's "Easter Wings."

Connotation Meaning that a word suggests beyond its literal, explicit meaning, carrying emotional associations, judgments, or opinions. Connotations can be positive, neutral, or negative. For example, *family* has a positive connotation when it describes a group of loving relatives; a neutral connotation when it describes a biological category; and a negative connotation when it describes an organization of criminals.

Conventional symbol See **Symbol**.

Couplet See **Stanza**.

Dactyl See **Meter**.

Deconstruction Type of theory and analysis according to which no work of literature can mean what it seems to say because of the ambiguous nature of language itself.

Denotation Dictionary meaning of a word; its explicit, literal meaning.

Dialect Particular regional variety of language, which may differ from the more widely used standard or written language in its pronunciation, grammar, or vocabulary. Robert Burns's "John Anderson, My Jo, John" uses dialect.

Diction Word choice of an author, which determines the level of language used in a piece of literature.

Formal diction is lofty and elaborate; **informal diction** is idiomatic and relaxed. **Jargon** is the specialized diction of a professional or occupational group (such as computer hackers). **Idioms** are the colloquial expressions, including slang, of a particular group or society.

Didactic poetry Poetry whose purpose is to make a point or teach a lesson, particularly common in the eighteenth century.

Double entendre Phrase or word with a deliberate double meaning, one of which is usually sexual.

Dramatic irony See **Irony**.

Dramatic monologue Type of poem perfected by Robert Browning that consists of a single speaker talking to one or more unseen listeners and often revealing much more about the speaker than he or she seems to intend; Browning's "My Last Duchess" is the best known example of this form.

Elegy Poem commemorating someone's death, usually in a reflective or mournful tone, such as A. E. Housman's "To an Athlete Dying Young."

Elision Leaving out an unstressed syllable or vowel, usually in order to keep a regular meter in a line of poetry ("o'er" instead of "over," for example).

End rhyme See **Rhyme**.

End-stopped line Line of poetry that has a full pause at the end, typically indicated by a period or semicolon.

Enjambment See **Run-on line**.

Envoi Three-line conclusion to a sestina that includes all six of the poem's key words, three placed at the ends of lines and three within the lines. See **Sestina**.

Epic Long narrative poem, such as the *Iliad* or the *Aeneid,* recounting the adventures of heroes on whose actions depend the fate of a nation or race. Frequently the gods or other supernatural beings take active interest in the events presented in the epic.

Epigram Short witty poem or phrase that makes a pointed statement—for example, Dorothy Parker's comment on an actress's performance, "She runs the gamut of emotions from A to B."

Euphemism Word consciously chosen for its pleasant **Connotations**; often used for subjects like sex and death whose frank discussion is somewhat taboo in our society. For example, a euphemism for "to die" is "to pass away" or "to go to one's reward."

Euphony Pleasant spoken sound created by smooth consonants such as "ripple" or "pleasure."

Extended metaphor See **Metaphor**.

Extended simile See **Metaphor**.

Eye rhyme See **Rhyme**.

Falling meter Trochaic and dactylic meters, so called because they move from stressed to unstressed syllables. See **Rising meter**.

Falling rhyme *See* **Rhyme**.

Feminine rhyme See **Rhyme**.

Feminist criticism Theory and practice that seeks to do justice to female points of view, concerns, and values in literature by reorienting both women and men as readers, reconsidering the treatment of women as literary characters, re-evaluating women writers, revising the literary canon, and speculating about the relationships between gender and language.

Figures of speech Expressions that suggest more than their literal meanings. The primary figures of speech are **Hyperbole**, **Metaphor**, **Metonymy**, **Personification**, **Simile**, **Synechdoche**, and **Understatement**.

Foot See **Meter**.

Form General organizing principle of a literary work. In poetry, form is described in terms of the presence (or absence) in a particular work of elements like rhyme, meter, and stanzaic pattern. See **Open form** and **Closed form**.

Formal diction See **Diction**.

Formalism Type of theory and analysis that emphasizes the formal patterns and technical devices of literature rather than its subject matter and social values.

Free verse See **Open form poetry**.

Genre Category of literature. Fiction, drama, and poetry are the three major genres; subgenres include the novel, the farce, and the lyric poem.

Haiku Seventeen-syllable, three-line form of Japanese verse that almost always uses concrete imagery and deals with the natural world.

Hermeneutics Traditionally, the use of the Bible to interpret other historical or current events; in current critical theory, the principles and procedures followed to determine the meaning of a text.

Heroic couplet See **Stanza**.

Hyperbole Figurative language that depends on intentional overstatement; Mark Twain often used it to create humor; Jonathan Swift used it for **Satire**.

Iamb See **Meter**.

Iambic pentameter See **Meter**.

Imagery Words and phrases that describe the concrete experience of the five senses, most often sight. A **pattern of imagery** is a group of related images developed throughout a work. **Synesthesia** is a form of imagery that mixes the experience of the senses (hearing something visual, smelling something audible, and so on): "He smelled the blue fumes of her scent." **Static imagery** freezes the moment to give it the timeless quality of painting or sculpture. **Kinetic imagery** attempts to show motion or change.

Imagism Movement in modern poetry much influenced by **haiku**, stressing terseness and concrete imagery. Imagists were a group of American poets in the early twentieth century, such as Ezra Pound, William Carlos Williams, and Amy Lowell, who completely dispensed with traditional principles of English versification, creating new rhythms and meters.

Imperfect rhyme See **Rhyme**.

Informal diction See **Diction**.

Internal rhyme See **Rhyme**.

Irony Literary device or situation that depends on the existence of at least two separate and contrasting levels of meaning or experience. **Dramatic** or **tragic irony**, such as that found in *Oedipus the King*, depends on the audience's knowing something the protagonist has not yet realized (and thus experiencing simultaneously its own interpretation of the events and that of the protagonist). **Situational irony** exists when what happens is at odds with what the story's situation leads readers to expect will happen, as in Browning's "Porphyria's Lover." **Verbal irony** occurs when what is said is in contrast with what is meant. It can be expressed as **understatement**, **hyperbole**, or **sarcasm**.

Jargon Specialized language associated with a particular trade or profession.

Kinetic imagery Imagery that attempts to show motion or change. See, for example, William Carlos William's "The Great Figure."

Literary canon Group of literary works generally acknowledged to be the best and most significant to have emerged from our history. The canon tends to be conservative (it is difficult to add to or remove works from it), and it reflects ideological positions that are not universally accepted.

Literary convention Something whose meaning is so widely understood within a society that authors can expect their audiences to accept and comprehend it unquestioningly—for example, the division of plays into acts with intermissions, or the fact that stepmothers in fairy tales are likely to be wicked.

Literary criticism Descriptions, analyses, interpretations, or evaluations of works of literature by experts in the field.

Literary symbol See **Symbol**.

Lyric Form of poetry, usually brief and intense, that expresses a poet's subjective response to the world. In classical times, lyrics were set to music. The Romantic poets, particularly Keats, often wrote lyrics about love, death, and nature.

Marxist criticism Readings of literature based on the social and economic theories of Karl Marx, who in conjunction with Frederick Engels predicted that the dominant capitalist middle class will eventually be challenged and overthrown by the working class, from whose labor the middle class profits unfairly.

Masculine rhyme See **Rhyme**.

Meditation Lyric poem that focuses on a physical object—for example, Keat's "Ode on a Grecian Urn"—using this object as a vehicle for considering larger issues.

Metaphor Concise form of comparison equating two things that may at first seem completely dissimilar, often an abstraction and a concrete image—for example, "My love's a fortress." Some people consider metaphor to be the essential element of poetry. An *extended metaphor* is a comparison used throughout a work; in John Donne's "Valediction Forbidding Mourning" two lovers are compared to two legs of a compass. See **Simile**.

Meter Regular pattern of stressed and unstressed syllables, each repeated unit of which is called a **Foot**: an **Anapest** has three syllables, two unstressed and the third stressed; a **Dactyl** has three syllables, the first stressed and the subsequent ones unstressed. An **Iamb** has two syllables, unstressed followed by stressed; a **Trochee** has a stressed syllable followed by an unstressed one; a **Spondee** has two stressed syllables; and a **Pyrrhic** has two unstressed syllables. A poem's meter is described in terms of the kind of foot (anapest, for example) and the number of feet found in each line. The number of feet is designated by the Greek prefix for the numbers, so one foot per line is called *monometer,* two feet is *dimeter,* followed by *trimeter,* *tetrameter, pentameter, hexameter,* and so on. The most common meter in English is *iambic pentameter.* See also **Rising meter** and **Falling meter**.

Metonymy Figure of speech in which the term for one thing can be applied to another with which it is closely associated—for example, using "defend the flag" to mean "defend the nation."

Mimesis Aristotle's term for the purpose of literature, which he felt was "imitation" of life; literature represents the essence of life and we are affected by it because we recognize (perhaps in another form) elements of our own experiences.

Mood Atmosphere created by the elements of a literary work (setting, characterization, imagery, tone, and so on).

Myth Anonymous story reflecting the religious and social values of a culture or explaining natural phenomena, often involving gods and heroes.

New historicism Type of theory and analysis that concentrates on the historical and cultural context of literary works in terms of both production and, later, interpretation and evaluation.

Octave See **Sonnet**.

Ode Relatively long lyric poem, common in antiquity and adapted by the Romantic poets, for whom it was a serious poem of formal diction, often addressed to some significant object (such as a nightingale or the west wind) that has stimulated the poet's imagination.

Onomatopoeia Word whose sound resembles what it describes: "snap, crackle, pop." Lewis Carroll's "Jabberwocky" uses onomatopoeia.

Open form Sometimes called *free verse* or *vers libre,* open form poetry makes use of varying line lengths, abandoning stanzaic divisions, breaking lines in unexpected places, and even abandoning any pretense of formal structure. See **Form**.

Ottava rima See **Stanza**.

Oxymoron Phrase combining two seemingly incompatible elements: "crashing silence."

Paradox Seemingly contradictory situation. Adrienne Rich's "A Woman Mourned by Daughters" uses paradox.

Parody "Take-off" or exaggerated imitation of a serious piece of literature for humorous effect.

Pastoral Literary work, such as Christopher Marlowe's lyric poem "The Passionate Shepherd to His Love," that deals nostalgically and usually unrealistically with a simple, preindustrial rural life; the name comes from the fact that traditionally pastorals feature shepherds.

Pattern of imagery See **Imagery**.

Perfect rhyme See **Rhyme**.

Persona Narrator or speaker of a poem or story; in Greek tragedy, the persona was a mask worn by an actor.

Personification Attributing of human qualities to things that are not human: "the river wept."

Petrarchan sonnet See **Sonnet**.

Poetic rhythm See **Rhythm**.

Prose poem Open form poem whose long lines appear to be prose set in paragraphs—for example, Walt Whitman's "Cavalry Crossing a Ford."

Psychoanalytic criticism Readings of literature based on the theories and methods of Sigmund

Freud, particularly those concerning family relationships and dream analysis.

Pyrrhic See **Meter**.

Quatrain See **Stanza**.

Reader response criticism Type of theory and analysis according to which some or all of the meanings of a literary work are the creation of the reader, and hence no single "correct" reading of a text exists.

Rhetoric Organization, strategy, and development of literary works, guided by an eye to how such elements will further the writer's intended effect on the reader.

Rhyme Repetition of concluding sounds in different words, often intentionally used at the ends of poetic lines. In **Masculine rhyme** (also called **rising rhyme**) single syllables correspond. In **Feminine rhyme** (also called **double rhyme** or **falling rhyme**) two syllables correspond, the second of which is stressed. In **Triple rhyme**, three syllables correspond. **Eye rhyme** occurs when words look as though they should rhyme but are pronounced differently ("cough, tough"). In **Perfect rhyme** the corresponding vowel and consonant sounds of accented syllables must be preceded by different consonants—for example, the *b* and *h* in "born" and "horn." **Imperfect rhyme**, also called *near rhyme*, *off rhyme*, or *slant rhyme*, occurs when consonants in two words are the same but intervening vowels are different—for example, "pick/pack," "lads/lids." The most common type of rhyme within a poem is **End rhyme**, where the rhyming syllables are placed at the end of a rhyme. **Internal rhyme** consists of rhyming words found within a line of poetry. **Beginning rhyme** occurs in the first syllable or syllables of the line.

Rhyme royal See **Stanza**.

Rhythm Regular recurrence of sounds in a poem. Ordinarily rhythm is determined by the arrangement of metrical feet in a line, but sometimes an alternate form of "sprung" rhythm, introduced by Gerard Manley Hopkins, is used. In this type of rhythm the number of strong stresses in a line determines the rhythm, regardless of how many weak stresses there might be.

Rising rhyme See **Rhyme**.

Romanticism Eighteenth- and nineteenth-century literary movement that valued subjectivity, individuality, the imagination, nature, excess, the exotic, and the mysterious.

Run-on line Line of poetry that ends with no punctuation or natural pause and consequently runs over into the next line; also called *enjambment*.

Sarcasm Form of irony in which apparent praise is used to convey strong, bitter criticism.

Satire Literary attack on folly or vanity by means of ridicule; usually intended to improve society.

Scansion Process of determining the meter of a poem by analyzing the strong and weak stresses in a line to find the unit of **Meter** (each recurring pattern of stresses) and the number of these units (or **Feet**) in each line.

Sestet See **Sonnet**.

Sestina Poem composed of 6 six-line stanzas and a three-line conclusion called an **Envoi**. Each line ends with one of six key words. The alternation of these six words in different positions—but always at the ends of lines—in the poem's six stanzas creates a rhythmic verbal pattern that unifies the poem.

Shakespearean sonnet See **Sonnet**.

Simile Comparison of two seemingly unlike things using the words *like* or *as*: "My love is like an arrow through my heart." See **Metaphor**.

Situational irony See **Irony**.

Sociological criticism Type of theory and analysis according to which a literary work cannot be separated from the social context in which it was created.

Sonnet Fourteen-line poem, usually a **Lyric** in *iambic pentameter* (see **Meter**). It has a strict rhyme scheme in one of two forms: the *Italian,* or **Petrarchan sonnet** (an octave rhymed abba/abba with a sestet rhymed cdc/cdc or a variation) and the *English,* or **Shakespearean sonnet** (three quatrains rhymed abab/cdcd/efef with a concluding couplet rhymed gg). The English sonnet developed partly because the Italian rhyme scheme was so difficult to achieve in English, where end rhymes are less frequent than they are in Italian. Modern poets often exploit the rigorous sonnet form by contrasting its restraints with violent content or imagery, as in Yeats's "Leda and the Swan."

Speaker See **Persona**.

Spenserian stanza See **Stanza**.

Spondee See **Meter**.

Stanza Group of lines in a poem that forms a metrical or thematic unit. Each stanza is usually separated from others by a blank space on the page. Some common stanzaic forms are the **Couplet** (two lines), the **Tercet** (three lines), **Quatrain** (four lines), **Sestet** (six lines), and **Octave** (eight lines). The **Heroic couplet**, first used by Chaucer and especially popular throughout the eighteenth century, as in Alexander Pope's poetry, consists of two rhymed lines of iambic pentameter, with a weak pause after the first line and a strong pause after the second. **Terza rima**, a form used by Dante, has a rhyme scheme (*aba, bcb, ded*) that creates an interlocking series of stanzas. The **Ballad stanza** alternates lines of eight and six syllables. Typically only the second and fourth lines rhyme. **Common measure** is a four-line stanzaic pattern closely related to the ballad stanza. It differs in that its rhyme scheme is *abab* rather than *abcb*. **Rhyme royal** is a seven-line stanza (*ababbcc*) set in iambic pentameter. **Ottava rima** is an eight-line stanza (*abababcc*) set in iambic pentameter. The **Spenserian stanza** is a nine-line form (*ababbcbcc*) with the first eight lines in iambic pentameter and the last line in iambic hexameter.

Static imagery Imagery that freezes a moment to give it the timeless quality of painting or sculpture. Much visual imagery is static.

Stress Accent or emphasis, either strong or weak, given to each syllable in a piece of writing, as determined by conventional pronunciation (cárpĕt, not cărpét) and intended emphasis ("going dŏwn, dówn, dówn tŏ thĕ bóttŏm ŏf thĕ ócean"). Strong stresses are marked with a ´ and weak ones with a ˘; stress can be an important clue in helping determine a poet's intended emphasis.

Structuralism Type of theory and analysis that applies the concepts of linguistics to the interpretation of literature.

Surrealism Literary movement that allows unconventional use of syntax, chronology, juxtaposition, and bizarre, dreamlike images in prose and poetry.

Symbol Person, object, action, or idea whose meaning transcends its literal or denotative sense in a complex way. For instance, if someone wears a rose in a lapel to a dance, the rose may simply be a decoration, but in Blake's "The Sick Rose" it becomes a symbol because it takes on a range of paradoxical and complementary meanings. A symbol is invested with significance beyond what it could carry on its own: A swastika, for instance, is a powerful and frightening symbol as a result of Hitler's Nazism. **Universal symbols**, such as the grim reaper, may be called **Archetypes**; **Conventional symbols**, such as national flags, evoke a general and agreed-upon response from most people. There are also **Private symbols**, such as the "gyre" created by Yeats, which the poet himself invested with extraordinary significance.

Synechdoche Figure of speech in which a part of something is used to represent the whole—for example, "hired hand" represents a laborer.

Synesthesia See **Imagery**.

Tercet See **Stanza**.

Terza rima See **Stanza**.

Theme Central or dominant idea of a piece of literature, made concrete by the details and emphasis in the work itself.

Tone Attitude of the speaker or author of a work toward the subject itself or the audience, as can be determined from the word choice and arrangement of the piece.

Tragic irony See **Irony**.

Triple rhyme See **Rhyme**.

Trochee See **Meter**.

Understatement Intentional downplaying of a situation's significance, often for ironic or humorous effect, as in Mark Twain's famous comment on reading his own obituary, "The reports of my death are greatly exaggerated."

Universal symbol See **Symbol**.

Verbal irony See **Irony**.

Villanelle First introduced in France in the Middle Ages, a nineteen-line poem composed of five tercets and a concluding quatrain; its rhyme scheme is *aba aba aba aba aba abaa*. Two different lines are systematically repeated in the poem: line 1 appears again in lines 6, 12, and 18, and line 3 reappears as lines 9, 15, and 19. Thus each tercet concludes with an exact (or close) duplication of either line 1 or line 3, and the final quatrain concludes by repeating both line 1 and line 3.

ACKNOWLEDGMENTS

Leonard Adamé, "My Grandmother Would Rock Quietly and Hum" by Leonard Adamé. Copyright © 1973 and reprinted by permission of Leonard Adamé.

Anna Akmatova, "He Love Three Things Alone" from *Anna Akmatova: Selected Poems,* by Anna Akmatova, translated by D. M. Thomas. Copyright © 1911 Anna Akmatova. Translation copyright © by D. M. Thomas. Originally published by Viking Penguin 1988. Reprinted by permission of John Johnson, Ltd.

Maya Angelou, "My Arkansas" from *And Still I Rise* by Maya Angelou. Copyright © 1978 by Maya Angelou. Reprinted by permission of Random House, Inc.

Margaret Atwood, "The City Planners" from *The Circle Game* by Margaret Atwood. Copyright © by and reprinted by permission of Stoddart Publishing Company Limited, Don Mills, Ont. "You Fit into Me" from *Power Politics* by Margaret Atwood. Copyright by and reprinted by permission of Stoddart Publishing Company Limited. Don Mills, Ontario.

W.H. Auden, "Look, Stranger on This Island Now" from *Auden: Collected Poems* by W.H. Auden, compiled and edited by Edward Mendelson. Copyright © 1940 and renewed 1968 by W. H. Auden. Reprinted by permission of Random House, Inc. "Musee des Beaux" from *W. H. Auden: Collected Poems* by W. H. Auden, compiled and edited by Edward Mendelson. Copyright © 1949 and renewed 1968 by W. H. Auden. Reprinted by permission of Random House, Inc. "The Unknown Citizen" from *W. H. Auden: Collected Poems* by W. H. Auden, edited by Edward Mendelson. Copyright © 1949 and renewed 1968 by W. H. Auden. Reprinted by permission of Random House, Inc.

Houston A. Baker, Jr., "The Achievement of Gwendolyn Brooks" by Houston A. Baker, Jr. from *A Life Distilled: Gwendolyn Brooks, Her Poetry and Fiction,* edited by Maria K. Mootry and Gary Smith. Copyright © 1987 by and reprinted by permission of The University of Illinois Press.

Imamu Amiri Baraka, "Watergate" from *Selected Poetry of Imamu Amiri Baraka/LeRoi Jones* by Imamu Amiri Baraka. Copyright © 1979 by Imamu Amiri Baraka. Reprinted by permission of Sterling Lord Literistic, Inc.

Matsuo Basho, "Four Haiku," "Silent and Still" by Matsuo Basho from THE PENGUIN BOOK OF JAPANESE VERSE translated by Geoffrey Bownas and Anthony Thwaite. Copyright © 1964 by Geoffrey Bownas and Anthony Thwaite. Reprinted by permission of Penguin Books, Ltd.

Suzanne E. Berger, "The Meal" from *Legacies* by Suzanne E. Berger. Originally published by Alice James Books, then again in *Tendrill*. Copyright © 1984 by and reprinted by permission of Suzanne E. Berger.

John Berryman, "Dream Song #14" from *The Dream Songs* by John Berryman. Copyright © 1959, 1962, 1964, 1966, 1969 by John Berryman. Reprinted by permission of Farrar, Straus, & Giroux, Inc.

Elizabeth Bishop, "The Fish" and "Sestina" from *The Complete Poems* by Elizabeth Bishop. Copyright © 1940, 1956, 1978 by Elizabeth Bishop. Copyright © 1979, 1983 by Alice Helen Meathfessel. Reprinted by permission of Farrar, Straus, & Giroux, Inc.

Robert Bly, "Snowfall in the Afternoon" from *Silence in the Snowy Fields* by Robert Bly. Originally published Wesleyan University Press, 1962. Copyright © 1962 by Robert Bly. Reprinted by permission of Robert Bly.

Louise Bogan, "Women" from *The Blue Estuaries* by Louise Bogan. Copyright © 1968 by Louise Bogan. Reprinted by permission of Farrar, Straus, & Giroux, Inc.

Richard Brautigan, "The Window's Lament" from *The Pill Versus The Springhill Mine Disaster* by Richard Brautigan. Copyright © 1968 by Richard Brautigan. Reprinted by permission of The Helen Brann Agency, Inc.

Joseph Brodsky, "Star of the Nativity" by Joseph Brodsky. Copyright © 1988 by Joseph Brodsky. Reprinted by permission of Farrar, Straus, & Giroux, Inc.

Gwendolyn Brooks, "The Ballad of Chocolate Mabbie," "The Ballad of Ruldolph Reed," "The Bean Eaters," "The Blackstone Rangers," "The Chicago Defender Sends a Man to Little Rock," "First Fight. Then Fiddle," "Meagers Evers," "People Who Have No Children Can Be Hard," "Sadie and Maud," "A Song in the Front Yard," "We Are Cool," "What Shall I Give My Children" from BLACKS by Gwendolyn Brooks. Reprinted by permission of Gwendolyn Brooks, Copyright © 1991. Publisher, Third World Press, Chicago, 1991. "The Boy Who Died in My Alley" from BECKONINGS by Gwendolyn Brooks. Reprinted by permission of Gwendolyn Brooks, Copyright © 1991. Publisher, Third World Press, Chicago, 1991. "Interview with Gwendolyn Brooks" from *Tri-Quartley*. Copyright © by and reprinted by permission of Gwendolyn Brooks. "Discussions of Your Poems: 'We Real Cool,' and 'Ballad of Rudolph Reed'" from Gwendolyn Brooks: *Report From Report One,* Broadside Press, 972. Reprinted by permission of the author.

Dennis Brutus, "On the Island" from *A Simple Lust* by Dennis Brutus. Copyright © 1973 by Dennis Brutus. Reprinted by permission of Heinemann Educational Books, Ltd.

Christopher Buckley, "Why I'm in Favor of a Nuclear Freeze" from *Dust Light, Leaves* by Christopher Buckley. Copyright © 1986 and reprinted by permission of Christopher Buckley.

Charles Bukowski, "Dog Fight" by Charles Bukowski. Copyright © 1980 by Charles Bukowski. Reprinted with the permission of Black Sparrow Press.

Raymond Carver, "Gravy" from the book *A New Path to the Waterfall* by Raymond Carver. Copyright © 1989 by the estate of Raymond Carver. Used here with the permission of the Atlantic Monthly Press. "Photograph of My Father in His Twenty-Second Year" from *Fires* by Raymond Carver. Copyright © 1983 by Raymond Carver. Reprinted by permission of the Capra Press, Santa Barbara.

Geoffrey Chaucer, Excerpt from THE COMPLETE POETRY AND PROSE OF GEOFFREY CHAUCER, Second Edition, by Geoffrey Chaucer, compiled and edited by John H. Fisher, pp. 9–10, Prologue. Copyright © 1989 by Holt, Rinehart, and Winston. Reprinted by permission of Harcourt, Brace, and Company.

Eric Chock, "Chinese Fireworks Banned in Hawaii" from *Last Days Here* by Eric Chock. Copyright © 1990 by Eric Chock. Reprinted by permission of Eric Chock.

Michelle Cliff, "A Visit to the Secret Annex" from *The Land of Look Behind* by Michelle Cliff. Copyright © 1985 by Michelle Cliff. Reprinted by permission of Firebrand Books, Ithaca, New York.

Lucille Clifton, "my mama moved among the days" Copyright © 1987 by Lucille Clifton. Reprinted from *good woman: poems and a memoir 1969–1980* by Lucille Clifton with the permission of BOA Editions, Ltd., 92 Park Ave., Brockport, NY 14420.

Judith Ortiz Cofer, "Lessons of the Past" from Judith Ortiz Cofer is reprinted with permission of the publisher from *Silent Dancing* (Houston: Arte Publico Press-University of Houston, 1990). "My Father in the Navy" from *Triple Crown* by Judith Ortiz Cofer. Copyright © 1987 by Bilingual Press. Reprinted by permission of Bilingual Press, Arizona State University Press, Tempe, Arizona.

Countee Cullen, "For A Lady I Know" and "Yet Do I Marvel" from *On There I Stand* by Countee Cullen. Copyright © 1925 by Harper & Brothers. Copyright renewed 1953 by Ida M. Cullen. Reprinted by permission of GRM Associates, Inc., agents for the Estate of Ida M. Cullen.

Victor Hernandez Cruz, "Anonymous," by Victor Hernandez Cruz is reprinted here with permission of the publisher from *Rhythm, Content, & Flavor* (Houston: Arte Publico Press-University of Houston, 1989).

E. E. Cummings, "anyone lived in a pretty how town" and "l)a" from *Complete Poems, 1913–1962,* by E. E. Cummings, by permission of Liveright Publishing Corporation. Copyright © 1923, 1925, 1931, 1935, 1938, 1939, 1940, 1944, 1945, 1946, 1947, 1948, 1949, 1950, 1951, 1952, 1953, 1954, 1955, 1956, 1957, 1958, 1959, 1960, 1961, 1962, by the Trustees for the E. E. Cummings Trust. Copyright © 1961, 1963, 1968 by Marion Morehouse Cummings. "Buffalo Bill's," "in Just—," and "the sky was can dy." Reprinted from *Tulips & Chimneys* by E. E. Cummings, Edited by George James Firmage, by permission of Liveright Publishing Corporation. Copyright © 1923, 1925 and renewed 1951, 1953 by E. E. Cummings. Copyright © 1973, 1976 by the Trustees for the E. E. Cummings Trust. Copyright © 1973, 1976 by George James Firmage. "next to of course god america i" is reprinted from *IS 5 Poems* by E. E. Cummings, Edited by George James Firmage, by permission of Liveright Publishing Corporation. Copyright © 1985 by E. E. Cummings Trust. Copyright © 1926 by Horace Liveright. Copyright © 1954 by E. E. Cummings. Copyright © 1985 by George James Firmage.

James Dickey, "Adultery" from *James Dickey Poems 1957–1976* by James Dickey. Copyright © 1966 by James Dickey. Reprinted by permission of The University Press of New England.

Emily Dickinson, "Because I Could Not Stop for Death," "I Heard a Fly Buzz-When I Died," "I Like to See It Lap the Miles," "I Taste a Liquor Never Brewed," and "The Soul Selects Her Own Society" by Emily Dickinson. Reprinted by permission of the Publishers and the Trustees of Amherst College from THE POEMS OF EMILY DICKINSON, Thomas H. Johnson, ed., Cambridge, Mass.: The Belknap Press of Harvard University Press, Copyright © 1951, 1955, 1983 by the President and Fellows of Harvard College.

Ariel Dorfman, "Hope" from *Last Waltz in Santiago and Other Poems of Excile and Disappearance"* by Ariel Dorfman. English translation Copyright © 1988 by Ariel Dorfman and Edith Grossman. Reprinted by permission of Viking Penguin, a division of Penguin Books USA, Inc.

Rita Dove, "Satisfaction Coal Company". Reprinted from Rita Dove: *Thomas and Beulah* by permission of Carnegie Mellon University Press © 1986 by Rita Dove.

T. S. Eliot, "Journey of the Magi" from THE COLLECTED POEMS, 1909–1962 by T. S. Eliot, Copyright © 1936 by Harcourt Brace Jovanovich, Copyright © 1964, 1963 by T. S. Eliot, reprinted by permission of the publisher. "The Love Song of J. Alfred Prufrock" from COLLECTED POEMS 1909–1962 by T. S. Eliot, Copyright 1936 by Harcourt Brace and Company, Copyright © 1964, 1963 by T. S. Eliot, reprinted by permission of the publisher.

James A. Emanuel, "Emmett Till" by James A. Emanuel. Copyright © 1968 by James A. Emanuel. Reprinted by permission of James A. Emanuel.

Russell Endo, "Susumu, My Name" by Russell Endo. Copyright © by Russell Endo. First published by *The Philadelphia Inquirer,* March 15, 1988. Reprinted by permission of the Haverford College Poetry Competition/Russell Endo.

Louise Erdrich, "Windigo" from *Jacklight* by Louise Erdrich. Copyright © 1984 by Louise Erdrich. Reprinted by permission of the author. "Dear John Wayne" from JACK LIGHT by Louise Erdrich, Copyright © 1984 Louise Erdrich, reprinted by permission of Harcourt Brace and Company.

Lawrence Ferlinghetti, "Constantly Risking Absurdity" and "Don't Let That Horse Eat That Violin" from *A Coney Island of the Mind* by Lawrence Ferlinghetti. Copyright © 1958 by Lawrence Ferlinghetti. Reprinted by permission of New Directions Publishing Corporation.

Jane Flanders, "Cloud Painter." Reprinted by permission of the University of Pittsburgh Press. Copyright © 1988 by Jane Flanders.

Robert Francis, "Pitcher" from *The Orb Weaver* by Robert Francis. Copyright © 1960 by Robert Francis. Reprinted by permission of The University Press of New England.

Robert Frost, "Acquainted With the Night," "Birches," "Design," "Fire and Ice," "For Once, Then, Something," "Stopping by Woods on a Snowy Evening," and "Out, Out—" from *The Poetry of Robert Frost* edited by Edward Connery Lathem. Copyright © 1916, 1923, 1928, 1969 by Holt, Rinehart, and Winston. Copyright © 1936, 1944, 1951, 1956 by Robert Frost. Copyright © 1964 by Lesley Frost Ballantine. Reprinted by permission of Henry Holt and Company, Inc. "In White" from *The Dimensions of Robert Frost* by Reginald L. Cook. Copyright © 1958 by Reginald L. Cook. Reprinted by permission of Henry Holt and Company, Inc.

Allen Ginsberg, "A Supermarket in California" from COLLECTED POEMS 1947–1980 by Allen Ginsberg. Copyright © 1955 by Allen Ginsberg. Reprinted by permission of Harper & Row Publishers, Inc.

Nikki Giovanni, "Nikki Rosa" from BLACK FEELING, BLACK TALK, BLACK JUDGMENT by Nikki Giovanni. Copyright © 1968, 1970 by Nikki Giovanni. Reprinted by permission of William Morrow & Company. "Poetry" from THE WOMEN AND THE MEN by Nikki Giovanni. Copyright © 1970, 1974, 1975 by Nikki Giovanni. Reprinted by permission of William Morrow and Company.

Louise Gluck, "Gretel in Darkness," © 1971, 1972, 1973, 1974, 1975 by Louise Gluck. From *The House on Marshland,* first published by Ecco Press in 1975. Reprinted by permission. "Life is a Nice Place" from *Mademoiselle* by Louise Gluck. Courtesy of Mademoiselle. Copyright © 1966 by The Conde Nast Publications, Inc.

Nadine Gordimer, "Once Upon a Time" from JUMP by Nadine Gordimer. Copyright © 1991 Felix Licensing, B. V. Reprinted by permission of Farrar, Straus, & Giroux, Inc.

Barbara L. Greenberg, "The Faithful Wife" by Barbara L. Greenberg in *Poetry Northwest,* V. 19, No. 2, 1979. Copyright © and reprinted by permission of Barbara Greenberg.

Donald Hall, "My Son, My Executioner" from *Old and New Poems* by Donald Hall. Copyright © 1990 by Donald Hall. Reprinted by permission of Ticknor & Fields, a Houghton Mifflin Co.

Robert Hayden, "Homage to the Empress of the Blues," "Monet's Waterlilies," "Those Winter Sundays" reprinted from *Angle of Ascent, New and Selected Poems* by Robert Hayden, by permission of Liveright Publishing Corporation. Copyright © 1975, 1972, 1970, 1966 by Robert Hayden.

Seamus Heaney, "Digging" from *Death of a Naturalist* by Seamus Heaney. Copyright © by Seamus Heaney. Reprinted by permission of Faber & Faber, Ltd.

Robert Hollander, "You Too? Me Too—Why Not Soda Pop" from *The Massachusetts Review* by Robert Hollander. Copyright © 1986 by Robert Hollander. Reprinted by permission of the Massachusetts Review, The University of Massachusetts at Amherst.

Garret Kaoru Hongo, "The Hongo Store 29 Miles Volcano Hilo, Hawaii" from *Yellow Light* by Garret Kaoru. Copyright © 1982 by Garret Kaoru Hongo. Reprinted by permission of The University Press of New England.

David Huddle, "Holes Commence Falling." Reprinted from *Paper Boy* by David Huddle by permission of The University of Pittsburgh Press. Copyright © 1979 by David Huddle.

Langston Hughes, "Dream Deferred" from *The Panther and The Leash* by Langston Hughes. Copyright © 1951 by Langston Hughes. Reprinted by permission of Alfred A. Knopf, Inc. "Island" and "Negro" from *Selected Poems of Langston Hughes* by Langston Hughes. Copyright © 1959 by Langston Hughes. Reprinted by permission of Alfred A. Knopf, Inc.

Randall Jarrell, "The Death of the Ball Turret Gunner" from *The Complete Poems* by Randall Jarrell. Copyright © 1945 and renewal Copyright © 1972 by Mrs. Randall Jarrell. Reprinted by permission of Farrar, Straus, & Giroux, Inc.

Donald Justice, "On the Death of Friends in Childhood" from *Summer Anniversaries* by Donald Justice. Copyright © 1981 by Donald Justice. Reprinted by permission of The University Press of New England.

Faye Kicknosway, "Gracie" first appeared in *All These Voices* by Faye Kicknosway, Coffee House Press, 1986. Reprinted by permission of the publisher. Copyright © 1986 by Faye Kicknosway.

Carolyn Kizer, "After Basho" Copyright © 1984 by Carolyn Kizer. Reprinted from *Yin: New Poems* by Carolyn Kizer with the permission of BOA Editions, Ltd., 92 Park Avenue, Brockport, NY 14420.

Etheridge Knight, "For Malcolm, a Year After." Reprinted from *The Essential Etheridge Knight* by permission of the University of Pittsburgh Press. Copyright © 1986 by Etheridge Knight.

Maxine Kumin, "Morning Swim" from *Our Ground Time Here Will Be Brief* by Maxine Kumin. Copyright © 1965 by Maxine Kumin. Reprinted by permission of Viking Penguin, a division of Penguin Books USA, Inc.

Philip Larkin, "Aubade" from COLLECTED POEMS by Philip Larkin. Copyright © 1988, 1989 by the Estate of Philip Larkin. Reprinted by permission of Farrar, Straus, & Giroux, Inc.

Denise Levertov, "The Ache of Marriage" and "What Were They Like?" from *Poems 1960–1967* by Denise Levertov. Copyright © 1964, 1966 by Denise Levertov Goodman. Reprinted by permission from New Directions Publishing Corporation.

Stephen Shu-ning Liu, "My Father's Martial Arts." Copyright © 1981 by The Antioch Review, Inc. First appeared in *The Antioch Review*, Vol. 39, No. 3, (Summer 1981). Reprinted by permission of the Editors.

Audre Lorde, "Rooming Houses Are Old Women" is reprinted from *Chosen Poems, Old and New* by Audre Lorde, by permission of W.W. Norton & Company, Inc. Copyright © 1982, 1976, 1974, 1973, 1970, 1968 by Audre Lorde.

Amy Lowell, "Patterns" from *The Complete Poetical Works of Amy Lowell* by Amy Lowell. Copyright © 1955, Copyright © 1983 renewed by Houghton Mifflin Company, Brinton P. Roberts, Esquire, and G. Beeline. Reprinted by permission of Houghton Mifflin Company.

Robert Lowell, "For the Union Dead" from FOR THE UNION DEAD by Robert Lowell. Copyright © 1960, 1964 by Robert Lowell. Reprinted by permission of Farrar, Straus, & Giroux, Inc.

Archibald MacLeish, "Ars Poetica" from *New and Collected Poems 1917–1982* by Archibald MacLeish. Copyright © 1985 by the Estate of Archibald MacLeish. Reprinted by permission of Houghton Mifflin Company.

Colleen McElroy, "My Father's Wars" from *Queen of the Ebony Isles* by Colleen McElroy. Copyright © 1984 by Colleen McElroy. Reprinted by permission of The University Press of New England.

Claude McKay, "If We Must Die" and "The White City" from *Selected Poems of Claude McKay* by Claude McKay. Copyright © 1981 by Mrs. Hope McKay Virtue. Reprinted by permission of the Archives of Claude McKay, Carl Jowl, Administrator.

William Meredith, "Dreams of Suicide" and "In Memory of Donald A. Stauffer" from PARTIAL ACCOUNTS: NEW AND SELECTED POEMS by William Meredith.

Copyright © 1987 by William Meredith. Reprinted by permission of Alfred A. Knopf, Inc.

Edna St. Vincent Millay, "Elegy Before Death" by Edna St. Vincent Millay. From COLLECTED POEMS, HarperCollins. Copyright © 1921, 1948 by Edna St. Vincent Millay. Reprinted by permission of Elizabeth Barnett, Literary Executor. "What My Lips Have Kissed, and Where and Why" by Edna St. Vincent Millay. From COLLECTED POEMS, HarperCollins. Copyright © 1923, 1951 by Edna St. Vincent Millay and Norma Millay Ellis. Reprinted by permission of Elizabeth Barnett, Literary Executor.

Janice Mirikitani, "Breaking Silence" and "Suicide Note" from *Shredding Silence* by Janice Mirikitani. Copyright © 1978, reprinted by permission of Celestial Arts, Berkeley, California.

N. Scott Momaday, "Comparatives" by N. Scott Momaday. Copyright © 1976 by and reprinted by permission of N. Scott Momaday. "Earth And I Gave You Turquoise" by N. Scott Momaday. Copyright © 1975 by and reprinted by permission of N. Scott Momaday.

Marianne Moore, "Poetry." Reprinted with permission of Macmillan Publishing Company from COLLECTED POEMS OF MARIANNE MOORE. Copyright © 1935 by Marianne Moore, renewed 1963 by Marianne Moore and T. S. Eliot.

Maria K. Mootry, "'Chocolate Mabbie' and 'Pearl May Lee': Gwendolyn Brooks, and the Ballad Traditions" from the *CLA Journal,* 30 (March 1987), 278–93. Copyright © 1987 by and reprinted by permission of The College Language Association.

Pat Mora, "Elena" by Pat Mora is reprinted with permission of the publisher from *Chants* (Houston: Arte Publico Press-University of Houston, 1984).

Ogden Nash, "The Llama" from *Verses from 1929 On* by Ogden Nash. Copyright © 1931 by Ogden Nash. Copyright © renewed 1985 by Frances Nash, Isabel Nash Eberstadt, and Linnell Nash Smith. Reprinted by permission of Little, Brown, and Company.

Howard Nemerov, "The Air Force Museum at Dayton" from *Inside the Onion* by Howard Nemerov. Copyright © 1984 by Howard Nemerov. Reprinted by permission of Ms. Howard Nemerov. "The Goose Fish" from *The Collected Poems of Howard Nemerov* by Howard Nemerov. Copyright © 1977 by and reprinted by permission of Mrs. Howard Nemerov.

Pablo Neruda, "The United Fruit Company" translated by Robert Bly. Copyright © 1950 by and reprinted by permission of Robert Bly.

Hilton Obenzinger, "Yes, We Have No Bananas" from *This Passover Or The Next I Will Not Be in Jerusalem* by Hilton Obenzinger. Copyright © 1980 by Hilton Obenzinger. Reprinted with the permission of Momo's Press.

Sharon Olds, "The One Girl at the Boys Party" from *The Dead and the Living* by Sharon Olds. Copyright © 1983 by Sharon Olds. Reprinted by permission of Alfred A. Knopf, Inc.

Simon J. Ortiz, "My Father's Song" by Simon J. Ortiz. Copyright © by Simon J. Ortiz. Reprinted by permission of the author. "Speaking" by Simon J. Ortiz. Copyright © by Simon J. Ortiz. Reprinted by permission of the author.

Wilfred Owen, "Dulce et Decorum Est" from *The Collected Poems of Wilfred Owen* by Wilfred Owen. Copyright © 1963 by Chatto & Windus, Ltd. Reprinted by permission of New Directions Publishing Corporation.

Linda Pastan, "Ethics" is reprinted from WAITING FOR MY LIFE, POEMS by Linda Pastan, by permission of W. W. Norton & Company, Inc. Copyright © 1981 by Linda Pastan.

Boris Pasternak, "In Everything I Want To Get" by Boris Pasternak and translated by Richard McKane. Translation Richard McKane, from *Post-War Russian Poetry,* ed. Daniel Weissbort, Penguin 1974.

Lucia Perillo, "Jury Selection" from *Ironwood* by Lucia Perillo. Copyright © 1985 by and reprinted by permission of Lucia Perillo.

Marge Piercy, "The Secretary Chant" from *Circles on the Water* by Marge Piercy. Copyright © 1982 by Marge Piercy. Reprinted by permission of Alfred A. Knopf, Inc.

Sylvia Plath, "Daddy" from *The Collected Poems of Sylvia Plath* by Sylvia Plath edited by Ted Hughes. Copyright © 1963 Ted Hughes; Copyright © 1981 by the estate of Sylvia Plath. Reprinted by permission of Harper & Row, Publishers, Inc. "Metaphors" from *The Collected Poems of Sylvia Plath,* edited by Ted Hughes. Copyright © 1960, 1965, 1971, 1981 by the Estate of Sylvia Plath. Reprinted by permission of Harper & Row, Publishers, Inc. "Morning Songs" by Sylvia Plath, Copyright © 1961 Ted Hughes from *Sylvia Plath: The Collected Poems* by Sylvia Plath. Copyright © 1960, 1965, 1971, 1981 by the Estate of Sylvia Plath; editorial material Copyright © 1981 by Ted Hughes. Reprinted by permission of Harper & Row, Publishers, Inc.

Ezra Pound, "In a Station of the Metro" and "The River Merchant's Wife" from *Personae* by Ezra Pound. Copyright © 1926 by Ezra Pound. Reprinted by permission of New Directions Publishing Corporation.

Dudley Randall, "Ballad of Birmingham" by Dudley Randall. Copyright © 1969 by and reprinted by permission of Dudley Randall.

John Crowe Ransom, "Bells for John Whiteside's Daughter" from *Selected Poems,* Third Edition, by John Crowe Ransom. Copyright © 1924 by Alfred A. Knopf, Inc. and renewed 1952 by John Crowe Ransom. Reprinted by John Crowe Ransom, by permission of Alfred A. Knopf, Inc.

Henry Reed, "Naming of Parts" by Henry Reed. Copyright © 1946 by Henry Reed. Reprinted by permission of Literary Executor of the Estate of Henry Reed, John Tydemann.

Adrienne Rich, "Aunt Jennifer's Tigers," "Driving into the Wreck," "Living in Sin," "A Woman Mourned by Daughters," and "The Roofwalker" reprinted from *The Fact of a Doorframe, Poems Selected and New, 1950–1984,* by Adrienne Rich, by permission of W. W. Norton & Company, Inc. Copyright © 1984 by Adrienne Rich. Copyright © 1975, 1978 by W. W. Norton & Company, Inc. Copyright © 1981 by Adrienne Rich.

Alberto Alvaro Rios, "Nani" from *Whispering to Fool the Wind* by Alberto Alvaro Rios. Copyright © 1982 Alberto Alvaro Rios. Reprinted by permission of the author.

Edwin Arlington Robinson, "Mr. Flood's Party," "Miniver Cheevy," and "Richard Cory" reprinted with permission of Macmillan Publishing Company from COLLECTED POEMS OF EDWIN ARLINGTON ROBINSON. Copyright © 1921 by Edwin Arlington Robinson, renewed 1949 by Ruth Nivision.

Theodore Roethke, "Child on Top of a Green House" and "My Papa's Waltz" from *The Collected Poems of Theodore Roethke* by Theodore Roethke. Copyright © 1942, 1946 by Hearst Magazines, Inc. Reprinted by permission of Doubleday, a division of Bantam, Doubleday, Dell Publishing Group, Inc. "I Knew a Woman" from *The Collected Poems of Theodore Roethke* by Theodore Roethke. Copyright © 1954 Theodore Roethke. Reprinted by permission of Doubleday, a division of Bantam, Doubleday, Dell Publishing Group, Inc. "Night Crow" from *The Collected Poems of Theodore Roethke* by Theodore Roethke. Copyright © 1944 by The Saturday Review Association, Inc. Reprinted by permission of Doubleday, a division of Bantam, Doubleday, Dell Publishing Group, Inc. "The Waking" from *The Collected Poems of Theodore Roethke* by Theodore Roethke. Copyright © 1953 by Theodore Roethke. Reprinted by permission of Doubleday, a division of Bantam, Doubleday, Dell Publishing Group, Inc.

Jim Sagel, "Baca Grande" by Jim Sagel from *Hispanics in the United States, An Anthology of Creative Literature,* Volume II, edited by Francisco Jimenez and Gary D.

Keller. Copyright © 1982 by Bilingual Press. Reprinted by permission of Bilingual Press, Arizona State University Press, Tempe Arizona.

Sonia Sanchez, "On Passing Through Morgantown, Pa." from *Homegirls and Handgrenades* by Sonia Sanchez. Copyright © 1984 by and reprinted by permission of Sonia Sanchez. "Right On: White America" from *We are BaddDDD People* by Sonia Sanchez. Copyright © 1970 by and reprinted by permission of Sonia Sanchez and Broadside Press.

Carl Sandburg, "Chicago" and "Fog" from *CHICAGO POEMS* by Carl Sandburg, Copyright © 1916 by Holt, Rinehart, & Winston, Inc., and renewed 1944 by Carl Sandburg, reprinted by permission of Harcourt Brace Jovanovich, Inc.

Delmore Schwartz, "The True-Blue American" from *Selected Poems: Summer Knowledge* by Delmore Schwartz. Copyright © 1959 by Delmore Schwartz. Reprinted by permission from New Directions Publishing Corporation.

Sipho Sepamla, "Words, Words, Words" by Sipho Sepamla. Copyright © by Sipho Sepamla. Reprinted by permission of Rex Collings, Ltd.

Mongone Wally Serote, "For Don M.—Banned" by Mongone Wally Serote. Copyright © 1982 by Wally Serote. Reprinted by permission of the Jane Gregory Agency.

Anne Sexton, "Cinderella" from *Tranformations* by Anne Sexton. Copyright © 1971 by Anne Sexton. Reprinted by permission of Houghton Mifflin Company.

Karl Shapiro, "Auto Wreck" by Karl Shapiro. Copyright © 1978 by Karl Shapiro. Reprinted by permission of Weiser & Weiser, Inc.

Leslie Marmon Silko, "Where Mountain Lion Lay Down with Deer" by Leslie Marmon Silko. Copyright © 1973 Leslie Marmon Silko. Reprinted with the permission of Wylie, Aitken & Stone, Inc.

Charles Simic, "Birthday Star Atlas" from UNENDING BLUES, POEMS, Copyright © 1986 by Charles Simic, reprinted permission of Harcourt Brace Jovanovich, Inc.

Jim Simmerman, "Child's Grave, Hale County, Alabama" by Jim Simmerman. Copyright © 1983 by Jim Simmerman. Originally published by Dragon Gate, Inc. Reprinted by permission of David K. Miller, Literary Agent, Inc.

Boris Slutsky, "How Did They Kill My Grandmother?" by Boris Slutsky and translated by Elaine Feinstein. Translation Copyright © by Elaine Feinstein, from *Post-War Russian Poetry*, ed. Daniel Weissbort, Penguin 1974.

Gary Smith, "Gwendolyn Brooks's *A Street in Bronzeville*, the Harlem Renaissance and the Mythologies of Black Women" from MELUS 10.3 (Fall 1983) by Gary Smith. Copyright © 1983. "Gwendolyn Brooks's Children of the Poor Metaphysical Poetry and the Inconditions of Love" by Gary Smith from *A Life Distilled: Gwendolyn Brooks, Her Poetry and Fiction*, edited by Maria K. Mootry and Gary Smith. Copyright © 1987 by and reprinted by permission of The University of Illinois Press.

Stevie Smith, "Not Waving but Drowning" from *Collected Poems of Stevie Smith* by Stevie Smith. Copyright © 1959 by Stevie Smith. Reprinted by permission of New Directions Publishing Corporation.

Gary Snyder, "Some Good Things to be Said for the Iron Age" by Gary Snyder. Copyright © 1970 by and reprinted by permission of Gary Snyder.

Cathy Song, "Lost Sister" from *Picture Bride* by Cathy Song. Copyright © 1983 by and reprinted by permission of Yale University Press.

Gary Soto, "Black Hair." Reprinted from *Black Hair* by Gary Soto, by permission of the University of Pittsburgh Press. Copyright © 1985 by Gary Soto. "History." Reprinted from *The Elements of San Joaquin* by Gary Soto, by permission of the University of Pittsburgh Press.

Wole Soyinka, "Future Plans" and "Telephone Connection" from *A Shuttle in the Crypt* by Wole Soyinka. Copyright © 1972 by Wole Soyinka. Reprinted by permission of Farrar, Straus, & Giroux, Inc.

Barry Spacks, "Finding a Yiddish Paper on the Riverside Line" from *Imaging a Unicorn* by Barry Spacks. Copyright © 1978 by and reprinted by permission of The University of Georgia Press.

Stephen Spender, "An Elementary School Classroom in a Slum" from COLLECTED POEMS 1928–1953 by Stephen Spender. Copyright © 1942 and renewed 1970 by Stephen Spender. Reprinted by permission of Random House, Inc.

Bruce Springsteen, "My Hometown" by Bruce Springsteen. Copyright © 1984 by Bruce Springsteen. Reprinted by permission of Jon Landau Management/Columbia Records, Inc.

William Stafford, "For the Grave of Daniel Boone" from *Stories That Could Be True: New and Collected Poems* by William Stafford. Copyright © 1947 and 1966 by William Stafford. Reprinted by permission of William Stafford. "Traveling Through the Dark" from *Stories That Could Be True: New and Collected Poems* by William Stafford. Copyright © 1960 and 1977 by William Stafford. Reprinted by permission of William Stafford.

George Stavos, "An Interview With Gwendolyn Brooks" from *Contemporary Literature*, Winter 1970 by George Stavos. Reprinted by permission of University of Wisconsin Press.

Dona Stein, "Putting Mother By" from *Ploughshares and Children of the Mafiosi* by Dona Stein. Copyright © 1977 by Dona Stein. Reprinted by permission of the author, Dona Stein.

Wallace Stevens, "Anecdote of the Jar," "Disillusionment at Ten O'Clock," and "The Emperor of Ice-Cream" from *The Collected Poems of Wallace Stevens* by Wallace Stevens. Copyright © 1923 and renewed 1951 by Wallace Stevens. Reprinted by permission of Alfred A. Knopf, Inc.

Mark Strand, "Pot Roast" from *Selected Poems* by Mark Strand. Copyright © 1979, 1980 by Mark Strand. Reprinted by permission of Alfred A. Knopf, Inc.

Andrew Suknaski, "The Bitter Word" from *Wood Mountain Poems* by Andrew Suknaski. Copyright © 1976 by and reprinted by permission of Andrew Suknaski.

May Swenson, "Women" from *Iconographs* by May Swenson. Originally published by Charles Scribner's Sons/Macmillan, 1970. Copyright © 1970 by May Swenson. Reprinted by R. R. Knudson, Executrix of the Estate of May Swenson.

Dylan Thomas, "Do Not Go Gentle into That Good Night," "Fern Hill," and "The Hand That Signed the Paper" from *Poems of Dylan Thomas* by Dylan Thomas. Copyright © 1945 by the Trustees for the Copyrights of Dylan Thomas, 1952 by Dylan Thomas. Reprinted by permission of New Directions Publishing Corporation.

Jean Toomer, "Reapers" is reprinted from *Cane* by Jean Toomer, by permission of Liveright Publishing Corporation. Copyright © 1923 by Boni & Liveright. Copyright © renewed 1951 by Jean Toomer.

Anne Tyler, "Teenage Wasteland" by Anne Tyler from *Seventeen*, 1984. Copyright © 1984 by Anne Tyler. Reprinted by permission of Russell Volkening.

John Updike, "Ex-Basketball Player" from *The Carpentered Hen and Other Stories* by John Updike. Copyright © 1957, 1982 by John Updike. Reprinted by permission of Alfred A. Knopf, Inc. "A & P" from *Pidgeon Feathers and Other Stories* by John Updike. Copyright © 1962 by John Updike. Reprinted by permission of Alfred A. Knopf, Inc.

Diane Wakoski, "Sleep" by Diane Wakoski. Copyright © 1966 by and reprinted by permission of Diane Wakoski.

Derek Walcott, "Sea Grapes" from *Sea Grapes* by Derek Walcott. Copyright © 1976 by Derek Walcott. Reprinted by permission of Farrar, Straus, & Giroux, Inc.

Alice Walker, "Revolutionary Petunias" from REVOLUTIONARY PETUNIAS & OTHER POEMS by Alice Walker, Copyright © 1972 by Alice Walker, reprinted by permission of Harcourt Brace Jovanovich, Inc.

Margaret Walker, "Lineage" from *This Is My Sensory* by Margaret Walker. Copyright © 1942 by and reprinted by permission of Margaret Walker.

Tom Wayman, "Wayman in Quebec" by Tom Wayman. Copyright © 1978 by and reprinted by permission of Tom Wayman.

Richard Wilbur, "For the Student Strikers" from THE MIND READER, Copyright © 1970 by Richard Wilbur, reprinted by permission Harcourt Brace Jovanovich, Inc. "Museum Piece" from CEREMONY AND OTHER POEMS by Richard Wilbur, Copyright © 1950 and renewed 1978 by Richard Wilbur, reprinted by permission of Harcourt Brace Jovanovich, Inc. "A Sketch" from THE MIND READER by Richard Wilbur, Copyright © 1975 by Richard Wilbur, reprinted by permission of Harcourt Brace Jovanovich, Inc. "Sleepless at Crown Point" from THE MIND READER, Copyright © 1973 by Richard Wilbur, reprinted by permission of Harcourt Brace Jovanovich, Inc.

William Carlos Williams, "The Great Figure," "Red Wheelbarrow," "Spring and All," and "This Is Just to Say" from *Collected Poems Volume I 1909–1939* by William Carlos Williams. Copyright © 1938 by and reprinted by permission of New Directions Corporation.

James Wright, "A Blessing" from *Collected Poems* by James Wright. Copyright © 1961 by James Wright. Reprinted by permission of The University Press of New England.

Richard Wright, "Hokku Poems" from RICHARD WRIGHT READER, edited by Ellen Wright and Michel Fabre. Copyright © 1978 by Ellen Wright and Michel Fabre. Reprinted by permission of HarperCollins Publishers, Inc.

William Butler Yeats, "An Irish Airman Foresees His Death." Reprinted with permission of Macmillan Publishing Company from THE POEMS OF W. B. YEATS: A NEW TRADITION, edited by Richard J. Finneran. Copyright © 1919 by Macmillan Publishing Company, renewed 1947 by Bertha Georgie Yeats. "The Second Coming." Reprinted with permission of Macmillan Publishing Company from THE POEMS OF W. B. YEATS: A NEW TRADITION, edited by Richard J. Finneran. Copyright © 1924 by Macmillan Publishing Company, renewed 1952 by Bertha Georgie Yeats. "Sailing to Byzantium" and "Leda and the Swan." Reprinted with permission of Macmillan Publishing Company from THE POEMS OF W. B. YEATS: A NEW TRADITION, edited by Richard J. Finneran. Copyright © 1928 by Macmillan Publishing Company, renewed 1956 by Bertha Georgie Yeats. "Crazy Jane Talks with the Bishop." Reprinted with permission of Macmillan Publishing Company from THE POEMS OF W. B. YEATS: A NEW TRADITION, edited by Richard J. Finneran. Copyright © 1933 by Macmillan Publishing Company, renewed 1961 by Bertha Georgie Yeats.

Yevgeny Yetushenko, "Lies" from *Yetushenko: Selected Poems* by Yevgeny Yetushenko, translated by Robert Milner-Gulland and Peter Levi, S. J. Copyright © 1962 by Robin Milner-Gulland and Peter Levi. Reprinted by permission of Penguin Books, Ltd.

Louis Zukofsky, "I Walk in the Old Street" from *Not "A": Complete Short Poetry* by Louis Zukofsky. Copyright © 1991 by and reprinted by permission of Louis Zukofsky and The John Hopkins University Press, Baltimore, London.

Index of Authors, Titles, and First Lines of Poetry

Titles of works are in italics. First lines of poetry are in regular type. Authors names are in small caps.

"A cold coming we had of it, **304**
A dented spider like a snowdrop white, **118**
A line in long array where they wind betwixt green islands, **393**
A noiseless patient spider, **184**
A poem should be palpable and mute, **34**
A ringing tire iron, **142**
A sudden blow: the great wings beating still, **268**
A sweet disorder in the dress, **201**
About suffering they were never wrong, **270**
Ache of Marriage, The, **208**
Achievement of Gwendolyn Brooks, The, **421-427**
Acquainted with the Night, **312**
ADAMÉ, LEONARD
   My Grandmother Would Rock Quietly and Hum, **75-76**
Adultery, **296-297**
After Basho, **153**
Again I hold these holy letters, **379**
Air Force Museum at Dayton, The, **352**
AKHMATOVA, ANNA
   He Loved Three Things Alone, **274**
All night, this headland, **153**
Almost midnight, and the aunties, **150**
Among the rain, **144**
And if I lived in those olden times, **294**
Anecdote of the Jar, **383**
ANGELOU, MAYA
   My Arkansas, **18**
Anonymous, **294**
anyone lived in a pretty how town, **132-133**

anyone lived in a pretty how town, **132-133**
Armed with an indiscriminate delight, **226**
Ars Poetica, **34-35**
As virtuous men pass mildly away, **168**
Astrophel and Stella, **371**
At eight I was brilliant with my body, **376**
At first, as you know, the sky is incidental, **138**
ATWOOD, MARGARET
   City Planners, The, **120-121**
   You Fit into Me, **179**
Aubade, **339-340**
AUDEN, W. H.
   Look, Stranger, **135**
   Musée des Beaux Arts, **270**
   Unknown Citizen, The, **98-99**
August and the drive-in picture is packed, **310**
Aunt Jennifer's Tigers, **196**
Aunt Jennifer's tigers prance across a screen, **196**
Auto Wreck, **114-115**

Baca Grande, **121-123**
BAKER, HOUSTON A., JR.
   Achievement of Gwendolyn Brooks, The, **421-427**
Ballad of Birmingham, **102-103**
Ballad of Chocolate Mabbie, The, **405-406**
Ballad of Rudolph Reed, The, **412-413**
BARAKA, IMAMU AMIRI
   Watergate, **277**
BASHO, MATSUO
   Four Haiku, **152**

Batter My Heart, Three-Personed God, **300**
Batter my heart, three-personed God, for You, **300**
Bean Eaters, The, **407-408**
Because I Could Not Stop for Death, **297-298**
Because I could not stop for Death—, **297**
Because there was a man somewhere in a candystripe silk shirt, **323**
Because we were 18 and still wonderful in our bodies, **285-286**
Bells for John Whiteside's Daughter, **359-360**
Bent double, like old beggars under sacks, **155**
BERGER, SUZANNE E.
    Meal, The, **143**
BERRYMAN, JOHN
    Dream Song #14, **278**
Between my finger and my thumb, **50, 54**
Birches, **312-314**
Birthday Star Atlas, **371-372**
BISHOP, ELIZABETH
    Fish, The, **278-280**
    Sestina, **223-224**
Bitter Word, The, **386-387**
Black Hair, **376-377**
Black reapers with the sound of steel on stones, **154**
Blackstone Rangers, The, **410-411**
BLAKE, WILLIAM
    Chimney Sweeper, The, **280-281**
    Her Whole Life Is an Epigram, **228**
    Lamb, The, **281**
    London, **281-282**
    Tyger, The, **282**
Blessing, A, **397-398**
BLY, ROBERT
    Snowfall in the Afternoon, **283**
BOGAN, LOUISE
    Women, **283-284**
Bonny Barbara Allan, **274-275**
Boy Died in My Alley, The, **414-415**
BRADSTREET, ANNE
    To My Dear and Loving Husband, **175**
BRAUTIGAN, RICHARD
    Widow's Lament, **229**
Breaking Silence, **347-350**
BRODSKY, JOSEPH
    Star of the Nativity, The, **266**

BROOKS, GWENDOLYN
    Ballad of Chocolate Mabbie, The, **405-406**
    Ballad of Rudolph Reed, The, **412-413**
    Bean Eaters, The, **407-408**
    Blackstone Rangers, The, **410-411**
    Boy Died in My Alley, The, **414-415**
    Chicago Defender Sends a Man to Little Rock, The, **408-410**
    First Fight. Then Fiddle, **221**
    Interview with Myself, An, **415-419**
    Medgar Evers, **413-414**
    People Who Have No Children Can Be Hard, **407**
    Report from Part One, **419-421**
    Sadie and Maud, **188**
    Song in the Front Yard, A, **406-407**
    We Real Cool, **130**
    What Shall I Give My Children?, **407**
BROWNING, ELIZABETH BARRETT
    How Do I Love Thee?, **284**
BROWNING, ROBERT
    My Last Duchess, **78-79**
    Porphyria's Lover, **93-94**
BRUTUS, DENNIS
    On the Island, **146-147**
BUCKLEY, CHRISTOPHER
    Why I'm in Favor of a Nuclear Freeze, **285-286**
Buffalo Bill's, **295**
Buffalo Bill's, **295**
BUKOWSKI, CHARLES
    Dog Fight, **126**
BURNS, ROBERT
    John Anderson, My Jo, John, **129**
    Oh, My Love Is Like a Red, Red Rose, **163**
But if I *were* to have a lover, it would be someone, **124**
By the road to the contagious hospital, **238**
BYRON, GEORGE GORDON, LORD
    She Walks in Beauty, **286**

Call the roller of big cigars, **384**
CAMPION, THOMAS
    There Is a Garden in Her Face, **287**
from *Canterbury Tales, The,* **288-289**
CARROLL, LEWIS
    Jabberwocky, **210-211**

CARVER, RAYMOND
    Gravy, **287-288**
    Photograph of My Father in His Twenty-Second Year, **44**
Cavalry Crossing a Ford, **393**
Cement-grey floors and walls, **146**
Channel Firing, **321-322**
CHAUCER, GEOFFREY
    from *Canterbury Tales, The*, **288-289**
Chicago, **231-232**
Chicago Defender Sends a Man to Little Rock, The, **408-410**
Child on Top of a Greenhouse, **364-365**
childhood remembrances are always a drag, **316**
Child's Grave, Hale County, Alabama, **250-251**
Chimney Sweeper, The, **280-281**
Chinese Fireworks Banned in Hawaii, **150-151**
CHOCK, ERIC
    Chinese Fireworks Banned in Hawaii, **150-151**
"Chocolate Mabbie" and "Pearl May Lee": Gwendolyn Brooks and the Ballad Tradition, **439-446**
Cinderella, **99-102**
City Planners, The, **120-121**
CLIFF, MICHELLE
    Visit to the Secret Annex, A, **147-150**
CLIFTON, LUCILLE
    My Mama Moved among the Days, **50**
Cloud Painter, **138-139**
COFER, JUDITH ORTIZ
    Lessons of the Past, **290-291**
    My Father in the Navy: A Childhood Memory, **45**
COLERIDGE, SAMUEL TAYLOR
    Kubla Khan, **291-292**
    Metrical Feet, **192**
    What Is an Epigram?, **228**
Come live with me and be my love, **344**
Comparatives, **199-200**
Compose for Red a proper verse, **197**
Composed upon Westminster Bridge, **396**
Constantly risking absurdity, **160**
Constantly Risking Absurdity, **160-161**
CRANE, HART
    To Brooklyn Bridge, **293-294**

Crazy Jane Talks with the Bishop, **398-399**
Cruising these residential Sunday, **120**
CRUZ, VICTOR HERNÁNDEZ
    Anonymous, **294**
CULLEN, COUNTEE
    For a Lady I Know, **295**
    Yet Do I Marvel, **265**
CUMMINGS, E. E.
    anyone lived in a pretty how town, **132-133**
    Buffalo Bill's, **295**
    in Just—, **115-116**
    l(a, **39**
    next to of course god america i, **295-296**
    the sky was can dy, **234**

Daddy, **170-172**
"Dead Crow" is an ol ugly, **277**
Dear John Wayne, **310-311**
Death Be Not Proud, **300**
Death be not proud, though some have called thee, **300**
Death of the Ball Turret Gunner, The, **166**
Delight in Disorder, **201**
Design, **119**
DICKEY, JAMES
    Adultery, **296-297**
DICKINSON, EMILY
    Because I Could Not Stop for Death, **297-298**
    I Heard a Fly Buzz—When I Died, **298**
    I Like to See It Lap the Miles, **193**
    I Taste a Liquor Never Brewed, **298-299**
    I'm Nobody! Who Are You?, **72**
    Soul Selects Her Own Society, The, **299**
    Volcanoes Be in Sicily, **252**
    Wild Nights—Wild Nights!, **299-300**
Did the people of Viet Nam, **340**
Digging, **50, 54-55**
Disillusionment of Ten O'clock, **383-384**
Diving into the Wreck, **257-259**
Do not go gentle into that good night, **47**
Do Not Go Gentle into That Good Night, **47**

Does the road wind uphill all the way?, **256**
Dog Fight, **126**
DONNE, JOHN
    Batter My Heart, Three-Personed God, **300**
    Death Be Not Proud, **300**
    Song, **301**
    Valediction: Forbidding Mourning, A, **168-169**
Don't let that horse, **239**
Don't Let That Horse Eat That Violin, **239-240**
DORFMAN, ARIEL
    Hope, **96-97**
DOVE, RITA
    Satisfaction Coal Company, The, **301-303**
DRAYTON, MICHAEL
    Since There's No Help, **303**
Dream Deferred, **159-160**
Dream Song #14, **278**
Dreams of Suicide, **261-262**
Drink to me only with thine eyes, **330**
Dulce et Decorum Est, **155**
DUNBAR, PAUL LAURENCE
    We Wear the Mask, **304**
Eagle, The, **199**

Earth and I gave you turquoise, **350**
Earth and I Gave You Turquoise, **350-351**
Earth has not anything to show more fair, **396**
Easter Wings, **244**
Elegy before Death, **134**
Elegy Written in a Country Churchyard, **71-321**
Elementary School Classroom in a Slum, An, **379-380**
Elena, **351**
ELIOT, T. S.
    Journey of the Magi, **304-305**
    Love Song of J. Alfred Prufrock, The, **306-309**
EMANUEL, JAMES A.
    Emmett Till, **310**
Emmett Till, **310**
Emperor of Ice-Cream, The, **384**
ENDO, RUSSELL
    Susumu, My Name, **112**
ERDRICH, LOUISE
    Dear John Wayne, **310-311**
    Windigo, **267**

Ethics, **356**
Ex-Basketball Player, **164-165**

Faithful Wife, The, **124**
Far far from gusty waves, these children's faces, **379**
Farewell, thou child of my right hand, and joy, **330**
Fear no more the heat o' the sun, **209**
Fear No More the Heat o' the Sun, **209**
FERLINGHETTI, LAWRENCE
    Constantly Risking Absurdity, **160-161**
    Don't Let That Horse Eat That Violin, **239-240**
Fern Hill, **389-390**
Finding a Yiddish Paper on the Riverside Line, **379**
Fire and Ice, **84**
First Fight. Then Fiddle, **221**
First fight. Then fiddle. Ply the slipping string, **221**
First having read the book of myths, **257**
Fish, The, **278-280**
FLANDERS, JANE
    Cloud Painter, **138-139**
Fog, **366**
For a Lady I Know, **295**
For Don M.—Banned, **366**
For Malcolm, A Year After, **197**
For Once, Then, Something, **249**
For the Grave of Daniel Boone, **110**
For the Student Strikers, **125**
For the Union Dead, **342-344**
Four Haiku, **152**
FRANCIS, ROBERT
    Pitcher, **311-312**
from fort walsh, **386**
From my mother, the antique mirror, **323**
From my mother's sleep I fell into the State, **166**
FROST, ROBERT
    Acquainted with the Night, **312**
    Birches, **312-314**
    Design, **119**
    Fire and Ice, **84**
    For Once, Then, Something, **249**
    In White, **118-119**
    Mending Wall, **314-315**
    "Out, Out—," **177-178**
    Road Not Taken, The, **315**

Stopping by Woods on a Snowy Evening, **315-316**
Future Plans, **260**

Gather ye rosebuds while ye may, **92**
GINSBERG, ALLEN
    Supermarket in California, A, **183-184**
GIOVANNI, NIKKI
    Nikki-Rosa, **316-317**
    Poetry, **33-34**
Glory be to God for dappled things, **207**
GLÜCK, LOUISE
    Gretel in Darkness, **73-74**
    Life Is a Nice Place, **233**
Go and catch a falling star, **301**
Go, lovely rose, **391**
Go, Lovely Rose, **391**
Go talk with those who are rumored to be unlike you, **125**
God's Grandeur, **326**
Goose Fish, The, **254-255**
Gracie, **127-128**
Grandma lit the stove, **377**
Gravy, **287-288**
GRAY, THOMAS
    Elegy Written in a Country Churchyard, **317-321**
Great Figure, The, **144**
GREENBERG, BARBARA L.
    Faithful Wife, The, **124**
Gretel in Darkness, **73-74**
Gwendolyn Brooks's A Street in Bronzeville, the Harlem Renaissance and the Mythologies of Black Women, **446-453**
Gwendolyn Brooks's "Children of the Poor," Metaphysical Poetry and the Inconditions of Love, **430-439**

"Had he and I but met," **639**
Had I the Choice, **187**
Had I the choice to tally greatest bards, **187**
Had we but world enough and time, **175**
HALL, DONALD
    My Son, My Executioner, **178-179**
Hand That Signed the Paper, The, **181**
HARDY, THOMAS
    Channel Firing, **321-322**
    Man He Killed, The, **85**
HAYDEN, ROBERT
    Homage to the Empress of the Blues, **323**
    Monet's "Waterlilies," **237**
    Those Winter Sundays, **50, 54**
He clasps the crag with crooked hands, **199**
he draws up against my rear bumper in the fast lane, **126**
He loved three things alone, **274**
He Loved Three Things Alone, **274**
He was found by the Bureau of Statistics to be, **98**
HEANEY, SEAMUS
    Digging, **50, 54-55**
Her whole life is an epigram: smack, smooth & neatly penned, **228**
Her Whole Life Is an Epigram, **228**
HERBERT, GEORGE
    Easter Wings, **244**
Heritage, **323-324**
HERRICK, ROBERT
    Delight in Disorder, **201**
    To the Virgins, to Make Much of Time, **92**
His art is eccentricity, his aim, **311**
History, **377-379**
Hog Butcher for the World, **231**
HOGAN, LINDA
    Heritage, **323-324**
Hokku Poems, **229-230**
Holes Commence Falling, **173-174**
HOLLANDER, ROBERT
    You Too? Me Too—Why Not? Soda Pop, **245**
Homage to the Empress of the Blues, **323**
HONGO, GARRETT KAORU,
    Hongo Store 29 Miles Volcano Hilo, Hawaii, The, **325**
Hongo Store 29 Miles Volcano Hilo, Hawaii, The, **325**
Hope, **96-97**
HOPKINS, GERARD MANLEY
    God's Grandeur, **326**
    Pied Beauty, **207**
    Windhover, The, **326-327**
HOUSMAN, A. E.
    Terence, This Is Stupid Stuff, **327-329**
    To an Athlete Dying Young, **329-330**
How did they kill my grandmother?, **373**
How Did They Kill My Grandmother?, **373-374**
How Do I Love Thee?, **284**

How do I love thee? Let me count the ways, **284**
How many dawns, chill from his rippling rest, **293**
How many notes written, **82**
HUDDLE, DAVID
    Holes Commence Falling, **173-174**
HUGHES, LANGSTON
    Dream Deferred, **159-160**
    Island, **253**
    Negro, **77**

I am, **245**
I am a Negro, **77**
I am nobody, **229**
I caught a tremendous fish, **278**
I caught this morning morning's minion, kingdom of daylight's, **326**
I celebrate myself, and sing myself, **393**
I climb the black rock mountain, **80**
I doubt not God is good, well-meaning, kind, **265**
I found a dimpled spider, fat and white, **119**
I gaze upon the roast, **384**
I have been one acquainted with the night, **312**
I have eaten, **395**
I hear a whistling, **310**
I Heard a Fly Buzz—When I Died, **298**
I heard a Fly buzz—when I died—, **298**
I Knew a Woman, **116-117**
I knew a woman, lovely in her bones, **116**
I know that I shall meet my fate, **399**
I like to see it lap the Miles, **193**
I Like to See It Lap the Miles, **193**
I mean, I'm a no shoes hillbilly an' home, **127**
I met a traveler from an antique land, **95**
I met the Bishop on the road, **398**
I placed a jar in Tennessee, **383**
I reach for the awkward shotgun not to disarm, **261**
i say you', **182**
I take him outside, **89**
I Taste a Liquor Never Brewed, **298-299**
I taste a liquor never brewed—, **298**
I, too, dislike it: there are things that are important beyond all this, **35**
I wake to sleep, and take my waking slow, **225**
I walk down the garden paths, **86**
I Walk in the Old Street, **38-39**
I walk in the old street, **38**
I wander through each chartered street, **281**
I wandered lonely as a cloud, **396**
I Wandered Lonely as a Cloud, **396-397**
I was born later, **148**
I was born the year my father learned to march, **290**
I was eight years old and running with a dime in my hand, **380**
I will arise and go now, and go to Innisfree, **399**
I will not toy with it nor bend an inch, **219**
I work all day, and get half-drunk at night, **339**
If all the world and love were young, **359**
If by dull rhymes our English must be chained, **213**
If ever two were one, then surely we, **175**
If they only could have put that in the papers, how the winter, **240**
If We Must Die, **345-346**
If we must die, let it not be like hogs, **345**
I'm a riddle in nine syllables, **357**
I'm Nobody! Who Are You?, **72**
I'm Nobody! Who are you?, **72**
In a Station of the Metro, **141**
In China, **374**
In ethics class so many years ago, **356**
In Everything I Want to Get, **356-357**
In everything I want to get, **357**
in her house, **75**
in Just—, **115**
In Little Rock the people bear, **408**
in Just—, **115-116**
In Memory of Donald A. Stauffer, **226**
In the cold season, in a locality accustomed to heat more than, **266**
In White, **118-119**
In Xanadu did Kubla Khan, **291**
Interview with Gwendolyn Brooks, An, **428-429**
Interview with Myself, An, **415-419**
Into my empty head there come, **338**

Into the lower right, **204**
Irish Airman Foresees His Death, An, **399**
Island, **253**
It began simply enough, as an invitation, **392**
it is a dry white season, **366**
It little profits that an idle king, **387**
It was in and about the Martinmas time, **274**
It was Mabbie without the grammar school gates, **405**
It was nearly a miracle, **122**
It's not quite cold enough, **229**
Its quick soft silver bell beating, beating, **114**
I've stayed in the front yard all my life, **406**

Jabberwocky, **210-211**
JARRELL, RANDALL
  Death of the Ball Turret Gunner, The, **166**
Jeremiah Dickson was a true-blue American, **262**
John Anderson my jo, John, **129**
John Anderson, My Jo, John, **129**
JONES, LEROI. *See* BARAKA, IMAMU AMIRI
JONSON, BEN
  On My First Son, **330**
  To Celia, **330-331**
Journey of the Magi, **304-305**
Jury Selection, **240-242**
Just off the highway to Rochester, Minnesota, **397**
JUSTICE, DONALD
  On the Death of Friends in Childhood, **331**

KEATS, JOHN
  La Belle Dame Sans Merci: A Ballad, **331-333**
  Ode on a Grecian Urn, **333-335**
  Ode to a Nightingale, **335-338**
  On First Looking into Chapman's Homer, **220**
  On the Sonnet, **213**
  When I Have Fears, **338**
KICKNOSWAY, FAYE
  Gracie, **127-128**
KIZER, CAROLYN
  After Basho, **153**
KNIGHT, ETHERIDGE
  For Malcolm, A Year After, **197**

Kubla Khan, **291-292**
KUMIN, MAXINE
  Morning Swim, **338-339**

l(a, **39**
l(a, **39**
La Belle Dame Sans Merci: A Ballad, **331-333**
Lake Isle of Innisfree, The, **399**
Lama, The, **203**
Lamb, The, **281**
LARKIN, PHILIP
  Aubade, **339-340**
Leda and the Swan, **268**
Lessons of the Past, **290-291**
Let me not to the marriage of true minds, **366-367**
Let Me Not to the Marriage of True Minds, **366-367**
Let us go then, you and I, **306**
LEVERTOV, DENISE
  Ache of Marriage, The, **208**
  What Were They Like?, **340-341**
Lies, **401-402**
Life, friends, is boring. We must not say so, **278**
Life Is a Nice Place, **233**
Life is a nice place (They change, **233**
Lineage, **390-391**
Little Lamb, who made thee?, **281**
LIU, STEPHEN SHU-NING
  My Father's Martial Art, **341-342**
Living in Sin, **113**
London, **281-282**
Look, Stranger, **135**
Look, stranger, at this island now, **135**
Lord, who createdst man in wealth and store, **244**
LORDE, AUDRE
  Rooming Houses Are Old Women, **162**
Lost Sister, **374-376**
Love set you going like a fat gold watch, **91**
Love Song of J. Alfred Prufrock, The, **306-309**
LOVELACE, RICHARD
  To Lucasta Going to the Wars, **180**
LOWELL, AMY
  Patterns, **86-88**
LOWELL, ROBERT
  For the Union Dead, **342-344**

MACLEISH, ARCHIBALD
   Ars Poetica, **34-35**
Man He Killed, The, **85**
MARLOWE, CHRISTOPHER
   Passionate Shepherd to His Love, The, **344-345**
MARVELL, ANDREW
   To His Coy Mistress, **175-176**
Maud went to college, **188**
MCELROY, COLLEEN J.
   My Father's Wars, **48-49**
MCKAY, CLAUDE
   If We Must Die, **345-346**
   White City, The, **219**
Meal, The, **143**
Medgar Evers, **413-414**
Mending Wall, **314-315**
MEREDITH, WILLIAM
   Dreams of Suicide, **261-262**
   In Memory of Donald A. Stauffer, **226**
Metaphors, **357**
Metrical Feet, **192**
MILLAY, EDNA ST. VINCENT
   Elegy before Death, **134**
   What Lips My Lips Have Kissed, **346**
MILTON, JOHN
   When I Consider How My Light Is Spent, **346-347**
Miniver Cheevy, **361-362**
Miniver Cheevy, child of scorn, **361**
MIRIKITANI, JANICE
   Breaking Silence, **347-350**
   Suicide Note, **81-83**
MOMADAY, N. SCOTT
   Comparatives, **199-200**
   Earth and I Gave You Turquoise, **350-351**
Monet's "Waterlilies,," **237**
MOORE, MARIANNE
   Poetry, **35-36**
MOOTRY, MARIA K.
   "Chocolate Mabbie" and "Pearl May Lee": Gwendolyn Brooks and the Ballad Tradition, **439-446**
MORA, PAT
   Elena, **351**
Morning Song, **91**
Morning Swim, **338-339**
"Mother dear, may I go downtown,", **102**
Mr. Flood's Party, **362-364**

Much have I traveled in the realms of gold, **220**
Musée des Beaux Arts, **270**
Museum Piece, **395**
My Arkansas, **18**
My Father in the Navy: A Childhood Memory, **45**
My Father's Martial Art, **341-342**
My Father's Song, **47-48**
My Father's Wars, **48-49**
My Grandmother Would Rock Quietly and Hum, **75-76**
My grandmothers were strong, **390**
My heart aches, and a drowsy numbness pains, **335**
My hips are a desk, **167**
My Hometown, **380-381**
My Last Duchess, **78-79**
My Mama Moved among the Days, **50**
My Mama moved among the days, **50**
My Mistress' Eyes Are Nothing Like the Sun, **367**
My mistress' eyes are nothing like the sun, **367**
My Papa's Waltz, **46**
My parents felt those rumblings, **325**
My son has been, **96**
My Son, My Executioner, **178-179**
My son, my executioner, **178**
My Spanish isn't enough, **351**

Naming of Parts, **360-361**
Nani, **222-223**
NASH, OGDEN
   Lama, The, **203**
Negro, **77**
NEMEROV, HOWARD
   Air Force Museum at Dayton, The, **352**
   Goose Fish, The, **254-255**
NERUDA, PABLO
   United Fruit Co., The, **353-354**
next to of course god america i, **295-296**
"next to of course god america i, **295**
Night Crow, **253**
Nikki-Rosa, **316-317**
No other word will do. For that's what it was. Gravy, **287-288**
Nobody heard him, the dead man, **374**
Noiseless Patient Spider, A, **184**
Not Marble, Nor the Gilded Monuments, **367-368**

Not marble, nor the gilded monuments, 367
Not Waving But Drowning, 374
Now as I was young and easy under the apple boughs, 389
Now, not a tear begun, 42
Nymph's Reply to the Shepherd, The, 359

O what can all thee, knight at arms, 331
O wild West Wind, thou breath of Autumn's being, 368
OBENZINGER, HILTON
    Yes, We Have No Bananas, 354-355
October. Here in this dank, unfamiliar kitchen, 44
Ode on a Grecian Urn, 333-335
Ode to a Nightingale, 335-338
Ode to the West Wind, 368-370
Oh, My Love Is Like a Red, Red Rose, 163
Oh, my love is like a red, red rose, 163
Old Eben Flood, climbing alone one night, 362
OLDS, SHARON
    One Girl at the Boys Party, The, 355
On Being Brought from Africa to America, 392-393
On the Death of Friends in Childhood, 331
On First Looking into Chapman's Homer, 220
On the Island, 146-147
On the long shore, lit by the moon, 254
On My First Son, 330
On Passing thru Morgantown, Pa., 182
On the Sonnet, 213
Once he followed simple rules, 48
One Day I Wrote Her Name upon the Strand, 131
One day I wrote her name upon the strand, 131
One Girl at the Boys Party, The, 355
ORTIZ, SIMON J.
    My Father's Song, 47-48
    Speaking, 89
Others taunt me with having knelt at well-curbs, 249
Out of the Cradle Endlessly Rocking, 235-236
Out of the cradle endlessly rocking, 235
"*Out, Out*—," 177-178
Over the half-finished houses, 165
OWEN, WILFRED
    Dulce et Decorum Est, 155
Ozymandias, 95

Passionate Shepherd to His Love, The, 344-345
PASTAN, LINDA
    Ethics, 356
PASTERNAK, BORIS
    In Everything I Want to Get, 356-357
Patterns, 86-88
Pearl Avenue runs past the high-school lot, 164
People Who Have No Children Can Be Hard, 407
People who have no children can be hard, 407
PERILLO, LUCIA
    Jury Selection, 240-242
Photograph of My Father in His Twenty-Second Year, 44
Pied Beauty, 207
PIERCY, MARGE
    Secretary Chant, The, 167
Pitcher, 311-312
PLATH, SYLVIA
    Daddy, 170-172
    Metaphors, 357
    Morning Song, 91
Poetry (Giovanni), 33-34
Poetry (Moore), 35-36
poetry is motion graceful, 33
Porphyria's Lover, 93-94
Pot Roast, 384-385
POUND, EZRA
    In a Station of the Metro, 141
    River-Merchant's Wife, The: A Letter, 358
Putting Mother By, 382-383

RALEIGH, SIR WALTER
    Nymph's Reply to the Shepherd, The, 359
RANDALL, DUDLEY
    Ballad of Birmingham, 102-103
RANSOM, JOHN CROWE
    Bells for John Whiteside's Daughter, 359-360
Reapers, 154

Red Wheelbarrow, **140**
REED, HENRY
  Naming of Parts, **360-361**
Report from Part One, **419-421**
Revolutionary Petunias, **206-207**
RICH, ADRIENNE
  Aunt Jennifer's Tigers, **196**
  Diving into the Wreck, **257-259**
  Living in Sin, **113**
  Roofwalker, The, **165-166**
  Woman Mourned by Daughters, A, **42-43**
Richard Cory, **364**
right on: white america, **365**
RIOS, ALBERTO ALVARO
  Nani, **222-223**
River-Merchant's Wife, The: A Letter, **358**
Road Not Taken, The, **315**
ROBINSON, EDWIN ARLINGTON
  Miniver Cheevy, **361-362**
  Mr. Flood's Party, **362-364**
  Richard Cory, **364**
ROETHKE, THEODORE
  Child on Top of a Greenhouse, **364-365**
  I Knew a Woman, **116-117**
  My Papa's Waltz, **46**
  Night Crow, **253**
  Waking, The, **225**
Roofwalker, The, **165-166**
Rooming Houses Are Old Women, **162**
Rooming houses are old women, **162**
ROSSETTI, CHRISTINA
  Uphill, **256**
Rudolph Reed was oaken, **412**

Sadie and Maud, **188**
SAGEL, JIM
  Baca Grande, **121-123**
Sailing to Byzantium, **400**
Sammy Lou of Rue, **206**
SANCHEZ, SONIA
  On Passing thru Morgantown, Pa., **182**
  right on: white america, **365**
SANDBURG, CARL
  Chicago, **231-232**
  Fog, **366**
Satisfaction Coal Company, The, **301-303**

SCHWARTZ, DELMORE
  True-Blue American, The, **262-263**
Sea Grapes, **269**
Second Coming, The, **401**
Secretary Chant, The, **167**
SEPAMLA, SIPHO
  Words, Words, Words, **106-107**
September rain falls on the house, **223**
SEROTE, MONGONE WALLY
  For Don M.—Banned, **366**
Sestina, **223-224**
SEXTON, ANNE
  Cinderella, **99-102**
SHAKESPEARE, WILLIAM
  Fear No More the Heat o' the Sun, **209**
  Let Me Not to the Marriage of True Minds, **366-367**
  My Mistress' Eyes Are Nothing Like the Sun, **367**
  Not Marble, Nor the Gilded Monuments, **367-368**
  Shall I Compare Thee to a Summer's Day?, **158**
  That Time of Year Thou Mayst in Me Behold, **38**
  When, in Disgrace with Fortune and Men's Eyes, **218**
Shall I Compare Thee to a Summer's Day?, **158**
Shall I compare thee to a summer's day?, **158**
SHAPIRO, KARL
  Auto Wreck, **114-115**
She Dwelt among the Untrodden Ways, **397**
She dwelt among the untrodden ways, **397**
She even thinks that up in heaven, **295**
She had thought the studio would keep itself, **113**
She Walks in Beauty, **286**
She walks in beauty, like the night, **286**
SHELLEY, PERCY BYSSHE
  Ode to the West Wind, **368-370**
  Ozymandias, **95**
SIDNEY, SIR PHILIP
  Astrophel and Stella, **371**

SILKO, LESLIE MARMON
  Where Mountain Lion Lay Down with Deer, **80-81**
SIMIC, CHARLES
  Birthday Star Atlas, **371-372**
SIMMERMAN, JIM
  Child's Grave, Hale County, Alabama, **250-251**
Since There's No Help, **303**
Since there's no help, come let us kiss and part, **303**
Sir Patrick Spence, **275-277**
Sitting at her table, she serves, **222**
Sketch, A, **204-205**
Sleep, **236**
Sleepless at Crown Point, **153**
SLUTSKY, BORIS
  How Did They Kill My Grandmother?, **373-374**
SMITH, GARY
  Gwendolyn Brooks's A Street in Bronzeville, *the Harlem Renaissance and the Mythologies of Black Women,* **446-453**
  Gwendolyn Brooks's "Children of the Poor," Metaphysical Poetry and the Inconditions of Love, **430-439**
SMITH, STEVIE
  Not Waving But Drowning, **374**
Snowfall in the Afternoon, **283**
SNYDER, GARY
  Some Good Things to Be Said for the Iron Age, **142**
so much depends, **140**
Some Good Things to Be Said for the Iron Age, **142**
Some say the world will end in fire, **84**
Someone drove a two-by-four, **250**
Something there is that doesn't love a wall, **314**
SONG, CATHY
  Lost Sister, **374-376**
Song (Donne), **301**
Song in the Front Yard, A, **406-407**
from *Song of Myself,* **393-394**
SOTO, GARY
  Black Hair, **376-377**
  History, **377-379**
Soul Selects Her Own Society, The, **299**
SOYINKA, WOLE
  Future Plans, **260**
  Telephone Conversation, **6**

SPACKS, BARRY
  Finding a Yiddish Paper on the Riverside Line, **379**
Speaking, **89**
SPENDER, STEPHEN
  Elementary School Classroom in a Slum, An, **379-380**
SPENSER, EDMUND,
  One Day I Wrote Her Name upon the Strand, **131**
Spring, **152**
Spring and All, **238-239**
SPRINGSTEEN, BRUCE
  My Hometown, **380-381**
STAFFORD, WILLIAM
  For the Grave of Daniel Boone, **110**
  Traveling through the Dark, **381-382**
Star of the Nativity, The, **266**
STAVROS, GEORGE
  Interview with Gwendolyn Brooks, An, **428-429**
STEIN, DONA
  Putting Mother By, **382-383**
STEVENS, WALLACE
  Anecdote of the Jar, **383**
  Disillusionment of Ten O'clock, **383-384**
  Emperor of Ice-Cream, The, **384**
Stiff and immaculate, **45**
Stopping by Woods on a Snowy Evening, **315-316**
STRAND, MARK
  Pot Roast, **384-385**
Suicide Note, **81-83**
SUKNASKI, ANDREW
  Bitter Word, The, **386-387**
Sundays too my father got up early, **50**
Sunlit sea, **199**
Supermarket in California, A, **183-184**
Susumu, My Name, **112**
SWENSON, MAY
  Women, **243**
  Women Should Be Pedestals, **247**

Telephone Conversation, **6**
Tell me not, Sweet, I am unkind, **180**
Telling lies to the young is wrong, **401**
TENNYSON, ALFRED, LORD
  Eagle, The, **199**
  Ulysses, **387-389**

Tentatively, you, **153**
Terence, This Is Stupid Stuff, **327-329**
"Terence, this is stupid stuff, **327**
That is no country for old men. The young, **400**
That night your great guns, unawares, **321**
That sail which leans on light, **269**
That Time of Year Thou Mayst in Me Behold, **38**
That time of year thou mayst in me behold, **38**
That's my last Duchess painted on the wall, **78**
the, **234**
The ache of marriage, **208**
The apparition of these faces in the crowd, **141**
The buzz saw snarled and rattled in the yard, **177**
The curfew tolls the knell of parting day, **317**
The farther he went the farther home grew, **110**
The fog comes, **366**
The good gray guardians of art, **395**
The grass is half-covered with snow, **283**
The hand that signed the paper felled a city, **181**
The houses are haunted, **383**
The king sits in Dumferling toune, **275**
The lead & zinc company, **173**
The man whose height his fear improved he, **413**
The meeting is called, **260**
The mole, **236**
The old South Boston Aquarium stands, **342**
The one-l lama, **203**
The price seemed reasonable, location, **6**
The rain set early in to-night, **93**
the sky was can dy, **234**
The Soul selects her own Society—, **299**
The time you won your town the race, **329**
The whiskey on your breath, **46**
The wind billowing out the seat of my britches, **364**

The world in charged with the grandeur of God, **326**
The world is too much with us; late and soon, **90**
There are miracles that happen, **347**
There is a deep brooding, **17**
There Is a Garden in Her Face, **287**
There is a garden in her face, **287**
There they are, **410**
There was such speed in her little body, **359**
There will be rose and rhododendron, **134**
They eat beans mostly, this old yellow pair, **407**
They have washed their faces until they are pale, **143**
this country might have, **365**
This Is Just to Say, **395-396**
This is the world we wanted. All who would have seen us dead, **73**
THOMAS, DYLAN
   Do Not Go Gentle into That Good Night, **47**
   Fern Hill, **389-390**
   Hand That Signed the Paper, The, **181**
Those Winter Sundays, **50**
Thou still unravish'd bride of quietness, **333**
To an Athlete Dying Young, **329-330**
To Brooklyn Bridge, **293-294**
To Celia, **330-331**
To His Coy Mistress, **175-176**
To Lucasta Going to the Wars, **180**
To My Dear and Loving Husband, **175**
To the Virgins, to Make Much of Time, **92**
Today as the news from Selma and Saigon, **237**
Today we have naming of parts. Yesterday, **360**
TOOMER, JEAN
   Reapers, **154**
Traveling through the Dark, **381-382**
Traveling through the dark I found a deer, **381**
Trochee trips from long to short, **192**
True-Blue American, The, **262-263**
Turning and turning in the widening gyre, **401**
'Twas brillig, and the slithy toves, **210**

'Twas mercy brought me from my
    Pagan land, **392**
Two roads diverged in a yellow wood,
    315
Tyger, The, **282**
Tyger! Tyger! burning bright, **282**

Ulysses, **387-389**
Under the barrel roof in solemn
    gloom, **352**
United Fruit Co., The, **353-354**
Unknown Citizen, The, **98-99**
UPDIKE, JOHN
    Ex-Basketball Player, **164-165**
Uphill, **256**

Valediction: Forbidding Mourning, A,
    168-169
Visit to the Secret Annex, A, **147-150**
Volcanoes Be in Sicily, **252**
Volcanoes be in Sicily, **252**

Waking, The, **225**
WAKOSKI, DIANE
    Sleep, **236**
WALCOTT, DEREK
    Sea Grapes, **269**
WALKER, ALICE
    Revolutionary Petunias, **206-207**
WALKER, MARGARET
    Lineage, **390-391**
WALLER, EDMUND
    Go, Lovely Rose, **391**
Wanting to say things, **47**
Watergate, **277**
Wave of sorrow, **253**
Wayman in Quebec, **392**
WAYMAN, TOM
    Wayman in Quebec, **392**
We are in her kitchen, **382**
We don't speak of tribal wars
    anymore, **106**
We have all been in rooms, **296-297**
We Real Cool, **130**
We real cool. We, **130**
We shall not ever meet them bearded
    in heaven, **331**
We Wear the Mask, **304**
We wear the mask that grins and lies,
    304
Western Wind, **277**
Western wind, when wilt thou blow,
    277

Whan that Aprill with his shoures
    soote, **288**
What happens to a dream deferred?,
    159
What Is an Epigram?, **228**
What is an epigram? a dwarfish
    whole, **228**
What Lips My Lips Have Kissed, **346**
What lips my lips have kissed, and
    where, and why, **346**
What Shall I Give My Children?, **407**
What shall I give my children? who
    are poor, **407**
What thoughts I have of you
    tonight, Walt Whitman, for I
    walked, **183**
What to do with a day, **301**
What Were They Like?, **340-341**
WHEATLEY, PHYLLIS
    On Being Brought from Africa to
    America, **392-393**
When, in Disgrace with Fortune and
    Men's Eyes, **218**
When, in disgrace with Fortune and
    men's eyes, **218**
When he came home Mother said he
    looked, **341**
When I Consider How My Light Is
    Spent, **346-347**
When I consider how my light is
    spent, **346**
When I Have Fears, **338**
When I have fears that I may cease to
    be, **338**
When I Heard the Learn'd Astronomer,
    108
When I heard the learn'd astronomer,
    108
When I saw that clumsy crow, **253**
When I see birches bend to left and
    right, **312**
When I take my girl to the swimming
    party, **355**
When my mother died I was very
    young, **280**
When the trumpet sounded, it was,
    353
Whenever Richard Cory went down
    town, **364**
Where Mountain Lion Lay Down with
    Deer, **80-81**
While my hair was still cut straight
    across my forehead, **358**

White City, The, **219**
WHITMAN, WALT
   Cavalry Crossing a Ford, **393**
   Had I the Choice, **187**
   Noiseless Patient Spider, A, **184**
   Out of the Cradle Endlessly Rocking, **235-236**
   from *Song of Myself,* **393-394**
   When I Heard the Learn'd Astronomer, **108**
Who will in fairest book of Nature know, **371**
Whose woods these are I think I know, **315**
Why I'm in Favor of a Nuclear Freeze, **285-286**
Widow's Lament, **229**
WILBUR, RICHARD
   For the Student Strikers, **125**
   Museum Piece, **395**
   Sketch, A, **204-205**
   Sleepless at Crown Point, **153**
Wild Nights—Wild Nights!, **299-300**
Wild Nights—Wild Nights!, **299-300**
Wildest dream, Miss Emily, **371**
WILLIAMS, WILLIAM CARLOS
   Great Figure, The, **144**
   Red Wheelbarrow, **140**
   Spring and All, **238-239**
   This Is Just to Say, **395-396**
Windhover, The, **326-327**
Windigo, **267**
Without my having known, **414**
Woman Mourned by Daughters, A, **42-43**
Women, **243**
Women (Bogan), **283-284**
Women (Swenson), **243**
Women have no wilderness in them, **283**
Women Should Be Pedestals, **247**
Women should be pedestals, **247**

Words, Words, Words, **106-107**
WORDSWORTH, WILLIAM
   Composed upon Westminster Bridge, **396**
   I Wandered Lonely as a Cloud, **396-397**
   She Dwelt among the Untrodden Ways, **397**
   World Is Too Much with Us, The, **90**
World Is Too Much with Us, The, **90**
WRIGHT, JAMES
   Blessing, A, **397-398**
WRIGHT, RICHARD
   Hokku Poems, **229-230**

YEATS, WILLIAM BUTLER
   Crazy Jane Talks with the Bishop, **398-399**
   Irish Airman Foresees His Death, An, **399**
   Lake Isle of Innisfree, The, **399**
   Leda and the Swan, **268**
   Sailing to Byzantium, **400**
   Second Coming, The, **401**
Yes, We Have No Bananas, **354-355**
"Yes, we have no bananas,", **354**
Yet Do I Marvel, **265**
YEVTUSHENKO, YEVGENY
   Lies, **401-402**
You always read about it, **99**
You are entitled to overhear, **112**
You do not do, you do not do, **170**
You Fit into Me, **179**
you fit into me, **179**
You knew I was coming for you, little one, **267**
You Too? Me Too—Why Not? Soda Pop, **245**

ZUKOFSKY, LOUIS
   I Walk in the Old Street, **38-39**

KEY TERMS

Abstract word, 107
Allegorical framework, 256
Allegory, 53, 255-256, 272, 504
Alliteration, 199-200, 211, 504
Allusion, 53, 259-262, 272, 504
Anapest, 190, 504
Annotating, 18-19, 53
Apostrophe, 181-182, 504
Archetype, 250, 504
Assonance, 200-201, 211, 504
Atmosphere, 139
Aubade, 41, 504
Audience, 19-20

Ballad, 41, 504
Ballad stanza, 41, 216, 504
Beginning rhyme, 202, 505
Blank verse, 191, 215, 505
Brainstorming, 22-23, 56-57

Cacophony, 198, 505
Caesura, 194, 505
Canon, literary, 4-5, 489
Carpe diem, 42, 505
Closed form, 213-215, 505
Common measure, 217, 505
Conclusion, 30, 70
Concrete poetry, 242-247, 505
Concrete word, 107
Connotation, 108, 139, 505
Conventional symbol, 249, 505
Conventional word order, 131-132
Couplet, 215-216, 505
Critical thinking, 7-9

Dactyl, 190, 505
Deconstruction, 501-503, 505
Denotation, 108, 505
Dialect, 127-128, 505
Dialogue with your instructor, 28
Diction, 52, 119-123, 505
Dimeter, 191
Documentation, 32, 461-475
Double rhyme, 202
Draft(ing), 26-27, 58-71
Dramatic irony, 93, 506
Dramatic monologue, 41, 77-78, 94-95, 506

Editing, 32
Elegy, 41, 192, 506
Emblem poem, 242
End rhyme, 202, 506
End-stopped lines, 195, 506

Enjambment, 195, 506
Enlightenment, 477-478
Envoi, 221, 506
Epic, 41, 506
Epigram, 84, 192, 227-229, 506
Euphony, 198, 506
Explanatory notes, 468-469
Eye rhyme, 202, 506

Falling rhyme, 202, 506
Feminine rhyme, 202, 506
Feminist criticism, 489-491, 506
Figures of speech, 52, 158-163, 185, 507
Foot, 190-191, 507
Form, 52-53, 213-247, 507
Formal diction, 119-121, 507
Formalism, 483-485, 507
Free verse, 214, 507

Genre, 2, 507
Greeks, Ancient, 476

Haiku, 229-230, 507
Heptameter, 191
Heroic couplet, 206, 215-216
Hexameter, 191
Highlighting, 16-17, 53
Hyperbole, 169-174, 507

Iamb, 190, 507
Iambic pentameter, 191, 225
Imagery, 52, 138-145
Imagism, 214, 507
Imperfect rhyme, 202, 507
Informal diction, 121-123, 507
Internal rhyme, 202, 507
Introduction, 29-30
Inverted word order, 131-132
Irony, 92-98, 507

Journal keeping, 23

Kinetic imagery, 144, 508

Listing, 23-24
Literary canon, 4-5, 489, 508
Literary criticism, 13, 27, 508
Literary symbols, 249-252, 508
Literary theories, 483-503
Lyric poetry, 41, 508

Marxist criticism, 491-493, 508
Masculine rhyme, 202, 508
Meaning, 7

537

Meditation (poem form), 41, 508
Metaphor, 159-163, 508
Meter, 189-196, 211, 508
Metonymy, 180, 509
Middle Ages, 476-477
Modern Period, 480-482
Monometer, 191
Mood, 139, 509
Myth, 53, 264-265, 272, 509

Narrative poetry, 40-41
New historicism, 493-495, 509

Octameter, 191
Octave, 217, 509
Ode, 41, 509
Onomatopoeia, 198, 509
Open form, 189, 214, 235-242, 509
Ottava rima, 217, 509
Outline, 25-26, 57-58

Paradox, 43, 509
Parenthetical references, 461-465
Pastoral, 41, 509
Peer review, 28
Pentameter, 191
Perfect rhyme, 202, 509
Persona, 73, 509
Personification, 159-163, 509
Petrarchan sonnet, 217, 509
Plagiarism, 461
Poetic form, 213
Poetic rhythm, 189, 509
Poetry, 36-37
Previewing, 15-16, 53
Private symbol, 250
Psychoanalytic criticism, 495-498, 509
Purpose, 20
Pyrrhic, 190, 510

Quatrain, 216, 510

Reader-response criticism, 485-488, 510
Reception theory, 486
Renaissance, 477
Revising, 28-32
Rhyme, 202-206, 211, 510
Rhyme royal, 217, 510
Rhythm, 187-189, 211, 510
Rising rhyme, 202, 510
Roman theater, 476
Romantic Period, 478-479
Run-on lines, 195, 510

Sarcasm, 96, 510
Scansion, 189-192, 510
Scratch outline, 26
Sestet, 217, 510
Sestina, 215, 221-224, 510
Shakespearean sonnet, 217-218, 511
Simile, 159-163, 511
Situational irony, 95, 511
Sociological criticism, 488-489, 511
Sonnet, 215, 217-218, 511
Sound, 52, 187-211
Source material, 32
Speaker, 72, 511
Specific word, 107
Spondee, 190, 511
Stanza, 215-217, 511
Static imagery, 144, 511
Stress, 189, 511
Structuralism, 498-501
Supporting ideas, 29
Symbol(-ism), 53, 248-252, 271-272, 512
Synaesthesia, 145
Synecdoche, 180, 512
Syntax, 130-133

Tercet, 216, 512
Terza rima, 41, 216, 512
Tetrameter, 191
Theme, 3-4, 42-46, 53, 512
Thesis, 25, 57, 67
Thesis and support, 26-27
Thinking critically, 7-9
Tone, 83-89, 104, 512
Topic, 20-22, 55-56
Topic sentence, 30-31, 69
Transitions, 31
Trimeter, 191
Triple rhyme, 203, 512
Trochee, 190, 512

Understatement, 169-174, 512
Universal symbol, 249-250, 512

Verbal irony, 96, 512
Victorian period, 479-480
Villanelle, 215, 225-227, 512
Voice, 52, 72-80, 104

Word choice, 107-111
Word order, 130-133
Works cited, list of, 465-468, 475